New England Encounters

New England Encounters

INDIANS AND EUROAMERICANS
CA. 1600–1850

Essays Drawn from
The New England Quarterly

Edited by Alden T. Vaughan

Northeastern University Press
BOSTON

Northeastern University Press

Library of Congress Cataloging-in-Publication Data

New England encounters : Indians and Euroamericans ca.
1600–1850 / edited by Alden T. Vaughan.
p.   cm.
Includes bibliographical references and index.
ISBN 1-55553-404-X (alk. paper)
1. Indians of North America—First encounter with
Europeans—New England.   2. Indians, Treatment of—
New England—History.   3. Indians of North America—
Wars—New England.   4. Frontier and pioneer life—New
England—History.   5. New England—History—Colonial
period, ca. 1600–1775.   6. New England—Race relations.
7. New England—Social conditions.
I. Vaughan, Alden T., 1929–   .
E78.N5N48   1999
974.004'97—dc21   99-28893

Designed by Ann Twombly

Composed in Caslon by Graphic Composition, Inc., Athens,
Georgia. Printed and bound by Maple Press, York,
Pennsylvania. The paper is Maple Eggshell, an acid-free sheet.

MANUFACTURED IN THE UNITED STATES OF AMERICA
03   02   01   00   99   5   4   3   2   1

Contents

Foreword

*W*HILE IT MAY SEEM somewhat ironic, editors of historical journals rarely look back. The press of daily business—soliciting essays, evaluating manuscripts, editing, production—places a premium on the present and future and not, alas, on the past. It was in the course of conducting our "daily business" that we noticed an interesting development. We seemed to be receiving an increasing number of essays focusing on Native Americans in New England. This recognition prompted us to break from our normal routine and look back at the enormous archive of essays published in *The New England Quarterly* since 1928. What we found was that, indeed, this was a relatively new phenomenon. Although the journal had published in the area of Native American studies before, the topic had been occasional whereas not it was persistent. Clearly, this was an area of intense scholarly interest. The moment struck us as opportune to bring together the distinguished essays we had published to date for a wider audience, including students.

Since neither of us specializes in Native American history, we consulted with Alden Vaughan, a renowned scholar in the field. He enthusiastically endorsed our plan to issue a collection of essays drawn fro mthe *NEQ* archive; and to our great joy, he agreed to edit *New England Encounters*. Thanks to his work and that of the fifteen other contributors, *NEQ* is pleased to present this volume.

WILLIAM M. FOWLER, JR.
LINDA SMITH RHOADS
Co-Editors, *The New England Quarterly*

Preface

*P*OPULAR AND SCHOLARLY enthusiasm for Native American history has flourished in recent decades. In part, this development reflects a genuine curiosity by non-Indians about the earliest of America's many "racial" groups. It also signals an awakened concern, among both Indians and non-Indians, about the centuries-long encounter between the peoples who once controlled all of America and those who almost completely and often brutally displaced them. The "new social history" emerging in the 1960s coalesced those generalized motivations into one of its more significant goals: to represent American minorities with heightened accuracy and empathy. The new history of Indian-white relations is accordingly often bitter, often sad, but sometimes uplifting, and always important. That story—or, rather, thousands of interlocking stories—needs to be told and retold, as new generations of storytellers, both amateur and professional, grapple with a major issue of the American past, present, and future.

Both historically (what happened) and historiographically (what has been written about what happened), New England has held a special place in Indian-white relations in North America. It was not, despite popular notions to the contrary, the scene of the first post-Columbian encounters between Indians and Europeans, which likely happened on a Portuguese voyage to Newfoundland in 1501 or on an unrecorded visit to the northern coast by Bristol fishermen even earlier. Nor did the first encounters between Native Americans and English colonists take place in New England. Coastal Carolina claims primacy in the 1580s, nearly two decades before the settlement at Jamestown, Virginia, took root while, almost simultaneously, another was aborted in Maine, and more than three decades before Samoset greeted the Pilgrims at Plymouth. But once New England became a viable outpost of the first British Empire, the interaction between natives and newcomers was frequent, intense, and widely publicized.

A large and growing literature recounts those manifold interactions for modern readers. Much of that literature centers on the seventeenth century, when the two populations were fairly evenly balanced and their cultural contacts more varied and abundant than they later would be. Indians and Euroamericans (mostly, but not exclusively, English) encountered each other in work, play, battle, barter, prayer, and virtually all other aspects of life. After about 1675, as New England's native population declined precipitously while Euroamericans prospered, and as the power of the Indians to resist encroachment and impoverishment rapidly waned, encounters between the two groups—who both increasingly perceived themselves to be racially distinct—continued to be important and often poignant. Indian-Euroamerican contact in the eighteenth century and beyond occurred less frequently on the battlefield or at diplomatic conferences; its settings—farmlands, Indian reservations, and (escalating from their origins in the 1650s–1670s) missionary communities—were now prosaic. Increasingly, too, Indian-Euroamerican encounters entered new realms of human interconnectedness, such as literary representation and political debate, where the natives of New England remained a vital presence despite their paucity of power or numbers. The story does not end in the middle of the nineteenth century, of course, as the essays in this volume perforce do; encounters between Native Americans and European Americans are ongoing and newly invigorated, as the daily newspapers often remind us.

New England Encounters presents selected episodes of Indian-white contact through fifteen essays that appeared originally in *The New England Quarterly: A Historical Review of New England Life and Letters.* Under the auspices of the Colonial Society of Massachusetts and, more recently, of Northeastern University (since 1981) and of the Massachusetts Historical Society (since 1998), *NEQ* has been published continuously since 1928. Although manuscripts about Native American history rarely arrived at the *Quarterly's* editorial office during its early decades, that situation changed gradually in the 1950s and 1960s and rapidly in the 1970s through 1990s, as scholars concerned with Indian-white encounters generated a small flood of well-researched and well-argued essays. The mounting numbers and dynamic content of such manuscripts inspired the *Quarterly's* editors to propose this book.

The criteria for selecting the fifteen articles which follow were twofold. First, an inviolable prerequisite, was outstanding research and effective presentation (which most articles in the pool readily met); second, the articles were collectively to form a fairly comprehensive account of Indian-white relations in New England from the early seventeenth century to the mid nineteenth—the latest date among the many articles published in the *Quarterly's* pages. Predictably, most of the articles here reprinted (with revisions) are of fairly recent vintage; nearly two-thirds are from the 1980s and 1990s, but one was first published in the 1950s, when an interest in Native Americans began tentatively to emerge, and five appeared in the 1970s, when the boom was palpably underway.

The wide range of publication dates is paralleled by the authors' varied scholarly interests. Most of the authors are historians of early New England, but several—as befits a rapidly expanding scholarly genre—are historians of other periods or regions, two are specialists in American literature, one is an anthropologist, one is currently an attorney and another a physician (both hold advanced degrees in history), yet all have written with skill and enthusiasm about the specific ethnohistorical encounters presented here. The result is an anthology of unusual diversity of topics and perspectives, of authorial backgrounds and styles.

These essays examine a wide range of highlights in the region's Indian-white relations during its first two and a half centuries: from Abenaki territory in northern Maine to Pequot lands in southern Connecticut; from profitable commerce to devastating warfare; from religious persuasion to labor exploitation; from cultural mixing to non-violent resistance; from literary representation to political argumentation. Not every major encounter between Native Americans and Euroamericans in New England's long history is addressed by these essays, of course, but taken as a whole their breadth and depth of coverage is extensive. To help readers place these disparate topics into the broad sweep of New England ethnohistory, the editor's introduction presents an overview of the region's first two and a half centuries of "encounters," with suggested readings on topics not covered by the fifteen authors.

SCHOLARLY INTERPRETATIONS, as almost everyone knows, can vary sharply. Each author assesses the surviving clues to the past in the light of his or her own particular assumptions, experiences, and accumulated knowledge—much as judges and jurors weigh legal evidence and physicians assess clinical symptoms. And like those of their counterparts in other endeavors, historians' judgments are often influenced by the broad social and intellectual climates in which they are formed. To make the point differently: each author is a craftsman, fashioning from diverse and often disparate materials a unique object—in this case a verbal reconstruction. Because of their varying preferences and disparate skills, no two craftsmen create quite the same object, and any craftsman's labors may produce a somewhat different result on a later occasion, even if the fundamental construction remains nearly constant. In the historical scholar's hands, these circumstances not only produce conflicting interpretations by different authors using the same evidence but, in some instances, different interpretations by the same author at different times. Scholars learn from new evidence, new perspectives, and further reflection.

In that spirit, the contributors to *New England Encounters* were invited to make two kinds of changes to their previously published articles: (1) minor adjustments to improve the text and notes, such as substituting or adding words or phrases where appropriate, citing new books and articles, correcting ambiguous or erroneous statements; and (2) general reflections on the original essay in the form of a brief postscript addressing other scholars' subsequent work and—if the author deemed it appropriate—broad historical issues as well. Older articles, obviously, are more likely to have amendments and postscripts; recent articles are reprinted almost unchanged. In either case, *New England Encounters* offers each author's current thinking, both substantive and historiographic, on his area of expertise.

The editors of *The New England Quarterly* and the contributors to this volume hope that *New England Encounters: Indians and Euroamericans, ca. 1600–1850* will be especially useful to students and general readers who have had little previous exposure to the rich literature on early New England ethnohistory. The fifteen essays introduce a remarkably diverse, dynamic, and often contested intellectual terrain; they will have served their intended purpose if they inspire further reading in these or related fields and, ultimately, encourage new contributions to the burgeoning study of Indian-European encounters of every kind in every era.

Worcester, Massachusetts
June 1999

New England Encounters

INTRODUCTION

Indian–European Encounters in New England
An Annotated, Contextual Overview

ALDEN T. VAUGHAN

LONG BEFORE Captain John Smith dubbed the northeastern corner of the future United States "New England," and even longer before shiploads of English Puritans and other European colonists forever changed its ethnic and cultural composition, the region was homeland to vibrant cultures of distant Asian origin.[1] As early, perhaps, as 10,000 B.C., aboriginal pioneers from the west probed the region's good land and, more important, good waters. The native communities that evolved during the next several millennia clustered along rivers, lakes, and harbors, where bountiful supplies of fresh- and salt-water seafood, supplemented by hunting, gathering, and eventually horticulture, fostered good health and procreation.[2] By the sixteenth century, when European explorers began to frequent New England's craggy coast, the native population numbered perhaps one hundred thousand and possibly far more.[3]

Although the native bands along the region's coast and waterways shared many customs and beliefs, they were far from homogeneous, as historical and archeological evidence increasingly reveals.[4] New England's natives all spoke dialects of the Algonquian language group, but local variations often stymied cross-band communication. All Indians subsisted primarily on fish, shellfish, wild game, and cultivated vegetables, but the dietary mix varied considerably from the coast to the interior and from south to north, as determined largely by topography and climate.[5] All lived in self-sufficient, sometimes palisaded, communities, but their sizes ranged from one or two houses to several score. All have subsequently been designated Algonquians, but they identified themselves with kinship groups or—especially after contact with Europeans—with chieftainships that the English called "nations" or (much later) "tribes" rather than with a modern anthropological category or geographic boundary.[6]

New England Indian culture differed significantly from the colonists' imported culture, often in ways that increased the likelihood of mutual misunderstanding and conflict. Cultural differences need not produce conflict, of course, but given the Euroamericans' determination to change Algonquian customs and beliefs and to acquire vast amounts of native territory, and given the Algonquians' overwhelming preference for their own cultural, political, and territorial autonomy, the contentiousness of many New England encounters is lamentable but not surprising. Not surprising either is the necessity, in the absence of native writings, of drawing heavily on colonial descriptions of seventeenth-century Algonquian culture when attempting to reconstruct Algonquian society as a background for early Indian-European encounters.

Despite considerable imprecision in colonial reports "Of *their Government* and *Justice*" (Roger Williams's phrase), the general outlines of Algonquian political forms and functions can be summarized, as can their dissimilarity to English colonial government and justice. In England's aristocratic, hierarchical, and bureaucratic government, the monarch and imperial officials had immense authority, although their influence in North America was sharply diminished by distance and often by local resistance; in the New England colonies, governors, legislators, and numerous local officers created and administered a wide range of rules, usually written and disseminated in print. At whatever level, authorities were to be obeyed; violators faced legal action and stiff penalties.

Algonquian political life was far less centralized, hierarchical, and coercive. Each Indian nation had a supreme chief, occasionally two (one civil, the other military); an advisory council of varying number, composition, and influence; and lesser chiefs in local communities. Although European observers often applied familiar terms for the Indians' political ranks— emperor, king, queen, prince, and captain, for example—such titles misrepresented native leaders' functions and degrees of authority. Some *sachems* (called *sagamores* in northern New England) "ruled" clusters of communities totaling, before the precipitous population losses of the early seventeenth century, perhaps thirty thousand; petty sachems presided over much smaller units. Although native customs of governance were not uniform, leaders generally inherited their offices, often through the maternal line, and tenure was usually for life, though occasionally a leader was ousted for failing to serve his (or, sometimes, her) people adequately.[7]

The relation between a sachem and his followers and between lesser and greater sachems was not as fixed as some English observers assumed. The sachem's power varied according to his or her persuasiveness, to the traditions of the specific community or nation, and to local circumstances.

In times of peace and plenty, the sachem's authority might diminish; during war or other community crises, it was likely to increase substantially, unless a separate war leader assumed the added burdens. But the sachem's power was never absolute. In 1674, the Massachusetts colony's superintendent of Indian affairs, Daniel Gookin, argued that although the Algonquians' "government is generally monarchial, . . . [t]heir sachems have not their men in such subjection, but that very frequently their men will leave them upon a distaste or harsh dealing, and go and live under other sachems."[8]

The sachem's role in enforcing community rules was also apparently limited. "The most usuall Custome amongst them in executing punishments," according to Roger Williams of Rhode Island, "is for the *Sachim* either to beat, whip, or put to death [the culprit] with his owne hand." William Wood, an early New England publicist, thought the punishments much less diverse: except for the death penalty in extreme cases, "[o]ther means to restrain abuses they have none, saving admonition or reproof; no whippings, no prisons, stocks, bilboes, or the like." Whatever the form of punishment in Algonquian society, it was often administered not by sachems but by the victim's kin; and the perpetrator's kin, in turn, might be held liable for the original infraction. Williams observed that "They hold the band of brother-hood so deare, that when one had commited a murther and fled, they executed his brother; and 'tis common for a brother to pay the debt of a brother deceased." It was common too, and wholly legitimate in Algonquian culture, for the victim of a crime, or his kin, to take revenge against the perpetrator or, if necessary, against the perpetrator's kin.[9] The contrast of Algonquian jurisprudence to the English state's monopoly of judicial authority and its restriction of punishment to the convicted party is too evident to belabor, as is the potential it held for intercultural misunderstanding and resentment.[10]

Differences between Algonquians and Angloamericans in religious beliefs, practices, and personnel abounded as well. English colonists, with some notable exceptions, were zealous, proselytizing Protestants, whose religious beliefs and rituals derived from a single book; Puritans, especially, insisted on their own brand of Christianity and on its acceptance to the exclusion of all other faiths. The natives' equally sincere attachment to their traditional cosmology and its associated practices and rituals derived from oral precepts and, perhaps partly for that reason, was far more tolerant of disparate views. Roger Williams observed the Narragansetts' "modest Religious perswasion not to disturb any man, either themselves *English, Dutch,* or any [others] in their Conscience, and worship."[11] A corollary to

the Algonquians' reluctance to coerce or proselytize was their openness
to syncretism, to adopting aspects of other faiths without relinquishing
their own.

Algonquian theology, like Puritanism, defies easy summary, and surely
(as Williams implied) not all New England natives shared the same beliefs. But probably all Algonquians acknowledged the existence of supernatural qualities—*manitou*—in a wide range of animate objects. As
Williams observed, "there is a generall Custome amongst them, at the
apprehension of any Excellency in Men, Women, Birds, Beasts, Fish, &c
to cry out *Manittoo,* that is, it is a God." Inanimate objects and acts could
also possess *manitou,* Williams added: "[W]hen they talke amongst themselves of the *English* ships, and great buildings, of the plowing of their
Fields, and especially of Bookes and Letters, they will end thus: *Manitto-
wock* They are Gods."[12] Propitiating certain *manitou,* especially important
animal spirits, Algonquians believed, assured good fortune in hunting and
other aspects of life; offending such spirits predictably brought misfortune.
Algonquians simultaneously respected the superior powers of Cautantowwit, in whose house good souls would dwell for eternity, and Abbomocho
(Hobbomok), who possessed great curative powers but also great potency
to do harm. Mediating with the spirits, both good and evil, were a variety
of human religious figures whose functions bore little resemblance to English clergymen's, although English chroniclers often likened *powwows* to
priests, wizards, or medicine men.[13] Except for occasional parallels to
Christianity, colonial observers usually emphasized the differences rather
than the similarities of native and colonial faiths.

Similarly, although Indian and colonial economies had much in common, most obviously their primary dependence on agricultural and marine
crops, most early Euroamerican descriptions of Indian economies focused
on dissimilarities, especially in gender roles. The colonists' domestic economy, like the Algonquians', divided tasks between the genders, but the
differences between colonial and Indian patterns were profound. Indian
men disdained agricultural labor; instead, they demonstrated their re-
sourcefulness and stamina, and made crucial contributions to the kin group's
well-being, on expeditions for wild game, skins, and deep-water fish. At
home, Algonquian men cleared fields, built canoes, crafted weapons and
tools, and repaired nets, weirs, and other semi-durable equipment. Wom-
en's work was as hard, if not harder: planting and tending the fields, gathering shellfish, making clothing and utensils, raising children. Many colonial commentators (all men) charged their Algonquian counterparts with
being lazy much of the time and with virtually enslaving their wives. But
because Indian men's work was largely performed away from the villages

and thus seldom observed by the English, and because widely divergent cultural contexts and the observers' palpable biases often clouded English perceptions, meaningful comparison is difficult, if not impossible. In any event, leisure in the seventeenth century was rare for either sex in either society, although male Algonquians' penchant for using whatever spare time they had in games—among a few participants (dice games, for example) or many ("football" and other team contests)—often offended Puritan sensibilities.[14]

If labor in Algonquian society was shared equally by the sexes, warfare was not. In Indian and English cultures alike, men did the fighting, and, by and large, noncombatants were not intended to be either victims or spoils of war. Such intentions notwithstanding, women and children were repeatedly enmeshed in seventeenth-century New England's armed conflicts. Civilian casualties were heavy, on both sides, in the battles of the 1630s and 1670s; and civilian captives were often kept by the victors for ransom (by both sides), servitude (primarily by the English), or adoption (exclusively by the Indians).[15] On both sides, too, torture was sometimes a captive's fate, although colonial writers usually overlooked such actions by their countrymen.

The reasons for warfare also varied: whereas the English most often fought for territory and jurisdiction, Indians rarely resorted to war for outright domination. Rather, they sought to show courage, to avenge injury or insult, to improve their position in commerce, to settle dynastic disputes, and, especially in the face of their sharply declining population, to acquire adoptees. Whatever the motive, the ensuing conflicts were, as Roger Williams pointed out, "farre lesse bloudy and devouring then the cruell Warres of *Europe*."[16]

FOR MANY MILLENNIA, the natives of northeastern North America developed their customs and beliefs in a hemisphere largely isolated from its other half until transatlantic exchanges proliferated after 1492. During the long separation, a few Europeans and possibly some Africans reached New England by accident or, less likely, by design; little is known about the number or nature of such early encounters. They undoubtedly involved few Europeans and American natives, and they were widely spread over time and space. The lasting impact of pre-Columbian encounters on the area that became New England seems to have been insignificant.[17]

That situation changed dramatically in the sixteenth and early seventeenth centuries, when explorers from Spain, Portugal, France, the Netherlands, and England probed the coastline for fish or furs (which they often acquired) or for gold or a passage to Asia (which, of course, eluded them). Among the Algonquians, the arrival of exotic strangers induced amazement—at their ships, their weapons, their trade goods—but also skepticism and, in some cases, disapproval. American natives generally disliked Europeans' pale complexions and abundant facial hair as well as their excessive clothing, fastidious eating, and, more seriously, their almost fanatical possessiveness of material goods. Natives were suspicious too of the religion called Christianity, which seemed to vary widely between Europeans from different nations and even among Englishmen but was advocated with unseemly vigor by its proponents of whatever denomination. Yet if the encounter with cultural strangers did not persuade Algonquians to emulate the newcomers, neither did it convince most natives to shun them. There was much to be gained from an exchange of goods and information and, in some situations, from military alliances.[18]

Among Europeans, at the same time, word-of-mouth reports from voyagers and written accounts by leaders of expeditions or their publicists offered fascinating glimpses of northeastern North America's peoples and commercial potential. Still more important to some English visionaries was the region's suitability as a Puritan refuge. To promoters of New England colonization, land seemed abundant, resources bountiful, the native population sparse and malleable. But while England's published accounts often praised the Indians' physical stature and physiognomy and predicted their religious and social conversion, promotional literature also revealed the Europeans' scant regard for Indian culture, rights, and even, sometimes, their lives—a foreshadowing of the troubled encounters of the seventeenth century and beyond.[19]

The most traumatic episodes for American natives in their initial confrontations with Europeans must have been the frequent and unprovoked kidnappings that disrupted, if they did not terminate, the lives of many Indians and sowed distrust among the rest of the coastal population. In the early seventeenth century, several English expeditions seized New England natives to be guides and interpreters or to display as curiosities back home. As the jester in Shakespeare's *Tempest* quipped, English audiences would pay to see even a dead Indian. Captain Thomas Hunt's 1614 seizure of twenty or more Algonquians from Cape Cod, whom he then sold into slavery in Spain, was especially detrimental to early Indian-English harmony. Hunt was roundly denounced in England, and at least some of the captives were eventually freed, but he had done serious damage to the reputation of English explorers and early colonists.[20] Earlier, five Indians from the Maine coast were seized by Captain George Waymouth and carried to England.[21] After two years of exposure to the English language, two Abenakis—named in the surviving records as Skidowares and Tahando (or variations on those spellings)—played significant roles in the founding, and perhaps in the demise, of the first English outpost in New England, established in 1607 at the mouth of the Sagadahoc River (see chap. 1).

In 1616, Captain John Smith's map of the region changed the name of the Indian village of Accomack to New Plymouth and, with Prince Charles's imprimatur, recast the whole region—previously known, loosely, as northern Virginia or Norumbega—as New England.[22] A year or so later, a devastating epidemic swept coastal New England, killing natives by the tens of thousands, disrupting political and economic relations, and undermining the survivors' health and often their confidence in traditional deities. Earlier waves of infectious disease brought unwittingly by European explorers and fishermen may already have sharply reduced the native population in some parts of New England; the records are silent on this matter. On the ravages of disease in 1616–19, however, the evidence is appreciable. Colonial commentators were aghast at the loss of Indian life, although they usually interpreted the tragedy as God's means of clearing the land for His chosen people.[23]

Close on the heels of the epidemic came the first wave of English settlers. The "saints and strangers" who arrived in Cape Cod Bay in November 1620 and soon settled at New Plymouth would prove more persistent than their counterparts in 1607–8 at Sagadahoc but no less dependent on good relations with neighboring Algonquians for their physical survival and commercial success, especially during the colony's tenuous first decade. Plymouth's durability in its early years owed much to the friendly assistance of a survivor of the epidemic: Tisquantum, a Patuxet native better known to history as Squanto, who was in England when the plague hit his homeland.[24] Like Indian-white relations elsewhere, however, the equity of Plymouth's dealings with its native neighbors—from its founding in 1620 until its incorporation into Massachusetts Bay in 1691—is endlessly arguable. Although relations were fragile between the colony and the Narragansetts, especially in the 1640s and 1650s, and the Wampanoags, especially in the 1660s and 1670s, armed conflict was avoided until the outbreak of King Philip's War in 1675 (see chap. 2).[25]

Plymouth's modest success as an English refuge encouraged emulation. Beginning in 1629, a small English community at Naumkeag, renamed Salem, and its nearby coastal and river locations attracted thousands of migrants, mostly Puritans, from old England under the aegis of the Massachusetts Bay Company; in 1630, many of the new colonists settled on the Shawmut Peninsula and established Boston as the colony's capital. The natives near Massachusetts Bay, diminished by the plague and eager to acquire metal tools, cloth, and other useful goods, generally welcomed and often aided the newcomers. In the wake of a frightful smallpox epidemic throughout New England in 1633–34, which may have been as deadly as the earlier plague, land appeared to be plentiful enough for both the diminishing Algonquians and the proliferating English.[26]

As the Euroamerican population around Boston boomed during the peaceful and prosperous early 1630s, colonists fanned out to new locations, especially on the major bays, rivers, and tributaries, often on land that had recently been well populated by natives. By the end of the decade, centers of colonial political and territorial expansion had been established at Hartford, on the Connecticut River; Providence, at the head of Narragansett Bay; and New Haven, at the mouth of the Quinnipiac River, in the separate colony (until 1664) of New Haven. From the colonists' perspective, such expansion was desirable and, they assumed, beneficial to the surviving Indians, who would adopt English farming, herding, housing, law, and, especially, religion. Most Algonquians were less sanguine. They resented colonial rules, colonial courts, colonial punishments, colonial arrogance, and especially the inexorable colonial acquisition of land (see chap. 3).

Partly because of contrasting cultural assumptions about the very nature of property, partly because of differences in methods of land conveyance, and partly because of linguistic barriers, territorial transactions caused major misunderstandings between Puritans and Indians. Such was the case even in Rhode Island, where Roger Williams and his followers supposedly acquired their initial plots by gift from the Narragansetts and further parcels by what they construed as purchase or present.[27] Land ownership, conveyance, and especially political jurisdiction caused far greater furor in the Connecticut Valley, where the founding of several English towns in the mid-1630s unsettled existing patterns of Indian suzerainty and commercial relations among various Indian groups and with Dutch traders from New Netherland.[28] In 1637, New England's first substantial clash of arms between colonists and Indians—pitting the Pequots and Western Niantics against the Connecticut and Massachusetts colonies, assisted by the Mohegans, Narragansetts, and Eastern Niantics—followed closely on the Puritans' expansion into the Connecticut Valley. The precise causes and character of the Pequot-Puritan War have spurred a remarkably contentious historical debate (see chap. 4).[29]

Not debatable is the war's immense cost in Indian lives. Several hundred men, women, and children died in the Mystic Fort massacre, and many others, mostly warriors, were killed in subsequent battles or executed by their captors, either English or Algonquian. Even the Narragansetts, who assisted the colonial army, were appalled at the brutality of Euroamerican warfare: "it is too furious," they complained, "and slays too many men."

The total Pequot mortality, according to John Winthrop of Massachusetts, was eight to nine hundred. The English retained an appreciable but undetermined number of survivors, mostly women and children, as involuntary servants and shipped a dozen Pequot boys to the English colony at Providence Island in exchange for African slaves.[30]

At the Treaty of Hartford in 1638, the victorious colonies imposed harsh terms on the losers: surviving Pequots were assigned to the allies (mostly to the Mohegans and Narragansetts, a few to the colonists) and Pequot territory was appropriated (mostly by the English). The other Indian nations, aghast at the fury of English warfare and the severity of its aftermath, had serious concerns about their aggressive colonial neighbors, who in 1643 gave them additional and ample cause. To counter potential native coalitions and to promote Christian proselytizing among the Algonquians, the four Puritan jurisdictions—Massachusetts, Plymouth, Connecticut, and New Haven—created a Confederation of New England. Confident of its military potential, the New England colonies, except Rhode Island, dealt with most major Indian-Euroamerican issues for the next several decades through this intercolonial organization.[31]

By mid-century, the ethnocultural map of southern New England had radically altered. Except in the territory north of Massachusetts, traditional Indian territories were far smaller than before, and in some cases—most notably the Pequots'—had disappeared altogether, although the dispersed nation would later regroup.[32] Lands under colonial control had vastly expanded. Scores of Puritan villages and a few large towns now dotted the landscape, especially along the very coasts and waterways that the Indians had long inhabited, as the leading edge of English expansion pushed slowly westward, northward, and (in Maine) eastward. When Mohawks raids in the 1660s dispersed the Pocumtucks of the central Connecticut River Valley, still further lands opened for Euroamerican settlement. Colonists and Indians now encountered each other at scores of old and new villages, trading posts, and along the paths between settlements. Occasionally the encounters were acrimonious, even lethal, but more often they were amicable, if sometimes grudgingly so on both sides, as a flourishing commerce exchanged Algonquian game, furs, wampum, and land for English hoes, hatchets, bolts of cloth, and—even when colonial laws excluded them from legitimate trade—firearms and alcoholic beverages.[33] Increasingly, however, Algonquian resentments festered as the English accumulated population, power, and territorial control. In 1675, half a century of gathering grievances erupted in New England's most catastrophic war (see chap. 5).

King Philip's War[34] began in New England's southeastern corner but soon spread throughout the region and prompted fears of a general Indian uprising from Massachusetts to Virginia.[35] For more than a year, the fortunes of war vacillated, with the initial momentum favoring the Wampanoags. As colonial blunders pushed more Indian nations to join Philip's uprising, the field of battle broadened to include most of southern New England and eventually the coastal regions of New Hampshire and Maine. Not until the colonies mobilized all their resources, largely under Captain Benjamin Church's leadership, and enlisted the aid of Algonquian allies— mostly Christian Indians who sided with their religious brethren against their ethnic kin—did the pendulum of battle swing to the English side. Even then, the colonists needed a major assist from the Mohawks of northern New York, who refused to help the Wampanoag sachem and closed off his potential escape route to the northwest. The war ended soon after colonial troops captured Philip's wife and son and one of Church's Indian scouts killed the Wampanoag sachem with a well-aimed musket shot.[36]

The human carnage of the Puritan-Algonquian war was horrendous: more than four thousand Indian deaths from battle, disease, and exposure; probably two thousand voluntary exiles from New England; and perhaps as many as one thousand sold into slavery. English losses were also high. Approximately one tenth of New England's adult males died in combat; the total loss of Euroamerican lives, both military and civilian, exceeded six hundred. Many other colonists were wounded or captured, some never to be repatriated.

The war's material cost was also immense. There is no way to calculate the devastation to Indians' crops, livestock, wigwams, and other goods; surely their losses were catastrophic for most communities and nations. More measurable was the destruction of colonial property: at least a dozen towns so thoroughly destroyed that they were abandoned, some for many years, and dozens of others heavily damaged; elsewhere the toll of homes, barns, mills, crops, and livestock—an estimated eight thousand head of cattle alone—was huge. The Confederation of New England estimated the monetary loss at £100,000. Decades would pass before New England's Euroamerican community recovered its material health and recouped its population; the native community never did.[37]

The "Indian wars" did not end with King Philip's death. Whereas the war of 1675–76 primarily involved the Algonquians of southern New England and the colonies of Plymouth, Massachusetts, and Connecticut, by late 1676 it had spread northeastward to the territories that would soon become the separate jurisdictions of New Hampshire and, much later, Vermont and Maine. Throughout the late 1670s, while the southern portions of New England gradually recovered from King Philip's War, sporadic fighting along the northern fringe of colonial settlement pitted the Abenakis against colonial outposts (all under Massachusetts Bay jurisdiction) at Saco, Wells, Kittery, Dover, Exeter, and other coastal hamlets. To a large extent, these clashes stemmed from local issues, but after Philip's defeat, some of his followers took refuge among the northeastern bands and continued fighting until the spring of 1678. Again the human and material cost was high on both sides: several hundred more casualties and uncounted losses of homes and livestock.

In 1689, a new type of war enveloped New England. Heretofore its Indian-Euroamerican clashes had been internal affairs, reflecting tensions between certain Algonquian nations and English colonies. With the outbreak of King William's War (named for the reigning English king), New England became a pawn as well as a player in the imperial contest between England and France for control of North America, an ongoing struggle that ended only with the demise of New France in 1763. The Indians' involvement was so varied, complex, and changing as to defy brief summary, but for them, as for the colonists, armed conflict was frequent and often destructive of life and property. The prolific Puritan author and cleric Cotton Mather dubbed the decade from 1688 to 1697 "Decennium Luctuosum" (dolorous decade) for its relentless warfare. Many northern outposts that had barely recovered from the previous war suffered devastating raids, and the colonial response was equally baneful as the military forces destroyed Indian villages and fields. In one of the few episodes of the "Tedious war" that Mather could celebrate, Hannah Dustan (Dustin), who had been seized in an Abenaki raid on Haverhill, Massachusetts, in 1697, returned triumphant from New Hampshire with the scalps of ten of her captors.[38]

This was, of course, a highly atypical event, but it provides another example of mounting Indian casualties in the intermittent international warfare that began in 1689. Whether, by siding with the French, Algonquians were the colonists' enemies or, as were many Indians for a variety of individual reasons, Angloamerican allies, they perished in disproportionate numbers in battle or (like their colonial counterparts) from war-related epidemics. Largely as a result of those losses but partly too from other lethal diseases, from selling their lands to clear debt, and from migration to friendlier places to work and live, the New England Algonquian population shrank dramatically during the eighteenth century.[39]

MATHER'S *Decennium Luctuosum* and its brief account of Hannah Dustan's experience among her Abenaki captors exemplify two New England literary genres that featured and demonized Native Americans: narratives of Indian-Euroamerican warfare, and narratives, often autobiographical, of individual or group captivities among the Indians. Indians had occasionally appeared in other types of Puritan literature, of course, including promotional tracts, sermons, and epic poems. But beginning with contemporary accounts of the Pequot-Puritan War of 1637, and stimulated especially by King Philip's War, histories of wars and narratives of captivity became the dominant New England literary reflection of Native Americans.

Sometimes the two genres overlapped. Because most captivities occurred during wartime, they were integral to military history and served as poignant reminders of how civilians might suddenly be drawn into the action. The Pequot War narratives are cases in point: both Philip Vincent's *A True Relation of the late Battell fought in New-England, between the English and the Pequet Salvages* (1637) and John Underhill's *Newes from America* (1638) recounted the capture and release of two young women from Wethersfield, Connecticut.[40] Four decades later, most histories of the war against King Philip gave at least passing reference to the captivity of Euroamerican civilians and their sometimes gruesome fate.

But New England historians, most of them clergymen-scholars, were primarily concerned with explaining the causes of conflict and the Lord's omnipresent hand in the Puritans' eventual victory over "the devil's instruments." Although the two most notable histories of King Philip's War— Increase Mather's *Brief History of the War with the Indians in New-England* and William Hubbard's *The Present State of New-England, being a Narrative of the Troubles with the Indians*—differed in emphasis and sometimes in interpretation, both books generally excoriated Indians. Repeated clashes with the French and their Indian allies along New England's northern frontier during Queen Anne's War (1702–13) and, after a brief spell of peace, during "Governor Dummer's War" in the east and "Grey Lock's War" in the west (1723–27) were recounted by Samuel Penhallow, who took up Mather's and Hubbard's mantle as quasi-official chronicler of the colonists' perspective, in *The History of the Wars of New-England, with the Eastern Indians or, A Narrative of Their Continued Perfidy and Cruelty* (1727).[41]

The other war-spawned literary genre, the captivity narrative, came into its own with the publication in 1682 of Mary White Rowlandson's *The Soveraignty & Goodness of God . . . Being a Narrative of the Captivity and Restauration of Mrs. Mary Rowlandson*. Between her abduction from Lancaster, Massachusetts, in early 1676 and her release nearly three months later, Rowlandson had opportunity for an unusually close look at the

Wampanoag's side of King Philip's War; her narrative, written a few years later at the urging of friends, offered rare insights into native New England, although the book's popularity owed more to her message of religious hope and redemption than to its relatively benign ethnography. In any event, New England colonists—and readers in England as well—now had a story of adventure among the Indians.[42]

Rowlandson's phenomenal success (it was perhaps colonial New England's most popular publication) was never matched but often emulated. Among the most successful were the Reverend John Williams's *The Redeemed Captive Returning to Zion* (1707), which highlighted the fate of captives, especially his own family, in Canada, and John Gyles's *Memoirs of Odd Adventures, Strange Deliverances, etc.* (1736), which gave far more attention to Algonquian culture than did most captivity narratives. The number of captives taken by the Indians to replenish the group's population, which had been diminished by war and disease, to exchange for their own captured members, or to ransom for much-needed currency or goods grew rapidly during King George's War (1744–48) and (in English terminology) the "French and Indian War" (1754–63; known subsequently as the Seven Years War [1756–63] outside North America). The captivity genre flourished, and although the later narratives increasingly berated the French, Indians continued to bear the brunt of most authors' invective.[43] In combination with the war histories, captivity narratives reflected and contributed to New England colonials' mounting disaffection from Native Americans and their intensifying perception of the Indians as a separate, inferior race.

Some colonists had been deeply prejudiced from the outset. Much of Europe's sixteenth-century exploration literature portrayed Indians as monstrous creatures, sometimes bestial, an impression that apparently took deep root in some early settlers' minds. Although New England's subsequent literature often attempted to offset notions of Indians' physical inferiority—while, at the same time, deprecating their culture—and although Euroamerican leaders tried to thwart some colonists' efforts to abuse Indians and to ignore their rights to property and even to life, a substantial and apparently increasing portion of the colonial population had nothing but contempt for Native Americans. As Daniel Gookin complained during King Philip's War, many English colonists were "filled with animosity against all Indians without exception," a prejudice that grew more prevalent in the succeeding century's protracted warfare.[44]

Signs of that prejudice, especially its widespread association of Indians with satanic practices, emerged in the Salem witchcraft episode of 1692. The Reverend Samuel Parris thought his community's troubles began when "diabolical means were used, by the making of a cake by my Indian man"; and crucial to the government's prosecution of the first several "witches" was the confession of Tituba, an Indian slave from the West Indies who was married to Parris's John Indian.[45] Among the earliest accusers was seventeen-year-old Mercy Short, who two years before had been captured by Indians, and although she had soon been ransomed back to English society, Short bore severe psychological scars from witnessing the murder of her parents and three siblings. Not surprisingly, Mercy Short imagined the devil to be of "an Indian colour" and had spectral visits from Indian chiefs. Throughout the Salem witchcraft proceedings, many parties to the frenzy—accusers, victims, judges—connected Indian devil-worship with the sins of the accused, either as assumed facts or as insidious metaphors.[46] A presumed connection between Indians and Satan's henchmen that had heretofore played a minor role in Puritan thought was now magnified and widely articulated (see chap. 6). In the year of the Salem trials, for example, Cotton Mather inveighed against "those Tawny Pagans, than which there are not worse Divels Incarnate upon Earth!"[47] Demonization of the Algonquians long persisted as a staple of Euro-american attitudes.

A THIRD NEW ENGLAND literary genre that portrayed Indian-Euroamerican encounters was missionary writing—tracts, translations, and the gospel—published in the second half of the seventeenth century and beyond. Beginning in the 1640s, John Eliot, Thomas Mayhew, Jr., and several other colonial spokesmen launched a promotional campaign to raise funds in England and consciences in New England to bolster the proselytizing program that had ostensibly been a major goal of Puritan colonization. The common thread in the dozen or so early pamphlets was, as a typical title proclaimed, "the Progress of the Gospel amongst the Indians in New-England." When the number of converts grew fairly impressively in the 1650s and 1660s, Eliot increasingly directed his publications at the Indians themselves, mostly through phonetic translations from English to Algonquian (Massachusetts dialect) of selected religious texts. With essential help from Cochenoe, a Long Island native captured in the Pequot War, who for several years served Eliot as teacher and interpreter, and from James Printer, Job Nesutan, and other bilingual Algonquians employed at the Cambridge press, Eliot had translated and published an Algonquian version of the whole King James Bible by 1663. During the next decade he produced catechisms, psalters, devotional tracts, and books of language instruction. Most of the texts were only in Algonquian; some were in both Algonquian and English. By the time Eliot died in 1690, he and his collaborators had issued more than a score of books, including a revised edition of the Bible in 1685, for distribution to actual or potential Algonquian converts.[48]

Despite the missionary program's severe curtailment after King Philip's War, the publishing program continued, fueled by contributions from England and the determination of a few zealous preachers, both English and Algonquian. They issued almost as many missionary titles after 1690 as before that date, most of them in translations by John Cotton, Jr., or Samuel Danforth. The last New England Indian tract intended for Algonquians appeared in 1720.

By that time, many Algonquians were writing too, either in English or in their own language, using the phonetic system devised jointly by colonial and native linguists. Examples of Algonquian writings are now scarce, for their purposes were largely local and practical—deeds of sale and other commercial transactions. More abundant are English-language works by Indian authors, especially the missionary writings of Samson Occom and other Christian Indians.[49] For most of the colonial era, however, the missionaries' principal means of communication remained oral/aural, while the transition to a reliance on reading/writing only gradually emerged.[50]

In the first half-century of Euroamerican settlement, missionaries persuaded more than two thousand Algonquians to become at least nominal Christians, although many of them may have retained substantial portions of their traditional beliefs. From the late 1640s, when Thomas Mayhew, Jr., on Martha's Vineyard (see chap. 7) and John Eliot in eastern Massachusetts (see chap. 8) launched their campaigns to convert New England's natives, until the outbreak of King Philip's War in 1675, perhaps one fourth of all Indians in southern New England adopted, in whole or in part, Puritan precepts and practices, and scores of converts became full church members. Some also became preachers to their fellow Indians or rulers within the fourteen Praying Towns that Eliot and his fellow missionaries, aided by early Algonquian converts, established before 1675 as centers of Christian living. The towns' principal purpose was to isolate neophytes from two major obstacles to effective proselytizing: discouragement from Indians who disapproved of Christian beliefs and customs—many of the converts' friends, relatives, political and religious leaders; and corruption by colonial reprobates, especially on the fringes of settlement, whose example of "unChristian" behavior undermined the missionaries' message. In most Praying Towns, converts adopted English customs of housing, agriculture, craftsmanship, and education as well as worship.[51]

The colonists' bloody conquest of the Algonquians in 1676 owed much to the timely assistance of Christian Indians, yet in the war's aftermath, the Puritans' missionary program was bitterly opposed by disillusioned Indians and disgruntled Euroamericans. Except for the few Indian converts whose faith withstood the frightful war against their ethnic kin, the natives no longer admired or trusted the colonists. The missionary message usually fell on deaf ears. Yet efforts to convert Algonquians did not terminate with the war of 1675, as is often assumed. Although few Christian Indian communities survived the rapid expansion of the colonial population and the post-war resentment against Indians, Christian or not, the actual number of Indian congregations in the region, including the offshore islands, remained at fifteen to seventeen until 1760, and the number of Euroamerican missions was consistently a few more than that. On the other hand, the number of practicing Indian ministers declined from highs of about forty or more in 1674 and again in 1698 to fewer than ten after 1725, although in every year until at least 1760 several Indian preachers served the missionary cause.[52]

As missionary fervor in established colonial areas waned in response to the shrinking native population and rising Euroamerican prejudice, New England's proselytizers increasingly gravitated toward the region's outer edges and beyond (see chap. 9). The most notable of the eighteenth-century missionary outposts were at Lebanon, Connecticut, and Stockbridge, Massachusetts. At the former, the Reverend Eleazar Wheelock offered a blend of religious indoctrination and social discipline that appealed to few Indian students; only a handful were together in his mission school at any one time. Yet before Wheelock forsook his role as teacher-missionary to assume the presidency of Dartmouth College (ostensibly an institution to educate Indians but in fact overwhelmingly for Euroamerican youths), he had trained several successful Indian preachers, most notably the Mohegan Samson Occom. Occom's eventual estrangement from Wheelock's college weakened that already fragile missionary enterprise.[53]

By then, the religious fervor of New England's Great Awakening had brought many natives into the Christian fold, especially into evangelical denominations. Indians within communities that had long since embraced Christianity—Natick, for example—remained largely unaffected by the religious clamor. Elsewhere—among the Mohegans and Pequots of Connecticut and the Narragansetts of Rhode Island, for example—excitement ran high, conversions were numerous, and the shared experience enhanced community identity and cohesion. Among the most effective preachers serving the Indians were several Algonquian ministers, some of them recent converts themselves, including Occom.[54]

While religion provided employment for a few Indians in eighteenth-century southern New England, the vast majority performed menial labor in colonial households and enterprises. As Indians' landholdings through-out New England drastically diminished, thereby reducing the opportunities to fish and hunt and raise crops, and as traditional Indian skills eroded from lack of practice and able instruction, many Algonquians—men and women alike—became voluntary or involuntary servants, even slaves, in the burgeoning colonial economy. Some Indians were thrown into servitude as war captives, but many others were forced to it by poverty or by legal action for debt or other infractions of Angloamerican law. In some instances Indian laborers were also the objects of Christian proselytizing, which meshed their economic and religious statuses in the emerging new world order. Although far too little is known about this aspect of the story, it has been well documented for eighteenth-century Rhode Island (see chap. 10).[55]

The machinations that deprived some Indians of their labor or free-dom were used in other circumstances to dispossess them of their land. In 1670, Roger Williams had complained of the colonists' "depraved Appetite after . . . great Portions of Land," an appetite not sated a century later.[56] Even the remote western Massachusetts missionary center at Stockbridge fell victim to Euroamerican land-hunger. That community's inexorable metamorphosis from an Indian mission to a vast Williams family (no relation to Roger Williams) estate illustrates with disturbing clarity the on-going displacement of New England natives, even in areas that were initially designated as Christian Indian enclaves (see chap. 11).

FEW INDIANS in Britain's North American colonies were keen partisans of either side in the empire's civil war of the 1770s and early 1780s. In New England, most Christian Indians favored the American cause, to which the region's Euroamerican clergymen were overwhelmingly committed. On the other hand, many Algonquian traditionalists, smarting from abuse by colonial frontiersmen and indifference by colonial governments, hoped for a British victory to preserve the imperial government's slightly more benign policies for Native Americans. Most Algonquians probably pre-ferred completely to avoid an Angloamerican clash that held no long-run advantages for Indians, regardless of the military outcome.

Given the tensions that had often characterized New England's Indian-white encounters, the extent of Algonquian participation and sacrifice on the rebel side is surprising. Stockbridge Indians, for example, formed a pro-American company in 1775, and others, individually, enlisted in the Provincial army. In addition to the usual soldiers' duties, many Stockbridge Indians were emissaries, assigned by the Americans to urge other Indian groups to remain neutral or join the rebels. As the war spread, Stockbridge contingents fought on several fronts: at Valcour Bay on Lake Champlain, at White Plains in southern New York, and, disastrously, at Kings Bridge on the Harlem River. More than thirty Stockbridge volunteers joined General John Sullivan's invasion of Iroquois country. Other southern New England Indian communities—including the Pequots, Mohegans, Mashpees, and Naticks—contributed comparably high portions of their able-bodied men to the Revolutionary forces.[57]

Many Eastern Abenakis, most of them pro-French and pro-Catholic if not themselves Catholics, favored the American insurgents—despite abundant grievances against them—because America was allied with France and because Britain's recent policies in Canada were anti-Catholic. The alignment was, then, more anti-English than pro-Yankee. Other Eastern Abenakis moved north, out of harm's way, or aided the British. A somewhat different pattern obtained among Western Abenakis. Most were probably neutral, but some fought on the American side (several held commissions from Congress), and a substantial number—most of them recent migrants to Canada from northern New England—served with the British forces.[58]

Algonquians who supported the American cause suffered extremely heavy losses. Stockbridge fatalities numbered perhaps thirty or more. Most of Natick's participants died in service or soon after from war-related wounds or diseases. Approximately half of the Pequots who went off to war never returned, and Mohegan losses were similarly high. Of twenty-six Mashpee soldiers, "all but one," according to a nineteenth-century account, "fell martyr . . . in the struggle of Independence." Abenaki losses, largely unrecorded, must have been substantial on both the American and British sides.[59]

New England Indians fared poorly in the aftermath of the American victory, too, no matter which side, if either, they had aided in the conflict. Euroamerican veterans clamored for frontier territory as a reward for their services, and the cash-strapped new American governments generally acquiesced. With Algonquian populations diminished by wartime deaths and migrations out of the region, the survivors were under intense pressure to sell their land; those who did not sell often lost their property to squatters anyway. And as more territory fell into Euroamerican hands, more Algonquians, especially Abenakis, migrated to upstate New York, where they were usually welcomed by the Iroquois, or to Canada, where they often joined kinfolk who had preceded them to havens in the St. Lawrence Valley. Further complicating the lives of Western and Eastern Abenakis was the arbitrary (from an ethnic standpoint) international boundary that after 1783 ostensibly divided them into Canadian and American components—a boundary that Algonquians usually ignored, as they continued to move back and forth in response to their own economic and familial needs.[60]

BY THE END of the eighteenth century, a distinctly American literature was emerging, largely in New England. Here and there in the literary out-pouring that would eventually be dubbed "the flowering of New England" Native Americans were acknowledged as a major force in New England's and the nation's past and—by a few authors—as a contemporary presence as well. Not that Euroamerican authors often wrote with knowledge or compassion about Indians; quite the contrary. With few exceptions, most notably Henry David Thoreau, New England's Euroamericans romanti-cized the region's Indians in the early years of encounter, disapproved of their subsequent rejection of Euroamerican culture and Christianity, and finally deplored the largely impoverished remnant of the present day. Many writers of fiction and supposed nonfiction mixed ethnic prejudice with demographic error in sentimental laments for "the vanishing Indian."

The Reverend Timothy Dwight, soon to be president of Yale, epito-mized prevailing attitudes. His historical poem about the war of 1637, "Greenfield Hill" (1794), mixed excoriation with, to a lesser extent, glori-fication of seventeenth-century Pequots; later, Dwight's *Travels in New England and New York* (1821–22) complained that in his time "the whole body of these Indians are a poor, degraded, miserable race of beings. The former, proud heroic spirit of the Pequot . . . is shrunk into the tameness and torpor of reasoning brutism. All the vice of the original is left. All its energy has vanished."[61]

The Pequots, usually as tragic victims, were a favorite character type for New England authors, and the captivity experience that had been so cen-tral to seventeenth-and eighteenth-century portrayals of Algonquians was a popular theme. Probably the most famous literary invocation of the Pequots is Herman Melville's name for Ahab's ill-fated ship (in its alterna-tive spelling "Pequod"), although several less notable authors accorded the Pequots greater prominence.[62] Catharine Maria Sedgwick's *Hope Leslie: or, Early Times in Massachusetts* (1827) is a case in point. In defiance of popu-lar literary conventions, her novel featured not only the standard fare of captivities, torture, and executions but also a romance between a Pequot woman and a colonial man and the marriage of a Pequot man with a colo-nial woman. In *Hope Leslie,* however, neither pairing proves fortunate, as Sedgwick succumbed to standard Euroamerican assumptions about the Indians' inevitable, irreversible savagery.[63]

Those assumptions were prevalent but not universal. Lydia Maria Child was not wholly free of her era's biases, but her *Hobomok* (1824) had more in common with Thoreau's generally supportive views of New England Indians than with Dwight's contempt. Many years later, Child's "Appeal for the Indians" (1868) would be a landmark of Indian rights advocacy. As a literary scholar recently proposed, it was "about as liberal . . . as could be expected of any white American of her background and generation."[64] Few other New England authors of any literary genre matched Child's level of understanding and empathy, but several, including the Vermont poet and essayist James Elliot, avoided their era's most blatant biases (see chap. 12). So too, to varying degrees, did some authors who were not themselves from New England but who set one or more of their stories in the area and featured its native population. James Fenimore Cooper, from upstate New York, placed most of his novels in his own region or farther west; an exception was his *The Wept of Wish-ton Wish* (1829), set in the Connecticut Valley in the era of King Philip's War. Later in the century, New Jersey author Edward S. Ellis featured as the hero of his shallow but popular dime novel *Seth Jones; or, The Captive of the Frontier* (1860) a New Hampshire man who, predictably in that time and genre, described Indians with scathing epithets.[65]

Even Thoreau, that "most Indian-like of classic American authors," whose dying words were reputed to have been "moose" and "Indians," could not entirely shake his era's belief in the Indians' innate savagism. As the principal authority on this aspect of Thoreau's life concludes, "Indians, to the savagist, might be noble or base, but they were always simple hunters who were not Christian and not civilized."[66] Still, as Thoreau demonstrated in his retelling of the Hannah Dustan captivity narrative, he could move beyond Child's relatively benign ambiguity. Largely as a result of extended encounters with Penobscot guides in the Maine woods, Thoreau came to believe deeply that American Indians were central to a full understanding of American life, and had he lived several years longer, he would probably have fulfilled his intention to write a book about Native Americans. Thoreau's work as a whole, especially his later writings, reflects a minor trend in early nineteenth-century New England literature about Native Americans that relied on personal knowledge of a few Indians and attempted to record their perspective as well as—or instead of—white society's stereotypes.[67] Subsequent writings about Native Americans in a New England context were, however, sparse; the focus of Eastern literary attention shifted increasingly westward.

THE NINETEENTH CENTURY brought remarkable demographic and social transformations to New England's Euroamerican and Indian populations. The region's rapid industrialization and the concomitant growth in its population from European, especially Irish, immigration is a familiar story. Well known too is the emergence of New Englanders on the national stage as political, intellectual, and social leaders, sometimes with important ramifications for Indians in other parts of the country (see chap. 13).[68]

Less familiar are the changes in Indian communities that had begun a century and a half earlier with the devastation of King Philip's War and accelerated in the international conflicts of the next century. With Algonquians often participating as allies or enemies of the New England colonies in the wars of 1675 to 1783, mortality, generation upon generation, was especially heavy among adult males, which over time created Indian communities with disproportionate numbers of adult women. Almost simultaneously, African Americans, predominantly males, were migrating into New England in increasing numbers. White prejudice against both peoples encouraged what the gender disparities suggested: marriages between Algonquian women and African American men, although a smaller but significant number of white men also married into Indian communities.[69]

One widespread result of this biological and cultural mixing was the emergence of Algonquian enclaves in which some members identified themselves as Indian, some as African American, a few as white, and an increasing number as mixed blood and mixed culture. By the 1830s, according to a contemporaneous report, only seven of nearly two hundred Narragansetts at the Charlestown, Rhode Island, reservation were "full-blood" Indians, all of them elderly women. Roughly similar estimates were reported for other Algonquian communities in southern New England. Even if those figures were exaggerated by the white reporters' prejudice and the innate imprecision of such data gathering, the general point remains valid: most of New England's Indian communities were now racially, ethnically, and culturally diverse, with varying implications for their subsequent characteristics and survival. In an era in which notions of "race" were perhaps most self-conscious and charged with prejudice (foreshadowed by the Massachusetts law of 1786 that prohibited Indian-white marriages), this development in Native American communities had profound implications for both internal dynamics and external treatment.[70]

Most of New England's multicultural communities remained emphatically Indian throughout the first half of the nineteenth century and often beyond. In keeping with Algonquian traditions of tolerance and assimilation, the outsiders (often called "foreigners") were generally accepted and their children almost always wholly so, even though a "foreign" newcomer was rarely accorded full rights of land ownership. Yet matters of identity sometimes intervened. Families or individuals who chose to emphasize their African American or Euroamerican affinities often migrated out of the reservation, since elsewhere opportunities for land ownership were usually greater and paternalistic values more widely accepted. Other non-Indian families and individuals remained in the Indian community and worked subtle changes on its collective character. For example, as African American men became increasingly numerous and prominent in some Indian enclaves, they undercut earlier customs of female leadership and land proprietorship, and they sometimes also accelerated the shift of land ownership from communal to individual. In some instances, intracommunity tensions stemmed from male Indians' resentment of African American or Euroamerican men who married into the reservation or Indian enclave in a predominantly Euroamerican town. In retaliation, "foreign" members of the Indian community and their mixed-blood children might be denied full tribal membership. Some of those outsiders moved away, some acceded to traditional patterns of ownership and leadership, while others remained in the Indian communities and helped to modify traditional ways. Whatever the individual actions, Indian communal lands were often further reduced as some members of the community opted to sell lands over which they had legal control. Still, remnants of many Algonquian nations clung tenaciously to their original homelands, however constricted. Throughout the region, native peoples and native cultures persisted.[71]

The Mashpee community on Cape Cod is a prime example of the New England Algonquians' altered situation. Its numbers had long hovered around three hundred fifty individuals, most of them with Indian ancestry but not necessarily Mashpee. Immigrants from neighboring Indian nations had sought refuge on the Cape after King Philip's War in the 1670s; nearly a century later, in 1763, when the Massachusetts government granted substantial "tribal" autonomy to the community, other Indians—Narragansetts, Mohegans, even Montauks from Long Island—were attracted to the Mashpee reservation. By the nineteenth century, the town's non-Indians included a sizable minority of African Americans and people of mixed ancestry; it also included some whites, even a few Hessian veterans from the American Revolution, as well as one Mexican, and an East Indian from Bombay.[72]

During the 1830s, New England's Euroamericans and Indians alike, though usually harboring differing sentiments, fixed their attention on the Mashpees' forceful protest for greater autonomy (see chap. 14). In keeping with nineteenth-century trends toward ethnic and cultural variety within Algonquian communities, the leading figure in that revolt against outside authority was William Apess, a remarkable Pequot and Christian preacher whose own heritage combined multiple ethnic and cultural strands (see chap. 15).

Encounters between Euroamericans and Indians in New England did not, of course, end in the middle of the nineteenth century, as do the essays in this book, but in many respects they had reached a temporary plateau. Most Algonquians lived in long-established reservations or, with varying degrees of autonomy, in enclaves within Euroamerican towns, while some Indians or individuals of part-Indian ancestry merged with the general population. The vastly greater Euroamerican population largely ignored the Indian communities; in southern and eastern New England especially, booming industry, lucrative markets, and expanding (male) political opportunities kept the Euroamericans' eyes on their own hoped-for prizes. Indians were left to their own devices. In northern New England, they often took jobs in the fur trade (on the decline), lumbering, fishing, or guiding (on the incline); in southern New England, especially on Nantucket island, many men labored in the whaling industry. But with very few exceptions, Indians were unwelcome in the factories or at the ballot box. Prosperity and democracy passed by the region's marginalized men and women.[73] At no time since the arrival of the first Europeans in New England had the two peoples been so separate or so unequal in territory, resources, and power.

But major changes would come later in the nineteenth century, as state governments sought to dismantle Indian reservations by distributing the land to individuals and granting them citizenship, including the political franchise. The Massachusetts Indian Enfranchisements Act of 1869, for example, declared "Indians and people of color, heretofore known and called Indians," to be full-fledged citizens of the commonwealth. This post–Civil War effort by the government to extend democratic rights, especially to African Americans but also to Native Americans, included not only the political franchise but also the right to acquire and alienate real estate. Many Indian communities welcomed such changes as steps toward their integration into mainstream America; others resisted innovations that threatened tribal autonomy, cohesion, and traditional social organization.[74]

The Massachusetts act foreshadowed the federal government's Dawes Severalty Act of 1887, named for Senator Henry L. Dawes of Massachusetts, and reflected a national trend toward disbanding Indian nations and promoting individual land ownership. Yet despite the prominence of Dawes and other New Englanders in the formation of United States Indian policy from the Revolutionary era onwards, national policies rarely had much direct impact on New England. Federal and state authorities assumed the region's Indian nations to have long since expired or succumbed to state control. Accordingly, the New England states continued to fashion laws and regulations as they saw fit, which were, almost invariably, to the advantage of the Euroamerican majority.[75]

In the twentieth century, national decisions had greater impact, though rarely to the extent that they were felt in other parts of the nation. By the Indian Citizenship Act of 1924, Native Americans throughout New England and elsewhere in the United States acquired full national membership; legislation and administrative policies of the New Deal, especially the Indian Reorganization Act of 1934, reversed the objectives of the Dawes Act by promoting the preservation of Indian traditions and collective communities; and, after a partial reversion in national priorities from about 1947 to the 1960s, the federal government gave renewed encouragement to Indian community revival and cultural persistence.[76] In recent decades, federal courts have—with some notable exceptions—ruled favorably on Indian suits to recapture territory illegally taken from the tribes over the centuries and to reestablish economic independence. Here again, the impact of national policy has been felt more forcefully in other parts of the nation, but New England has not been entirely unaffected, especially in the last quarter of the twentieth century.[77]

The resurgence of tribal identity and pride that has been exhibited during those years by the Wampanoags, Narragansetts, Nipmucs, Penobscots, and others has helped to enlighten non-Indians about the region's natives, past and present. And as the Mashantucket Pequots have demonstrated remarkably, New England's Native Americans are determined not only to preserve their culture, their territory, and their autonomy but, wherever possible, to generate prosperity.[78] Although vast areas of inequality remain between Indian and non-Indian communities in wealth, health, and political influence, and although old prejudices persist, the real progress of some tribes gives hope for further gains. So too does the resurgence of scholarly interest in New England's Indian-white encounters, which this collection of essays seeks to promote and enhance.

Notes

1. I am reversing the usual formula for anthology introductions, in which the book's disparate chapters are summarized while their historical context is left largely unstated. Instead, I present a synthesis of recent scholarship on Indian-white relations in New England *minus* explicit coverage of the topics addressed by the fifteen contributors. Their essays—all of them recently published or updated—need no summaries, yet readers unfamiliar with the two and a half centuries of Indian-white

encounters addressed by this book may benefit from a historical and literary survey. Some readers may profit too from the suggested readings on numerous topics that made early New England a dynamic, if often disturbing, stage for intercultural encounters. The most appropriate point in the contextual overview to read each of the fifteen essays in this anthology is indicated by a parenthetical reminder.

The author gratefully acknowledges the improvements in this essay suggested by James Axtell, Robert S. Grumet, Daniel R. Mandell, Neal Salisbury, William S. Simmons, and Virginia M. Vaughan.

2. For the early history of native New England, see esp. Bruce G. Trigger, ed., *Northeast*, vol. 15 of *Handbook of North American Indians*, gen. ed. William C. Sturtevant (Washington, D.C.: Smithsonian Institution, 1978); Dean R. Snow, *The Archeology of New England* (New York: Academic Press, 1980); and Bruce G. Trigger and Wilcomb E. Washburn, eds., *The Cambridge History of the Native People of the Americas*, vol. 1: *North America* (New York: Cambridge University Press, 1997). A concise summary of pre-contact North America is Brian Fagan's "The First Americans," in *Encyclopedia of the North American Colonies*, ed. Jacob E. Cooke, 3 vols. (New York: Scribner's, 1993), 1:15–45; and, more recently, Neal Salisbury's, "The Indians' Old World: Native Americans and the Coming of Europeans," *William and Mary Quarterly*, 3d ser. 53 (1996): 435–58. Much of the region covered by this volume is examined in Dena F. Dincauze's "A Capsule Prehistory of Southern New England," in *The Pequots in Southern New England: The Fall and Rise of an American Indian Nation*, ed. Laurence M. Hauptman and James D. Wherry (Norman: University of Oklahoma Press, 1990), pp. 19–32. A comprehensive guide to books and articles published through 1981 is Neal Salisbury's *The Indians of New England: A Critical Bibliography* (Bloomington: Indiana University Press for the Newberry Library, 1982); for titles published between 1982 and 1992, see the "Selected Bibliography of Algonkian Peoples in New England," in *Algonkians of New England: Past and Present*, Dublin Seminar for New England Folklife, Annual Proceedings 1991, ed. Peter Benes (Boston: Boston University, 1993), pp. 144–51.

3. Estimates of the aboriginal population of New England have varied widely in the past few decades. Higher figures for the pre-contact population are now generally accepted. See Sherburne Cook, *The Indian Population of New England in the Seventeenth Century* (Berkeley: University of California Press, 1976); Trigger, *Northeast*, p. 169; Snow, *Archeology of New England*, pp. 31–42; Neal Salisbury, *Manitou and Providence: Indians, Europeans, and the Making of New England, 1500–1643* (New York: Oxford University Press, 1982), pp. 22–30; and Kathleen J. Bragdon, *Native People of Southern New England, 1500–1650* (Norman: University of Oklahoma Press, 1996), pp. 25–26.

4. Recent important integrations of historical and archeological evidence are Bragdon's *Native People*; William A. Haviland and Marjory W. Power's *The Original Vermonters: Native Inhabitants Past and Present* (Hanover, N.H.: University Press of New England, 1981); and Robert S. Grumet's *Historic Contact: Indian People and Colonists in Today's Northeastern United States in the Sixteenth through Eighteenth Centuries* (Norman: University of Oklahoma Press, 1995), esp. pt. 2. See also Bruce G.

Trigger, "American Archeology as Native History: A Review Essay," *William and Mary Quarterly,* 3d ser. 40 (1983): 413–52. Anthropologists disagree whether "bands," "tribe," or some other term best describes the region's pre-contact Indian groups.

5. On Algonquian food consumption, see M. K. Bennett, "The Food Economy of the New England Indians, 1605–1675," *Journal of Political Economy* 58 (1955): 369–97; and—more recent and from a different perspective—Barrie Kavasch's "Native Food of New England," in *Enduring Traditions: The Native Peoples of New England,* ed. Laurie Weinstein (Westport, Conn.: Bergin and Garvey, 1994). Indian and colonial land usages are compared in Peter A. Thomas's "Cultural Subsistence Strategies and Land Use as Factors for Understanding Indian-White Relations in New England," *Ethnohistory* 23 (1976): 1–18.

6. For pre-contact and early post-contact native society, see esp. Bragdon, *Native People;* Howard S. Russell, *Indian New England before the Mayflower* (Hanover, N.H.: University Press of New England, 1980); and the relevant essays in *History of Indian-White Relations,* ed. Wilcomb E. Washburn, vol. 4 of *Handbook of North American Indians* (Washington, D.C., 1988), and Trigger, *Northeast.* Most early English writers designated the major Indian groups as "nations"; the widespread shift to "tribe" occurred in the third quarter of the eighteenth century, when Angloamericans increasingly challenged Indian sovereignty in theory and fact. The Federal Constitution of 1787 referred to "tribes," as did almost all government documents thereafter. Most historians and many anthropologists have applied "tribe" retroactively to the pre-Revolutionary era, as the essays in this volume attest.

7. The most recent brief description of Algonquian leaders is Bragdon's *Native People,* pp. 25–26. On the role of Indian women, see Robert S. Grumet, "Sunksquaws, Shamans, and Tradeswomen: Middle Atlantic Coastal Algonkian Women during the 17th and 18th Centuries," in *Women and Colonization: Anthropological Perspectives,* ed. Mona Etienne and Eleanor Burke Leacock (New York: Praeger, 1980), pp. 43–62; and Ann Marie Plane, "Putting a Face on Colonization: Factionalism and Gender Politics in the Life History of Awashunkes, the 'Squaw Sachem' of Sconet," in *Northeastern Indian Lives, 1632–1816,* ed. Robert S. Grumet (Amherst: University of Massachusetts Press, 1996), pp. 140–65.

8. Daniel Gookin, *Historical Collections of the Indians in New England* (Boston: Belknap and Hall, 1792; reprinted, New York: Arno Press, 1972), p. 14.

9. Roger Williams, *Key into the Language of America* (1643), ed. John J. Teunissen and Evelyn J. Hinz (Detroit: Wayne State University Press, 1973), pp. 203, 115; and my edition of William Wood's *New England's Prospect* (1634) (Amherst: University of Massachusetts Press, 1977), p. 99. Williams was more knowledgeable than Wood, yet his observations were confined almost wholly to the Narragansetts. There were surely variations among and within Indian nations in New England, much as there were among and within European nations, including England.

10. A thorough analysis of Algonquian legal concepts and practices has yet to be published, but important implications emerge from John Phillip Reid's *A Law of Blood: The Primitive Law of the Cherokee Nations* (New York: New York University Press, 1970). An extensive literature examines the treatment of Algonquians in Euroamerican jurisprudence. See, e.g., Yasahide Kawashima, *Puritan Justice and the In-*

dian: White Man's Law in Massachusetts, 1630–1763 (Middletown, Conn.: Wesleyan University Press, 1986), and "The Pilgrims and the Wampanoag Indians, 1620–1691: Legal Encounters," *Oklahoma City University Law Review* 23 (1998): 115–31; Lyle Koehler, "Red-White Power Relations and Justice in the Courts of Seventeenth-Century New England," *American Indian Culture and Research Journal* 3:4 (1979): 1–31; Kathleen Bragdon, "Crime and Punishment among the Indians of Massachusetts, 1675–1750," *Ethnohistory* 28 (1981): 23–32; and James Warren Springer, "American Indians and the Law of Real Property in Colonial New England," *American Journal of Legal History* 30 (1986): 25–58.

11. Williams, *Key into the Language,* p. 193.

12. Williams, *Key into the Language,* p. 191.

13. Important modern studies of Algonquian religion include William S. Simmons's *Cautantowwit's House: An Indian Burial Ground on the Island of Conanicut in Narragansett Bay* (Providence: Brown University Press, 1970), *The Spirit of the New England Tribes: Indian History and Folklore, 1620–1984* (Hanover, N.H.: University Press of New England, 1986), and "Southern New England Shamanism: An Ethnographic Reconstruction," *Papers of the Seventh Algonquian Conference, 1975,* ed. William Cowan (Ottawa: Carleton University, 1978), pp. 190–97; Frank Shuffleton's "Indian Devils and Pilgrim Fathers: Squanto, Hobomok, and the English Conception of Indian Religion," *New England Quarterly* 49 (1976): 108–16; and Bragdon's *Native People,* chaps. 8–9. The powwow's role is summarized in Henry Warner Bowden's *American Indians and Christian Missions: Studies in Cultural Conflict* (Chicago: University of Chicago Press, 1981), pp. 104–5; and, more recently and extensively, in Bragdon's *Native People,* chap. 9.

14. The best early colonial description of Algonquian leisure activities is found in Wood's *New England's Prospect,* pp. 103–5. See also Williams, *Key into the Language,* pp. 229–32. Russell (*Indian New England,* pp. 111–15) offers a brief modern commentary.

15. A lively debate concerning the similarities of and differences between Indian and European warfare often focuses on New England. Among the relevant works are Francis Jennings's *The Invasion of America: Indians, Colonialism, and the Cant of Conquest* (Chapel Hill: University of North Carolina Press for the Institute of Early American History and Culture, 1975); Patrick Malone's *The Skulking Way of War: Technology and Tactics among the New England Indians* (Baltimore: Johns Hopkins University Press, 1991); and Adam J. Hirsch's "The Collision of Military Cultures in Seventeenth-Century New England," *Journal of American History* 64 (1988): 1187–212. Regarding civilian casualties: during the Pequot War (1636–37), Indians killed some colonial women and children in the Connecticut Valley; English forces killed many Indian women and children at the Mystic Fort massacre. In King Philip's War (1675–76), scores of women and children were killed on each side. After both wars, many captured Indian women and children were forced into servitude or (by sale out of the colony) into slavery. During both wars, and especially later wars, some captured English men, women, and children were held for ransom, servitude, torture, or adoption.

16. Malone, *Skulking Way of War,* pp. 9–10; Williams, *Key into the Language,* p.

237. The relative ferocity of Indian and English warfare and the separate but integral issue of European warfare's varieties and applications of cruelty continue to be intensely debated. See, e.g., Jennings, *Invasion of America,* esp. chap. 9; Hirsch, "Collision of Military Cultures"; James Drake, "Restraining Atrocity: The Conduct of King Philip's War," *New England Quarterly* 70 (1997): 33–56; Jill Lepore, *The Name of War: King Philip's War and the Origins of American Identity* (New York: Alfred A. Knopf, 1998); and Ronald Dale Karr, "'Why Should You Be So Furious?': The Violence of the Pequot War," *Journal of American History* 85 (1998): 876–909.

17. The evidence on Norse voyagers to northern North America is concisely summarized by Thomas Howatt McGovern, in Cooke's *Encyclopedia of the North American Colonies,* 1:105–11. For other possible pre-Columbian contacts, see Samuel Eliot Morison, *The European Discovery of America: The Northern Voyages,* A.D. 500–1600 (New York: Oxford University Press, 1971); David B. Quinn, *North America from Earliest Discovery to First Settlements: The Norse Voyages to 1612* (New York: Harper & Row, 1977); and, most recently, Kirsten A. Seaver, *The Frozen Echo: Greenland and the Exploration of North America, ca.* A.D. 1000–1500 (Stanford: Stanford University Press, 1996), which revises several earlier assumptions. For claims of African contact with the Americas before 1492, see Ivan Van Sertima, *They Came before Columbus* (New York: Random House, 1976); and Jack D. Forbes, *Black Africans and Native Americans: Color, Race and Caste in the Evolution of Red-Black Peoples* (Oxford: Basil Blackwell, 1988). Skeptical responses to such claims include Nigel Davies's *Voyagers to the New World: Fact or Fantasy?* (Albuquerque: University of New Mexico Press, 1979); and Bernard Ortiz de Montellano, Gabriel Haslip-Viera, and Warren Barbour's "They Were NOT Here before Columbus: Afrocentric Hyperdiffusionism in the 1990s," *Ethnohistory* 44 (1997): 199–234.

18. In the absence of written native sources for the early contact period, conclusions about their reactions to Europeans is largely conjectural. Important clues are imbedded in the early European accounts, although they must be used with caution. Among the best early English accounts are Wood's *New England's Prospect;* Thomas Morton's *New English Canaan* (Amsterdam: printed by Jacob Frederick Stam, 1637; reprinted New York: Arno Press, 1972); and esp. Williams's *Key into the Language.* For an overview of North American Indian perceptions, see James Axtell, "Through Another Glass Darkly: Early Indian Views of Europeans," in his *After Columbus: Essays in the Ethnohistory of Colonial North America* (New York: Oxford University Press, 1988), pp. 125–43; several essays, more specific in focus, appear in *American Beginnings: Exploration, Culture, and Cartography in the Land of Norumbega,* ed. Emerson W. Baker et al. (Lincoln: University of Nebraska Press, 1994), pt. 2.

19. On European, especially English, reactions to the Indians in the sixteenth and early seventeenth centuries, see Bernard Sheehan, *Savagism and Civility: Indians and Englishmen in Colonial Virginia* (Cambridge: Cambridge University Press, 1980); Karen Ordahl Kupperman, *Settling with the Indians: The Meeting of English and Indian Cultures in America, 1580–1640* (Totowa, N.J.: Rowman and Littlefield, 1980); Alfred A. Cave, Jr., "Richard Hakluyt's Savages: The Influence of 16th Century Travel Narratives on English Policy in North America," *International Social Science*

Review 60 (1985): 3–24; and my "Early English Paradigms for New World Natives," in my *Roots of American Racism: Essays on the Colonial Experience* (New York: Oxford University Press, 1995), pp. 34–54. Euroamerican visual images of Algonquians from 1605 to 1879 are reproduced and analyzed in William S. Simmons's "The Earliest Prints and Paintings of New England Indians," *Rhode Island History* 41 (1982): 73–85.

20. English kidnapping in New England is documented by David B. Quinn and Alison M. Quinn, eds., in *The English New England Voyages, 1602–1609* (London: Hakluyt Society, 1983), pp. 283–85; and in *The Complete Works of Captain John Smith (1580–1631)*, ed. Philip L. Barbour, 3 vols. (Chapel Hill: University of North Carolina Press for the Institute of Early American History and Culture, 1986), 1:433; 2:399, 401.

21. On the abduction, see my *New England Frontier: Puritans and Indians, 1620–1675*, 3d ed. (Norman: University of Oklahoma Press, 1995), pp. 3, 8–13; Salisbury, *Manitou and Providence*, pp. 90–93; and Axtell, "The Exploration of Norumbega: Native Perspectives," in Baker's *American Beginnings*, pp. 160–65.

22. On English efforts to change place names, some of them unsuccessful, see *Complete Works of John Smith*, esp. 2:401–2, 407–8, 416–19; 3:221, 278; Wood, *New England's Prospect*, pp. 123–24; and J. B. Harley, "New England Cartography and the Native Americans," in Baker's *American Beginnings*, chap. 13.

23. The epidemic has never been satisfactorily diagnosed. It was almost certainly not smallpox—a familiar and frightening disease to the English. Most contemporary commentators called the epidemic of 1616–19 simply "the plague," an ambiguous label at the time. Two recent surveys of the evidence are helpful: Dean R. Snow and Kim M. Lanphear's "European Depopulation in the Northeast: The Timing of the First Epidemics," *Ethnohistory* 35 (1988): 15–33; and William A. Starna's "The Biological Encounter: Disease and the Ideological Domain," *American Indian Quarterly* 16 (1992): 511–19, although Starna errs (p. 513) in asserting that Snow and Lanphear attribute the 1616–19 epidemic to smallpox; rather, those authors conclude that smallpox first struck New England in 1633. For the plague's effects on the Indians and English interpretations of its import, see Alfred A. Crosby, Jr., "God . . . Would Destroy Them, and Give Their Country to Another People," *American Heritage*, October/November 1978, pp. 39–42. Demographic aspects are addressed in Sherburne Cook's "The Significance of Disease in the Extinction of the New England Indians," *Human Biology* 45 (1973): 485–508.

24. For Squanto's complicated career, see the biographical sketch by Samuel Eliot Morison, in *Dictionary of American Biography*, 20 vols. plus supplements (New York: Scribner's, 1928–95); and Neal Salisbury, "Squanto: Last of the Patuxets," in *Struggle and Survival in Colonial America*, ed. David G. Sweet and Gary B. Nash (Berkeley: University of California Press, 1981), pp. 228–46. The evidence for Squanto's various sojourns in Europe is murky; Salisbury, unlike Morison, does not include him among Waymouth's captives in 1605. On Squanto's escape from the plague, see *Complete Works of John Smith*, 2:448. On the controversy over Squanto's supposed mundane but important contribution to Euroamerican agricultural practices, see Nanepashemet, "It Smells Fishy to Me: An Argument Supporting the Use of Fish

Fertilizer by the Native People of Southern New England," in Benes's *Algonkians of New England*, pp. 42–50.

25. For a range of interpretations of Indian-white relations in Plymouth Colony, see (in addition to chap. 2 in this volume), George F. Willison, *Saints and Strangers: Being the Lives of the Pilgrim Fathers* . . . (New York: Reynal and Hitchcock, 1945); my *New England Frontier;* George D. Langdon, Jr., *Pilgrim Colony: A History of New Plymouth, 1620–1691* (New Haven: Yale University Press, 1966); and Salisbury, *Manitou and Providence.*

26. On the smallpox outbreak of 1633–34, see Snow and Lanphear, "Timing of the First Epidemics," p. 23.

27. See the sophisticated analysis in Anne Keary's "Retelling the History of the Settlement of Providence: Speech, Writing and Cultural Interaction on Narragansett Bay," *New England Quarterly* 69 (1996): 250–86.

28. On English expansion into the Connecticut Valley, there is much useful information (though marred by the biases of its time), in John W. De Forest's *History of the Indians of Connecticut: From the Earliest Known Period to 1850* (1851; Hamden, Conn.: Archon Books, 1964).

29. For widely differing reconstructions of the war itself, see my *New England Frontier;* Jennings, *Invasion of America;* Salisbury, *Manitou and Providence;* Hirsch, "Collision of Military Cultures"; and Alfred A. Cave, *The Pequot War* (Amherst: University of Massachusetts Press, 1996).

30. John Underhill, *Newes from America* (London, 1638; reprinted in *Massachusetts Historical Society Collections,* 3d ser. 6 [1837]), p. 27. The Pequot boys were intended for Bermuda but were instead sold at Providence Island by Captain William Pierce, whose return cargo included slaves. See John Winthrop to William Bradford, 28 July 1637, *Winthrop Papers,* 6 vols. (Boston: Massachusetts Historical Society, 1929–92): 3:456–58; Patrick Copland to John Winthrop, 4 December 1639, *Winthrop Papers,* 4:157–59; *The Journal of John Winthrop, 1630–1649,* ed. Richard S. Dunn, James Savage, and Laetitia Yeandle (Cambridge: Harvard University Press, 1996), pp. 229, 246.

31. The confederation's career is thoroughly recounted in Harry M. Ward's *The United Colonies of New England, 1643–1690* (New York: Vantage Press, 1961). For the confederation's inept handling of its first crisis, stemming from a rivalry between the Narragansetts and Mohegans, see John A. Sainsbury, "Miantonomo's Death and New England Politics, 1630–1645," *Rhode Island History* 30 (1971): 111–23.

32. For the revival of the Pequots after the war, see Jack Campisi, "The Emergence of the Mashantucket Pequot Tribe, 1637–1975," in Hauptman and Wherry's *The Pequots,* pp. 117–40.

33. For a brief analysis of Indian-white relations, mostly commercial, in the post–Pequot War period, see Neal Salisbury, "Indians and Colonists in Southern New England after the Pequot War," in Hauptman and Wherry's *The Pequots,* pp. 81–95; on the Mohawk defeat of the Pocumtucks and colonial settlement of their area, see Richard I. Melvoin, *New England Outpost: War and Society in Colonial Deerfield* (New York: Norton, 1989). Peter A. Thomas examines various aspects of economic exchange in "Cultural Change on the Southern New England Frontier, 1630–1665,"

in *Cultures in Contact: The Impact of European Contacts on Native American Cultural Institutions, A.D. 1000–1800,* ed. William W. Fitzhugh (Washington, D.C.: Smithsonian Institution, 1985), pp. 131–57. The ecological consequences of English expansion are examined perceptively in William Cronon's *Changes in the Land: Indians, Colonists, and the Ecology of New England* (New York: Hill and Wang, 1983); and Carolyn Merchant's *Ecological Revolutions: Nature, Gender, and Science in New England* (Chapel Hill: University of North Carolina Press, 1989). Peter Mancall exposes the uses and abuses of the liquor trade in *Deadly Medicine: Indians and Alcohol in Early America* (Ithaca, N.Y.: Cornell University Press, 1995).

34. I use the traditional nomenclature for the war, which has prevailed in historical writings for more than two centuries. In the past few decades, historians have frequently renamed the conflict Metacom's War, on the assumption that applying the sachem's native name in lieu of the English name that he requested and used, at least in negotiations with the colonists, somehow corrects an ethnocentric misnomer. See also Lepore, *Thr Name of War,* pp. xv–xxi. Francis Jennings signified his belief in the colonists' responsibility for the war by renaming it "the Second Puritan Conquest" (*Invasion of America,* p. 298).

35. The prospect of a wider war—beyond the confines of southern New England—is discussed in Wilcomb E. Washburn's "Governor Berkeley and King Philip's War," *New England Quarterly* 30 (1957): 363–77.

36. The standard works on the war are Douglas Edward Leach's *Flintlock and Tomahawk: New England in King Philip's War* (New York: Macmillan, 1958), and, more recent and with a very different focus, Lepore's *The Name of War.* A lively account, but less scholarly, is Russell Bourne's *The Red King's Rebellion: Racial Politics in New England, 1675–1678* (New York: Oxford University Press, 1990). Some aspects of the war and immediate postwar period are illuminated in Michael J. Puglisi's *Puritans Besieged: The Legacies of King Philip's War in the Massachusetts Bay Colony* (Lanham, Md.: University Press of America, 1991). Wartime losses are analyzed in Sherburne F. Cook's "Interracial Warfare and Population Decline among the New England Indians," *Ethnohistory* 20 (1973): 1–24. The role of Christian Indians in the conflict and the hostility toward them by large segments of the Euroamerican population during and after the war were poignantly described at the time in Daniel Gookin's *An Historical Account of the Doings and Sufferings of the Christian Indians in New England in the Years 1675, 1676, 1677,* first published in the American Antiquarian Society's *Transactions and Collections* (Worcester, Mass., 1836); modern assessments include Leach, *Flintlock and Tomahawk,* esp. chap. 8; and Jenny Hale Pulsipher, "Massacre at Hurtelberry Hill: Christian Indians and English Authority in Metacom's War," *William and Mary Quarterly,* 3d ser. 53 (1996): 459–86.

37. The war's human and material costs are discussed in Cook's "Interracial Warfare"; Leach's *Flintlock and Tomahawk;* and Puglisi's *Puritans Besieged.*

38. Cotton Mather's account of the war, *Decennium Luctuosum: An History of Remarkable Occurrences in the Long War . . . with the Indian Salvages* (Boston: printed by B. Green and J. Allen for Samuel Phillips, 1699), is reprinted in *Narratives of the Indian Wars, 1675–1699,* ed. Charles H. Lincoln (New York: Scribner's, 1913), pp.

169–300; the Hannah Dustan story is on pp. 263–66. For the evolution of attitudes toward Dustan, see Kathryn Whitford, "Hannah Dustin: The Judgment of History," *Essex Institute Historical Collections* 108 (1972): 304–25.

39. The best work on eighteenth-century New England Algonquians is Daniel R. Mandell's *Behind the Frontier: Indians in Eighteenth-Century Eastern Massachusetts* (Lincoln: University of Nebraska Press, 1996), esp. chaps. 5–6; on Natick, see Jean M. O'Brien, *Dispossession by Degrees: Indian Land and Identity in Natick, Massachusetts* (New York: Cambridge University Press, 1997). Excellent biographies of several Algonquians of the seventeenth and eighteenth centuries are in Grumet's *Northeastern American Lives*.

40. The four principal narratives of the Pequot War are conveniently published together in *History of the Pequot War: The Contemporary Accounts of Mason, Underhill, Vincent and Gardener*, ed. Charles Orr (Cleveland: Helman-Taylor Company, 1897; reprinted, New York: AMS Press, 1980).

41. The most extensive analysis of New England's literary attention to Indians is Richard Slotkin's *Regeneration through Violence: The Mythology of the American Frontier, 1600–1860* (Middletown, Conn.: Wesleyan University Press, 1973). The eighteenth-century wars and other aspects of northern New England ethnohistory are examined in two very useful books: Colin G. Calloway's *The Western Abenakis of Vermont, 1600–1800: War, Migration, and the Survival of an Indian People* (Norman: University of Oklahoma Press, 1990), and *Dawnland Encounters: Indians and Europeans in Northern New England*, ed. Calloway (Hanover, N.H.: University Press of New England, 1991). Governor Dummer's War and its diplomatic aftermath are examined in David L. Ghere's "Mistranslations and Misinformation: Diplomacy on the Maine Frontier, 1725 to 1755," *American Indian Culture and Research Journal* 8 (1984): 3–26. For "Grey Lock's War," see Calloway, *Western Abenakis*, chap. 6; for the Eastern Abenakis, see Kenneth M. Morrison, *The Embattled Northeast: The Elusive Ideal of Alliance in Abenaki-Euroamerican Relations* (Berkeley and Los Angeles: University of California Press, 1984). Six major New England texts are reprinted in *So Dreadfull a Judgment: Puritan Responses to King Philip's War, 1676–1677*, ed. Richard Slotkin and James K. Folson (Middletown, Conn.: Wesleyan University Press, 1978).

42. Rowlandson's narrative has been reprinted scores of times in the three centuries since its publication in 1682 in Boston (twice) and London and has been the centerpiece of many captivity narrative anthologies. For Rowlandson's and other New England captivity texts, and an analysis of the genre, see *Puritans among the Indians: Accounts of Captivity and Redemption, 1676–1724*, edited by me and Edward W. Clark (Cambridge: Harvard University Press, 1981). The most recent separate edition of Rowlandson's narrative, enriched by an ethnohistorical introduction, is *The Sovereignty and Goodness of God by Mary Rowlandson, with Related Documents*, ed. Neal Salisbury (Boston: Bedford Books, 1997). An excellent collection with a complementary geographic focus is *North Country Captives: Selected Narratives of Indian Captivity from Vermont and New Hampshire*, ed. Colin G. Calloway (Hanover, N.H.: University Press of New England, 1992). Scholarly literature about the narratives is abundant. Perceptive modern studies include June Namias's *White Captives:*

Gender and Ethnicity on the American Frontier (Chapel Hill: University of North Carolina Press, 1993); Mitchell Robert Breitwieser's *American Puritanism and the Defense of Mourning: Religion, Grief, and Ethnology in Mary White Rowlandson's Captivity Narrative* (Madison: University of Wisconsin Press, 1990); and Roy Harvey Pearce's "The Significances of the Captivity Narrative," *American Literature* 19 (1947): 1–20. For a comprehensive list of published narratives and of modern studies of narratives (published before 1982), with an interpretive essay by Wilcomb E. Washburn, see my *Narratives of North American Indian Captivity: A Selective Bibliography* (New York: Garland, 1983). In recent years, the volume of writings about captivity narratives has not abated. Many of the scholarly articles have appeared in the journal *Early American Literature.*

43. The captivity experience in general is best described in James Axtell's "The White Indians of Colonial America," in his *The European and the Indian: Essays in the Ethnohistory of Colonial North America* (New York: Oxford University Press, 1981), pp. 168–206. For New England captivities, see "Crossing the Cultural Divide: Indians and New Englanders, 1605–1763," an essay by me and Daniel K. Richter in my *Roots of American Racism*, pp. 213–52. The Williams family's experience is dramatically recounted in John Demos's *The Unredeemed Captive: A Family Story from Early America* (New York: Knopf, 1994), which should be supplemented by Evan Haefeli and Kevin Sweeney's "Revisiting *The Redeemed Captive:* New Perspectives on the 1704 Attack on Deerfield," *William and Mary Quarterly*, 3d ser. 52 (1995): 3–46.

44. The evolution of Euroamerican attitudes toward Indians in New England can be traced through a number of essays and articles. See esp. William S. Simmons, "Cultural Bias in the New England Puritans' Perception of Indians," *William and Mary Quarterly*, 3d ser. 38 (1981): 239–54; James Axtell, "The Vengeful Women of Marblehead: Robert Roule's Deposition of 1677," *William and Mary Quarterly*, 3d ser. 31 (1974): 647–52; and my *Roots of American Racism*, chaps. 1–2, 8–10. The quotation is from Gookin's *Doings and Sufferings of the Christian Indians*, p. 434.

45. For conflicting views of Tituba's ethnicity, see Chadwick Hansen, "The Metamorphosis of Tituba, or Why American Intellectuals Can't Tell an Indian Witch from a Negro," *New England Quarterly* 47 (1974): 3–12; Elaine G. Breslaw, *Tituba, Reluctant Witch of Salem: Devilish Indians and Puritan Fantasies* (New York: New York University Press, 1996); and Peter C. Hoffer, *The Devil's Disciples: Makers of the Salem Witchcraft Trials* (Baltimore: Johns Hopkins University Press, 1996). Breslaw comments on several of the earlier interpretations in "Tituba's Confession: The Multicultural Dimensions of the 1692 Salem Witch-Hunt," *Ethnohistory* 44 (1997): 535–56, and Bernard Rosenthal contributes an important summation of interpretive shifts and the surviving evidence in "Tituba's Story," *New England Quarterly* 71 (1998): 190–203.

46. For the myriad connections in the Puritan mind between Indians and witchcraft, see esp. Breslaw, *Tituba;* Slotkin, *Regeneration through Violence*, pp. 128–45; Richard Godbeer, *The Devil's Dominion: Magic and Religion in Early New England* (Cambridge: Cambridge University Press, 1992), pp. 191–201; and Alfred A. Cave, "Indian Shamans and English Witches in Seventeenth-Century New England," *Es-*

sex Institute Historical Collections 128 (1992): 239–54. Mercy Short's testimony is available in *Narratives of the Witchcraft Cases, 1648–1706,* ed. George Lincoln Burr (New York: 1914), quotation p. 261. The quotation from Samuel Parris appears in Breslaw, *Tituba,* p. 89.

47. Cotton Mather, *Fair Weather: or Considerations to Dispel the Clouds, & Allay the Storms, of Discontent* (Boston: printed by Bartholomew Green and John Allen for Benjamin Harris, 1692), p. 86.

48. For convenient lists of the missionary publications, both those aimed at English backers (and hence published in English in London) and at potential converts (hence published in Cambridge or Boston in Algonquian or in bilingual editions), see Frederick L. Weis, "The New England Company and Its Missionary Enterprises," *Colonial Society of Massachusetts Transactions,* vol. 38 (Boston, 1947–51), pp. 213–14, 216–18.

49. For insights into Indian literacy and transcriptions of numerous Algonquian documents, see Ives Goddard and Kathleen J. Bragdon's *Native Writings in Massachusetts,* 2 vols. (Philadephia: American Philosophical Society, 1988); Bragdon offers a comparative perspective in "Vernacular Literacy and Massachusett World View, 1650–1750," in Benes's *Algonkians of New England,* pp. 26–34. A perceptive examination of literacy's problematic role in seventeenth-century Indian-white encounters is Jill Lepore's "Dead Men Tell No Tales: John Sassamon and the Fatal Consequences of Literacy," *American Quarterly* 46 (1994): 479–512.

50. The standard studies of literacy in early New England are Kenneth A. Lockridge's *Literacy in Colonial New England: An Enquiry into the Social Context of Literacy in the Early Modern Period* (New York: Norton, 1974); and E. Jennifer Monaghan, "Literacy Instruction and Gender in Colonial New England," *American Quarterly* 40 (1988): 18–41. For Algonquian literacy, see Goddard and Bragdon, *Native Writings.* Two articles address literacy among Indian females: Margaret Connell Szasz's "'Poor Richard' Meets the Native American: Schooling for Young Indian Women in Eighteenth-Century Connecticut," *Pacific Historical Review* 49 (1980): 215–35; and E. Jennifer Monaghan's "'She loved to read in good Books': Literacy and the Indians of Martha's Vineyard, 1643–1725," *History of Education Quarterly* 30 (1990): 493–521.

51. Chapters 7 and 8 in this volume present in-depth views of New England's two most important seventeenth-century missionary centers, Martha's Vineyard and Natick. For overviews of the missionary movement throughout the region, see my *New England Frontier,* chaps. 9–11; and James Axtell, *The Invasion Within: The Contest of Cultures in Colonial North America* (New York: Oxford University Press, 1985). On Eliot's missionary efforts, see also Richard W. Cogley, "John Eliot in Recent Scholarship," *American Indian Culture and Research Journal* 14 (1990): 77–92, and his "Idealism vs. Materialism in the Study of Puritan Missions to the Indians," *Method and Theory in the Study of Religion* 3 (1991): 165–82. More extensive analyses are Dane Anthony Morrison's *A Praying People: Massachusetts Acculturation and the Failure of the Puritan Mission, 1600–1690* (New York: Peter Lang, 1995), and, esp., Richard W. Cogley's *John Eliot's Mission to the Indians before King Philip's War* (Cambridge: Harvard University Press, 1999). The status of the missionary campaign on the eve of King Philip's War is described in Gookin's *Historical Collections.*

52. For the post-1676 history of missions in New England, see William Kellaway, *The New England Company: Missionary Society to the American Indians, 1649–1776* (New York: Barnes and Noble, 1962); and Weis, "New England Company," pp. 134–218; the latter work is particularly useful for its several appendices, which list more than 100 praying towns, 25 Indian churches, nearly 120 Euroamerican missionaries (including 20 "Occasional Preachers and Missionaries"), and 159 native preachers. For tables summarizing Weis's data, see my *Roots of American Racism,* p. 224.

53. On Wheelock's missionary career, see James Axtell, "Dr. Wheelock's Little Red School," in his *The European and the Indian,* pp. 87–109; on Occom, see Harold Blodgett, *Samson Occom: The Biography of an Indian Preacher* (Hanover, N.H.: Dartmouth College, 1935); and Laurie Weinstein, "Samson Occom: A Charismatic Eighteenth-Century Mohegan Leader," in her *Enduring Traditions.* The most thorough assessment of the Stockbridge mission is Patrick Frazier's *The Mohicans of Stockbridge* (Lincoln: University of Nebraska Press, 1992); a briefer look at the mission's efforts at schooling Indians is James Axtell's "The Scholastic Frontier in Western Massachusetts," in his *After Columbus,* pp. 58–72. An extensive but uneven overview of its topic is Margaret Connell Szasz's *Indian Education in the American Colonies, 1607–1783* (Albuquerque: University of New Mexico Press, 1988).

54. William S. Simmons has written extensively on Algonquians in the Great Awakening. See "The Great Awakening and Indian Conversion in Southern New England," in *Papers of the Tenth Algonquian Conference,* ed. William Cowan (Ottawa: Carleton University, 1979); "Red Yankees: Narragansett Conversion in the Great Awakening," *American Anthropologist* 10 (1983): 253–71; and, edited with Cheryl L. Simmons, *Old Light on Separate Ways: The Narragansett Diary of Joseph Fish, 1765–1776* (Hanover, N.H.: University Press of New England, 1982).

55. The changing circumstances of Algonquian economies are outlined in Daniel R. Mandell's "'Habits of Industry and Good Morals': Indians in Southern New England from the Encounter to the Industrial Age," paper (revised) presented to the Second Mashantucket Pequot History Conference, Mystic, Conn., October 1993.

56. *The Correspondence of Roger Williams,* ed. Glenn W. LaFantasie, 2 vols. (Hanover, N.H.: Brown University Press and the University Press of New England, 1988), 2:614.

57. The best examination of Native American participation in the war is Colin G. Calloway's *The American Revolution in Indian Country: Crisis and Diversity in Native American Communities* (New York: Cambridge University Press, 1995). Calloway devotes chap. 3 to the Stockbridge Indians, who are also addressed in Frazier's *Mohicans of Stockbridge,* chaps. 16–18. A concise regional overview is Calloway's "New England Algonkians in the American Revolution," in Benes's *Algonkians of New England,* pp. 51–62. For stimulating and contested interpretations of Indians and the Revolution, see the essays by Edward Countryman, Philip J. Deloria, Sylvia R. Frey, and Michael Zuckerman in the forum on "Rethinking the American Revolution," *William and Mary Quarterly,* 3d ser. 53 (1996): 341–86.

58. Calloway, *Western Abenakis,* chap. 11; Dean R. Snow, "Eastern Abenaki," and Gordon M. Day, "Western Abenaki," in Trigger's *Northeast.*

59. Calloway, *Western Abenakis,* chap. 12; Calloway, *American Revolution in Indian*

Country, p. 34; Mandell, *Behind the Frontier*, p. 167; *Our Own Ground: The Complete Writings of William Apess, A Pequot*, ed. Barry O'Connell (Amherst: University of Massachusetts Press, 1992), p. 240.

60. Calloway, *Western Abenakis*, chaps. 12–13.

61. Timothy Dwight, *Greenfield Hill: A Poem in Seven Parts* (New York, 1794), in *Travels in New England and New York*, ed. Barbara Miller Solomon, 4 vols. (Cambridge: Harvard University Press, 1969), 3:14. A perceptive recent analysis is Eve Kornfeld's "Encountering 'the Other': American Intellectuals and Indians in the 1790s," *William and Mary Quarterly*, 3d ser. 52 (1995): 287–314. Still valuable for context is Roy Harvey Pearce's *Savagism and Civilization: A Study of the Indian and the American Mind* (Baltimore: Johns Hopkins University Press, 1965).

62. *Moby-Dick; or, The Whale* (1851). For Melville's familiarity with Pequot history and his reasons for borrowing their name, see the 1952 edition of *Moby Dick*, ed. Luther S. Mansfield and Howard P. Vincent (New York: Hendricks House), pp. 68, 631–33. In other works, especially *The Confidence Man* (1857), Melville wrote more extensively about Indians and about prevailing prejudices against them. In addition to the New England writers who featured New England Indians in one or more of their stories, many authors incorporated them tangentially or in relatively minor roles, as in several novels and short stories by Nathaniel Hawthorne.

63. For a variety of perspectives on Sedgwick's novel, see Slotkin, *Regeneration through Violence*, pp. 451–54; Klaus Lubbers, *Born for the Shade: Stereotypes of the Native American in United States Literature and the Visual Arts, 1776–1894* (Amsterdam: Editions Rodopi, 1994), pp. 269–71; and Michelle Burnham, *Captivity and Sentiment: Cultural Exchange in American Literature, 1682–1861* (Hanover, N.H.: University Press of New England, 1997), pp. 105–17. See also Philip Gould's *Covenant and Republic: Historical Romance and the Politics of Puritanism* (New York: Cambridge University Press, 1996).

64. Slotkin, *Regeneration through Violence*, p. 451; Lubbers, *Born for the Shade*, pp. 71–72, 303–5; quotation p. 72. See also Carolyn L. Karcher's introduction to her edition *Hobomok and Other Writings on Indians*, by Lydia Maria Child (New Brunswick, N.J.: Rutgers University Press, 1986).

65. Limitations of space preclude further discussion of literature by non-New Englanders, of epic poems such as James Wallis Eastburn and Robert Sands's *Yamoyden, A Tale of the Wars of King Philip: In Six Cantos* (1820), or of theatrical dramas, such as John Augustus Stone's *Metamora; or, The Last of the Wampanoags* (1829), that focused on New England characters or locations; on that play, see esp. Lepore, *The Name of War*, chap. 8. For an early but still useful discussion of its topic, see Albert Keiser's *The Indian in American Literature* (New York: Oxford University Press, 1933).

66. Robert F. Sayre, *Thoreau and the American Indians* (Princeton, N.J.: Princeton University Press, 1977), quotations pp. lx, xi, 214. On Thoreau's view of Indians and the experiences on which he based them, see also Lubbers, *Born for the Shade*, pp. 69–71; Slotkin, *Regeneration through Violence*, pp. 518–38; and Philip F. Gura, "Thoreau's Maine Woods Indians: More Representative Men," *American Literature* 49 (1977): 366–84.

67. *The Writings of Henry D. Thoreau,* ed. Walter Harding (Princeton, N.J.: Princeton University Press, 1971–).

68. For the contributions of two early nineteenth-century New Englanders to Indians outside the region, see William G. McLoughlin, "Two Bostonian Missions to the Frontier Indians, 1810–1860," in *Massachusetts and the New Nation,* ed. Conrad Edick Wright (Boston: Massachusetts Historical Society, 1992), pp. 152–201.

69. Daniel Mandell, "Shifting Boundaries of Race and Ethnicity: Indian-Black Intermarriage in Southern New England, 1760–1880," *Journal of American History* 85 (1998): 466–501.

70. Mandell, "Indian-Black Intermarriage," discusses the growing racial mixtures and their long-range effects. Notably, in the 1880s, when state and federal governments campaigned to end tribal communities, they often had the active support of African American members of those communities who perceived greater benefits from United States citizenship and individual land ownership than from continued, traditional Indian communalism. On the complex dynamics of New England's native communities in mid-century, see esp. Ann Marie Plane and Gregory Button, "The Massachusetts Indian Enfranchisement Act: Ethnic Contest in Historical Context, 1849–1869" *Ethnohistory* 40 (1993): 587–618.

71. For the dispersal of one of New England's largest pre-contact nations, see Paul R. Campbell and Glenn W. LaFantasie, "Scattered to the Winds of Heaven— Narragansett Indians, 1676–1880," *Rhode Island History* 37 (1978): 67–83; for Narragansett persistence in the face of local white antagonism, see Ruth Wallis Herndon and Ella Wilcox Sekatau, "The Right to a Name: The Narragansett People and Rhode Island Officials in the Revolutionary Era," *Ethnohistory* 44 (1977): 433–62. Native persistence, especially among the Nipmucks, is documented in Donna Keith Baron, J. Edward Hood, and Holly V. Izard's "They Were Here All Along: The Native American Presence in Lower-Central New England in the Eighteenth and Nineteenth Centuries," *William and Mary Quarterly,* 3d. ser. 53 (1996): 561–86. See also several of the essays in *After King Philip's War: Presence and Persistence in Indian New England,* ed. Colin G. Calloway (Hanover, N.H.: University Press of New England, 1997), esp. Thomas L. Doughton's "Unseen Neighbors: Native Americans of Central Massachusetts: A People Who Had 'Vanished'" (pp. 207–30).

72. The history of the Mashpees is recounted in Francis G. Hutchins's *Mashpee: The Story of Cape Cod's Indian Town* (West Franklin, N.H.: Amarta Press, 1979), chaps. 1–6; James Clifford's *The Predicament of Culture: Twentieth-Century Ethnography, Literature, and Art* (Cambridge: Harvard University Press, 1988), chap. 12; and Jack Campisi's, *The Mashpee Indians: Tribe on Trial* (Syracuse, N.Y.: Syracuse University Press, 1991), chaps. 4–5.

73. Mandell, "Habits of Industry"; Plane and Button, "Massachusetts Indian Enfranchisement Act"; Trigger, *Northeast,* pp. 145–46, 152; Daniel Vickers, "The First Whalemen of Nantucket," *William and Mary Quarterly,* 3d ser. 40 (1983): 560–83.

74. Plane and Button, "Massachusetts Indian Enfranchisement Act."

75. For a concise summary of federal Indian policy from 1776 to the twentieth century, see the essays by Reginald Horsman, Francis Paul Prucha, and William T. Hagan in Washburn's *History of Indian-White Relations,* pp. 29–65.

76. Philleo Nash, "Twentieth-Century United States Government Agencies," in Washburn's *History of Indian-White Relations,* pp. 264–75.

77. On an early New England land case, see Francis J. O'Toole and Thomas N. Tureen, "State Power and the Passamaquoddy Tribe: 'A Gross National Hypocrisy?'" *University of Maine Law Review* 23 (1973): 1–39. Several cases are poignantly recounted in Paul Brodeur's *Restitution: The Land Claims of the Mashpee, Passamaquoddy, and Penobscot Indians of New England* (Boston: Northeastern University Press, 1985).

78. Laurie Weinstein, "'We're Still Living in Our Traditional Homeland': The Wampanoag Legacy in New England," in *Strategies for Survival: American Indians in the Eastern United States,* ed. Frank W. Porter (Westport, Conn.: Greenwood Press, 1989); Jack Campisi, "The New England Tribes and Their Quest for Justice," in Hauptman and Wherry's *The Pequots.*

PART ONE

Early Intercultural Contact

I

Why Was the Sagadahoc Colony Abandoned?
An Evaluation of the Evidence

ALFRED A. CAVE

Modern accounts of Indian-European relations in New England customarily begin when the Pilgrims arrive in 1620 and are welcomed early the next year by Samoset and, subsequently, by Squanto and Massasoit. Often overlooked is the encounter half a generation earlier between English colonists and Eastern Abenakis on the coast of Maine, which, historians have lately argued, brought the short-lived British outpost to its speedy demise.

Or did it? The handful of historians who have given more than passing attention to England's northern counterpart to the barely successful 1607 venture at Jamestown, Virginia, have offered disparate interpretations of the relations between the Abenakis and incipient New Englanders. In some retellings, the Indians are friendly to the newcomers—eager for their manufactured goods and unconcerned over their appropriation of a small, uninhabited peninsula. Other retellings focus on the Abenakis' initial suspicion of their new neighbors and the growing hostility that within a year, according to one contemporaneous source, dealt a deathblow to the inept imperial project.

Alfred A. Cave takes a fresh look at the evidence. He especially questions the reliability of the French document that, for historians who attributed the Sagadahoc Colony's downfall to Abenaki resistance, has heretofore been crucial, indeed almost unimpeachable. Cave also resurrects an English document, often ignored by scholars, that may provide the most accurate account of inter-ethnic events in 1607–8. But whatever version of the colony's fate prevails, a major lesson embodied in Cave's meticulous reconstruction of the Sagadahoc episode is the centrality of Native Americans to the colony's brief existence and, simultaneously, the apparently disruptive impact of the colony's several-score Englishmen on the lives of the local natives. As early as 1607—just as to the south Powhatan and Pocahontas were getting acquainted with Captain John Smith—Indians and Englishmen were also learning to understand, and misunderstand, each other on the coast of New England.

*I*N 1612, the French Jesuit missionary Pierre Biard reported to his superiors in Paris that during a visit to the Sagadahoc River country (now called the Kennebec) he had learned that hostile Indians had forced the abandonment of a substantial English settlement on the Maine coast several years earlier. Biard's Indian informants claimed that even though the newcomers at first had treated their Native American neighbors in a kindly manner, a local chieftain, using witchcraft, had killed the commander of the English expedition. After that incident, Biard related, "the English, under another captain, changed their tactics. They drove the Savages away without ceremony; they beat, maltreated and misused them outrageously and without restraint; consequently these poor abused people, anxious and dreading still greater evils, in the future, determined to kill the whelp ere its teeth and claws became stronger." After an Indian attack on three fishing shallops in which eleven Englishmen were killed, the remaining settlers, according to Biard, fled New England in panic.[1]

Biard's account of the circumstances surrounding the evacuation of Sagadahoc has generally been either ignored or discounted by historians. It cannot be confirmed, for none of the contemporary English accounts mention Indian hostility as a factor in the decision to abandon the venture. The Sagadahoc Colony, a privately sponsored undertaking mounted in 1607 under the authority of the Plymouth Company, was intended to serve both as a permanent trading colony and as a base for the ongoing search for the Northwest Passage. Sagadahoc's founders, numbering between 100 and 120 men, set sail for Maine on 1 June in two vessels, the *Gift of God,* under the command of George Popham, and the *Mary and John,* commanded by Raleigh Gilbert. Soon after disembarking on 8 August, the party built a sturdy fortified village on the Sabino peninsula. Named Fort St. George, the new English settlement was protected by several cannons mounted on the log palisade. Within the walls were a storehouse, a chapel, and "lodges" to house the colonists. George Popham served as first president of the colony's governing council. He died in February and was succeeded by Raleigh Gilbert. Sagadahoc was evacuated late the following summer.[2]

In correspondence outlining the problems that plagued the venture, Sir Ferdinando Gorges, one of the principal underwriters, blamed "the malice of the Divell." In tracing the means Satan presumably used to foil English efforts to settle in Maine, Gorges surprisingly made no mention of Indian hostility. He spoke instead of inept leadership and internal dissension. Fort St. George, he related, was populated by "ignorant, timorous and ambitouse persons" and plagued with "childish factions." Popham, the colony's first leader, was, in Gorges's view, too old and indecisive to provide the necessary direction. But Popham's death in February 1608 only exacerbated the colony's problems, for Gilbert, his successor, portrayed by Gorges as a man "of small judgment and experience," proved to be headstrong, undisciplined, and self-indulgent. The elements, as Gorges explained, also aided the devil's efforts. A severe winter, unanticipated by the colonists, sapped their strength. A fire in the early spring of 1608, which destroyed most of the village, including the supply house, completed their demoralization.[3]

William Strachey's summary of explanations of the abandonment of Sagadahoc in his *Historie of Travell into Virginia Britania* (1612) made no mention of an Indian attack either. Instead, the colonists, as Strachey paraphrased their testimony, complained that the Indian trade had yielded no gold or silver and expressed fears of another harsh winter. Their decision to abandon Sagadahoc was, however, directly attributed not to these factors per se but to Raleigh Gilbert's return to England to claim his inheritance.[4] The Council of New England, in a pamphlet published in 1622, stated that while "Captain Popham . . . was the only man indeed that died there that winter," still all "endured the greater extremities; for that in the depth thereof, their lodges and stores were burnt and they were thereby wondrously distressed." When the supply ships brought word of the death in England of Chief Justice Popham, principal underwriter of the venture and uncle of the late president, George Popham, the colonists were further disheartened. The Council's account explained that "this calamity and evil news together with the resolution that Captain Gilbert was forced to take for his own return (in that he was to succeed his brother in the inheritance of lands in England), made the whole company to resolve upon nothing but their return with the ships."[5] Captain John Smith repeated this explanation of the colony's abandonment in his *Generall History of Virginia, the Somer Isles and New England,* published in 1624.[6]

Only one contemporary English publication mentioned Indian hostility. In 1614, the Reverend Samuel Purchas, a compiler of travel narratives included in the second edition of *Purchas, his Pilgrimage* an account of the Sagadahoc venture that reported that "Mr. Patterson was slain by the savages of Nanhoe, a river of the Tarrentines."[7] Purchas's report, which has generally been overlooked by historians, casts doubt on the accuracy of official accounts of mortality at Sagadahoc but otherwise offers no substantial confirmation of Biard's claims.

With few exceptions, Maine historians have given no credence to Biard's story.[8] From the mid-nineteenth century through the early twentieth, the Sagadahoc Colony was the object of a sustained and sometimes acrimonious controversy, but that dispute focused on Sagadahoc's claim to be the first true English colony in New England. Defenders of Plymouth's primacy charged that the Sagadahoc settlers were an irresponsible and dissolute lot who, by abandoning the colony without good reason, had forfeited their right to the honor. Indian hostilities were rarely mentioned in the voluminous literature generated by that debate.[9] Until recently, historians in general have accepted Herbert L. Osgood's conclusion that "in the main friendly relations seem to have been established" between the Sagadahoc colonists and the Indians.[10] Since the colony's survival and success depended on the good will and cooperation of potential Indian trading partners, the French priest's claim that the English "drove the savages away without ceremony" struck most historians as illogical. However, a few recent writers, more sensitive to English abuse of Native Americans, accept Biard's version as the authentic explanation of the failure of Sagadahoc. While acknowledging that the problems enumerated by Gorges were undoubtedly very real, these critics argue that the failure "after the demise of Popham to treat the natives of the area with justice and good will" was "the most significant shortcoming of the Sagadahoc colonists."[11]

Although contemporary English reports on the Popham colony, with the exception of Purchas's, made no mention of any Indian violence against colonists, some support for Biard's claim may be found in two later English accounts of Indian testimony. One comes from the Puritan historian William Hubbard. Writing in 1680, Hubbard declared that prior to the evacuation of Sagadahoc, "the English were some of them killed by said Indians and the Rest all driven out of the Fort." Relating the episode to his grand theme of divine providence in human history, Hubbard added that Indian informants revealed that when they took possession of the abandoned fort, they found large quantities of gun powder stored in barrels. "After they had opened them, not knowing what to do therewith, they left the Barrels carelessly open, and so scattered the Powder about, so as accidentally it took Fire, and blew up all that was within the Fort, burnt and destroyed many of the Indians, upon which they conceived their god was angry with them for doing hurt to the English."[12]

A more detailed, and curious, story of racial conflict was reported by an eighteenth-century antiquarian. "There was a tradition amongst the Norridgwalk [Norridgewock] Indians," wrote James Sullivan, "that these planters invited a number of the natives, who had come to trade with them, to draw a small cannon by a rope, and that when they were arranged in a line in this process, the white people discharged this piece, and thereby killed and wounded several of them. . . . The resentment of the natives, consequent on this treacherous murder, obliged the English to re-embark the next summer."[13]

Neither Hubbard's story nor Sullivan's can be confirmed. Hubbard's credibility as a historian is suspect, for his work is in many instances both biased and inaccurate. Sullivan wrote long after the event, and the atrocity he relates, while not impossible, is rather unlikely. But while we must recognize that the precise details contained in Hubbard's and Sullivan's accounts are somewhat problematic, we must not disregard the fact that both provide evidence of a tradition independent of Biard that regarded Indian hostility as instrumental in the abandonment of the English outpost on the Kennebec. An early-nineteenth-century historian of Maine remarked that while we cannot determine whether these stories have a "foundation in truth, both were believed to be true by the ancient and well informed inhabitants on Sagadahock river."[14] The Reverend Henry O. Thayer, editor of a collection of documents relating to the Sagadahoc Colony published in 1892, differed from most of his contemporaries in rejecting the notion that "the silence of English writers" constituted a persuasive refutation of Biard's report. "The long infamous record of injustices and unkindness toward the Indian, provoking his terrible retaliation," Thayer mused, "may have had some of its shaming and bloody lines written at Sagadahoc, as the kidnapping processes of that period bear proof."[15]

Thayer's observation deserves our consideration. Given the propensity of colonial promoters to understate or suppress evidence of difficulties and dangers in the New World, the absence of reports of Indian hostilities in Gorges's account and in Strachey's and Smith's summaries of the survivors' testimony may be less significant than many historians have believed. Indeed, a review of all of the evidence relating to the Popham/Raleigh expedition indicates that the relations between the Sagadahoc colonists and the indigenous inhabitants of the Maine coast were both complex and ambiguous. To understand fully the reasons for the colony's failure, then, we must first analyze the patterns of interracial contact on the New England coast prior to the landing of the Sagadahoc expedition at the Kennebec River in the summer of 1607.

ALTHOUGH promotional literature written to encourage investment in New World ventures sometimes spoke of Native Americans as gentle and tractable, popular accounts of the Americas read by Englishmen on the eve of colonization more commonly portrayed Indians as bestial and diabolical.[16] A survey of world geography that went through several editions in the early seventeenth century claimed that the inhabitants of the New World were worshipers of "vile spirits" and regularly engaged in witchcraft, incest, sodomy, and cannibalism.[17] The colonial promoter Sir Ferdinando Gorges complained that it was difficult to persuade Englishmen to venture into regions inhabited by such "savage people."[18] The records of the exploratory probes led by Bartholomew Gosnold in 1602, Martin Pring in 1603, and George Waymouth in 1605, as well as those of the Popham/Gilbert expedition of 1607, reveal that the savage stereotype played a decisive role in shaping English contact with Native Americans in the formative years of colonization.[19] Quite simply, both perception and treatment of the Indians were conditioned by a priori assumptions about their basic nature. James Rosier, chronicler of Waymouth's voyage, wrote: "We little expected any sparke of humanity." Surprised by the friendly reception they received from Indians intent on trade, the visitors remained wary and seized upon the slightest intimation of hostility as proof that they were indeed in constant danger from natives, who, according to Rosier, were presumed to be like "other salvages who have beene by travellers in most discoveries found very trecherous."[20] English behavior, predicated on the assumption that such bestial and vicious people could be taught to "love and fear" the settlers only if they showed strength, was often heavy handed and provocative.[21] Captain Pring used two ferocious mastiffs to intimidate the local inhabitants. The dogs were unleashed whenever he wanted to drive curious Indians away from his encampment on Cape Cod.[22] Waymouth responded to the sighting of a large group of Indians armed with bows and arrows by taking several captives whom he transported back to England.[23]

Experience did little to modify preconceptions. Despite their preoccupation with the dangers presumably posed by savages, Waymouth and his predecessors seldom encountered any sign of Indian hostility. The Indians they met on the New England coast were generally not only friendly but often avidly interested in trade as well. The English voyagers found that the locals already possessed a number of European trade goods, knew some French words, and traveled along the coast in Basque shallops. Some New England natives proved to be sharp traders who knew the value of their peltry to Europeans and were accustomed to receiving a higher price than the English expected to offer. Even so, they remained interested in the acquisition of metal implements, glass beads, and other trade commodities from the newcomers. Isolated expressions of hostility, such as a skirmish with two members of Gosnold's party who had gone on a hunting expedition, probably motivated by a concern to define the boundaries of a restricted game preserve, were invariably followed by renewed Indian overtures of friendship. There is no tangible evidence that the Indians had any intention of mounting an all-out attack on any of the English probes. Even after Waymouth's abductions, the Indians sought to maintain trade with his party. But the English, persuaded that they were in danger of ambush, on occasion refused to respond to Indian appeals that they exchange goods. Nonetheless, the voyages yielded both furs, provided by Indian traders, and sassafras, a reputed cure for syphilis, gathered with Indian aid.[24]

Despite wariness about Indian character, English interest in New England was stimulated by false expectations of the imminent discovery of gold, silver, and spices as well as a northwest passage to the orient in the regions north of Cape Cod. Misled by vague and garbled Indian testimony, Sir Ferdinando Gorges was persuaded that the natives of Maine were in contact with China.[25] Acting under the authority of the Plymouth Company, Gorges in 1606 sent Henry Challons and thirty-nine prospective colonists to New England. His orders were to establish a New England trading post. Challons, disregarding his instructions, chose the southern route across the Atlantic and, along with his crew and two of Waymouth's Indian captives attached to the expedition as guides and interpreters, was captured in the West Indies by the Spanish. A second vessel, under command of Thomas Hanham, did reach the New England coast. It carried another of Waymouth's captives, a local sagamore named Tahenedo, sometimes called Nahanada. Tahenedo remained behind after the return of the Hanham expedition. In the following year, Popham and Gilbert established the Sagadahoc Colony. They were accompanied by Skidwarres, also a former Waymouth captive.

In assessing the controversy over the failure of the Sagadahoc venture, Gorges's testimony is of particular value, for it articulates the attitudes that guided the colonists' dealings with Native Americans. He shared commonplace assumptions about Indians, describing them in a letter to Sir Robert Cecil as a "people daungerouse to bee dealt with."[26] But Gorges was persuaded that exposure to English power and wealth would completely overawe savages. If treated with proper firmness, he held, captives could be transformed into agents of British expansionism. In planning the Sagadahoc venture, Gorges assumed that two of Waymouth's former captives whom he had taken into his household and educated would be of great use in promoting peace and trade with the Indians. "After I had these people sometime in my custody," Gorges wrote, "I observed in them an inclination to follow the example of the better sort." He questioned them closely about their homeland. "I made them able to set me down what great rivers ran up into the land, what men of note were seated on them, what power they were of, how allied, what enemies they had." Believing that those captives would not only provide information vital to the success of a New England colonial venture, but would also urge their compatriots to extend a warm welcome to the English, Gorges declared the kidnappings part of God's preordained plan for "giving life to all our plantations."[27]

The surviving records of the expedition indicate that the plan soon went awry. Although incomplete, a revealing narrative appears in a long-lost manuscript found in 1876 at Lambeth Palace. It was unsigned, but internal evidence suggests that the author is James Davies, a naval officer who served under Gilbert on the *Mary and John*.[28] Davies related that shortly after his party landed on the Maine coast in early August, Skidwarres, who was serving as an interpreter, was asked to escort his English companions to his village. At first, he refused, claiming that the village was now deserted. He denied any knowledge of his people's present whereabouts but, under pressure, finally led the company to "whear they did inhabytt whear we found near a hundredth of them men wemen and Children." Approaching the village, the Englishmen saw Tahenedo, who, after his repatriation in 1606, had resumed his position as a Pemaquid sagamore. In response to his "howlinge or Cry," a number of Indians armed with bows and arrows rushed toward the startled English party. Skidwarres then intervened, speaking to Tahenedo and the men in their own language. It is not known just what he said, but Tahenedo ordered his men to put down their weapons and then embraced the Englishmen.[29]

Despite his belated display of friendship, Tahenedo's anxieties were not allayed. Two days later, when a party of some fifty Englishmen, including Popham and Gilbert, tried to visit his village, they were once again confronted by armed warriors. Although the English tried once again to reassure Tahenedo of their peaceful intent, the sagamore demanded that most of them remain aboard ship. After further parlay, Tahenedo, as Davies related, appeared "well contented that all should Land So all landed we ussinge them with all kindnesse that possibell we Could." Appearances were deceiving, however, for the Indians soon "withdrew them Selves from us into the woods & Lefte us." Intensifying the settlers' perplexity, Skidwarres, on whom they depended, now refused to return with the English. Hearing their plea, Skidwarres agreed to rejoin them at their encampment on the following day, but, as the chronicler noted, "he heald not his promysse" (pp. 59–60). The Sagadahoc colonists had no contact with any of the indigenous inhabitants of the region until 1 September, when a canoe approached the newly constructed English fort. With two large brass kettles aboard the vessel, its occupants were obviously familiar with European trade goods, but they refused to trade with the English. Indeed, they were so wary of the newcomers that they permitted only one Englishman at a time "to com near unto them" (p. 71). After a short parley, they departed abruptly.

In September, Tahenedo and Skidwarres, accompanied by forty tribesmen, called at Fort St. George. The Lambeth manuscript relates that "they

Cam & parled wth us & we aggain ussed them in all frindly manner We Could & gave them vytaills for to eatt" (p. 71). Skidwarres and Tahenedo promised to assist their former masters in opening up trade relations with the powerful Abenaki sagamore Bashaba.[30] But they did not keep that promise. Three days later, Gilbert and a party of twenty-two Englishmen bearing trade goods journeyed to Pemaquid, where they had agreed to rendezvous with Skidwarres and Tahenedo prior to their visit to Bashaba. The English had been delayed by bad weather, but on arriving, and after searching diligently, they "found no Lyvinge Creature They all wear gon from thence" (p. 73). Despite the contrary opinion of some historians, it seems reasonable to assume that Skidwarres and Tahenedo never intended to keep their appointment.[31]

English efforts to open trade relations with the local Indians were even less auspicious. The last week of September, an exploratory party led by Gilbert had encamped upstream on the Sagadahoc (Kennebec) River. They were approached by five Indians, one of whom announced himself as "Sabenoa . . . Lord of the River Sagadahock." The Indians displayed goods already received from earlier European contact—"Beades, Knives, and some Copper of which they seemed very fond." The commodities the Indians then presented for trade with the English, however, turned out to be quite unattractive—"some Tobacco and certaine small Skynnes which were of no value." Gilbert broke off bartering and ordered his men to re-embark. Alarmed by the withdrawal, the Indians feared that the English would bombard them from the shallop. Apparently quite familiar with European cannons, Sabenoa's men disabled the ship's guns by dispatching a warrior who quickly boarded the vessel, grabbed the firebrand held by one of the gunners, and threw it into the water. Gilbert ordered his men to take up their muskets and cover a sailor who went ashore "for more fier," but the Indians barred his way and also grabbed hold "of the boate-roape that the Shallop could not putt off." On Gilbert's order, muskets were leveled at the Indians hanging onto the rope, who then let go and "ran into the bushes." The shallop sailed to the other side of the river, where it was hailed by the occupants of an Indian canoe who sought to excuse "the fault of the others." Gilbert "entertaynd them kyndly" for a short time, then returned to Fort St. George.[32]

This episode reveals a great deal about the ambiguity and misunderstanding that plagued English efforts to establish a productive trade relationship with Maine's native peoples. Sabenoa's followers had obviously had earlier experiences with Englishmen, as evidenced by their ability to understand and speak some English.[33] Those experiences had left them anxious and wary. The natives also already had access to European trade goods and had no need to enter into a relationship with the English, let alone accept them as overlords.[34] The expectation of Gorges and other armchair travelers and entrepreneurs about the beneficial effect the English presence was supposed to have on "savage" peoples was, at the very least, unrealistic.

In early October, Skidwarres and Tahenedo reappeared at Fort St. George, bringing with them Bashaba's brother. In response, the English, hoping to open a lucrative trade "in the River of Penobscot," sent a present to Bashaba. We do not know the exact outcome of that initiative, but it must have been unsuccessful, since the colony did not prosper.[35] Unfortunately, the surviving documentary evidence provides few details about Fort St. George's interactions with the Indians after 6 October 1607.[36] In Gorges's correspondence, however, we find hints of serious difficulties, particularly in the ongoing relationship with the former captives. The colonists complained that whenever prospective Indian clients approached Fort St. George, Skidwarres and Tahenedo "instantly carry them away, and will not suffer them to come neere any more." They also reported that the Indians had resorted to hiding the goods the colonists needed.[37] We do not know precisely why they took that step, nor have we any clear evidence on the nature of the English response. It is possible that the English at Sagadahoc, frustrated in their efforts to use their former captives to secure trade and angered by the passive resistance of the local inhabitants, sought to secure Indian compliance with their demands by force, thereby deepening the resentments and anxieties that began with the abductions of 1605.

Strachey's sketchy account of the later months at Sagadahoc claims that at the time of the evacuation of Sagadahoc, the colonists had obtained "many kyndes of Furrs" through trade with the Indians and also had a "good store of sasparilla."[38] Strachey is not to be trusted on this point, however, for contemporary evidence contradicts him. Gorges noted in the fall of 1607 and again the following winter that the investors were "much discouraged" by the fact that the ships sent to Sagadahoc returned "without any commodity."[39] In none of his correspondence or later writings do we find support for the view that the Sagadahoc colonists succeeded in their efforts to open a profitable commerce with the local inhabitants. One recent historian who has reviewed the evidence reports that the backers of Sagadahoc "lost everything," and no subsequent statement in Gorges's writings disputes this finding.[40] His efforts to find new underwriters for another prospective Maine colony were fruitless.[41] The Sagadahoc experience suggested that such a colony would be a financial liability.

It is clear from his writings and his actions that Gorges never really understood why his strategy had failed. In his correspondence, he alluded to the possibility that the French were inciting the Indians against the settlers at Fort St. George, but his harshest criticism was that the colonists were undisciplined and had displayed inappropriate "familiarity" with the "savages." He charged, for example, that the colonists had gossiped with Indians about the squabbling within the small English community. His comments reveal a fundamental lack of understanding of the prerequisites for cordial relations with Native Americans. Gorges, who had no first-hand experience in the New World, assumed that the Indians, being igno-rant and primitive, were "a people tractable," easily managed by a "discrete" show of force and resolution.[42] Accordingly, he concluded that the Sagada-hoc settlers' inability to obtain bountiful trade goods from the locals re-flected the absence of a firm hand. Gorges was particularly astounded that Tahenedo and Skidwarres, exposed to the marvels of England, refused to play the roles assigned to them. Unwilling to consider the possibility that his assumptions about Indian character were in error, even though he had grudgingly acknowledged Tahenedo's and Skidwarres's independent be-havior and semi-covert hostility, Gorges stubbornly maintained that a little coercion would have resolved a problem that only a change in attitude could have rectified. The French, whose success in the Indian trade Gorges envied and resented, had quickly learned the importance of understanding and respecting Native American customs and expectations. The documen-tary evidence on Sagadahoc discloses no such effort on the part of the En-glish. In that omission, I believe, lies the key to the failure of Sagadahoc.

We do not, of course, know the full story. Did the English at Fort St. George coerce or abuse their prospective Indian trading partners? Did the Indians then retaliate by seeking to drive the English from New England? Did the sponsors of the Sagadahoc Colony conceal the fact that a number of colonists were massacred by the Indians? We have ample evidence of Indian resistance to English demands, but the facts at our disposal do not support Biard's claim that the killing of eleven Englishmen precipitated the evacuation of Fort St. George. Granted, Gorges and other colonial promoters had good reason to seek to suppress information about Indian hostility, but we should remember that the English were avid gossip-mongers. The survivors of other colonial catastrophes were seldom mute. News about the high casualty rate at Jamestown in the same period spread throughout England and prompted Jamestown's founders to embark on a major propaganda campaign to promote the colony.[43] But we comb the records in vain for any indication that the erstwhile Sagadahoc colonists carried back stories of Indian massacre. It is therefore likely that, although there may have been some altercations between Indians and settlers, the

Indians made no effort to annihilate the colony. While we cannot totally disprove Biard's claim of eleven deaths, the evidence we do have indicates that those casualties were so few in number (probably no more than the one reported by Purchas) that in and of themselves they did not undermine confidence in the English ability to maintain a viable outpost in New England. Indeed, Gorges continued to send trading ships to the Maine coast. His ventures did not prosper, but he ascribed their failure not to Indian violence against Englishmen but rather to European diseases that decimated his prospective Indian trading partners.[44]

Sagadahoc ultimately failed because from the outset the venture was unrealistic. The colonists had little understanding of the climate and resources of the region and were even more misguided in their expectations of their Indian trading partners. Not only did they assume erroneously that the indigenous peoples of the Maine coast could supply them with precious metals, but their belief that kidnapped Indians were in thrall to the superior race, that English power would invariably overawe the Indians, and that fear would lead to both submission and love set the stage for failure. In the final analysis, Indian relations are indeed at the heart of the problem. But it is important to note that the Sagadahoc colonists complained not that their lives were endangered by Indian attacks but rather that Indian leaders on whom they relied refused to cooperate in their economic ventures. The evidence on balance thus suggests that the Indians' passive resistance, their refusal to serve as English agents and trading partners, was the decisive factor in turning back this first wave of English settlement in New England.

Notes

1. Reuben Gold Thwaites, ed., *The Jesuit Relations and Allied Documents*, 73 vols. (New York: Pageant, 1959), 2:45, 47. Biard erred by one year in claiming the colony was founded in 1608 and abandoned in 1609.

2. Our information about the Sagadahoc Colony comes from only a handful of sources, since much of the documentary evidence relating to this venture has disappeared. Samuel Purchas, who wrote a short account of the colony for the second, enlarged edition of *Purchas his Pilgrimage* ([London, 1614], p. 756), mentioned in a later edition that he had access to a number of sources that cannot now be located, specifically, journals written by Raleigh Gilbert, John Eliot, and others he does not identify, as well as "divers letters from Capt. Popham and others." See Henry O. Thayer, ed., *The Sagadahoc Colony* (Portland, 1892), pp. 89–90. An incomplete copy of a journal, originally found in the papers of Sir Ferdinando Gorges, was discovered

in Lambeth Palace in 1876. William Strachey had access to the journal and para-phrased parts of it, including portions that now are missing, in *The Historie of Travell into Virginia Britania* (London, 1614). See also the edition by Louis B. Wright and Virginia Freund (London: Hakluyt Society, 1953), the version of *Virginia Britania* that will be cited henceforward. The writings of Sir Ferdinando Gorges are equally important. His correspondence, which includes several letters dealing very candidly with the problems of the Sagadahoc venture, has been published in *Sir Ferdinando Gorges and His Province of Maine*, James P. Baxter, 3 vols. (Boston, 1890). Also of value are Gorges's two short memoirs of his New World promotional efforts: "A Brief Relation of the Discovery and Plantation of New England," reprinted in *Massachusetts Historical Society Collections*, 2d ser. 9 (1823): 1–25; and "Brief Narration of the Original Undertakings of the Advancement of Plantations into the Parts of America," reprinted in *Maine Historical Society Collections*, 1st ser. 2 (1847): 1–65. For other documentary evidence relating to Sagadahoc, see "A Letter from George Popham, President of the Sagadahoc Colony, to King James I, dated December 13, 1607," *Maine Historical Society Collections* 5 (1857): 343–60, and Charles W. Banks, "New Documents Relating to the Popham Expedition, 1607," *Proceedings of the American Antiquarian Society*, n.s. 39 (1930): 307–34. Information about the design of Fort St. George is found in a drawing, discovered in Spain in the late nineteenth century, labeled "The draught of St. George's fort, first erected by Captain George Popham, Esquire, on the entry of the famous river of Sagadahoc in Virginia, taken out by John Hunt the VIII of October in the year of our Lord 1607." This map was first published in Alexander Brown's *The Genesis of the United States*, 2 vols. (Boston, 1890), 1:190. Many of the primary sources relating to Sagadahoc have been reprinted, with useful commentaries, in Thayer's *The Sagadahoc Colony*. The most detailed sec-ondary account remains Henry S. Burrage, *The Beginnings of Colonial Maine, 1602–1658* (Portland: State of Maine, 1914), pp. 63–99.

3. Gorges to the Earl of Salisbury, 3 December 1607, and Gorges to Sir Robert Cecil, 7 February 1607/8, in Baxter, *Gorges and Maine*, 3:158–60, 161–68; Gorges, "Brief Relation," pp. 8–10. Raleigh Gilbert was a son of the celebrated navigator and colonial promoter Sir Humphrey Gilbert. While the exact date of his birth is not known, he was probably in his late twenties or early thirties in 1607. Gorges's preju-dice against him probably was the outgrowth of a dispute over the patent. As Thayer explains, the ship that returned from Sagadahoc in early 1608 "brought report that Gilbert's aspiring claims were threatening the plans and interests of the company. He proposed to revive his father's patent, and to demand supposed rights accruing to him under it, which he believed could not be superseded by the charter of James in 1606; and was endeavoring to form a party to support his designs, sending mes-sages to England to friends to come over and join him. Gorges sought at once to checkmate these plans, and it is inferred that Gilbert soon learned that his revolu-tionary scheme was hopeless" (*Sagadahoc Colony*, p. 31). On better acquaintance, Gorges later modified his assessment of Raleigh Gilbert's character, writing in the *Brief Narration*, published in 1658, that he was "a man worthy to be beloved of them all for his industry, and care for their well being" (p. 22). Baxter believes that Gorges

modified his judgment after becoming better acquainted with Gilbert. See also Baxter, *Gorges and Maine*, 2:16.

4. Strachey, *Virginia Britania*, pp. 172–73.

5. "Relation of the Discovery and Plantation of New England," in Thayer's *Sagadahoc Colony*, p. 92.

6. *The Complete Works of Captain John Smith*, ed. Philip L. Barbour, 3 vols. (Chapel Hill: University of North Carolina Press, 1986), 2:299.

7. *Purchas his Pilgrimage*, p. 756.

8. See, e.g., Louis Clinton Hatch, ed., *Maine: A History* (1919), 4 vols. in 1 (Somerville, N.H.: New Hampshire Publishing Company, 1973), pp. 5–6; Marion Jacques Smith, *A History of Maine* (Portland, Maine: Falmouth, 1949), pp. 32–40; Charles E. Clark, *Maine: A Bicentennial History* (New York: Norton, 1992), p. 17; Royer F. Duncan, *Coastal Maine: A Maritime History* (New York: Norton, 1992), pp. 41–42.

9. In Edward Ballard's *Memorial Volume of the Popham Celebration, August 20, 1862* (Portland, Maine, 1863), a voluminous collection of speeches, testimonials, toasts, and documents, the Sagadahoc colonists are celebrated, but their Indian neighbors and erstwhile trading partners receive little mention. An exception is a piece by Rufus K. Sewell that alluded to Biard's testimony and commented in passing that "collisions, more or less disastrous to the colonists, aided in hastening the abandonment of Sagadahoc" (p. 145). However, in a later article on "Popham's Town of Ft. St. George," *Collections of the Maine Historical Society* 7 (1876): 306, Sewell concluded that the Jesuit account was inaccurate, on grounds that "such a bloody catastrophe could not possibly have escaped the record of incidents at Sagadahoc, before and at the time of its abandonment, made by the English historians Gorges and Strachey."

10. Herbert L. Osgood, *The American Colonies in the Seventeenth Century*, 3 vols. (New York: Macmillan, 1904), 1:335.

11. Quotation from Alden T. Vaughan, *New England Frontier: Puritans and Indians, 1620–1675* (New York: Norton, 1979), p. 14. Neal Salisbury, *Manitou and Providence: Indians, Europeans and the Making of New England, 1500–1643* (New York: Oxford University Press, 1982), p. 94, and Kenneth M. Morrison, *The Embattled Northeast: The Elusive Ideal of Alliance in Abenaki-Euramerican Relations* (Berkeley: University of California Press, 1984), p. 24, also give credence to Biard's account.

12. William Hubbard, *The History of the Indian Wars in New England*, ed. Samuel G. Drake, 2 vols. (New York: Kraus Reprints, 1969), 2:251–52.

13. [James Sullivan], "A Topographical Description of Georgetown," *Massachusetts Historical Society Collections*, 1st ser. 1 (1792): 251. Oddly, Sullivan did not mention this incident in his *History of the District of Maine* (Boston, 1795) but rather attributed the evacuation to the severe winter.

14. William D. Williamson, *A History of the State of Maine from Its First Discovery, A.D. 1602, to the Separation, A.D. 1820, Inclusive*, 2 vols. (Hallowell, 1832), 1:201.

15. Thayer, *Sagadahoc Colony*, p. 204.

16. See the examples in my "Richard Hakluyt's Savages: The Influence of Sixteenth-Century Travel Narratives on English Indian Policy in North America," *International Social Science Review* 60 (1985): 1–24.

17. George Abbot, *A Briefe Description of the Whole World* (London, 1605).

18. Gorges, "Brief Narration," p. 58.

19. For contemporary reports from those expeditions, see George Parker Winship, ed., *Sailors' Narratives of Voyages along the New England Coast* (Boston: Houghton Mifflin, 1905); Charles Herbert Levermore, ed., *Forerunners and Competitors of the Pilgrims and Puritans*, 2 vols. (Brooklyn: New England Society of Brooklyn, 1912); Henry S. Burrage, ed., *Early English and French Voyages* (New York: Charles Scribner's Sons, 1906).

20. James Rosier, "A True Relation of the most Prosperous Voyage made this present yeere 1605 by Captaine George Weymouth in the Discoverie of the land of Virginia" (1605), in Winship's *Sailors' Narratives*, pp. 116, 127.

21. The formula "love and fear" as a guide to policy concerning the Indians is found in numerous travelers' reports from the ill-fated Roanoke Colony in the 1680s through the colonial enterprises of the eighteenth century. For an example of its use in an early account of New England, see Rosier, "A True Relation," p. 119.

22. "A Voyage set out from the Citie of Bristoll at the Charge of the chiefest Merchants and Inhabitants of the Said Citie with a small Ship and Barke for the discourie of the North Part of Virginia," in Winship's *Sailors' Narratives*, p. 57.

23. Rosier, "A True Relation," p. 127.

24. John Brereton, "A Briefe and True Relation of the Discourie of the North Part of Virginia," in Winship's *Sailors' Narratives*, pp. 31–49; "A Voyage set out from the Citie of Bristoll," pp. 51–63; Rosier, "A True Relation," pp. 99–151; "Documents Relating to Captain Bartholomew Gosnold's Voyage to America, A.D. 1602," *Massachusetts Historical Society Collections*, 3d ser. 8 (1843): 69–123.

25. Baxter, *Gorges and Maine*, 2:80. Vaughan, *New England Frontier*, p. 10.

26. Gorges to Cecil, 7 August 1607, in Baxter, *Gorges and Maine*, 3:149.

27. Gorges, "Brief Narration," pp. 17–18.

28. On the question of authorship of the Lambeth manuscript, see Thayer, *Sagadahoc Colony*, pp. 17–20.

29. [James Davies], "The Relation of a Voyage unto New England," in Thayer, *Sagadahoc Colony*, pp. 57–58. Further page citations will appear in the text. For a more recent edition of the Davies journal, see David B. and Alison M. Quinn, *The English New England Voyages, 1602–1608* (London: Hakluyt Society, 1983), pp. 397–443.

30. Bashaba had earlier tried unsuccessfully to persuade Waymouth to send a trading party to the Penobscot. Waymouth suspected his motives and thus missed an opportunity to open Maine to English trade. See Salisbury, *Manitou and Providence*, pp. 90–91.

31. For those who attribute the failed rendezvous to English tardiness see, e.g., Burrage, *Beginnings of Maine*, pp. 83–84; Salisbury, *Manitou and Providence*, p. 93.

32. The Lambeth manuscript contains only the beginning of the account of the meeting with Sabenoa. Strachey continues the story, apparently drawing on a portion of the Davies chronicle that is now lost. Strachey, *Virginia Britania*, p. 171.

33. It is now believed that there were numerous contacts between English fishermen and New England Indians from the mid-sixteenth century onward.

34. Indian middlemen provided links with trade centers to the north. See Bruce

J. Bourque and Ruth Holmes Whitehead, "Tarrantines and the Introduction of European Trade Goods in the Gulf of Maine," *Ethnohistory* 32 (1983): 337–41.

35. Strachey, *Virginia Britania,* p. 171.

36. The chronicle contained in the Lambeth manuscript breaks off at the end of September 1607. Strachey's excerpts from portions of the lost manuscript, possibly supplemented by other sources, carry the detailed narrative forward to 6 October, a probable date for Davies's return to England.

37. Gorges to Cecil, 7 February 1607/8. Samuel Purchas later claimed that Indian informants related that an "evil spirit" threatened to kill them if they had dealings with the English and promised to kill the settlers if the Indians stayed away from Fort St. George (*Purchas his Pilgrimage,* p. 756).

38. Strachey, *Virginia Britania,* p. 177.

39. Gorges to Sir Robert Cecil, 7 August 1607 and 7 February 1607/8.

40. A. L. Rowse, *The Elizabethans and America* (London: Macmillan, 1959), p. 101.

41. Gorges, "Brief Narration," pp. 23–24.

42. Gorges to Cecil, 7 August 1607.

43. Louis B. Wright, *Religion and Empire: Piety and Commerce in English Expansion, 1558–1625* (Chapel Hill: University of North Carolina Press, 1943), pp. 84–113.

44. Gorges, "Brief Narration," p. 24.

2

The Treatment of the Indians in Plymouth Colony

DAVID BUSHNELL

For approximately a decade after the Sagadahoc remnant sailed back to England, Europeans on voyages of exploration and commerce intermittently visited the New England coast. Many of those visits were beneficial to natives and Europeans alike for the mutual knowledge gained and the goods exchanged. A notable exception were the expeditions which kidnapped natives for transport to Europe, where they were trained to be guides and interpreters or, in a few instances, were sold into slavery. Even more damaging to the native population at large were the diseases unwittingly brought by fishermen and other transient voyagers, especially the devastating epidemic that erupted in 1616.

The now-famous "saints and strangers" who arrived at Cape Cod Bay in the fall of 1620 were the unexpected beneficiaries of a kidnapping and of the epidemic. Squanto, seized in 1614 by Captain Hunt, was back in New England by 1621 to serve the Pilgrims as interpreter and guide, yet no other Indians survived at Plymouth harbor to challenge the new settlement. The land the Pilgrims chose for their first town had fields already cleared but no residents, and the nearest tribe of any size, the Wampanoags, needed allies against the Narragansetts, who had been relatively unharmed by the epidemic. In many respects, then, Plymouth had far less to fear from Indian resentment than did most other European outposts, in New England and elsewhere. And at this early stage of Indian-English encounters, a few European neighbors with goods to trade and curious customs to observe were apparently of minor concern to the natives of southeastern New England. For several decades, most encounters were peaceful.

David Bushnell's article of 1953 was an early attempt to summarize Plymouth's Indian policy from 1620 to 1675, a topic long neglected. After 1630, Plymouth would be overshadowed by the Massachusetts Bay Colony, but as long as it remained a separate political entity, its Indian policies were, essentially, generated internally. Although Plymouth would subsequently work in close alliance with the other Puritan colonies, in its early years it established patterns of Indian-white relations that provided useful precedents for those colonies yet to come. Thus the Plymouth story is a crucial plot in the grander tale of New England's Indian-Euroamerican encounters.

In the several decades since 1953, some historians have taken issue with aspects of Bushnell's analysis, while others have fleshed out some of the topics—legal and commercial relations, for example—that he touches upon briefly. His article remains, nonetheless, an excellent starting point for any discussion of Indian-white relations in the Old Colony.

IN THE POPULAR TRADITION concerning Plymouth Colony, the Indian Squanto has acquired a place almost as prominent as the first Thanksgiving, and it can fairly be said that Massasoit does not lag far behind. This is as it should be, for the Compact could easily have remained a dead letter and Thanksgiving might never have become a holiday if the Indians of southeastern Massachusetts had chosen to pounce upon the Pilgrim settlement in the dreary winter of 1621. Despite the obvious importance of Indian relations, however, it does not appear that the Pilgrim Fathers carried with them a preconceived Indian policy when they set out from Holland. We know from Bradford that the lurid tales of Indian savagery then circulating through Europe had prepared them to expect the worst,[1] but they seem to have trusted in Captain Miles Standish to improvise a system of defense after their arrival in America. For their other relations with the natives, they trusted in the Ten Commandments. They would attempt to behave with Christian charity toward the Indian, and they intended to be treated with similar decency in return.

Thus the Pilgrims did not doubt for a moment that they should ultimately pay the Indians for the corn and utensils that they found abandoned on Cape Cod and at New Plymouth, nor did they hesitate to demand the promptest restitution whenever the natives stole property of their own. When Squanto was found guilty of petty intrigues inimical to Massasoit, the Pilgrims agreed in principle to hand him over to justice, although they were naturally delighted to see the Wampanoag envoys return home before the extradition of the interpreter was finally decreed.[2] On the other hand, the Pilgrims insisted that all Indian grievances should be pressed through proper channels. They did not deny the Massachusetts Indians' grievances against Weston's men, but the Indians were fully justified in their fear that Plymouth would not permit the Wessagusset settlement to be wiped out by force. And when the natives apparently determined to wipe out the Pilgrims as well, Captain Standish hurried off to stage a preventive massacre at Massachusetts Bay. No further punishment was inflicted however, and no action whatever was taken against the Cape sachems who had been implicated in the Massachusetts' conspiracy.[3] The natives were given to understand that treachery would not be tolerated, and the English settlers were consequently spared much future trouble. But it was also made clear that the Pilgrims bore the Indians no ill will and that the latter had nothing to fear so long as they behaved amicably.

From the battle of Wessagusset to the outbreak of King Philip's War few spectacular events mark the history of Plymouth Colony, and fewer still concern the Pilgrims' relations with the Indians. During these fifty years of peace, both peoples were learning little by little to know each other better. The Indians had much to teach about New England geography, while the superior technical knowledge of the English soon worked great changes in the natives' way of living. This intercourse was, however, rather one-sided. Squanto deserves full credit for his first lessons in corn cultivation, but the Pilgrims more than repaid the favor by introducing the Indians to the use of metal farm instruments and other European tools.[4] It is certain that for a time the settlers were very glad to buy Indian basketwork.[5] But other than this the Indians had nothing to offer save their labor, their land, and a few furs. Their labor, moreover, was never economical in terms of English cost accounting. It was occasionally used for cutting firewood and even for ordinary farm work, but the Town of Plymouth expressly forbade the employment of Indians in the former occupation because of their wasteful methods.[6]

The Indians' land was a different matter. In the strictest legal sense no "land question" ever existed, for the Pilgrims recognized that in English and also in Divine law the sole title to landed estate in New England belonged to the English crown. Even on a practical level, Indian claims to the greater part of Plymouth Colony were weak, since most of their territory was used only intermittently as a game preserve. Along the western shore of Cape Cod Bay, furthermore, the native inhabitants had been almost entirely wiped out by the recent plague, so that the Pilgrims scarcely needed Massasoit's gracious permission to take all the land they could use.[7]

Nevertheless, the Pilgrims were scrupulously careful to extinguish Indian rights of "occupancy" whenever they pressed beyond the vacant tract on which they raised their first settlements. This was done by means of hoes, cloth, fencing, wampum, or a day's plowing; and since the Indians commonly recognized a joint title to lands, the settlers often attempted to have as many Indians as possible affix their marks to the deed of transfer (2:131, 3:145).[8] There was, however, no strict rule. At times the sachem and his son sealed the transaction alone; often both the sachem and the Indians who had enjoyed immediate use of the purchased tract would sign the deed; and occasionally individual Indians were reputed to have full power to sell the land they occupied. At the eastern end of Cape Cod, there even lived a certain "Paumpmunitt alias Charles" who seems to have made a business of buying land from his fellow Indians in order to resell it to the Plymouth planters (4:152, 12:227–28, 235–36, 238–42).[9] On still other occasions lands were granted outright by the Indians. Massasoit's gift to the original settlers is the most notable example, but later donations were also made in recognition of "kindness, respect, and love" shown an Indian's parents or perhaps to win the favor of an influential politician.[10] But if, at the other extreme, the Indians resolutely refused to part with their lands, the colonial government simply instructed prospective purchasers to look elsewhere. Under Plymouth law it was apparently necessary to pay for totally unoccupied lands if an Indian claimant presented himself, and at least one Indian was able to make good his claim twenty-two years after the English established themselves on his property (2:164, 4:109).[11]

Since these transactions seem to have been almost invariably open and aboveboard, it would be unnecessary to discuss the process of purchasing land at any length if it were not for the common opinion that land was constantly contended between colonists and Indians and a direct cause of King Philip's War. For one thing, it has often been claimed that the English cheated the Indians unmercifully by paying far less than their lands were actually worth, and at first glance this charge appears to have some basis in fact. Since early colonial deeds were often vague in setting down the boundaries of the tracts purchased, and since the money value of corn, shoes, kettles, and other legal tender varied with both time and place, it is impossible to construct a table showing the average price per acre of land bought from the Indians. Even if a precise scale in pounds, shillings, and iron hoes were available, it would not greatly clarify the problem, for just as land was less valuable to the Indians than to the Pilgrims, all metal artifacts were more highly prized by the natives than by the English settlers. Nevertheless, the Indians can hardly have failed to grasp the fact that a Pilgrim syndicate could buy native lands at Freetown and resell them within a few years at a five hundred per cent profit,[12] and it is likely that even sharper rises in land values were not uncommon.

In defense of the Pilgrims, it can fairly be said that they were no more to blame than the Indians themselves for what was a natural consequence of economic forces. Lands effectively incorporated into the North Atlantic economy by the expansion of English settlement were obviously worth more, monetarily, than a native hunting reservation, and the profit was not necessarily speculative when lands were improved before being resold. King Philip himself, who cited land "injuries" as one motive for his hostilities against Plymouth Colony, did not hesitate to continue his sales of tribal land almost until the outbreak of war, at least in part the better to enjoy luxuries brought by the English.[13] As a matter of fact, the sums paid by the English were often far from insignificant; in 1672 Philip sold sixteen square miles to Taunton for £190,[14] and similarly high prices were not infrequent after the early years of settlement.

Still another line of attack on the Pilgrims' land purchases has to do with the Indians' supposed reservations about transferring their lands to the English. In particular, it has been charged that whereas the Indians imagined they were transferring a mere right of usufruct, the English were no less convinced that they were acquiring absolute ownership. Although it is impossible to reconstruct exactly what went on in the Indians' minds, their notions of landed property were so indefinite that some such confusion may easily have existed both in Plymouth and elsewhere in New England. However, it seems unreasonable to assume that the Pilgrims' interpreters were never able to find an intelligible rendering of the word "forever" which constantly appeared in the deeds of purchase, and when the Indians actually did attempt to reassert a right of ownership over land they had already sold, the English were generous in buying off their pretensions. A long list could be made of the so-called "quit-claim" or "confirmatory" deeds that a new sachem would issue, for a slight compensation, for the purpose of renouncing any rights in tracts of land that had been formally alienated by his predecessors. The Pilgrims were equally reasonable with regard to lands claimed by more than one tribe or band of Indians.[15] Multiple purchases of one sort or another became so frequent that in 1659 the colony saw fit to issue firm orders against the practice, on the plausible grounds that such transactions cast doubt on the legality of the original purchase (11:124).

Whatever the Indians may have thought regarding the length of tenure accorded to English purchasers, there is no doubt that they frequently intended to continue hunting or fishing or gathering rushes on their former lands after the English had moved in. Certain Cape Indians likewise desired the right to continue taking blubber from whales washed up on the shore (2:131).[16] Indeed, the fact that such conditions were carefully written into the terms of purchase is one reason to doubt that the Indians were entirely unaware of what they were doing in parting with their lands. The specific recognition of Indian rights, moreover, must have spared the Pilgrims much controversy in later years. The records of Plymouth Colony contain numerous instances of Indians prosecuted for "trespass" on English property, and at times a township felt compelled to issue special orders for the purpose of excluding unwelcome Indians from its land.[17] But it would be rash to assume that such misdemeanors resulted simply from the natives' theory of property, for Englishmen were frequently charged with exactly the same offense.

Unfortunately land prices and terms of occupancy were not the only questions capable of causing friction between Pilgrims and Indians. The vague boundaries established in the first land deeds inevitably led to difficulties, although it seems that an amicable settlement was usually reached. While there may well have been instances of obtaining an Indian's "signature" to a deed while he was drunk or other cases of swindling the "poore Indians," the Plymouth authorities were more zealous than most colonial governments to prevent such abuses. From the very start of the settlement a legal permit from the colony was required before land could be purchased from the natives (11:41, 183), and this rule protected the Indians quite as much as it furthered the cause of an orderly English settlement. The law was not always enforced with equal severity, but at least one Pilgrim was actually disfranchised for the offense (3:101).

Even more significant is Plymouth's readiness to guarantee the Indians a full legal title to their lands. At times an Indian would request the government to register his property; in such cases the required document was promptly drawn up and the Indian's possession was secured on the same terms as those applied to English lands (see, e.g., 12:225, 242). The official registration of Indian wills, which became increasingly frequent as the natives learned the ways of English judicial procedure, and which often amounted to a virtual entail, had exactly the same effect (12:228, 231, 233–34).[18] In the case of Mount Hope, Pocasset, and other leading sites of Indian settlement it seems that the Pilgrims anticipated the natives' wishes, for it was ordered that such lands might not be purchased even if the Indians agreed to sell.[19] Despite a general disinclination to mingle socially with the natives, the colonists did not necessarily object if the Indians desired to live and farm alongside the English. They acquiesced when the Indians insisted on retaining a reservation for their own use within the bounds of a township that had otherwise extinguished the native titles; and the records of the Town of Plymouth contain more than one instance of land rented or granted outright to individual Indians.[20]

For the main body of Pilgrim settlers, trade was far less important than land. Indian corn was found necessary for the survival of the colonists during their first years in New England, and it was the fur trade that allowed the struggling colony to win its financial independence from the London adventurers. But as soon as the colony became agriculturally self-sufficient, it did not need Wampanoag corn. The fur resources of the Pilgrims' immediate neighbors were always limited, so that Plymouth fur traders were soon compelled to look farther afield, in Maine and Connecticut. The local trade nevertheless throws considerable light on the Pilgrims' relations with the Indians. Official policy was to organize it as a monopoly on somewhat the same lines as the fur trade on the Kennebec. To make matters more certain, the colonists were strictly forbidden to do any trading whatever that involved paying the Indians in money, arms, or liquor (1:54, 11:33, 184). But the monopoly system does not seem to have been rigorously enforced, and the holders of the concession were not always very active. In 1640, therefore, it was decided that any colonist might "trade for corne, beades, venison, or some tymes for a beaver skine" without violating Plymouth laws (1:50–51, 130, 2:4).[21]

A more effective limitation on the local trade was the continuing prohibition of giving the Indians money, liquor, or arms. The first of these prohibitions was finally lifted in 1669, only to be restored eight years later on the plea that the Indians might use their money for liquor (11:184, 244). And this excuse is not at all improbable, for the Pilgrims felt very strongly indeed on the subject of "drinking Indians." "They drinke themselves drunke," it was observed, "and in their drunkenes committ much horred wickednes, as murthering theire nearest relations, &c, as by sadd and woefull experience is made manifest" (3:60). Even for medical purposes, a permit was required before liquor could be given to a native (11:184), and few crimes appear so often in the Plymouth court records as the sale of liquor to the Indians.

The colonists were almost as adamant on the subject of arming the natives. It is well known that one of their strongest objections to Thomas Morton of Merrymount was the fact that he supplied his Indian friends with arms and ammunition.[22] This concern is understandable. Whereas the liquor traffic was frowned upon as much because it endangered the Indians' souls as because it threatened to disturb public order, the sale of guns to the Indians was deemed to strike at the very basis of the colonists' security. It is thus remarkable that throughout the 1660s and up to the eve of King Philip's War, the prohibition was repeatedly suspended for powder and shot and then put back in full force (11:184–85, 215, 219, 237); but on the whole it was strictly enforced, and precautions were taken to prevent the transfer of arms to the natives under the pretense of lending them guns to hunt game in English employment (11:185).[23]

Despite the list of prohibited articles, the Indians remained eager to trade with the Pilgrims. They were gradually replacing their traditional clothing, tools, and household utensils with the English products,[24] and their sudden awakening to the benefits of European civilization is strikingly illustrated by the growing use of wampum as a medium of exchange. Before the coming of the Pilgrims, the Wampanoags and their satellites had felt little need for either large-scale commerce or a form of money. But soon after the Dutch instructed the Pilgrims in the potential value of shell beads, the situation changed abruptly. Even so, wampum did little more than facilitate the act of trading; it did not provide the Indians with a favorable trade balance. The Indians of Plymouth Colony could satisfy some of their needs by turning to the manufacture of wampum themselves, but in this industry they never attained the proficiency of the Narragansetts and Pequots.[25]

To obtain English manufactures, therefore, the Wampanoags and Nausets had to supplement their meager stocks of furs and wampum with the one thing that they had in abundance and that the English ardently desired: their lands. It is thus easy to understand why the relative values of land and iron kettles were very different among the Indians from what they were among the Pilgrims, and one consequence of this relation was that the trade and land questions tended to merge together. The clearest examples of the process are to be found among the sachems themselves, who combined the greatest ambition for personal improvement with the greatest territorial resources. Massasoit's son Alexander, for instance, sold land to redeem a debt which he owed to a Plymouth tavernkeeper who was later convicted of repeatedly selling liquor to the natives; another of Alexander's deeds could not be recognized as valid in later years until it was established by witnesses that he had been fully sober when affixing his mark to the paper.[26] There is no evidence, however, that the liquor traffic was a major factor in the land problem. A better example of the connection between trade and land sales is offered by Alexander's brother and successor, King Philip, who is said to have been exceedingly fond of elegant apparel. As a result of this weakness—over and above the need to pay off a heavy fine levied against him by Plymouth Colony—Philip surpassed all other Indians in the number of his land sales.[27]

The problems of land tenure and trade with the Indians, strictly speaking, could not be separated from the broader question of English authority over the native tribes of New England. The territorial claims of the King of England were more modest in extent than those of the Crown of Castile, and they were based on the sighting of new lands by Cabot and his successors rather than on discovery and a papal bull. From the point of view of the original inhabitants, however, all this made little difference; and other claims were duly reinforced by the prior clearing of so much of the land through epidemic disease. In any case, the entire process of acquiring land from the natives was based on the assumption that property rights in New England resided ultimately in the English crown. Similarly the granting of fur monopolies and the careful regulation of all Indian trade reflected a firm belief that the only legitimate government in New England was that of the English king and the colonial authorities acting in his behalf. In his first treaty with the Pilgrims, to be sure, Massasoit obtained the anomalous status of "friend and ally" to his ultimate sovereign, James I, but such glaring inconsistencies do not appear in subsequent treaties (1:133, 4:25–26).[28] The mere fact of agreeing, tacitly or otherwise, to become His Majesty's subjects did not, however, place the Indians in the same category as his English vassals. On one occasion, the town of Rehoboth asked Plymouth Court to approve the admission of "Sam, the Indian that keeps the cows," as an inhabitant, but the absence of any further reference to Sam suggests that the petition was not granted.[29] Nor did any Indian ever obtain political rights in Plymouth Colony.

The status of the Indians was further differentiated by the existence of a distinct system for their immediate government. Though willing to assert their jurisdiction over the entire native population of the colony, the Plymouth authorities were not equally willing to accept the responsibilities and the nuisance of regulating all the Indians' affairs. As a result, the Pilgrims were slow to part with the services of the sachems. When a group of Sandwich Indians asked the colony court in 1665 for permission to organize "some orderly way of government," apparently under the supervision of the missionary Richard Bourne, the colony agreed only on condition that the new arrangement in no way interfere with the prerogatives of their "superior sachem" (4:80). Respect for the sachems was not, however, an invariable rule. As the Indians grew more familiar with English ways and brought their own disputes into Plymouth courts, the authorities sometimes bluntly told them to refer them to their sachems (5:102). But the colonial government increasingly saw fit to intervene in such cases, and this was particularly true whenever English interests were indirectly involved. It is not surprising that Plymouth Court agreed to hear a case in which an Indian sued squaw sachem Awashunks of Saconet for illegally retaining lands that he desired to sell to the English settlers, nor that the court found in favor of the plaintiff (7:191).[30] Neither was there ever any doubt regarding jurisdiction in disputes between Englishmen and Indians. The procedure in such cases was not clearly formulated before 1670, when Plymouth enacted that all ordinary disputes between the two races should be heard first by the selectmen of the towns, but the principle had never been questioned. Indeed, the colony court seems to have handled disputes directly in many instances, despite the order of 1670, and it reserved the right to treat all cases involving land titles or capital crimes. And needless to say, when Plymouth magistrates became involved, they normally followed the principles of English law and conducted proceedings in the language of the settlers, not that of the Indians, whether plaintiffs or defendants (11:227–28).[31]

The separate status of the Indian population was also emphasized by the special legislation that affected the native but not his white neighbor. The best-known examples of such laws are those already mentioned regarding the sale of arms and liquor, but many more restrictions were imposed upon the Indians. The Indian could not buy a horse without a permit from the colony, nor could he acquire any boat except a canoe (11:65, 184). He could not be trusted with sales on credit (11:259), nor could he shoot his gun or make other unpleasant commotion on the Sabbath day or at night. Indeed, the pagan Indian was arbitrarily required to keep the Sabbath as quietly as the Christian settler (11:60–61, 66). Since the conglomeration of Indians in the capital during court sessions was distasteful to the Pilgrims, the natives were forbidden to draw near on such occasions (6:113, 11:243).

Even regulations that held good for members of both races were not always equally applied. Thieves of either race could be compelled to make amends by labor; but in the case of at least five Indian thieves, servitude was made perpetual when they were sold as slaves. Where the law allowed either corporal punishment or a fine to be imposed, Indian offenders were far more likely than English to receive the lash (at least in part because they were less often in a position to pay fines) (5:151–52, 270, 6:108, 153).[32] However, even though the penalties against Indians were often different from those decreed for English criminals, they were not necessarily harsher. It was suggested to one group of Indians that they might pay for killing an English mare by destroying wolves for the colony (4:17). Moreover, an "ingenuous" confession sufficed more than once to win easy terms for an Indian culprit. A striking case is that of an Indian who had readily confessed to raping a white woman. The statutory penalty was death, but the Indian was let off with a whipping and an order to leave the colony "considering hee was but an Indian, and therefore in an incapacity to know the horiblenes of the wickednes of this abominable act, with other cercomstances considered" (6:98).[33]

Reasonableness is also shown in the law of 1674, which held that Indians should not be bound by English rules of sworn testimony in court but instead should testify as in a court of chancery; the Plymouth judges were to use their own discretion in assessing the value of their declarations (11:236). Likewise, Indian jurors were occasionally impaneled in cases involving their fellows (5:167–68),[34] although this was not a frequent occurrence. But the Pilgrims' interest in fair treatment of the natives is shown best of all by the willingness of Plymouth courts to grant the Indians redress when they were wronged by their white neighbors. The most common offense of the English was negligence in pasturing their cattle, pigs, and horses, with the result that the Pilgrims' animals repeatedly trampled down the Indians' cornfields. The frontier settlement of Rehoboth was the most "unsufferable" offender. Year after year Indian complaints reached the Plymouth court, which ordered the townspeople to build fences around Indian fields at their own expense and to construct a pound where the Indians might keep delinquent animals until proper compensation was paid. The chief exception was made in the case of Rhode Island horses, which were to be seized outright (3:21, 106, 167, 192, 222).[35] In 1671 the Colony went so far as to name officers in each town to view the damage done to Indian fields, and only in the case of Indians living within an English township did the responsibility for fencing rest entirely with the natives (5:62, 11:143).

The same protection was accorded Indians who suffered burglary, false witness, and abuse at the hands of the English, or even those who found that their kettles had been penetrated by a hunter's stray bullet (2:20, 89, 5:152, 6:24, passim). Recourse was had to intercolonial diplomacy when a Boston man failed to pay a Cape Indian for his services in catching fish.[36] The most spectacular instance of Pilgrim justice, however, was the execution of three English servants for the murder of an Indian bearing wampum. Bradford relates that "some of the rude and ignorant sort murmured" in protest, but exemplary justice was inflicted.[37]

The Plymouth authorities were not content with mere protection of the Indian against English settlers; they were no less eager to save him from the devil. With the friendly Massasoit, surprisingly enough, the Christian gospel found no acceptance. The Wampanoag sachem was primarily interested in the material advantages that a new religion had to offer,[38] and it seems that he never received a satisfactory answer in this respect. Shortly before his death, Massasoit unsuccessfully attempted to write a clause against further missionary efforts into the terms of a sale of land.[39] With the Indians of Cape Cod, however, the Pilgrims had better luck. The Cape Indians, like Mayhew's charges on Martha's Vineyard, were relatively isolated from their fellow pagans, and the Cape was the scene of the earliest and most vigorous missionary activity. It appears that Richard Bourne, a wealthy merchant of Sandwich, and Captain Thomas Tupper, a Pilgrim soldier, began their work among the natives even before John Eliot's first visits to the Indians of Massachusetts Bay,[40] but Eliot himself turned his attention to the Cape as early as 1648. In that year he was sent by the United Colonies to end dissension within the English church at Yarmouth; and Eliot did not miss the opportunity to preach to the local

Indians. One deceitful sachem promised to bring his subjects to hear the Apostle's lesson and then sent them off on a fishing expedition instead. Other Indians, however, were more amenable, and Eliot was happy to learn of a vague local tradition that the natives had once known the true God but had somehow lost contact with Him in the course of time.[41]

The most intensive missionary work, on the other hand, had to await the formation of the Corporation for the Propagation of the Gospel in New England by act of Parliament in 1649.[42] It is possible that Plymouth received less than its due share of the Corporation's remittances, but Bourne and his associates obtained regular grants for the hiring of interpreters and miscellaneous expenses, while the Plymouth authorities were generally assigned a few pounds a year to distribute among "well deserving Indians" (10:183, 205, 219, 246, 263, 277, 296, 317, 331, 356, 367). Richard Bourne continued to lead the way; in 1670 he was formally ordained as pastor of the colony's first Indian church, and to assure the permanence of his efforts, he secured a grant of land for his converts at Mashpee. Similar reservations of "Praying Indians" were established elsewhere.[43] On the eastern side of the Cape, the Reverend Samuel Treat rivaled Bourne in the number of his conversions, becoming especially popular with the natives through the visits that he made to their wigwams.[44] By the outbreak of King Philip's War, progress had even been made in the center of the colony, in the vicinity of Middleborough; here John Sassamon, a Harvard alumnus and protégé of Eliot, was established as the first regularly settled Indian minister in New Plymouth.[45]

As a result of these combined efforts, Plymouth contained well over 1,000 Indian converts in 1674; in addition, 142 of these had learned to read their own language, and nine had been taught to read English.[46] By 1685 the total was approaching 1,500. Naturally a small proportion of these Indians were fully accredited members of a Christian church; the lists merely included "such as do, before some of their magistrates or civil rulers, renounce their former heathenish manners, and give up themselves to be Praying Indians. . . ."[47] But neither could all the English settlers be enrolled as Visible Saints. The fact remains that the Indian population of Plymouth Colony was almost as thoroughly christianized in 1685 as the Pilgrims themselves, particularly as the most obstinate had meanwhile been eliminated by King Philip's War.[48]

The extent of the missionaries' success is further shown by the fact that the natives had come to shoulder the greater part of their own spiritual guidance. From the very start, the missionaries had been assisted by Indian "teachers" and interpreters, and by 1686 a friend of the natives could complain that Indian teachers received £3–4 a year for constant work, whereas

English missionaries were paid up to £20 for preaching to the Indians only three or four times.[49] Equally significant was the loyalty of the Praying Indians to Plymouth Colony during King Philip's War.

The long years of peace with the Indians that had distinguished Plymouth Colony came to an abrupt end in the reign of Philip, the third Wampanoag sachem known to the Plymouth settlers. In view of the generally fair treatment that had been accorded to the Plymouth Indians, in particular as compared to the situation in other American colonies, it is surprising that an Indian war should begin in New Plymouth; and it is more so that the Indians should attribute the entire guilt to the Pilgrim Fathers. Yet Philip himself did not hesitate to remind the people of Massachusetts Bay that they were shedding the blood of their sons merely to pull Plymouth chestnuts out of the fire.[50] Moreover, the bitter controversy between Philip and Plymouth Colony has given rise to a strong tradition that pictures Philip as a veritable Indian statesman who saw the impending doom of his race at the hands of his grasping neighbors and staked the redress of countless legitimate grievances on a carefully laid conspiracy against English rule in New England. If the war was well planned, however, the evidence does not seem to support it. Philip appears to have begun the struggle with a wholly inadequate store of arms, and despite both threats and entreaties, many of his immediate neighbors had not yet decided which side to support when war broke out.[51]

Philip's unpreparedness can probably be explained by the hypothesis that he had only begun his scheming when his hand was forced by premature revelation of the plot. The necessity for his supreme effort is less easily established. Philip laid greatest stress on the unfair absorption of the Indians' "planting lands," both by unjust arbitration of land disputes and by such practices as getting an Indian drunk in order to purchase his lands for a fraction of their worth,[52] but the general land policy of Plymouth Colony would suggest that he can have had no very serious grievances in this respect. In particular there is no specific mention in Plymouth records or in contemporary narratives of major land disputes with Philip; and though the English settlers would hardly leave a fair statement of Philip's complaints, one would at least expect a passing reference. Likewise it has never been shown that the Wampanoags lacked sufficient farm land; by the time of Philip's War, in fact, they could get along with much less than before, thanks to new methods learned from the English. Nor could the reduction of their hunting lands have disastrous effects for a primarily agricultural people. Philip further complained of the damages done to Indian corn by English cattle and of the sale of liquor to the natives.[53] In both cases, however, the Plymouth government was quite as anxious as he was to correct the abuse. The frontier settlements found some difficulty in enforcing the colony's orders, yet probably neither abuse was so serious as to explain a recourse to arms.

Thus it is not impossible that Palfrey was right in regarding the war as a wanton and even irrational attack by the Indians upon Plymouth Colony; such a hypothesis is indirectly supported by reports that Philip himself opposed war but that his policy was influenced by young braves chafing under an unwelcome peace.[54] A wild venture of this sort would naturally be encouraged by the various petty irritations which arose along the frontier and for which both Englishmen and Indians were to blame. In fairness to Philip, however, it must be said that the trampling of cornfields and the sale of liquor were not the only irritations. There were also political grievances that the sachem for some reason failed to emphasize. It has already been seen that the Indians' nominal acceptance of Plymouth authority became increasingly real as the English settlements were consolidated, and during the last years before the conflict in particular, there was a tendency to tighten control over the Indian population and impose harsher penalties against those convicted of crime.[55] It also appears that the Plymouth authorities were somewhat tactless in their dealings with the later Wampanoag rulers.

Only once was there any serious doubt of the loyalty of Massasoit; it was cast by Squanto, and the white man's good friend nearly lost his life when his falseness was discovered. In return for the chief's friendship, the English more than once came to his support against Indian rivals (9:15).[56] On the accession of Massasoit's son Alexander in 1662, however, rumors of treachery at once began to gain credence, and the sachem was ordered to come to Plymouth to explain his conduct. After a probably justifiable delay he appeared at the Pilgrim capital, satisfied the authorities of his loyalty, and was immediately dismissed. Despite the romantic tale that Alexander died of chagrin soon afterwards, there is no real evidence that he was mistreated by the English settlers during this episode.[57] Yet no sooner had he been succeeded by his younger brother than exactly the same process was repeated with Philip. Again it seems that there was no basis for Plymouth's suspicions, and the incident was closed with a renewal of the treaty between the English and the Wampanoags. New suspicions arose in 1667. Once more the authorities recognized in the end that they possessed no concrete evidence and let the matter drop, although they compelled Philip to pay the cost of the proceedings (4:25–26, 151, 164–66). Nevertheless relations with Philip were, on the whole, friendly during the first part of his rule. On one occasion, he apparently vowed to suspend land sales for a seven-year period, but the exact circumstances of this decision are by no means clear.[58] He did not keep his pledge, and it is probable that his need for English money to live in royal state was as much responsible for his change of heart as pressure from the Plymouth authorities.

In 1671, however, graver troubles arose. The usual rumors had arisen, in part because of a murder near Boston in which Philip was rumored to have had a hand;[59] but it is quite possible that the English had more important grounds for their suspicions, since they viewed the matter in a much more serious light than any of the preceding "conspiracies." Philip ultimately agreed to meet Plymouth envoys at Taunton on 10 April, provided a Massachusetts delegation went along to ensure fair play, but far from showing remorse over his recent activities, he countered by accusing Plymouth of certain unspecified injuries to his "planting land." According to the colonists, it was then shown that his charges were absurd, whereupon Philip admitted his military preparations but claimed they were directed against the Narragansetts. This, too, is said to have been disproved, and Philip finally admitted that he had been conspiring against the English "from his own naughty heart." He reaffirmed his allegiance to the English crown and to New Plymouth and agreed to deposit his arms as security for future good behavior (5:63).[60]

Peace now seemed to have returned, and at this juncture the Praying Indians of Cape Cod came loyally to the government's support with a spate of treaties couched in the most picturesque phrases:

> forasmuch as the English, and wee, the poor Indians, are as of one blood, as Acts 17th, 26, for wee doe confess wee poor Indians in our lives were as captives under Sathan, and our sachems, doeing theire wills whose breath perisheth, as Psalmes 146, 3, 4; Exodus 15, 1, 2, &c; but now wee know by the word of God, that it is better to trust in the Great God and his strength. Psalm 188, 8, 9; and besides, wee were like unto wolves and lyons, to destroy one another; but wee hope and believe in God; therefore wee desire to enter into covenant with the English respecting our fidelitie, as Isai: 11, 6. [5:66–67]

Not all Indians, however, showed this humility. Since the alarm had been general, Plymouth also attempted to disarm many of Philip's friends and subjects, and in this endeavor the authorities met with some resistance. Awashunks of Saconet, for instance, was bullied into accepting the English demands, but she could induce only forty-two of her subjects—not including her two sons—to obey the order for surrender of arms (5:75).[61] Nor was this truly surprising, since even a largely sedentary people such as the Indians of Plymouth Colony still derived at least part of their livelihood from hunting, and it would seem that the bow and arrow had long gone out of fashion. Philip himself, moreover, bluntly refused to meet the full demands of the colonial government. He insisted, probably with some justification, that the treaty of Taunton referred only to arms that he and his men had left outside when they entered to confer with the English, and he refused to hand over any more. Moreover, he appealed to the government of Massachusetts Bay which strangely informed Plymouth that the Taunton agreements did not make Philip a subject of the colony but merely a friend. Nevertheless Philip was finally brought to terms in much the same manner as before. A general conference was arranged, although this time Connecticut, too, sent a delegation; a full confession was obtained; and Philip agreed to pay a fine of £100 and to kill a yearly quota of five wolves in payment for the trouble he had caused (5:76–79).

The fine which was thus levied against Philip was clearly unreasonable, even for an Indian chief; indeed it may well be connected with the fact that one year later Philip was compelled to mortgage a small tract of land in view of his inability to pay certain monies that he owed to the colony (5:101). This time, however, peace really did return to New Plymouth, and it lasted until early in 1675. The English chroniclers, to be sure, were convinced that Philip began plotting a general war immediately after the humiliation at Taunton, but conditions were outwardly so calm that the embargo on giving arms and ammunition to the Indians was partially lifted in 1674 (11:237).[62] Then in February of the following year new reports of Philip's impending treachery were carried to Plymouth by John Sassamon, the Indian preacher at Middleborough. Following the traditional procedure, Philip came to court, but no conclusive evidence was found against him, and he was allowed to return home with a mere admonition (10:362–63). Yet the problem was not so easily solved, for a week after his own visit to Plymouth, Sassamon had been found dead beneath the ice of Assowamsett Pond. There were at once some suspicions of foul play, and later in the spring of 1675, "by a strange Providence, an Indian was found, that by Accident was standing unseen upon a Hill [and had seen three of Philip's men] murder the said Sassamon."[63]

The tardy appearance of such a witness seems somewhat suspicious, and the Indians had a story that the informer was merely trying to avoid payment of a gambling debt by having his creditors executed for murder. Still another version implied that Sassamon was murdered because of his missionary activities.[64] On the other hand, it is not impossible that the Indian was telling the truth. There is nothing inherently implausible in the explanation that he had refrained from doing his duty sooner for fear that the same thing would happen to him that had happened to Sassamon and that the truth was finally divulged when he shared his knowledge with a Praying Indian.[65] Be that as it may, the three Indian culprits were haled before Plymouth Court, tried by a jury to which certain of the "most indifferentest, gravest, and sage Indians" had been added, and duly executed (5:167–68).[66]

Nothing was done, however, about Philip himself, for Plymouth showed a laudable dislike of proceeding against him on mere suspicion. Plymouth hoped that as soon as the Wampanoag sachem observed that no action was intended against him for lack of evidence, he would desist from his warlike intentions; around the middle of June a conciliatory message was sent off in which he was merely requested to disband his forces (10:363–64).[67] But, unfortunately, the authorities were too optimistic. Whether Sassamon had been correct in February or not, by June there was no doubt that Philip was engaged in a general conspiracy. The hostile nature of his activities was amply confirmed by so trustworthy a witness as Benjamin Church, who obtained his information directly from meetings with his good friend Awashunks and with other Indians, including the very envoys sent out by Philip to win support for his cause.[68] After the middle of the month, border incidents became frequent, and after an English settler had been goaded into firing the first shot, the Indians launched their war with the Swanzey massacre of 24 June.[69]

The military history of King Philip's War is too well known to require retelling, and the most important engagements took place outside Plymouth Colony. The struggle, nevertheless, had a profound effect upon the condition of Plymouth's Indian inhabitants. The Praying Indians, to begin with, were subjected to considerable suspicion despite their unwavering loyalty to the English. This distrust was unfounded, but it is easily understandable in view of the aroused feeling of the English settlers and the common report that an Indian's chief delight was to "rob, kill and roast, lead captive, slay . . . blaspheme."[70] It was some time before the Pilgrims could realize that such things were not going to happen on Cape Cod; and hence it was only in the face of a rapidly deteriorating military situation that the colony finally agreed to a general enlistment of loyal Indians (5:186–87).[71] But such slights as this were nothing compared with the lot of the hostile Indians. An indeterminate number perished as casualties of war or fled from the colony never to return; a relatively small number, including Church's friends from Saconet, were permitted to make a timely submission and resettle in Plymouth Colony on much the same terms as before. The rest of Philip's followers, however, were classed as prisoners of war and formally enslaved. Many Indians who had been encouraged to surrender in the hope of kinder treatment probably met exactly the same fate (5:173–74, 210, 215).[72]

The General Court of November, 1676, determined that all adult male captives must be sold out of the colony (11:242), but the rule did not apply in every case. Ringleaders of the revolt and any Indians who had taken part in major atrocities were summarily tried and executed; nor did the authorities spare certain war criminals who had been given quarter by Captain Church, for his commission did not authorize an indiscriminate show of mercy (5:204–6).[73] Likewise Philip's young son, though scarcely an adult male Indian, was condemned to be sold as a slave to Bermuda; but this might almost be termed an act of generosity, since several Plymouth clergymen, citing scriptural precedents, had advised that he be put to death for the future security of the state.[74] Women and children, on the other hand, were allowed to remain in the colony, where they were employed as domestic servants or perhaps taught some useful craft. Indeed, a few male prisoners were similarly favored; Captain Church, for instance, was allowed to retain some of his own captives on the interesting condition that they should perform military service under his command if need arose (5:207, 225).[75]

The fate of the defeated thus varied rather widely. There were certainly many excesses committed against them, but at least by twentieth-century standards their treatment can hardly be termed genocidal. Moreover, since the hostile Indians were all but eliminated as an independent factor in the life of Plymouth Colony, the problem of Indian relations was decidedly eased in many respects. Military preparedness could be comfortably forgotten as far as any internal danger was concerned. Similarly the land question was greatly simplified by the confiscation of rebel territory, and, in fact, one group of loyal Indians was asked to accommodate a few English settlers on their lands in payment for the colony's services in defending them against King Philip (5:224–25, 6:63, 10:407–8). The decline of the pagan population, moreover, brought the first phase of missionary activity to its close.

The elimination of the stronger sachems, however, finally compelled the colony to devise a regular system of Indian government. This was done by a law of July 1682, which ordered that every ten adult Indians should unite to elect one of their number as a "tithingman" for the general supervision of their affairs. All the Indian "tithingmen" of a given township, in turn, were to gather together to hold courts among the natives, to name Indian constables, and to assess the Indians' taxes. In these functions they were to be assisted by a specially appointed English overseer, who was instructed to collect his charges and once each year read aloud the laws of Plymouth Colony (11:252–53).

Otherwise there was no major change in the treatment of the Indians; they were about as well cared for in Plymouth courts as before, and they continued to be protected against guns and liquor. Instead it was the Indians who had changed, for Plymouth was now truly a Christian commonwealth, and in the fight for survival the lowly Praying Indians had shown themselves fitter than King Philip. Their descendants, in fact, are still living in the Old Colony today. They are, of course, much fewer in number, but this results in part from a natural process of race mixture. In any case, it would be unfair to put sole blame on the Pilgrim Fathers for the drastic decline of the Indian population. Their principal contribution to that end result was the fact that they, along with other English people, introduced new diseases and a societal system to which the Indians could not fully adjust for several generations. It is not even certain that the battle casualties of the Wampanoags should be blamed purely on the English. It is true that the Pilgrims generally treated the natives as a race apart, but they made a conscious effort to deal fairly with them, and except for the repression triggered by King Philip's War, they were not notably harder on the Indians than on each other.

Author's Postscript

The preceding article had its inception in the Harvard seminar of Samuel E. Morison a half century ago. I was then and have remained a Latin Americanist, who was drawn to the topic of Plymouth's Indian policy because of the critical importance of Indian relations for colonial Spanish America. From a comparative perspective, I was struck more by the similarities than by the differences in official policy and objectives between English America, as represented by the Pilgrims, and Spanish America; and having been taught that Spanish policy, if not practice, toward the natives was informed by Christian humanism, that parallel did not in my view tarnish the Pilgrims' reputation. The article thus took its place within the relatively benign current of interpretation of New England's Indian relations that is best exemplified by Alden T. Vaughan's *New England Frontier: Puritans and Indians, 1620–1675*, 3d ed. (Norman: University of Oklahoma Press, 1995).

In the years since the essay was written and then first revised for publication in *NEQ*, the fate of the New England Indians has been the topic of some frequently polemical general works and a good many monographic articles. With a few exceptions, this body of literature has not focused explicitly on Plymouth Colony, although both general overviews and the works devoted primarily to Massachusetts Bay tend to assume that there were common features to the Indian policies of all New England colonies.

In no case does later research appear to overturn the specific factual details presented in the earlier version. Neither do additional details included in more recent writings (some of which have now been incorporated in the reference notes) significantly alter the picture presented, save in the matter of crime and punishment. However, in the revisionist school that initially came to the fore in the 1960s and set much of the tone of discussion at least through the quincentennial in 1992 of discovery/encounter, all those details either received a radically different interpretation or (from the standpoint of benign interpreters) were conveniently overlooked. Thus, in explaining the origins of King Philip's War, all emphasis was placed on the settlers' misdeeds vis-à-vis the Indians, which no one had seriously denied, while efforts of the Plymouth authorities to curb the excesses tended to be portrayed as ineffective if not downright hypocritical. The brutal punishment of the defeated enemy, which again no one had denied, became one more part of a supposedly genocidal campaign of extermination rather than just overreaction to a perceived danger. In the treatment of peacetime relations, special emphasis was placed on the land question, stressing the incorporation of ever greater amounts into the settlers' possession while ignoring the accumulated evidence both of voluntary alienation on the part of individual Indians and the limitations placed on the process of alienation/acquisition by colonial statutes and officials. Missionary activity appeared to the revisionists as nothing more than a form of cultural aggression, with doubts cast even on the sincerity of the "Apostle," John Eliot. And the administration of justice to the Indian in Plymouth courts has been depicted as clearly skewed against the Indian, with my article singled out by no less than two authors (James Ronda and Lyle Koehler as cited in n. 31) in their very first reference notes as an example of what needs to be revised in this connection.

As Vaughan has suggested in the introduction to the third edition of his own study, the tenets of the revisionists are typically found in general works such as that of Francis Jennings, *The Invasion of America: Indians, Colonialism, and the Cant of Conquest* (Chapel Hill: University of North Carolina Press for the Institute of Early American History and Culture, 1975), while monographic studies of particular aspects of Indian relations more often have supported the benign interpretation of Puritan motives, if not in all instances Puritan actions. As this revised version of my article will show, I continue to hold much the same interpretation as I did four decades ago. Greater sensitivity has caused me to expunge such terminology as "red man," which to be sure was sparingly used in the earlier version. I also have come to realize more fully than before that the transaction of legal proceedings in English, for example, was a serious limitation upon the fairness of treatment that the natives received in Plymouth courts. Neither had I attempted a systematic comparison of the punishments meted out to English and Indians for similar crimes, and scholars who have done just that—Koehler in particular—have made a strong case that there was greater harshness shown to the natives. At various points, in fact, I have felt compelled to insert a qualifier in what now strikes me as an overly dogmatic statement of the Pilgrims' neighborly good will. At the same time, with advancing age I have no doubt become more cynical about humankind generally, which makes me less surprised to observe the failings of Plymouth justice. And I do wonder how the Wampanoags might have fared, in practice, in sixteenth-century Hispaniola or twentieth-century Europe.

Notes

1. William Bradford, *History of Plymouth Plantation* (Boston, 1898), pp. 33–34.

2. Alexander Young, ed., *Chronicles of the Pilgrim Fathers* (Boston, 1841), p. 292.

3. Bradford, *History of Plymouth Plantation*, pp. 155–59; Young, *Chronicles of the Pilgrim Fathers*, pp. 298–302, 309–12, 327–45.

4. Bradford, *History of Plymouth Plantation*, p. 123.

5. Charles C. Willoughby, *Antiquities of the New England Indians* (Cambridge, 1935), p. 252. The fundamental importance of Squanto's teaching is not really at stake in the recent controversy as to whether the use of fish for fertilizer, conventionally listed as the greatest of his contributions, was in fact an Indian invention. See William Cronon, *Changes in the Land: Indians, Colonists, and the Ecology of New England* (New York: Hill and Wang, 1983), p. 45, and sources cited there. A recent contribution to the debate is Nanepashemet, "It Smells Fishy to Me: An Argument Supporting the Use of Fish Fertilizer by the Native People of Southern New England," in *Algonkians of New England: Past and Present*, Dublin Seminar for New England Folklife, Annual Proceedings 1991, ed. Peter Benes (Boston: Boston University, 1993), pp. 42–50.

6. *Records of the Colony of New Plymouth*, 12 vols. (Boston, 1855–61), 4:183; 7:161. All further references to this collection will appear parenthetically in the text by volume and page number. *Records of the Town of Plymouth*, 3 vols. (Plymouth, 1889), 1:172–73.

7. Young, *Chronicles of the Pilgrim Fathers*, p. 245.

8. See also Donald G. Trayser, *Barnstable* (Hyannis, Mass.: F. B. & F. P. Goss, 1939), p. 29; Ronald Oliver MacFarlane, "Indian Relations in New England, 1620–1760" (M.S. thesis, Harvard University, 1933), p. 21. On the question of Indian lands in New England generally, see James Warren Springer, "American Indians and the Law of Real Property in Colonial New England," *American Journal of Legal History* 30 (January 1986): 25–58.

9. See also Alice Austin Ryder, *Lands of Sippican* (New Bedford: Reynolds Printing, 1934), p. 21.

10. See Josiah Paine, *A History of Harwich* (Rutland, Vt., 1937), pp. 40, 64n, 82–83.

11. See also Francis Baylies, *An Historical Memoir of the Colony of New Plymouth*, 2 vols. (Boston, 1866), 2:219–20.

12. Richard LeBaron Bowen, *Early Rehoboth*, 4 vols. (Rehoboth, 1945–46), 1:80.

13. John Easton, "A Relacion of the Indyan Warre," in *Narratives of the Indian Wars, 1675–1699*, ed. Charles H. Lincoln (New York: Scribner's, 1913), pp. 9–11; Samuel G. Drake, *The Old Indian Chronicle* (Boston, 1867), pp. 58–62.

14. Samuel H. Emery, *History of Taunton* (Syracuse, N.Y., 1893), pp. 114–20.

15. Baylies, *Memoir of New Plymouth*, 2:225; 4:90–91.

16. See also Paine, *History of Harwich*, p. 84; Enoch Pratt, *A Comprehensive History Ecclesiastical and Civil of Eastham, Wellfleet, and Orleans* (Yarmouth, 1844), p. 11.

17. *Plymouth Town Records*, 1:94; Leonard Bliss, *History of Rehoboth* (Boston, 1836), p. 49.

18. See also Paine, *History of Harwich*, p. 393.

19. William Hubbard, *A Narrative of the Troubles with the Indians* (Boston, 1677), p. 13.

20. *Plymouth Town Records*, 1:41, 97, 172.

21. See also MacFarlane, *Indian Relations*, pp. 377–79.

22. Bradford, *History of Plymouth Plantation*, pp. 287–91. The Pilgrims clearly exaggerated the extent of this practice, but there is little reason to doubt that there was at least some basis for their complaint. See Neal Salisbury, *Manitou and Providence: Indians, Europeans and the Making of New England, 1500–1643* (New York: Oxford University Press, 1982), pp. 157–58.

23. On the enforcement of these regulations, see the index to the first six volumes of *Plymouth Colony Records;* during King Philip's War, giving arms to the Indians became a capital offense (5:173).

24. Daniel Gookin, *Historical Collections of the Indians in New England, Massachusetts Historical Society Collections*, 1st ser. 1 (1792): 152, 153.

25. Bradford, *History of Plymouth Plantation*, p. 282; Willoughby, *Antiquities*, pp. 265–66.

26. Bowen, *Early Rehoboth*, 1:79–83.

27. Drake, *Old Indian Chronicle*, pp. 58–62; Russell Bourne, *The Red King's Rebellion: Racial Politics in New England 1675–1678* (New York: Oxford University Press, 1990), p. 102.

28. Young, *Chronicles of the Pilgrim Fathers*, p. 193; Nathaniel Morton, *New Englands Memoriall* (New York, 1937), p. 29.

29. Bliss, *Rehoboth*, p. 60.

30. The details of this case are not entirely clear. See also Thomas (Benjamin) Church, *Entertaining Passages Relating to Philip's War*, ed. S. G. Drake (Boston, 1875), p. 6 n. 12; Samuel G. Drake, *The Aboriginal Races of North America* (New York, 1880), p. 251; Baylies, *New Plymouth*, 4:63–67.

31. For general treatment of judicial proceedings, see James P. Ronda, "Red and

White at the Bench: Indians and the Law in Plymouth Colony, 1620–1691," *Essex Institute Historical Collections* 110 (July 1971): 200–215; and the passages relating to Plymouth in Lyle Koehler's "Red-White Power Relations and Justice in the Courts of Seventeenth-Century New England," *American Indian Culture and Research Journal* 3 (1979): 1–31, and in Yasuhide Kawashima's *Puritan Justice and the Indian* (Middletown, Conn.: Wesleyan University Press, 1986).

32. Koehler, "Red-White Power Relations and Justice," pp. 14–18, 29 n. 108.

33. Koehler points out that despite the law, Plymouth did not execute white rapists either ("Red-White Power Relations and Justice," p. 14), but it is easy to recall other times and places when interracial rape, with the white as victim, regularly led to savage retribution.

34. See also Paine, *History of Harwich*, p. 435.

35. The Indians were likewise instructed to build pounds, possibly because the frontiersmen were slow to carry out the colony's orders.

36. John A. Goodwin, *The Pilgrim Republic* (Boston, 1888), p. 545.

37. Bradford, *History of Plymouth Plantation*, pp. 432–35; John Winthrop, *History of New England*, 3 vols. (Boston, 1853), 1:321–23. For modern analyses of this episode, see Glenn W. LaFantasie, "Murder of an Indian, 1638," *Rhode Island History* 38 (1979): 67–77; and Alden T. Vaughan, *Roots of American Racism: Essays on the Colonial Experience* (New York: Oxford University Press, 1995), pp. 205–12.

38. Henry Whitfield, "The Light Appearing More and More Towards the Perfect Day," *Massachusetts Historical Society Collections*, 3d ser. 4 (1834): 117.

39. Hubbard, *Narrative of the Troubles*, p. 8.

40. Morton, *New Englands Memoriall*, p. 180; Delores Bird Carpenter, *Early Encounters—Native Americans and Europeans in New England: From the Papers of W. Sears Nickerson* (East Lansing: Michigan State University Press, 1994), pp. 170–73.

41. Thomas Shepard, "The Clear Sun-shine of the Gospel Breaking Forth upon the Indians in New-England," *Massachusetts Historical Society Collections*, 3d ser. 4 (1834): 42–44.

42. George Parker Winship, ed., *The New England Company of 1649 and John Eliot* (Boston: Prince Society, 1920), pp. xiv–xxii.

43. *Plymouth Church Records 1620–1859*, 2 vols. (Boston: Colonial Society of Massachusetts, 1920–23), 1:146; Baylies, *New Plymouth*, 2:283; Gookin, *Historical Collections of the Indians in New England*, p. 198.

44. "A Description and History of Eastham," *Massachusetts Historical Society Collections*, 1st ser. 8 (1802): 170, 174.

45. Goodwin, *Pilgrim Republic*, pp. 536–38.

46. Gookin, *Historical Collections of the Indians in New England*, pp. 197–98.

47. *The Hinckley Papers, Massachusetts Historical Society Collections*, 4th ser. 5 (1861): 133–34.

48. No truly reliable data are available on the size of the Indian population at the time of the Pilgrims' arrival or in the aftermath of the war. It was long customary to estimate their numbers around 1620 as about 2,000, generally following the lead of James Mooney, *The Aboriginal Population of North America North of Mexico* (Wash-

ington: Smithsonian Institute, 1928), p. 4. Some recent revisionist authors have suggested much higher totals for southern New England, generally without offering a separate figure for the territory of Plymouth Colony—e.g., Salisbury, *Manitou and Providence*, pp. 22–30—but the weight of opinion is against them. See Kathleen J. Bragdon, *Native People of Southern New England, 1500–1650* (Norman: University of Oklahoma Press, 1996), pp. 25–26. As for the postwar figures, Sherburne F. Cook does not discriminate between Plymouth and adjoining territories in his "Interracial Warfare and Population Decline among the New England Indians," *Ethnohistory* 20 (Winter 1973): 15–21. However, Cook's estimate of a 60–80 percent decline due to battle casualties, disease, flight, and other causes during and just after King Philip's War (p. 21) would certainly apply to Plymouth and further suggests that the number of its "Praying Indians" in the 1680s must have been close to that of its total Indian population.

49. *The Hinckley Papers*, pp. 131–32.

50. John Gorham Palfrey, *History of New England*, 5 vols. (Boston, 1858–90), 3:188 n. 2; Goodwin, *Pilgrim Republic*, p. 551.

51. Church, *Entertaining Passages*, pp. 5–14; Thomas Hutchinson, *History of Massachusetts*, 3d ed., 2 vols. (Salem, 1795), 1:267. For recent overviews of the question, see Philip Ranlet, "Another Look at the Causes of King Philip's War," *NEQ* 61 (March 1988): 79–100, (chap. 5 in this volume); and Bourne, *Red King's Rebellion*, pp. 94–108 and passim.

52. Easton, *Narratives of the Indian Wars*, pp. 9–11.

53. Easton, *Narratives of the Indian Wars*, pp. 10–11.

54. Palfrey, *New England*, 3:222–29; John Callendar, *An Historical Discourse on . . . Rhode Island* (Providence, 1838), pp. 126–28.

55. Ronda, "Red and White at the Bench," pp. 210–12.

56. See also Frank G. Speck, *Territorial Subdivisions and Boundaries of the Wampanoag, Massachusetts, and Nauset Indians* (New York: Museum of the American Indian, 1928), pp. 33–35; John H. Humins, "Squanto and Massasoit: A Struggle for Power," *NEQ* 60 (March 1987): 54–70.

57. Drake, *Old Indian Chronicle*, pp. 32–42; Hubbard, *Narrative*, pp. 9–10; Goodwin, *Pilgrim Republic*, pp. 542–43.

58. Drake, *Aboriginal Races*, pp. 198–99.

59. Drake, *Old Indian Chronicle*, pp. 65–66.

60. See also Drake, *Old Indian Chronicle*, pp. 64–72; Hubbard, *Narrative*, pp. 11–12; Bourne, *Red King's Rebellion*, pp. 100–102.

61. See also Drake, *Old Indian Chronicle*, pp. 74–75, 81–82.

62. See also Hubbard, *Narrative*, p. 13.

63. Hubbard, *Narrative*, p. 15; Increase Mather, *History of King Philip's War* (Boston, 1862), pp. 47–48; Douglas Edward Leach, *Flintlock and Tomahawk: New England in King Philip's War* (New York: Macmillan, 1958), pp. 30–33.

64. Easton, *Narratives of Indian Wars*, pp. 7–8; "The Present State of New England with Respect to the Indian War," in Drake, *Old Indian Chronicle*, p. 122.

65. Hubbard, *Narrative*, p. 15; Increase Mather, *King Philip's War*, pp. 47–48.

66. See also Drake, *Old Indian Chronicle*, p. 96.

67. See also Hubbard, *Narrative*, pp. 16–17.

68. Church, *Entertaining Passages*, pp. 5–14.

69. "The Present State of New England," in Drake, *Old Indian Chronicle*, pp. 123–27; Leach, *Flintlock and Tomahawk*, pp. 35–38.

70. From "Upon the Elaborate Survey," by B. H., in Hubbard, *Narrative;* no page number in original, p. 24 in Drake ed. (Roxbury, 1865).

71. See also Church, *Entertaining Passages*, pp. 67–69. It is not true, however, that Plymouth used no Indian troops until the spring of 1676; acting apparently on his own authority, Church had made use of them at the very start of the war.

72. See also Church, *Entertaining Passages*, pp. 45–47, 79–92; Easton, *Narratives of the Indian Wars*, p. 13.

73. See also Hubbard, *Narrative*, pp. 98, 109; Church, *Entertaining Passages*, pp. 100, 101, 178–79.

74. Baylies, *New Plymouth*, 3:190–91.

75. MacFarlane, *Indian Relations*, p. 631.

3

"A Melancholy People"
Anglo-Indian Relations in Early Warwick, Rhode Island, 1642–1675

JOSHUA MICAH MARSHALL

Most studies of Indian-white relations in early New England purport to be about the whole region. In practice, however, they are usually confined to the actions of Massachusetts, with occasional glances at neighboring colonies (but seldom Rhode Island) toward the several Indian nations of southern New England. The major players are the magistrates (e.g., John Winthrop, John Endecott) and leading sachems (e.g., Sassacus, Uncas, Miantonomo), and their script is everything that strikes the author as broadly significant, especially commerce, wars, and missionary activity. But as useful as such works often are for understanding the cultural dynamics of early New England, they usually ignore the important everyday encounters of natives and newcomers in the region's numerous villages and byways. There the interaction of ordinary individuals and small groups formed the core of Indian-white contact for most natives and colonists, often with significant cumulative impact on the larger scene as well. This chapter is a prime example of local history's important, clarifying revelations.

Joshua Micah Marshall examines the interaction of the growing, and changing, white population of Warwick, Rhode Island, with the shrinking, and also changing, Indian groups, the Shawomets and Pawtuxets. From the town's origins in 1642 until the outbreak of King Philip's War in 1675, almost every facet of the colonists' apparent success boded ill for the neighboring natives, whether the issue was land or law or the markings of hogs.

Marshall's analysis of one small colonial community and two Indian bands is in many respects a microcosm of New England's early ethnohistory. The specifics of Indian-white relations differed from town to town, of course, but most communities probably shared Warwick's broad pattern of misunderstandings, mistreatments, and the mounting tensions that culminated in King Philip's War.

OBSERVING WARWICK, RHODE ISLAND, from a few miles north at Providence, Roger Williams fretted over "the slipperie and dangerous condition of [the town's] intermingled cohabitation" and thanked God for "restraining and preventing very great fires, of mutuall slaughters, breaking forth." Surely, Williams insisted in this year of 1656, no town in New England had suffered "such molestation from the natives as this one towne and people."[1] Williams's fears were not exaggerated. In time, the conflicts and animosities he witnessed in Rhode Island would explode in King Philip's War. Much has been written on that war, but if we are interested in understanding the history of Anglo-Indian relations at its heart, we are largely forced to rely on studies covering the treatment of Indians in Massachusetts, where Englishmen outnumbered Indians by fifteen to one as early as 1633 and settlers subjected many to the coercive paternalism of the assimilating Praying Towns.[2] We know much less about conditions in Rhode Island where Indians vastly outnumbered colonists.

Englishmen's first contacts with Rhode Island Indians were commercial. The powerful Narragansett tribe owed much of its prosperity and political dominance to the fur trade. That trade connected southern New England Indians to the markets of Europe and funneled European goods and technical skills back to the Native Americans. The fur trade was, however, dynamic and transitory, based on unstable European markets and an unsustainable overharvesting of beaver pelts. As the fur trade began to decline in the 1640s, an Anglo-Indian economy slowly gave way to a thoroughly English one centered on European agriculture.[3] The tribes were cut off from the source of wealth and the goods upon which they had become dependent. Indian political structures, which the tribes had transformed to accommodate European trade, crumbled as their economies contracted. The once powerful Narragansett confederation splintered into numerous petty tribes.

In the period of time between the onset of English settlement in 1636 and the outbreak of war in 1675, however, these overarching trends were far from obvious. Because their numbers were so few and their religious and political interests so diverse, the exiles who streamed into the first four Rhode Island towns lacked both the ability and the desire to make the Indians over into Christian Englishmen. The ambitious program of cultural assimilation the Puritans were implementing in Massachusetts was never even considered. Many Rhode Islanders traded actively with the Indians, but in matters of culture and religion, they were content to let the Indians live however they chose. Because of the colony's peculiar demographic setting, where Indians were relatively strong and Englishmen relatively weak, the two peoples lived among one another on a greater level of equality than elsewhere in New England.

The followers of Puritan eccentric Samuel Gorton founded Warwick in 1642. Hated by orthodox Puritans for their countless heresies, the Gortonists sought refuge in Rhode Island. Throughout the town's early history, conflicts with other colonies and other Rhode Island towns frustrated Warwick's efforts to control the local Indian population. The earliest antagonisms between the Gortonists and the local Shawomet and Pawtuxet Indians arose from the political disorder surrounding the decline of the Narragansett confederation. Rather than purchasing the "Shawomet tract" from the Pawtuxets and Shawomets who lived on the land (see map), the Gortonists bought it from the tribes' former overlord, the Narragansett sachem Myantonomy.[4] Pomham and Socononoco, the sachems of the Shawomets and Pawtuxets, resented having their land sold out from under them, and after Myantonomy was murdered at the behest of Massachusetts in 1643, they resolved to fight. After subjecting the settlers to a campaign of intimidation, Pomham and Socononoco traveled to Boston and struck an alliance with Massachusetts. The pact gave Massachusetts a pretext to harass the Gortonists and claim their land, while it gave the tribes a protective ally with which to overawe the settlers. The Indians told the settlers that "Massachusetts is all one with them, let the Villanie they doe bee what it will, they thinke themselves secure."[5] The dispute with Massachusetts eventually boiled over into armed conflict, and several Gortonists were temporarily enslaved in Massachusetts.[6] The Gortonists finally returned to their town in 1646–47 with a formal patent from the Earl of Warwick, but Massachusetts still refused to relinquish its claim to the land and the Bay magistrates continued to supply Pomham and Socononoco with guns and powder at least until the late 1650s.[7]

The very tolerance the Gortonists championed soon overwhelmed them as new settlers arrived and altered the character of the town. The predominantly Gortonist "purchaser" group, which had a proprietary interest in the hundred-odd square miles of town land, constantly disagreed with the "inhabitants," who owned only house lots and undivided shares of the town's Four Mile Common (see map). Between 1647 and 1660 Warwick was integrated into the coastal trade, and the town's leadership passed from the hands of the founding Gortonists into those of a new, more trade-oriented group of settlers. The economic development of the town further undermined the local Indian communities, and individual Indians were gradually subordinated in relations of trade, labor, and criminality.

The engine driving the confrontation between the two peoples and the process of subordinating one to the other was the basic incompatibility

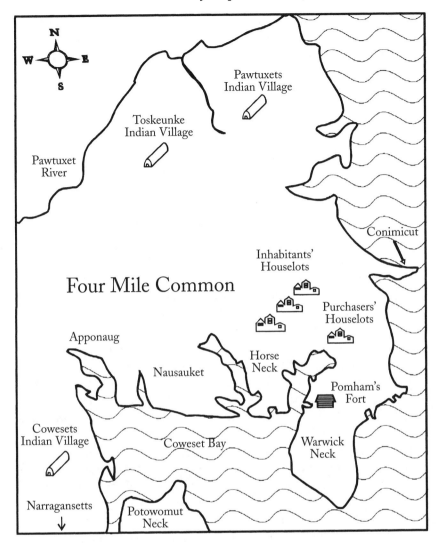

between English and Indian agriculture. As the settlers fenced more land, grew more crops, and raised more livestock, they exerted increasing pressure on Indian agriculture. Until the outbreak of King Philip's War, the colonists were in no position to evict Indians from their lands and thus had to "keepe and mingle fields" with them.[8] But the English disrupted Indian hunting and planting in other, more subtle ways that they rarely intended or understood. The tribes rotated crops to prevent soil exhaustion and periodically burned meadows and forests to enhance hunting. When the English "improved" apparently unused land, they wrought havoc on Indian economies that relied on those lands remaining available for future use. It was this kind of disruption to which the Narragansett sachem Myantonomy referred when he called for a general war against the English in which the Indians would "kill men, women, and children, but no cows, *for they will serve to eat till our deer be increased again.*"[9]

The source of the most heated conflict was the management of livestock. The Indians had never before seen the fecund and destructive beasts that now trampled and ate their crops. Hogs despoiled so many Indian crops that as early as 1648 the Shawomets and Pawtuxets began fencing their corn fields.[10] The hogs also ruined the tribes' shellfish harvesting sites, a vital source of food and raw material for the Indians' "wampum factories."[11] As early as 1647 Pomham had to appeal for relief to his Massachusetts patrons because his crops had been "spoyled by those of Mr Gortons society." Massachusetts sent him one hundred bushels of corn, but fifty more were needed six months later.[12] A typical confrontation took place in the summer of 1648. The Pawtuxet sachem Socononoco was using the gun his Massachusetts allies had loaned him to pick off hogs in his cornfields when Gortonist John Wickes approached. Wickes rushed Socononoco and with "a Cudgle in his hand laid on him and 2 Indians more that were with him and strocke one of them in the backe with his foot."[13] In short order, Pomham's men and the Warwick settlers congregated, and a general melee ensued. These encounters became the flashpoints of Anglo-Indian contact and furnished the context in which economic and legal relations were defined.

The management of livestock also set the English community at odds with itself. Hogs aligned the poorer settlers against their wealthier neighbors. Wealthy settlers could hire English or Indian "keepers" for their hogs and pen up the beasts on large tracts of fenced land, just as they did their cows and horses. Because hogs could fend for themselves among the large wolf populations that then roamed over southern New England, on the other hand, a settler with little land could subsist, and even make substantial profits, by marking his hogs' ears and letting them run and forage without restraint. The same qualities that made the hogs so resilient in the wild, however, also made them extremely destructive to crops. Free-running hogs were a nuisance both to the Indians who grew corn and to settlers who had substantial acreage under cultivation. As was often the case, these economic tensions within the English community were eventually resolved at the expense of the Indians.[14]

Warwick's wealthier "purchasers" favored restrictive livestock regulation not only out of economic self-interest but also because they were wary of their powerful Indian neighbors. The settlers' first solution was to pen up the hogs during the planting season. In 1648 the town meeting ordered that "no man is to turne swine into the woods between planting time and Harvest without sufitient keepers to prevent dangers to Indeans and Inglish Corne." On more than one occasion the settlers paid the Indians west of town to fence their lands or paid Englishmen to do the job for them.[15] In negotiations over land sales, the settlers even included guarantees to protect Indian crops. In 1659 one local sachem agreed to allow the settlers to graze their animals on his land "provided, they wrong not ye Indeans Corne, in the Sommer time, from the time of ye plantinge of ye Corne, till it be gathered In."[16]

Although a prudent and enlightened self-interest moved the town's leaders to provide a degree of protection for Indian crops, these dictates were routinely ignored because they worked to the disadvantage of the majority of the settlers, particularly the "inhabitants." Never effectively enforced, the regulations were eventually repealed. The town oscillated between more and less restrictive practice during the first decade of settlement, but the clear trend was toward less restriction. In June 1656 the town forbade settlers to let "any Hoggs goe abroad upon the Common after" the planting of corn in early March, under threat of confiscation. But just before the beginning of planting the following year, the town repealed the law because "*the generalitie of the inhabitants* of the Towne of Warwicke does plead that there is no subsisting by keeping up of hoggs in their penns." The town decided simply to confine troublesome hogs and fine the owners of animals that were "apt to trespas in breaking of fences."[17]

The changed emphasis reflected the shifting balance of power between "purchasers" and "inhabitants" as well as more fundamental imperatives of commercial animal husbandry. By the early 1650s the generally poorer "inhabitants" outnumbered the "purchasers," who were more sensitive to the threat of the Indians and their Massachusetts allies. By 1653 "inhabitants" had effectively gained control of the town.[18] Relentless economic pressures also accelerated the trend toward less restriction. Placing the emphasis of the law on seeking redress for damages already committed rather than trying to prevent damages in the first instance was an improvement for Englishmen. It was economically more rational to mete out fines for individual offenses than to stymie the whole system by penning countless hogs for months. On their part, the Indians were particularly disadvantaged because they were less able to use the legal system for their own benefit. Hogs, therefore, became a dynamic force of territorial expansion. They fanned out in advance of English colonists and prepared the way for later settlement by disrupting the Indians' use of land the English had not yet sought to acquire. Hogs became a source of conflict and the vehicle of English expansion.

For the Warwick settlers, the law was a tool to control tensions emerging between Englishmen and Indians. For every new conflict, they enacted an ordinance that settled the matter in their favor. There was nothing new about this. Colonists all over New England used the courts as an instrument of social control.[19] But the Warwick settlers were never fully successful because they lacked effective mechanisms to enforce their laws. They had to be able to compel Indians to appear in English courts, but since Indians had little to gain by appearing as defendants, they did so only when they were physically constrained or when they were economically and politically dependent upon the local English community. After the 1648 cornfield brawl, the Warwick settlers obtained a warrant from the colony's General Assembly ordering Pomham "to come to this Court," but the sachem simply ignored it. When the settlers went out to fetch him there was "a great Fray . . . and blood spilt and many Cuts on both sides."[20] The settlers had followed a customary procedure but, with no force behind it, it remained mere pretense.

The English saw every brawl and broken fence as evidence that the Indians were a lawless and uncontrollable people. The devolution of political power that accompanied the murder of Myantonomy only heightened the settlers' anxieties. The great sachems upon whom the English had once relied to exert control over and exact justice from their Indian subjects could no longer command fealty from the lesser tribes who were asserting their independence. The English found themselves contending with innumerable petty tribes who were under no "law" and represented no "legitimate" authority. One of the sharpest complaints against the Shawomet sachem Pomham was that he was "under the command of no Sachim," that he was, as Roger Williams put it, "living without all exercise of actual authoritie."[21] Those the English most wanted in some way accountable were, however, those nearest to them: Indian laborers.

While the Warwick settlers recognized the danger of bringing displaced Indians into their households, they did so from an early date. New England's chronic labor shortage left them little choice. In Massachusetts, Emanuel Downing had complained to John Winthrop that he did "not see how wee can thrive until wee gett into a stock of slaves suffitient to doe all our busines." Rhode Islanders knew that they could not enslave the Narragansetts *en masse*, but they soon learned that that extreme was unnecessary. Commercial and ecological dislocations were churning up a vast pool of cheap Indian labor. Daniel Gookin observed a similar process in Massachusetts when he noted that driving the Indians from their fields "turned the Indians from idleness." In other words, disruptions in tribal economies forced displaced Indians to sell their labor to the English simply to survive. Gookin called the "Narragansitt and Warwick Indians . . . active, laborious [and] ingenious" and thought they performed more labor for English settlers than "any other Indian people."[22] Indeed, Indians in and around Warwick worked as house servants, guides, mail carriers, keepers of livestock, wolf killers, and fence builders.[23] By the 1660s, some Indians may even have worked as skilled artisans in nearby Providence.[24] Indian labor had become so widespread in Warwick that when the town needed men to rebuild the town fence in 1666, it had to ask specifically for "one Englishman" from each household. But while Indian labor was becoming more prevalent, much of it remained temporary and transient. Many Indian laborers were like the Pawtuxet Indian Nanhegin, who testified in his 1649 theft trial that he had labored and boarded at the homes of no fewer than four English families in the previous three weeks.[25]

The flourishing market in Indian labor was a great boon for the town's economy, but it came at a cost. Indian laborers bore little attachment to Warwick or its English population; instead, they maintained strong ties to their nearby villages, where resentments against the English were profound. When the settlers drew Indians into town life, the anarchic and uncontrollable elements that caused the English such anxiety were both literally and figuratively incorporated within their community. While such proximity increased dangers, it also increased opportunities for social control. Indian servants, although paid and not bound to service, became their master's charges in the eyes of English law. As it had required of Indian sachems, the legal system demanded that English masters produce Indian servants in court.[26] Because the English valued family government, they exempted Indian servants from many laws supposedly applied to all Indians. Just as Massachusetts had prohibited gun sales to all Indians except those who "have bin servants of divers years, and are in good measure Civilliced," the Rhode Island General Assembly allowed Roger Williams to give his Indian servant a gun to shoot fowl. Benedict Arnold was allowed to "imploy that Indian wch he keepeth as his servant to shoote [game] *so long as hee shall continue in his family.*" The General Assembly also exempted Indian servants from the colony's strictures on Indian drinking. A 1659 law stated that "any man that keeps an Indian servant for refreshment, may give him a dram, *if he can make it apeare he is his hyred servant.*"[27] The fact, even the appearance, of subordination calmed English anxieties. For the settlers, family government defined a space where reassuring rituals of authority and obedience could be exercised. The most rigorous laws regulating Indian behavior, though nominally addressed to all Indians, were actually reserved for those who were not "in good measure Civ-illiced," those who were not clearly governed by the dictates of English family government.

The town sought to control the "uncivilized" Indians with an ever in-creasing variety of restrictive laws. But as the laws directed toward Indians multiplied, their legal personhood diminished proportionately. Legislation regulating Indian drinking exemplifies the trend.

In 1648 the first recorded Warwick law concerning alcohol stipulated that "no man in the towne is to *sell* strong lickers or sack to the Indians for to drink in there houses." The penalty to be exacted was five shillings. Only in 1652 did the town order that drunken Indians "be dealt with ac-cordinge to the General lawe for English."[28] Through the following decade the fines for selling spirits gradually increased to the quite substantial sum of five pounds, but profits were so heady that penalties proved no deter-rent. Selling alcohol to the Indians seemed to carry little social stigma, and Roger Williams claimed that the "bloody trade of Liquors to the Indians" was worse in Rhode Island than in any other colony. By 1651 John Eliot's Praying Indians already knew that Warwick was the place to "buy much strong water . . . and have a great drinking."[29] A familiar pattern was estab-lishing itself: the desire for security was giving way to the quest for profit.

By the late 1650s the town was passing increasingly coercive laws not against selling alcohol to Indians but against their consumption of it. The difficulty of enforcing these laws simply confirmed the settlers' belief that Indians were inherently lawless and thus required more vigorous regula-tion. Before 1657 the law had allowed, and often required, Indian testimony in Indian drinking trials. That year the Warwick town meeting decided that "Indians are such fraudulent persons that their Testimony cannot be taken." "[S]ome few Inglish" and their Indian clients had dealt "so fraudu-lently" that the Indians were better supplied than ever. Recognizing the futility of outright prohibitions, the town allowed Englishmen to sell the Indians alcohol as long as they took it a mile from town to drink it. The town would confiscate the liquor of any Indians found "within a mile of the Towne without an Englishman to help him Convey it away." They would prosecute drunken Indians. And any Indian found drinking within the town limits they fined five shillings, which any Englishman could col-lect, or "*plunder them and have the pay to themselves.*"[30] Not only had the Indians become more vulnerable to English law, the law now operated upon them in a unique manner. Any Englishman could exact personal jus-tice from any Indian under the color of law.

Increasingly restrictive legislation reflected more than a concern for In-dian drunkenness. The numerous English and Dutch traders who gladly sold the Indians alcohol also sold them guns. Warwick's first settlers, wary of outside interference and vexed by Pomham's villagers, quickly recognized the danger and tried to prevent the Indians from trading with the Dutchmen from Manhattan who sailed their sloops into Narragansett Bay. The Plymouth Colony had suppressed this illicit commerce with a "rigid control" of the fur trade, but with so many irregular traders and a weak government, Warwick could never do the same.[31]

The Gortonists' continued efforts to cut off the Dutch trade eventually caused them to lose control of the town. The "inhabitants," who entered Warwick only a few years after its founding, at first acquiesced in the benign rule of the Gortonists, but in time they became disgruntled over the unequal distribution of land and the Gortonists' opposition to the Dutch trade. Tensions finally erupted in 1652 in a dispute over Dutch trader John Garreardy's unpaid debts. When the Gortonists overplayed their hand, the once docile "inhabitants" cast the Gortonists aside and asserted control over the town's affairs. The leading Gortonists were excluded from town politics until 1656. The mantle of leadership passed into the hands of Ezekiel Holliman and John Greene, Jr., two "received purchasers" who were actively involved in the fur trade. The new non-Gortonist commissioners to the General Assembly quickly joined the movement to open the colony's trade to all foreign nationals.[32]

After 1652, the guns and alcohol so feared by the Gortonists flowed more easily into Indian hands. Roger Williams insisted that he could have made "thousands by such a murtherous trade" and declared that there was "no law yet extant . . . secure enough against such a villanie." Since the English around Narragansett Bay had no monopoly on the Indian trade, however, if they enforced the laws too strictly, Indians would simply patronize less scrupulous traders. Even John Winthrop had criticized overly rigid laws because he thought they would give "the greater portion of the beaver trade to the Dutch and French." The folly of selling guns to a hostile and numerically superior Indian tribe may today seem self-evident, but the trade expanded according to an inexorable economic logic. The "perfidious English all the land over"—many Warwick settlers included—sold guns to the Indians, and when they were caught, English courts treated them with surprising leniency.[33] In short, when the interests of trade conflicted directly with the interests of security, the interests of trade won out.

By the middle 1650s this flourishing trade with the Indians was threatening to destabilize Warwick. The tribes were well armed. Indians' technical ability had progressed so rapidly that they could repair their own guns and cast their own bullets. Roger Williams, who negotiated endless disputes between Pomham and Warwick during the 1650s, complained that the Indians around Warwick and Providence were "filled with artillerie and ammunition . . . [and] dayly consult and hope and threaten to render us slaves." He called Pomham's village "a very den of wickedness [and] a confluence and rendezvous of all the wildest and most licentious natives and practices of the whole country."[34]

The town's precarious position became clear as early as 1653 when the fear of a Dutch invasion gripped Warwick and the rest of Rhode Island. While the town placed itself in a state of readiness, the settlers, questioning the loyalty of the town's Indian servants, promptly ordered that "what Indian guns are in this Towne shalbee reserved, in the Towne untill the liklihoode of this trouble be past concerning the Indians." Another instance of the town's peril came in 1655, when the resident Dutch trader Garreardy, an associate of Holliman and Greene, committed an outrage against the Narragansetts. Garreardy and his crew—"one Samuel a Hatter and one Jones a Seaman and an Irishman persons infamous"—broke into Pessacus's sister's grave looking for jewels and other fineries. The settlers had learned how to manage the Narragansett sachems by playing one off against another, but now the Indians marched on Warwick "unanimous and (as Union strengthens) . . . were so bold as to talke often of Mens lives and of fighting with us and demaunded an English child for Hostage."[35] Roger Williams finally stepped in to calm the angry sachems, but disaster had been narrowly averted.

The five years surrounding 1660 marked a turning point in the history of Warwick. The Rhode Island towns were swept up in a burgeoning commerce that was transforming New England and indirectly connecting small towns like Warwick with ports throughout the Atlantic world. The resolution of many of Warwick's political and legal entanglements also enhanced the climate for trade. In 1658 Massachusetts renounced its claim to the "Shawomet tract." In 1663 Rhode Island received a new charter that greatly strengthened the colony's legal standing. In 1664 the English assumed control of New Amsterdam and thus greatly reduced the threat of Dutch attacks, if not the nuisance of Dutch traders. The settlers' access to new markets stimulated demand and dramatically increased the value of land and staple commodities on the Narragansett Bay.[36] This commercial expansion markedly intensified the pressures trade had exerted on Indians during the first years of settlement.

As the possibilities for agricultural wealth grew, the original frontier trading economy gradually disappeared. This transformation was strikingly manifest in Rhode Island's currency. The colonists' use of wampum as a medium of exchange had symbolized not only their lack of metallic money but also the pivotal role of the Indian trade in the early

Rhode Island economy. But as the profits of the Indian trade began to diminish, the value of wampum sharply declined. In 1662 the Rhode Island General Assembly disestablished wampum because it had "fallen to so loe a ratte . . . [that] it is unreasonable that it should be forced upon any man." Pork, which symbolized the increasing role of agriculture, was now much in demand. When the Newport Quaker merchant Peleg Sanford sent a bill to Warwick's James Greene, he wrote that he would accept payment in "pease or good Indian Corne though by convenant it is to be in porke." By 1670, pork had become such a pivotal part of the Rhode Island economy that the General Assembly made it an official colony staple, acceptable as payment for town or colony taxes.[37]

Warwick's economy was changing in ways that made the Indians not simply irrelevant but a decided obstacle to exploiting the profit potential of the land. The settlers began to take control of acreage they had earlier "purchased" but had hitherto left untouched. They no longer allowed Indians to live on land they believed they owned. Even so sympathetic an observer as Roger Williams signaled this growing impatience with the Indian presence when he insisted that the Shawomets should vacate their lands because they could do so "with little more trouble and dammage than the wild beasts of the wilderness." In 1662 the town responded to the expanding appetite for grazing land by distributing among the settlers equal shares to Potowomut Neck and Toskeunke Meadows, where there was a small Indian village. The escalating value of land also added heat to the long-standing controversy over the land rights of Warwick's "purchasers" and "inhabitants." Defining the precise boundaries of the "inhabitants'" Four Mile Common became an increasingly contentious matter.[38] The town curtailed the grants of land routinely offered to every new settler and in 1660 ordered that even those inhabitants who had not yet "layd out" their six-acre lots do so within three months or forfeit the land. Shortly thereafter the town declared that any new "inhabitants" would receive land not "accordinge to any former Order but so much onely as the Towne shall by particular order grant."[39]

As the towns grew, so did pressure to settle disputes over conflicting and overlapping land titles. In 1662 the Rhode Island General Assembly established clear guidelines for judging rival land claims, including giving preference to men who had made "improvements" on the land and setting a statute of limitations. But the emphasis on possession did not extend to Indians because it was their "usuall manner . . . [to] deny the sale and keepe the lands in [their] possestion." Suits against Indians were not practical because "ther potency, faction, [and] combination with some others" caused "great inconveniences" in bringing them to a "speedye course of tryall." This rationale for not evicting Indians, which was a testament to the tribes' continuing military power, also reflected the English belief that Indian land ownership was inherently temporary. The General Assembly stipulated that Englishmen settle disputes over Indian-occupied lands on paper until the advent of a "convenient season, when ther may be a *more cleare power* to cause ther due obedience to law."[40]

During the 1660s, the Warwick town government issued a spate of new orders designed to rationalize the perpetually vexed process of regulating livestock. Central to this effort was the settlers' campaign to ban Indians from the practice of animal husbandry. In 1657 Warwick had given "notice unto the Indians and espeshally to Pomham that he nor they marke swine" and further commanded them to "keep them up or els the Inglish will seaze them." By 1666 the matter had become so serious that both the General Assembly and Warwick passed laws forbidding Indians to own or sell "any swine with markes in ther eares." Since the English marked their hogs at birth, and since all hogs in New England had an English ancestry, the effect of the law was that most hogs would be confiscated and that others would become legally suspect.[41] The English had practical reasons for such punitive regulations. Their crops had been despoiled by Indian hogs, and they believed that Indians' animal husbandry often involved livestock theft. But the more fundamental motive concerned the necessity of subordinating Indians' rights to colonial interests. Indian efforts to carve out a permanent and independent role in the colonial economy simply could not be tolerated.

The intensifying contact between Indians and Englishmen—in matters of labor, law, and trade—multiplied sources of conflict and spurred the English toward ever stricter legal controls. The Warwick settlers were still unable to dominate entire tribes, like the Shawomets, but they were increasingly successful in punishing individual Indians. They accused more Indians of thievery and vandalism and brought more defendants before English courts. The settlers' ability to compel attendance in court was still circumscribed, but their economic and social dominance, as well as their willingness to use physical coercion, was expanding. The Indian thieves who had "Voyolenly" stolen the goods of William Arnold in the late 1650s finally found themselves in "Fetters" before the court in 1661. When Warwick's Francis Derby accused "Ahogshake and Wawisum two Indean Inhabitant in or about ye towne or township of Warwicke" of torching his home in 1662, the two brothers failed to present themselves in court. Three years later they were finally captured.[42]

By 1664 Indian trials were becoming so common that the town petitioned the General Assembly to establish an inferior court to hold "Trialls of small matters here upon ye maine[land] as allso some Course for of trialls of Indians in pettey matters." Indians were becoming more familiar with English court practices. Sachems, long accustomed to the indignity of having to supply a bond against an Indian's appearance in court, learned to use proxies. At one trial, Wamsitta, the brother and predecessor of King Philip, sent his "Counselor caled by the English Thomas," who placed the bond on his behalf. Yet for every case like this, there was a glaring example of ignorance of the English law. When Warwick's John Knowles sued Wawenockshott "for burning his hay" in 1670, the judge stopped the trial halfway through "because the Indians could not understand the way of our proceedings."[43]

While more Indians were appearing in court, a surprising number were escaping from prison. In 1661, when the Indian Cajontoosuck was about to face trial for theft in Warwick, the sheriff had to inform the court that the "Indian had made an Escape." This was a common occurrence. But while some Indians escaped English oppressions by absconding from custody, the very ease of their escapes only hardened English suspicions about Indian lawlessness and strengthened their belief that Indian barbarism could only be checked by a sterner and more exacting form of justice. English courts responded by granting Englishmen ever widening powers to exact their own justice on Indian offenders. The General Assembly even authorized Richard Pray *"to take by Authority* the indian that hath wronged them in any Township in this Collony if he can be Fownd."[44] In this way judges gradually legitimated the practice of personally settling accounts with Indians by giving these actions the sanction of law.

The new aggressiveness of the English was also evident in their treatment of Indian sachems. Those great sachems whom the English had once approached through diplomacy were now summoned with high-handed warrants. In 1659 the Rhode Island General Assembly threatened the Narragansett sachem Pessacus that if he did not pay his just debts the Court would "Fetch him in to macke Restitution" and take other steps that would "prove troublesome . . . unto him."[45]

English legal power was most keenly felt when Indians' economic opportunities contracted. The English had long since held Indian sachems accountable for various debts they supposedly owed to the English, but after 1660 debts were more widespread and more effectively collected. Some debts arose from accidental or intentional damage to English property, others from English products purchased. English juries did not always grant the amounts sought by English plaintiffs, but judgments could still be quite high. When the Gortonist Randall Holden sued Moeallike, the jury awarded only slightly more than half the "fiftie pound Starlinge" he had requested, but this was an astonishing figure when English labor could be bought for a few shillings a day and several hundred pounds made a substantial estate. After 1664 the special court, which had been established in Warwick that year, heard more and more cases of "debt and damage." What the damages were is seldom clear, but in most cases the defendants appear to have been familiar to the settlers and within the economic orbit of the town. One Indian servant named "John" was sued twice in five years, once by James Greene in 1667 and again by the Dutch trader John Garreardy in 1672.[46]

In the changing colonial economy, Indians found it ever more difficult to clear their debts. The decline in fur trading and the value of wampum, as well as restrictions on swine herding, sharply curtailed the Indians' ability to make money and led to greater penury and thievery among them. At the same time, more extensive use of the land prompted more lawsuits over broken fences, butchered livestock, and despoiled orchards. The need to repay debts forced Indians, already intermittently employed in English homes, into "voluntary" servitude. Indians who lacked this source of meager income were unable to satisfy their debts at all. Caught in a vise of contracting opportunities, many Indians in this increasingly market-oriented economy felt their superfluity all too acutely. As the English experienced a rising tide of Indian "vandalism" and "thievery" and found many Indians unable to repay "debts," they again reacted with a special set of laws for the Indians. As early as 1659 the General Assembly had ruled that Indians who "spoyle or damnify the cattel, fence or fruite trees, corne house or other goods of . . . the English [or] feloniously take away the[ir] goods, monies, [and] cattell" would be "sould as a slave to any forraigne country of the English," if they could not satisfy their just debts.[47]

While some individual Indians were vulnerable to the threats of trial, whippings, and exorbitant fines, many organized Indian groups remained safely beyond the grasp of English law. Members of Pomham's Shawomet tribe continually foiled Warwick's attempts to force them into English courts. In 1659 Warwick imprisoned a Shawomet felon. When Pomham got word of this capture, he "made an insurrection" and "by a royat and rescuinge" liberated the captured Indian. The angry settlers procured a warrant from the General Assembly, then meeting at Warwick, authorizing them to arrest Pomham and "any . . . that have been guiltie in the royat and rescue." But they could never catch him. In fact, the settlers still appeared more frightened of Pomham than he of them. Warwick and the Shawomet villages were so proximate and socially intertwined that the General Assembly had to devise its plans quietly for fear that "the Indians will be made acquainted with the matter . . . and soe escape."[48]

The persistence of Indian power was pointedly dramatized in 1666 and 1667 when the "purchasers" and the "inhabitants" made separate attempts to evict the Indians from town lands. The "purchasers" believed their chance had finally come to expel the nettlesome Shawomets when they were promised aid from Sir Robert Carr, leader of the royal commission Charles II had sent to New England to discipline Massachusetts and to reestablish royal authority. Both the settlers and the commissioners soon found, however, that Pomham would have little truck with royal commissioners. After Pomham refused to meet with Carr, the commissioner was obliged to negotiate with the sachem's son Cheesachamut at Richard Smith's fur trading outpost in the Narragansett country. Cheesachamut first stalled the commissioners but finally accepted thirty pounds in exchange for Warwick Neck. Although he acknowledged that the Indians had "seemed dissatisfied about" the deal, Carr still thought he had resolved the matter; the Shawomets, however, had not the slightest intention of leaving their lands.[49]

The "purchasers'" hopes began to dim. Sympathetic Englishmen spoke up on Pomham's behalf. Cheesachamut's insistence on meeting Carr at Smith's outpost suggests that the fur trader was an ally and supporter of the sachem. The Massachusetts evangelist John Eliot, a friend and adviser to Pomham who had preached to the Shawomets, sent Carr a letter demanding that the commissioner end his efforts to evict the oppressed Shawomets. Roger Williams explained to Carr that the situation was more complicated than it seemed. Williams insisted that evicting the Shawomets "not only without consent, which feare may extort, but without some satisfying consideration" would be unwise as well as unjust. "They are a melancholy people and judg themselves . . . oppressed and wronged" by the English as well as their former Narragansett overlords. "You may knock out their braines, and yet not make them peaceably to surrender." The Gortonists were despised, Williams continued, not only by the Puritans but also by powerful factions within Rhode Island. The Shawomets knew "that it is but one partie [the "purchasers"] which claim this Neck," and they played on divisions among the English to great effect. The matter could not be accomplished simply. "The business as circumstantiated will not be effected without bloudshed, Barbarians are barbarians." And, "if it come to bloud," other sachems like Philip would join the fight against the English. The advice was sound, but it was lost on Carr. He moved on to other business, dispatched Pomham a few threatening letters, and assumed that Shawomets had departed. But the tribe remained on Warwick Neck until 1675, when they joined forces against the English in King Philip's War.[50]

In 1667 Warwick's "inhabitants" tried to rid their lands of the Indians. Since 1664 the "inhabitants" had received assurances from the Coweset Indians, who lived at Coweset and Nausauket, that they would cease planting corn on the southwestern corner of Four Mile Common; each year the promise was broken. In February 1667, the "inhabitants" decided to press the eviction before a new round of planting forced another year's delay. The town constable Edmund Calverly and four "inhabitants" walked off toward the Indian villages with a warrant from the commissioners ordering the Indians "to depart, And come no moor one [*sic*] the towns lands, to plant or inhabit." Realizing the significance of accepting the written document, the "Indians did peremptoryly aver that they would take no notice thereof, some of them throwing ye Copie away." About forty Indians surrounded the small English group, "threatening that they would make them Carry the said Copie back againe." Making a virtue of necessity, Calverly decided to consider the mob "witness of ye delivery of the wrighting" and stopped pressing his point.[51]

The matter was not, however, so easily dismissed, for there in the crowd stood Pomham and a group of his men. The Indians were behaving "very ryotously & in A Scornfull manner did deryd the King's Athoryty represented in ye Constable when he charged them to keep ye kings peace." Motioning to "Pomham & his Company," Calverly charged the formerly pliant Cowesets "not to Adhear to Any that did deny to yeeld obedyence" to the king. In the end, only the intervention of Awashkooke secured the settlers' safe departure, but this "pretended sachime" had produced a letter from Thomas Willet of Plymouth which obliged the settlers to suspend their efforts to evict Indians.[52] Thus, for all of the trappings of English law and a warrant from a commissioner of Charles II, the settlers who set out to expel the Indians barely managed to escape without a severe pummeling.

In the final, anxious years before the outbreak of King Philip's War, the Rhode Islanders stepped up measures to place the Indians firmly under English domination, even adopting strategies of social control first practiced in the orthodox colonies. More Indian crimes were being punished by periods of involuntary servitude. In 1673 the General Assembly enacted a new law against Indian drinking that combined this trend towards enforced labor with the colony's vigilante enforcement tactics. Indians found drinking or drunk were "indebted one weeks worke, or six shillings to him or they that" caught them.[53] But despite renewed attempts to seize control, settlers still seemed caught in a cycle of expanding commerce and persistent Indian power.

The increasing volatility and instability of Anglo-Indian relations were everywhere evident. Frequent incidents of theft and violence between the races had been common since the early 1660s. In the late 1660s, however, the balance shifted when the intertribal divisions that had allowed the settlers to play one tribe off against another diminished. The Niantic sachem Ninigret reportedly attended a powwow with his former enemy the Mohegan sachem Uncas, a supposed client of Massachusetts. The settlers seem to have realized, even if unconsciously, that a storm was brewing. A rapid succession of real or imagined Indian conspiracies convulsed the colony. Every suspected conspiracy included a different list or varied order of conspirators. Would the instigators be the Dutch, the French, or the Indians themselves? No one seemed to know. In 1667 there was "a great occasion of suspicion of [the Indians] and their treacherous designs . . . especially of Philip." The General Assembly alerted Providence and Warwick to apprehend any Indians wandering about at night, and they forced Indians on Aquidneck to carry "licenses" from the governor. A month later Pessacus and Ninigret were summoned to Warwick to discuss the conspiracy. In 1669 Ninigret was again suspect. In August of that year the settlers set up watches and seized "the armes of Indians that are in the hands of the English." In 1671 there were once more "apparent grounds to expect" Indian violence, but no specific suspect was identified.[54]

The conspiracy panics that gripped Warwick and the other Rhode Island towns in these final years before the war colored reality with hysteria. The times seemed out of joint. The signs of growing Indian restiveness were heightened by the even more worrisome evidence that in the developed section of the colony surrounding Newport some poor English men and women were making common cause with the Indians. Indians and Englishmen in Newport frequently broke one another out of prison during the late 1660s and early 1670s. The most notorious incident occurred in 1671 when John Carr and several Indian convicts escaped from prison in Newport and fled into the Narragansett country to establish a base of operations for waging guerrilla raids against the English.[55]

The outbreak of King Philip's War in 1675 was less the result of Philip's schemes than of the changing economic and social conditions that had bedeviled relations between Indians and Englishmen for decades. The tensions leading to this war—Indians struggling against the transformation of a partially beneficial trading economy into an agricultural economy in which they could maintain only a degraded existence—were similar to those at play in other parts of North America during the first century of settlement.[56] These forces of economic change, which the colonists created but never fully controlled nor comprehended, produced very different effects in Rhode Island, however, than they did in the rest of New England. In this sparsely populated and loosely governed colony, economic dynamism placed the desire for safety at odds with the quest for profits. Particularly in Warwick, the settlers were too divided among themselves and too reviled and harassed by their English neighbors ever to restrain the dangerous consequences of the town's bumptious trade. Though these changes ripped apart the Indian society that had existed prior to settlement, the settlers could never truly dominate the colony's Indian population. English settlement thus created tensions, animosities, and hatreds that could only end in war.

Author's Postscript

The last decade has witnessed a remarkable cross-fertilization of ideas between ethnohistory and environmental history, which has transformed our vision of New England's Native American past. We now better understand the full complexity of the process by which settlers dispossessed the Indians of their land. The land sales that once typified the process of dispossession can now be seen in a much larger context. An intricate combination of economic pressures, epidemiological disasters, and environmental changes wrecked Indian economies and paved the way for the alienation of land on a massive scale. We need now to ask what happened to those displaced Indians. What role did they take, voluntarily or under coercion, in the New England economy that expanded so rapidly after 1660?

Warwick, Rhode Island, was but one town in a small colony. But if its difficulties were extreme, they were not unique. The dynamics at work there could be found in many other mid-seventeenth-century New England villages, particularly those in the broad arc of outlying settlements stretching from Cape Cod through the Connecticut Valley. Indian involvement in the settler economy did not end, but rather intensified, with the demise of the fur trade. Indians sold all manner of corn, fish, and livestock to the colonists and in increasing numbers worked for the English as agricultural laborers. Nor was this phenomenon confined to "frontier" towns. The acute labor demand in the most densely settled sections of eastern Massachusetts drew many Indians from southern New England to work in those areas—often for wages, sometimes through indentures, and occasionally as slaves. But the significance of Indian labor transcends the sheer number of hours they toiled in English fields or the quantity of Native American corn, fish, or pork that made its way to distant ports. The ubiquity of Indian labor attests to a seldom appreciated degree of interpenetration between the lives and experiences of the two peoples.

This evidence of the commingled lives of Englishmen and Indians radically alters the standard image of early New England society and culture. Just as the settlers could not build New England without the Indians, we cannot understand what they built or why they built it without placing Indians at the center of the story.

In recent years scholars have waged a contentious and illuminating debate over the origins of American capitalism. As that debate now focuses on the seventeenth century, it must reckon with the implications of this early Anglo-Indian economy. We should not, as the literature generally has, frame the question in terms of whether the settlers were basically peasant-like or entrepreneurial. Early colonial economies possessed a dynamism that neither of these models can fully convey. The wrenching process of settling New England, though often clothed in precociously modern economic instrumentalities, was after all a matter of conquest. Our approach to the early New England economy must recognize this fact and focus on the principal imperatives of colonization: how the settlers changed the early Anglo-Indian economy into a European one, how the settlers remade the region's human and physical environment, and how that process of remaking shaped New England's economy, society, and culture. Failure to take this fact into consideration simply masks the economic abundance, the anxiety, and the creative violence of early New England life with false visions of either static village communities or an orderly, enterprising, and "middling" society.

Bringing Native American history into contact with the transition-to-capitalism debate should free New England history from its long-standing preoccupation with how expanding commerce rotted away the fibers of community and left religion lifeless and stale, a theory underlying not only Perry Miller's much vaunted declension model but also the community studies of the 1970s and much of the transition-to-capitalism literature of the early 1990s. This preoccupation has not only obscured the role of Indians. It has also sustained the erroneous belief that New England was somehow sui generis—fundamentally set apart from the larger context and imperatives of New World colonization. A deeper attention to Native American history should alter this mistaken view.

Notes

1. Roger Williams to General Court of Massachusetts Bay, 12 May 1656, *Roger Williams Papers*, ed. Glenn LaFantasie, 2 vols. (Hanover, N.H.: Brown University Press, 1988), 2:450–51.

2. Yushide Kawashima, *Puritan Justice and the Indian: White Man's Law in Massachusetts, 1630–1673* (Middletown, Conn.: Wesleyan University Press, 1986) and "Jurisdiction of the Colonial Courts over the Indians in Massachusetts, 1689–1763," *New England Quarterly* 42 (1969): 532–50; James P. Ronda, "Red and White at the Bench: Indians and the Law in Plymouth Colony, 1620–1691," *Essex Institute Historical Collections* 110 (1974): 165–215; Lyle Koehler, "Red-White Power Relations and Justice in the Courts of Seventeenth-Century New England," *American Indian Culture and Research Journal* 3 (1979): 1–31. For a notable exception, see John A. Sainsbury, "Indian Labor in Early Rhode Island," *New England Quarterly* 48 (1975): 378–93. For the Anglo-Indian ratio, see Neal Salisbury, *Manitou and Providence: Indians, Europeans and the Making of New England, 1590–1643* (New York: Oxford University Press, 1982), p. 183.

3. Daniel H. Usner describes a similar process at work in the eighteenth-century Gulf Coast region in his *Indians, Settlers, and Slaves in a Frontier Exchange Economy: The Lower Mississippi Valley before 1783* (Chapel Hill: University of North Carolina Press, 1992).

4. For a discussion of the merits of the relative "land rights" of Pomham and Myantonomy, see Oliver Payson Fuller, *The History of Warwick, Rhode Island, from Its Settlement in 1642 to the Present Time* (Providence: Angell, Burlingame & Co., Printers, 1875), p. 11; see also, Williams to Mass. General Court, 12 May 1656, *Williams Papers*, 2:450–53.

5. See Edward Winslow, *Hypocrosie Unmasked: A True Relation of the Proceedings of the Governor and Company of the Massachusetts against Samuel Gorton of Rhode Island* (London, 1646; reprinted, Providence: Club for Colonial Reprints, 1916), pp. 32–33, quotation p. 33; *Records of the Governor and Company of The Massachusetts Bay in New England*, ed. Nathaniel B. Shurtleff, 5 vols. (Boston: William White Press, 1853–54), 2:38, 48, 72, 112, 117, 128–29, 198–99, 227–28, 231, 240, 263, 275, and 3:96, 116; *John Winthrop Papers*, ed. Allyn B. Forbes, 5 vols. (Boston: Merrymount Press, 1929–44), 5:177–78.

6. Howard M. Chapin, *Documentary History of Rhode Island*, 2 vols. (Providence: Preston and Rounds Co., 1916), 1:192–99.

7. *Mass. Records*, 2:72, 48, 61; Howard M. Chapin, "Pomham and His Fort," *Rhode Island Historical Society Collections*, vol. 11 (Providence, 1918), pp. 31–36; Williams to Mass. General Court, 15 November 1655, *Williams Papers*, 2:445.

8. Williams to Mass. General Court, 12 May 1656, *Williams Papers*, 2:450–52; *Warwick First Book*, 1 October 1649. The *Warwick First Book* is available at the Rhode Island Historical Society in typescript and on microfilm; it was also published as *The Early Records of the Town of Warwick*, ed. Howard M. Chapin (Providence, 1926).

9. William Cronon, *Changes in the Land: Indians, Colonists, and the Ecology of New England* (New York: Hill and Wang, 1983), pp. 50–51, 127–56; Salisbury, *Manitou and Providence*, p. 231.

10. *Winthrop Papers*, 5:246–47.

11. Roger Williams, *Key to the Language of America*, printed in *The Complete Writ-*

ings of Roger Williams, 7 vols. (New York: Russell & Russell, 1963), p. 140; Fuller, *History of Warwick,* pp. 5–6.

12. *Mass. Records,* 2:198–99, 227–28, 231, and 3:116.

13. *Mass. Records,* 2:48; *Winthrop Papers,* 5:246–47.

14. Cronon, *Changes in the Land,* pp. 135–37; *Warwick First Book,* 23 January 1648 and 22 December 1666; *Records of the Colony of Rhode Island and Providence Plantations in New England,* ed. John Russell Bartlett, 10 vols. (Providence, 1856–65), 2:172–73.

15. *Warwick First Book,* 23 January 1648, 15 January 1651, 8 February 1658, 2 May 1653, 9 May 1653, 17 May 1656, and 20 July 1666.

16. Deed of sale between Cauhanaquanack and Samuel Gorton and Randall Houlden, *Warwick First Book,* 27 May 1659.

17. *Warwick First Book,* 2 June 1656 and 5 February 1657.

18. Dennis Allen O'Toole, "Exiles, Refugees, and Rogues: The Quest for Civil Order in the Towns and Colony of Providence Plantations, 1636–1654," 2 vols. (Ph.D. diss., Brown University, 1973), 1:260.

19. Kawashima, *Puritan Justice,* passim; David Bushnell, "The Treatment of the Indians in Plymouth Colony," *New England Quarterly* 26 (1953): 193–218 (see chap. 2 of *New England Encounters*); Kawashima, "Jurisdiction of the Colonial Courts," pp. 532–50; Lyle Koehler, "Red-White Power Relations," pp. 1–31; Ronda, "Red and White at the Bench," pp. 165–215.

20. *Rhode Island Records,* 1:218–19; *Rhode Island Court Records: Records of the Court of Trials of the Colony of Providence Plantations: 1647–1670,* 2 vols. (Providence: Rhode Island Historical Society, 1920), 1:5; Williams to John Winthrop, Jr., 10 November 1649, *Williams Papers,* 1:301–3.

21. Sir Robert Carr to Lord Arlington, 9 April 1666, *Rhode Island Records,* 2:137–38; Williams to Mass. General Court, 12 May 1656, *Williams Papers,* 1:450–52.

22. Emanuel Downing to John Winthrop, August 1645, *Winthrop Papers,* 5:38–39; Daniel Gookin, "Historical Collections of the Indians of New England," *Massachusetts Historical Society Collections,* 1st ser. 1 (1792): 162–210.

23. On servants, see *Records of the Court of Trials of the Town of Warwick,* ed. Helen Capwell (Providence: Shepply Press, 1922), p. 12; *Rhode Island Court Records,* 1:53–54; *Mass. Records,* 2:61, 3:64. On guides, see *Mass. Records,* 2:24; on mail carriers, see *Williams Papers,* 1:150–51; on keepers of livestock, see *Rhode Island Records,* 2:172–73, and *Warwick First Book,* 22 December 1666. On wolf killers, see *Warwick First Book,* 5 March 1662. On fence builders, see Gookin, "Indians of New England," p. 210; Wood, *New England's Prospect,* as quoted by William B. Weeden, "Indian Money as a Factor in New England Civilization," *Johns Hopkins University Studies in Historical and Political Science,* 2d ser. 8–9 (1884): 7; *Warwick First Book,* 2 and 9 May 1653.

24. In the aftermath of King Philip's War, Providence, like many other New England towns, decided the fate of those Indians who remained. They shot some, deported others, and allowed still more to remain in various degrees of dependency.

During this process of selection, the town records refer to two Indian women, "ye old Women & ye old Women Peter ye Smiths mother," implying that this Indian woman's son was a "Smith." *The Early Records of the Town of Providence,* ed. Horatio Rogers et al., 21 vols. (Providence, 1892), 15:152. For other evidences of Indian technical ability, see Patrick M. Malone, "Changing Military Technology among the Indians of Southern New England, 1600–1677," *American Quarterly* 25 (1973): 48–63.

25. *Warwick First Book,* 20 July 1666; *Providence Records,* 15:22–25.

26. The *Warwick First Book,* which contains numerous English indentures, has none for Indians. Furthermore, while there are no records of payments received by servants, they were able to begin and terminate their employment at will. For similarities between the treatment of Indians and the treatment of servants in the New England colonies, see Lawrence W. Towner, "A Fondness for Freedom: Servant Protest in Puritan Society," *William and Mary Quarterly* 21 (1964): 256–69, esp. 208–9. For sachems' legal "responsibilities," see *Rhode Island Court Records,* 1:44–45, 57; for English "masters," see *Rhode Island Court Records,* 2:64.

27. Kawashima, *Puritan Justice,* p. 81; *Rhode Island Records,* 1:219, 413–14; *Mass. Records,* 2:61.

28. *Warwick First Book,* 23 January 1648 and 10 May 1652.

29. Williams to John Throckmorton, 30 July 1672, *Williams Papers,* 2:671–75. See also *Rhode Island Judicial Records* (located at the Rhode Island Judicial Archives, Pawtucket, R.I.), 22 October 1673, p. 18; Francis Moloney, *The Fur Trade in New England, 1620–1676* (Cambridge: President and Fellows of Harvard College, 1931), pp. 102–3; Henry C. Dorr, "The Narragansetts," *Rhode Island Historical Society Collections,* vol. 7 (Providence, 1885), pp. 178–210; Williams to Mass. General Court, 12 May 1656, *Williams Papers,* 2:451. John Eliot, "Strength Out of Weakness Or a Glorious Manifestation of the Further Progresse of the Gospel among the Indians in New England," *Massachusetts Historical Society Collections,* 3d ser. 4 (1834): 173.

30. *Warwick First Book,* 15 May 1656 and 5 February 1657.

31. *Rhode Island Records,* 1:243, 245–46; O'Toole, "Exiles, Refugees and Rogues," pp. 495–96; Moloney, *Fur Trade,* pp. 102–3.

32. For Holliman's and Greene's involvement in the fur trade, see Carl Bridenbaugh, *Fat Mutton and Liberty of Conscience: Society in Rhode Island, 1636–1690* (Providence: Brown University Press, 1974), p. 23. For lists of town officers and colony commissioners dominated by Gortonists from 1647 to 26 October 1652, and by Holliman, Greene, and their allies from 19 December 1652 to 1655, see *Warwick First Book.* Gortonists were again represented in the town government after March–May 1656, but Holliman kept tight control of the town moderatorship until his death in 1659. On deregulating the colony's trade, see *Providence Records,* 15:41–46, and O'Toole, "Exiles, Refugees, and Rogues," pp. 498–501, 503–4.

33. *Williams Papers,* 2:445, and Kawashima, *Puritan Justice,* p. 82. See also Moloney, *Fur Trade,* pp. 102–3; Williams to Mass. General Court, 12 May 1656, *Williams Papers,* 2:450–52; *Rhode Island Court Records,* 1:25–26; *Warwick First Book,* 4 March 1659 and 4 May 1652.

34. *Mass. Records,* 2:48; Malone, "Indian Military Technology," pp. 48–63; Wil-

liams to Mass. General Court, 15 November 1655 and 12 May 1656, *Williams Papers*, 2:443–45 and 2:450–52.

35. *Warwick First Book*, 5 April 1653; *Rhode Island Records*, 2:282; Bridenbaugh, *Fat Mutton*, p. 23; Williams to John Winthrop, Jr., 15 February 1655, *Williams Papers*, 2:425.

36. *Mass. Records*, 4:356; Bridenbaugh, *Fat Mutton*, pp. 22–23, 93–126; William B. Weeden, *Rhode Island: A Social History of the People* (New York, Grafton Press, 1910), p. 68.

37. William B. Weeden, *Economic and Social History of New England, 1620–1789*, 2 vols. (Cambridge: Riverside Press, 1890), 1:39–40, 42–43, and Weeden, "Indian Money," pp. 5–51; *Rhode Island Records*, 1:474; Williams, *Key to Language*, pp. 174–75; Peleg Sanford to James Greene, 12 February 1667, *The Letter Book of Peleg Sanford of Newport, Merchant (late Governour of Rhode Island) 1666–1668*, ed. Howard W. Preston and G. Andrews Moriarty, Jr. (Providence: Rhode Island Historical Society, 1920), p. 53; Bridenbaugh, *Fat Mutton*, p. 41.

38. Williams to Mass. General Court, 12 May 1656, *Williams Papers*, 2:450–52; Harold P. Curtis, "Warwick Proprietors Divisions," *Rhode Island Historical Society Collections*, vol. 20 (Providence, 1927), pp. 35–39; Frank Green Bates and Charles M. Perry, "The Shawomet Purchase in the Colony of Rhode Island and Providence Plantations in New England" (unpublished typescript located at the Rhode Island Historical Society), pp. 21, 61, 96. These transactions were also tied to disputes over land ownership between contending groups in Providence and Warwick.

39. *Warwick First Book*, 14 February and 9 April 1660.

40. *Rhode Island Records*, 1:477–78.

41. *Warwick First Book*, 11 March 1661, 24 June 1666, 5 February 1657, 22 December 1666; *Rhode Island Records*, 2:172–73.

42. *Rhode Island Court Records*, 1:64, 73; *Rhode Island Records*, 1:484; *Warwick First Book*, 22 May 1662 and 22 February 1665.

43. *Rhode Island Records*, 2:51, 362; *Warwick First Book*, 20 February 1664; *Rhode Island Court Records*, 1:57.

44. *Rhode Island Court Records*, 1:72–73, 55; *Rhode Island Judicial Records*, pp. 6–7; *Warwick First Book*, 31 December 1662.

45. *Rhode Island Records*, 1:403, 425–26; *Rhode Island Court Records*, 1:54.

46. *Rhode Island Court Records*, 1:76 (see also Benedict Arnold's suit against Cocaunaguant on the same day); *Warwick Court of Trials Records*, pp. 9–14.

47. *Rhode Island Records*, 1:412–13.

48. *Rhode Island Records*, 1:405–6; *Rhode Island Court Records*, 1:54–55.

49. See William Greene Roelker, "Samuel Gorton's Master Stroke," *Rhode Island History* 2 (1943): 1–10; *Williams Papers*, 2:554n; *Rhode Island Records*, 2:314, 133.

50. *Rhode Island Records*, 2:134–35 (for previous records of the connection between Eliot and Pomham, see *Mass. Records*, 3:96, and *Williams Papers*, 2:550–51, 553n).

51. *Warwick First Book*, 24 April 1666 and 12 February 1667.

52. *Warwick First Book*, 12 February 1667; *Warwick Court of Trials Records*, 20 October 1666. There were several notable Indians in western Rhode Island and Con-

necticut whose names were phonetically similar to "Awashkooke." But since the Indians at Nausauket were part of the Coweset Tribe, it is most probable that the "pretended sachime" Awashkooke was the son of the Coweset sachem Taccomanan, whose name appears in the 1654 Potowomut deed (13 July 1654) as "Awashocnss" (*Rhode Island Records*, 2:132–38).

53. *Rhode Island Records*, 2:269–78, 284–86, 500–502.

54. *Rhode Island Records*, 2:191–93, 194–95, 198–99, 264–65, 267, 282, 408–10.

55. *Rhode Island Judicial Records*, pp. 6–7; *Rhode Island Records*, 2:295, 336–37.

56. Usner, *Indians, Settlers, and Slaves*, passim.

PART TWO

Debates on the "Indian Wars"

4

The Pequot War Reconsidered

STEVEN T. KATZ

A cataclysmic war between colonists and Indians, as the two previous essays make abundantly clear, was the tragic climax to New England's intercultural contact from 1607 to 1675. In some parts of the region, war came much sooner. If the Pequot War of 1637 did not match King Philip's War in breadth of scope or number of participants, it exhibited, on a smaller scale, a similar ferocity. It also demonstrated the fragility of relations between the Puritan colonies and their Indian neighbors, which had begun with high prospects for peaceful coexistence in the Plymouth-Wampanoag alliance of 1621 and continued in the Bay Colony's early relations with the Indian bands of eastern Massachusetts.

The war that pitted the Pequots and their few allies against the combined forces of Connecticut, Massachusetts, the Mohegans, and the Narragansetts generated a lively literature. Beginning in 1637, a spate of tracts, memoirs, and correspondence set forth the war's causes and its place in God's plans for New England. Historians ever since, especially in recent decades, have attempted to fashion persuasive explanations of the "Pequot War" from the surviving documents. Few topics in early American history have produced such conflicting, often rancorous, interpretations.

Several flash points mark the debate. One is the assignment of responsibility for the war—were the Puritans or Pequots primarily (or solely) at fault? A second, related, question concerns the colonists' motives for battle—did they arise from cupidity, aggression, self-defense, or some combination of these and perhaps other impulses? A third, vociferously argued, question interrogates the Puritans' ultimate objective—did they want a quick, if bloody, tactical victory, or a genocidal destruction of the foe? Steven T. Katz's essay addresses all of these controversial issues but especially the paramount question of genocide, on which his postscript adds a forceful rebuttal to his critics.

*I*T IS WELL KNOWN that in the 1970s and 1980s traditional scholarly analyses and judgments of the motives and events surrounding the Pequot War of 1637[1] came to be revised. In place of the view that the English were simply protecting themselves by preemptively attacking the Pequots, the revisionists argued that the Europeans used earlier, limited threats against them as cause to bring mass destruction on the Pequots.[2] That assault is then taken to be a harbinger, a symbol of a larger, premeditated exterminatory intent that characterized the invasion of the New World. While there is surely room for a more penetrating critical reconstruction of the meaning of America's conquest and settlement than has yet appeared, one must be cautious in allowing legitimate moral outrage at the treatment of the Indians to substitute for a careful sorting of the evidence about the Pequot War. If we examine the facts closely and try to analyze them within their particular historical context, our judgments of the wrongs done the Native Americans will be more nuanced, balanced, and discriminating than radicalizing polemics allow and thus ultimately will better serve our efforts to understand the processes and consequences of colonization.

I

My first cautionary comment regarding the war is that it should not be viewed in strictly racial or ethnic terms of Red vs. White. I do not dispute that the colonists viewed the Indians through racial stereotypes or that those stereotypes affected their behavior, but the particular circumstances of the Pequot War certainly seem to argue against the charge that it was a universal offensive against "Indianness" per se. The most telling of these circumstances is the presence of rival Indian groups on the side of the colonists. The crucial role of the Narragansetts, first in rejecting Pequot overtures to join a pan-Indian front against the English and then, in October 1636, in allying with the English against the Pequot, is but the earliest and most prominent case of European-Indian collaboration in the conflict.[3] Following this alliance, the Mohegans, the Massachusetts and River Tribes, and later the Mohawks all sided with the British.[4] Although the reasons for these alliances have been disputed for three centuries, seventeenth-century evidence—for example, the "Remonstrance of New Netherland," John Winthrop's *History of New England,* and John De Forest's *History of the Indians*[5]—is clear that at least intermittent hostility between the Pequots and the Narragansetts and their tributaries preceded the war.

Once we are able to hold our charges of racism in reserve, we can attend to the specifics of the war. Our distance from the events obviously blurs our vision. Many facts about the war have been contested, including the particular causes for the outbreak of hostilities; however, there can be no doubt that both sides had cause to feel aggrieved. From the perspective of most Indians, exceptions notwithstanding, the very presence of the European was an act of aggression. Filling in the outlines of this generalized aggression was an already considerable and well-documented body of particular crimes committed by unscrupulous individuals like John Oldham, whose murder in 1636 by Indians of uncertain provenance set in motion the events that led to the war.[6] Oldham was not, moreover, the only Englishman the Pequots or their tributaries had murdered. In 1634 they had killed two English captains, including the notorious and disreputable John Stone (and his crew), who had kidnapped and held several Indians for ransom,[7] and in the next two years they had killed at least six more colonists. Alternatively, the English leadership was disturbed that the Pequots had taken no action against the guilty among them and disheartened that the Pequots had abrogated the terms of the treaty they had signed. Fears increased when Jonathan Brewster, a Plymouth trader, passed word that Uncas, sachem of the Mohegans, had reported that

> the Pequents have some mistrust, that the English will shortly come against them (which I take is by indiscreet speeches of some of your people her to the Natives) and therefore out of desperate madnesse doe threaten shortly to sett upon both Indians [Mohegans] and English, joyntly.[8]

Uncas may well have fabricated the rumor, but the colonists were certainly in a frame of mind to take it seriously. Their numbers were small, and news of the Virginia uprising of 1622, with its 350 casualties, had still not faded from memory.[9] What the Puritans sought was a stratagem that would put an end to unpredictable, deadly annoyances as well as forestall any larger, more significant Indian military action like that suggested by Uncas's report. However one estimates the "good faith" or lack thereof of the Massachusetts leadership, efforts were made to negotiate, but these efforts failed, or at least were perceived to have failed. The colonists then chose as their best course of action a retaliatory raid, intended both to punish and to warn, on the Indians of Block Island, who were specifically charged with Oldham's murder. The Pequots were involved, according to William Hubbard, because the murderers had "fled presently to the Pequods, by whom they were sheltered, and so became also guilty themselves of his blood."[10]

Ninety Englishmen participated in the raid commanded by John Endecott. John Winthrop noted that Endecott was ordered

> to put to death the men of Block Island, but to spare the women and
> children, and to bring them away, and to take possession of the Island;
> and from thence to go to the Pequods to demand the murderers of Capt.
> Stone and other English, and one thousand fathom of wampon for dam-
> ages, etc., and some of their children as hostages.[11]

None of the mainland Pequot at Pequot Harbor were to be harmed if they capitulated to his demands. In the event, the raid on Block Island turned into an extensive assault, and the Indian settlement there was looted and burned. However, although property was destroyed and several Indians were wounded, "the Bay-men killed not a man, save that one Kichomi-quim, an Indian Sachem of the Bay, killed a Pequit."[12] The fact that only one Indian was killed seems to confirm John Winthrop's belief that the colonists "went not to make war upon [the Pequots] but to do justice." Not all colonists defined "justice" as Winthrop did, however, for the Endecott raid on the Harbor Indians was condemned by the colonial leaders of Plymouth, Connecticut, and Fort Saybrook.[13]

In response to Endecott's assaults, the Pequots plagued the settlers with a series of raids, ambushes, and annoyances. On 23 April, Wethersfield, Connecticut, was attacked. Nine were killed, including a woman and child, and two additional young women were captured.[14] A number of other raids claimed the lives of thirty Europeans, or five percent of all the settlers in Connecticut.[15] In addition to these offensive actions, the Pequots set about developing alliances, particularly with the Narragansetts, to galvanize support for a war to destroy European settlement in their territory, if not in New England entirely.[16] Many colonists who learned of the plan for a broad effort against them, which was frustrated only at the last minute through the intervention of Roger Williams,[17] rightly felt, given their demographic vulnerability, that their very survival was threatened.[18] Even Francis Jennings, the most severe critic of Puritan behavior, acknowledges that "Had these [Pequot] proposals [for alliance with the Narragansetts] been accepted by the Narragansetts, there would have without a doubt arisen a genuine Indian menace. . . . Whether the colonies could long have maintained themselves under such conditions is open to serious question."[19]

The Pequot War was the organized reaction of the colonists of Connecticut and Massachusetts to these intimidating events. In choosing to make war, they were choosing to put an end to threats to their existence as individuals and as a community. They did not decide to fight out of some a priori lust for Indian blood based on some metaphysical doctrine of Indian inferiority, however much they may have held that view, or some desire for further, even complete, control over Indian territory, much as they coveted such land. They fought, initially, a defensive war. They may well have provoked events, as even Winthrop tacitly acknowledged,[20] by their over-reactive raid on Block Island, but, in the early stages of the conflict, they did not intend to enter into a full-scale war with the Pequots until the Pequots raised the stakes with their response to the events at Block Island and Pequot Harbor. Of course the Indians cannot be blamed for so replying, for they too saw themselves as acting legitimately in self-defense, both narrowly and more generally in defense of traditional Indian rights to their own native lands. In effect, both sides acted to defend what they perceived as rightly theirs. In this context, if either side can be said to have harbored larger geopolitical ambitions, it was the Pequots, though defeat would certainly bury those desires.

The major action of the war was an attack by 70 Connecticut and 90 Massachusetts colonists along with 60 Mohegans, plus some scattered Narragansett and Eastern Niantics, against the Pequot Fort at Mystic, which held an Indian population of between 400 and 700, including women and children.[21] The colonists and their Indian allies surprised the Pequots and burned their fort to the ground. During the battle 2 English soldiers were killed and about 20 were wounded, while almost half the Indians allied with them were killed or wounded; almost all the Pequots were killed.[22]

Richard Drinnon, in his *Facing West: The Metaphysics of Indian Hating and Empire Building* (1980), has argued that the unusual violence of the operation signals the colonists' "genocidal intentions."[23] In evaluating the behavior of the English in this particular instance, however, it should be recognized that the tactics employed were neither so unconventional nor so novel that they can be taken to mark a turning point in Puritan-Indian relations, nor were they so distinctive as to indicate a transformation in Puritan awareness of the otherness of their adversaries. Given the relative strength of the enemy, the inexperience of the colonial forces, and the crucial fact that Sassacus, chief of the Pequot, and his warriors were camped only five miles from Mystic Fort and were sure to arrive soon, as in fact they did, one need not resort to dramatic theories of genocidal intentionality to explain the actions of the English. The simple, irrefutable fact is that had the battle been prolonged, Sassacus would have had time to reach Mystic and deflect the English attack.

II

Although he does not use the term *genocide* per se,[24] it is clear from the rhetorical thrust of his argument and his use of phrases like "deliberate massacre" that Francis Jennings is an insistent advocate of the genocidal thesis. Given the force of his prose, the popularity of his work, and its long-standing influence, it is useful to deconstruct Jennings's argument to evaluate the legitimacy of the heinous charge leveled against the English colonists.

Jennings attributes to Capt. John Mason, the expedition's leader, an overt, *ab initio* desire to massacre the Indians. "Mason proposed," he writes,

> to avoid attacking Pequot warriors, which would have overtaxed his unseasoned, unreliable troops. Battle, as such, was not his purpose. Battle is only one of the ways to destroy an enemy's will to fight. Massacre can accomplish the same end with less risk, and Mason had determined that massacre would be his objective.[25]

Ignoring all other reports of Mason's intentions and actions, Jennings bases his conclusions on Mason's own terse account of the event. Jennings cites Mason's reasons for his strategy, with special reference to his concluding "'and also some other [reasons],'" which he says "'I shall forebear to trouble you with'" (p. 220). Even Jennings labels this comment cryptic, but he still does not forebear using it as unambiguous evidence of a hidden, premeditated plan to massacre all the Indians at Fort Mystic.

Jennings also refers to Mason's discussion with his colleagues Lt. Lion Gardiner and Capt. John Underhill as well as with the expedition's Chaplain Stone. He takes Mason's request that the chaplain "'commend our Condition to the Lord, that night, to direct how in what manner we should demean our selves'" (p. 220) to be a covert reference to the existence of a plan to massacre the Indians the next day. But on the eve of such a battle, especially given Puritan sensibilities, such a request is neither surprising nor, given the text before us, indicative of any special intent; to read it as an implicit confession of genocidal desire, Jennings has to over-interpret the brief original source dramatically.

Jennings charges that "all the secondary accounts of the Pequot conquest squeamishly evade confessing the deliberateness of Mason's strategy, and some falsify to conceal it" (p. 220). What Jennings adduces as confirmation of both the premeditated plot to massacre and the later conscious suppression of that fact emerges in the course of a curious argument, which I quote in full.

> Mason's own narrative is the best authority on this point. The Massachu-setts Puritans' William Hubbard brazened out his own misquotation by telling his readers to "take it as it was delivered in writing by that valiant, faithful, and prudent Commander Capt. Mason." With this emphatic claim to authority he quoted Mason as saying, "We had resolved a while not to have burned it [the village], but being we could not come at them, I resolved to set it on fire." Despite Hubbard's assurance, these were not Mason's words. His manuscript said bluntly, "we had formerly concluded to destroy them by the Sword and save the Plunder." [Pp. 220–21]

Jennings's conclusion does not follow logically from the texts he cites nor from his juxtaposition of them. They neither suggest premeditation to massacre nor falsification of the record; instead, Hubbard's paraphrase of Mason's words accords perfectly with his stated intent to plunder the set-tlement. Jennings himself recognizes that such economic motives were central to the Block Island raid, as well as other actions by the English. Burning Fort Mystic would, of course, severely limit its economic poten-tial; the sword was a less efficient tool of human destruction but would preserve goods of value to the English. In fact, Mason's vow to "destroy" the Pequots "by the Sword" is a phrase not at all unusual to the language of military conflict and in that context such comments almost always signal not the annihilation of the enemy but the disruption of its capacity to fight. This understanding of Mason's comment is supported by the Puritans' fur-ther prosecution of the war.

Jennings continues to press home his point in his increasingly confused and confusing reconstruction of events. I quote:

> The rest of Mason's manuscript revealed what sort of inhabitants had been occupying the Mystic River village and proved conclusively that mere victory over them was not enough to satisfy Mason's purpose. After telling how the attack was launched at dawn of May 26, and how entrance to the village was forced, the account continued thus:
> At length William Heydon espying the Breach in the Wigwam, sup-posing some English might be there, entred; but in his Entrance fell over a dead Indian; but speedily recovering himself, the Indians some fled, others crept under their Beds: the Captain [Mason] going out of the Wig-wam saw many Indians in the Lane or Street; he making towards them,

they fled, were pursued to the End of the Lane, where they were met by Edward Pattison, Thomas Barber, with some others; where seven of them were Slain, as they said. The Captain facing about, Marched a slow Pace up the Lane he came down, perceiving himself very much out of Breath; and coming to the other End near the Place where he first entred, saw two Soldiers standing close to the Pallizado with their Swords pointed to the Ground: The Captain told them that We should never kill them after that manner: The Captain also said, WE MUST BURN THEM: and immediately stepping into the Wigwam where he had been before, brought out a Fire Brand, and putting it into the Matts with which they were covered, set the Wigwams on Fire. [P. 221]

From this sparse, unsophisticated description, Jennings concludes that "It is terribly clear . . . that the village, stockaded though it was, had few warriors at home when the attack took place" (p. 222). Mason himself, however, asserts that just the day before the English attack, 150 braves had reinforced the Indian garrison holding the fort, but Jennings cavalierly dismisses this claim in a marvelous display of selective reading. The reasons he musters for denying Mason's express testimony on such a vital matter are offered both in Jennings's text and in a dizzying footnote (p. 222). The burden of the main argument is that insofar as Mason's account portrays Indians fleeing and creeping under their beds for protection, those so described could only have been "women, children, and feeble old men," who had no other recourse but to resort to such cowardly stratagems. Surely 150 warriors—and the Pequots had already well demonstrated "their willingness to fight to the death"—would not have "suddenly and uncharacteristically turned craven." At the end of this convoluted denial of part—and only part, indeed the most straightforward and factual part—of Mason's account is Jennings's assumption that Mason marched on Fort Mystic because he had received advance intelligence from Narragansett allies that "there were no 'reinforcements.'" Destroying the "wretches" would be easily accomplished.

But the original narratives of the battle suggest a very different reading. Mason indicates that he found his first plan unworkable, that only after the attack had begun did he realize how costly it might prove for the English; only then, in self-protection, did he make the decision to burn rather than to plunder the settlement. This analysis of events is confirmed by Underhill's record of the battle, which also has the virtue of emphasizing the bravery of the Indians involved. "Most courageously," he writes, "these Pequots behaved themselves." Only when the battle grew too intense did the British, out of necessity, torch the fort. Even then, Underhill states, "many courageous fellows were unwilling to come out and fought most desperately through the palisadoes . . . and so perished valiantly. Mercy did they deserve for their valor, could we have had opportunity to bestow it."[26] Jennings does not cite Underhill's crucial and disarming testimony; instead, he engages in some more verbal sleight of hand, carefully choosing the texts he wishes to manipulate.

In a footnote (n. 57, p. 222) he replays his charge against Mason. Leaving out only the citations, I quote in full:

> . . . Underhill and Hubbard omitted the reinforcements assertion. Winthrop assigned as Pequot casualties "two chief sachems, and one hundred and fifty fighting men, and about one hundred and fifty old men, women, and children." . . . Mason's and Winthrop's "reinforcements" thus became Winthrop's total of warrior casualties. Even if this is true, it means that Mason planned the attack before those warriors arrived, but the likelihood of its truth is remote. No matter how these wriggly texts are viewed, they testify to Mason's deliberate purpose of massacring noncombatants. He had advance information of the Pequot dispositions.

First, it should be recognized that because Underhill and Hubbard do not mention the 150 Indian reinforcements, Jennings uses their silence as confirmation of the dishonesty of Mason's account. But arguments from silence "say" very little, and extreme caution should be exercised in employing them, especially in the face of explicit testimony to the contrary. Jennings next uses Winthrop's narrative, which supports Mason's claim about reinforcements, to diminish that claim by impugning Winthrop's veracity. But such double-think will not do, for if Winthrop is unreliable, the truth of his account "remote," he cannot serve to discredit Mason; if he is reliable, his depiction of events cannot be taken lightly. Then, out of this morass of conflicting facts and conclusions, Jennings draws the non sequitur that Mason was intent on massacring noncombatant Pequots; in fact, all contemporary accounts simply state that noncombatants were massacred, not that there was any premeditated plan to do so. It appears that Jennings would have us believe that his highly ambiguous, contradictory reconstruction of the facts proposed 340 years after the event and premised on a dubious dialectical analysis of silence, a great deal of hermeneutical confusion, and a series of non sequiturs is to be given precedence over the description of circumstances provided by several contemporary and first-person accounts in our possession. Assuredly, the Connecticut militiamen acted reprehensibly and with unnecessary severity against non-combatants that spring day in 1637, but they did not do so for the reasons, nor in the manner, advanced in Jennings's moving, but untrue, retelling of the tale.

III

Following the destruction of Mystic Fort, the colonists and their Indian allies pursued the surviving Pequots. In the first major encounter of this subsequent stage in the conflict, approximately 200 Indians were captured, of whom 22 or 24 were adult males; these braves were executed. The remaining women and children, almost 80 percent of the total captured, were parceled up about evenly, as was common Indian practice, among the victorious Indian allies and the colonists of Massachusetts Bay.[27] A second and larger engagement took place on 14 July near modern Southport, Connecticut, where Sassacus and the majority of the remaining Pequots, numbering several hundred, were surrounded. In the ensuing battle, women, children, and old men, again a majority of the Pequots present, were allowed to seek sanctuary while about 80 warriors fought to their death. In the final phase of the war, various Indian tribes in the area, vying for English friendship and seeking to settle old tribal debts, hunted down and murdered Pequot braves while dispersing their womenfolk and children. Sassacus was killed, and in early August the Mohawks sent his head to the British in Hartford.[28]

Alden Vaughan describes the aftermath of these events:

> Toward the end of 1637 the few remaining sachems begged for an end to the war, promising vassalage in return for their lives. A peace convention was arranged for the following September. With the Treaty of Hartford, signed on September 21, 1638, the Pequots ceased to exist as an independent polity.[29]

The treaty arrangement as well as the previous pattern of killing all adult males suggests that the anti-Pequot forces, both Indian and European, were determined to eliminate the Pequot threat once and for all. The 180 Pequots captured in the assault on Sassacus were parceled out among the victors: 80 to the Narragansetts, 80 to the Mohegans, and 20 to the Eastern Niantics.[30] The survivors were now no longer to be known as Pequots or to reside in their tribal lands, and the Pequot River was renamed the Thames and the Pequot village, New London. These treaty stipulations, which required the extinction of Pequot identity and the assignment of Pequot survivors to other tribes, and some to slavery,[31] suggest an overt, unambiguous form of *cultural* genocide, here employed in the name of military security. However, the dispersion of the remaining communal members—the elderly, the women, and the children, almost certainly a majority of the tribe as a whole—directly contradicts the imputation of any intent to commit *physical* genocide, as some revisionists insist.[32]

A more restrained reading of events would not deny that the Puritans, as their post-war writings reflect, were conscious that they had acted with great, perhaps even excessive, destructive force. Almost certainly composed as responses to English and Indian critics, these after-the-fact appraisals should not, however, be misconstrued as evidence of either genocidal intent prior to the event or even of genocidal behavior during and after the war. Rather, given the Puritan mentality, saturated as it was with concerns to detect God's providential design in temporal matters, these post-hoc accountings, even were we to call them rationalizations, were attempts to satisfy the Puritans' own internal axiological demand that their taking of lives on such a large scale, and in such a bloody way, was justified. Puritans had to know, and they wanted their critics to know, that what they had done was sanctioned by heaven. This concern for ethical legitimation should not be mistaken as evidence that the Puritans, however aware they were *after the event* of the contentious nature of the massacre they had wrought, looked upon this happening as signaling some fundamental re-orientation in their relationship either to their New World surroundings in general or with their New England Indian neighbors in particular. Neither Edward Johnson's approval of the Puritan preachers' exhortation to "execute vengeance upon the heathen," nor William Bradford's description of the burning of the inhabitants at Fort Mystic as a "sweet sacrifice" to the Lord, nor Underhill's appeal to scriptural precedent that in conquering a grossly evil people, such as the Pequot, "women and children must perish with their parents" are proof to the contrary.[33] Indeed, they are exactly the sort of theological pronouncements one would expect within the Puritan conceptual environment, fed as it was by recycled scriptural paradigms.

In general, the English did not relish their victory in an unseemly way. John Mason, for example, "refused to publish his accounts of his exploits, deeming them too immodest and likely to detract from the glory ascribed to God in those events." Captain Underhill, by contrast, did publish his version of the tale, but as Richard Slotkin has written, "Captain Underhill was a man clearly out of step with the Massachusetts way and one proscribed and exiled by the Puritan community." Underhill's "enthusiasms," in fact, were repeatedly met with censure rather than emulation. Mason, by contrast, the modest, self-effacing, God-extolling leader, was considered a worthy model in early American literature.[34]

IV

When the actions of the Puritans are placed in their appropriate context, when they are deconstructed as part and parcel of the historical reality of the seventeenth century, the accusations of genocide leveled against them are recognized to be exaggerations. However excessive the force wielded by the colonists, they had already seen—and would continue to see—their own die at the hands of the Indians. The Virginia Indian uprisings of 1622 have already been mentioned. In April 1644, a second uprising took the lives of approximately 500 whites, and in 1675, 300 more colonists were killed.[35] The bloody events of King Philip's War (1675–76) would certainly have intensified the fears that had long plagued those living at the edge of the frontier. Much Indian violence was, of course, a response to English greed, but for those charged with protecting the members of expanding English communities, the violence had to be stopped at all costs. In the New World—an environment so uncertain, so hostile—the colonists' need to limit threats to their survival was intense. Their responses could be excessive, but their fears were not unfounded.

From our point of view, it is easy to sympathize with the Pequots and to condemn the colonists' actions, but the scope of our condemnation must be measured against the facts. After the Treaty of Hartford was signed, Pequots were not physically harmed. Indeed, in 1640 the Connecticut leadership "declared their dislike of such as would have the Indians rooted out," that is, murdered.[36] Before the Pequots capitulated, many of their tribe had died, but the number killed probably totaled less than half the entire tribe. Sherburne Cook's estimate is even lower: "If the initial population [of Pequots] was 3,000 and 750 were killed, the battle loss was twenty-five percent of the tribe."[37]

While many Pequots were absorbed by other tribes—it is estimated that Uncas's Mohegan tribe, for example, received hundreds—evidence clearly indicates that soon after the conclusion of the war, the Pequot began to regroup as a tribe. By 1650 four special towns were created to accommodate them, each ruled by a Pequot governor, and in 1667 Connecticut established permanent reservations for the tribe, which by 1675 numbered approximately 1,500–2,000 members.[38] That year, no more than two generations after the Pequot War had ended, the Pequots allied with the colonists to fight King Philip's War. As recently as the 1960s, Pequots were still listed as a separate group residing in Connecticut.[39] Such factors suggest that while the British could certainly have been less thorough, less severe, less deadly in prosecuting their campaign against the Pequots, the campaign they actually did carry out, for all its vehemence, was not, either in intent or execution, genocidal.

This revision of the revisionists is not meant to deny the larger truth that the conquest of the New World entailed the greatest demographic tragedy in history. The wrongs done to the Native Americans, the suffering they experienced, the manifest evil involved in the colonial enterprise is in no way to be deflected or minimized. However, this sorry tale of despoliation and depopulation needs to be chronicled aright, with an appropriate sense of the actuality of seventeenth-century colonial existence. False, if morally impassioned, judgments cannot substitute for carefully nuanced and discriminating appraisals. Thus, while it is appropriate to censure the excesses, the unnecessary carnage, of the Pequot War, to interpret these events through the radicalizing polemic of accusations of genocide is to rewrite history to satisfy our own moral outrage.

Author's Postscript

Since the appearance of my original essay in 1991, four works have appeared that bear directly on the issues I originally raised: Alfred A. Cave's essay "Who Killed John Stone? A Note on the Origins of the Pequot War," *William and Mary Quarterly*, 3d ser. 49 (1992): 509–21; the revised version of Alden T. Vaughan's "Pequots and Puritans: The Causes of the War of 1637," in his volume of collected essays entitled *Roots of American Racism: Essays on the Colonial Experience* (New York: Oxford University Press, 1995), pp. 177–99; David E. Stannard's *American Holocaust: Columbus and the Conquest of the New World* (New York: Oxford University Press, 1992); and Michael Freeman's "Puritans and Pequots: The Question of Genocide," *New England Quarterly* 68 (1995): 278–93. Each of the above requires some brief comment in this context.

Alfred A. Cave's essay is important to my argument because it establishes, quite conclusively, that the Pequots were involved in the murder of Captain John Stone (whether in consort with the West Niantics or on their own is still an open question; see Cave's discussion p. 516). Cave's evidence thus rebuts the claim of Francis Jennings that those responsible for the death of Stone were West Niantics, a small tribe that was a tributary of the Pequots, and that the colonists knew this to be the case yet still laid the blame on the Pequots in order to justify war against them in aid of their territorial ambitions in the Connecticut Valley (*Invasion of America* [Chapel Hill: University of North Carolina Press, 1975]).

Beyond this not unimportant fact, Cave's essay also has the virtue of revealing, as I argued at some length, that, to quote Cave, "a close reading of the relevant sources does not support Jennings's verdict, which is grounded in a highly selective use of evidence" (p. 511). Given Jennings's position as the foundation stone for almost all of the revisionist essays of the last twenty years—e.g., Neal Salisbury's *Manitou and Providence* (New York: Oxford University Press, 1982); Karen Kupperman's *Settling With the Indians* (Totowa, N.J.: Rowman and Littlefield, 1980); Richard Drinnon's *Facing West* (Minneapolis: University of Minneapolis Press, 1980); and Stannard's *American Holocaust*—a recognition of the fundamental hermeneutical failures inherent in Jennings's work is of major consequence for all reconsiderations, including my own, of what actually occurred in seventeenth-century New England in general and in the Pequot War in particular.

Alden T. Vaughan's revised essay argues, as I did, that the Pequot War was a "synthesis" of Pequot and Puritan aggression (p. 190). However, the contribution made by Vaughan's recent revision of his well-known essay lies in his new emphasis on the implications of the colonists' increasing "assertion of ultimate jurisdiction over the region that colonists and Indians increasingly shared" (p. 192). It was this "assertion of authority" that led the Puritan leadership to demand that the Pequot punish those responsible for the murder of whites and to the costly belief that questions of inter-ethnic justice be settled according to European rules. "The magistrates' arrogation to themselves of the right to regulate and discipline neighboring Indians made war almost inevitable in 1636–37, especially when Endecott's enforcement—like so many subsequent 'police actions'—was brutally overreactive and ultimately counterproductive" (p. 194). This judicial-political factor was under-emphasized in my original paper, and I would now wish to incorporate this insight into any account of the causes of the Pequot War that I offered. (In fact, it has been incorporated into my revised discussion of the Pequot War that forms part of my analysis of early Indian-European contacts in volume 2, chapter 5 of my *Holocaust in Historical Context* (New York: Oxford University Press, forthcoming). More broadly, as already made evident in my original essay, I concur with Vaughan's seminal and judicious conclusion on the responsibility for the conflict: "the Pequot War, like most wars, cannot be attributed solely to the unmitigated bellicosity of one side and the righteous response of the others" (p. 194). Both Pequots and Puritans must share the blame for the tragedy that occurred in 1637.

David E. Stannard's recounting of the Pequot War is a very different matter. His *American Holocaust* is based on an inadequate and misleading use of primary sources, a misreading of secondary works, and several methodological misconceptions, the most seriously debilitating of which is his a priori belief that the correct way to decipher the interaction of Indians and European colonizers is by way of the Nazi murder of the Jews—thus the exploitative title of his book. This false analogy leads to gross misunderstandings of both the early American and the mid-twentieth-century European experience. Stannard apparently believes that his outraged feelings about the tragedy that befell the Native Americans—a tragedy of world-historical proportions but of a very different phenomenological sort than that which he (mis)describes—can substitute for careful reconstruction of the historical events.

Primarily dependent on Francis Jennings's tendentious reading of the Pequot War but going far beyond Jennings in the emotional character of his polemic, Stannard accounts for the war in this simplistic way:

> The brutish and genocidal encounter to which Mason was referring was the Pequot War. . . . Even in light of the colonists' grossly disproportionate sense of retribution when one of their own had been killed by Indians, this should have been sufficient revenge, but it was not. The colonists simply wanted to kill Indians. Despite the pledge of the Narragansetts' chief to mete out punishment to Oldham's murderers—a pledge he began to fulfill by sending 200 warriors to Block Island in search of the culprits—New England's Puritan leaders wanted more. [P. 112]

Moreover, Stannard, though he cites my essay, contends that after the destruction of the Pequot fort at Mystic River,

> the surviving Pequots were hunted into near-extermination. Other villages were found and burned. Small groups of warriors were intercepted and killed. Pockets of starving women and children were located, captured, and sold into slavery. If they were fortunate. Others were bound hand and foot and thrown into the ocean just beyond the harbor. And still more were buried where they were found, such as one group of three hundred or so who tried to escape through a swampland, but could make "little haste, by reason of their Children, and want of Provision," said Mason. When caught, as Richard Drinnon puts it, they "were literally run to ground," murdered, and then "tramped into the mud or buried in swamp mire."
>
> The comparative handful of Pequots who were left, once this series of massacres finally ended, were parceled out to live in servitude. [Pp. 114–15]

As my essay and most responsible recapitulations of the war make clear, this is not what happened: the errors of fact and interpretation in Stannard's account are legion. For example, contrary to Stannard's claim that a "comparative handful of Pequots . . . were left," approximately 75 percent of the tribe survived the conflict, as I indicated in my original essay, based on the basic research of Sherburne Cook. And contrary to Stannard's assertion that the colonists "virtually eradicated an entire people," by 1650–51 the Pequot were reconstituted as a people and resettled in four Indian towns with Pequot governors. Stannard's recycling of Richard Drinnon's claim that all the Pequots "were literally run to ground, murdered and then tramped into the mud or buried in swamp mire" (p. 115) is simply false. The majority of the pursued Pequot encircled by the colonial forces were *not* murdered. Pequot women, children and old men—the majority of the Pequots present—were allowed to seek sanctuary. The fighting then continued, and 80 Pequot warriors were killed in a final battle on 14 July 1637.

Such basic information on the final stages of the war is not the only relevant data ignored by Stannard. In his explanation of the cause of the war, for example, he mentions the murder of John Oldham by Indians (p. 112) but conveniently fails to mention all the other murders of settlers (at least 39 or 6.5 percent of all the colonists in Connecticut at the time); nor does he remind his readers that events in Connecticut in 1637 occurred against the backdrop of the Virginia uprising of 1622 that claimed 350 lives (out of 1,240 settlers); nor does he convey any sense of the general vulnerability of the colonists—given the immense demographic asymmetry that existed between the white and Indian populations. His partial description of events also ignores the pan-Indian alliance that the Pequots attempted to organize in order to drive all the settlers out of Connecticut. Even Francis Jennings allows that this possibility could have had catastrophic consequences had it materialized: "Had these [Pequot] proposals [for alliance] been accepted by the Narragansetts, there would have been without doubt a genuine Indian menace. . . . [W]hether the colonies could have long maintained themselves under such conditions is open to serious question" (*Invasion of America*, p. 213). In effect, nothing of the actual historical context, as perceived by the colonists, is presented, and nothing is allowed to count against Stannard's a priori certainties.

One last matter needs to be addressed. Referring to my original article on p. 318, n. 11, of *American Holocaust*, Stannard asserts, in a total misrepresentation of my argument:

> Professor Katz concludes his essay by observing that *some* Pequots survived the English colonists' efforts to annihilate them as a people, adding: "As recently as the 1960s, Pequots were still listed as a separate group resid-

ing in Connecticut. . . . [W]hile the British could certainly have been less thorough, less severe, less deadly in prosecuting their campaign against the Pequots, the campaign they actually did carry out, for all its vehemence, was not, either in intent or execution, genocidal." In other words, because the British did not kill *all* the Pequots they did not commit a genocide. This is not the place for a detailed critique of Professor Katz's flimsy thesis, but one can only wonder (actually, one need *not* wonder) at what his response might be to a Professor of Native American Studies taking the trouble to write an essay claiming that the Holocaust was not an act of genocide ("although the [Nazis] could certainly have been less thorough, less severe, less deadly in prosecuting their campaign against the [Jews]") because, after all, some Jews survived—a number of whom even live in Connecticut today.

The basic logical error in Stannard's argument is this: the Pequot survived the 1637 war because the colonists allowed them, indeed helped them, to survive. The Puritans had no intention of murdering all the Pequots. In stark contrast, the Jews survived the Nazi assault against them despite Nazi intentions. Only the defeat of Germany in World War II permitted Jewish survival. Had the Third Reich won World War II, as the British won the Pequot War, all of Europe's Jews (and, depending on the scale of Hitler's eventual victories, potentially all the Jews of the world) would have been exterminated by design. Stannard is blind to this essential difference.

Finally, there is the essay by Michael Freeman written in direct reply to my original essay. Freeman raises many issues that require comment, and I have responded at some length to his argument in a paper entitled, "'Pequots and the Question of Genocide': A Reply to Michael Freeman," *New England Quarterly* 68 (1995): 641–49. Here I concentrate on the main points of disagreement between us.

Freeman claims that "Katz conflates two different questions: the first concerns English motives for going to war; the second is whether the war was genocidal. Katz conflates these questions because he holds that the Puritans acted in self-defense and defensive wars cannot be genocidal" (p. 289). This argument, however, is simply false. Nowhere do I claim that defensive wars cannot be genocidal; defensive wars can, according to my definition, become as genocidal as offensive wars. Freeman produces no text in support of this mistaken reading of my essay—indeed, there is no such text to be quoted—and instead produces an erroneous version of my position.

While I acknowledged in my original essay that Uncas "may well have fabricated" his report of Pequot intentions to make war, this does not mean that independently of this report the Puritans did not have cause for authentic concern as to their safety. My wording regarding the rumor passed on by Brewster was purposely cautious: I wrote that Uncas "may well have fabricated" rather than "Uncas fabricated"; that is, at this remove of 350 years we have to be cautious and allow that Uncas might have been telling the truth about Pequot intentions, though it seems to me more likely that he was not. The Puritans had plenty of other evidence, described by me on p. 209 of my original piece, suggesting that they were in danger. I repeat here, for emphasis, that after John Endecott's initial raid on Block Island, the Pequots mounted a series of raids of differing sorts that claimed thirty lives, or 5 percent of all the settlers in Connecticut, and set about to develop alliances with other Indian nations such as the Narragansett (which failed to materialize) in order to create a common front capable of driving the English from their territory.

I do not deny, indeed I make very clear in my original essay, as Freeman cites, that Puritan actions were "excessive." But this judgment is not, as Freeman suggests, in contradiction to my further assertion that "the Pequot had geopolitical ambitions and that the Puritans did not" (p. 289, and see my original discussion on p. 211). In making the claim as to the respective geopolitical ambitions of the two sides in the Pequot War in the careful and balanced way that I did, I simply meant to indicate that the specific actions undertaken by the Puritans in this military conflict were unconnected to territorial aggrandizement, while the destruction of the Puritan settlement meant the recapture of territory by the Pequot. Moreover, as a logical matter, there is no necessary link between the "excesses" of the colonists and the control of territory, that is, the excesses can have been, as I believe they were, the product of motives unrelated to territorial expansion. In other words, Freeman sees the punitive excesses and territorial gain as motives necessarily connected when in fact they are only contingently so.

Again, Freeman misunderstands my position when he argues that I mistakenly hold that because the war was fought by the Puritans out of "fear for their survival . . . their actions were not genocidal." I never make such a claim, and Freeman therefore quotes no pertinent portion of my text. Of course, wars fought out of "fear for survival" can become genocidal. The relevant question is: was *this* war genocidal? The answer, I still maintain, is no.

To sum up to this point: Freeman has offered a series of faulty inferences and non sequiturs to my carefully argued paper. He has not shown that the Pequot War was genocidal, nor has he, thus far, attempted an independent demonstration that it was.

On p. 290 of his essay, Freeman gets to the heart of the issue: my definition of genocide vs. Raphael Lemkin's and, later, that of the United Nations, based on Lemkin's work. Freeman is correct that my definition is more "stringent" (my term, p. 213, n. 24) than Lemkin's and the United Nations' (for reasons I explain at length elsewhere, in volume 1 of my *Holocaust in Historical Context* [New York: Oxford University Press, 1994], chapter 1, and that were explained briefly in n. 24, p. 213, of my original essay). However, with the definitional matter in place, Freeman plays a verbal game by calling attention to my conclusion that the Pequot War led to "an overt, unambiguous form of cultural genocide" (p. 291) and then concluding that "cultural genocide is, of course, a form of genocide." The *essential* point here is this: there are two types of intentions and related activities that must be distinguished in the analysis of the notion of genocide: (a) those that entail *physical* genocide, that is, the physical destruction of a people; and (b) those that entail *cultural* genocide, that is, the loss of a people's identity. ("Ethnocide," as Lemkin earlier noted in *Axis Rule in Occupied Europe* [Washington, D.C.: Carnegie Foundation, 1944], p. 79, n. 1, is a roughly parallel term for this second phenomenon.) In the debate about whether the Pequot War is genocidal, the argument, as advanced by those I criticized in my original essay, is always related to *physical* genocide, which they demonstrate by analogies to the Holocaust, where the Nazi "Endlösung" has everything to do with the complete physical extermination of the Jewish people and nothing to do with their religious or cultural transformation, loss of territory, or incorporation in whatever form into other groups or sociopolitical structures and entities. Thus, for Freeman to think that he has shown my argument to be in error by noting what I myself note, and what is self-evident in the context of my essay, accomplishes nothing substantive.

As to my reading of Mason's statement on the eve of the battle, I believe that the historical and ideological circumstances, and a knowledge of language such as Mason's in comparable military contexts, supports my view that such language is conventional and does not indicate genocidal intent. Even if one were to agree that belligerent rhetoric "admits of a genocidal interpretation" (p. 291), the admission of possibility does not establish that the specific statements presently at issue were so intended. It merely establishes that such a reading is one possible alternative. In order to decide whether it is the correct reading, one has to bring other independent evidence to bear—evidence notably absent from Freeman's account.

Freeman is wrong when he claims: "Katz does not dispute that the goal of the Treaty of Hartford was to annihilate the Pequot people as such" (p. 291; cf. my pp. 222–23). Note that I was careful to indicate in my original essay that the remaining Pequots were not killed after the cessation of hostilities but were instead subjected to a form of *tribalcide*, that is, the dismantling of the tribe as a functioning entity. Put another way, one must be extremely cautious in evaluating what Freeman means when he claims that the Treaty of Hartford sought to "annihilate the Pequot people as such." What the Treaty of Hartford sought to *annihilate* was the *identity* of the Pequot people as such—the end of their distinctive tribal identity and political organization; it did not seek or legitimate their physical extermination.

Freeman objects to my claim that "the identification of the Puritan attack upon the Pequots as 'genocide' is a polemical, radical rewriting of history to satisfy a sense of moral outrage" (p. 292). This, he contends, "is a polemical and implausible thesis" (p. 292). In response, I suggest that readers, independent of Katz or Freeman, re-read, for example, the main target of the critique in my original paper, namely, Francis Jennings's review of the war (*The Invasion of America*, pp. 187–201) or the more recent, emotion-laden misdescription of David Stannard (*American Holocaust*, pp. 112–15) and judge for themselves whether or not my position is correct. (For other historical cases where the term "genocide" has now been employed in a questionable way see my *The Holocaust in Historical Context* [1:18, n. 40]).

Here I call particular attention to the grounds of Freeman's objection to my not calling the Pequot War genocidal: "the *outcome* of the Pequot War," he writes, "fits the definition of genocide originally proposed by Lemkin as well as that incorporated into international law" (p. 292, emphasis added). However, Lemkin's definition, the definition of the United Nations Convention on Genocide, and my definition of genocide all involve *intention* (to commit genocide); none involves *outcomes*. The notion of genocide as used by myself, consistent with Lemkin's position and that of international law, is not judged by the *outcome* of a conflict, for one can have *un*intended outcomes that are catastrophic. Lemkin, for example, writes that the term genocide is "intended to signify a coordinated plan of different actions aiming at the destruction of essential foundations of the life of national groups, with the aim of annihilating the groups themselves" (*Axis Rule*, p. 79). Likewise, Article II of the United Nations' definition explicitly involves "intent to destroy." The specific crime of genocide involves actualized intentions, not, as Freeman redefines it, without notifying his readers of this critical change of meaning, results. (Freeman similarly emphasizes *outcome* in the top paragraph of p. 292 of his essay.)

Freeman is correct to argue that:

Acts of unprovoked aggression were probably committed by both sides. Both sides took revenge in very destructive forms. Thus, each had reason to fear the other. The Pequot War may have seemed to the Puritans a justified preemptive strike, but the suspicions, fears, and calculations of the

Puritans were of a kind common in ethnic conflicts, including those that result in genocide. [P. 292]

However, this is not to prove the case that the Pequot War was actually genocidal. That there were ingredients present in the Puritan milieu that are also found in genocidal conflicts (as well as other sorts of conflicts, as Freeman testifies) does not yet establish that the Pequot War was such a conflict *in fact*. One would have to show that this had been the case, that the potential became actual, something that Freeman has certainly *not* done in his reply to my paper.

Freeman's polemical paraphrase—similar to the malicious distortion of my view of the Pequot War in Stannard's *American Holocaust* (p. 318, n. 11)—that "the survival of some Pequots, even their survival as a people, does not refute the charge of genocide, for if it did we would have to say there was no Nazi genocide of the Jews" (p. 291), must be rejected, as already argued above in my discussion of Stannard's work, for the nonsense it is.

Finally, Freeman concludes, "[to call the Pequot War genocide is] to register the Pequot War for what it historically was: one of the many cases in which nation-destruction was part of the process of nation-building" (p. 293). Again I must demur, given the gross ambiguity in Freeman's language. His use of the term "nation-destruction" can mean physical destruction or ethnocidal elimination and reconstitution (remember, ethnocide involves the assumption of a new identity and continued physical existence rather than physical extermination and all that such extermination entails). If he means the latter, then there is no disagreement between us regarding what occurred during the period immediately following the end of the war itself, but then there is no physical genocide either—the real point at issue. If he means ethnocide rather than genocide, which appears to be what he does mean, then he has made a *totally* different case from mine (and indeed from Jennings's, Drinnon's, Stannard's, etc.), and his argument turns out to be a case of verbal gymnastics. I am concerned, in contrast, to make relevant historical distinctions in order to understand the complex and turbulent past.

Notes

1. See, e.g., Alden T. Vaughan, *New England Frontier: Puritans and Indians, 1620–1675* (Boston: Little Brown, 1965), and *The History of the Pequot War: The Contemporary Accounts of Mason, Underhill, Vincent and Gardiner,* ed. Charles Orr (Cleveland: Helman-Taylor Company, 1897).

2. See Francis Jennings, *The Invasion of America: Indians, Colonialism, and the Cant of Conquest* (New York: Norton, 1976), pp. 202–28; Richard Slotkin, *Regeneration Through Violence: The Mythology of the American Frontier, 1600–1860* (Middletown, Conn.: Wesleyan University Press, 1973), pp. 69–78; Anna R. Monguia, "The Pequot War Reexamined," *American Indian Culture and Research Journal* 1 (1975): 13–21; Larzer Ziff, *Puritanism in America: New Culture in a New World* (New York: Viking Press, 1973), pp. 90–93; Neal Salisbury, *Manitou and Providence: Indians, Europeans, and the Making of New England, 1500–1643* (New York: Oxford University Press, 1982), pp. 203–35; Richard Drinnon, *Facing West: The Metaphysics of Indian-Hating and Empire-Building* (Minneapolis: University of Minnesota Press, 1980), pp. 41–67; Charles M. Segal and David Stineback, *Puritans, Indians and Manifest Destiny* (New York: Putnam, 1977), pp. 110–12; and Wilcomb E. Washburn, *The Indian in America* (New York: Harper and Row, 1975), pp. 129–30.

3. See Elisha R. Potter, *The Early History of Narragansett* (Providence: Rhode Island Historical Society, 1835), pp. 245–48; Increase Mather, *Early History of New England* (1677), ed. Samuel G. Drake (Boston, 1864), pp. 169–71; and, for a recent review of the relevant evidence, Salisbury, *Manitou and Providence*, pp. 209–10. On the failed Indian and successful European negotiations, see John Winthrop, *Journal: "History of New England, 1630–1649,"* ed. James Kendall Hosmer, 2 vols. (New York: C. Scribner's Sons, 1908), 1:177–78, 233–35, and *The Winthrop Papers*, ed. Allyn B. Forbes, 5 vols. (Boston: Massachusetts Historical Society, 1929–43), vol. 1, passim; Edward Johnson, *Johnson's Wonder-Working Providence* (1654), ed. J. Franklin Jameson (New York: Scribner's, 1910), pp. 161–64; Roger Williams, *The Complete Writings of Roger Williams*, 7 vols. (New York: Russell and Russell, 1963), 6:231–32, 338–39; and Salisbury, *Manitou and Providence*, pp. 213–15.

4. P. Richard Metcalf, "Who Should Rule at Home? Native American Politics and Indian-White Relations," *Journal of American History* 61 (1973–74): 651–65.

5. "Remonstrance of New Netherland," in *Documents Relative to the Colonial History of New York State*, ed. E. B. O'Callaghan and B. Fernow (Albany: Weed Parsons Printers, 1856), p. 287; Winthrop, *The History of New England from 1630 to 1649*, ed. James Savage, 2 vols. (Boston: Brown & Co., 1853), 1:52, 105; and John De Forest, *History of the Indians of Connecticut from the Earliest Known Period to 1850* (Hartford: Hammersley, 1851), p. 73.

6. The seventeenth-century evidence is ambiguous about the circumstances of the murder. See Winthrop, *Journal: "History of New England,"* 1:176–77. Jennings's claim (*Invasion of America*, p. 207) that the murderer was a Narragansett rather than a Pequot is at best unproven and directly disconfirmed by a 1640 letter to Winthrop that specifically identifies the killer as a Niantic (*Winthrop Papers*, 4:269–70). Alfred A. Cave argues "that Oldham was killed by Block Islanders tributary to the Narragansetts," in "Who Killed John Stone? A Note on the Origins of the Pequot War," *William and Mary Quarterly*, 3d ser. 49 (1992): 511, n. 7. There is, however, enough confusion and uncertainty in the contemporary Puritan sources to leave this question open.

7. On Stone, see William Hubbard, *The Present State of New England, Being a*

Narrative of the Troubles with the Indians in New England (London, 1671–72), p. 118; Winthrop, *Journal: "History of New England,"* 1:104, 111, 123, 148; William Bradford, *Of Plymouth Plantation, 1620–1647,* ed. Samuel Eliot Morison (New York: Knopf, 1952), pp. 268–70, 291. Jennings argues that Western Niantics, not Pequots, killed Stone, though he does acknowledge, in a convoluted way, that the Niantics were tributaries of the Pequots (*Invasion of America,* p. 195); Neal Salisbury, *Manitou and Providence,* p. 211 and p. 218, mistakenly supports Jennings's position, as do Segal and Stineback, *Puritans, Indians and Manifest Destiny,* p. 108; and Laurence M. Hauptman, "The Pequot War and Its Legacies," in *The Pequots in Southern New England: The Rise and Fall of an American Indian Nation,* ed. Laurence M. Hauptman and James D. Wherry (Norman: University of Oklahoma Press, 1990), p. 72. Cave, in "Who Killed John Stone?," pp. 509–21, convincingly argues, after a review of all the relevant primary evidence that, *contra* Jennings, the Pequots were responsible for Stone's murder. See also Alden T. Vaughan's revised version of his article "Pequots and Puritans: The Causes of the War of 1637," in his *Roots of American Racism: Essays on the Colonial Experience* (New York: Oxford University Press, 1995), wherein he points out (p. 193) that not only was Stone killed but also, according to Winthrop's testimony, Stone's "company, being eight." Likewise, Vaughan calls attention to Bradford's mention of the murder of two captains (one of which was Stone) "and some others," while Gardiner reports the death of "Captain Stone, with his bark's crew." Altogether, the murder of Stone was part of a larger attack that claimed the lives of nine colonists.

8. *Winthrop Papers,* 3:270–71.

9. Gary B. Nash, "The Image of the Indian in the Southern Colonial Mind," *William and Mary Quarterly,* 3d ser. 29 (1972): 218; William S. Powell, "Aftermath of the Massacre: The First Indian War, 1622–1632," *Virginian Magazine of History and Biography* 66 (1958): 44–75; Wesley Frank Craven, "Indian Policy in Early Virginia," *William and Mary Quarterly,* 3d ser. 1 (1944): 65–82; Alden T. Vaughan, "'Expulsion of the Salvages': English Policy and the Virginia Massacre of 1622," *William and Mary Quarterly,* 3d ser. 35 (1978): 57–84; and J. Frederick Fausz, "The Powhatan Uprising of 1622: A Historical Study of Ethnocentrism and Cultural Conflict" (Ph.D. diss., College of William and Mary, 1977).

10. Hubbard, *Present State of New England,* p. 119.

11. Winthrop, *Journal: "History of New England,"* 1:186–87.

12. John Underhill, "Newes from America" (1638), and Lion Gardiner, "Relation of the Pequot Warres," in *History of the Pequot War,* pp. 60, 127–28. There is a discrepancy in the early sources on the exact number of casualties, ranging from one to fourteen.

13. Gardiner, "Relation of the Pequot Warres," p. 126; Winthrop, *Journal: "History of New England,"* 1:194, 212.

14. John Mason, "Brief History of the Pequot War," in *History of the Pequot War,* pp. 131–32; Underhill, "Newes from America," p. 12; Winthrop, *Journal: "History of New England,"* 1:213.

15. Winthrop, *Journal: "History of New England,"* 1:312–31; John W. De Forest,

History of the Indians of Connecticut (1853; reprinted Hamden, Conn.: Archon Books, 1964), pp. 105–15. The total colonial population of Connecticut in this period was only 600; see Evarts Greene and Virginia Harrington, *American Population before the Federal Census of 1790* (New York: Columbia University Press, 1932), p. 473.

16. This reading of Pequot policy seems to me justified by the sources, though I recognize that it is not self-evident. See Winthrop, *Journal,* 1:190; Mason, "Brief History," p. 123; Bradford, *Of Plymouth Plantation,* 2:247; Hubbard, *Present State of New England,* p. 16.

17. *The Complete Writings of Roger Williams,* 6:231–32, 338.

18. Colonial accounts vividly reveal concern, even panic, over the possible escalation of hostilities with the Pequot and their potentially annihilatory outcome. See, e.g., Underhill, "Newes from America," p. 66, and Bradford, *Of Plymouth Plantation,* p. 294. Given the vast demographic disparity between Europeans and Indians on the North American Continent at this time, it is appropriate to ponder the possibility that Europeans, rather than Indians, could have been eradicated. It is estimated that there were only 21,200 colonists in all of New England (Greene and Harrington, *American Population,* p. 473).

19. Jennings, *Invasion of America,* p. 213. For more on the colonists' perceptions of their exposed situation, see Karen Kupperman, "English Perceptions of Treachery," *Historical Journal* 20 (1977): 263–88, and *Settling with the Indians: The Meeting of English and Indian Cultures in America, 1550–1640* (Totowa, N.J.: Rowman and Littlefield, 1980).

20. Winthrop, *Journal: "History of New England,"* 2:115–16.

21. Sherburne Cook, "Interracial Warfare and Population Decline among the New England Indians," *Ethnohistory* 20 (1973): 6–8. Neal Salisbury puts the lower limit at 300 (*Manitou and Providence,* p. 221). Figures of participants on the English side are cited from the revised edition of Vaughan's *New England Frontier* (New York: W. W. Norton & Co., 1979), p. 141.

22. Vaughan, *New England Frontier* (1979), p. 145.

23. Drinnon, *Facing West,* p. 44.

24. I shall take the term "genocide" to mean an intentional action aimed at the complete physical eradication of a people. This is a more stringent use of the term than that encoded in the United Nations Treaty on Genocide. The recent use of the term "genocide" by American historians and others to describe various persecutions past and present is undoubtedly tied to the emotive power the notion has acquired because of its connection with Auschwitz.

25. Jennings, *Invasion of America,* p. 220. Further page citations will appear in the text.

26. Underhill, "Newes from America," pp. 21–26.

27. See Vaughan, *New England Frontier* (1979), p. 148; cf. Jennings's estimates in *Invasion of America,* pp. 225–26. Roger Williams reports that "(as they say is their general custome) [these transferred Indians] were used kindly, ha[ving] howses and goods and friends given them" (Williams to Winthrop, in *Winthrop Papers,* 3:427, 434, quoted by Adam J. Hirsch, "Collision of Military Cultures in Seventeenth-

Century New England," *Journal of American History* 74 [1978]: 1198). The fate of those delivered to the colonists was less benign; many were sold into slavery.

28. Vaughan, *New England Frontier,* p. 150.

29. Vaughan, *New England Frontier,* p. 150.

30. Vaughan, *New England Frontier,* p. 151.

31. On the deportation of a small number of Pequots to Bermuda to be sold as slaves, see Ethel Boissevain, "Whatever Became of the New England Indians Shipped to Bermuda to be Sold as Slaves," *Man in the Northeast* 11 (1981): 103–14.

32. When Larzer Ziff speaks of the Pequots as being "exterminated" and "an entire tribe . . . obliterated," he evokes powerful contemporary images of "extermination" that are, at least in part, inappropriate. Again, he fails to distinguish between cultural and physical "extermination" or "obliteration" and thus confuses rather than clarifies the issue (*Puritanism in America,* pp. 90–92).

33. On these, and like, sentiments, see the various accounts of the war reprinted in *The History of the Pequot War.*

34. Slotkin, *Regeneration Through Violence,* pp. 92, 183–87.

35. Richard L. Morton, *Colonial Virginia,* 2 vols. (Chapel Hill: University of North Carolina Press, 1960), 1:152ff; Wilcomb E. Washburn, *The Governor and the Rebel: A History of Bacon's Rebellion in Virginia* (Chapel Hill: University of North Carolina Press, 1957), pp. 20–21. It should be emphasized that these casualty figures represent a considerable percentage of the European population in seventeenth-century Virginia.

36. Winthrop, *Journal: "History of New England,"* 2:218–19.

37. Cook, "Interracial Warfare," p. 9.

38. Vaughan, *New England Frontier* (1979), pp. 177–80.

39. *State of Connecticut Census* 1965 (Hartford, Connecticut).

5

Another Look at the Causes of King Philip's War

PHILIP RANLET

The Pequot-Puritan War was unusual in its alignments: most of the Indians sided with the colonists or remained neutral, yet the English colonies did not themselves always see eye to eye. King Philip's War, like Indian-Euroamerican conflicts elsewhere in British America, came closer to an absolute face off of Indians against English. Once the war spread from its local origins in Plymouth Colony to encompass all of southern New England, most Indians apparently considered all Euroamericans to be enemies, although the Mohegans and reconstituted Pequots and, near the end of the war, a substantial number of Christian Indians, aided the Puritans. And while some dissension surfaced among the colonies over the war's onset and execution, the colonies generally put forth a united front. It was fundamentally, though not exclusively, an intercultural battle for New England.

As with the Pequot War, the causes of King Philip's War are endlessly arguable. Even before the war ended, Puritan spokesmen found handy scapegoats: Indian treachery, or colonial immorality, or the devil himself. Almost no Euroamericans attempted to explain, much less champion, the Indians' side, although Quaker John Easton of Rhode Island persuasively (in the eyes of many modern historians) argued the Wampanoags' case, and the Massachusetts Colony's superintendent of Indian affairs, Daniel Gookin, lamented his compatriots' widespread prejudice. In recent years, not surprisingly, historians have agreed to disagree. Many are now sympathetic to the Indian position, sometimes wholeheartedly; most historians, at the very least, paint a complex causal picture. There are few easy explanations.

In the following essay, Philip Ranlet reviews the events of the 1660s and 1670s, when Wampanoag leaders and Plymouth magistrates increasingly misunderstood and maligned each other. Ranlet also summarizes a variety of viewpoints with which he emphatically disagrees. And, in keeping with the current diversity of interpretations, Ranlet's emphases are not wholly congruent with some of this book's other chapters.

IN 1676 King Philip's War resulted in a resounding victory for the colonists, a victory that largely eliminated the Indian threat to English expansion in New England. The obvious importance of the war has drawn the attention of historians, but it has also had the curious effect of arousing their biases. In the nineteenth century, John Gorham Palfrey stated that King Philip, chief of the Wampanoag tribe, was "an unreasoning and cruel barbarian" who had no cause to war against the Puritan settlers. Palfrey's attitudes, at times blatantly racist, were not unique among his contemporaries' or his predecessors'.[1] In the turbulent 1960s and 1970s, historians of the New Left arose to champion the cause of the Indians, but they too have since been accused of sympathizing so totally with the natives that they have failed to appreciate the settlers' experience.[2] As historical assessments of the war continue to see-saw, it seems appropriate to return once again to contemporary accounts and to view the participants as well as the probable motives for their actions objectively in a search for the origins of this crucial event.[3]

Soon after the *Mayflower* arrived in the New World, the Pilgrims and the Wampanoag tribe began to live in peace. Both societies honored a treaty sealed in 1621 which spelled out their relationship. Because of the peace enjoyed in the colony of New Plymouth, Americans were given one of their best-known events, the first Thanksgiving.

While Massasoit, the friend of the Pilgrims, was the chief sachem of the Wampanoags, the two cultures remained friendly. As he grew older, however, Massasoit showed signs of concern for the future. He expressed the hope that relations between his grandsons, Wamsutta and Metacom, and the English would be as amicable after he died as when he lived. His concern was well placed. After his death in 1660, the two societies seemed to be on a collision course.[4]

Wamsutta, Massasoit's eldest grandson, succeeded him as chief sachem. In 1659 as well as in 1660 Wamsutta, apparently being primed to assume his grandfather's authority, had been selected to complain to the English about damage done to Indian crops by stray horses and pigs. He also brought an Indian land dispute to the attention of the Pilgrim leaders and asked their advice on the matter.[5]

In June 1660 Wamsutta, in recognition of having become chief sachem, decided to change his name. He asked the Plymouth leaders for an English name, and they dubbed him Alexander Pokanokett. Alexander also asked that they do the same for his brother, Metacom. The Plymouth officials, again drawing upon classical Greek history, called him Philip. Despite Francis Jennings's assertion, the English were not trying to mock Metacom by naming him Philip.[6] On the contrary, both the Indians and

Plymouth's leaders were apparently pleased with each other. Having an English name was popular among the Indians at this time.[7] As for the colonists, they were undoubtedly honored by Alexander's gesture, for they selected regal names for the two sachems who were so important to the well-being of the colony. Plymouth's leaders were reluctant, however, to grant another of Alexander's requests: he wanted permission to buy some gunpowder. Preferring to avoid a precedent, they gave him the small amount he had asked for as a gift.[8]

Alexander's cordial relations with the English ended abruptly. In 1662 Plymouth heard rumors that Alexander was plotting against the colony. Alexander did not come to the colony to discuss the reports, as requested, so Josiah Winslow, with an armed force, was sent to bring him to Plymouth. When Winslow found Alexander, the sachem satisfactorily explained why he had been delayed and then voluntarily accompanied Winslow to Plymouth, where he justified his conduct. The worried colonists were mollified. As Alexander was returning to his territory, however, he became ill; a few days later he died.[9]

Alexander's youthful brother, Philip, now became chief sachem of the Wampanoags. Many Indians flocked to Mount Hope, the tribe's most favored area, to celebrate his accession. As John Cotton, Jr., later wrote, there was "great feasting and rejoycing" among the assembled natives.[10]

Because the Wampanoags were now headed by a new sachem, Plymouth decided to investigate more thoroughly various rumors that the Indians were going to make war against the colony. The rumors proved to be groundless. On 6 August 1662, Philip and Plymouth agreed upon the terms of a new pact. The Wampanoags accepted that they were subjects of the English Crown, and Philip promised not to break any treaty signed by his predecessors. Nor would he sell land to "strangers," English settlers not acceptable to the colony. (Alexander had sold land to whom he pleased.) King Philip also vowed that he would "not att any time needlesly or unjustly provoake or raise warr with any other of the natives." In return, the colony promised that all settlers would treat the Indians as friends. In addition, it would advise the sachem and aid him, presumably with military force.[11]

About this time, Philip and Plymouth came to another understanding. Philip wanted to stop selling land for seven years, and Governor Thomas Prence agreed to discourage any potential buyers, either Indian or English. The sachem was not moved by a fear that the Wampanoags were being cheated out of their land; rather, he was simply tired of being bothered by the legal problems land sales had caused. In 1662, for example, an Indian accused Alexander of selling land that was not his to sell. Alexander and

Philip were also involved in a land dispute with the Narragansetts, which in 1663 the colonists decided in the Wampanoags' favor.[12] In 1665, however, Philip made an exception and sold land to the town of Rehoboth, a deal that had the full approval of Plymouth's General Court.[13]

During the 1660s, Philip and his tribe came in contact with the Reverend John Eliot, of Roxbury, in Massachusetts Bay, who sought to convert them to Christianity. Eliot's life-long mission to spread the Protestant religion earned him the title "Apostle to the Indians." In that capacity, he became a special target of New Left historians. Neal Salisbury has called Eliot a cultural aggressor, who by converting Indians opened their land to seizure by the Puritans. Jennings, also finding Eliot opportunistic, has argued—without any evidence—that his mission to and efforts to learn the language of the Indians were motivated solely by a desire to impress London.[14] Such judgments are unwarranted.

Despite Eliot's determined efforts, the Indians were slow to accept Christianity. In 1657 he wrote that the natives "so disliked" the Christian faith "that if any began to speake of God and heaven and hell and religion unto them they would presently be gone." This distaste soon became a "knowne thing to all English that if they were burdensome, and you would have them gone, speake of religion and you were . . . rid of them." By 1668 the Praying Indians—those who accepted Christ—were still few in number.[15]

The English settlers themselves gave the Indians little encouragement. When Eliot established new towns—called "Praying Towns"—for the converts, many colonists near the sites reacted hostilely.[16] To make Eliot's task even more difficult, in 1652 wild charges spread that the Praying Indians were conspiring with the pagan natives and the Dutch against New England. Although colonial leaders tried to encourage the spread of Christianity, the common people had little regard for Indian converts.[17]

Still, with all these discouragements, Eliot somehow got converts. An Indian who professed Christianity had to leave the society of the unconverted and dwell in a Praying Town, because Eliot believed that the natives should accept Western culture as well as Christianity.[18] Eliot may also have wanted the Indians to emulate Christ's apostles, who had to abandon their former lives to follow Christ. The Praying Indians, like the apostles, were expected to try to convert nonbelievers as well.[19]

Not surprisingly, Eliot was anxious to convert King Philip. If such an important sachem embraced Christianity, others could be expected to follow his example. Eliot's efforts were at first rebuffed. As Cotton Mather later wrote, Philip treated the offer of "everlasting salvation . . . with contempt and anger, and, after the Indian mode of joining signs with words, he took a button upon the coat of the reverend man, adding, 'That he cared for his gospel, just as much as he cared for that button.'" Eliot was not dissuaded. According to his *Indian Dialogues,* written in 1671, Philip gradually took an interest in Christianity although he still had objections to converting.[20]

Of course a wary historian, knowing that Eliot stated that the *Indian Dialogues* were "partly historical, of some things that were done and said, and partly instructive, to show what might or should have been said," would tend to discount his record of events. Indeed, if the *Dialogues* were the only evidence for Philip's interest in Eliot's teachings, then little stock could be placed in it. But more evidence exists. As late as 1674, Daniel Gookin, a civil magistrate who assisted Eliot, wrote:

> There are some that have high hopes of their greatest and chiefest sachem, named Philip. . . . Some of his chief men, as I hear, stand well inclined to hear the gospel: and himself is a person of good understanding and knowledge in the best things. I have heard him speak very good words, arguing that his conscience is convicted: but yet, though his will is bowed to embrace Jesus Christ, his sensual and carnal lusts are strong bands to hold him fast under Satan's dominions.

Eliot himself gave still further witness to Philip's interest. In 1664 he observed that "Phillip and his people of Sowamset [Mount Hope] . . . did this winter past, upon solicitations and means used, send to me for books to learne to read, in order to praying unto God."[21]

In the end, Eliot failed to bring Philip and his tribe into the fold; the Wampanoags as a whole rejected the Christian faith. Philip's motive, as Gookin suggested, may have centered on his distaste for the Christian practice of monogamy. More important, however, were the political consequences of his conversion. Philip may have feared losing authority over any Praying Indian from his tribe, and he may have disdained becoming "a common man among them"; in addition, those Indians who rejected Christianity would certainly reject the authority of a Christian sachem. As King Philip reportedly said, according to the *Indian Dialogues,* if he became "a praying sachem, I shall be a poor and weak one, and easily be trod upon by others . . . and I shall be a great loser by praying to God."[22]

In the early 1660s, however, Eliot could, with good reason, be hopeful about the religious future of the Wampanoags. He was optimistic that an Indian missionary assigned to teach Philip to read could thereby encourage his conversion. For this important task, Eliot selected John Sassamon, whose Indian parents had also been Christians. Sassamon, whom Eliot thought to be a sincere believer, had been educated at the Indian school at Harvard.[23] Despite Sassamon's Christianity, he attained a position of influence among the Wampanoags. In 1662, for example, he witnessed the treaty between Philip and Plymouth; he also served as Philip's secretary and was an advisor. Yet Sassamon eventually left the tribe, probably in the late 1660s, when Philip finally decided against becoming a praying sachem. Sassamon then settled at Middleborough, in Plymouth Colony, where he served as an Indian minister.[24]

Sassamon's departure is indicative of a steady deterioration of the once friendly relations between the two different cultures. By the late 1660s many of the natives had undoubtedly experienced the growing hostility of the English settlers. As early as 1645, Roger Williams complained that he had often heard scurrilous comments, such as:

> These Heathen Dogges, better kill a thousand of them then [*sic*] that we Christians should be indangered or troubled with them; Better they were all cut off, and then we shall be no more troubled with them: They have spilt our Christian blud, the best way to make riddance of them, cut them all off, and so make way for Christians.

Slowly but surely this hostility grew, and not surprisingly, it hindered the spread of Christianity among the Indians.[25] Men of good will such as Eliot, Gookin, and Williams became increasingly isolated as the original settlers died, for the next generation of Puritans generally cared little for the Indians.

Other problems surfaced during the 1660s. The royal commission of 1664–67 found evidence that some English colonists had obtained Indian land by devious means. The natives also were annoyed when the colonists' untended animals wandered onto the Indians' planted fields and destroyed their crops. Straining relations still more, the colonists sometimes hurt the Indians' animals.[26]

By May and June 1667, the Wampanoags' growing hostility towards the English forced Philip to reassess his interest in English culture. In May of that year, Philip's actions led Rhode Islanders to believe he had "treacherous designes." Just a few weeks later, in June, Plymouth's leaders received information that stirred their suspicions as well. According to a Wampanoag source, Philip and the French were plotting against the New Englanders. In front of some of his warriors, he had reportedly announced that he wished to regain the Indians' old lands as well as seize some of the colonists' property. Some settlers at Rehoboth brought Philip's accuser to the sachem, and the informer "freely and boldly did avouch it to his face, and soe to particularise time [and] place."[27]

The General Court insisted that Philip explain his actions, and in July he did so. Realizing that he was in a difficult position, Philip insisted that the whole report had been fabricated by Ninigret, a Narragansett sachem, to discredit him. To prove his innocence, Philip presented a letter from another Narragansett sachem that supported his story, but that sachem soon denied having sent any such letter. Finally, Philip asserted that forming an alliance with the Dutch or French made little sense since they had killed or kidnapped eighteen of his tribe in 1666. Having sifted through the evidence, the Plymouth leaders decided that "there was great probabillitie that his tongue had bine runing out," but there was no sound proof of a plot. Still, the Court fined Philip £40 as partial reimbursement for expenses incurred in investigating the affair.[28] Quite likely, Philip had been boasting to his tribesmen and never thought his words would be carried to the English. This incident was surely both an insult and an embarrassment for the sachem.

In June and July 1669 the colonists had another scare. Some of Philip's chief advisors spent over a week visiting Ninigret. An Indian from Long Island spread a rumor that the two Indian leaders were planning an attack against the English. Ninigret, however, rejected the charge: ever since he had met with the royal commissioners of 1664–67 a few years before, he had considered himself a loyal subject of Charles II. Ninigret insisted that he had sent one of his followers to the Wampanoags simply because Philip had asked "for an old man to teach or informe his men in a certaine dance." The Rhode Islanders were not satisfied with this explanation but took no further action.[29]

Since Ninigret became an ally of the colonists during King Philip's War, it is unlikely that he was conspiring with the Wampanoags. A more reasonable explanation would involve the border dispute that the Narragansetts and the Wampanoags had brought to the royal commissioners. Relying upon the testimony of Roger Williams, the commissioners settled the dispute in Philip's favor.[30] Perhaps the two tribes were engaging in some form of ceremonial acceptance of the decision and were trying to establish peace among themselves. If so, they wanted no further participation by their English neighbors.

By 1671 the Wampanoags' hostility towards the English had grown markedly. In that year Eliot wrote that he could not recall "such violent opposition" to the preaching of Christianity. At this time, as well, damage to Indian property by stray farm animals may have reached a high point, for on 5 June 1671, the Plymouth General Court appointed people in eleven different towns to examine such cases.[31]

Undoubtedly, Philip was being pressured by a number of elements within the Wampanoags. The tribe's religious leaders, the powwows, for example, had always resented Eliot's preaching—especially when he was successful—and they can be assumed to have been eager for a confrontation with the English colonists and their missionaries. Although Philip had calmed their agitation before, by 1671 he had another problem—his younger brother, Takamunna, had come of age.[32] This young sachem, who was to take an active military role in the upcoming war, probably wanted to fight the English, as did the other youthful Wampanoag warriors.

Whatever the cause of worsening relations, Philip was clearly persuaded to prepare for war. During the early months of 1671, the natives were spotted sharpening their tomahawks and repairing their firearms. In March 1671 Philip made a gesture that probably signaled his intention to fight. Assembling a group of fully-armed warriors, he and his men marched to the town of Swansea in Plymouth Colony but did not attack.[33]

The Plymouth General Court quickly summoned Philip to explain his actions. Instead of following through on his threat, he came to Plymouth in peace and, incredibly, admitted that his tribe had been preparing for war against the colonists. He gave no reason why except that the Indians' desire for war came from within "theire owne naughty harts." Suddenly, despite their avowed aim, the Wampanoags lost interest in war. On 10 April 1671, they signed a peace treaty at Taunton, by which Philip pledged to surrender to the colonists "all my English Armes to be kept by them for their security, so long as they shall see reason."[34]

Peace seemed to have been restored. In May, when an Indian murdered an Englishman in Massachusetts Bay, Philip was "industriously active" in bringing the culprit to justice. Relations soon soured again, however, over a difference in the interpretation of the new agreement. Apparently, Philip had assumed that only the guns he and his men had carried to Taunton were to be surrendered. Plymouth, on the other hand, insisted upon a literal interpretation: all guns meant every single firearm the Wampanoags possessed.[35] With this attempt to disarm Philip's tribe totally, the Plymouth leaders began blundering their way into a bloody war.

The Wampanoags refused to comply with Plymouth's interpretation. In retaliation, on 5 June the colony announced that it would confiscate all the guns that had been surrendered at Taunton. Furthermore, the colonists insisted that other Indians, including the Saconetts, who were associated with the Wampanoags, also had to surrender their guns. To back up these demands, on 8 July the Plymouth General Court made plans for a military expedition that would "proceed by force to reduce [the Saconetts] to reason." The Saconetts quickly backed down and surrendered their six guns, which satisfied the colony's leaders.[36]

Before Plymouth could turn its attention to Philip, John Eliot intervened, in a role that has been neglected by historians. The Praying Indians, under Eliot's guidance, sent three former missionaries—Anthony, William, and John Sassamon—back to the Wampanoags. Despite the Wampanoags' failure to accept Christ, the Natick Indians wanted to try to head off war. They believed that the best way to settle the disagreement was to ask Massachusetts Bay to arbitrate it. The missionaries were also to remind Governor Thomas Prence of Plymouth that arbitration was far superior "to kill or be killed, when no capital sin hath been committed or defended by them, (that we hear of)."[37]

On 23 August 1671, Plymouth's council of war charged Philip with trying to mislead Massachusetts Bay about its conduct. The sachem was also "insolent" because he had entertained hostile Saconetts and also "many strange Indians which might p[or]tend danger towards us." These mysterious strangers were Narragansett sachems, probably solicited for aid. John Sassamon, who had seen the Narragansetts while on his mission with the Natick Indians, had reported their presence to the English colonists.[38]

Although Plymouth's leaders believed that Philip had to be subdued by force, their resolve had been weakened by Eliot's intercession. They decided to ask the advice of both Rhode Island and Massachusetts Bay, a small concession to Eliot's arbitration plan. But Plymouth still reserved the right to go to war against Philip on 20 September even if the other two colonies disapproved of the use of arms. Meanwhile, Philip was again summoned to Plymouth to explain himself. The colony's order was in a letter to be conveyed by James Brown of Swansea and others.[39]

The messengers arrived at a bad time: Philip and his advisors had been drinking. After "some words" passed between the sachem and Brown, Philip knocked off the Englishman's hat. When Philip sobered the next day, he was more courteous but refused to indicate whether or not he would obey Plymouth's summons. He also expressed his anger at John Sassamon for informing the English about the visit of the Narragansetts.[40]

King Philip had been deliberately evasive with Plymouth's messengers because Eliot had invited him to Boston to talk with the Bay's leaders. Philip decided to go since he had been unable to muster the help of other Indians necessary to wage war against Plymouth. The Narragansetts had apparently decided not to get involved, and the Saconetts could not be depended upon. Although the sons and brother of Awasuncks, the queen of the Saconetts, were hostile to the English, both she and her husband wanted peace, and she had enough support among her warriors to keep her tribe off the warpath. Other smaller groups, such as the Dartmouth Indians, also favored peace.[41]

When Philip came to Boston, he talked not only with the Bay's leaders but also with John Winthrop, Jr., Connecticut's governor, who happened to be in the city. Philip stated his side of the dispute and the prominent colonists seemed sympathetic. Offering their aid in arranging a peaceful settlement, they wrote to Governor Prence that "they resented not his offence soe deeply" as did Plymouth and that no previous agreement had made the Wampanoags subject to Plymouth. Plymouth was bound to accept arbitration from John Leverett of Massachusetts Bay, Winthrop of Connecticut, and other prominent men from both colonies, including some who were not delegates to the Confederation of New England, a league of all the Puritan colonies except Rhode Island. No one from Rhode Island—a colony not on good terms with the others—was invited.[42]

On 24 September 1671, the arbitrators met at Plymouth and were joined by Philip and a host of interpreters. Disinterested inquiry soon gave way. The arbitrators were simply too tied to the interests they shared with Plymouth colonists, who called the arbitrators "our good friends and naighbors." Deciding that Philip was totally at fault, the arbitrators ordered him "to amend his wayes, if hee expected peace, and that if hee went on in his refractory way, he must expect to smart for it." The hapless Philip now faced three united foes.[43]

King Philip had little choice but to accept the imposed treaty of 29 September 1671, which made him subject to Plymouth. He could not sell land or go to war against another tribe without the approval of Plymouth's governor. The sachem also had to do some service for the colony—each year five wolves had to be killed. But the harshest part of the treaty involved a fine. For his various offenses, Philip had to pay the colony £100 within three years. In November 1671 Takamunna signed a similar agreement which made him subject to Plymouth and required that he kill one wolf every year.[44]

Seemingly, Plymouth had triumphed. Philip had to endure the taunt of one of his advisors, who called him "a white-liver'd Cur" because he had not made war. Most galling, however, was the heavy fine. As late as June 1675, Philip mentioned his resentment about it to John Easton of Rhode Island.[45] Despite his anger, Philip did pay up, with money he received from, reluctantly, selling land. After paying the fine, Philip still had cash left.[46] The surplus was probably used to replace the guns lost at Taunton and to buy more gunpowder. Plymouth's victory in 1671 was clearly Pyrrhic.

The situation remained outwardly calm, though, until March 1674, when the Indians reacted against land sales. Even though one of her tribesmen had cleared his title, Awasuncks and her husband had him tied up and threatened for intending to sell land to the English. Among the Wampanoags, concern over land surely increased in July 1674, when Philip was sued for £800 in the Plymouth courts by a Rhode Islander who produced a bond from Alexander, dated 1661, which entitled him to a large amount of the natives' land. Although land was still plentiful in New England, such events surely set disturbing precedents.[47] Yet, despite the hints of some historians, Indian anxieties about future land loss were not the direct provocation for King Philip's War.[48] Instead, the conflict was ignited by the death of John Sassamon.

At the end of 1674, Philip and his tribe were near Middleborough, and Sassamon went to the campsite. Exactly why is not known, but perhaps he had continued to hope that the sachem might be converted. While there, the Indian minister somehow determined that Philip was planning a war against the colonists. Sassamon, fearing for his life, then journeyed to Plymouth and told the English about his suspicions, but he failed to convince them. Other Christian Indians had recently given similar warnings and had also been ignored.[49]

On 29 January 1675, soon after Sassamon left Plymouth, he was killed by three Wampanoags, one of whom, Tobias, was an important advisor to Philip. Sassamon's murder was made to look accidental: his body was found in a pond, where he had presumably fallen while fishing. He was buried and, at first, little attention was paid to his death. But Tobias and the others did not know that another Indian, Patuckson, had seen the murder and could not resist talking about it. When William Nahauton, a Praying Indian, heard the story, he informed the English. Only then did they credit Sassamon's warnings.[50]

Tobias and the others were tried for Sassamon's death in June 1675. Despite their denials, all three were found guilty by an English jury. In addition, Plymouth had sworn in six Indians besides the twelve regular jurymen. The Indians agreed with the regular jury's decision. Plymouth's leaders had no doubts about who had killed Sassamon, but they could not determine whether Philip had known about or ordered the murder. In March 1675 he had come to the General Court, without being summoned, and denied any role in Sassamon's death. Although the colonists were suspicious, they had no proof that implicated Philip, so he was allowed to leave.[51]

It is unlikely that Philip ordered Sassamon's death. There is no evidence that any of the Wampanoags knew that Sassamon had recently given information to the English. Moreover, when Sassamon had done so before, in 1671, Philip had not retaliated even though bitterly angry.

Instead, Sassamon's death was probably planned solely by Tobias and his confederates. The killing may have been motivated purely by hatred. There was, of course, much about Sassamon to detest: he was a Christian, a minister, and a loyal follower of the English. He had been close to King Philip, and this closeness had surely earned him the envy of many. His role in the events of 1671 added to such ill feelings. After that incident, Tobias and the others may have been waiting for the right time to kill Sassamon. Although a wait of four years to exact revenge may seem unbelievable, an Indian revenge killing once took place after a delay of thirteen years. The attempt to conceal Sassamon's murder—an act unusual for Indians—may have been intended to protect the perpetrators not only from the English but also from the wrath of Philip.[52]

Shortly before Tobias's trial, the Wampanoags appeared armed in public. The colonists assumed that Philip felt guilty about Sassamon's death. From the great interest the colonists were showing in Sassamon's demise, Philip may have guessed that Sassamon had told them about his plans. The Wampanoags may therefore have been armed out of suspicion that a preemptive strike, like the one urged upon the Pilgrims by Massasoit in 1623 against the Massachusetts tribe, might be used against them. But Plymouth's leaders were not planning an attack, nor was Philip questioned again about Sassamon's death. In fact, the colony's leaders later claimed that they had hoped "the cloud might blow over"; on 13 June 1675, Roger Williams believed that it had.[53]

The storm, though, had not yet gathered strength. Plymouth Governor Josiah Winslow knew of no *causus belli* committed by his colony, except possibly in having executed Tobias and his accomplices. Philip reportedly claimed that the executions had started the war. Without doubt, they had inflamed young warriors of the Wampanoag and other tribes. Much evidence suggests that the young braves pressured other sachems, who preferred peace, into fighting the English. King Philip, also pressured, probably had another, more compelling reason for deciding upon war, however. He realized that the power of the Indians was fast declining, that New England was becoming the domain of the English. If there was to be war, it had to be fought before the odds got worse and while there was still a chance for an Indian victory.[54]

Without the support of the other Indians, the Wampanoags had no chance at all against the colonists. Various emissaries were sent to neighboring tribes to urge them to join with the Wampanoags. Those sachems, such as Awasuncks, who were still reluctant to join them, were threatened.

In another effort to gain support, the Wampanoags held special dances for the young warriors of other tribes. The enthusiasm of the youthful Wampanoags infected their peers.[55]

Despite these efforts and the dedication of the young men, Philip's decision for war seems to have been grudging. He tried to give special protection to certain colonists who had been friendly or kind to him. Even as late as 17 June 1675, he invited certain settlers to retrieve their stray horses, but some Wampanoags pointed guns at the colonists when they came to the Indian camp; the Englishmen were clearly not welcome. Perhaps Philip was moved by memories of his grandfather's good feelings towards the colonists. William Harris, for one, had reminded Philip that "had it not bin for the plimoth old planters . . . the narragansets [would have] cut of[f]" Massasoit's head in 1632.[56] Whatever the reason, Philip was once more willing to consider peace.

About 13 June, a week or so before the war erupted, John Easton, the deputy governor of Rhode Island, and some others from that colony approached the Wampanoags to urge Philip to accept arbitration of his complaints against the English. At first, the Indians rejected the suggestion: if all the arbitrators were English, as in 1671, the Indians were sure to suffer. But Easton and the others suggested that there be only two arbitrators: an Indian sachem, to be chosen by the Wampanoags, and Edmund Andros, then the governor of New York. Judging from Andros's later career, he would not have hesitated to find against the New Englanders if he felt that the natives' grievances were valid. The Wampanoags were surprised by the suggestion, and Easton thought the idea was agreeable to them.[57]

Some Wampanoags still wanted war and had no intention of waiting for arbitration to be tried first. They were also mindful, however, of the powwows' prediction that if they began the war, they would be beaten. Both to prevent arbitration and to avoid fulfilling the prophesy, the Indians had to force the English to open hostilities. Ironically, Easton and the Rhode Islanders may have encouraged that strategy when they told the Wampanoags: "when in war against [the] English[,] blud was spilt that ingadged all Englishmen for we wear to be all under one king."[58]

A few days after the Rhode Island conference, some Wampanoags approached the town of Swansea in Plymouth Colony and looted some abandoned homes. A young Englishman fired at the Indians and killed one. With that shot, King Philip's War had begun. On 20 June the Indians attacked Swansea and killed some colonists. A delegation from Massachusetts Bay, which had also planned to propose arbitration, returned home, its mission hopeless. There could now be no turning back for either the Wampanoags or the English.[59]

Some circumstances suggest that the timing of the war was not Philip's. First of all, the Indians had not yet amassed enough guns and ammunition; nor had the other tribes been firmly recruited into a general alliance against the colonists. At the very least, Philip may have hoped to use arbitration as a means of delaying any attack the English might be contemplating until these important matters had been accomplished. In fact, the sachem seems to have been unable to control the ardor of his warriors, not only in June 1675 but earlier as well. During the spring of 1675, some of them decided to settle some old scores with Ninigret's men and killed eleven of his followers. After that attack, Philip could not even ask for Ninigret's aid, aid he sorely needed.[60]

When the accumulated biases of centuries are rolled away, King Philip appears to have been a cautious leader of his people. Philip's reputation is not aided by scholars who go to the other extreme and are biased against the colonists. John Easton, who was one of the few fair observers of the time, put the blame for the war in perspective. Peace was "best" for everyone, Easton declared, "but the English dear not trust the indians promises nether the indians to the Englishes promises and each have gret Case therfore."[61]

Author's Postscript

Those interested in following King Philip's life to its conclusion should examine my book, *Enemies of the Bay Colony* (New York: Peter Lang Publishing, Inc., 1984). Other accounts include Stephen Saunders Webb's controversial *1676: The End of American Independence* (New York: Knopf, 1984), and Russell Bourne's *The Red King's Rebellion: Racial Politics in New England, 1675–1678* (New York: Atheneum, 1990), which, although not really scholarly, is generally fair. Also of interest are James Drake's article "Restraining Atrocity: The Conduct of King Philip's War," *New England Quarterly* 70 (1997): 33–56, and Jill Lepore's book *The Name of War* (see n. 3).

Notes

1. John Gorham Palfrey, *History of New England,* vol. 3 (Boston: Little, Brown, and Company, 1885), pp. 216–27. Some modern scholars have sought to achieve a more balanced view; see, e.g., Douglas Edward Leach, *Flintlock and Tomahawk: New England in King Philip's War* (New York: W. W. Norton and Company, Inc., 1958), and Alden T. Vaughan, *New England Frontier: Puritans and Indians, 1620–1675,* 3d

ed. (Norman: University of Oklahoma Press, 1995). Some of Vaughan's conclusions went too far in defending the Puritans, but his book should nonetheless be the starting point for those pursuing the subject.

2. Francis Jennings, *The Invasion of America: Indians, Colonialism, and the Cant of Conquest* (New York: W. W. Norton and Company, Inc., 1975), pp. vi, 11, 295, 298, is the leading New Left scholar in the field. The bias in Jennings's views has been pointed out by Bernard Bailyn et al., *The Great Republic: A History of the American People*, 2 vols., 3d ed. (Lexington, Mass.: D.C. Heath and Company, 1985), 1:59, and Carl Bridenbaugh and Juliette Tomlinson, eds., *The Pynchon Papers*, 2 vols. (Boston: Colonial Society of Massachusetts, 1982–85), 1:xiii. Neal Salisbury, "Red Puritans: The 'Praying Indians' of Massachusetts Bay and John Eliot," *William and Mary Quarterly*, 3d ser. 31 (1974): 27–54, has been aligned with Jennings and attacked by, among others, James Warren Springer, "American Indians and the Law of Real Property in Colonial New England," *American Journal of Legal History* 30 (January 1986): 54n–55n.

3. I should clarify my use of two terms. The New Left has popularized alternative ways of referring to the Indians: the word "Indian" is often frowned upon, although the natives used it themselves, as I will here. (See Roger Williams, *A Key into the Language of America* [1643], in *The Complete Writings of Roger Williams*, 7 vols. [New York: Russell and Russell, Inc., 1963], 1:22–23). King Philip's War has been dubbed "Metacom's War," after the chief's original name (Gary B. Nash, *Red, White, and Black: The Peoples of Early North America*, 3d ed. [Englewood Cliffs, N.J.: Prentice-Hall, Inc., 1992], pp. 118–23). Yet the Indians often changed their names (Jennings, *Invasion of America*, p. 290n), and Metacom was no exception; he appears to have changed his at least three times after he became the Wampanoags' leader. During May 1666 he was "Eleise Pokonoahkit." In 1671 John Eliot called him "Philip Keitasscot," and three years later the Pilgrims referred to him as "Phillip, allies Wewasowannett" (see Eleise Pokonoahkit to chief officer, 7 May 1666, Public Record Office, *Calendar of State Papers, Colonial Series, America and West Indies*, ed. W. Noel Sainsbury et al., 44 vols. [London, 1860–1969], 5:380, and *John Eliot's Indian Dialogues: A Study in Cultural Interaction* [1671], ed. Henry W. Bowden and James P. Ronda [Westport, Conn.: Greenwood Press, 1980], p. 120, and Nathaniel B. Shurtleff and David Pulsifier, eds., *Records of the Colony of New Plymouth*, 12 vols. [Boston, 1855–61; reprinted, New York: AMS Press, 1968], 8:190–91). Calling the conflict "Wewasowannett's War" would be historically precise but confusing. Renaming King Philip's War, then, seems to be of dubious value. Similarly, the issue of his "kingship" is moot. The English settlers believed that the Indians favored a monarchical government and therefore at first treated the chiefs (also called sachems) as petty princes. Those few sachems who controlled large territories were, hence, kings (see Williams, *Language of America*, 1:163; Thomas Hutchinson, *The History of the Colony and Province of Massachusetts-Bay* [1764–67], ed. Lawrence Shaw Mayo, 3 vols. [Cambridge: Harvard University Press, 1936], 1:235; Edward Winslow, *Good News from New England* [1624], in *The Story of the Pilgrim Fathers*, ed. Edward Arber [London, 1897], pp. 586–87). Metacom was named King Philip when the Indians and the colonists

were on friendly terms (see Richard Slotkin, *Regeneration Through Violence: The Mythology of the American Frontier, 1600–1860* [Middletown, Conn.: Wesleyan University Press, 1973], p. 79). There is no reason not to use the name. It has been suggested that Keitasscot, for example, is really an Indian word for king and so could not have been Philip's name. However, the English-speaking world has numerous titles that also serve as names: king, queen, bishop, duke, lord, and so on. Keitasscot surely was a name. Its Indian meaning strongly suggests that Philip enjoyed being called king (see Jill Lepore, *The Name of War: King Philip's War and the Origins of American Identity* [New York: Knopf, 1998], pp. 252–53 n. 38).

4. William Hubbard, *A Narrative of the Troubles with the Indians in New-England* (1677), ed. Samuel G. Drake, 2 vols. in 1 (New York: Kraus Reprint Co., 1969), pp. 46–47; *Plymouth Records*, 3:192; Betty Groff Schroeder, "The True Lineage of King Philip (Sachem Metacom)," *New England Historical and Genealogical Register* 144 (1990): 211–14. Massasoit's date of death is uncertain.

5. *Plymouth Records*, 3:167, 192. On pigs, see Virginia DeJohn Anderson, "King Philip's Herds: Indians, Colonists, and the Problem of Livestock in Early New England," *William and Mary Quarterly*, 3d ser. 51 (1994): 601–24, and also the exchange of letters between Anderson and myself that was published in *William and Mary Quarterly*, 3d ser. 52 (1995): 575–80.

6. *Plymouth Records*, 3:192; Jennings, *Invasion of America*, p. 290n.

7. John Josselyn, *An Account of Two Voyages to New-England* (London, 1674), p. 128.

8. *Plymouth Records*, 3:192.

9. John Cotton to Increase Mather, 20 March 1676/77, *The Mather Papers, Massachusetts Historical Society Collections*, 4th ser. 8 (1868): 233–34. Cotton Mather gave a very different version of events; see his *Magnalia Christi Americana; Or, The Ecclesiastical History of New-England* (1702), ed. Thomas Robbins, 2 vols. (New York: Russell and Russell, 1967), 2:558–59.

10. Hutchinson, *History of Massachusetts-Bay*, 1:235n: John Cotton to Increase Mather, c. 20 March 1676/77, *Mather Papers*, pp. 232–34.

11. *Plymouth Records*, 4:8, 25–26. Philip's letter, printed as "Sachem Philip, His Answer to the Letter Brought to Him from the Governor of New-Plymouth," *Massachusetts Historical Society Collections*, 1st ser. 6 (1799): 94, may have been written at this time.

12. *Plymouth Records*, 3:192, 4:16–17, 24–25; "A Letter from King Philip to Governour Prince," n.d., *Massachusetts Historical Society Collections*, 1st ser. 2 (1793): 40. The dating of this letter is disputed, but it was probably written in late 1662 or early 1663 (see Jennings, *Invasion of America*, pp. 290n–291n, and, for another interpretation of the letter, p. 290).

13. *Plymouth Records*, 4:109–10.

14. Jennings, *Invasion of America*, pp. 233, 238; Salisbury, "Red Puritans," pp. 29, 33–34, 54. For Eliot, see Ola Elizabeth Winslow, *John Eliot: "Apostle to the Indians"* (Boston: Houghton Mifflin, 1968); Timothy J. Sehr, "John Eliot, Millennialist and Missionary," *The Historian* 46 (1984): 187–203; Richard W. Cogley, "Idealism vs. Ma-

terialism in the Study of Puritan Missions to the Indians," *Method and Theory in the Study of Religion* 3 (1991): 165–82; Cogley, "John Eliot and the Millennium," *Religion and American Culture* 1 (1991): 227–50; Cogley, "John Eliot and the Origins of the American Indians," *Early American Literature* 21 (1986–87): 210–25, and Cogley, "John Eliot in Recent Scholarship," *American Indian Culture and Research Journal* 14 (1990): 77–92.

15. Richard Baxter to John Eliot, 20 January 1656/57, Eliot to Baxter, 7 October 1657, and 22 January 1667/68, in *Some Unpublished Correspondence of the Reverend Richard Baxter and the Reverend John Eliot, the Apostle of the American Indians, 1656–1682*, ed. F. J. Powicke (Manchester, England: Manchester University Press, 1931), pp. 21, 22–23, 32.

16. John Eliot to Humphrey Atherton, 4 June 1657, *Massachusetts Historical Society Collections*, 1st ser. 2 (1793): 9. For the dispute between Dedham and the Praying Indians, see Don Gleason Hill, ed., *The Early Records of the Town of Dedham, Massachusetts*, 6 vols. (Dedham, 1894), 4:241–85.

17. John Eliot, *A Late and Further Manifestation of the Progress of the Gospel in New-England* (1655), *Massachusetts Historical Society Collections*, 3d ser. 4 (1834): 271.

18. James P. Ronda, "'We Are Well As We Are': An Indian Critique of Seventeenth-Century Christian Missions," *William and Mary Quarterly*, 3d ser. 34 (1977): 67.

19. Despite what James Axtell has asserted, Eliot did not equip the Praying Indians with guns to intimidate the other natives. Some pagan Indians did think they were threatened with war if they did not convert, but they misunderstood the biblical story of Armageddon, the great battle marking the end of the world during which believers in Christ would be protected while pagans were doomed. See Axtell, *The Invasion Within: The Contest of Cultures in Colonial North America* (New York: Oxford University Press, 1985), pp. 147–48; Rev. 3:10, 16:14–16.

20. Mather, *Magnalia*, 1:566; *Eliot's Indian Dialogues*, p. 121.

21. *Eliot's Indian Dialogues*, p. 61; Daniel Gookin, *Historical Collections of the Indians in New England* (1674), *Massachusetts Historical Society Collections*, 1st ser. 1 (1792): 200; Eliot to Commissioners of United Colonies, 25 August 1664, *Plymouth Records*, 10:383. Jennings, although he cites Eliot's letter, does not mention Philip's interest in Christianity. See Jennings, *Invasion of America*, pp. 294–95, 295 n. 40.

22. Daniel Gookin, *An Historical Account of the Doings and Sufferings of the Christian Indians in New England, in the Years of 1675, 1676, 1677* (1677?), *American Antiquarian Society Transactions and Collections* 2 (1836): 438–39; *Eliot's Indian Dialogues*, pp. 121, 123.

23. Mather, *Magnalia*, 2:559; Eliot to Commissioners of United Colonies, 25 August 1664, *Plymouth Records*, 10:384; Increase Mather, *Diary, March 1675–December 1676, Together with Extracts from Another Diary by Him, 1674–1687* (Cambridge: J. Wilson, 1900), p. 42; *The Present State of New-England with Respect to the Indian War* (1675), in *Narratives of the Indian Wars, 1675–1699*, ed. Charles H. Lincoln (New York: Charles Scribner's Sons, 1913), p. 24. For Sassamon, see Jill Lepore, "Dead Men Tell No Tales: John Sassamon and the Fatal Consequences of Literacy," *Ameri-*

can Quarterly 46 (December 1994): 479–512. Jennings depicts Sassamon as a spy planted among the Indians by Eliot and also accepts a wild charge that Sassamon tried to defraud Philip of Indian land (see *Invasion of America*, pp. 294–95).

24. Hubbard, *Troubles with the Indians*, 1:60–61; *Plymouth Records*, 4:25–26; David Bushnell, "The Treatment of the Indians in Plymouth Colony," *New England Quarterly* 26 (1953): 208 (see *New England Encounters*, chap. 2).

25. Roger Williams, *Christenings make not Christians, or a Briefe Discourse concerning that name Heathen, commonly given to the Indians* (1645), in his *Complete Writings*, 7:31; Alden T. Vaughan and Daniel K. Richter, "Crossing the Cultural Divide: Indians and New Englanders, 1605–1763," *American Antiquarian Society Proceedings* 90, pt. 1 (1980): 45.

26. "Cartwright's Answer," 5 January 1665/66, *The Clarendon Papers, New-York Historical Society Collections* 2 (1869): 90–91, 102; George D. Langdon, Jr., *Pilgrim Colony: A History of New Plymouth, 1620–1691* (New Haven: Yale University Press, 1966), pp. 157–58; Bushnell, "Treatment of Indians," p. 211; *Plymouth Records*, 5:6.

27. John Russell Bartlett, ed., *Records of the Colony of Rhode Island and Providence Plantations in New England*, vol. 2 (Providence, 1857), p. 193; *Plymouth Records*, 4:151, 164–66.

28. *Plymouth Records*, 4:151, 164–66.

29. *Rhode Island Records*, 2:266–78; Louis B. Mason, *The Life and Times of Major John Mason of Connecticut: 1600–1672* (New York: G. P. Putnam's Sons, 1935), pp. 310–14; J. Hammond Trumbull, ed., *The Public Records of the Colony of Connecticut*, 15 vols. (Hartford, 1852; reprinted, New York: AMS Press, 1968), 2:548–51.

30. Roger Williams to Massachusetts General Court, 7 May 1668, and to Commissioners of United Colonies, 18 October 1677, in his *Complete Writings*, 6:326, 387–88; Increase Mather, *A Brief History of the Warr With the Indians in New-England* (1676), in *So Dreadfull a Judgement: Puritan Responses to King Philip's War*, ed. Richard Slotkin and James K. Folsom (Middletown, Conn.: Wesleyan University Press, 1978), p. 107.

31. Eliot to Baxter, 27 June 1671, *Baxter Correspondence*, pp. 62–63; *Plymouth Records*, 5:62.

32. Frank Shuffelton, "Indian Devils and Pilgrim Fathers: Squanto, Hobomok, and the English Conception of Indian Religion," *New England Quarterly* 49 (1976): 116. On Philip's younger brother, see *Plymouth Records*, 4:25. Identification of the brother as Takamunna, based upon one Takamunna having signed on 3 November 1671 a treaty resembling Philip's agreement of September 1671, remains speculative. Described as "a sachem att Saconett," Takamunna was clearly under Philip, referred to as "chiefe sachem" (*Plymouth Records*, 5:80).

33. John Pynchon to John Winthrop, Jr., or John Allyn, 6 August 1675, *Pynchon Papers*, 1:139; Hutchinson, *History of Massachusetts-Bay*, 1:247n, 237; Langdon, *Pilgrim Colony*, p. 159. The maneuver violated European military strategy because it alerted the colonists that war was possible. It may have been a traditional ceremonial gesture, perhaps the last step before war. In 1675 the Narragansetts marched on Warwick, Rhode Island, in the same fashion. Roger Williams to John Winthrop, Jr.,

27 June 1675, *Winthrop Papers, Massachusetts Historical Society Collections*, 4th ser. 6 (1861): 302–3.

34. *Plymouth Records*, 5:63; Taunton treaty in Mather's *Brief History*, p. 151.

35. John Pynchon to John Winthrop, Jr., 10 May 1671, *Pynchon Papers*, 1:87; Leach, *Flintlock and Tomahawk*, p. 27.

36. Leach, *Flintlock and Tomahawk*, p. 27; *Plymouth Records*, 5:63–64, 73–75; "A Letter from Awasuncks to Governor Prince," 11 August 1671, *Massachusetts Historical Society Collections*, 1st ser. 5 (1798): 195–96.

37. "Instructions from the Church at Natick to William and Anthony," 1 August 1671, *Massachusetts Historical Society Collections*, 1st ser. 6 (1799): 201–3. These instructions were written by "John Eliot, with the consent of the church." Jennings, for one, makes no mention of Eliot's attempt to bring about a peaceful solution (see *Invasion of America*, p. 293).

38. *Plymouth Records*, 5:76; "James Walker's Letter to Governor Prince," 1 September 1671, *Massachusetts Historical Society Collections*, 1st ser. 6 (1799): 198.

39. *Plymouth Records*, 5:76–77.

40. "James Walker's Letter to Governor Prince," p. 198.

41. "James Walker's Letter to Governor Prince," p. 198; Prence to Awasuncks, 20 October 1671, "Articles of Agreement Between the Court of New Plymouth and Awasuncks, the Squaw Sachem of Saconett," and "Dartmouth Indians' Engagement," 4 September 1671, all in *Massachusetts Historical Society Collections*, 1st ser. 5 (1798): 197, 193–94, 194–95.

42. *Plymouth Records*, 5:76–77.

43. *Plymouth Records*, 5:77–79.

44. *Plymouth Records*, 5:79–80 and 10:362; Langdon, *Pilgrim Colony*, p. 161.

45. Hubbard, *Troubles with the Indians*, 1:58; William Harris to Sir Joseph Williamson, 12 August 1676, *Harris Papers, Rhode Island Historical Society Collections* 10 (1902): 163–64; Bushnell, "Treatment of Indians," pp. 213–14.

46. *Plymouth Records*, 5:97–98, 101, 106–7, 180; Langdon, *Pilgrim Colony*, p. 155. In 1671 Philip also sold some land in Massachusetts Bay. See Nathaniel B. Shurtleff, ed., *Records of the Governor and Company of the Massachusetts Bay in New England*, 5 vols. (Boston, 1853–54), vol. 4, pt. 2, p. 498.

47. *Plymouth Records*, 8:190–91; Vaughan, *New England Frontier*, p. 238.

48. See, e.g., Salisbury, "Red Puritans," pp. 52–53; Axtell, *Invasion Within*, p. 168.

49. Hutchinson, *History of Massachusetts-Bay*, 1:242; James P. and Jeanne Ronda, "The Death of John Sassamon: An Exploration in Writing New England History," *American Indian Quarterly* 1 (1974): 92; *Plymouth Records*, 10:362; Hubbard, *Troubles with the Indians*, 1:62; Gookin, *Doings and Sufferings*, pp. 440–41.

50. Mather, *Magnalia*, 2:559–60; Hubbard, *Troubles with the Indians*, 1:63; *Plymouth Records*, 5:167; Ronda, "Death of Sassamon," p. 92; Mather, *Brief History*, p. 87.

51. *Plymouth Records*, 5:159, 167–68, and 10:362–63; Ronda, "Death of Sassamon," p. 93. Jennings tries to explain away the Indian jury by using twisted logic (see *Invasion of America*, pp. 295–96).

52. Gookin, *Doings and Sufferings*, p. 440; John Easton, "A Relacion of the Indyan

Warre," in *Indian Narratives,* p. 7; Francis Jennings, "Francis Parkman: A Brahmin among Untouchables," *William and Mary Quarterly,* 3d ser. 42 (1985): 309. On the importance of revenge among the natives, see Wilcomb E. Washburn, *The Indian in America* (New York: Harper and Row, 1975), pp. 17, 138, and John Phillip Reid, *A Law of Blood: The Primitive Law of the Cherokee Nation* (New York: New York University Press, 1970), pp. 85–112.

53. *Plymouth Records,* 10:363; Josiah Winslow to John Leverett, 4 July 1675, in Hutchinson, *History of Massachusetts-Bay,* 1:242n–243n; Roger Williams to John Winthrop, Jr., 13 June 1675, in his *Complete Writings,* 6:364; Winslow, *Good News,* pp. 545, 555–56, 568–69.

54. Winslow to John Winthrop, Jr., 29 July 1675, *Winthrop Papers, Massachusetts Historical Society Collections,* 5th ser. 1 (1871): 428; Benjamin Church, *Entertaining Passages Relating to Philip's War* (1716), in Slotkin and Folsom, *So Dreadfull a Judgement,* p. 400; George Madison Bodge, *Soldiers in King Philip's War* (Leominister, Mass., 1896), p. 104; Richard Smith, Jr., et al., *Further Letters on King Philip's War* (Providence: Society of Colonial Wars, 1923), p. 12; Vaughan, *New England Frontier,* pp. 312–13.

55. Church, *Entertaining Passages,* pp. 397–400.

56. George W. Ellis and John E. Morris, *King Philip's War* (New York: Grafton Press, 1906), pp. 60–61; *Plymouth Records,* 10:364; William Harris to Sir Joseph Williamson, 12 August 1676, *Harris Papers,* pp. 164–65; Mason, *John Mason,* p. 38; James K. Hosmer, ed., *Winthrop's Journal: "History of New England," 1630–1649,* 2 vols. (New York: Charles Scribner's Sons, 1908), 1:76.

57. Easton, "Relacion," pp. 8–12.

58. Easton, "Relacion," pp. 10, 14; Leach, *Flintlock and Tomahawk,* pp. 42–43.

59. Easton, "Relacion," p. 12; *Plymouth Records,* 10:364; *A Continuation of the State of New England* (1676), in *Indian Narratives,* p. 62; Hubbard, *Troubles with the Indians,* 1:64.

60. Bushnell, "Treatment of Indians," p. 210; Ellis and Morris, *King Philip's War,* p. 46; Tobias Sanders to Fitz-John Winthrop, 3 July 1675, *Winthrop Papers, Massachusetts Historical Society Collections,* 5th ser. 1 (1871): 426–27; Hubbard, *Troubles with the Indians,* 1:59.

61. Easton, "Relacion," p. 16.

6

Indian John and the Northern Tawnies

JOHN MCWILLIAMS

Probably no aspect of New England's history has been more thoroughly and diversely debated than the attempt by Puritan authorities to identify and elimi-nate—by reformation or, in extreme cases, by execution—Satan's agents. The obsession with witches was not an exclusively New England phenomenon, of course: in the British Isles and Continental Europe between 1500 and 1700, hundreds of thousands of people (mostly women) were accused of practicing witchcraft, and tens of thousands, perhaps far more, were found guilty and exe-cuted. Even in Britain's other American colonies, presumed witches were occa-sionally accused and harassed. But only in the New England colonies—Con-necticut and New Haven (during its brief separate colonial existence) as well as Massachusetts—were lives snuffed out in accordance with the biblical injunc-tion (Exodus 22:18) that "Thou shalt not suffer a witch to live."

Among the many problems that historians have long sought to resolve is the connection, both in actuality and in the Puritan mind, between the increase in witchcraft cases in the 1660s through 1690s and the simultaneous rise in friction among the region's Euroamericans and Indian nations. It began, perhaps, with a growing assumption that Indians were God's chosen instrument of affliction. In the 1660s, the clergyman-poet Michael Wigglesworth's "God's Controversy with New England" predicted that the Lord would punish his people for their failure to follow His rules and for backsliding from the first generation of New Englanders' high standards of belief and performance. King Philip's War seemed to fulfill Wigglesworth's prediction and to identify the method of divine retri-bution.

With the war still in progress, the Massachusetts General Court in the fall of 1675 announced that "the righteous God hath . . . given commission to the barba-rous heathen to rise up against us, and to become a smart rod and severe scourge to us." Four years later, the colony's leaders lamented that "Christians in this land have become too like unto the Indians, and then we need not wonder if the Lord has afflicted us by them." With warfare continuing along the ambiguous

northern border between Euroamerican settlements and Indian territories,
New England Puritans were more prone than ever to link their own social
and religious shortcomings with Indian depredations and, increasingly, with
Satanic explanations of ordinary events.

Adding to the Puritans' collective paranoia were plausible fears deriving from
political upheavals of the 1680s, especially the revocation of the Massachusetts
charter, England's imposition of the unpopular Dominion of New England,
and the threat of French and Indian military assault from the North. New
England was ripe for an outburst of accusation and persecution spurred by no-
tions of "Divels Incarnate."

In the following essay, John McWilliams demonstrates the close but hereto-
fore unappreciated connection between the infamous Salem witchcraft hysteria
of 1692 and Puritan perceptions of Indians, especially those on the northern
frontier.

*E*VEN FOR INDIVIDUALS far removed in time and space—say
twentieth-century Europeans—Salem, Massachusetts, inevitably con-
jures a specific, still disgraceful association: "witch trials." The word
"witch" has, to be sure, drawn some historians back into British folklore
and seventeenth-century British court practices or into Puritan concepts
of divine and diabolic agency. In general, however, the cluster of events
labeled "the trials of 1692" has been associated less with the British empire,
or with colonial America, or even with New England than with a specific
location: the individual community of Salem itself. The common phrase
"Salem witch trials" continues to focus our attention upon the local conditions—economic, spiritual, and political—of Salem town and Salem village (Danvers). Salem still lures the summer tourist dollar by claims upon
its presumably unique notoriety.

"Witchcraft belonged, first and last, to the life of the little community,"
John Demos concluded in *Entertaining Satan.* In Massachusetts' isolated
communities, the roles of accused, accuser, and victim initially evolved
from intra-village conflict: "Suspicion and gossip, charge and counter-
charge, the resort to private magic and/or formal proceedings in court; all
were geared to local conditions."[1] As Demos's careful statistics and biographical narratives, as well as those of Carol Karlsen, have shown, the
accused witch in seventeenth-century New England was most likely to be
a woman over forty years of age, without a secure social position or a male
heir, but known to have a sharp tongue, skills at midwifery, familiarity
with tavern life and/or a reputation for having practiced white or black
magic.[2] But by the late summer of 1692, as I shall show, a much more

evasive, and more harrowing, spectre-devil had passed through Essex County. It was the figure of the male Indian, who might look like the Black Man, the Red Man, or a "Tawny." "Seen" either as a warrior or a powwow, his spectral presence in Salem village and to the north was a sure sign of the devil's impending war against New England. So widespread a fear of Indian spectral visitation cannot be adequately explained by ascribing it to neighbors' jealousies, to the lurid imagination of adolescent girls, or to Puritan racial superstition. The origin of Salem's fear was regional as well as local, historical as well as imagined—a more pressing and immediate threat than post-Enlightenment skeptics have wished to entertain.

I. The Fears: Warriors and Powwows

Paul Boyer and Stephen Nissenbaum are certainly correct in their assessment that the faltering rural economy of Salem village, in contrast to the booming maritime trade in neighboring Salem town, energized, perhaps even caused, the initial accusations of witchcraft.[3] But such complaints do not surface as such in the trial transcripts, nor do they explain the speed or geographical range with which popular fear spread. The explanation may be sought in Cotton Mather's often scorned view of the witch trials, for Mather shows us how village accusations could, in the 1680s and 1690s, rapidly transcend local confines. His three narratives of the "grievous" decade that had begun in 1685 all specify that Indian powwows, thought to be the devil's agents, if not devils themselves, had been leading the assault of Satan's legions against New England from the Pequot War of 1636, to the intertribal conspiracy of King Philip's War, and, most recently, to the north and east of God's commonwealth. Fear of Indian invasion from without was aggravated by circumstances of political drift from within. Because Massachusetts had remained an unchartered colony for two years after the revolt against Andros ("between government and no government," in Robert Calef's words),[4] witchcraft accusations were allowed to multiply and jails allowed to fill during the spring of 1692, a time when, in anticipation of the new charter, no colony-wide trial could be held. The authority to name judges, granted to the appointed governor of the province by the new charter, enabled William Phips not only to create the special Court of Oyer and Terminer and to appoint William Stoughton as its chief justice but also to disband the special court five months later and then to reconstitute it. As Edmund Andros had done in March 1689, William Phips left Massachusetts at a time of gathering inner turmoil, June 1692, to lead a New England army against the northern Indians and the French. While the two governor-generals were fighting their frontier battles, the not unrelated crises within coastal communities exploded behind and to the south of them.

Without the contexts of the northern Indian war and the turmoil over the new charter, Salem witchcraft is thus historically inconceivable. King Philip's War, it must be understood, did not in fact end the Indian military threat to English settlement in Massachusetts, despite the claims of William Hubbard, Thomas Hutchinson, George Bancroft, and Samuel Eliot Morison. Although the Wampanoags to the south and the Nipmucks to the west had at great cost been defeated by 1676, many of the northern tribes, including the Pennacooks, the Nashaways, the Sacos, the Androscoggins, and the Penobscots, were soon preparing to continue the fight.[5] In 1688, while Massachusetts was struggling with its continuing war debt, its depleted treasury, the loss of its charter, and a royally appointed governor, the western and eastern Abnaki peoples put aside their internecine hostilities and formed the Wabanaki Confederation to drive the English down from the north, much as Metacomet ("Philip") had done to the south and west. With the organizational assistance of resettled Narragansett veterans and the support of the French, the Abnaki began a ten-year war so devastating in its raids as far south as the Merrimack River, and even into Massachusetts, that Cotton Mather's book about the war, *Decennium Luctuosum* (1699), opens with a citation of Aeneas's famous outburst expressing his horror at having to recount the grief of the Trojan War: "Infandum, regina, iubes renovare dolorem."[6] Mather's epigraph assumes that the "grievous decade" of battling the Abnaki will readily be understood as New England's Trojan War. Salem's geographical position made it critical to this fearsome, prolonged conflict. Although not on the frontier line in 1692, Salem was the largest English community north of Boston, the port of embarkation for the northern wars against the French and the Abnaki, and a major source of the Essex County militia who would fight in those sporadic, seemingly endless wars from 1688 until 1763.

To grasp the crucial importance of geography to developing patterns of witchcraft accusations, it is useful to place the chronologies of the wars against witches and the wars against northern Indians side by side. In 1689, Saco Falls, Dover, and Casco Bay were attacked by Indians and/or French. That same year, John Bishop and Nicholas Reed of Salem village were killed while fighting Indians. In 1690, Schenectady, Salmon Falls, Casco, Berwick, Exeter, and Amesbury were attacked; Godfrey Sheldon of Salem village was killed. In 1691, Wells, York, Berwick (again), Rowley, and Haverhill were attacked. At least thirty-five men from Essex County were then serving in the northern forces while at least twenty-one of their fellows were on militia-alert back home. In January 1692, just as Tituba, Abigail Williams, Betty Parris, and Ann Putnam were playing with white magic in Reverend Parris's household, the French and Indians attacked York again, burning the town, killing at least fifty people, including Reverend Shubael Dummer, and capturing about eighty more. Northern service for select, able-bodied Essex County men was to continue throughout the summer. On 20 June, ten days after Bridget Bishop was hung and ten days before Sarah Good, Rebecca Nurse, Suzannah Martin, Elizabeth How, and Sarah Wildes were sentenced to death, the French and Indians attacked the town of Wells. The minister of Wells, a man of reputation most unlike that of the revered Dummer, was apparently not present. He had recently been "cried out" as a wizard in Salem village by Ann Putnam and Abigail Hobbs; his name was George Burroughs.[7]

The direction in which accusations spread shows the special locus of the province's collective apprehension. Of the 141 suspected witches against whom legal action was initiated during the Salem trials, 107 resided in towns from Salem village north, while only 31 resided in towns from Salem town south, even though at least 80 percent of the population of the province lived south of Salem. Even more telling are the figures for legal actions begun before and after 20 June 1692, the date of the French and Indian attack on Wells:

	Before 20 June	After 20 June
Residents of Salem village	27	0
Residents of Salem town	9	1
Residents north of Salem village	23	59
Residents south of Salem village	17	4
Total		140

NOTE: John Lee's residence is unknown.
SOURCE: Richard Weisman, "List of Persons against Whom Legal Actions Were Initiated during Salem Prosecutions," app. C of his *Witchcraft, Magic and Religion in Seventeenth-Century Massachusetts* (Amherst: University of Massachusetts Press, 1984), pp. 208–16.

Although witchcraft accusations began in Salem village and Salem town, they almost immediately, during the months of May and June, spread somewhat more to the north than to the south. But after mid June, when accusations against residents of Salem town and Salem village had virtually ceased, accusations of witchcraft spread almost entirely toward the north, despite the thinness of the population there. Of the 59 accusations after 20

June, 39 were from Andover (Martha Carrier being the only Andover resident accused before that date); the remaining 20 were scattered among northern towns as dispersed as Rowley, Reading, Gloucester, and Haverhill.

Andover's importance in the seeing of spectres was second only to Salem's. During the years immediately preceding 1692, the town of Andover, some twenty miles northwest of Salem, had been blessedly spared any Indian attack. As the hysteria in Andover spread, however, eleven of the Andover witches confessed that they had been communicants in the black masses conducted by Reverend Burroughs, either recently in Reverend Parris's pasture in Salem village or as long ago as three years before, somewhere in more northerly forests. The court transcripts suggest that these Andover suspects had agreed among themselves to focus attention on Burroughs, the devil's agent. Their court accusations against him were to begin immediately after the French and Indians attacked Wells and were to concentrate upon his presumed association with northern Indians.

II. The Transcripts: Red Blood, Red Wine, and Black Books

Whether Tituba and her husband John, the two household slaves Reverend Parris had purchased in Barbados, were of West Indian, African, or Native American origin, or some combination thereof, is not known.[8] In seventeenth-century Massachusetts, such discriminations among unregenerate peoples of color were neither usual nor considered necessary, especially for slaves. Throughout the records of the preliminary witchcraft hearings, Tituba's race is referred to only as "Indian" and her husband is referred to only as "Indian John" or "John Indian"; in the warrant for her arrest she is referred to as "titibe an Indian Woman servant."[9] By 1692 (exactly two centuries after first contact), Columbus's misnaming had yielded a catchall term variously applied to the Guanahani, the Carribe, the Aztecs, and West Indies Africans, as well as to the Iroquois and the Abnaki "Tarratines."

According to the first narrative account of the Salem accusations, written by Reverend Deodat Lawson in April 1692, the witchcraft practiced by Reverend Parris's two "Indians" led to the investigations that culminated in the accusations, trials, and convictions:

For introduction to the discovery of those that afflicted them, It is reported Mr. Parris's Indian Man and Woman made a Cake of Rye Meal, and the Childrens water, baked it in the Ashes, and gave it to a Dogge, since which they have discovered, and seen particular persons hurting of them.[10]

Shifting responsibility away from Tituba, Parris would note in his church record book that "diabolical means were used by the making of a cake by my Indian man, who had his direction from this our sister, Mary Sibley."[11] Samuel P. Fowler, commenting on the use of the word "Indian," long ago advanced an explanation that has been too little considered: "By some Persons, these Indians have been supposed to belong to the Aborigines of our Country and to have obtained their knowledge of Witchcraft from the Indian Powows."[12] Lawson, Parris, and Fowler all agreed, however, on one crucial point. The purpose of preparing the witch-cake was not to afflict but to discover the afflicter. Practicing white, not black, magic, Parris's two "Indians" were appealing to supernatural powers, generally associated by Christians with the powwows of New England tribes, to identify and exorcise diabolical spirits from a household suddenly overrun with afflicted young women.[13]

Even though the witchcraft had been set in motion by Indian John, it was Tituba, not her husband, who was summoned to be examined, along with Sarah Good and Sarah Osborne, at the first preliminary hearing. As soon as Tituba confessed to practicing witchcraft in order to protect the "children," the associations of race and maleficium became overpoweringly strong. The accuser quickly became the accused. Under force of the "cross and swift questions"[14] recommended for witchcraft cases, Tituba was soon confessing to having ridden on a pole behind "a tall man of Boston": "He goes in black clothes a tal man with white hair I thinke." That an Indian woman had been in the company of a devil with white hair was far less impressive to the judges, though, than Tituba's attempt to shift her suddenly emerging responsibility onto three other suspects: Sarah Good, Sarah Osborne, and a man with a yellow bird who had ordered her indiscriminately to "kill the children." On the second day of examination, Tituba confessed to signing a six-year covenant with the devil unwillingly and to having made "a marke in the Booke & made itt with Red Bloud." Once an indictment was issued contending that Tituba was "A detestable Witch," a pattern of confessing to certain rituals of black covenant, while crying out upon yet more afflicting spectres, had been established. When Tituba testified that the others who had signed the devil's book were to be found "some in Boston & Some herein this Towne," however, she expanded the geographical scope of the accusations—but in a direction contrary to the pattern that would develop.[15]

Of the 141 suspected witches summoned to court, there was to be—despite Tituba's fingerpointing—only one resident of Boston, and he was a tall man with northern associations. Captain John Alden, son of John and Priscilla, had served with steady distinction in the northern Indian wars during the two years before he was cried out as a witch. Alden's testimony was considered to be so important that Chief Justice William Stoughton attended his preliminary examination. Although the afflicted young women could not identify Alden until he was presented to them, once they knew him, they knew him well. During court recess "a Ring was made" around Alden in the public street. According to his own account, "the same Accuser [probably Mercy Lewis] cried out, 'there stands Aldin, a bold fellow with his Hat on before the Judges, he sells Powder and Shot to the Indians and French, and lies with the Indian Squaes, and has Indian Papooses.'" Like almost every accused witch, Alden then failed the touch test, a ritual cleansing of spirit intended both to calm the afflicted and to reveal the probable guilt of the afflicter. Beyond Alden's presumed dealings with the French and the Indians, no other evidence was brought forward against him. Even though Bartholomew Gedney testified on Alden's behalf, Samuel Sewall wrote for him, and Cotton Mather prayed with him, Alden's only recourse for avoiding trial was to escape from jail three months later. Had he not fled, Alden's service in the Indian wars, together with Tituba's reference to the Tall Man, might have been sufficient to condemn him.[16]

Crucial moments of court testimony repeatedly emerged in the context of either a suspected witch's misuse of Indian power or an afflicted person's confrontation of Indian deviltry. Although aged, ailing Sarah Osborne stoutly denied ever seeing the devil, harming children, or even knowing her accuser (Sarah Good), she did acknowledge having had one possibly supernatural experience:

> shee said this morning that shee was more like to be bewitched than that she was a witch Mr Harthorn asked her what made her say so shee answered that shee was frighted one time in her sleep and either saw or dreamed that shee saw a thing like an indian all black which did pinch her in her neck and pulled her by the back part of her head to the dore of the house.

Any woman who had read Mary Rowlandson's recently published, celebrated captivity narrative, especially an honest, bedridden woman like Sarah Osborne living near the frontier, might well have told Judge Hathorne how she "saw or dreamed that shee saw a thing like an indian" who proceeded to drag her by the hair to the door of her house. The Indian's spectral visitation—if that is, indeed, what it was—came to an abrupt close only moments before the threatened scalping. Given her failing finances and inability to attend church, Sarah Osborne's subsequent challenge to Judge Hathorne's probing for spectral evidence ("I doe not know that the devil goes about in my likeness to doe any hurt") was more likely to condemn than to exonerate her. The jury's assessment of her dreamlike Indian associations was never to be known, however: Sarah Osborne was to die in prison before she could be brought to trial.[17]

Suzannah Martin, convicted 30 June and executed 19 August, came from the frontier town of Amesbury, which had been attacked by Indians in 1690 and then again fleetingly in July 1692. Martin was condemned largely on the testimony of twenty-seven-year-old Joseph Ring of nearby Salisbury. Returning from military service against the Indians under Captain Shadrach at Casco Bay, Ring had met the devil while passing through the forest near Hampton, where Martin's spectre assisted in serving the red wine and red bread,[18] a rite of incorporation the young soldier heroically resisted.

Much as Suzannah Martin succumbed to the evidence marshaled by Joseph Ring, so Bridget Oliver Bishop fell prey to the testimony of John Louder of Salem, although the poppets found in her house provided physical evidence of witchcraft. Louder testified that Bishop's likeness had sat on his chest during the night. Shortly after the spectre vanished, Louder saw "a black thing Jump into the window." He valiantly struck it with a stick, whereupon the evil creature "sprang back and flew over the apple tree." Louder barred his doors, then looked up to see his neighbor Bridget Bishop in her orchard, hurrying home. Testimony like Louder's surely suggested to the court that the spectre of a suspected witch could attack households in an instant and then disappear with supernatural speed— exactly as Indians were feared to do.[19]

Examiners Corwin and Hathorne had obtained their first voluntary confession from a white Christian in April, when the court heard the spectacular revelations of Abigail Hobbs and her mother Deliverance, both from Topsfield, a community just north of Salem village. Attempting to exonerate herself, Abigail adopted a strategy of showing how she had "seen sights and been scared and . . . been very wicked." She had seen the devil only once, had signed his book only once, and it had all happened three or four years ago "at the Eastward at Casko-bay" when she had lived in Maine. Once Abigail was examined in prison, however, she recalled details. She had consented to afflict families living near the Casco Bay fort, where she had known Reverend George Burroughs. Indeed, Burroughs had brought her a poppet in the likeness of Mary Lawrence (since dead) and had urged her to stick thorns into it. From prison, Abigail's mother, Deliverance, would soon confess to having long been a "Covenant Witch." Like many of the accused who would confess during the next five months, Deliverance admitted that she had first partaken of the devil's supper in Reverend Parris's pasture in Salem village, where the service had been conducted by "Mr. Burroughs the Preacher," even though he was then living in Maine. Casco Bay's importance in the Indian Wars was evidently enhancing, rather than diminishing, Reverend Burroughs's spectral traveling abilities. The "Red Bread and Red Wine Like Blood," Deliverance said, had been distributed by five women, all of them already accused as witches, together with "a Man in a long crowned white Hat, next the Minister."[20]

III. Satan's Design and George Burroughs's Heathen Ministry

The centrality of George Burroughs's conviction in extending the prosecution of witchcraft is evident in the sheer volume and length of the materials (30 pages) devoted to his case. Sixteen people testified at his 9 May preliminary examination before Chief Justice William Stoughton; four subsequent indictments, a lengthy physical examination, oral testimony by six individuals, four letters to the court, and seven additional depositions followed—all before the trial even began. A corrupted minister was, of course, the leader needed to conduct the Black Mass, to offer and elevate the red Host, and, in general, to organize and proselytize on behalf of the devil's New England congregation, especially because the Old Boy still had to spend prime time in France. Burroughs's qualifications, however, well exceeded the minimum for his evil role. Not only had he, ten years before, resigned the Salem village pulpit after being arrested for debt by Captain John Putnam. Not only had he never received nor offered communion thereafter, nor baptized any of his children beyond the eldest. Not only had Mercy Lewis, one of the afflicted young women, served as Burroughs's maidservant. And not only had he acquired a reputation, probably deserved, for cruelly mistreating his three wives. Reverend Burroughs had, after leaving Salem village, moved north to Wells, near the bloodied heart of tawny territory in Casco Bay.

At the center of the case against Burroughs were the many documents filed by the Putnam family, most of which developed the inflammatory deposition of the younger Ann Putnam describing her experiences on the evening of 20 April 1692. As soon as Ann saw the apparition of a minister, she instantly comprehended its significance: "oh dreadfull; dreadful here is a minister com; what are Ministers wicthes to: whence com you and What is your name for I will complaine of you; tho you be A minister." After revealing that it was George Burroughs's spectre that had tortured her and had offered her the book to sign, Ann Putnam charged Burroughs with monstrous perversion of duty: "It was a dreadfull thing: that he which was a Minister that should teach children to feare God should com to perswad poor creatures to give their souls to the divill." Ann then tallied three specific charges against Burroughs, all apparently conveyed to her by his spectre: 1) he had bewitched his first two wives to death; 2) he had "killed Mr. Lawsons child because he went to the eastward with Sir Edmon and preached soe"; and 3) "he had bewicthed a grate many souldiers to death at the eastword, when Sir Edmon was their." Historians of Salem witchcraft have had much to say about George Burroughs's wives, but they have neglected the other two charges. Ann Putnam was accusing George Burroughs of bewitching the soldiers in Edmund Andros's army, which can only have meant that Burroughs was a spiritual agent of the French and Indians, who were still killing New England Christians.[21]

As Thomas Putnam wrote to Hathorne and Corwin the next day, the unmasking of Burroughs provided authorities the "wheel within a wheel at which our ears do tingle." Benjamin Hutchinson was soon testifying that, on the very day of that discovery, the spectre of the "lettell black menester that Lived at Casko bay" had appeared twice to Abigail Williams. On its second pass, Abigail was able to identify the spectre as that of George Burroughs, even though it had appeared amid a "roome full of them" in Lieutenant Ingersoll's tavern. Burroughs's spectre was so terrifying that Abigail was overjoyed when Benjamin Hutchinson and Ely Putnam pulled out their rapiers and stabbed two of the accompanying spectral invaders, "a great black woman of Stonintown, and an Indian that comes with her." By 1 June, Abigail Hobbs would explain that the ever expanding number of witches were all able to gather and conspire at one communion because "Mr. Burroughs had a trumpett & sounded it." This image would recur in many Andover depositions, with confessed witch William Barker, Sr., finally claiming that the blasts of Burroughs's trumpet were able to summon "about 307 witches in the country" ranging from Maine to Connecticut.[22]

Although Mercy Lewis testified that on 7 May "mr Burroughs caried me up to an exceeding high mountain and shewed me all the kingdoms of the earth," it was not until August that William Barker revealed the full revolutionary intent of Devil Burroughs's ministry:

Satan's design was to set up his own worship, abolish all the churches in the land, to fall next upon Salem and soe goe through the countrey. He sayth the devil promeised that all his people should live bravely; that all persones should be equall; that their should be no day of resurrection or of judgment, and neither punishment nor shame for sin.—He sayth there was a Sacrament at that meeting, there was also bread & wyne Mr. Burse [Burroughs] was a ringleader in that meeting.[23]

William Barker's testimony perfectly illustrates John Demos's claim that witchcraft accusations involved "a vicarious indulgence of forbidden wish and fantasy" together with, "at the end, a decisive act of repudiation."[24] In Barker's view, Salem was merely Satan's secondary target; the demon's real aim was to "goe through the countrey" destroying everything that had proven so demanding in New England communal life. A new life of bravery and equality, free of the last judgment, and somewhat like the imagined world of the savage, might await all New England. Although the forbidden desires of the 1692 Essex County witches may have begun in young girls' anxieties to discover the names of future marital partners, the aims of forbidden desire had certainly undergone a remarkable expansion.

While Barker's vision of Satan's grand mission exposed inner constraints of the Puritan spirit, the recently widowed Mary Toothaker from Billerica (a town considerably to the west of Salem and many miles from Maine) finally saw the devil directly in the face of the feared Indian outsider. Examined by Gedney, Hathorne, Corwin, and Captain Higginson on 30 July, Toothaker's resistance was broken when she was confronted by her accuser. She admitted that, until the afflicted had just now penetrated her secrecy, the devil's chokings had been so severe as to prevent her from speaking out. "The truth in this matter" was that, ever since last May, "she was under great Discontentedness & troubled w'h feare about the Indians, & used to dream of fighting with them." Now, however, "she is convinced she is a witch" because, at the time of her worst fears, "the Devil appeared to her in the shape of a Tawny man and promised to keep her from the Indians and she should have happy dayes with her sone." The devil's emissary had repeated that "she should be safe from the Indians" if only she would sign his book by rubbing off the "white scurff" on "a piece of burch bark." Not considering that the tawny man who had come to her was clearly able to use Indian powers, Mary signed the birch bark. Now, however, she has been shocked to discover that in Salem village 305 witches convene at "the Beating of a drum" and "the sound of a trumpet" under the leadership of "a minister, a little man whose name is Burroughs" and who promises to set up "the Kingdom of satan." Mary Toothaker, who had bargained with an Indian to be saved from his fellows, had found that Satan, true to his nature, had tricked her after all. Attempting to escape one set of demons, she had fallen prey to another, for through Reverend

Burroughs, Satan was setting up some sort of heathen ministry throughout the country. Satan's promise to defend her from Indians had been his lure to persuade her to join them.[25]

Although George Burroughs was not to be executed until 19 August, no one appears to have ever spoken out in his defense. After the French and Indian attack on Wells in June, it is probable that nothing could have saved him. Because Burroughs was not in Wells at the time of the attack, he could not be directly accused of conspiracy. But the contrast between his conspicuous inaction and the heroic resistance of Shubael Dummer, minister of York, could hardly have been more plain. Despite repeated advice to flee south, Dummer—whom Cotton Mather described as a man of "Exemplary Holiness, Humbleness, Modesty, Industry and Fidelity . . . a Gentleman Well-Descended, Well-Tempered, Well-educated"[26]—had refused to leave his flock. When the northern tawnies attacked York in January 1692, Dummer had been shot dead in his own doorway.

The shooting led to a telling reversal of ministerial role. "On the next Lord's Day," according to Mather, "one of those Tawnies chose to Exhibit himself unto them, (A Devil as an Angel of Light!) in the Cloaths, whereof they had Script the Dead Body of this their Father."[27] If Francis Parkman is correct, this Abnaki warrior wished to taunt the conquered by displaying his booty and by preaching "a mock sermon to captive parishioners."[28] In the absence of the minister who might have served as an Angel of Light, the Indian devils were soon to be found "toiling and Moiling in the Mud, and blacken'd with it, as if Mud could add Blackness to such Miscreants." By means of such phrasings and within such settings does the Red Man become the Black. Indeed, no atrocity in New England's frequent retellings of its Indian wars was to exceed Cotton Mather's account of how the "Diabolical" tawnies had castrated, further mutilated, and slowly burned the body of John Diamond at Wells, Maine, in June 1692.[29]

During the weeks immediately preceding George Burroughs's execution, Satan appeared to be planning a coastal attack. Reverend John Emerson carefully recorded five different occasions during July 1692 when various citizens of Gloucester saw small groups of armed Indians and armed Frenchmen, usually together and usually crossing salt marshes. The enemy was always speechless; the Gloucestermen's guns always misfired. After the executions of 19 August, however, there were no more sightings. When attempting to account, nine months later, for the "wonderful and Surprising Things which happened in the Town of Glocester," Emerson would not for a minute consider that the sightings had been delusions. "I hope the Substance of what is written, will be enough to Satisfy all Rational

Persons, that Glocester was not Alarumed last Summer, for above a Fortnight together, by real French and Indians, but that the Devil and his Agents were the cause of all the Molestation, which at this time befel the Town."[30] The fact that no attack had occurred did not suggest to Emerson that the diabolic spectres were mere figments of men's imaginations; instead, he assumed that New England's prompt resistance to the French and Indian threat had rendered those spectres ineffectual.

IV. An "Hysterical" Indian

The slave whom everyone called "Indian John" played a curious and important role in apprehending and examining suspected witches. Like his wife Tituba, John must have aroused suspicions of witchery, if not deviltry, himself. However, unlike her, he was never accused, and therefore never examined, even though, according to Parris's account, it was Indian John who had prepared the witch-cake. John succeeded in protecting himself not by avoiding but by regularly attending the hearings; in fact, he became a periodic witness. As a waiter at Lieutenant Ingersoll's tavern, he had ample opportunity to overhear the conversations of those residing beyond Salem village who had been summoned to the court examinations nearby. Although Indian John was careful to absorb whatever information he could, his strategy was not to impart it, for his court testimony, like the witnessing of the afflicted women, was usually wordless. He too displayed convulsive symptoms of demonic possession or hysteria when suspected witches were brought into court; he too was periodically called upon to perform the touch test.

In a remarkable display of marital dissociation, Indian John's first hysterical fit occurred in court shortly after his wife's second examination was concluded. In all probability, it was this sign of affliction that enabled this black-Indian-slave-waiter to be listed as one of the two afflicted persons in the first complaint against Elizabeth Proctor and Sarah Cloyse. The examination of Sarah Cloyse before Deputy Governor Thomas Danforth opened with questions posed to Indian John, who revealed that Goody Proctor and Goody Cloyse had brought him the book. When a clearly suspicious judge asked "John! tell the truth, who hurts you? have you been hurt?" John forthrightly replied that Goody Proctor had choked him and then brought him the book and that Goody Cloyse had bit him "yesterday at meeting." Despite Sarah Cloyse's outburst ("Oh! you are a grievous liar"), Indian John's testimony seems to have been convincing to the court, because he was allowed the uncontested last word. The examining judges then asked a similar set of questions of Mary Walcott, Abigail Williams, Mercy Lewis, and Ann Putnam, Jr., all of whom gave answers remarkably similar to those just provided by John.[31]

The frequency and severity of the young women's symptoms of afflic-tion, together with their physical proximity to sometimes skeptical exam-ining judges, make it difficult for any careful reader of the transcripts to believe that their fits of "hysteria" were feigned. Indian John's convulsive fits, on the other hand, seem all too precisely timed. When Mary Warren, formerly an accuser, recanted her accusation and therefore found herself accused, Indian John appears to have been momentarily perplexed. As he looked on, Elizabeth Hubbard testified against Mary Warren by recalling that Mary had recently said "the afflicted persons did but dissemble." Sam-uel Parris, who recorded this particular court summary, then adds, "Now they were all but John Indian grievously afflicted & mrs. Pope also, who was not afflicted before hitherto this day; & after a few moments John Indian fell into a violent fit also." "Hysteria" may be contagious, but one wonders whether Indian John's delayed response does not reveal that he had misunderstood the word "dissemble" until the afflicted women gave him his cue. At Suzannah Martin's hearing, his first attack of hysteria seems to have been genuine: "John Indian fell into a violent fit, & said it was that woman, she bites, she bites." A few minutes later, however, he reacted to the request for a touch test in a manner that smacks of calcula-tion: "John Indian said he would kill her, if he came near her, but he fell down before he could touch her."[32]

Captain Nathaniel Cary, a Charlestown shipbuilder, accompanied his accused wife Elizabeth to Salem village for her hearing late in May. Unable to meet with her accuser, Abigail Williams, Elizabeth and her husband made their way to Ingersoll's tavern. The captain recorded the curious ex-periences that followed:

> We went therefore into the Alehouse, where an Indian Man attended us, who it seems was one of the afflicted; to him we gave some Cyder, he shewed several Scars, that seemed as if they had been long there, and shewed them as done by witchcraft, and acquainted us that his Wife, who also was a Slave, was imprison'd for Witchcraft.

Converting the whipping scars of slavery into witch marks was but the first of Indian John's nice touches. Shortly after the Carys' first encounter with him, three afflicted women came into the room, "began to tumble down like Swine," and cried out upon "Cary." Following this event, Eliza-beth was summoned to court almost immediately. Before the justices began their questioning, "The Indian before mentioned, was also brought in, to be one of her Accusers; being come in, he now (when before the Justices) fell down and tumbled about like a Hog, but said nothing." When the justices ordered the touch test, Indian John seems at first to have played the unknowing savage: "The Indian took hold on her hand, and pulled her down on the Floor, in a barbarous manner." When the test was performed in the approved manner, however, John's spirit was restored to calm, thus convincing the court that Elizabeth's demon spirit had returned from John's body to its proper home in hers. No additional evidence of her witchery was offered, apparently because none was needed. Elizabeth Cary was committed to a local prison and remained there for about two months until, thanks to her husband's efforts, she escaped to Rhode Island.[33]

Although we need not accept Nathaniel Cary's premise that the Salem village hearings were staged brutalities, it is evident that Indian John had been accorded a very special status in the pre-trial examinations. His was a role of carefully limited authority not unlike that of the Praying Indians who had served as scouts for white troops during King Philip's War. With his presumed special knowledge of the wildness beyond, Indian John could lend special insight to the search for the devil's spirit. To trust too much to the spiritual scouting of an Indian would obviously be folly. To ignore him, however, would be more so. Convinced that the devil's evidence could be used to discover the devil, the Court of Oyer and Terminer was to proceed as if Indian powers could be both used and triumphed over simultaneously.

V. Cotton Mather's Devil

Perhaps the most vivid of all George Bancroft's historical narratives is his error-ridden account of how Cotton Mather's supposed credulity, infatuation, and "boundless vanity" led him to promote the Salem witch trials. To Bancroft, the guilty verdicts were explicable only as the temporary victory of a backward-looking Puritanism worriedly defended by Calvinist ministers and a few appointed justices in face of the growing opposition of New England's commonsensical people.[34] Many pages have been needed to challenge, though they have yet to dispel, the seductive power of Bancroft's thesis.[35] Mather's writings on witchcraft, especially his 15 June advisory letter to the court on behalf of the ministry, have been mined in an attempt to determine the exact degree of responsibility he bore for the outcome of events. None of these publications, however, including even *The Wonders of the Invisible World*, was conceived as a factual recollection designed for historical self-defense. Instead, as was his wont, Mather intended his narratives to represent the voice of New England, to explain to the world New England's shifting viewpoint about Salem witchcraft.

The Salem trials were not to be regarded, Mather believed, as a Salem or even an Essex County affair; in compiling *The Wonders of the Invisible World*, he announced, "I have indeed set my self to Countermine the whole Plot of the Devil against New England." Observing that no people have ever wished to be "more free from the debauching and the debasing Vices of Ungodliness" than New Englanders, Mather cites Richard Baxter to explain the extremity of the devil's exertions: "Where will the Devil show most Malice, but where he is hated, and hateth most?" And Salem, the very site of New England's origins, is therefore the logical choice for Satan's first attack: "An Army of Devils is horribly broke in upon the place which is the center, and after a sort the First-born of our English Settlements." The "army" of invading spectres would surely have reminded Mather's Massachusetts readers of the army of French and Indians still presumably hovering not far north of Salem village. To help a worried citizenry recognize the devil's legions and the powers of the air, Mather suggests that his readers "think on vast Regiments of cruel and bloody French Dragoons, with an intendant over them, overruning a pillaged Neighbourhood, and you will think a little what the Constitution among the Devils is."[36]

New Englanders are presently enduring the northernmost, perhaps the last, of the devil's attacks. Just as in the time of our forefathers "First the Indian Powawes, used all their Sorceries to molest the first planters here," so now "The Tawnies among whom we came, have watered our Soil with the Blood of many Hundreds of our inhabitants." No one should wonder, Mather insists, that so many of the convicted or confessed witches have recently referred to the devil as the black man. Witches know their own kind, and the afflicted have come to know them too. At any time, at any gathering, but especially in New England's present extremity, one can perceive an agent of "the Black Man (as the Witches call the Devil; and they generally say he resembles an Indian)."[37] By the time he published *Decennium Luctuosum* seven years later, Mather was to be even more explicit about the precipitating events of "the Prodigious War made by the Spirits of the Invisible World upon the People of New-England, in the year 1692": "this inexplicable War might have some of its Original among the Indians, whose chief Sagamores are well known unto some of our Captives, to have been horrid Sorcerers, and hellish Conjurers, and such as Conversed with Daemons."[38]

Cotton Mather's understanding of demonic possession proceeded out of a fear of communal disintegration broadly shared among New Englanders. During the winter of 1692–93, he would witness the ravages of dispossession directly as he helped treat a neighbor's young servant woman, Mercy Short, for mental distress. During the Indian attack on Salmon Falls at the onset of the northern wars in 1690, Mercy had watched her house burn and both of her parents and three siblings die; she had then suffered months of captivity.[39] Among the "cursed Spectres" that afflicted her (spirits Mather was too wary of spectral evidence to name) was the demon who had controlled them:

> The Divel that visited her was just of the same Stature, Feature, and complexion with what the Histories of the Witchcrafts beyond-sea ascribe unto him; he was a wretch no taller than an ordinary Walking-Staff; hee was not of a Negro, but of a Tawney, or an Indian colour; hee wore an high-crowned Hat, with strait Hair; and had one Cloven-Foot.

Mather found it "remarkable" that Mercy's devil should so closely resemble European descriptions he knew she could not have read. What seems much more remarkable, however, is that Mercy's devil had "Indian" qualities no beyond-sea history would have enumerated. Mercy saw a particularly New England devil "not of a Negro, but of a Tawney, or an Indian Colour." She told Mather how this devil spoke to her in a foreign tongue, asked her to sign the book with red characters, threatened her with burning flames, and inflicted fasts upon her until she felt all "the Agonies of One roasting a Faggot at the Stake."[40]

Mercy's most severe afflictions, Mather noted, dated not from her arrival in Boston but more recently, from the summer of 1692, when "that most Horrid and Hellish Witchcraft . . . had brought in the Divels upon several parts of the Country."[41] Unlike beggarly Sarah Good of Salem village, Mercy Short had known the devil's most savage attacks, yet she had continued to resist covenanting with either the black man or the red. And therein lies the English maiden's true triumph—as well as her special value—for Mather: Mercy's accusations led the determined devil searcher directly back to the Indian rather than to an inexplicably corrupted Englishman who had made covenant with Satan and his tawny associates. Cotton Mather was never to finish his narrative of Mercy's afflictions, yet one wonders whether the act of writing about the young woman, without ever calling out upon the spectres that invaded her, did not serve him, by March 1693, as the best way he now knew to keep New England from its own continued burning.

VI. Afterquestions

What should be concluded from the preceding selection of the extant evidence? First, I do not mean to suggest that the northern Indian war should be regarded as the cause of the Salem witch trials. Such mono-causal explanations, though we continue to seek them, are the bane of all historical understanding. Should we consider the northern war to be the major reason why accusations took hold so firmly and spread so rapidly beyond Salem village? Probably, although the suspension of charter government may have been of equal importance. The point of this essay, however, is that neither the extent nor the intensity of Salem's experience of witchcraft is at all explicable without continuing reference to the northern war and the communal spectre of the Indian devil. There were, indeed, plausible historical reasons for such spectres to arise; widespread hallucination can be based upon real and pressing fears.

A last nagging authorial worry. Are studies of Salem witchcraft likely to give due consideration to the impact of the northern Indian war? Here a self-protective skepticism may be in order. As long as we continue to identify and conceive of the subject as "The Salem Witch Trials," the significance of the Puritans' fear of northern tawnies is likely to remain slighted, especially because the scholarship of Salem witchcraft has become so voluminous that no one can be expected to master all of it. The most that can be hoped for may be the remembering of one caveat: the trials may have been held in Salem and Salem village, but they were regarded at the time, and should be regarded by us, as a trial with militant import for all New England. *Pace* Cotton Mather.

Author's Postscript

Since this essay was written, there have been three books published on the Salem witch trials: Bernard Rosenthal's *Salem Story: Reading the Witch Trials of 1692* (New York: Cambridge University Press, 1993); Elaine Breslaw's *Tituba, Reluctant Witch of Salem* (New York: New York University Press, 1996); and Peter Charles Hoffer's *The Devil's Disciples: Makers of the Salem Witchcraft Trials* (Baltimore: Johns Hopkins University Press, 1996). These books demonstrate an increasing, much-needed interest in the historiography of the Salem trials, in particular the ways in which Tituba and the young women of Samuel Parris's household have been made scapegoats by assumptions about Tituba's race and about the "hysteria" of adolescent girls.

Notes

1. John Putnam Demos, *Entertaining Satan: Witchcraft and the Culture of Early New England* (New York: Oxford University Press, 1982), p. 275.

2. See Demos, *Entertaining Satan,* pp. 93–94, and Carol F. Karlsen, *The Devil in the Shape of a Woman: Witchcraft in Colonial New England* (New York: Random House, 1987), pp. 39–40, 51, 65–66, 116–18.

3. Paul Boyer and Stephen Nissenbaum, *Salem Possessed: The Social Origins of Witchcraft* (Cambridge, Mass: Harvard University Press, 1974), pp. 81–83, 109, 180. Other single community studies of inland Massachusetts towns during the colonial period include Philip Greven, *Four Generations: Population, Land and Family in Colonial Andover, Massachusetts* (Ithaca: Cornell University Press, 1970), Robert Gross, *The Minutemen and Their World* (New York: Hill and Wang, 1976), Kenneth A. Lockridge, *A New England Town: The First Hundred Years* (New York: W. W. Norton, 1970; enlarged, 1985), and Sumner Chilton Powell, *Puritan Village: The Formation of a New England Town* (Middletown, Conn.: Wesleyan University Press, 1963). In comparing these studies, the differences underlying the institutional and economic similarities seem particularly striking. The volatility and contentiousness of Boyer's and Nissenbaum's Salem village little resemble the staid quality of Lockridge's Dedham or the generational anxieties of Greven's Andover. These differences suggest that, in order to account for the rapid spread of Salem witchcraft, one should look beyond the particular conditions of Salem town and Salem village.

4. Robert Calef, *More Wonders of the Invisible World* (1700), in *Narratives of the Witchcraft Cases, 1648–1706,* ed. George Lincoln Burr (New York: Charles Scribner's Sons, 1914), p. 349.

5. On the northern aftermath of King Philip's War, see chap. 6 of Russell Bourne's *The Red King's Rebellion: Racial Politics in New England, 1675–1678* (New York and Oxford: Oxford University Press, 1990).

6. Cotton Mather, epigraph to *Decennium Luctuosum* (1699), in *Narratives of the Indian Wars: 1675–1699,* ed. Charles H. Lincoln (New York: Charles Scribner's Sons, 1913), p. 179. A literal translation of Aeneas's words (*The Aeneid,* bk. 2, l. 3) would be: "It is a horrible thing, Queen Dido, for you to command me to retell all that grief!"

7. Information about the war service and deaths of Salem area residents during the Indian wars of 1689–93 is derived from Samuel G. Drake's *The Witchcraft Delusion in New England,* 3 vols. (Roxbury, Mass.: W. Elliot Woodward, 1866) and Charles W. Upham's *Salem Witchcraft* (Boston: Wiggin and Lunt, 1867). For the history of the war, see Mather's *Decennium Luctuosum;* Jeremy Belknap's *The History of New-Hampshire* (Boston: J. Mann & J. Remick, 1812); William D. Williamson's *History of the State of Maine* (Hallowell, Me.: Glazier & Masters, 1832); Francis Parkman's *Comte Frontenac and New France* (Boston: Little, Brown, 1877); and chap. 5 of Charles E. Clark's *The Eastern Frontier: The Settlement of Northern New England: 1610–1763* (New York: Knopf, 1970).

8. On the sequence of literary and historical renderings of Tituba's race, see Chadwick Hansen, "The Metamorphosis of Tituba, or Why American Intellectuals

Can't Tell an Indian Witch from a Negro," *New England Quarterly* 47 (March 1974): 3–12. Elaine G. Breslaw has recently made the fascinating discovery that a slave whose name was spelled "Tattuba" was listed in a contract enabling Barbadian planter Samuel Thompson to lease his plantation to Bridgetown merchant Nicholas Prideaux in 1676 ("The Salem Witch from Barbados: In Search of Tituba's Roots," *Essex Institute Historical Collections* 128 [October 1992]: 217–38). Arguing that Parris's Tituba was most likely an Arawak, Breslaw nonetheless acknowledges that "There is no clear indication in the Barbadian papers that Hothersall or Prideaux sold the slave Tattuba from the Thompson plantation to Parris or even that she was an Amerindian" (p. 223). Breslaw shows that Arawak slaves were few in number in Barbados by the 1670s; many had been assimilated within the prevailing African slave culture.

Because there is no known connection between Thompson's "Tattuba" and Parris's "Tituba" or "Titibe," her race and origin must remain a matter of conjecture. I thank William Hart for the suggestion, earlier implied by Richard S. Dunn, that Tituba might well have been a Native American rather than a West Indian "Indian" (see Dunn, *Sugar and Slaves: The Rise of the Planter Class in the English West Indies, 1624–1713* [Chapel Hill: University of North Carolina Press, 1972], pp. 74, 335, 337). It remains at least possible that Tituba and Indian John were Wampanoags or, more likely, Nipmucks who had been, like many others, sold into slavery into the West Indies at the end of King Philip's War. In 1676 the aged John Eliot protested the selling of captive Indians as slaves to Jamaica and Barbados. In the same year Barbados banned further importation of New England Indian slaves, perhaps because Massachusetts Indians were not proving to be an efficient agricultural slave labor force.

9. *The Salem Witchcraft Papers: Verbatim Transcripts of the Legal Documents of the Salem Witchcraft Outbreak of 1692,* ed. Paul Boyer and Stephen Nissenbaum, 3 vols. (New York: Da Capo Press, 1977), 3:745.

10. Deodat Lawson, "A Brief and True Narrative," in *Narratives of the Witchcraft Cases,* p. 152.

11. Samuel Parris's church record book, quoted by Upham, in *Salem Witchcraft,* 2:95.

12. Samuel P. Fowler, "An Account of the Life and Character of the Rev. Samuel Parris," in Drake, *Witchcraft Delusion,* 3:204.

13. On the distinction between white and black magic, see Chadwick Hansen, *Witchcraft at Salem* (New York: New American Library, 1969), pp. 25–26. The New England Protestants' long-standing association of the powwow (shaman) with the devil is discussed by William S. Simmons, in *Spirit of the New England Tribes: Indian History and Folklore, 1620–1984* (Hanover and London: University Press of New England, 1986), pp. 49–64.

14. Cotton Mather to John Richards, May 1692, in *Selected Letters of Cotton Mather,* ed. Kenneth Silverman (Baton Rouge: Louisiana State University Press, 1971), p. 38.

15. *Salem Witchcraft Papers,* 3:747, 749; 2:361; 3:748, 754, 755.

16. *Salem Witchcraft Papers,* 1:52. Among the accusers present, Mercy Lewis of

Casco Bay, who had been George Burroughs's maidservant, would have been the most likely and most convincing witness to Indian warfare. Carol Karlsen notes that the fathers of thirteen of the afflicted young women accusers had died before 1692, many of them in the northern Indian wars. Among them were two prominent accusers, Sarah Churchill and Mercy Lewis. (See Karlsen, *Devil in the Shape of a Woman*, pp. 226–28.)

17. *Salem Witchcraft Papers*, 2:611, 610.

18. The frequent mention of "red bread" in confessional testimony about witch communions needs explanation. If ergot turned rye red, Linda B. Caporeal's now discredited explanation of the Salem trials (that ergot in rye caused hallucinations) might deserve a rehearing. However, Caporeal nowhere mentions that rye infected with ergot shows any such coloration. (See Caporeal, "Ergotism: The Satan Loosed in Salem?" *Science* 192 [April 1976]: 21–26). The explanation for the red bread may lie in Old World folklore, in New World fears of the Indian, or in a combination of both.

19. *Salem Witchcraft Papers*, 2:99, 100.

20. *Salem Witchcraft Papers*, 2:405, 410, 411, 423.

21. *Salem Witchcraft Papers*, 1:164.

22. *Salem Witchcraft Papers*, 2:165, 171, 172, 66.

23. *Salem Witchcraft Papers*, 1:66.

24. Demos, *Entertaining Satan*, p. 130.

25. *Salem Witchcraft Papers*, 3:767, 768, 769.

26. Mather, *Decennium Luctuosum*, p. 230.

27. Mather, *Decennium Luctuosum*, p. 231.

28. Parkman, *Comte Frontenac and New France*, 2:213–14.

29. Mather, *Decennium Luctuosum*, pp. 230, 238–39.

30. John Emerson, "A Faithful Account of many Wonderful and Surprising Things which happened in the Town of Glocester, in the Year 1692" (1693), in Mather, *Decennium Luctuosum*, pp. 246–47.

31. *Salem Witchcraft Papers*, 2:659.

32. *Salem Witchcraft Papers*, 3:793; 2:554.

33. *Salem Witchcraft Papers*, 1:208, 209.

34. George Bancroft, *History of the United States From the Discovery of the American Continent*, 6 vols. (Boston: Little, Brown and Co., 1883), 3:85; vol. 3 was first published in 1840.

35. Although there are important differences and qualifications, the following historical surveys of the Salem witch trials retain the two essential elements of Bancroft's interpretation: faith in the people's reason and dwelling upon the benighted credulity of the Puritan ministry: Upham's *Salem Witchcraft* (1867); James Russell Lowell's "Witchcraft," *North American Review* 106 (January 1868): 170–224; John Gorham Palfrey's *History of New England*, 4 vols. (Boston: Little, Brown, 1858–1890); John Fiske's *The Beginnings of New England* (Boston: Houghton Mifflin, 1889); and James Truslow Adams's *The Founding of New England* (Boston: Atlantic Monthly Press, 1921). Bancroft's view has remained readily adaptable to more contemporary

ends. Selma R. Williams, for example, concludes that "For all practical purposes the Great Witch Hunt petered out at Salem in 1692, laid to rest by the onset of the scientific revolution and the Age of Reason. But not before it had subordinated women to men with a vengeance—and with effects still felt today." Williams remains convinced that Cotton Mather still deserves to be called "New England's intellectual witch hunter" and "intellectual inquisitor" (*Riding the Nightmare: Women and Witchcraft from the Old World to Colonial Salem* [New York: HarperCollins Publishers, 1978], pp. 202, 125, 200). David Levin's two essays "The Hazing of Cotton Mather" and "Historical Fact in Fiction and Drama: The Salem Witch Trials," neither of which is listed in Williams's bibliography, define the kinds of historiographical distortion she is repeating. See Levin's *In Defense of Historical Literature* (New York: Hill and Wang, 1967).

36. Cotton Mather, *The Wonders of the Invisible World* (1693) (London: John Russell Smith, 1862), pp. 4, 10, 11, 14, 45.

37. Mather, *Wonders of the Invisible World*, pp. 74, 126.

38. Mather, *Decennium Luctuosum*, p. 242.

39. Richard Slotkin has vividly reconstructed the historical circumstances and Puritan responses to the Salmon Falls raid. See chap. 5 of his *Regeneration Through Violence: The Mythology of the American Frontier, 1600–1860* (Middletown: Wesleyan University Press, 1973), pp. 117–28.

40. Cotton Mather, "A Brand Plucked out of the Burning," in *Narratives of the Witchcraft Cases*, pp. 261, 266.

41. Mather, "A Brand Plucked," p. 259.

PART THREE

Missionaries and Indians

7

Conversion from Indian to Puritan

WILLIAM S. SIMMONS

Massachusetts Bay Colony's John Eliot has garnered most of the credit for the Puritans' modest missionary success. Often overlooked are the other clergymen who took time from their pastoral duties in Puritan villages to proselytize neighboring Algonquians; every New England colony, even relatively nonproselytizing Rhode Island, had several such missionaries. The earliest and most successful was Thomas Mayhew, Jr., of Martha's Vineyard, an island off the south coast of Cape Cod that later became part of Massachusetts but for most of the seventeenth century was an independent proprietorship. Anthropologist William S. Simmons examines Mayhew's early achievements and briefly compares his missionary strategy to Eliot's and Roger Williams's.

Simmons is as concerned with the Indians' beliefs as he is with the Christian alternative, for missionaries did not encounter tabulas rasa. New England's natives had deeply cherished ideas abut deities, death, good and ill fortune, and medical cures; they practiced time-honored rituals to promote health, happiness, and longevity; they respected the spirituality and special skills of their traditional priesthood. Simmons draws on fragmentary but revealing sources to reconstruct the Martha's Vineyard Indians' religious culture.

He also narrates the circumstances in which the earliest conversions took place. Before Algonquians could be persuaded to embrace Christian doctrine, they had to question their faith in traditional beliefs and rituals and in their spiritual leaders. During the early years of Mayhew's proselytizing, the logic of his message gained immeasurably from epidemic diseases, bolts of lightning, and medically inexplicable recoveries and deaths, which all seemed to work in the missionary's favor. The Puritan's god and his ministers seemed infinitely more powerful than the Algonquians' gods and their powwows. The result was gratifying to the Reverend Mayhew and to the English and American promoters of Puritan missions. The overwhelmingly peaceful, if occasionally contentious, interaction of Indians and colonists on Martha's Vineyard is also a prime example of how Indian-Euroamerican encounters could be mutually satisfying to large segments of both peoples.

*A*T THE IDEOLOGICAL LEVEL, New England Puritan society in the seventeenth century renewed itself, not through birth, as had been true for most of humanity in its earlier existence, but through rebirth experienced as religious conversion. Membership in the community of living saints was determined through an analysis of the preparation of one's soul for salvation and not by kinship, territorial, or class relationships. What the convert experienced as an emotional transition in the construction of his or her identity was simultaneously a passage from one sphere or traditional social relationships perceived as sinful into a new sphere perceived as saintly. Some New England clergymen, notably John Eliot of Roxbury and Thomas Mayhew, Jr., of Martha's Vineyard, took seriously the responsibility that many Puritans felt to impart the means of salvation to the Indians they encountered in the New World. In their hands, conversion became the instrument for the total reconstitution of Indian cultures. Although both succeeded in converting Indians to the symbolic and social forms of English Puritan culture, the converts themselves never became fully assimilated members of Puritan society. They formed separate Indian congregations and for the most part lived in separate Indian Praying Towns, married among themselves, and constituted an isolated segment of Puritan society which drew boundaries between the saved according to race. This essay concerns one case of conversion across distinct cultural boundaries from American Indian to English Puritan which occurred on Martha's Vineyard under the guidance of the Reverend Thomas Mayhew, Jr., during the earliest years of English settlement of that island. It is an analysis of the conflict between those symbolic forces through which the missionary and his adversaries, the Indian shamans, were conscious of themselves and in terms of which they peacefully fought out the historical relationship between their cultures. This conflict resulted in the most successful cross-cultural transference of English Puritan identity to have been documented in seventeenth-century New England.

Throughout southern New England the highest political status was that of sachem, which was hereditary within certain privileged male lineages. The sachem owned bounded territories, collected tribute from persons who farmed or hunted his lands and waters, exercised authority and administered justice over subjects within, and directed policy without. Within each maximal sachemdom, or tribe, a paramount sachem ruled a hierarchy of lesser sachems who presided over territorial subdivisions within the larger domain. The principal religious status was that of powwow or shaman. Shamans differed from other human beings because one or several forms of a spirit known as Hobbomock or Chepian had entered them in a vision. When John Eliot of Roxbury asked two Massachusetts

Indians how one became a powwow, they told him "that if any one of the Indians fall into any strange dreame wherein *Chepian* appeares unto them as a serpent, then the next day they tell the other *Indians* of it," whereupon the others "dance and rejoyce for what they tell them about this Serpent, and so they become their *Pawwaws*."[1]

The powwow functioned mainly as diviner, curer, and sorcerer. His divination techniques included inducing visions, which he then read as good or bad omens, direct encounters between his soul and other spirits, and insight available through his helping spirits. One or more shamans, the patient, an audience, and a variety of spirits participated in the cure, which sometimes took several hours. The powwow and audience commenced with a musical invocation, and throughout the ritual he sang and the onlookers responded and sometimes joined with him "like a Quire."[2] He removed sickness from the patient's body by the invisible cooperation of his spirits, which was seen by others as laying on hands, sucking, and spitting or blowing the objects away. If a wound proved to be curable, "he toucheth it not, but *askooke,* that is, the snake, or *wobsacuck,* that is, the eagle, sitteth on his shoulder, and licks the same. This none see but the powah, who tells them he doth it himself."[3] A successful powwow would show his spirit to the audience:

> The *Pawwaws* counted their Imps their Preservers, had them treasured up in their bodies, which they brought forth to hurt their enemies, and heal their friends; who when they had done some notable Cure, would shew the Imps in the palm of his Hand to the Indians who with much amazement looking on it, Deified them.[4]

Their methods succeeded with what might be described as emotional as well as physical disorders, and included skills such as bone setting and wound binding.[5]

Although the powwow was not responsible for all the misdeeds that Indians and Englishmen attributed to him, he directed his sorcery against enemies and political rivals in his own behalf and in behalf of clients both within and outside the sachemdom. Magical intrusion and dream-soul capture best describe his techniques. In the former case he prepared a physical object such as a leather arrowhead, a hair, or a bone from a dead creature, which his spirit conveyed to the victim's body:

> The mischief that the Pawwaws and Devils usually do to the common Indian this way, is both by outward and bodily hurt, or inward pain, torture, and distraction of mind, both which I have seen my self. To accom-

plish the first, the Devil doth abuse the real body of a Serpent, which comes directly towards the man in the house or in the field, looming or having a shadow about him like a man, and do shoot a bone (as they say) into the Indians Body, which sometimes killeth him.[6]

Dream-soul capture was the second sorcery technique: "by their Seizing something of the *Spirit* (as the Devil made *them* think) of such they intended to Torment or kill, while it wandered, in their Sleep: this they kept being in the Form of a Fly, closely imprisoned; and according as they dealt with this, so it Fared with the *Body* it belonged to."[7]

In contrast to the shamanistic beliefs of the Indians, the Puritan settlers in early New England did not believe that their God communicated directly with mortals. In their view, although "God of old did call and summon our fathers by predictions, dreams, visions, and certain illuminations . . . now there is no such calling to be expected . . . God having such a plentiful storehouse of directions in his holy word, there must not now any extraordinary revelations be expected."[8] Following John Calvin, they interpreted the prophets of enthusiastic religion, including enthusiastic Protestantism, as instruments of the devil and opposed to the needs of orderly Christian society.

Although conversion of the Indians to Christianity was among the several reasons why English Puritans emigrated to the New World, their first advances were inadvertent. In 1623 the planters at Plymouth feared losing their crops because of a drought which began in May and intensified during the summer. They appointed a day upon which they assembled for eight or nine hours to fast and pray for rain. In the morning and during the greater part of that day, the sky continued to be clear, but before they disassembled clouds appeared and the next morning rain fell and continued for fourteen days. This rain revived the corn and other fruits, "and made the Indians astonished to behold"[9] with the result that "all of them admired the goodness of our God towards us . . . showing the difference between their conjuration, and our invocation on the name of God for rain."[10]

The English God also performed in war. The Puritan victory over the Pequot stronghold at Mystic in 1637 was sudden and complete. Before that clash, a party of Pequot warriors taunted the English garrison at Saybrook to "come out and fight, if you dare. . . . we have one amongst us that if he could kill but one of you more, he would be equal with God, and as the *English* man's God is, so would he bee."[11] As John Mason's tiny army made its way overland toward the Pequot stronghold, his Narragansett allies trembled at the mention of the Pequot sachem Sassacus's name, "saying, *he was all one a God, nobody could kill him.*"[12] After the English victory, some three hundred Niantic warriors suspected of harboring Pequot refugees refused a challenge from forty of Mason's English, saying "*they would not Fight with* English Men, *for they were* Spirits."[13] Wequash, a Pequot or Niantic who lived among the Narragansetts and assisted the English as a scout, and later lived among the English, saw a message for himself in these events:

> before that time he had low apprehensions of our God, having conceived him to be (as he said) but a *Musketto* God, or a God like unto a Flye; and as meane thoughts of the English that served this God, that they were silly weake men; yet from that time he was convinced and perswaded that our God was a most dreadfull God . . . he could have no rest or quiet because he was ignorant of the *Englishman's God:* he went up and down bemoaning his condition, and filling every place where he came with sighes and groans.[14]

Hobbomock in the meantime appeared to Indians in the midst of Puritan Boston, some of whom may have been Pequot slaves, and warned them against acculturation to English ways:

> About this time the Indians, which were in our families, were much frighted with Hobbamock (as they call the devil) appearing to them in divers shapes, and persuading them to forsake the English, and not to come at the assemblies, nor to learn to read.[15]

Perhaps as many as twenty English families first settled on Martha's Vineyard in 1642 under the civil and religious leadership of Thomas Mayhew, Sr., who bought the patent that included Martha's Vineyard, Nantucket, and the Elizabeth Islands. Although the Pokanoket sachem Massasoit and his heirs considered the four sachemdoms and the three thousand or so native inhabitants of the island to be within their protectorate, the elder Mayhew did not seek their agreement in possessing their domains. He did intimate, however, to an important and probably Pokanoket sachem in a way that respected the proprieties of Indian culture that he considered himself to be superior to the Indian rulers:

> This Prince coming to *Martha's Vineyard,* with his usual attendants, being about *Eighty* Persons, well Armed, came to Mr. *Mayhew's* House, and being admitted, sat down; Mr. *Mayhew* entred the Room, but being acquainted with their Customes, took no notice of the Prince's being there

(it being with them in point of Honour incumbent on the Inferiour to Salute the Superiour:) a considerable time being past the Prince broke Silence, and said, *Sachem* (a word importing in their language not more than, Noble, or Worshipful) *Mr. Mayhew, are you well?*[16]

The patriarch's son, Thomas Mayhew, Jr., minister to the small English congregation of the island, developed an interest in converting the neighboring Indians. The father, having asserted his authority to the Indian ruler from the mainland, reassured the local island sachems that he would respect their rights in land transactions and would not challenge their internal power structure. He then proposed a separation between political and religious authority which offered the sachems security in the promise of indirect rule and opened the way for his missionary son to challenge the symbolic basis of Indian culture:

> and seeing his Son as aforesaid in a zealous indeavor for their Conversion, he judged it meet that *Moses* and *Aaron* joyn hands; he therefore prudently lets them know, that by order from his Master the King of *England,* he was to Govern the *English* which should inhabit these Islands; that his Master was in Power far above any of the *Indian Monarches;* but that as he was powerfull, so was he a great lover of *Justice;* that therefore he would in no measure invade their *Jurisdictions;* but on the contrary Assist them as need required; that *Religion* and *Government* were distinct things. Thus in no long time they conceived no ill Opinion of the *Christian Religion.*[17]

Thomas Jr. learned to speak the Algonquian language and made a number of friends with individual Indians and their families. Although he was aware of the supernatural categories of Indian culture such as manitou, the many deities they worshiped, and the spirits controlled by shamans, he interpreted these as variations of the devil. According to his understanding, the Indians of Martha's Vineyard were descended from Adam, but having lived apart from knowledge of God and Christ, they lived in captivity to the devil, who ruled over them through the shamans:

> When the Lord first brought me to these poor Indians on the *Vinyard,* they were mighty zealous and earnest in the Worship of False gods and Devils; their False gods were many, both of things in Heaven, Earth, and Sea: And there they had their Men-gods, Women-gods, and Children-gods, their Companies, and Fellowships of gods, or Divine Powers, guiding things amongst men, besides innumerable more feigned gods belong-

ing to many Creatures, to their Corn, and every Colour of it: The Devil also with his Angels had his Kingdom among them, in them; account him they did the terror of the Living, the God of the Dead.[18]

He perceived Indian social and religious practices as sin, which would destroy them unless he revealed what must be done for their salvation.

Thomas Jr. first converted a man named Hiacoomes, who was a marginal, low-ranking person in Indian society and who befriended the English at the time of their arrival. "His Descent was but mean, his Speech but slow, and his Countenance not very promising. He was therefore by the *Indian Sachims,* and others of their principal Men, looked on as but a mean Person, scarce worthy of their Notice or Regard."[19] Having noticed Hiacoomes's interest in English culture and religion, Thomas "invited him to come to his House every *Lord's-day* Evening, that so he might then more especially have a good Opportunity to treat with him about the things of GOD, and open the Mysteries of his Kingdom to him."[20] Hiacoomes welcomed this attention and absorbed Thomas's instruction "as a new-born Babe."[21] As Moses spoke to Aaron, the missionary instructed his convert on how to teach Christianity to his people. Thereafter, a number of sachems and powwows resented this once obscure person's increased intimacy with the English. In 1643 Hiacoomes with a company of English men visited a sachem named Pakeponesso at Chappaquiddick who "reproached him for his fellowship with the English, both in their civil and religious wayes, railing at him for his being obedient to them: *Hiacoomes* replyed that he was gladly obedient to the English, neither was it for the Indians hurt he did so; Upon which the Sagamore gave him a great blow on the face with his hand; but there being some English men present, they would not suffer the Sagamore to strike him again."[22] In this incident the English communicated that, although they would not invade Indian jurisdictions, they would protect their convert's well-being from Indian authorities. Hiacoomes concluded, *"I had one hand for injures, and the other for God, while I did receive wrong with the one, the other laid the greater hold on God."*[23]

That same year, 1643, a strange disease startled the Indian inhabitants of Martha's Vineyard: "they ran up and down as if delirious, till they could run no longer; they would make their Faces as black as a Coal, and snatch up any Weapon, as tho they would do Mischief with it, and speak great swelling Words, but yet they did no Harm."[24] The majority perceived this disease "and all other Calamities" as a warning not to depart from tradition. Hiacoomes, however, who did not contract the illness, saw his immunity as cause for increasing his commitment to the English.[25]

The sachem Pakeponesso confronted Hiacoomes with the argument that Christian conversion would deprive him of the sources within Indian culture of health and healing:

> I wonder (said he) *that you that are a young man, having a wife and two children, should love the English and their wayes, and forsake the Pawwawes; what would you do if any of you should be sick? whither would you go for help? I say, if I were in your case there should be nothing draw me from our gods and Pawwawes.*[26]

In his own opinion, Thomas Mayhew, Jr.'s success as a missionary owed in part to what he described as "several providences which hath advantaged my progresse."[27] The sachem Pakeponesso who once previously had hit Hiacoomes and who asked him what he would do if he were sick, took a prominent part in one of these providences by being struck by lightning through the smoke hole of his wigwam: "there fell a great judgment of God on this Sagamore . . . a great flash of lightning . . . full of the vengeance of God . . . strook *Pakeponesso* down dead for a long time."[28] Hiacoomes, protected by Englishmen on earth and lightning from heaven, concluded that "God did answer him."[29]

What Mayhew described as a universal sickness afflicted the Vineyard Indians in 1645, and because Hiacoomes and his family escaped its effects, and those who listened to his teaching suffered less, it proved to be a breaking point in openness to Christian instruction. In contrast to the interpretation of the sickness of 1643 as a warning against departure from traditional ways, the sickness of 1645 seemed to many to be a sign of the Christian God's favor to his Indian believers. A sachem named Myoxeo invited Hiacoomes to explain the ways of the English God, and . . . asked him how many gods the English worshiped:

> he answered one God, whereupon *Myoxeo* reckoned up about 37 principal gods he had, and shall I (said he) throw away these 37 gods for one? *Hiacoomes* replyed, what do you think of your self? I have throwne away all these, and a great many more some yeers ago, yet am preserved as you see this day; you speak true said *Myoxeo;* therefore I will throw away all my gods too, and serve that one God with you.[30]

Having persuaded Myoxeo of the greater power of his God, Hiacoomes explained the sacrificial meaning of Christ's death and assured him that since Christ had died for humanity's sins, they could shed them without fear and with hope for a new life. He thereby conveyed the missionary's reinterpretation of Indian culture as sin and referred to the anger in store from the Father for those who did not seek deliverance from their sins through the Son:

> *Hiacoomes* told them all, he did fear this great God only, and also in a speciall manner that the Son of God did suffer death to satisfie the wrath of God his Father, for all those that did trust in him, and forsake their sinnes. . . . He reckoned up to them many of their sins, as having many gods, going to Pawwawes; and *Hiacoomes* told me himself, that this was the first time that ever he saw the Indians sensible of their sins.[31]

Another sachem, Towanquattick, invited Mayhew to preach to him and his people, and the missionary agreed to do so on two Sundays each month. Towanquattick confessed that his culture had lost something which it once possessed and which Mayhew translated as wisdom. The sachem told Mayhew that he and his people were as empty jars waiting to be filled:

> *a long time agon; they had wise men, which in a grave manner taught the people knowledge; but they are dead, and their wise-dome is buried with them.* . . . *he hoped that the time of knowledge* was now come. . . . *I should be to them, as one that stands by a running River, filling many vessels* . . . with everlasting knowledge.[32]

Mayhew prevailed over shamans in several curing situations. In the first case he prayed for and restored to health an old man whom the powwows had given up for dead. Mayhew persuaded the old man of the "weaknesse and wickednesse of the *Pawwaws* power; and that if health were to be found, it must be had from him that gave life, and breath, and all things."[33] On another occasion he prayed for and revived the son of Pakeponesso who happily thanked God for his recovery, fell ill again, and sought the aid of shamans, whereupon Mayhew predicted that he would die. "I also added," wrote Mayhew, "the example of Ahaziah, who because he had the knowledge of the Great God, and sought unto an inferiour God, God was angry with him and killed him: And so for that [the sick Indian] was informed of the true God, and is fallen from him to the earthen gods here below; that God will kill him also; and so it shortly came to Passe."[34] On a later occasion the powwows warned the son of Towanquattick, who was feverish, that if he did not seek their help he would die. He ignored their warning and sent for Mayhew who prayed for him in the Indian language and bled him a little, whereupon he recovered. In another case a convert refused help offered by a shaman for his wife who was in labor and she nevertheless "obtained a merciful deliverance by prayer."[35] When Hiacoomes's five-day-old infant died, Mayhew comforted those at the burial by speaking of the Resurrection and reassured them that good children and adults would be with God.[36]

The Indians of southern New England explained disease in two principal ways.[37] First there were those diseases diagnosed by the shaman as incurable which were thought to have been sent by the creator Cautantowwit because of anger. Over these the shaman had no control. Second there were those diagnosed as curable which were believed to be caused by the shaman's sorcery and which were potentially curable by shamans. In his first curing success with the old man whom the powwows had given over for dead, Mayhew proved that his God could cure in a situation where the shamans had declared they had no power. In the other cases he demonstrated that his God could heal converts as well as the powwows could heal their followers. He stressed further that the shamans' sorcery was ineffective against Christians, and thus converts were protected against a major source of physical affliction. Hiacoomes dealt a dramatic blow to the powwows' confidence that they could injure Christian Indians by sorcery when, one Sunday after meeting, a shaman announced to the Indians present that he could kill all of them through sorcery. Hiacoomes replied, "that he would be in the midst of all the Pawwawes of the Iland that they could procure, and they should do their utmost they could against him, and when they did their worst by their witchcrafts to kill him, he would without feare set himself against them."[38] The shaman, intimidated by the challenge, acknowledged that it was true.

Thus, to continue to believe in shamans denied one the greater healing power of the English God and made one vulnerable to the injuries believed to be caused by shamans to which Christians were immune. Furthermore, Mayhew interpreted all suffering among nonbelievers as punishment from God for their sins, which included foremost the refusal to accept God's way. Mayhew thereby usurped the shamans' final power, the ability to cure sorcery victims, by interpreting sorcery as an expression of God's displeasure with those who continued to believe in shamans:

An instance [of magical intrusion sorcery] whereof I can give, whereby it may the more plainly appear, that it is a great mercy to be delivered therefrom; and it is of a youth, who living with his Parents upon a neck of Land, They did not pray unto *Jehovah*, yet their Neighbours who lived there with them, did: This Youth was hurt after the same manner, and then presently his Parents pulled down the house they lived in, and fled to an Island near by, where I saw the Indian thus hurt in his Thigh, he was greviously tormented, and his Kindred about him mourning, not knowing where to find any comfort, or help, for cure could not be had from their gods or Pawwaws: I then took the opportunity to reason with them about their way, with the best wisdom God gave me, but all in vain, for they would not hear to seek the true God, notwithstanding he had shewn his displeasure so apparently against them for their former refusing of Him, but they still followed in their wonted Serpentine Machinations: The Pawwaws, and their devillish train, with their horrible outcries, hollow bleatings, painful wrestlings, and smiting their own bodies, sought deliverance, but all in vain, for he died miserably.[39]

Mayhew checked the shaman's advantages as healer and sorcerer at all points. His God could cure sicknesses the shamans believed to be beyond their curative powers. The shamans found themselves unable to injure Christians through sorcery, and the missionary offered conversion as a cure to persons afflicted by sorcery. Only those who steadfastly followed the shamans could be harmed by sorcery. Although shamans retained the power to bewitch pagans, God made their sorcery incurable for those who refused to convert, thus denying shamans the ability to cure what they could cause. Finally, Mayhew thanked Providence that during the first seven years of his efforts, his converts enjoyed good health.[40] The shamans felt a loss in their ability to cure and to inflict sorcery and concluded that their deities were inferior and subservient to the God of the English:

This *Pawwaw* declaring by what means the Lord took him off this devillish Trade . . . had many searchings of heart about his *Pawwawing,* and did think it was not a good way, and that God was angry with him for it; for said he my Wife hath been a long time sick, and the more I *Pawwaw* for her, the sicker she is; And this doth agree with an observation of the *Indians* of this Island, *viz.* that since the Word of God hath been taught unto them in this place, the *Pawwaws* have been much foiled in their devillish tasks, and that instead of curing have rather killed many.[41]

. . . a converted *Sachim,* who was before a *Pawwaw,* did in his publick Protestation afterwards declare as followeth . . . That having often employed his God, which appeared unto him in the Form of a Snake, to kill, wound, or lame such as he intended Mischief to, he employed the said Snake to kill, and that failing, to wound or lame *Hiacoomes,* the first *Indian* Convert on the Island; all which prov'd ineffectual. And that, having seriously considered the said *Hiacoomes's* Assertion, that none of the *Paw-*

waws could hurt him, since his God whom he now served was the great God to whom theirs were subservient, he resolved to worship the true God.[42]

By 1650 two shamans had rejected their spirits and with great emotion converted to Christianity. In converting they confessed to Mayhew the mysteries of their calling in terms of the Puritan model of Indian culture as sin. These statements, offered at the moment of surrender to the missionary, are the most explicit expressions by Indians of their world view to have been recorded in New England in the seventeenth century:

> One of them did then discover the bottom of his witchcraft, confessing that at first he came to be a *Pawwaw* by Diabolical Dreams, wherein he saw the Devill in the likenesse of four living Creatures; one was like a man which he saw in the Ayre, and this told him that he did know all things upon the Island, and what was to be done; and this he said had its residence over his whole body. Another was like a Crow, and did look out sharply to discover mischiefs coming towards him, and had its residence in his head. The third was like to a Pidgeon, and had its place in his breast, and was very cunning about any businesse. The fourth was like a Serpent, very subtile to doe mischiefe, and also to doe great cures, and these he said were meer Devills, and such as he had trusted to for safety, and did labor to raise up for the accomplishment of any thing in his diabolicall craft, but now he saith, that he did desire that the Lord would free him from them, and that he did repent in his heart, because of his sin.[43]
>
> And as himself said he had been possessed from the crowne of the head to the soal of the foot with *Pawwawnomas,* not onely in the shape of living Creatures, as Fowls, Fishes, and creeping things, but Brasse, Iron, and Stone. It was therefore the more to be acknowledged the work of God, that he should forsake this way, his friends, his gain, to follow the Lord, whose wayes are so despisable in the eyes of devillish minded men.[44]

When they rejected their spirits, they did so in a dramatic and literal way:

> . . . and they came much convinced of their sinnes that they had lived in, and especially of their *Pawwawing,* saying, I throw it from me with hatred of it, being sorry that ever I medled with it. And now I have heard of *Jehovah,* by his help I put it under my feet, and hope to trample it down in the dust with the Devill and *Pawwawnomas* (or Imps) I throw it into the fire, and burn it.[45]

By 1652 eight more *powwows* converted. Some felt their spirits struggling for several years afterwards. The shaman who spoke of his attempt to injure Hiacoomes with the help of a magical snake told Mayhew that the snake continued to appear to him for seven years after his conversion. As these spirits slipped away, God and Christ took their place:

> A Pawwaw told me . . . That after he had been brought by the Word of God to hate the Devil, and to renounce his Imps . . . his Imps remained still in him for some months tormenting of his flesh, and troubling of his mind . . . he asked me . . . That if a Pawwaw had his Imps gone from him, what he should have instead of them to preserve him? Whereunto it was Answered . . . he should have the Spirit of Christ dwelling in him . . . and that if he did set himself against his Imps, by the strength of God they should all flee away like Muskeetoes: He told me . . . That ever since that very time God hath in mercy delivered him from them, he is not troubled with any pain (as formerly) in his Bed, nor dreadful visions of the night, but through the blessing of God, he doth lie down in ease.[46]

Conversion ritual was not described in great detail. A convert took the hand of Reverend Mayhew or one of the members of the Christian Indian community and said, *"I do love you, and do greatly desire to go along with you for God's sake."*[47] Mayhew and Hiacoomes gave their lectures and prayers and sang Psalms in the Indian language. On occasion an elderly convert would remind younger Indians of the worthiness of "the old customes of the ancient Heathen, preferring them before those wayes of their own they were now in, yet acknowledging they were farre inferior to those wayes of God they had now begun."[48] By 1651 the convert community had grown to 199 men, women, and children, divided between two meetings, each under an Indian minister.[49] Mayhew built a school to teach reading to the converts and began plans for a separate Christian Indian town. By 1652 the convert population exceeded three hundred persons in addition to numerous nonconverts who came for religious instruction. In 1652 the converts requested a covenant which Mayhew wrote and which established the foundation for civil and religious authority among the Christian Indians:

> *Wee the distressed* Indians *of the Vineyard (or* Nope the Indian name of the Island) *That beyond all memory have been without the True God, without a Teacher, and without a Law, the very Servants of Sin and Satan, and without Peace, for God did justly vex us for our sins; having lately through his mercy heard of the Name of the True God, the Name of his Son Christ Jesus, with the holy Ghost the Comforter, three Persons, but one most Glorious God, whose Name is* JEHOVAH: *We do praise His Glorious Greatness, and in the sorrow of*

our hearts, and shame of our faces, we do acknowledg and renounce our great
and many sins, that we and our Fathers have lived in, do run unto him for
mercy, and pardon for Christ Jesus sake; and we do this day through the bless-
ing of God upon us, and trusting to his gracious help, give up our selves in this
Convenant, Wee, Our Wives, and Children, to serve JEHOVAH: *And we do this*
day chuse JEHOVAH *to be our God in Christ Jesus, our Teacher, our Law-giver*
in his Word, our King, our Judg, our Ruler by his Magistrates and Ministers;
to fear God Himself, and to trust in Him alone for Salvation, both of Soul and
Body, in this present Life, and the Everlasting Life to come, through his mercy
in Christ Jesus our Savior, and Redeemer, and by the might of his Holy Spirit;
to whom with the Father and Son, be all Glory everlasting. Amen.[50]

By 1657 the Christian Indian community included several hundred fully
converted men and women and many hundred more who attended services
but whose conversion was incomplete.[51] In that year, 1657, Mayhew made
a voyage to England on business related to his wife's brother's death and
took with him a young Indian minister to testify to the clergyman's success
as a missionary. The ship and all its passengers disappeared at sea: "It was
never known what disaster overtook her, but it only came to be known that
she was long and then longer overdue."[52] The bereaved Indians of Martha's
Vineyard built a little monument on the place where Mayhew last met
with them before leaving on his voyage: "It is a part of the legendary lore
of this spot, that no Indian passed by it without casting a stone into a heap
that, by their custom, had thus grown like a cairn, in remembrance of him,
to be a great monument to this sad event in their lives."[53] The father took
over the missionary program in his son's place and continued the process
of institutional change through religious conversion. Neither the father
nor the son nor the converts themselves discussed the possibility of inte-
grating converts within the English Christian community. All thought
only of the creation of Christian Indian towns and churches which would
be similar to those of the English, subordinate to them, and geographically
separate. Although the father once emphasized that religion and government were distinct things, change in one enabled change in the other:

When afterwards the number of the *Christian Indians* were increased
among them, he perswaded them to admit of the *Counsils* of the *Judicious*
Christians among themselves, and in cases of more than ordinary consequence of a *Jury* for Tryal; when likewise he promised his assistance and
direction with the *Prince;* when notwithstanding the *Princes assent* was to
be obtained, though he were *no Christian.* Thus within a few years there
was a happy Government settled among them, and *Records* kept of all Ac-

tions and *Acts* passed in their several Courts, by such who having learned to *Write* fairly were appointed thereto. The *Princes* with their *Sachims* (or Nobles) made Publick acknowledgment of their Subjection to the King of *England,* being notwithstanding mindful to be understood as Subordinate Princes, to Govern according to the Laws of God and the King.[54]

The Martha's Vineyard conversion is an example of deep and rapid voluntary change to colonial ideology and thus differs from the majority of religious movements studied among colonized people which are characterized by their departure from the ideology of the dominant group. Of all the Puritan missionaries who worked among New England Indians in the seventeenth century, Thomas Mayhew, Jr., was one of if not the most successful in the thoroughness and permanence of his conversions and in the number of converts and the longevity of the Christian Indian communities that he helped create. The conversion process began with the existence in the missionary's mind of a model of Indian culture that was accurate and informed in its comprehension of detail but that formulated these details in a way that reflected the missionary's world view. Mayhew perceived Indian symbols and institutions as examples of false gods, devils, and sinful living, which brought unhappiness to those who adhered to them and punishment from his God to those who, when offered the opportunity to convert, refused to do so. The fact that the missionary provided Indians with an alternative interpretation of their culture in itself did not motivate them to convert. Acceptance at the emotional level by the Indians of this outside perspective on themselves required a mutually understood expression of social dominance by the English and an active but not coercive effort by the missionary to offer the symbols of his culture. A brief consideration of the missionary impact of Roger Williams in Narragansett country and John Eliot in Massachusetts Bay suggests that a shift in authority in favor of the English was a precondition for Indian populations to be open to religious persuasion and that the more implicit and less threatening this shift, the more favorably Indian subjects responded to religious assimilation.

At one extreme, when Roger Williams as a political fugitive spoke of his God to the powerful Narragansetts, they accepted that *"Englishmans* God made *English* Men, and the heavens and Earth there!" yet concluded confidently that "their Gods made them and the Heaven, and Earth where they dwell."[55] In a situation of relative equality the Narragansetts understood the English perspective but maintained their own. At the other extreme, a catastrophic change in power relationships also did not favor openness to the English world view. The United Puritan Colonies overwhelmed the Narragansetts in King Philip's War, and after their devastation the Narragansetts angrily rejected English religion for over half a century. When they did convert in the mid–eighteenth century, they redefined Christianity in their own terms.[56] John Eliot was more successful as a missionary than was Roger Williams but less successful than Mayhew. He aimed his efforts at Indian populations that had not been destroyed by war but had been more explicitly weakened by disease and dominated by colonial settlement than those of Martha's Vineyard, and his program involved more coercion. On 4 November 1646, shortly after Eliot began his missionary efforts in earnest, the Massachusetts General Court enacted legislation that forbade all persons within its jurisdiction both English and Indian to deny or ridicule the Christian God, with the harsh incentive that if any persons were to break that law they would be put to death. As Francis Jennings commented, "An Indian would think twice about heckling Eliot after learning about that law."[57] The court also forbade the practice of Indian shamanistic ritual and backed this up with heavy fines for offenders. In writing of Eliot's program, Neal Salisbury observed: "The missionaries moved in where traditional communities had been shattered. With English domination a fact of life, the praying towns seemed to offer many natives the only means of restoring a viable sense of community."[58] Consistent with the greater coerciveness of Eliot's missionary environment, his model of the conversion process stressed behavioral obedience to Puritan social form as a prerequisite to religious transformation. Indians, according to Eliot, "must have visible civility before they can rightly injoy visible sanctities."[59] Mayhew's approach was the reverse of Eliot's in this regard. Conversion for him began with the implanting of English religious symbols, after which the converts voluntarily restructured their families and political institutions in the direction of English models.

Without coercion, conversion appeared as a choice to the Martha's Vineyard Indians, who had been dominated gently at the political level and who consequently began to doubt the efficacy of their religious powers. Although the Mayhews assumed greater legitimacy than the Indian rulers, they offered to rule and to purchase land through intact native institutions and never threatened them with violence for not complying with their missionary program. Nevertheless, these Indians had seen from a distance a few years earlier the sudden, almost magical, destruction of the Pequot tribe by English soldiers, their island had been settled by colonists with no prior agreement, and the leader of these colonists, Thomas Mayhew the elder, insinuated his superiority to the paramount Indian ruler. Thus a healthy Indian community was colonized by what appeared to be a peaceful enclave from a more powerful culture. The missionary offered Indians the opportunity to participate in and enjoy the protection of this new order and let them know in their own language and through his talents as a healer that there was no wisdom in the customs that traditionally had guided them. In this context, a few and then increasingly more Indians accepted this alternative interpretation of themselves as followers of the devil and sin and experienced a profound weakening of confidence in the shamans and in the religious powers they controlled. In contrast to general expectations concerning social transformation through religion, where a new order is built from the collapse of the old, deep and integrated change occurred here among a people whose health, culture, and institutions were relatively undisturbed at the moment of conversion. In comparison with other cases where Indian conversion occurred in seventeenth- and eighteenth-century New England, the Martha's Vineyard conversions indicate that where the traditional culture was most intact, the transference of the dominant culture was most complete.

Author's Postscript

"Conversion from Indian to Puritan" is an account of a turning point in the religious consciousness and social history of the native peoples of Martha's Vineyard, or *Nope*, as the island was known to its Indian inhabitants. The essay was intended to be a close-to-the-sources interpretation of the conversion to Reformed Christianity on the part of the indigenous Massachusett-speaking Indians following English colonization in 1642 under the leadership of Thomas Mayhew, Sr. In this account I attempted to understand, event by event, the interactional process through which the missionaries, Thomas Mayhew, Jr., and Thomas Mayhew, Sr., persuaded the local sachems, shamans, and their followers to lose confidence in or at least abandon aspects of their ancestral symbols, to internalize the English projection of Indian religion as sin, and to embrace certain important religious symbols of English culture. At the end of the first paragraph, I wrote that I was aiming at "an analysis of the conflict between those symbolic forces through which the missionary and his adversaries, the Indian shamans, were conscious of themselves and in terms of which they peacefully fought out the historical relationship between their cultures." I was interested in the arguments and strategies by which missionaries challenged Indian religious belief and practice and in the process whereby the native Massachusett of Martha's Vineyard reordered themselves socially and symbolically as Christians. I was and continue to be particularly interested in understanding both the Indian and the English perspectives on what occurred as well as in the bearing of colonization throughout the region on Indian self-consciousness. Then, as now, the task is complicated because the sources mainly reflect English colonial perspectives.

Two very important books, Alden T. Vaughan's *New England Frontier: Puritans and Indians, 1620–1675* (1965; revised ed., New York: W. W. Norton, 1979) and Francis Jennings's *The Invasion of America: Indians, Colonialism, and the Cant of Conquest* (Chapel Hill: University of North Carolina Press, 1975), dominated scholarly attention to seventeenth-century New England Puritan missionary activities in the 1960s and 1970s and continue to shape contemporary debate. Most recent scholarship, including this article, has moved with the direction of post-colonial intellectual currents in the humanities and social sciences and has suggested ways in which Native Americans used Christian affiliation to survive, resist, and protect themselves from the destructive impacts of colonization while attempting to preserve as much of their cultural and community identity as possible.[60] The American frontier historian James Axtell, for example, observed that: "By accepting the Christian minister or priest as the functional equivalent of a native shaman and by giving traditional meanings to Christian rites, dogmas, and deities, the Indians ensured the survival of native culture by taking on the protective coloration of the invaders' religion."[61] Some new work (including that of James Axtell and Richard W. Cogley) has greatly refined our understanding of the political and theological contexts that shaped seventeenth-century missionary theory and practice.[62] Charles L. Cohen, an American historian and authority on Puritan conversion experience, in an original reading of the Natick conversion testimonies, suggests ways in which Indians' cultural background influenced their ability to understand some aspects of Christian teaching more readily than others: "To be born again, Amerindians had to learn not only the dogmas of creation and Fall, Passion and resurrection, but also the behaviors of grace-piety and godly love. They grasped the former more readily than the latter."[63] In her analysis of a complex legal case involving a Punkapoag woman, Ann Marie Plane, also an American colonial historian, raises and illuminates the less-understood question of how Christian conversion affected Indian women.[64] A number of case studies (notably those by Mandell, Ronda, Van Lonkhuyzen, and Simmons) explore the long-term aftermaths of seventeenth-century missionary activities in southern New England.[65] To my knowledge, no other scholar of New England colonization has replicated this particular study, with its attention to Indian and English cultural perspectives and the processes of religious persuasion, abandonment, and conversion.

While viewing missionary and Indian interaction, "Conversion from

Indian to Puritan" addresses the question of how Europeans and Native Americans understood each other in the earliest settlement period and how these understandings affected their relationships. From the first moments of contact between Europeans and Native Americans, both peoples tried to explain the "others" to themselves in terms of internal mythic categories. Numerous Indian traditions attest to the symbolic ways in which they remembered the unprecedented ships, people, and technology that entered their lives in the sixteenth and seventeenth centuries. For example, early English accounts mention that Indians at first described their ships as floating islands, giant birds, and as the return from the sea of their culture-hero known as Wetucks or Maushop.[66] In two important essays and in the two-volume monograph with the North American linguist Ives Goddard, Kathleen Bragdon (an anthropologist and authority on the New England region) has provided original perspectives on continuity and change in the Indian world view and social institutions in the Christian Indian communities on Martha's Vineyard and throughout the Massachusett-speaking region of southeastern Massachusetts.[67] "It was in the Massachusett language," Goddard and Bragdon note, "that John Eliot produced his translation of the complete Bible." These two volumes, with their attention to "all known manuscript writings in the Massachusett language by native speakers," are an unparalleled achievement in New England ethnohistorical scholarship. The Massachusett writings "reflect aspects of everyday life among the Massachusett speakers from the 1660s to the 1750s, a period when they formed largely self-governing, self-sufficient Christian communities."[68]

Readers interested in new overviews of the Indian cultures of southern New England in the early and later historic periods will find an abundance of recent scholarship, including tribal histories,[69] regional overviews,[70] annotated reprints,[71] and richly documented edited collections that include anthropological, archaeological, historical, literary, and Native American perspectives on Indian life in this region.[72] Kathleen Bragdon's *Native People of Southern New England, 1500–1650* (Norman: University of Oklahoma Press, 1996) is the most comprehensive and authoritative ethnohistoric portrait of the region.

Interestingly, the Indian Christian converts of Martha's Vineyard maintained oral traditions, particularly of the indigenous culture-hero known as Maushop, that are known even today among persons of Indian descent on the island. I assembled all known published and manuscript texts of the Maushop legends as well as some I recorded from living Gay Head Wampanoag in *Spirit of the New England Tribes: Indian History and Folklore, 1620–1984*. In closing "Conversion from Indian to Puritan," I wrote that "In comparison with other cases where Indian conversion occurred in seventeenth-and eighteenth-century New England, the Martha's Vineyard conversions indicate that where the traditional culture was most intact, the transference of the dominant culture was most complete." Taking account of the unbroken continuity of the culture-hero legends on Martha's Vineyard, I would now add that here, where the transference of the dominant culture was most complete, aspects of the traditional culture persisted most intact.

Notes

1. John Eliot, in [John Wilson's] "The Day-Breaking if not The Sun-Rising of the Gospell With the Indians in New-England" (1647), *Massachusetts Historical Society Collections*, 3d ser. 4 (1834): 20.

2. Roger Williams, *A Key into the Language of America* (1643), ed. Howard Chapin (Providence: Rhode Island and Providence Plantations Tercentenary Committee, 1936), p. 198.

3. Edward Winslow, "Good News From New England" (1624), in *Chronicles of the Pilgrim Fathers of the Colony of Plymouth*, ed. Alexander Young (Boston, 1841), pp. 357–58.

4. Thomas Mayhew, in John Eliot and Thomas Mayhew's "Tears of Repentance: Or, A further Narrative of the Progress of the Gospel Amongst the Indians in New-England" (1653), *Massachusetts Historical Society Collections*, 3d ser. 4 (1834): 202.

5. For a more extended discussion of the shamans' healing powers, see my "Southern New England Shamanism: An Ethnographic Reconstruction," in *Papers of the Seventh Algonquian Conference, 1975*, ed. William Cowan (Ottawa: Carleton University, 1976), pp. 239–43.

6. Thomas Mayhew, in Eliot and Mayhew's "Tears of Repentance," p. 204.

7. Matthew Mayhew, *A Brief Narrative of the Success which the Gospel hath had among the Indians* (Boston, 1694), p. 14.

8. Robert Cushman, in Young's *Chronicles of the Pilgrim Fathers*, p. 240.

9. William Bradford, *Of Plymouth Plantation, 1620–1647*, ed. Samuel E. Morison (New York: Modern Library, 1952), p. 131.

10. Winslow, in Young's *Chronicles of the Pilgrim Fathers*, p. 350.

11. John Underhill, *Newes From America* (1638), ed. David H. Underhill (New York: Underhill Society of America, 1902), p. 16.

12. Cotton Mather, *Magnalia Christi Americana: or the Ecclesiastical History of New-England*, 2 vols. (Hartford, 1820), 2:481.

13. John Mason, *A Brief History of the Pequot War*, ed. Thomas Prince (Boston, 1736), p. 20.

14. *New England's First Fruits* (1643) (New York, 1865), pp. 11–12.

15. John Winthrop, *The History of New England*, ed. James Savage, 2 vols. (Boston, 1825), 1:254.

16. Matthew Mayhew, *A Brief Narrative*, p. 10.

17. Matthew Mayhew, *A Brief Narrative*, p. 33.

18. Thomas Mayhew, in Eliot and Mayhew's "Tears of Repentance," pp. 201–2.

19. Experience Mayhew, *Indian Converts: Or Some Account of the Lives and Dying Speeches of a considerable Number of the Christianized Indians of Martha's Vineyard, in New-England* (London, 1727), pp. 1–2.

20. Experience Mayhew, *Indian Converts*, p. 2.

21. Experience Mayhew, *Indian Converts*, p. 2.

22. Thomas Mayhew, in Henry Whitfield's "The Light appearing more and more towards the perfect Day, Or, A farther Discovery of the present state of the Indians in New-England" (1651), *Massachusetts Historical Society Collections*, 3d ser. 4 (1834): 109–10.

23. Thomas Mayhew, in Whitfield's "Light appearing," p. 110.

24. Experience Mayhew, *Indian Converts*, p. 3.

25. Experience Mayhew, *Indian Converts*, p. 3.

26. Thomas Mayhew, in Whitfield's "Light appearing," p. 110.

27. Thomas Mayhew, in Edward Winslow's "The Glorious Progresse of the Gospel amongst the Indians in New-England" (1649), *Massachusetts Historical Society Collections*, 3d ser. 4 (1834): 77.

28. Thomas Mayhew, in Whitfield's "Light appearing," p. 110.

29. Thomas Mayhew, in Whitfield's "Light appearing," p. 111.

30. Thomas Mayhew, in Whitfield's "Light appearing," p. 111.

31. Thomas Mayhew, in Whitfield's "Light appearing," p. 111–12.

32. Thomas Mayhew, in Whitfield's "Light appearing," p. 112.

33. Thomas Mayhew, in Winslow's "Glorious Progresse," p. 77.

34. Thomas Mayhew, in Winslow's "Glorious Progresse," p. 77.

35. Thomas Mayhew, in Whitfield's "Light appearing," p. 115.

36. Thomas Mayhew, in Whitfield's "Light appearing," p. 116.

37. For further discussion of the structure of the New England Indian world view, see my "Southern New England Shamanism," pp. 217–56, and *Spirit of The New England Tribes: Indian History and Folklore, 1620–1984* (Hanover and London: University Press of New England, 1986), pp. 37–64; and Frank Shuffelton's "Indian Devils and Pilgrim Fathers: Squanto, Hobomok, and the English Conception of Indian Religion," *New England Quarterly* 49 (1976): 108–16.

38. Thomas Mayhew, in Whitfield's "Light appearing," p. 116.

39. Thomas Mayhew, in Eliot and Mayhew's "Tears of Repentance," p. 204.

40. Thomas Mayhew, in Whitfield's "Light appearing," p. 116.

41. Thomas Mayhew, in Henry Whitfield's "Strength out of Weaknesse; Or a Glorious Manifestation Of the further Progresse of the Gospel among the Indians in New-England" (1652), *Massachusetts Historical Society Collections*, 3d ser. 4 (1834): 187.

42. Experience Mayhew, *Indian Converts*, p. 7.

43. Thomas Mayhew, in Whitfield's "Strength out of Weaknesse," p. 186.

44. Thomas Mayhew, in Whitfield's "Strength out of Weaknesse," p. 187.

45. Thomas Mayhew, in Whitfield's "Strength out of Weaknesse," pp. 185–86.

46. Thomas Mayhew, in Whitfield's "Strength out of Weaknesse," pp. 205–6.

47. Thomas Mayhew, in Whitfield's "Light appearing," p. 115.

48. Thomas Mayhew, in Whitfield's "Light appearing," p. 114.

49. Thomas Mayhew, in Whitfield's "Strength out of Weaknesse," p. 188.

50. Thomas Mayhew, in Whitfield's "Strength out of Weaknesse," p. 207.

51. Matthew Mayhew, *A Brief Narrative*, p. 19.

52. Charles Edward Banks, *The History of Martha's Vineyard*, 3 vols. (Boston, 1911), 1:228.

53. Banks, *History of Martha's Vineyard*, 1:229; Constance A. Crosby, "The Algonkian Spiritual Landscape," in *Algonkians of New England: Past and Present*, ed. Peter Benes, Dublin Seminar for New England Folklife Annual Proceedings for 1991 (Boston: Boston University, 1993), pp. 38–41, and my *Spirit of the New England Tribes*, pp. 251–55.

54. Matthew Mayhew, *A Brief Narrative*, pp. 33–34.

55. Williams, *A Key Into the Language of America*, p. 123. For a discussion by Williams concerning Indian conversion, see his *Christenings Make Not Christians* (1645), ed. Henry M. Dexter (Providence, 1881).

56. W. De Loss Love, *Samson Occum and the Christian Indians of New England* (Boston, 1899), pp. 190–95, and my "Red Yankees: Narragansett Conversion in the Great Awakening," *American Ethnologist* 10 (May 1983): 253–71; and my and Cheryl L. Simmons's *Old Light on Separate Ways: The Narragansett Diary of Joseph Fish, 1765–1776* (Hanover and London: University Press of New England, 1982).

57. Francis Jennings, *The Invasion of America: Indians, Colonialism, and the Cant of Conquest* (Chapel Hill: University of North Carolina Press, 1975), p. 241.

58. Neal Salisbury, *Conquest of the "Savage": Puritans, Puritan Missionaries and Indians, 1620–1680* (Ph.D. diss., University of California, Los Angeles, 1972), p. 205. The author's understanding of the Mayhew missionary approach has been aided by the discussion in chap. 5 of this dissertation, pp. 167–75. See also Salisbury, "Red Puritans: The Praying Indians of Massachusetts Bay and John Eliot," *William and Mary Quarterly* 29 (1972): 335–66.

59. John Eliot, in "Three Letters of John Eliot and a Bill of Lading of the *Mayflower*," ed. Rendel Harris, *Bulletin of the John Rylands Library* 5 (1918–20): 104. For a discussion of the implicit and explicit meanings of this phrase, see James Axtell's important chapter entitled "Reduce Them to Civility," in *The Invasion Within: The Contest of Cultures in Colonial North America* (New York and Oxford: Oxford University Press, 1985), pp. 131–78, and Richard W. Cogley, "John Eliot and the Millennium," *Religion and American Culture* 1 (1991): 244.

60. Relevant essays by James Axtell include "Reduce Them to Civility," "The Tribe of True Believers," and "Preachers, Priests, and Pagans," in *The Invasion Within*, and "Some Thoughts on the Ethnohistory of Missions" and "Were Indian Conversions Bonafide?" in *After Columbus: Essays in the Ethnohistory of Colonial North America* (New York: Oxford University Press, 1988). See also Elise M. Brenner, "To Pray or to Be Prey: That Is the Question: Strategies for Cultural Autonomy of Massachusetts Praying Town Indians," *Ethnohistory* 27 (1980): 135–52; Robert James Naeher, "Dialogue in the Wilderness: John Eliot and the Indian Exploration of Pu-

ritanism as a Source of Meaning, Comfort, and Ethnic Survival," *New England Quarterly* 62 (1989): 346–68; James P. Ronda, "Generations of Faith: The Christian Indians of Martha's Vineyard," *William and Mary Quarterly* 38 (1981): 369–94; and Harold W. Van Lonkhuyzen, "A Reappraisal of the Praying Indians: Acculturation, Conversion, and Identity at Natick, Massachusetts, 1646–1730," *New England Quarterly* 63 (1990): 396–428 (see chap. 8 of *New England Encounters*).

61. Axtell, *After Columbus*, p. 54.

62. Axtell, "Reduce Them to Civility," pp. 131–78; Cogley, "John Eliot and the Millennium," pp. 227–50, and "Idealism vs. Materialism in the Study of Puritan Missions to the Indians," *Method & Theory in the Study of Religion* 3 (1991): 165–82. In my article, I comment upon differences in missionary practice and effectiveness between Thomas Mayhew, Jr., and John Eliot. Richard Cogley explores this contrast at length in "Two Approaches to Indian Conversion in Puritan New England: The Missions of Thomas Mayhew Jr. and John Eliot," *Historical Journal of Massachusetts* 23 (1995): 44–60.

63. Charles L. Cohen, "Conversion among Puritans and Amerindians: A Theological and Cultural Perspective," in *Puritanism: Transatlantic Perspectives on a Seventeenth-Century Anglo-American Faith*, ed. Francis J. Bremer (Boston: Massachusetts Historical Society, 1993), pp. 233–56; passage quoted on p. 255.

64. Ann Marie Plane, "'The Examination of Sarah Ahhaton': The Politics of 'Adultery' in an Indian Town of Seventeenth-Century Massachusetts," in Benes's *Algonkians of New England*, pp. 14–25.

65. Daniel Mandell, "'To Live More Like My Christian Neighbors': Natick Indians in the Eighteenth Century," *William and Mary Quarterly* 48 (1991): 552–79; Ronda, "Generations of Faith"; Van Lonkhuyzen, "A Reappraisal of the Praying Indians"; and my "Red Yankees."

66. See my "Cultural Bias in the New England Puritans' Perception of Indians," *William and Mary Quarterly* 38 (1981): 56–72; Alden T. Vaughan, "Early English Paradigms for New World Natives," *Proceedings of the American Antiquarian Society* 102 (1992): 33–67. For Indian accounts of Europeans, see my *Spirit of the New England Tribes*, pp. 65–90, and "The Mystic Voice: Pequot Folklore from the Seventeenth Century to the Present," in *The Pequots in Southern New England: The Fall and Rise of an American Indian Nation*, ed. Laurence M. Hauptman and James D. Wherry (Norman: University of Oklahoma Press, 1990), and "Of Large Things Remembered: Southern New England Indian Legends of Colonial Encounters," in *The Art and Mystery of Historical Archaeology: Essays in Honor of James Deetz*, ed. Anne Elizabeth Yentsch and Mary C. Beaudry (Ann Arbor: CRC Press, 1992), pp. 317–30; James Axtell, *Beyond 1492: Encounters in Colonial North America* (New York: Oxford University Press, 1992), pp. 25–74; Kathleen J. Bragdon, *Native People of Southern New England, 1500–1650* (Norman: University of Oklahoma Press, 1996), pp. 29–31.

67. Bragdon, "Language, Folk History, and Indian Identity on Martha's Vineyard," in Yentsch and Beaudry's *The Art and Mystery of Historical Archaeology*, pp. 331–42, and "Vernacular Literacy and Massachusett World View, 1650–1750," in Benes's *Algonkians of New England*, pp. 26–34; Ives Goddard and Kathleen Brag-

don, *Native Writings in Massachusett,* pts. 1 and 2 (Philadelphia: American Philosophical Society, 1988).

68. Goddard and Bragdon, *Native Writings in Massachusett,* pt. 1, pp. xv, 1.

69. Jack Campisi, *The Mashpee Indians: Tribe on Trial* (Syracuse: Syracuse University Press, 1991); Russell M. Peters, *The Wampanoags of Mashpee: An Indian Perspective on American History* (Somerville, Mass.: Indian Spiritual and Cultural Training Council, 1987); my *The Narragansett* (New York and Philadelphia: Chelsea House, 1989); Laurie Weinstein-Farson, *The Wampanoag* (New York and Philadelphia: Chelsea House, 1989).

70. Henry Warner Bowden, *American Indians and Christian Missions: Studies in Cultural Conflict* (Chicago: University of Chicago Press, 1981); Kathleen J. Bragdon, "The Northeast Culture Area," in *Native North Americans: An Ethnohistorical Approach,* ed. Daniel L. Boxberger (Dubuque: Kendall/Hunt Publishing Company, 1990), pp. 91–133; Christian F. Feest, *Indians of Northeastern North America* (Leiden: E. J. Brill, 1986); J. C. H. King, *Thunderbird and Lightning: Indian Life in Northeastern North America, 1600–1900* (London: British Museum Publications Ltd., 1982); Neal Salisbury, *The Indians of New England: A Critical Bibliography* (Bloomington: Indiana University Press, 1982); Peter A. Thomas, "Cultural Change on the Southern New England Frontier, 1630–1665," in *Cultures in Contact: The Impact of European Contacts on Native American Cultural Institutions, A.D. 1000–1800,* ed. William W. Fitzhugh (Washington: Smithsonian Institution Press, 1985), pp. 131–61.

71. Henry W. Bowden and James P. Ronda, eds., *John Eliot's Indian Dialogues: A Study in Cultural Interaction* (Westport: Greenwood Press, 1980); Colin G. Calloway, ed., *The World Turned Upside Down: Indian Voices from Early America* (Boston and New York: Saint Martin's Press, 1994); *The Complete Writings of William Apess, A Pequot,* ed. Barry O'Connell (Amherst: University of Massachusetts Press, 1992); *The Correspondence of Roger Williams,* vols. 1 and 2 (1629–82), ed. Glenn W. LaFantasie (Hanover, N.H.: University Press of New England, 1988).

72. John L. Allen, ed., "Reshaping Traditions: Native Americans and Europeans in Southern New England," *Connecticut History* 35 (1994); Benes, *Algonkians of New England;* Susan G. Gibson, ed., *Burr's Hill: A Seventeenth-Century Wampanoag Burial Ground in Warren, Rhode Island* (Providence: Brown University/Haffenreffer Museum of Anthropology, 1980); Hauptman and Wherry, *The Pequots in Southern New England;* Ann McMullen and Russell G. Handsman, eds., *A Key into the Language of Woodsplint Baskets* (Washington, Conn.: American Indian Archaeological Institute, 1987); Laurie Weinstein, ed., *Enduring Traditions: The Native Peoples of New England* (Westport and London: Bergin and Garvey, 1994).

8

A Reappraisal of the Praying Indians
Acculturation, Conversion, and Identity
at Natick, Massachusetts,
1646–1730

HAROLD W. VAN LONKHUYZEN

Although the Mayhews and the Martha's Vineyard Indians had a significant role in the Puritans' missionary program, John Eliot's "Praying Towns" are more notable in their sheer numbers and in the share of attention they attracted in the seventeenth century and since. Of course religious motivation (to the extent that it can be separately discerned) is at the heart of the missionary process, but in Algonquian society other forces were at work that helped to shape an individual's response to the Christian message. Harold W. Van Lonkhuyzen examines those forces, especially at the Praying Town of Natick, from the community's inception until its ethnic composition changed drastically a century later.

A variety of characteristics in Eliot's Praying Towns attracted new Indian residents, and the converts, in turn, were expected to conform to new ways of thinking and acting. Few of those changes were immediate; old ways lingered, especially in housing and probably in agriculture, gender roles, and childrearing. But under gentle prodding from the principal Christian Indians, as well as from Eliot himself, the men and women of Natick and the other Christian Indian communities began to speak a new language and eventually, in many cases, to read it; to practice an unaccustomed degree of privacy in their homes and in public spaces; to wear new types of clothing and to cut and arrange their hair in new styles; to labor at new tasks and for new objectives; and, of course, to worship a new deity in new words and rituals. All Puritans, English and Algonquian, were expected to experience a spiritual rebirth; Indian converts were expected as well to practice and internalize a radically new lifestyle.

Natick was the prototype and the longest lasting of Eliot's Praying Towns. As Van Lonkhuyzen makes clear, however, Natick's decline from its intended role began with King Philip's War and accelerated in the early eighteenth cen-

*tury. From a bastion of missionary fervor it became, barely a century later, al-
most indistinguishable from other New England towns, where Indians were
scarce and most of their Euroamerican neighbors wished there were none.*

I N THE THIRTY YEARS before King Philip's War in 1675, nearly one
fourth of the Indians of southeastern New England pledged themselves
to Christianity, the first large-scale conversion of Native Americans
effected by English settlers in North America.[1] Because of the relative
wealth of sources about them, these Praying Indians, as they were known,
offer an opportunity to explore issues of acculturation, conversion, and
identity in the colonial period.

In the historical literature of the past twenty years, the Praying Indians
were at first depicted as a shattered remnant, so overcome by the stresses
of contact with the English and by the missionaries' insidious efforts to
convert them that they relinquished their Indianness and came to identify
completely with the dominant culture.[2] More recent interpreters, best represented by James Axtell, have still viewed the Indians' conversion as a
necessary—though rather grudging—response to the new conditions imposed upon them, but these critics have also focused on the positive aspects
of those adaptations. For example, Axtell has argued that conversion fore-
stalled the annihilation experienced by traditionalist Indian groups in New
England and that, as a form of protective coloration, Christianity also
helped preserve the Indians' "crucial ethnic core" or their "ethnic identity."
At the same time, however, it has also been suggested that conversion
nonetheless required "wholesale cultural change."[3]

While they have outlined the essential story of the New England conversions and offered tentative interpretations, recent studies of the Praying Indians are problematic in several respects. First, the literature argues
that conversion was forced, that it was a necessary adaptation to a changing environment—ecological, political, military, demographic, and economic—created by the English. Yet numerous bands living in close proximity to converted groups never adopted the English religion until decades
after King Philip's War. In addition, conversion has been viewed primarily
as an individual transformation of identity but is then generalized to the
experience of whole bands. Consequently, the relation of conversion to
Indian social relations has remained largely unexamined. Third, extremely
little attention has been paid to the process of Christianization over time,
with most studies abandoning the Praying Indians as early as 1675 and thus
neglecting to assess the impact and aftermath of King Philip's War. More-

over, "ethnic identity," which figures prominently in recent interpretations, has not been adequately defined or clearly related to behavioral and cultural changes. Finally, the acculturative adaptations of the unconverted have not been clearly related to those of the Praying Indians, thereby making traditionalism and conversion appear to be two wholly antithetical alternatives.

While the sources pertaining to the Praying Indians are comparatively rich, most were written by Puritan missionaries or their close associates, often for fundraising or promotional purposes. Given that intent, one must be especially critical when analyzing the missionaries' portraits of their proselytes. Yet these same sources contain many references to facets of Praying Indian life that were unimportant to the missionaries' purposes and that therefore may have been recorded with greater veracity than, say, claims about numbers of converts, their beliefs, or their reading ability. By focusing on these seemingly less important aspects of the life of Praying Indians—such as their material culture, rituals, and use of space—an alternate methodology for assessing actual behavior, social relations, and ethnic identity emerges. In addition, such an approach offers a means of comparing the converted with the unconverted, who can speak to us for the most part only through their artifacts.

Although our findings can be truly representative only if applicable to most of the Praying Towns, Natick seems the best place to begin an inquiry. By far the best-documented of the Praying villages, it was also the oldest and most thoroughly anglicized. The particular endeavor of John Eliot, the most ardent and dedicated of the Puritan missionaries, Natick is in many respects atypical, but because it offers the most extreme case of acculturation, it also offers the best opportunity to examine the conversion phenomenon in process, from the motivations of Eliot's earliest proselytes to the alterations in Indian culture evident by 1730.

I

In explaining conversion, historians have rightly focused on the fast-changing environment that challenged the Indian way of life and religion. Indeed, the new conditions created by the English were strong enough to produce significant, rapid transformations of identity in *some* individuals. The missionary records contain several instances of what one anthropologist has termed a "conversion syndrome," in which illness and abnormal behavior result from a conscious and thoroughgoing shift to a new religion.[4] Eliot himself considered his new converts to have crossed, however tentatively, a crucial boundary between savage pagans and civilized Christians.

Yet in the 1640s, when Eliot first started preaching, and indeed throughout the pre-war period, these forces do not seem to have been strong enough to *necessitate* any significant or rapid transformation in identity. In fact, relatively limited beliefs and behaviors seem to have dominated the concerns of Eliot's first converts. The very first, Waban, narrated the story of his conversion in 1652. Its content suggests a mild loss of cultural confidence but demonstrates Waban's larger interest in English modes of work; whatever transformation had occurred transpired over the course of nearly two decades: "After the great sickness [an epidemic in 1633–34], I considered what the English do; and I had some desire to do as they do; and after that I began to work as they work; and then I wondered how the English came to be so strong to labor." He then went on to relate his fear of death and how, after a time, God had indeed made him "strong to labor."[5] Similarly, one of the first aspects of English culture that the women of Waban's band wished to learn from Eliot was how to spin.[6] Indians' individual motivations in first adopting Christianity thus appear to have been highly specific, rather modest, and perhaps not at all what the missionaries might have wished. Moreover, only a minority of even the Natick band seems to have felt much changed by new beliefs. In 1652, after nearly a decade of work among several hundred Indians, Eliot dared bring only fourteen men to profess their faith before his Roxbury congregation, and a number of them were found wanting by their English examiners.

If Waban's conversion—and, indeed, the conversion of most Praying Indians—cannot really be seen as a sudden, wholesale transformation and adoption of English values, perhaps we should look beyond the locus of English-Indian interactions into the Indians' own social structure for clues of their attraction to Christianity. In traditional Algonquian society, band leadership was provided by a *sachem* or headman, who was assisted by several counselors or elders. These offices were loosely hereditary but also consensual. Sachems and counselors had to maintain their positions by charisma, wiliness, and the adept manipulation of social relationships. Competition for these leadership roles was often intense, and intrigue and factionalism were commonplace.

The other role of prime social importance was that of powwow or shaman, which depended on an individual's ability to converse with and marshal spirit beings. Powwows acted as healers and sorcerers and were greatly feared by those less well connected to the spirit world. Indian religion was not exclusive, and a new cult that could be used to advantage in the competition for prestige and leadership and that offered freedom from sorcery with no loss of communication to the spirit world would have been of keen interest.[7]

Inter-band hierarchies developed around trade networks and military alliances. Subordinate bands paid tribute to an important local sachem, who in turn might owe allegiance to a more powerful chief. Such alliances were problematic for most bands, for while they offered some protection and access to desired goods, at the same time they burdened the community with unwanted quarrels and tribute payments. A special relationship with the English could offer a means of altogether evading inconvenient ties or of manipulating them to advantage.[8]

A separate literature on unconverted New England Indians also hints at some of the reasons why contact with the English was desirable. These Indians were eager to make use of European goods and technologies as a means not of abandoning but of fulfilling their traditional way of life. Thoroughly selective, they used only those items that offered an advantage in native contexts, and they were highly ingenious in adapting the new goods and technologies to their own ends.[9] Praying to God would have been attractive for enhancing the traditional, internal cultural milieu, then, just as it might have been protective in the increasingly hostile external environment.

John Eliot was first invited to preach at Waban's wigwam at Nonantum, or Watertown Mill, in the fall of 1646. He had been attempting to convert the Indians for several years but had been rebuffed.[10] At the time, Waban seems to have been only a moderately influential member of the band, which was under the general sachemship of Cutshamekin, who headed another band nearby. Having sold much of the tribe's seaside land, Cutshamekin had made it difficult to exploit coastal food resources, which alienated some of his followers and fueled Waban's ambitions.[11] Moreover, in June 1646 Cutshamekin was particularly vulnerable, for he was being personally harassed by Uncas, the powerful Mohegan sachem. Thus, it was an opportune moment for challenging Cutshamekin's leadership. Waban organized a faction that, in showing an interest in Christianity, quickly attracted new adherents from outside the band. Increasing the size of the band not only gave it greater autonomy but also surely helped confirm individual members in their choice. By 1648, John Winthrop referred to Waban as a "new sachem."[12]

The story was much the same in other bands. Sometimes the motivation for praying to God was clearly related to destructive forces created by contact, as when alcohol unraveled the social fabric.[13] In at least as many cases, however, missionaries were sought out as a means of escaping traditional alliances, of gaining new ones with the English, or, within bands, as a means of subverting existing relationships. For example, Thomas Mayhew convinced some sachems on Martha's Vineyard to allow him to continue proselytizing by offering them an alliance with the English as a way of escaping the influence of a tributary hierarchy on the mainland. "Thus in no long time," he wryly noted, "they conceived no ill opinion of the Christian religion." Hiacoomes, Mayhew's first convert, was catapulted to an important leadership role in the Indian community when he converted.[14] Unconverted Indians often pointed to the continuing poverty of their Praying brethren as proof that the new ways were not beneficial, thereby indicating what they themselves took to be an important motivation for adopting the new cult.[15] There is also considerable evidence that one of the major attractions of praying to God was the protection it offered from the sorcery of the powwows. Eliot and other Puritan missionaries made every effort to root out the powwows and to assume their other functions, such as curing and prophesying.[16] In short, the Indians' traditional social context usually remained the operative framework within which individual Indians embraced or rejected the new cult.

Just as Indians most often sought out the missionaries for their own purposes, they also controlled the pace and timing of change. Eliot wished to isolate his proselytes in a village wholly their own, and toward that end he secured a reserve of several thousand acres for Waban's band in 1646. The actual move, however, did not take place for four years. Many of Waban's followers—as well as Cutshamekin—were not enthusiastic about the new religion or the removal, in large measure because they were still strongly attached to their home territory. When the band finally moved to Natick in 1650, it did so at the urging of Wampooas, a revered counselor and convert. Evidently in an effort to maintain control over the band, Cutshamekin himself reluctantly espoused Eliot's gospel in 1652.[17]

That the primary motivations for praying to God derived from issues of control within Indian society explains why conversion precipitated such exceptionally vicious factionalism among the Indians. Eliot's converts were scoffed, mocked, derided, bewitched, and threatened with death by their fellow Indians. James Axtell has argued that the bitter factionalism arising from conversion stemmed wholly from the dilemma of how to respond to the English.[18] It seems clear, however, that the disputes were equally inflamed because the new cult created an alternate social structure, essentially a new path to power within and among bands. While factionalism had always been an element of Indian social organization, the new cult threatened some of the most basic premises of native society which had gone unquestioned in earlier disputes.

Focusing on the social context of conversion thus helps to explain why praying to God took hold in nearly all bands in southeastern New England, including those relatively removed from the immediate pressures of settlement. It also explains why sachems and powwows, who had the most to lose if the social order were upset, were typically against Christianity. Eliot noted that Praying emissaries from Waban's band were scorned by Narragansett sachems but welcomed by lesser members of the tribe. Even Philip and Uncas, the two most powerful traditionalist sachems in New England, had Praying factions within their home and tributary bands, despite their efforts to exclude the cult.[19]

Looking at conversion from this perspective also helps to explain the Indians' piecemeal adaptation of the Puritans' gospel. The Natick band built a framed meetinghouse and elaborate fences around their fields but refused to live in English-style houses, despite Eliot's urgings. Likewise, in the 1660s, Philip—notwithstanding his antipathy to Christianity—asked Eliot to send him some books and a teacher so that he and his people could learn to read, as the Natick band was doing.[20] The Indians, seeking to enhance rather than abandon their traditional order, tried to take only what they wanted of the missionary program.

II

If the praying-to-God movement was at first motivated as much by traditional, internal cultural patterns as by external conditions, it nonetheless resulted in important changes. Before they even moved to Natick, Waban's band members changed the way they built their wigwams, and by 1674 they were attempting to set up a sawmill on the Charles River. A mere generation later, the band had nearly disintegrated. Praying to God, in concert with other changes in the Indians' surrounding environment, immediately altered, and then destroyed, the social relations that had first inspired its practice. The Natick band's relationship with John Eliot was central to this process.

Eliot, though not the only one, was by far the most important source of English culture at Natick, and his role within the band is best described as that of cultural patron. Peter Thomas has argued that patronage was essential to the smooth flow of desired goods and knowledge between what he calls "state" and "egalitarian" cultures. In frontier areas of New England in the seventeenth century, fur traders and certain Indians, or "big men," who controlled exchanges with them, had established patron-client relationships. In southeastern New England, the fur trade had been exhausted by the early 1640s, but missionaries quickly assumed the role of patrons. Indian preachers and teachers, such as Waban, Anthony, and John Speen at Natick, took over the role of "big men."[21] The patron-client relationship offered the Indians what they wanted in part, but at the same time it accelerated change in their social order.

Eliot believed that "civilizing" the Indians was a necessary function of, even prerequisite to, saving them. Thus, in addition to promulgating Puritan rituals and religious teachings, Eliot also provided a small but steady flow of English goods and technologies to the Natickites. He gave the Indians hoes, shovels, spades, mattocks, and crowbars; cast-off clothing as well as new trade cloth; ox bells; cards and spinning wheels; apple trees and English herbs; and also medicines. In 1652 he also obtained "winter supplies" for the new community. During the 1660s, when the Praying bands were under attack by the Mohawks, Eliot successfully urged the General Court to give them firearms and ammunition. He also distributed a considerable amount of money among the Indians, paying them to construct a meetinghouse and fences, to accompany him on preaching tours, and to act as missionaries themselves. Throughout the pre-war period, he also made yearly payments of £5 to £10 to native preachers and teachers and to "sundry deserving Indians," like Waban, whose influence was crucial to the success of the mission work.[22] Eliot hoped that the materials would contribute to the Indians' further "civilization," but he also recognized that his gifts helped make praying to God attractive to the Indians and increased his personal prestige among them.[23]

Eliot introduced the Indians to new technologies for the same reasons. In addition to teaching the women how to spin and supplying them with the necessary tools and raw materials to do so, Eliot hired an English carpenter for a few days to help frame the meetinghouse at Natick. Several of the Indian men either knew or learned enough that they completed the structure unassisted. By the 1670s at least some of the Natick Indians had adopted English farming methods, for a cart, plow, English grains, and fruit trees are mentioned in the sources. The Natickites' hogs were accounted the best at the Boston market, and they had a "store of cattle" as well. Eliot also encouraged the Indians to construct elaborate, ditched, rock-reinforced post-and-rail fences around their fields. Just how familiar the Natick group had become with complex English technologies is clear from their attempt that same decade to establish a sawmill.[24]

One "technology" that deserves special mention is Eliot's literacy program. He translated the Bible and other works into the Massachusett language and distributed the books to his converts. He arranged for Indians to attend dame and grammar schools, and a few even studied briefly at

Harvard. A large building, called the Indian College, was constructed there for their use. Eliot also set up schools at the Praying Towns, and at Natick he even conducted summer seminars in logic. By 1660 he claimed that one hundred of his converts, most of whom probably lived at Natick, could read.[25]

The new rituals Eliot introduced, however, had the greatest impact on Indian life. Foremost among these were Sabbath worship services and family prayer in the morning and evening and before and after meals. At Natick and some of the other Praying Towns, Eliot also introduced certain church practices: baptism, admonition and excommunication, communion, catechism, prophesying, and days of fasting and thanksgiving. He also initiated a tithing ceremony which bore a strong resemblance to tribute payment. Together with his civilian colleague Daniel Gookin, moreover, Eliot seems to have encouraged some of the practices associated with English judicial and governmental systems.[26] It was, above all, their participation in these new rituals that truly distinguished the Praying Indians from their unconverted neighbors.

Eliot's ideological message accompanied and explained his other importations. He preached at Natick every other week from 1646 until the early 1680s and visited other times, particularly in the summer. In an effort to root out the most obviously "savage" aspects of Indian life, Eliot concentrated on discouraging a fairly small, though important, range of behaviors, including polygamy, "idleness," drunkenness, and belief in the magic of the powwows. More generally, he exhorted his proselytes to act meekly toward the English and to live as much like them as they possibly could.[27]

Eliot's program had some beneficial effects for the Indians. New goods and technologies helped the band adapt to a rapidly changing environment. Farming, woodworking, and spinning technologies, along with hunting game for sale to the English, berry gathering, and basket and broom making, all enabled the Indians to be producers in the colonial economy rather than an exploited underclass.[28] His education program initially allowed Indian scholars access to situations where they interacted with the English in a positive way. Literacy provided a basis for continued group identity and an important means of acquiring knowledge about the English. On a more concrete level, the fences Eliot encouraged the Indians to build reduced one of the major sources of tension between natives and newcomers. Finally, the guns and ammunition, the meetinghouse, and the sawmill would also have functioned as symbolic reassurances that the Indians' own aspirations would be accorded fair scope by the increasingly powerful English.

The Praying faction at Natick found much in Eliot's program that could be used to gain and maintain control over the band. Money and clothing helped distinguish the elite. Eliot's educational endeavors also served to create a cohort of Indian preachers and teachers who functioned as the "big men" in the patron-client relationship. For example, while their earlier status within the band is uncertain, Anthony, John Speen, and Piambow clearly served as important counselors to Waban after they converted and became preachers. In addition, new rituals provided leading roles for the Praying faction and relegated formerly important players, like Cutshamekin, to bit parts. In some bands the praying movement seems to have subsumed the existing leadership within it; in others, praying to God functioned as an alternative organization.[29] Finally, Eliot's sermons no doubt reinforced the dominance of the Christian faction as well.

Praying to God also provided other advantages that could be exploited by the members of an otherwise powerless band. Natickites came to be particularly valued by other Indians for their familiarity with reading and writing. John Sassamon, a Natick native, became a scribe to Philip and later served as the teacher at Assowampsett, where he married the sachem's daughter. A Natick man gathered the Praying Town of Hassanamesit, and others preached to a variety of bands, particularly in Eliot's Nipmuck "new towns." In 1664 Eliot wrote that "sundry places in the country are ripe for laborers [i.e., teachers], and some places do intreat that some of their countrymen, by name, might be sent unto them."[30] The colony's efforts to protect the band's land reserve and to supply it with arms, both of which required Eliot to appear before the General Court as an advocate for the Indians, spoke loudly to other natives of the Natickites' close relationship with the powerful newcomers.

Yet although Eliot's introductions of English culture in some ways benefited the Natick community—by helping its members adapt to their changing environment and by serving the traditional social ends of men like Waban, Anthony, and John Speen—those same elements also changed the very context that had prompted their adoption. The alteration of the band's social relationships occurred gradually but affected the Indians' personal and collective identities profoundly and irreversibly.[31] The *sine qua non* of any discussion of the Indians' ethnic identity in this period, the band was an important economic unit, overwhelmingly the most significant political and military unit, the minimum unit for social ritual practice, and the basic unit within which social identities and status were defined. As the band changed, so did individual and corporate identities.

Although most southeastern New England bands were becoming increasingly sedentary during this period, Eliot's new technologies accelerated that process for his converts. Even before the band moved to Natick, its members built larger wigwams covered with thick bark rather than the portable rush mats typically used. Thomas Shepard remarked that the new wigwams were as big as sachems' houses elsewhere, a mark of status that may have enhanced the desirability of praying to God.[32] But more permanent dwellings impeded mobility and sedentariness disrupted traditional subsistence cycles of food gathering and production. Compensation for that loss required further change. The need for winter supplies in 1652 may have been a direct result of this spiraling process.

Precisely why and to what extent the Natick community shifted away from swidden to English plow agriculture cannot be determined from the sources, but it too promoted sedentariness. It also had other drastic consequences. As they became more reliant on domesticated cattle and swine, the Natick Indians seem to have conceived of animals and their relationships with animal spirit masters in new ways. Although a cast pewter button bearing the image of a turtle survives from Natick, zoomorphic images seem to have gradually disappeared from Praying Indian basketry, pipes, and possibly wooden bowls.[33] Moreover, English agriculture, which required that land be carefully divided and bounded, forced the Indians to see the earth in new ways. The fences Eliot encouraged the Natick men to build simply could not be integrated into the Indians' traditional ethos but instead required and simultaneously reinforced a new one. Many other bands never made the significant change in behavior and cognitive understanding such enclosures necessitated. Fences went unbuilt; those that were, were not maintained.[34]

Accompanying the change in agricultural systems came shifts in gendered work roles. In traditional Algonquian life, women were responsible for all aspects of agricultural production and processing except land clearing and tobacco cultivation.[35] As they were no doubt required to do when working for English masters, the Natick Indians adopted some English gender roles. Men fenced the fields, broke the land, and took charge of harvesting. In the traditional ethos women were responsible for housing, but converted Indian men built the meetinghouse and a wigwam for Cutshamekin. Women, on the other hand, extended traditional activities such as basket and mat making when they learned to spin.[36] In fact, there is evidence that the Praying movement's redefinition of gender roles, though resisted by men, was an important attraction among women especially because it discouraged wife beating and alcohol abuse.[37]

Like the goods and technologies he introduced, Eliot's educational program altered the converted Indians' cognitive appreciation of the world. Reading, together with Eliot's preaching, stimulated a multitude of questions about the English conception of reality. Indians wanted to know about the composition of the body, the origin of the Bible, the nature of spirits, the causes of rainbows, and a host of other phenomena. Although reading may have remained more a ritualistic than an intellectual activity, Natick Indians clearly wanted more books than Eliot could supply.[38]

The Puritan ideology Eliot communicated to the Indians also helped to undermine existing social relations. Offered a new group with which to identify, some Praying Indians came to refer to both unconverted natives and irreligious English settlers as "all one Indian." To show their respect for the governor of Massachusetts Bay, when he visited Natick with a large entourage, the Indians built a special awning under which the honored guests were seated. In gloating that runaway Indian servants found no protection or sympathy at Natick, Eliot revealed that his converts had internalized attitudes overtly injurious to any incipient ethnic solidarity. Moreover, out of his concern that they learn to work like the English, Eliot encouraged the Indians to engage themselves as day laborers, servants, and apprentices, but many of these relationships were exploitative, some even enslaving.[39]

Eliot's preaching on marriage and sexual relations also disrupted traditional social relationships, giving rise to a wholly new sexual modesty. Even before 1650 converts were erecting partitions in their wigwams to shield married couples from the view of their families. The usual places and orders prescribed—by rank and gender—for sitting and sleeping within the wigwam would have been subverted by partitions, which at the same time structurally reinforced a new primacy for the married couple. As part of his effort to implant a European concept of marriage, Eliot taught with some success that wife beating was wrong. Once a man and woman were married, they became one flesh, so to beat one's wife was to do violence to one's own body.[40] With such teachings, Eliot contributed not only to altering gender relationships but to redefining the social body through reconceptualizing the human body and domestic space.

Because Eliot was an integral member of the Natick community, his physical presence as well as his words altered traditional social relations. The Indians frequently asked him to settle disputes, so often, in fact, that he eventually had to decline to handle most of them. In the chamber over the main room of the meetinghouse, Eliot had a large closet constructed in which he put a bed. Here he stored his provisions and clothes and slept when visiting the village. The room became a sacred space for the Indians, and even though it had no lock, they stored their furs and other valuables there. The Indians' use of this room indicates not simply a new concern with personal possessions but the extension into the spatial realm of Eliot's prestige and his special role in the band.[41]

By far the most important agent altering traditional social relationships and identities, however, were the new rituals the Praying Indians adopted. As Sherry Ortner has argued, rituals are not epiphenomena, which reflect reality. Rather, in their enactment rituals help construct reality by transforming experience and meaning, as a funeral transfigures loss into a social and spiritual experience of solidarity. Rituals are not necessarily representational; they may precede and actually create social order. Because of their transformative, constructive power, rituals are therefore also crucial to identity formation and change, for they shape "actors in such a way that they wind up appropriating cultural meaning as a personally held orientation." Thus ritual is "a sort of two way transformer, shaping consciousness in conformity with culture, but at the same time shaping culture in conformity with the more immediate social-action and social-structural determinants of consciousness in everyday life."[42] By examining the performance of rituals at Natick, one can observe the shifts in social relationships that, in concert with the changing environment and balance of power in New England, gradually destroyed the band and radically altered traditional Indian identity.

The rituals adopted at Natick, used initially to secure the dominance of the Praying faction, implicitly contained a new differentiation of time. Unlike traditional Indian rituals which were seasonal and, like the Green Corn ceremony, closely tied to major subsistence cycle events, the Praying rites were tied to daily and weekly cycles. In keeping with Puritan practice, Eliot permitted no special holy days, like Christmas or Easter, save for occasional days of thanksgiving or fasting. The prayers Eliot taught the Indians also fostered in them a qualitatively new relationship with the Divine. The elaborate cycle of daily prayers contained in *The Practice of Piety,* a work Eliot translated for his converts in 1665, constantly recapitulated the Christian redemptive cycle. Moreover, the rituals overtly differentiated society in new ways, for the Indians seem to have adopted English seating arrangements at their meetings, the men sitting on one side, women on the other, by order of social rank. Praying to God at first modified the social order in many villages only slightly, but more significantly it supplied a new rationale for society, indeed, a new cosmos.[43]

A vignette may perhaps best serve to illustrate the process by which the essence of Indian society and identity was gradually altered through the new rituals. Eliot recorded, but did not participate in, a fast-day service conducted at Natick on 15 November 1658. Heavy rains had spoiled much of the band's hay and corn harvest, and many in the community were sick. Four Praying faction leaders, including Waban, addressed the band. Each speaker, in true Protestant fashion, exhorted his listeners to search out the sins in their hearts that might be responsible for the current manifestations of God's displeasure. While the Indian preachers had the books of Genesis and Matthew to draw from at this time, and probably many more metaphors of Christ that they had heard as well, at least two of the speakers chose to center their talks around the image of Christ the physician, clearly paralleling the shaman's traditional function of healing.[44] But however familiar the rhetoric may have seemed, its implications were not. Shamans had typically projected social tensions onto the natural world, but now each individual was being asked to look inside him- or herself to confront an integrally sinful human nature. This shift implied a new concept of human nature, of responsibility, and, ultimately, of community.[45] These subtle but pervasive new constructs—like new concepts of time, of the spirit world, and of the social order—sucked at the very marrow of Indian identity.

One important way in which rituals construct and legitimate a reality is through the strong emotional responses they evoke in their participants, which make what is happening seem true. Public weeping was strongly discouraged in traditional Indian society, but if observers' descriptions can be taken as accurate, it became fairly common in Christian rituals at Natick. A distraught eleven-year-old girl dying of consumption witnessed a baptism and was so moved that she persuaded her parents to join the church so that she could experience the rite herself. According to Eliot, the girl died contentedly soon after her own baptism.[46] These examples suggest the emotional efficacy of the new rituals at Natick and, therefore, their capacity to transform social reality and individual identity.

Because rituals can be a means of solving social problems, they are frequently the site of social tensions.[47] Another vignette illustrates not only how much was in contention at Natick but also how wrenching the changes in practice and identity could be. Three Indian men, unhappy about the Praying regime at Natick, took the eleven-year-old son of a prominent member of the Praying faction and got him drunk and then left him out all night. Uncertain how to respond to the matter, the father consulted Eliot and Indian church members. The traditional mechanism for settling differences, revenge or restitution by the kin of the parties involved, was no longer considered legitimate, so instead a characteristically English and Puritan resolution was attempted. It was determined not only that the three men should receive twenty lashes at the whipping tree but also that the boy should be punished, presumably for allowing himself to be led astray. Evidently to indicate his acceptance of this new conception of sin, the father overcame his own considerable misgivings and whipped his son in front of the child's schoolmates and then placed him in the town stocks. The Praying faction leaders used the opportunity to lecture the entire community, attempting to frighten unbelievers into joining the cult.[48] As in the fast-day example, the Praying faction utilized the new rituals for their own ends, but they could not escape the implications of the rites, with their attendant emotional costs. Within the traditional ethos, the boy probably would not have been held accountable at all.

III

However painful it effects, the process of social and psychological change proceeded. By 1675, the Praying Indians had made the most of the missionary program, although one source suggests that at least once they were almost overthrown.[49] The Natick band was much more favorably positioned than most to meet changing economic and ecologic realities and yet still maintain its basic social organization and ethnic identity. Yet, the very presence of a sawmill, cattle, a whipping tree, partitions in wigwams, and fences in the fields suggests that important changes in that identity had already taken place. New meanings replaced, quietly coexisted with, and powerfully contradicted old ones, but the dynamic tension that resulted was disrupted by King Philip's War, despite the best efforts of both Eliot and the Indians.

In fact, this tension may have been one of the primary causes of the war, which broke out in 1675. Historians have traditionally stressed Philip's role in provoking the conflict. Concerned about English encroachment on Indian lands and about his diminishing status with the Plymouth authorities, Philip was also undoubtedly concerned about his declining influence in the face of the accommodationist Praying movement.[50] Although in the 1660s he had solicited books and literacy instruction from Eliot and had allowed the missionary's son to preach at least twice to his band, by the 1670s Philip was reluctant to permit any further activity by the Praying faction in his village. Further evidence that the early 1670s saw increased tension between Praying and traditionalist Indians may be found in Eliot's recording that, after thirty years of hard-won progress, there was a sudden increase in backsliding among his converts and that his work had never encountered "such violent opposition by Satan."[51] The event that touched off the fighting was, of course, the murder of John Sassamon, a Praying Indian from Natick and Philip's erstwhile scribe.[52] While the evidence is inconclusive, it appears that Philip had Sassamon killed for betraying his plans to the English. In many ways, moreover, the conflict was a civil war among the Indians. Most Praying bands tried to stay out of the fighting, but the hostile Indians frequently attacked them, in part to get them to join the cause. The Praying Indians who served on the English side were particularly hated, and Philip ordered that if any were captured, they were to be reserved for special tortures.[53]

King Philip's War was devastating for the Praying Indians as well as the English. Many Natick men aided the English as scouts, messengers, and soldiers, perhaps out of necessity, pragmatism, or sincere identification with their co-religionists. Waban, as well as Sassamon, warned the Massachusetts Bay authorities of Philip's plans. Notwithstanding its contributions, which Daniel Gookin maintained were absolutely critical to the English victory, the Natick band only barely survived the war, suffering grave atrocities at the hands of its ally. Forcibly interned on Deer Island in October 1675, the band did not return to Natick until the fall of 1677, after two years of extreme privation.[54]

For the Praying Indians, King Philip's War had two important consequences: it both changed the context of English-Indian relations and terminated the special relationship that had allowed the two communities to derive mutual benefits from each other. Engendering a wave of vicious anti-Indian feeling, the war encouraged the English to believe that all Indians were "fiendish sons of Satan" and threats to God's people.[55] It also altered Indian attitudes. On their return to Natick in 1677, the Indians held a thanksgiving service at which Waban summed up the experience of the war. While he acknowledged that Gookin and Eliot had been instrumental in saving the band, it is clear from his remarks that the group's trust in the English had been irreparably damaged.[56] At the same time, Mohawks, incited by the English government to attack supposedly hostile Indians, harassed the Natick community until 1682. In the aftermath of the war, the colony government attempted to exert more direct and strict control over the Indians and ordered all unaffiliated persons to reside in one of the four remaining Praying Towns. The forced immigration of new Indians into the community threatened the patterns established at Natick, but the Praying faction still maintained its control. Yet, given the traditionalists' annihilation in the war, it is not surprising that throughout nearly all the remaining New England bands, praying to God superseded traditional religion.[57]

The patron-client relationship also came to an end with the war. Due to age, Eliot and Gookin had been obliged to reduce their involvement with the Indians after the war, and by 1690 both men were dead. Increasingly forced to sell off parcels off their own reserve to settlers intent on taking them, the Natick band searched for a new cultural mediator. In 1682 they permitted Daniel Gookin's son Samuel to build a sawmill and cut timber in exchange for his assistance in dealing with trespassers and exploiters. The younger Gookin betrayed the Indians' trust, however, and in 1695 they brought a complaint against him for encroaching beyond the boundaries of his grant. Nevertheless, by 1696 Gookin held 1,700 acres of the reserve. Eliot's image seems never to have been tarnished, though, and there is evidence that the Natick Indians continued to venerate him long after his passing.[58]

Natick in the aftermath of the war is difficult to reconstruct, but some formal aspects of Eliot's program seem to have been discontinued. Whereas in 1669 the Natick church had between thirty and forty full communicants, by 1698 there were only ten, even though the population of the village remained relatively constant. Moreover, by that year only one child in the community under the age of sixteen could read, and the town had no schoolmaster. Residents of Dedham complained of "proud and surly behavior" by the Natick Indians "in refusing to take notice of an Englishman if they meet him in the street." An English minister suggested that the Indians had, perhaps in reaction to the new status quo, "generally and in great measure returned to their former habits of indolence and improvidence, of intemperance and irreligion."[59]

Notwithstanding this analysis, the decline in church membership does not necessarily indicate a reactionary return to a more traditional way of life. Indeed, the Praying Indians at Natick continued their private and public devotions and maintained an Indian minister; they probably discontinued formal church membership because it was no longer relevant in the new context of relations with the English. On the other hand, if the evidence from other Praying Towns is representative, Natick at this time was probably anxious to continue schooling but lacked a qualified teacher.[60]

Meanwhile the external pressures, which had in part prompted praying to God, continued to mount after 1675. The numbers of English settlers grew, and in the 1680s the first whites moved onto the Natick reserve. Economic and ecologic change also proceeded apace, making traditional Indian life increasingly difficult. Massachusetts was forced to hold its first closed hunting season on deer in 1694, and in 1718 hunting was prohibited for the next three years. The Natick Indians passed their own ordinance prohibiting the sale of any more timber from their common lands, and by 1730 it was difficult to find material with which to build wigwams. Disease, too, continued to take a heavy toll. Between 1721 and 1753, 191 Indians were baptized at Natick, but 256 were buried.[61]

English racism also continued to harden. The same minister who had observed reactionary lapses in the Indians also noted that "they are generally considered by white people, and placed, as if by common consent, in an inferior and degraded situation and treated accordingly."[62] Even the English missionary movement succumbed to the new perspective. Embedded in the narrative of William Kellaway's *New England Company* is the final devolution of the missionaries' debate over which language to teach the Indians. Publications in Algonquian continued to appear in the early 1700s, although they conveyed more explicitly coercive material, such as a 1705 catalogue of twenty-one legal offenses to which Indians were thought particularly susceptible. Writing to the company's English board in 1710, Cotton Mather averred: "It is very sure the best thing we can do for our Indians is to Anglicize them in all agreeable instances; and in that of languages, as well as others. They can scarce retain their language, without a tincture of other savage inclinations, which do but ill suit, either with honor, or with the design of Christianity."[63] After 1720, no books in Massachusett appeared.

The continuing processes of internal and external change in the postwar period rapidly dissolved the social organization underpinning Indian identity. Exactly when the Natick Indians relinquished their communal village is uncertain, but the abandonment of the pattern of habitation probably occurred about 1700. A manuscript map made in 1749 indicates that by that date English and Indians both lived dispersed throughout the town on family farms.[64] During this half-century, and especially by 1730, the Indians' way of life, social structure, institutions, and identity were redefined far more drastically than ever before.

As the work of Ives Goddard and Kathleen Joan Bragdon has shown, the Natick reserve was gradually broken into private small holdings. A series of land divisions recorded about 1700 by Thomas Waban, the town clerk, indicates the adoption of an English "two-field" farming system, which suggests that by that date the Indians had largely internalized English conceptions of land ownership, its transmission, and its bounding. When the communal "two-field" system failed, individual farms, averaging about sixty acres in size, were granted in 1719. At that time, rights to proprietorship in common lands were assigned based on inheritance rather than membership in the Indian community, and Natick Indians began to bequeath real estate to their offspring either informally or in wills. Partible inheritance, favoring male children, was practiced, and land reverted to the common stock if no heir was found.[65]

The material culture of the Indians also changed rapidly around the turn of the century. Indian society became increasingly stratified, with some Indians living in frame houses by the 1720s, while others continued in wigwams at least until mid-century.[66] Probate inventories indicate a wide disparity in the value and amounts of real and personal property held by individual Indians. Josiah Speen's estate, valued at £1,100 in 1749, included a dwelling house worth £250, over 150 acres of land, a variety of tools, brass and pewter objects, four chairs, a table, and a chest. He also received an English-style burial, complete with gloves for the pallbearers, minister, and widow. By contrast, Moses Waban left only his "wearing apparel" when he departed this life in 1747.[67]

While the Indians' religious exercises seem to have become less formalized after the war, a succession of native preachers served the community in the second decade of the eighteenth century. Then in 1720 a Harvard College sophomore, Oliver Peabody, was induced by the offer of a stipend to preach at Natick; he later moved there and served as minister until 1753. During his first year among the Indians, a new frame meetinghouse was constructed for services. Peabody presided over a racially-mixed congregation, and there was some tension between the two groups. A report of conditions in the parish issued in 1729 indicates that the Indians prayed and read the Bible in their homes, that they were not averse to having the English attend their worship services, but that they wished to maintain control over the liturgy. While satisfied with Peabody's preaching, the Indians were reluctant to send their children to him for catechism. The report also states that they were no longer particularly interested in supporting a school and had grown lax in teaching their children. The eight families of English settlers, on the other hand, wanted a formal church reestablished at Natick so that "afterwards those of neighboring towns that desired admission . . . might be admitted into the church of Natick."[68] The Indians were obviously losing control of their own institution and, perhaps, some hope along with it.

The formal government of Natick was vested in English-style town officers, elected at annual meetings at least as early as 1712 and probably a decade before that. White men who moved to Natick or who lived nearby played important roles as guardians, trustees, and sureties. The first white held a town office in 1733, and by 1763 settlers held all offices.[69] A school teacher was hired in 1731, and animal pounds and roads were constructed during that decade. The Indians began to intermarry with blacks, and their language fell into disuse by 1750.[70]

Much of course remained the same, and it would be irresponsible to overdramatize the changes that took place over more than a generation. Yet, taken together, the changes that did occur reflect a more drastic redefinition of identity than any that had preceded them. And that process was not unique to Natick, for by 1762 Mashpee, the Praying Town established near Sandwich by Richard Bourne, had experienced a very similar pattern of acculturation.[71]

A reexamination of the story of Natick offers some sobering insights into a world increasingly characterized by the confrontation and commingling of cultures. Contact with Europeans did not drastically alter traditional Indian goals; it simply made their realization through traditional means more difficult and finally impossible. At the same time contact, especially adoption of the Praying cult, seemed to offer new means toward those old ends, but neither party gained precisely what it desired. The Indians were undone in their desire to interact with the English while still maintaining their traditional social structure and goals; the English were largely unsuccessful in achieving the renunciation of "savagery" that they had sought.

In some respects, Eliot's relationship with the Indians was positive.[72] Yet praying to God did not preserve the Indians' ethnic identity any more successfully than did rebellion; in effect, it intensified assimilation and subverted traditional patterns from the very start. By altering basic social relations within the band, and then by helping to destroy the band itself, the new cult changed the Indians' perception of themselves and reality. Thus praying to God did end in "wholesale cultural change" but only over several generations, and even then the process was incomplete. Marginalized and more strictly controlled after King Philip's War, the Natick Indians were no longer able to shape their lives as freely as before. The process of constant redefinition was neither smooth nor linear. Fraught with conflict, disruption, and suffering, it perhaps often remained beyond the grasp of understanding if not of feeling.

Notes

1. James Axtell, *After Columbus* (New York: Oxford University Press, 1988), p. 88; Neal Salisbury, *Manitou and Providence* (New York: Oxford University Press, 1982), p. 225; William Cronon, *Changes in the Land* (New York: Hill and Wang, 1983), p. 89.

2. Francis Jennings, *The Invasion of America* (Chapel Hill: University of North Carolina Press, 1975); Neal Salisbury, "Red Puritans: The 'Praying Indians' of Massachusetts Bay and John Eliot," *William and Mary Quarterly*, 3d ser. 31 (1974): 27–54, and "Conquest of the 'Savage': Puritans, Puritan Missionaries, and the Indians, 1620–1680" (Ph.D. diss., University of California, Los Angeles, 1972); William S. Simmons, "Conversion from Indian to Puritan," *New England Quarterly* 52 (1979): 197–218 (chap. 7 of *New England Encounters*); Henry W. Bowden, *American Indians and Christian Missions* (Chicago: University of Chicago Press, 1981).

3. The most perceptive and critical insights into the Praying Indians can be found in James Axtell's *The Invasion Within* (New York: Oxford University Press, 1985), *The European and the Indian* (New York: Oxford University Press, 1981), and *After*

Columbus (quotations from *After Columbus*, p. 51, and *European and Indian*, p. 89). Offering the same basic interpretation are Elise Brenner, "To Pray or to Be Prey: That Is the Question: Strategies for Cultural Autonomy of Massachusetts Praying Town Indians," *Ethnohistory* 27 (Spring 1980): 135–52, and James P. Ronda, "Generations of Faith: The Christian Indians of Martha's Vineyard," *William and Mary Quarterly*, 3d ser. 38 (1981): 369–94. Daniel Mandell, "'To Live More Like My Christian Neighbors': Natick Indians in the Eighteenth Century," *William and Mary Quarterly* 48 (1991): 552–79, offers the most complete examination of Natick after 1700. An interpretation more sympathetic to Eliot and the Puritans can be found in Robert James Naeher's "Dialogue in the Wilderness: John Eliot and the Indian Exploration of Puritanism as a Source of Meaning, Comfort, and Ethnic Survival," *New England Quarterly* 62 (1989): 346–68.

4. Raymond Firth, "Conversion from Paganism to Christianity," *Royal Anthropological Institute News* 14 (1976–77): 7; John Eliot and Thomas Mayhew, "Tears of Repentance" (1653), in *Collections of the Massachusetts Historical Society*, 3d ser. 4 (1834): 205; Matthew Mayhew, *A Brief Narrative of the Success which the Gospel hath had, among the Indians of Martha's Vineyard* (Boston, 1694), p. 44.

5. Eliot and Mayhew, "Tears of Repentance," pp. 231–32.

6. Thomas Shepard, "The Clear Sunshine of the Gospell, Breaking forth upon the Indians in New England" (1648), in *Collections of the Massachusetts Historical Society*, 3d ser. vol. 4 (1834): 59; John W. Ford, ed., *Correspondence of the New England Company* (London, 1896; reprinted, New York: Burt Franklin Publishing, 1970), p. 20.

7. Typically in indigenous religions, any cult that offers the hope of banishing witchcraft or sorcery will at least be entertained, "even if it is of foreign extraction and carries with it theological and conceptual aspects that do not altogether conform to local custom and belief." See Jack Goody, "Religion, Social Change, and the Sociology of Conversion," in *Changing Social Structure in Ghana: Essays in the Comparative Sociology of a New State and an Old Tradition*, ed. Goody (London: International African Institute, 1975), pp. 94–96; Salisbury, *Manitou and Providence*, pp. 33–43.

8. Salisbury, *Manitou and Providence*, pp. 41–43; Cronon, *Changes in the Land*, pp. 59–60; Daniel Gookin, *Historical Collections of the Indians in New England* (Boston, 1792; reprinted, New York: Arno Press, 1972), pp. 7, 9.

9. Christopher L. Miller and George R. Hamell, "A New Perspective on Indian-White Contact: Cultural Symbols and Colonial Trade," *Journal of American History* 73 (1986): 311–28; Cronon, *Changes in the Land*, pp. 98–99, 102; Patrick M. Malone, "Changing Military Technology among the Indians of Southern New England, 1600–1677," *American Quarterly* 25 (1973): 48–63; Charles A. Bishop, "Northeastern Indian Concepts of Conservation and the Fur Trade: A Critique of Calvin Martin's Thesis," in *Indians, Animals, and the Fur Trade: A Critique of "Keepers of the Game,"* ed. Shepard Krech (Athens: University of Georgia Press, 1981), pp. 39–58; Susan Gibson, ed., *Burr's Hill: A Seventeenth-Century Wampanoag Burial Ground in Warren, Rhode Island* (Providence: Brown University/Haffenreffer Museum of Anthropology, 1980), pp. 23–24.

10. "When I first attempted it, they gave no heed unto it, but were weary, and rather despised what I said" (Shepard, "Clear Sunshine," p. 50); John Eliot, "The Day-Breaking, if not the Sun-Rising of the Gospell with the Indians in New-England" (1647), in *Collections of the Massachusetts Historical Society*, 3d ser. 4 (1834): 4, 9.

11. In his conversion narrative, Waban recalls his desire to be a sachem or a pow-wow (Eliot and Mayhew, "Tears of Repentance," pp. 231–32). Gookin, who knew Waban personally, described him only as "one of their principal men" in the early 1640s (*Historical Collections*, p. 28). Eliot, "Day-Breaking," p. 3.

12. *Winthrop Papers*, vol. 5, ed. Allyn Forbes (Boston: Merrymount Press, 1947), p. 131; Eliot, "Day-Breaking," p. 17. Cutshamekin seems to have had a close relationship with John Winthrop, on whose behalf he was assisting some English settlers in Connecticut, thereby earning Uncas's displeasure. Eliot was a member of the anti-Winthrop faction in the Bay colony and consistently supported Waban against Cutshamekin (see John Winthrop, *The History of New England from 1630 to 1649*, 2 vols., ed. James Savage [Boston, 1825; reprinted, New York: Arno Press, 1972], 1:195; 2:120, 303). For a description of Waban's vigorous efforts to attract adherents to the new cult and an interesting example in which a Praying Indian preacher criticized Cutshamekin's wife, see Shepard, "Clear Sunshine," pp. 52, 62.

13. Gookin, *Historical Collections*, p. 54.

14. Matthew Mayhew, *Brief Narrative*, pp. 32–33; Henry Whitfield, "Strength out of Weaknesse" (1652), in *Collections of the Massachusetts Historical Society*, 3d ser. 4 (1834): 171, 191; Shepard, "Clear Sunshine," pp. 38–39, 58; Edward Winslow, "The Glorious Progresse of the Gospell, amongst the Indians in New-England" (1649), in *Collections of the Massachusetts Historical Society*, 3d ser. 4 (1834): 88; Henry Whitfield, "The Light appearing more and more towards the perfect Day" (London, 1651), in *Collections of the Massachusetts Historical Society*, 3d ser. 4 (1834): 110–12, 125, 131.

15. Shepard, "Clear Sunshine," p. 57; Henry Bowden and James Ronda, eds., *John Eliot's Indian Dialogues: A Study in Cultural Interaction* (Westport, Conn.: Greenwood Press, 1980), p. 66.

16. Gookin, *Historical Collections*, p. 14; Matthew Mayhew, *Brief Narrative*, p. 18; Winslow, "Glorious Progress," p. 78; Experience Mayhew, *Indian converts; or, Some account of the lives and dying speeches of a considerable number of the Christianized Indians of Martha's Vineyard, in New England* (London, 1727), p. 7; Experience Mayhew, *A Discourse Shewing that God Dealeth with Men* (Boston, 1720), p. 8; Shepard, "Clear Sunshine," pp. 50–51.

17. Whitfield, "Light appearing," pp. 139, 142; Eliot, "Day-Breaking," pp. 17, 20. Cutshamekin complained, evidently unjustly, that the new converts refused to pay him his tribute. John Eliot, *A late and further manifestation of the Progress of the Gospel amongst the Indians in New England* (London, 1655), pp. 2–3.

18. Eliot, "Day-Breaking," pp. 14, 22; Whitfield, "Light appearing," pp. 113, 142; Shepard, "Clear Sunshine," pp. 50–51, 57; Gookin, *Historical Collections*, pp. 14,

68–69; J. William T. Youngs, "The Indian Saints of Early New England," *Early American Literature* 16 (Winter 1981/82): 250; Axtell, *After Columbus*, p. 56.

19. Bowden and Ronda, *Indian Dialogues*, pp. 120, 127–29; William Kellaway, *The New England Company, 1649–1776* (New York: Barnes and Noble, 1961), p. 143; Winslow, "Glorious Progresse," p. 88; Whitfield, "Light appearing," p. 139.

20. Gookin, *Historical Collections*, pp. 41, 51, 60, 68–69; David Pulsifer, ed., *Records of the Colony of New Plymouth: Acts of the Commissioners of the United Colonies of New England* (Boston, 1859), p. 383.

21. Peter A. Thomas, "Cultural Change on the Southern New England Frontier, 1630–1665," in *Cultures in Contact*, ed. William W. Fitzhugh (Washington, D.C.: Smithsonian Institution Press, 1985), pp. 131–58. It is interesting to note that Waban is described in a nineteenth-century source as an "Indian merchant" (Oliver N. Bacon, *A History of Natick* [Boston, 1856], p. 28). In the 1630s, a trading post was built on the Merrimac, effectively eliminating the Massachusett Indians' mediation in the fur trade. Although trade goods had been thoroughly integrated into their way of life by this time, the Indians had little left to sell but their land or their labor (see Salisbury, *Manitou and Providence*, pp. 148–49, 185, 200–202).

22. Ford, *Correspondence of the New England Company*, pp. 13, 40, 45, 50; John Eliot to Jonathan Hammer, 19 July and 7 October 1652, ed. F. J. Powicke, *Bulletin of the John Rylands Library* 5 (1918–20): 104–8; Winslow, "Glorious Progresse," p. 87; Whitfield, "Light appearing," p. 143, and "Strength out of Weaknesse," p. 168; Kellaway, *New England Company*, pp. 33–69; Pulsifer, *Records of New Plymouth*, pp. 189, 245, 296, 331, 356; Gookin, *Historical Collections*, p. 58.

23. Eliot, "Day-Breaking," p. 9.

24. Unconverted Indians during King Philip's War constructed elaborate forts and also maintained several blacksmith forges, indicating a similar but somewhat less extensive and perhaps necessary rather than pro-active adoption of English technology (see Malone, "Changing Military Technology," pp. 58–59). Paul J. Lindholdt, ed., *John Josselyn, Colonial Traveler* (Hanover, N.H.: University Press of New England, 1988), p. 105; Daniel Gookin, "An Historical Account of the Doings and Sufferings of the Christian Indians in New England, in the Years 1675, 1676, and 1677," in *Transactions of the American Antiquarian Society*, vol. 2 (Cambridge, 1971), p. 512; Ford, *Correspondence of the New England Company*, p. 20; Winslow, "Glorious Progresse," pp. 80, 87; Kellaway, *New England Company*, pp. 112–18; Whitfield, "Strength out of Weaknesse," p. 167; Shepard, "Clear Sunshine," p. 59. Gookin, *Historical Collections*, p. 32, states that one Praying Indian became a carpenter and another a mariner.

25. Pulsifer, *Records of New Plymouth*, p. 242; Winslow, "Glorious Progresse," p. 88; Ford, *Correspondence of the New England Company*, pp. 19, 44.

26. Ford, *Correspondence of the New England Company*, pp. 87–88; Cotton Mather, *Bonifacius: An Essay . . . To Do Good* (Boston, 1710; reprinted, Gainesville, Fla.: Scholars' Facsimiles & Reprints, 1967), p. 197; Gookin, *Historical Collections*, pp. 37, 38, 53; John Eliot, "An Account of Indian Churches in New England," in *Collections*

of the Massachusetts Historical Society, 1st ser. 10 (1809): 125–26. At Natick a whipping tree and stocks were set up; Gookin and Eliot held periodic "courts" there and at other towns and attempted to institutionalize the choice of church officers and band leaders. See Eliot, "A late and further manifestation," pp. 6–9; Whitfield, "Strength out of Weaknesse," p. 178; Frederick L. Weis, "The New England Company of 1649," in *Transactions of the Colonial Society of Massachusetts*, vol. 38 (Boston, 1947–51), p. 138. Matthew Mayhew, in describing the political and legal system that had arisen among the Praying Indians of Martha's Vineyard, noted that they used a combination of their traditional precepts and English law, "the knowledge whereof they much aspire unto" ("Brief Narrative," p. 38).

27. Bowden and Ronda, *Indian Dialogues*, pp. 74–76, 110; Eliot, "Day-Breaking," pp. 20–27; Shepard, "Clear Sunshine," p. 50.

28. Eliot proudly described one woman who no longer went "to English houses abegging, as sundry do (though it is well reformed with many of them)" but instead stayed home with her children making baskets to sell to the settlers (Winslow, "Glorious Progresse," p. 80). By comparison, unconverted Indians in the Connecticut Valley were reduced to buying their food from the English by the 1670s (Thomas, "Cultural Change," p. 155).

29. It is clear from the biographies of Martha's Vineyard's Praying Indians that the churches there functioned as an alternative career ladder, with a hierarchy of positions that could be filled sequentially over a lifetime (Experience Mayhew, "Indian converts," p. 39).

30. Shepard, "Clear Sunshine," pp. 58, 62–63; Eliot and Mayhew, "Tears of Repentance," p. 231; Winslow, "Glorious Progresse," p. 80; Pulsifier, *Records of New Plymouth*, p. 383; Gookin, *Historical Collections*, pp. 40–55, and "Doings and Sufferings," p. 440. The Massachusett Indians had historically held sway over most of the Nipmuck bands but had lost influence during the early 1600s—due to disease and other factors—to the Narragansetts, the Pequots, and the Mohegans (Gookin, *Historical Collections*, pp. 7–8).

31. For a theoretical and well-documented exploration of this process among Canada's Cree Indians in this century, see A. Irving Hallowell, *Culture and Experience* (Philadelphia: University of Pennsylvania Press, 1955).

32. Shepard, "Clear Sunshine," pp. 59, 62; Gookin, *Historical Collections*, p. 11, noted wooden chests in Praying Indian wigwams, objects incompatible with a mobile lifestyle. A mobile subsistence cycle had helped to reduce human impact on the land (see Cronon, *Changes in the Land*, p. 53; Kevin A. MacBride and Nicholas F. Bellantoni, "The Utility of Ethnohistoric Models for Understanding Late Woodland-Contact Change in Southern New England," *Bulletin of the Archaeological Society of Connecticut* 45 [1982]: 51–64).

33. Gibson, *Burr's Hill*, p. 23; Charles C. Willoughby, *Antiquities of the New England Indians* (Cambridge, 1935; reprinted, New York: AMS Press, Inc., 1973), pp. 243, 259, 264. Willoughby notes that native manufactures rapidly declined among all New England Indians as European goods became available. He lists one dogs-head

bowl from the Praying Town of Hassanamesit, but it was not made until the 1840s, was commissioned by a collector, and was quite probably a re-creation of a nearly forgotten form. William A. Turnbaugh, *The Material Culture of R-1000* (Kingston: Department of Sociology and Anthropology, University of Rhode Island, 1984), concludes that from 1625 to 1720 there was a gradual expansion in both the number and variety of European goods among unconverted Narragansett Indians. The assemblages he analyzed contain several examples of zoomorphism. For the change in basketry, compare Gookin, *Historical Collections,* p. 11, with Sarah P. Turnbaugh and William A. Turnbaugh, *Indian Baskets* (West Chester, Pa.: Schiffer Publishing, Ltd., 1986), pp. 14, 67, 113. Since objects are symbolic as well as utilitarian, the increase in European goods would help to create new social identities for both converted and unconverted; see Lawrence E. Dawson, Vera-Mae Frederickson, and Nelson Graburn, *Traditions in Transition: Culture Contact and Material Change* (Berkeley: Lowie Museum of Anthropology, 1974), p. 4.

34. On bounding of land, see Cronon, *Changes in the Land,* pp. 138–39, 169. For a theoretical explanation of the relationship between acculturation and material culture, see Dawson, Frederickson, and Graburn, *Traditions in Transition,* pp. 3–5.

35. In southeastern New England, women provided about 90 percent of the calories in the Indians' diet. See Salisbury, *Manitou and Providence,* pp. 39–40; Cronon, *Changes in the Land,* pp. 37–53; Thomas, "Cultural Change," pp. 131–33.

36. Whitfield, "Light appearing," p. 141; Shepard, "Clear Sunshine," p. 59; Gookin, "Doings and Sufferings," p. 475.

37. Gookin, *Historical Collections,* p. 51; Shepard, "Clear Sunshine," pp. 41–42, 52–54.

38. Some theorists such as Jack Goody have argued that "the practice of literacy (with or without printing) and the experience of texts rather than oracles or incantations as embodiments of language profoundly change the nature of thought" (quoted in Wyatt MacGaffey's *Religion and Society in the Central Africa: The Ba-Kongo of Lower Zaire* [Chicago: University of Chicago Press, 1986], p. 251). John Eliot, *A further account of the progress of the Gospel* (London, 1659), pp. 8–12; Eliot and Mayhew, "Tears of Repentance," pp. 242–49; Shepard, "Clear Sunshine," pp. 44–47, 53; Winslow, "Glorious Progresse," pp. 78–91.

39. Eliot, "A late and further manifestation," pp. 6–9; Whitfield, "Strength out of Weaknesse," pp. 178, 181; Shepard, "Clear Sunshine," pp. 41, 58; Eliot and Mayhew, "Tears of Repentance," pp. 246–47; James P. Ronda, "Red and White at the Bench: Indians and the Law in Plymouth Colony, 1620–1691," *Essex Institute Historical Collections* 110 (1974): 211–15. In a similar vein, see Amanda Porterfield, "Witchcraft and the Colonization of Algonquian and Iroquois Cultures," *Religion and American Culture* 2 (1992): 103–24.

40. Shepard, "Clear Sunshine," pp. 41–42, 52–54, 62; Gibson, *Burr's Hill,* p. 13.

41. Whitfield, "Light appearing," p. 138, and "Strength out of Weaknesse," pp. 171–77; Shepard, "Clear Sunshine," p. 58. On Indian attitudes to property, see Cronon, *Changes in the Land,* p. 62.

42. Rituals are "primarily a manipulation of consciousness of, by, and for actors, through symbolic objects, constructions, and arrangements." Sherry B. Ortner, *Sherpas Through Their Rituals* (Cambridge: Cambridge University Press, 1978), pp. 1–9; all quotations from p. 5.

43. Christian F. Feest, *Indians of North America* (Leiden: E. J. Brill Publishing Co., 1986), pp. 19–20; John Witthoft, "Green Corn Ceremonialism in the Eastern Woodlands" (M.A. thesis, University of Pennsylvania, 1946), pp. 10–16; Cotton Mather, *Magnalia Christi Americana* (London, 1702), pp. 559, 563, 570, 572–73; Gookin, *Historical Collections*, p. 43; Charles E. Hambrick-Stowe, *The Practice of Piety* (Chapel Hill: University of North Carolina Press, 1982), pp. 267, 278; Lewis Bayley, *The Practice of Piety* (London, 1648). For an explicit connection between concepts of time and psychological identity, see Hallowell, *Culture and Experience*, p. 234.

44. Eliot, "A further account," pp. 9–19.

45. Dean R. Snow, "'Keepers of the Game' and the Nature of Explanation," p. 68.

46. Ortner, *Sherpas*, p. 5; Gookin, *Historical Collections*, p. 42; Shepard, "Clear Sunshine," pp. 45, 60; Eliot, "Day-Breaking," p. 9. One observer noted that the Indians sang psalms with "ravishing" beauty (Ford, *Correspondence of the New England Company*, p. 88).

47. Ortner, *Sherpas*, pp. 5–9. This aspect of Ortner's theoretical framework owes much to Godfrey Lienhardt's *Divinity and Experience*.

48. Eliot, "A late and further manifestation," pp. 6–9; Gookin, *Historical Collections*, p. 9.

49. Bowden and Ronda, *Indian Dialogues*, p. 123.

50. Douglas Edward Leach, *Flintlock and Tomahawk* (New York: Macmillan Co., 1958), pp. 1–29.

51. Eliot to Richard Baxter, 27 June 1671, *Bulletin of the John Rylands Library* 15 (1931): 462.

52. Gookin, "Doings and Sufferings," p. 440; Bowden and Ronda, *Indian Dialogues*, p. 120: Winslow, "Glorious Progresse," p. 88; Pulsifer, *Records of New Plymouth*, p. 384.

53. Gookin, "Doings and Sufferings," p. 489.

54. Gookin, "Doings and Sufferings," pp. 442–534.

55. Gookin, "Doings and Sufferings," p. 513; Richard Slotkin and James K. Folsom, eds., *So Dreadful a Judgement: Puritan Responses to King Philip's War, 1676–1677* (Middletown, Conn.: Wesleyan University Press, 1978), p. 62.

56. Gookin, "Doings and Sufferings," p. 523; Ford, *Correspondence of the New England Company*, pp. 27–28, 66, 76.

57. Despite these disruptions, the Natickites seem to have made the most of their influence over the Nipmucks by selling to the English much of the newly depopulated land that had been their neighbors' territory. Nathaniel Shurtleff, ed., *Records of the Governor and Company of the Massachusetts Bay in New England*, vol. 5 (Boston, 1854), pp. 353, 355, 361, 469, 510, 533. Kathleen Joan Bragdon, "Crime and Punishment among the Indians of Massachusetts, 1675–1750," *Ethnohistory* 28 (Winter 1981): 25.

By 1700 the missionaries could report that "almost all [Indians] that remain under the influence of the English . . . are so far Christianized as that they believe there is a God, and that Jesus Christ is the Son of God, and the Savior of the world." Of the 180 families on Martha's Vineyard, only 2 "remained in their paganism" (Ford, *Correspondence of the New England Company*, pp. 83–84).

58. Shurtleff, *Records of the Governor*, pp. 328–29, 353, 355, 361, 469, 510; *Acts and Resolves of the Province of the Massachusett Bay*, vol. 7 (Boston, 1892), pp. 81, 130; Ford, *Correspondence of the New England Company*, p. 74.

59. *Acts and Resolves of the Province of Mass. Bay*, 7:267, Bragdon, "Crime and Punishment," pp. 27, 29: Ford, *Correspondence of the New England Company*, pp. 27–28, 66, 76; Bacon, *History of Natick*, p. 27.

60. Mather, *Magnalia*, pp. 565, 572. Pre-war church covenant ceremonies had been important ritual occasions, where many of the English elite would attend and Indians were accorded at least symbolic equality (see John Eliot, "A Brief Narrative of the Progress of the Gospel amongst the Indians in New England in the Year 1670" [London, 1671], p. 3). "Account of an Indian Visitation, AD 1698," in *Collections of the Massachusetts Historical Society*, 1st ser. 10 (1809): 129–34; Experience Mayhew, *A Discourse*, pp. 4–7; Ford, *Correspondence of the New England Company*, p. 65.

61. Bacon, *History of Natick*, p. 63; Natick Town Records, microfilm roll 6, Morse Library, Natick, Massachusetts; Mandell, "To Live More Like My Christian Neighbors," pp. 552–79, covers the demographic decline of the Natick Indians in detail.

62. Quoted in Bragdon's "Crime and Punishment," p. 29.

63. Kellaway, *New England Company*, pp. 148, 156–57. In the 1650s Indian scholars studied at Harvard, whereas by the 1690s they were being hired as spit turners at college feasts (*Publications of the Colonial Society of Massachusetts*, vol. 16 [Boston, 1925], p. 830).

64. Ms., Natick Town Records, manuscript box, Morse Library, Natick, Mass. According to the scale of the map, only four Indian dwellings stood within a quarter mile of each other. The total Indian population at that time was 166 (Bacon, *History of Natick*, p. 125).

65. Ives Goddard and Kathleen Joan Bragdon, *Native Writings in Massachusett*, 2 vols. (Philadelphia: American Philosophical Society, 1988), 1:11, 15, 16, 18; 2:276–77, 280–87, 293, 308; Natick Town Records, microfilm roll 1.

66. Middlesex County Probate Records, microfilm box 1864, #23401–2, Middlesex County Probate Court, Cambridge, Mass.; Mandell, "To Live More Like My Christian Neighbors," p. 552.

67. Middlesex County Probate Records, microfilm box 1864, #23400, and box 1842, #21035–39.

68. Adam Winthrop et al., "Report on the Natick Indians, 1729," in *Publications of the Colonial Society of Massachusetts*, vol. 16 (Boston, 1925), pp. 575–77; Natick Town Records, microfilm rolls 1, 14.

69. Natick Town Records, microfilm roll 6.

70. Natick Town Records, microfilm roll 6; Goddard and Bragdon, *Native Writings*, p. 20.

71. Francis G. Hutchins, *Mashpee: The Story of Cape Cod's Indian Town* (West Franklin, N.H.: Amarta Press, 1979).

72. By comparison, as early as 1662, John Winthrop, Jr., proposed a forcible work farm scheme for the Praying Indians: they were to supply the labor and market that would make the project's investors a profit (Kellaway, *New England Company*, p. 107).

9

"Poor Indians" and the "Poor in Spirit"
The Indian Impact on David Brainerd

RICHARD W. POINTER

Almost simultaneous with the disintegration of the missionary program in eastern Massachusetts, new initiatives emerged in the western part of the colony. In 1734, several New England clergymen, led by Stephen Williams (a former captive of Canadian Indians), struck an agreement with sachem Konkapot and other members of the Housatonic band for the creation of a missionary community at Stockbridge, on the western edge of Massachusetts. Its first pastor/teacher was John Sergeant, originally from New Jersey but a graduate of Yale who was deeply committed to the conversion of Indians. One of Sergeant's early assistants was David Brainerd; he remained only briefly at Stockbridge but would become, thanks to a biographical memoir by the renowned Reverend Jonathan Edwards, one of eighteenth-century New England's most heralded missionaries.

Although Brainerd was born in Connecticut and died in Massachusetts, he did not confine his missionary work to New England natives. After a brief assignment on eastern Long Island—among Indians whose origins were mostly in southern Connecticut—and another brief term at an eastern New York outpost of the Stockbridge mission, Brainerd spent the few remaining years of his life (he died of tuberculosis at age twenty-nine) among the Delaware Indians of New Jersey and Pennsylvania—a New England missionary in the wider world.

Richard W. Pointer's article examines not so much what missionary Brainerd did for the Delawares as what the Delawares did for him. In ways somewhat reminiscent of the early Algonquian experience of turning to Christianity in the face of serious affliction, Brainerd's illness in 1745 renewed his faith and focused his pastoral energies. Thereafter he relied increasingly on his interpreter, Moses Tatamy, and other natives to reshape his preaching and his own dependence on saving grace. Brainerd's missionary efforts took on a new urgency and were increasingly successful.

If Brainerd's career had no close parallels among his contemporaries, it none-

theless demonstrates the persistence and the geographic expansion of the Protes-
tant missionary movement in the eighteenth century and the complexity of En-
glish-Indian religious encounters throughout New England's history.

𝓕RESH ON THE HEELS of his most successful month as a missionary
evangelist, Presbyterian David Brainerd headed off into the Pennsylvania interior in September 1745 to visit Indian villages along the Susquehanna River. There he spent nine days observing and conversing with natives more different than he had anticipated from the Indians he had lately
seen awakened to Christian faith at Crossweeksung, New Jersey. Brainerd
found his attempts "to instruct and Christianize" the inland Indians to be
"all to no purpose." Once back in Crossweeksung, however, his preaching
brought "a season of comfort to some in particular" and "numbers were
affected with divine truths." He could not help but take note of the contrast: "Oh, what a difference is there between these and the Indians I had
lately treated with upon Susquehanna! To be with those seemed like being
banished from God and all his people; to be with these like being admitted
into his family, and to the enjoyment of his divine presence!"[1]

Brainerd's distinction among varied native responses to his evangelism
reveals an understanding many other colonial preachers probably grasped
intuitively and modern Indian historians have recently emphasized: Native
Americans already living on the English-dominated side of the cultural
divide between Indians and colonists were far more likely to embrace
Christianity than those still living in "Indian Country."[2] That deceptively
simple insight nevertheless adds considerable sophistication to our current
appreciation of colonial Christianity's divergent appeal among Indian
peoples. But even something more can be gleaned from Brainerd's brief
reflection: his own emotional and spiritual conditions were apparently
affected by the character of his contact with Indians. Or, to put it another
way, Indians made some kind of difference, at least temporarily, in his life.
While this point may seem like nothing more than stating the obvious,
interpreters of Brainerd since Jonathan Edwards have minimized or ignored it. In spite of Brainerd's daily contact with Mahican and Delaware
Indians for much of his brief adult life, Edwards and later observers considered Native Americans irrelevant to the story of Brainerd's real historical significance.[3]

Pushing Indians aside in such a manner might seem surprising if it were
not part of a larger and long-standing tendency among historians of English colonial religion to treat natives as, at best, part of the set and, at
worst, entirely off stage in the colonial religious drama. Indians find very

little place in even the best recent syntheses of colonial religion.[4] And the analyses of English-Indian religious interaction that do exist focus over-whelmingly on the European's impact on the native.[5] While clearly help-ful, these studies need to be complemented by attempts to portray the other side: specifically, how the presence of Indians in British North America may have affected colonial religion.[6] Taking David Brainerd at his word, that Indians could and did influence him, seems a useful starting point for reintroducing Native Americans as the major actors they un-doubtedly were both in Brainerd's world and in the larger colonial world the English and Indians shared.

I

By the time Brainerd made that trip to the Susquehanna Indians, he was already an experienced Indian missionary by eighteenth-century colonial standards, even though he had been in the "field" only two and a half years. Evangelizing Indians had never been a major concern of the first colonial churches in English North America, and it was even less of one by the late 1600s. A generation later, the fledgling efforts of Anglican missionaries from the Society for the Propagation of the Gospel and the more focused initiatives of newly arrived Moravians had sparked increased Protestant competition for native souls; nonetheless, Indian missions were still a low priority for the colonial church, and few young men felt called to serve Christ's kingdom among Native Americans.[7] Such indifference stemmed from a host of factors, not the least of which was the broader culture's desire for expediency. Often, as James H. Merrell has commented, "it proved easier to kill Indians than convert them."[8] But Merrell and others have also pointed up that Indian resistance cannot be ignored as another crucial explanation for the scarcity of missionary ventures.[9] With compara-tively few exceptions, Indian peoples throughout the colonial era wished to shun rather than embrace the whites' religion. Missionaries and native converts both found themselves swimming upstream against powerful cul-tural currents. No wonder so little was happening.

And no wonder David Brainerd responded soberly when the prospect of evangelizing Indians was first presented to him in the fall of 1742. Hav-ing grown up in Haddam, Connecticut, a village along the Connecticut River where colonists had occasional contact with the surviving remnants of the neighboring southern New England Indians, young David un-doubtedly overheard more than one story about bothersome natives.[10] While studying at Yale College (1739–42), the young man absorbed accounts of John Eliot and the Mayhews, of the Pequot and of King Philip's Wars, all of which, however told, would have left their mark. Norman Pettit suggests that Brainerd inherited Eliot's view of Indians as "doleful creatures,"[11] and certainly the young man would have been aware that many Indians had notoriously little interest in the Christian gospel.

It is highly unlikely that David Brainerd's attitudes toward Indians could have been very sympathetic. Altered circumstances had prematurely forced him to choose a vocation, however, and working among Indians was one option that presented itself. In November 1742, Presbyterian pastor Ebenezer Pemberton invited him to New York City to meet the colonial commissioners of the Society in Scotland for Propagating Christian Knowledge. Since his expulsion from Yale ten months earlier for accusing tutor Chauncey Whittelsey of having "no more grace than a chair," Brainerd had spent much of his time agonizing over God's plan for him. Pemberton's offer left him "much concerned" and prompted intensified prayers for divine guidance. His New York meeting went well enough to generate a job offer, which he accepted. But far from relieving his anxiety, the prospect of a life spent "gospellizing the heathen" overwhelmed him with a sense of his own "great ignorance and unfitness for public service" (p. 188).[12]

Brainerd was depressed, not enthused, by his calling, a reaction explained largely by his melancholic spirit, lack of self-confidence, and ongoing disappointment over unfulfilled scholarly ambitions.[13] Yet his conception of Indian missions, a conception partially created by Indians themselves, seems also to have played a role. As he prepared to take up his first assignment for the Scottish society, a sense of doom settled over his farewell to loved ones: "Took an affectionate leave of friends, not expecting to see them again for a very considerable time, if ever in this world" (p. 193). So awesome was the task ahead that the already modest Brainerd was humbled, prostrated: "I saw I was not worthy of a place among the Indians, where I am going, if God permit: I thought I should be ashamed to look them in the face, and much more to have any respect shown me there. . . . I thought I should be ashamed to go among the very savages of Africa" (p. 195).

The Scottish society assigned Brainerd to be a supply preacher to white Christians at East Hampton, Long Island. He spent six weeks there pastoring the Congregational church. But he also saw firsthand the poverty of both the neighboring Indians (Niantics, Mahicans, Pequots, and Narragansetts) and Presbyterian minister Azariah Horton's attempts to convert them. In an oft-quoted passage from his diary, Brainerd admitted his sense of "flatness and deadness" after meeting Horton's parishioners at Montauk

Point. He struggled to preach to them twice that day but was preoccupied with the "blackness" of his own soul and the thought that he was not fit "to speak so much as to Indians" (pp. 199–200). While Brainerd's comments suggest a religious self-centeredness,[14] their focus is broader, for they encompass not only his private thoughts but the realities reflected in the faces of the natives who stared back at him. Indians were, without a doubt, "poor" in every sense of the word, and going among them meant not only moving to the geographic margins of colonial society but to the religious margins of the colonial church.[15] While Brainerd's obvious distaste—his flatness and deadness—at the prospect of working with Indians partakes of the racist sentiments typical of white colonists, he does not share the swelled pride that, according to James Axtell, characterized the English response to relations with Native Americans.[16] Brainerd departed from the Long Island Indians with a broken spirit rather than an inflated ego. Direct contact with natives had done far more to intensify his self-loathing than to deepen his cultural bias.

II

Not yet twenty-five, David Brainerd was poised to assume his first missionary post without benefit of formal training or experience. His uncompleted Yale education and his year as an itinerant preacher (he had spoken a few times to Indians) were all he could draw upon as he readied himself to embark on evangelistic work along the Delaware River. Now came word from the commissioners of the Scottish society that tensions on the Pennsylvania frontier were too high to risk sending a new missionary. Instead, Brainerd was to head north to extend the ministry of John Sergeant, missionary to the Indians at Stockbridge, Massachusetts.[17] Sergeant, veteran missionary, former Yale tutor, and the individual who had recommended that the society place a missionary among the Delaware Indians after his own visit with them in 1741,[18] was a logical mentor for Brainerd. Brainerd arrived in the Stockbridge vicinity in early April 1743, disheartened by the change in plans and ill prepared to minister to a small group of Mahican Indians living in Kaunaumeek, New York, about eighteen miles from Albany and twenty miles from Sergeant.

Over the course of the following twelve months, Sergeant taught Brainerd many of the standard strategies English missionaries traditionally employed in evangelizing Indians: establish a school to teach native youths Christian morals, manners, and doctrine; suppress any "heathenish" practices, such as "idolatrous sacrifices" and "savage" dances; tutor Indians in how to pray, how to sing the Psalms, and how to observe the Sabbath; gather your charges into a single town, keep them there year round, and instill in them the work ethic of the English yeoman farmer; garner the support of native political leaders and discredit the spiritual authority of powwows; and learn the Indians' language while also teaching them English as quickly as possible.[19] Always a good student, Brainerd rapidly absorbed and implemented the lessons Sergeant and the Stockbridge mission had developed. In the long run, however, much of what Brainerd learned from Sergeant proved useless. For example, Brainerd's arduous efforts to learn one Algonquian dialect were wasted, for it could not be understood by the Algonquian and Iroquoian speakers of New Jersey and Pennsylvania among whom he spent most of his career.[20]

If much of what Brainerd the student learned in his year at Kaunaumeek was ultimately irrelevant, the same cannot be said of what Brainerd the teacher drew from his students. Ever since the Pilgrims had arrived in 1620, Native Americans had offered the English numerous lessons of lasting value.[21] Most colonists, and Brainerd was among them, never plainly acknowledged their debts. With or without Brainerd's awareness or acknowledgment, however, his first sustained contact with Indians revealed a host of truths about himself, his work, his faith, and his "people."

Some of those truths merely confirmed what Brainerd had previously been told or seen for himself. Missionary evangelism was a lonesome task with few rewards. New England Indians had been "reduced" to economic want. Neighboring whites were unsympathetic both to natives and to native missions. And breaking down Indian "prejudices" against Christianity was prerequisite to planting the gospel.[22]

Other lessons were fresh and unexpected. Brainerd's experiences among the Housatonic Valley Indians altered his view of material plenty. Six weeks after his arrival, he noted that he lived "poorly with regard to the comforts of life: most of my diet consists of boiled corn, hasty pudding, etc. I lodge on a bundle of straw, and my labor is hard and extremely difficult" (p. 207). Even after moving into a cottage of his own, Brainerd's surroundings were spare by white standards. While at first a cause for complaint, Brainerd's own condition and the Mahicans' more straitened circumstances eventually prompted him to issue increasingly strident denunciations of lives devoted to "worldly pleasures."[23]

Feeling as if the world had rejected him, Brainerd now in turn rejected the world. Whether praying for his own death, which would free him for immortality, or for the advent of the millennium, which would free all of God's chosen,[24] one thing was clear: Brainerd desperately wanted to escape from the miserable world he then inhabited. How fully the Kaunaumeek

Indians shared in Brainerd's discontent is impossible to say. But sharing even partially in their impoverished lives clearly deepened his alienation from "all earthly pleasures and profits" (p. 234).

Naturally, what Brainerd desired most for the Mahicans was that they embrace Christianity. Their warm reception and willingness to listen to him preach initially provoked expectations of quick conversions.[25] When these failed to materialize, Brainerd gradually realized that native hospitality and deference to his spiritual leadership were no guarantees that regeneration (as he understood it) had or would take place in any individual Indian lives. Wishful thoughts about instant success gave way to more modest hopes that, slowly but surely, God "was preparing his way into their souls."[26] Ironically, when Brainerd decided to leave Kaunaumeek for the Forks of the Delaware, it was the Mahicans who warned him that the far distant tribes he now went to serve "were not willing to become Christians, as they were."[27] The truth of that lesson lay before him.

III

It was not long before Brainerd discovered on his own what the Mahicans had suggested about natives living on the other side of the cultural divide. On his way to Pennsylvania, he stopped at Minisink, New York, and met with a group of Munsees. His efforts to win a hearing for Christianity were mocked by the local "King" and rebuffed by a "rational" Indian who criticized Christianity as a corrupting rather than a purifying influence. They preferred to "live as their fathers lived and go where their fathers were when they died," the Indians informed Brainerd. To his request for a return engagement, they replied that they would be "willing to see me again as a friend, if I would not desire 'em to become Christians."[28]

Daunted by his failure to persuade the Munsees, a gloomy Brainerd arrived at the Forks of the Delaware and Lehigh Rivers unsure of how to proceed with his ministry. What he soon learned about the Indians he had waited a year and a half to evangelize only intensified his discouragement. Most immediately, only a smattering of Delawares still lived in this part of Pennsylvania. Most of the area's Lenape Indians had been forced in the previous seven years to migrate westward to native towns along the Susquehanna River. They had been no match for the combined forces of white land hunger, government deceit, and imperial politics. White encroachment on Indian lands had been legitimated in the infamous Walking Purchase of 1737. Five years later, the Pennsylvania government had demanded that its Six Nations allies exert additional pressure on the Delawares to move. The few dozen who remained at the Forks thereafter lived in scattered villages and struggled to maintain some semblance of the life previous generations had enjoyed.[29] What in recent memory had still been Indian Country was now rapidly being absorbed into the Anglo-american world.

David Brainerd was there, of course, to change, not to support, Indian ways. The extent of his "reform" agenda as well as the character of the Indians he encountered is revealed in a letter to Ebenezer Pemberton, written six months after Brainerd's arrival at the Forks. The evil influence of irreligious whites certainly compounded "the difficulties that attend the Christianizing of these poor pagans," Brainerd conceded, but most obstacles were erected by the Delawares. He enumerated them: the Delawares' strong attachment to "the customs, traditions, and fabulous notions of their fathers"; their ability to defend their religious faith; their awe for their powwows; and their "roving" lifestyle. Brainerd assumed that each of these features of native life would have to be altered if Christianity were to take hold among the Lenape.

Despite his discouragements, however, Brainerd was able to report some modest success. The Forks Indians had often been willing to listen to him preach, and some of them had renounced "their old idolatrous notions" and were trying to persuade others to do likewise.[30]

Yet such a simple account belies the intensity of Brainerd's struggle with the question of missionary "success," both in the six months preceding and in the six months following his correspondence with Pemberton. He arrived in Pennsylvania in May 1744, and ordination a month later by the Presbytery of New York confirmed his call. Living among whites at Hunter's Settlement, Brainerd had to ride up to twelve miles each way to visit the Indians in the Forks area. He would preach to them in the "King's house" or, more privately, converse with those "much disaffected to Christianity." When apart from those he had been called to serve, he labored to translate prayers into the Unami Delaware dialect and to locate lands where the natives "might live together and be under better advantages for instruction."[31] Notably absent from his activities were any sustained efforts simply to observe Delaware life, let alone participate in it, tactics used effectively by his Moravian competitors in Pennsylvania.[32] Instead, he felt compelled to disrupt native ceremonies and to dare local powwows to inflict their worst spells upon him.[33]

Feeling the "weight and difficulty" of his work, Brainerd understood that his "whole dependence and hope of success seemed to be on God." The task of Indian conversion "appeared 'impossible with men,' yet with God ... 'all things were possible.'" Divine possibility increasingly consumed Brainerd. As early as July, he wrote that "of late all my concern almost is for the conversion of the heathen; and for that end I long to live." By late July, he thought he could be content never to see any of his old friends again "if God would bless my labors here to the conversion of the poor Indians." In October he took his first trip inland to evangelize the Susquehanna Indians, again prompted by his growing passion for Indian converts.[34]

Still, with no sure signs that any native souls had been or were about to be won, Brainerd was plagued by doubts: perhaps God was "not able to convert the Indians before they had more knowledge"; perhaps He did not exist at all. Such thoughts were quickly repressed, but anxieties would occasionally reemerge and find expression. "I feel as if my all was lost and I was undone for this world if the poor heathen mayn't be converted," Brainerd confessed to one friend. As fall turned to winter, no real progress could be reported. The Delaware continued to participate in native feasts and dances, and some simply "refused to believe the truth of what I taught them."[35]

Indian recalcitrance, along with a developing case of tuberculosis, brought Brainerd to something of a breaking point in early February 1745. For two days he experienced hellish depression and confusion. Relief came on the third day in the form of a revised understanding of what it meant to be a successful missionary. Brainerd wrote in his diary,

> God was pleased to hear my cries, and to afford me great assistance; so that I felt peace in my own soul; and was satisfied that if not one of the Indians should be profited by my preaching, but should all be damned, yet I should be accepted and rewarded as faithful; for I am persuaded God enabled me to be so. [P. 285]

Selfless execution of missionary duties, in Brainerd's new view, was an appropriate criterion for judging his or any other evangelist's success, even in the absence of an impressive tally of born-again souls.

Six months later, in Crossweeksung, New Jersey, Brainerd finally witnessed that ingathering of repentant Indians for which he had long hoped. At that point, he reverted to his earlier position of valuing results over devoted service. Ironically, however, many of Brainerd's eighteenth- and nineteenth-century evangelistic successors adopted the view Brainerd had arrived at in despair. Joseph Conforti has persuasively argued that Brainerd's example and words inspired later missionaries to place as much, if not greater, emphasis on their personal quests for holiness as on the salvation of non-Christians. For them, a missionary's success was to be measured not by the number of his converts but by the faithfulness of his sacrificial service in the cause of Christ.[36]

But while Brainerd's influence on the evangelical missionary movement has been recognized by historians, that of the Delaware Indians has not. They were the chief cause of Brainerd's much-noted soul searching. Their occasional responsiveness fueled his zeal for converts. Their more frequent hostility sparked his long journeys into night. They prompted him to reassess why he was among them and what he could accomplish. They provoked him consciously and unconsciously to wonder about the nature of God and his power. They left him perplexed and perturbed about the workings of native life and thought. And they aroused in him feelings of love and hate toward himself and toward those he had come to serve. Through it all, forgotten Delaware men, women, and children molded the character of the young missionary. In so doing, they made their own inadvertent contribution to the spread of Christianity around the globe.

IV

In June 1745, David Brainerd visited the Delaware Indians at Crossweeksung. There he found a much more receptive audience for his Christian message, and within six weeks, a spiritual awakening had dawned among his native listeners. Indian conversions became a regular, if not quite commonplace, occurrence, and Brainerd poured himself into the work of pastoring and catechizing the new believers. He quickly sensed the need for a more permanent home for his emerging congregation, and he set about acquiring lands where the Christian Indians could live in peace and grow in faith. By the following May, he helped them move to Cranberry, New Jersey, and the work of creating a Christian Indian town began in earnest. Brainerd spent the next six months overseeing the community's spiritual and "worldly" concerns. Then, fighting ever worsening tuberculosis, he left Cranberry in November 1746, hoping to recuperate in New England so that some day he could return to his people. But apart from a brief visit the following March, Brainerd never again saw his congregation.[37]

Much of the story of the Christianization of the Crossweeksung Indians conforms with recent historical findings about natives and missionaries. As "Settlement Indians," these Delaware were more susceptible to Christian evangelism than their brethren at the Forks. By the 1740s, their ranks were depleted, their lands appropriated, and their culture in disarray. They lived in a colony where English ways dominated and where Indian ways were less and less visible. On the whole, the contest of cultures had inexorably pushed New Jersey's natives toward an increasing dependence upon whites. Within such a context, embracing Christianity was a logical, although not inevitable, choice for resident Indians and destroying native traditions a common practice among those doing the Christianizing.[38] Expressing a cultural arrogance all but universal among the English settlers, Brainerd publicly berated members of his own flock as ungrateful, indolent, slothful, and lacking "the spirit of a man."[39]

Still, the story of David Brainerd's sixteen months among the New Jersey Delaware has enough interesting twists and turns in it that it would be unwise, and unfortunate, to make it conform to type. For example, whereas most Native American groups more readily adopted the economic than the religious practices of the English, Brainerd's Indians found Christianity much more to their liking than the work ethic he tried to drill into them.[40] Repeatedly complaining about having to attend to the Indians' secular affairs, he bemoaned their reluctance to become the "laborious and industrious" self-sufficient farmers he envisioned. In fact, virtually all of Brainerd's virulent remarks about the Native Americans with whom he was acquainted concerned their work habits. What he saw were idle Indians too willing to depend upon him for their worldly well-being. What he failed to see was that such a willingness was likely a reluctance for, and an attempt to retard, a far more thoroughgoing dependence upon English ways.[41]

Brainerd's private diary and public journal for 1745 and 1746 suggest that he was often blind to another major twist in the story: his own growing dependence upon Indians. Hidden but not absent in his writings are clues that while he remained thoroughly English and Christian, his relationships with Indians increasingly shaped everything from his evangelistic method to his psychological health.

The most important of these relationships during his years in Pennsylvania and New Jersey was Brainerd's association with his Indian interpreter, Moses Tatamy, hired soon after Brainerd arrived in the Forks of the Delaware. Tatamy was an extraordinary Indian. He was well known in the area not only as a skilled interpreter but as a private landowner and an experienced "cultural broker" who facilitated negotiations between various Indian groups and the Pennsylvania government. He also knew the ways of Christian missionaries, having spent time with Moravian leader Count Zinzendorf two years earlier. Once employed, Tatamy soon became indispensable to Brainerd.[42] With little or no facility in the Delaware languages and committed to a brand of Christianity dominated by words rather than images, symbols, or rituals, Brainerd rightly saw his missionary effectiveness as directly dependent on his translator. On one occasion he acknowledged, "my interpreter being absent, I know not how to perform my work among the Indians" (p. 288).[43]

Tatamy's importance in Brainerd's life and ministry steadily grew in the two and a half years they spent together. A critical turning point came when Tatamy experienced the new birth. He and his wife were the first Indians Brainerd baptized; their children were sprinkled several days later, all in July 1745. With this event Brainerd's earlier frustrations that his interpreter's doctrinal knowledge was insufficient and his tone indifferent now gave way to an enthusiasm for his colleague's ability to appreciate and replicate the missionary's sermonic style and substance.[44] Soon Tatamy was extending his role. Amid the revival in Crossweeksung, the native had taken "pains night and day to repeat and inculcate upon the minds of the Indians the truths . . . taught them daily." Indeed, Tatamy was doing so much spiritual mentoring that Brainerd found it necessary to remind him frequently to avoid setting himself up as a "publick teacher."[45] By the last of the four evangelistic trips the two made together into the rugged Pennsylvania interior (August 1746), however, Brainerd had instructed Tatamy and five other Christian Indians to spend a day talking with the Delaware residents before the missionary began his evangelizing. Apparently, Brainerd had come to rely on Tatamy to clear a spiritual as well as a physical path through the alien forest.[46]

Brainerd's appreciation for Tatamy was, although limited, completely genuine. In his public journal, Brainerd described the native as a "great comfort" and a "great instrument of promoting this good work among the Indians."[47] He also referred to Tatamy by name, the only native so honored in any of his writings.[48] At the same time, Brainerd never thought of Tatamy as anything but an Indian. Brainerd's repeated attempts to recruit a white colleague to assist him and to provide the opportunity for Christian fellowship makes plain the limits of his friendship with Tatamy and thus with natives in general.[49] Still, the Indian interpreter was a crucial presence for Brainerd. Experientially acquainted with divine truths and highly assimilated to English ways, Tatamy represented precisely the kind of Christianized and Anglicized Indian Brainerd set out to create. No wonder Brainerd felt comforted by Tatamy. He was living proof that, with God's grace, the ideal could be realized.

As Tatamy helped translate Brainerd's message into Indian languages, other natives, individually and collectively, helped determine what that message would be. The evangelist noted immediately that he had struck a responsive chord with the Crossweeksung Indians in early August 1745 when he preached a "milder gospel," one devoid of terror and focused instead on "the compassion and care of the Lord Jesus Christ for 'those that were lost.'"[50] For the rest of the month, he drew on scriptural texts revealing the "comfortable" rather than the "awfull truths of God's word" in his daily revival preaching. As more and more Indian hearts were "melted," he became convinced that native spiritual concern "was never excited by any harangues of terror, but always appeared most remarkable, when I insisted upon the compassions of a dying Saviour, the plentifull provisions of the Gospel, and the free offers of divine Grace to needy distressed Sinners."[51] Not surprisingly, Brainerd used the same texts (and probably the same sermons) when he traveled in September to the Forks of the Delaware and on to Shamokin and Juniata, Indian towns on the Susquehanna.[52] Once back in Crossweeksung, he continued to reorient his preaching and teaching toward those themes natives preferred to hear.[53]

Studies of Delaware culture by Herbert Kraft, C. A. Weslager, and Anthony F. C. Wallace suggest that Lenape sensibilities were more suited to receiving a "milder gospel."[54] Just how clearly those sensibilities were communicated or how fully Brainerd understood them is impossible to say. At the very least, though, the Indians' words and actions made him aware that concepts of sin, guilt, divine anger, and eternal punishment were especially foreign to their vocabulary. And once aware, Brainerd made concerted efforts to tailor his evangelism accordingly.[55] He even tried to build on native religious beliefs occasionally. For instance, what "very aged Indians" taught him about their ancestors' notion that "something of the Man . . . would survive the Body" became a means for explaining the other-worldly focus of his own message to Indians who were otherwise accustomed to conversing with whites only about this-worldly matters.[56]

When native souls were saved, Brainerd, like any good Calvinist, was quick to credit God. But that is not to say that he did not derive deep personal satisfaction from his role in the process. For the first time, his ministry had borne tangible fruit, and he finally had a congregation he could truly call his own. Feelings of warm affection evolved on both sides, leaving Brainerd less emotionally disabled than perhaps at any other point in his adult life.[57] By December 1745, with twenty Indian families living within a quarter mile of his cottage, he had ample opportunity to nurture his flock. Individual Indians moved him with their struggles for faith, and he delighted in going from house to house teaching and counseling and in gathering Indians in his home for singing and Bible study. Emotions often ran high as pastor and laypersons wept together over the conditions of their souls.[58] By the following spring, Brainerd felt a wonderful closeness with his people: "My heart was knit to them . . . And I saw in them appearances of the same love. This gave me something of a view of the heavenly state; and particularly that part of the happiness of heaven which consists in the communion of saints: and this was very affecting to me" (p. 380).

The spiritual pilgrimages of the Indian conjurer, the woman in "great distress," and the "one who had been a vile drunkard" bespoke the amazing work of God's grace among the New Jersey Indians.[59] So, too, did the testimony of "one weary heavy-laden soul" whose account of "God's dealing with his soul" Brainerd found "abundantly satisfying" and "refreshing." This native described how he had often heard the missionary say that people must recognize their helplessness to do anything on behalf of their own salvation. He imagined that once he was humbled, God "would then be well pleased with him and bestow eternal life upon him." To his surprise, however, having become aware of his inability to save himself, he "felt it would be just with God to send him to eternal misery." Preoccupied thereafter with his own sinfulness, the Indian had come to one of Brainerd's evening services, and amid the invitation to sinners, his heart saw "something that was unspeakably good and lovely, and what he had never seen before." That "unspeakable excellence" was "the way of salvation by Christ." The regenerate native now believed that it was "unspeakably better to be saved altogether by the mere free grace of God in Christ, than to have had any hand in saving himself" (pp. 355–57).

In a real sense, Brainerd depended on this story and others like it to convince the Angloamerican religious world that the Crossweeksung awakening, and the Great Awakening in general, were truly God's work. His 1746 journal was very much an apologia for moderate evangelicalism.[60] Thus, several years before Brainerd's own religious autobiography was used for the same purpose by Jonathan Edwards, Brainerd himself had upheld some of his Indian converts as models of sinners saved by grace and living in faith. In fact, he thought they were such good models that no criticism of either their conversions or the evangelistic means employed to achieve them would be possible.[61] That these anonymous Indians should have been ignored by succeeding generations of white Christians, who preferred to cite David Brainerd as their model of true religion, comes as no surprise. That they continue to be ignored by students of colonial religion, including Brainerd scholars, is a historical oversight long awaiting correction.

V

The denouement of Brainerd's life took eleven months to play out. Housebound in Elizabethtown, New Jersey, and Northampton, Massachusetts, for most of that time, the twenty-nine-year-old missionary fought losing battles with physical affliction and emotional depression. As difficult as the previous four years of ministry had been at times, nothing seemed worse to him than his idle passing of days in 1747. Strong yearnings for death returned, mixed once again with present feelings of uselessness.[62]

Yet Brainerd's final year was not altogether dark. His physical strength ebbed and flowed, occasionally affording him enough "clearness of thought and composure of mind" to talk and write about those things he considered most vital to the colonial church (p. 451). High on his list was promoting Indian missions. Norman Pettit may be right that Brainerd's original desire was to be a scholar; but once he became a missionary, there is no denying that evangelizing Indians and watching God's kingdom descend among them became central concerns.[63] The fortunes of his congregation in Cranberry especially "lay much on his heart" during the last two weeks of his life. Edwards wrote that when Brainerd spoke of his people, "it was with peculiar tenderness; so that his speech would be presently interrupted and drowned with tears" (p. 471).

Those tears should not be discounted as simply signs of a dying man's agony. Brainerd had defended the healthy emotionalism of the Cranberry Indians, and following their bent, he had privileged a compassionate God over a stern one in his preaching to them. Perhaps that compassionate God is who Brainerd now contemplated meeting face to face as he was called to give an account of himself.

Ever since he had left Yale, Indians had been making important differences in Brainerd's life. Those "differences" varied depending on the character of the Native Americans he encountered and of the relationship he experienced with them. Brainerd no doubt felt closest to the Christian Indians in New Jersey, but his repeated trips to the Pennsylvania interior reflect how powerfully he was drawn to the far larger groups of unevangelized natives living there.[64] Both types of Indians influenced him and deserve to be acknowledged in any telling of his story. Such a comment seems little more than stating the obvious. All versions of his life rehearsed since the 1750s, however, have principally portrayed Brainerd as a model of true virtue, example of sacrificial missionary service, definer of missionary success, and defender of the moderate Awakening against rational Arminianism and religious enthusiasm. In his otherwise excellent introduction to Edwards's *Life of David Brainerd,* for example, Norman Pettit fails to include any Indians in his discussions of Brainerd's adversaries, friends, associates, and confidants. Brainerd is placed solely in the contexts of white New England religion, as though he had spent his abbreviated career as a pastor in New Haven rather than as a missionary to at least four different groups of Indians.[65]

Perhaps interpreters of Brainerd have overlooked native influence in part because of Brainerd's own imperviousness to it.[66] His recurrent self-absorption sealed him off from others, especially alien Indians. So, too, did a missionary strategy that featured preaching at natives he barely knew rather than becoming one of them and, in the process, earning the right to be heard. Likewise, his notion of evangelistic success provided personal solace but shifted attention back to his own soul and away from those of his charges. How willful or deliberate Brainerd was in shielding himself from any Indian impress is difficult to say. But in the end, what emerges as most striking in his story is that in spite of whatever conscious or unconscious efforts were made to avoid the native touch, he nevertheless felt it and was changed by it.

To leave Indians out, therefore, will not do. With Native Americans absent, the picture not only of Brainerd's life in particular but of early American religion in general is incomplete. If current historians are going to redress that problem, they will have to rediscover the Indian presence in colonial North America and look for clues in its historical record to find where and how Native Americans were actors and not just acted upon. Once that task is accomplished, then religious historians may begin to understand more fully how Indians made a difference in the complex drama of colonial religion.

Notes

1. Jonathan Edwards, *The Life of David Brainerd*, ed. Norman Pettit, vol. 7 of *The Works of Jonathan Edwards* (New Haven: Yale University Press, 1985), pp. 331, 332. Quotations from this edition will be cited in the text. It should be noted that Edwards's *Life* is primarily his edited version of Brainerd's private diaries.

2. James H. Merrell, "'The Customes of Our Countrey': Indians and Colonists in Early America," in *Strangers Within the Realm: Cultural Margins of the First British Empire*, ed. Bernard Bailyn and Philip D. Morgan (Chapel Hill: University of North Carolina Press, 1991), pp. 146–52; James Axtell, *The Invasion Within: The Contest of Cultures in Colonial North America* (New York: Oxford University Press, 1985), pp. 242–43.

3. See Norman Pettit, introduction to Edwards's *Life of Brainerd*, p. 13. Indians find little place in either older popular accounts or in more recent scholarly assessments of Brainerd's significance. For popular accounts, see Richard Ellsworth Day, *Flagellant on Horseback: The Life Story of David Brainerd* (Philadelphia: Judson Press, 1950); David Wynbeek, *David Brainerd, Beloved Yankee*, 2d ed. (Grand Rapids, Mich.: Eerdmans, 1964); and Clyde S. Kilby, "David Brainerd," in *Heroic Colonial Christians*, ed. Russell T. Hitt (Philadelphia: Lippincott, 1966), pp. 151–206. For

scholarly assessments, see Joseph Conforti, "David Brainerd and the Nineteenth-Century Missionary Movement," *Journal of the Early Republic* 5 (1985): 309–29; Joseph Conforti, "Jonathan Edwards's Most Popular Work: 'The Life of David Brainerd' and Nineteenth-Century Evangelical Culture," *Church History* 54 (1985): 188–201; David L. Weddle, "The Melancholy Saint: Jonathan Edwards's Interpretation of David Brainerd as a Model of Evangelical Spirituality," *Harvard Theological Review* 81 (1988): 297–318; and Pettit's introduction to Edwards's *Life of Brainerd*, pp. 1–71. Richard A. S. Hall, *The Neglected Northampton Texts of Jonathan Edwards* (Lewiston, N.Y.: Edwin Mellen Press, 1990), pp. 145–200, pays somewhat greater attention to Indians in a chapter on Brainerd's diary.

4. Patricia U. Bonomi, *Under the Cope of Heaven: Religion, Society, and Politics in Colonial America* (New York: Oxford University Press, 1986), and Jon Butler, *Awash in a Sea of Faith: Christianizing the American People* (Cambridge, Mass.: Harvard University Press, 1990), mention Indians briefly. I have borrowed the stage metaphor from James H. Merrell, "The Indians' New World: The Catawba Experience," *William and Mary Quarterly*, 3d ser. 41 (1984): 565. See James H. Merrell, "Some Thoughts on Colonial Historians and American Indians," *William and Mary Quarterly*, 3d ser. 46 (1989): 94–119, and Daniel K. Richter, "Whose Indian History?" *William and Mary Quarterly*, 3d ser. 50 (1993): 379–93, on the absence of Indians in studies of early American history in general.

5. Examples are too numerous to cite. James Axtell makes a similar point in "The Indian Impact on English Colonial Culture," in his *The European and the Indian* (New York: Oxford University Press, 1981), pp. 272–75.

6. James Axtell has taken the lead in providing serious consideration of this question. See "Indian Impact," pp. 272–315, *Invasion Within*, pp. 286, 302–33, and "Colonial America without the Indians: Counterfactual Reflections," *Journal of American History* 73 (1987): 981–96. Also see the group of articles on religious encounters by Daniel K. Richter, Helen C. Rountree, and Neal Salisbury in *American Indian Quarterly* 16 (1992): 471–509.

7. Pettit, introduction to Edwards's *Life of Brainerd*, pp. 25–32; Henry Warner Bowden, *American Indians and Christian Missions: Studies in Cultural Conflict* (Chicago: University of Chicago Press, 1981), pp. 111–41.

8. Merrell, "'Customes of Our Countrey,'" p. 152.

9. For discussions of Indian resistance, see Merrell, "'Customes of Our Countrey,'" pp. 152–56; James P. Ronda, "'We Are Well as We Are': An Indian Critique of Seventeenth-Century Missions," *William and Mary Quarterly*, 3d ser. 34 (1977): 66–82; and Francis Jennings, *The Invasion of America: Indians, Colonialism, and the Cant of Conquest* (New York: Norton, 1976), pp. 250–53.

10. Pettit, introduction to Edwards's *Life of Brainerd*, pp. 33–36; Wynbeek, *Beloved Yankee*, pp. 13–16.

11. Pettit, introduction to Edwards's *Life of Brainerd*, p. 26.

12. Brainerd's ill-fated career at Yale is explained by Norman Pettit, in "Prelude to Mission: Brainerd's Expulsion from Yale," *New England Quarterly* 59 (1986): 28–50.

13. Edwards, *Life of Brainerd*, p. 197; Weddle, "Melancholy Saint," pp. 298–301;

Pettit, introduction to Edwards's *Life of Brainerd*, p. 57; Wynbeek, *Beloved Yankee*, p. 55.

14. Wynbeek, *Beloved Yankee*, pp. 54–55.

15. Pettit, introduction to Edwards's *Life of Brainerd*, pp. 57–59, and "Prelude to Mission," p. 47. Numerous commentators have suggested that Brainerd was particularly struck by the squalid living conditions of the Long Island Indians.

16. Axtell, *Invasion Within*, pp. 329–33, bemoans the failure of European settlers to learn a greater measure of humility and tolerance from their interactions with Indians. Brainerd acknowledged his sense of inadequacy as a missionary on many occasions, but whether this stemmed more from his contact with natives or from his natural inclination toward self-condemnation is difficult to tell. In either case, he was a man "poor in spirit."

17. Edwards, *Life of Brainerd*, p. 201; "Related Correspondence," in Edwards, *Life of Brainerd*, pp. 588–89. See Patrick Frazier, *The Mohicans of Stockbridge* (Lincoln: University of Nebraska Press, 1992), for a general account of these Indians, and also Lion G. Miles, "The Red Man Dispossessed: The Williams Family and the Alienation of Indian Land in Stockbridge, Massachusetts, 1736–1818," *New England Quarterly* 67 (1994): 46–76 (see *New England Encounters*, chap. 11).

18. Pettit, introduction to Edwards's *Life of Brainerd*, pp. 59–61; Margaret Connell Szasz, *Indian Education in the American Colonies, 1607–1783* (Albuquerque: University of New Mexico Press, 1988), pp. 205–11; Samuel Hopkins, *Historical Memoirs, relating to the Housattunuk Indians* (Boston: S. Kneeland, 1753), pp. 89–90; Axtell, *Invasion Within*, pp. 197–204.

Sergeant's missionary trip had been largely unsuccessful. First visiting the Susquehanna Indians, he carried a letter from the Stockbridge Indians extolling the truth of Christianity. After hearing the message, the Indians deliberated and then responded with the following (as told by Sergeant): "It is true, we have one Father above, and we are always in his Presence. The Indians have one Way of honouring and pleasing him, and the White People have another; both are acceptable in Him. I am glad to hear from my Brother, and to cultivate Friendship with him. He shall always find me here if he has any Message to send: But Christianity need not be the Bond of Union between us." Sergeant met with a warmer welcome from natives along the Delaware River: thus his suggestion to Pemberton. See Hopkins, *Historical Memoirs*, pp. 89–90.

19. Edwards, *Life of Brainerd*, pp. 222, 228, 243–45; "Related Correspondence," pp. 570–77; Szasz, *Indian Education*, pp. 213–14. Some of Sergeant's methods had been publicly described in his *A Letter from the Rev. Mr. Sergeant of Stockbridge, to Dr. Colman of Boston* (Boston: Rogers and Fowle, 1743). See Axtell, *Invasion Within*, pp. 131–286, for a general discussion of English missionary strategies in colonial America.

20. David Brainerd, *Mirabilia Dei inter Indicos, or the Rise and Progress of a Remarkable Work of Grace amongst a number of Indians* (Philadelphia: William Bradford, 1746), pp. 79–80, 196–201. This is Brainerd's so-called public journal, covering the

period from June 1745 to June 1746. The published version contained two parts (the second part was entitled *Divine Grace Displayed* . . .) and an extensive appendix. The Yale edition of *The Life of David Brainerd* interweaves parts of this public journal with Edwards's version of Brainerd's private diaries. Omitted are several critical passages, especially Brainerd's "general remarks" at the end of parts one and two (*Mirabilia Dei*, pp. 65–80, 169–95) and the appendix (*Mirabilia Dei*, pp. 196–248). A manuscript copy of part one of the public journal, which appears to be in Brainerd's hand and which differs at numerous points from the printed version, may be found at the American Philosophical Society, Philadelphia (David Brainerd's Journal, 1745). See Pettit, introduction to Edwards's *Life of Brainerd*, pp. 71–84, and "Related Correspondence," pp. 561–62, on Brainerd texts and manuscripts.

21. James Axtell, "The Scholastic Philosophy of the Wilderness," in his *The European and the Indian*, pp. 131–67, discusses how Indians served as teachers to the New English.

22. Edwards, *Life of Brainerd*, pp. 204–8, 216–17, 221, 245; "Related Correspondence," pp. 571–72; "Some Further Remains of the Rev. Mr. David Brainerd," in Edwards, *Life of Brainerd*, pp. 484–86.

23. Brainerd's initial assessment of his circumstances in Kaunaumeek may be sampled in a letter to his brother John, dated 30 April 1743, in "Some Further Remains," pp. 484–85. His change in attitude may be traced in Edwards, *Life of Brainerd*, pp. 213–14, 216, 225, 228–29. His outcry against selfish ambition and worldly pleasures is evident in his letters to John Brainerd, 27 December 1743, and Israel Brainerd, 21 January 1744, in "Some Further Remains," pp. 486–88. One can only speculate about Brainerd's opinion of the relative opulence of John Sergeant's home in Stockbridge, where the missionary had married into the locally powerful Williams family.

24. On his longing for death, see Edwards, *Life of Brainerd*, pp. 201, 205, 215–17, 239; and on his millennial desires, pp. 203, 205, 225–26, 228. J. A. DeJong, *As the Waters Cover the Sea: Millennial Expectations in the Rise of Anglo-American Missions, 1640–1810* (Kampen, Netherlands: J. H. Kok, 1970), pp. 134–37, esp. p. 135, emphasizes Brainerd's interest in the expansion of the kingdom of God and argues that the "Indians, with whom he conversed daily, assumed a dominant place in his reflections on the kingdom."

25. Edwards, *Life of Brainerd*, pp. 202–3; "Some Further Remains," p. 485.

26. "Related Correspondence," pp. 574–75.

27. "Related Correspondence," p. 575.

28. "Related Correspondence," p. 576; Wynbeek, *Beloved Yankee*, pp. 86–87. Moravian A. G. Spangenberg's 1745 journal describes a similar native response to Brainerd at Shamokin, Pennsylvania, in June 1745. See William M. Beauchamp, ed., *Moravian Journals relating to Central New York, 1745–66* (Syracuse: Onondaga Historical Association, 1916), p. 7. Axtell, *Invasion Within*, pp. 242–82, recounts the Shamokin incident and similar vignettes to illustrate the largely fruitless efforts of eighteenth-century English missionaries.

29. Edwards, *Life of Brainerd*, pp. 249–51; "Related Correspondence," p. 577;

C. A. Weslager, *The Delaware Indians: A History* (New Brunswick, N.J.: Rutgers University Press, 1972), pp. 187–94; Francis Jennings, *The Ambiguous Iroquois Empire* (New York: Norton, 1990).

30. "Related Correspondence," pp. 577, 579–81.

31. Edwards, *Life of Brainerd*, pp. 251–60; "Related Correspondence," p. 577.

32. On Moravian missionary strategies, see Elma E. Gray, *Wilderness Christians: The Moravian Mission to the Delaware Indians* (1956; reprinted, New York: Russell and Russell, 1973), pp. 31–51, and Earl P. Olmstead, *Blackcoats among the Delaware: David Zeisberger on the Ohio Frontier* (Kent, Ohio: Kent State University Press, 1991), pp. 5–10, 35–36. A contemporary account of Moravian evangelism in Pennsylvania is provided in "Br. Martin Mack's Journal from the 13th Sept. 1745 N. S. of his Journey and visit in [?] Shomoko," in Records of the Moravian Mission among the Indians of North America, microfilm ed., reel 28, box 217, folder 12B, item 1, Archives of the Moravian Church, Bethlehem, Pennsylvania. I am indebted to James H. Merrell for this reference.

33. Edwards, *Life of Brainerd*, pp. 261–63, 265–66.

34. Edwards, *Life of Brainerd*, pp. 252, 254–55, 259, 267–69; "Related Correspondence," p. 490.

35. Edwards, *Life of Brainerd*, pp. 262, 274–75, 278–79; "Related Correspondence," p. 490. Herbert C. Kraft, in *The Lenape: Archaeology, History, and Ethnography* (Newark: New Jersey Historical Society, 1986), pp. 161–94, describes Delaware spirituality.

36. Conforti, "Brainerd and the Nineteenth-Century Missionary Movement," pp. 320–22, and "Edwards's Most Popular Work," p. 200.

37. Edwards, *Life of Brainerd*, pp. 298–440; Wynbeek, *Beloved Yankee*, pp. 145–235.

38. Merrell, "'Customes of Our Countrey,'" pp. 146–52; Weslager, *Delaware Indians*, pp. 261–63.

39. Brainerd, *Mirabilia Dei*, pp. 241–42. Bowden, *Indians and Christian Missions*, p. 154, and Conforti, "Brainerd and the Nineteenth-Century Missionary Movement," p. 320, cite these remarks as representative of Brainerd's view of the Indians, but I think they reflect but one of many, sometimes seemingly incompatible, attitudes.

40. Merrell, "'Customes of Our Countrey,'" pp. 131–37, 150–53. Brainerd tended to follow John Eliot and John Sergeant rather than the Mayhew family on the issue of how swiftly and how fully Indians should be expected to give up their own ways and become "civilized."

41. Edwards, *Life of Brainerd*, pp. 336, 358, 376–78, 390, 402–3, 414, 434, 435; Brainerd, *Mirabilia Dei*, pp. 199–200, 240–42; Thomas Brainerd, *The Life of John Brainerd* (Philadelphia: Presbyterian Publications Committee, 1865), pp. 98–105. John Brainerd, *A Genuine Letter from Mr. John Brainerd . . . to his Friend in London* (London: J. Ward, 1753), pp. 5–9, 14, indicates that the task of "civilizing" these Indians was still proceeding slowly six years later.

42. William A. Hunter, "Moses (Tunda) Tatamy, Delaware Indian Diplomat,"

in *A Delaware Indian Symposium,* ed. Herbert C. Kraft (Harrisburg: Pennsylvania Historical and Museum Commission, 1974), pp. 72–80. Norman Pettit notes Brainerd's dependence on Tatamy but does not develop the point. Edwards, *Life of Brainerd,* p. 254n.

43. Brainerd did make progress in understanding and using the Delaware languages during 1745–46, while at the same time his listeners became more familiar with English. Nevertheless, Tatamy remained vital to Brainerd's ministry. Brainerd, *Mirabilia Dei,* pp. 186, 196–201.

44. Brainerd, *Mirabilia Dei,* pp. 13–14, 71–72, 226–27.

45. Brainerd, *Mirabilia Dei,* p. 72.

46. Edwards, *Life of Brainerd,* p. 421. Brainerd had used a similar tactic a few months earlier in bringing six of his Indian converts from Crossweeksung to the Forks of the Delaware to speak to Indians there who had previously been hostile to Christianity. He hoped this would be "a means to convince them of the truth and importance of Christianity to see and hear some of their own nation discoursing of divine things." The strategy apparently worked, at least in persuading some of the Indians to pay closer attention. See Edwards, *Life of Brainerd,* p. 363.

47. Brainerd, *Mirabilia Dei,* p. 72.

48. Brainerd's aversion to recording Indian names contrasts with Moravian practice, as revealed in diaries. Brainerd may have been reluctant to record what he could not pronounce, but Indians were also reluctant to reveal their real names. See C. A. Weslager, "Delaware Indian Name Giving and Modern Practice," in *Delaware Indian Symposium,* pp. 135–45, and Weslager, *Delaware Indians,* pp. 71–72.

49. Edwards, *Life of Brainerd,* pp. 289–90, 338, 359; "Related Correspondence," pp. 582–83; Brainerd, *Mirabilia Dei,* pp. 77–78, 80, 238–39.

50. Edwards, *Life of Brainerd,* pp. 307, 310, 312. At the end of part one of his public journal (*Mirabilia Dei,* p. 73), Brainerd noted that "God saw fit to improve and bless milder means for the effectual awakening of these Indians." See Pettit, introduction to Edwards's *Life of Brainerd,* pp. 9–10, for a different interpretation of Brainerd's preaching methods.

51. Edwards, *Life of Brainerd,* pp. 312–21; Brainerd, *Mirabilia Dei,* pp. 73–75.

52. Edwards, *Life of Brainerd,* pp. 321–32. From the time the revival broke out, Brainerd made a point of noting his sermon texts in both his private diary and public journal. These texts emphasized God's invitation to the lost and lowly. Among the texts he used both in Crossweeksung and in the Pennsylvania interior were Luke 14:16–23, Isaiah 53:3–6, Matthew 13, and Acts 2:36–39. Brainerd explained in his public journal (*Mirabilia Dei,* p. 73) that he noted his scriptural texts to counter any criticisms that those "awakened" were "only frightened with a fearful noise of hell and damnation, and that there was no evidence that their concern was the effect of a divine influence."

53. Edwards, *Life of Brainerd,* pp. 332–45.

54. Kraft, *The Lenape,* pp. 161–69, 176–79, 189, 193–94; Weslager, *Delaware Indians,* pp. 55, 65–69, 107; Anthony F. C. Wallace, *King of the Delawares: Teedyuscung, 1700–1763* (Philadelphia: University of Pennsylvania Press, 1949), pp. 14–17, 43–44.

Robert Daiutolo, Jr., "The Early Quaker Perception of the Indian," *Quaker History* 72 (1983): 104–13, also describes the character of Delaware morality and religion in the context of explaining why Quakers had such a favorable view of them. Brainerd gives his own analysis of Indian religion in *Mirabilia Dei*, pp. 212–25.

55. Brainerd, *Mirabilia Dei*, pp. 232–34. Brainerd especially noted the difficulty he had in convincing all Indians that they were sinners. One tactic he used was to emphasize the scriptural command to love God with all of one's heart, strength, and mind to reveal to natives their failure to obey God.

56. Brainerd, *Mirabilia Dei*, pp. 230–31.

57. Based on his private diaries and public journal, Brainerd seems to have been less prone to periods of intense depression between August 1745 and October 1746 than at any other time from early 1742 (when he left Yale) to his death in October 1747. For examples of his growing affection for the Crossweeksung Indians, see Edwards, *Life of Brainerd*, pp. 332–33, 349–51, 367–68, 380, 386–87, 422, 432–33, 436.

58. Edwards, *Life of Brainerd*, pp. 350–51, 363, 390, 436; Brainerd, *Mirabilia Dei*, p. 137, commented on the effectiveness of this style of ministry: "I find particular and close Dealing with Souls in private, is often very successful."

59. On the Indian conjurer, see Edwards, *Life of Brainerd*, pp. 308, 359, 391–95; on the woman in "great distress," pp. 344, 346, 352–53, 362, 369–72, 373; on the "one who had been a vile drunkard," p. 362. For another account of an Indian spiritual pilgrimage, see Brainerd, *Mirabilia Dei*, pp. 94–98. For an example of a recent historian who has creatively attended to one of the Indians Brainerd encountered (the Indian "reformer"), see Gregory Evans Dowd, *A Spirited Resistance: The North American Indian Struggle for Unity, 1745–1815* (Baltimore: Johns Hopkins University Press, 1992), p. 29.

60. Brainerd wished to present the revival in Crossweeksung as an amazing work of God's grace but one free of the "enthusiastic" excesses that had drawn sharp criticism from opponents of the Great Awakening. He repeatedly explained that while his Delaware converts showed strong emotions, they never exhibited "any mental disorders . . . such as visions, trances, [or] imaginations of being under prophetic inspiration." See *Mirabilia Dei*, pp. 74–75, 187–88. On Brainerd's own rejection of religious enthusiasm, see Edwards, *Life of Brainerd*, pp. 448–52.

61. Brainerd, *Mirabilia Dei*, pp. 74–75. See Pettit, introduction to Edwards's *Life of Brainerd*, pp. 5–6, 11–24, and "Prelude to Mission," pp. 46–50, on Edwards's use of Brainerd. Weddle, "Melancholy Saint," pp. 297–318, finds that Edwards's use and interpretation of Brainerd was not altogether representative of who or what Brainerd was. Hall, *Neglected Northampton Texts*, pp. 145–200, offers the most thorough discussion of Edwards's use of Brainerd and argues that the missionary was Edwards's model of the good citizen in his ideal society.

62. Edwards, *Life of Brainerd*, pp. 438–41, 448–50.

63. Pettit, introduction to Edwards's *Life of Brainerd*, pp. 37–51, 57. Brainerd devoted most of his energies during the last months of his life to promoting Indian missions any way he could. See Edwards, *Life of Brainerd*, p. 459–76, and "Some Further Remains," pp. 496–99.

64. Even after Brainerd's success in Crossweeksung and his lack of success with inland Indians, he struggled over whether to settle down with his congregation of Christian Indians in Cranberry or to devote himself to itinerant evangelism among the far larger number of Indians on the frontier. Edwards, *Life of Brainerd,* pp. 397, 400–402. Another missionary's perspective on Brainerd's visits to the Pennsylvania interior is contained in "Br. Martin Mack's Journal." Moravian Mack contrasted the fruitlessness of Brainerd's strategy of periodic visits during which he tried to gather the resident Indians to hear him preach with the Moravian approach of living with the Delawares and patiently waiting for opportunities to speak to individual natives about "the Love of our Saviour."

65. Pettit, introduction to Edwards's *Life of Brainerd,* pp. 42–71.

66. The ideas of this paragraph owe much to Michael Zuckerman's helpful reading of my original article.

PART FOUR

Conflicts over Labor, Land, and Jurisdiction

IO

Indian Labor in Early Rhode Island

JOHN A. SAINSBURY

The chronic shortage of labor in England's southern colonies is widely recognized, as is their twofold solution: indentured servitude in the early years and, increasingly, racial slavery. New England colonists employed both forms of bound labor, almost from the outset, but the region's relatively light demand for unskilled workers produced a pattern of labor quite different from that of the South or even the Middle Colonies. The typical New England worker was either a free, wage-earning worker—a hired hand—or, if bound by an indenture, was an apprentice or servant who, for a specified number of years, lived in his or her master's home and was treated in most respects as a family member. That, at least, is the myth, and like most myths it contains some truth. What it overlooks, besides many non-English Euroamerican servants who were held at arms' length, and a smaller but significant number of African American slaves, especially in Rhode Island, are the hundreds of Indians who served long terms as bound servants (apprenticed or, more often, indentured) or who for their entire lives were slaves. Nor does the myth account for the manipulative methods that propelled Indians into that lot in life.

It might be thought that Rhode Island, with its strong Quaker influence and its tradition of religious and social toleration, would have the fewest Indians in subservient status. Perhaps a thorough, comparative analysis of the New England colonies would prove that to be the case, but the tentative findings suggest that Rhode Island was the leading employer of bound Indians. As John A. Sainsbury's article demonstrates, a large portion of the Indians in eighteenth-century Rhode Island labored, under duress, for white masters. The exact number of Indian servants and slaves at various times is unknown, but abundant evidence—censuses of households, colonial statutes, and travelers' comments, for example—reveals a widespread pattern of exploitation of Narragansetts and other natives of the area and of Indians imported from elsewhere in the Americas.

For some Indians, bound servitude may have been an acceptable and effective adjustment to the new world of Angloamerican dominance and disintegrating Indian culture. For most of them, surely, it was a coerced option that proved a poor substitute for traditional Indian patterns of work, habitation, and association.

*cA*s ETHNOHISTORIANS are at some pains to remind us, the history of relations between European settlers and Native Americans in early America is inadequately characterized as a saga of confrontation in which the two sides gazed at each other across an unbridgeable cultural gulf. Instead, we are encouraged to consider relations as a process of interaction and exchange, or cultural "conversation," in which Indians as well as whites sought advantage in what for both was a New World of opportunities and dangers.[1] This paradigm has encouraged fruitful analyses of trading arrangements, but there has been less emphasis on labor relations, a more intimate aspect of the shared economic and cultural nexus. Investigating various forms of Indian labor, from free to coerced, is also one way of evaluating the extent and character of Indian autonomy, individual as well as tribal, and the degree to which such autonomy was constrained over time.

This essay focuses on Indian labor in Rhode Island, where eighteenth-century commentators noted the emergence of an Indian labor force in service to whites. Dean George Berkeley, in a sermon before the Society for the Propagation of the Gospel in 1731, observed that the Rhode Island Indians were "nearly all servants or labourers for the English," and John Callender, seven years later, wrote that many of the local Narragansetts were "scattered about where the English will employ them." There was a comparable situation in neighboring coastal Connecticut. As a visiting Marylander, Dr. Alexander Hamilton, rode through that area in 1744, he noted that children were frightened by the sight of his black slave, "for here negroe slaves are not so much in use as with us, their servants being chiefly bound or indentured Indians."[2]

The phenomenon witnessed by these observers was undoubtedly a consequence of the rapid erosion of tribal autonomy in southern New England in the seventeenth century. Metacom's War of 1675–76 broke the power of the Narragansetts, the dominant tribe of Rhode Island and perhaps the most formidable in the area. The war ended their existence as a discrete tribal unit, though several hundred Narragansetts survived it. A remnant of them attempted to preserve a traditional life under King Ninigret, the sachem of the Niantic tribe, but with limited success. Although a covenant of 1709 between the Narragansetts and the Rhode Island government gave theoretical protection to those in possession of the reservation at Charles-town, the Ninigret family—most notoriously Thomas Ninigret, who be-came sachem in 1746—was allowed to sell the tribe's lands in order to pay its debts, thus further damaging the economic viability of the reservation.[3] As a result, many Indians were obliged to seek alternative employment elsewhere. In addition to the native Rhode Island Indians who were enter-ing a subservient association with whites, Indians were imported from out-side the colony, especially during the early eighteenth century. Indians from the Spanish colonies, seized in Queen Anne's War, and Tuscarora Indians, captured during their tribe's conflict with the Carolinas in 1711–13, were part of a movement of Indians from the southern to the New En-gland colonies—a flow that was eventually stemmed by legislative action from the New England governments.[4]

The extent to which Rhode Island Indians were integrated in various forms of servitude with white families toward the end of the colonial pe-riod is suggested by the fact that in 1774, 35.5 percent of all Indians in the colony were living with white families (see appendix). If the Indians still living on the Charlestown reservation are excluded, the figure rises to 54 percent. Since there is little evidence for marriages between Indians and whites,[5] and it is unlikely that many of the Indians living with white fami-lies were rent-paying lodgers,[6] it is clear that the overwhelming majority of them were held in service by the families with whom they are included in the census.

War and tribal upheaval thus furnished an Indian labor force, the dimensions of which, at least in Rhode Island, can be determined with reasonable accuracy. That much is evident. This essay seeks to answer three more complex questions relating to Indian labor in early Rhode Is-land: (1) Under what terms did Indians enter employment with whites? (2) How did the Rhode Island government seek to regulate the labor status of Indians and to what effect? And (3) what occupations did Indians en-gage in and what value was placed on their labor?

The earliest settlements of what was to become the colony of Rhode Island did not participate with the other New England colonies in the war against the Pequots in 1637 and thus did not share in the human spoils. Roger Williams of Providence did, however, enter the religious debate concerning the proper disposal of those Pequot captives who were to be spared execution, asking whether "after a due time of training up to labor, and restraint, they ought not to be set free." Williams himself requested and received from John Winthrop in Boston a Pequot boy for "keeping and bringing up."[7] Indian labor in Rhode Island's earliest years was usually voluntary and contractual, however. Indians were commonly employed in construction work of various kinds, demonstrating skills in nontraditional areas. Daniel Gookin, after lamenting the resistance of the Rhode Island Indians to Christianity, conceded

> by way of commendation of the Narragansett and Warwick Indians . . . that they are an active, laborious, and ingenious people; which is demonstrated in their labours they do for the English of whom more are employed, especially in making stone fences . . . than any other Indian people or neighbours.[8]

Local governments, as well as individuals, hired Rhode Island Indians. In May 1653, for example, the town of Warwick paid a group of Indians £12 10s. for building fences.[9] Such contracted labor was not incompatible with the integrity of tribal organization, but increasingly Indians were entering into closer and longer liaisons with the English by becoming indentured servants. Throughout the colonial period, the inventories of personal estates in those areas where the Indian population was greatest contain numerous entries for Indian apprentices, in which the unexpired term is specified or expressed in its monetary equivalent.[10]

Voluntary indentured servitude was, of course, an established system for whites as well as Indians, which, potentially at least, allowed for a return to independence with the possibility of having acquired a valuable skill. A disproportionate number of Indians, though, entered servitude involuntarily—as a result of their inability to pay debts or as restitution for felonies. As James Merrell has gloomily observed, "among Settlement Indians the road from free to forced labor was wide, slippery, and all downhill, with colonists often pushing from behind."[11] Because Indians could rarely pay cash or goods in lieu of service, they were especially vulnerable to servitude as a form of punishment. As early as 1649, Nanhegin, a Rhode Island Indian, having been found guilty of breaking into a house and stealing from it, was ordered to be whipped and was additionally sentenced to serve one John Downing until he had made two-fold restitution for his crime.[12] Similar practices continued into the eighteenth century. A felony committed by an Indian already in service to a colonist was punished by prolongation of his term.[13] The extent of Indian criminality was allegedly so great that Rhode Island's General Assembly decreed in 1659 that any Indian unable to "pay and discharge all the damages, costs and restitutions by law due," to the value of twenty shillings and above, for crimes he had committed, was liable "to be sold as a slave to any foreign country of the English subjects." Such a verdict was given, in 1727, in the case of an Indian boy who attempted to murder his master in Newport.[14]

The notion that the guilty should make restitution by compulsory service found its most important single application in Rhode Island with the refugees of Metacom's War—albeit that many of them were guilty only by association.[15] Rhode Island, however, disposed of its captives with more humanity than did the colonies of Massachusetts and Plymouth, which sold their Indian captives into perpetual slavery, both inside and outside their borders.[16] During the war (in March 1676), the Rhode Island Assembly ruled that "noe Indian in this Collony be a slave, but only to pay their debts or for their bringing up, or custody they have received, or to performe covenant as if they had been countrymen not in warr." This act, like the abortive attempt in 1652 to legislate against black slavery, was not permanently effective, though it did influence the disposal of refugees of the war. Its passage at a critical period for white settlement in New England possibly reflected the increasing influence of the Quaker party in Rhode Island politics.[17] As a consequence of the March legislation, captive Indians brought into Providence, and others who voluntarily submitted, were sold into servitude within the colony for limited periods only. At first the specified term was nine years, later modified on the basis of a sliding scale according to age, so that, for example, a child under five years old could serve a maximum term of servitude of thirty years.[18] Shares in the proceeds from the sale of the Indians were granted to the Rhode Island companies responsible for their capture and to the small group of citizens who had stayed in Providence during the war. Profits from the disposal of a small party of Indians, however, were to "be the right of all the Inhabitants of the Towne (of Providence) universally." The committee elected to supervise the disposal of the Indians, on behalf of those with a share in the sale, included Roger Williams, who was thus given an opportunity to put into effect those notions concerning limited servitude that he had expounded to John Winthrop in 1637.[19] The actual sale and delivery of the Indians were entrusted to three men, whose accounts have survived. Prices for the Indians varied considerably but averaged thirty-three shillings in silver. More eccentric currencies were clearly acceptable, though: some Indians sold for the appropriate quantity of "fatt sheepe" or "bushells of Indian corne."[20]

A further insight into the nature of the Indian war refugees' service is provided by the indentures for an Indian woman and her children made servants in Portsmouth. The documents specify the period to be served and the responsibilities of the master, as in a normal indenture of apprenticeship, but signatures of the Indians themselves or their representatives are not included, only those of the town agents "appointed and Impowered to dispose of Indians and place them out as apprentices."[21] This kind of

Indian servitude was not confined to the immediate aftermath of Meta-com's War; the tribal disintegration that the war accelerated was responsi-ble for an Indian pauper problem well into the eighteenth century. Town governments addressed the problem by binding as apprentices any Indians who threatened to become a burden to the community.[22] In addition, the General Assembly legislated an ingenious solution by incorporating into an act intended to make free Indians responsible for their own paupers, a clause that each "town Council Be . . . Impowered to hire or Bind out or rate such and so many . . . Indians as need shall require for the support of . . . [the Indian] poor."[23]

The apprenticeship system was regulated to prevent excessive exploita-tion. In 1730, the Assembly ordered that "no Indian shall be bound as Ap-prentice or Servant . . . in this Colony, without the Consent . . . of two justices of the peace, or Wardens of this Colony." Reflecting on the malign operation of the credit system, the preamble stated that the action was necessary because "evil minded Persons in this Colony, of a greedy and covetous Design, often draw Indians into their Debt, by selling them Goods at extravagant Rates, and get the . . . Indians bound to them for longer Time than is just or reasonable."[24] It has been plausibly suggested that this legislation was principally necessary to prevent the children of the captives of Metacom's War from being kept in service by the masters of their parents. It was also required to prevent recurrence of other abuses, typified by the case of Trugo, a Block Island Indian, who was sold into bondage by his brothers and sisters for a period of thirteen years in return for four cloth coats and thirteen annual installments of a gallon of rum.[25] Attempts at illegally inveigling Indians into servitude continued even after the 1730 legislation was passed. In 1732, Thomas Thornton, a constable of Providence, and his accomplice Zachariah Jones, fraudulently obtained from Grigory, an Indian, acknowledgment that he owed them ten pounds. Grigory was duly bound in service, with the required approval of two mag-istrates, but he eventually regained his freedom when a petition on his behalf to the General Assembly brought the imposition to light.[26]

Despite a continuing strain of humane paternalism displayed in the 1730 legislation, during the course of the eighteenth century, placing Indians in perpetual bondage became established and legally acceptable in Rhode Island. One anomalous instance of unlimited servitude, or its attempted implementation, appears even earlier—within months of the 1676 ban—with the sale of an Indian woman (condemned by the "Collony of New Plymouth to perpetual Servitude and Slavery") to William Wodell of Portsmouth, Rhode Island, "his Executors Administrators and assignes forever."[27] This purchase moreover contravened a ban on the importa-tion of Indians imposed in March 1675 by the town government of Portsmouth.[28] It is not recorded whether Wodell was permitted to keep the Indian under the terms specified in the bill of sale, yet within thirty years of this transaction, evidence for the bondage of Indians in perpetuity, the condition that defined enslavement, becomes much more apparent. Indian slaves are mentioned in an act of 1704 and continue to be referred to in legislation throughout the colonial period. In much of this legislation, "Indian slaves" are clearly differentiated from "Indian servants."[29] Advertisements for runaway Indian slaves recur in eighteenth-century newspapers. Possibly the first such fugitive was a "Spanish Indian Man Slave" who, in 1706, absconded from his master, Samuel Niles of Kingstown.[30] Indian slaves are also occasionally listed, alongside black slaves and white and Indian apprentices, in inventories of estates. In two such inventories, children are included with their mothers, confirming that hereditary Indian slavery existed in the colony. The estate of Benjamin Barton of Warwick, who died in 1720, lists an Indian boy, "Daniell," at a value of £10, beneath his mother, who is valued at £25. And the estate of Richard Green of Warwick, who died in 1724, includes, together with a black male valued at £70, a "Spanish Indian Woman and her Child" valued at £85.[31] A clue to this apparently blatant violation of the 1676 legislation is the fact that so many of those who were enslaved are described as "Spanish Indian" or of "Spanish Indian parentage." It is conceivable that the 1676 act applied, either by original intention or by subsequent interpretation, only to native Rhode Island Indians and that the considerable number of Indians imported from outside Rhode Island in the early eighteenth century—many of them originating from the Spanish colonies—were not accorded the same protection.

An erosion of religious scruples about slavery in Rhode Island during the early eighteenth century—which allowed the colony to become, relative to its population, the leading holder of black slaves in New England[32]—would have contributed to the *de facto* negation of the 1676 act. A further possibility is that a ban on Indian slavery could not be made to interfere with existing property relations in those areas where Rhode Island confirmed or acquired jurisdiction after 1676. This would help to explain the considerable development of Indian slavery in Narragansett, an area subject to a long-standing territorial dispute in 1676 and not firmly incorporated with Rhode Island until 1685.[33] Such an explanation is marginal, however, because Indian slavery also developed in those areas that were already attached to the colony and subscribed to the 1676 legislation.

Whatever ambiguities existed in the Rhode Island government's attitude toward Indian servitude, one position was consistently maintained: the determination with which the institution was controlled to prevent it from threatening colonial peace and security. Such action was particularly evident in times of war and social disruption. In August 1676, during Metacom's War, the General Assembly barred Indians from being brought into the colony "without leave and permit from the Governor, or two Assistants." In addition, half of the profit from Indians legally imported was to go "to the Treasurer for Newport."[34] More stringent precautions were exercised at the local level. Portsmouth, in March 1675, forbade outright the importation of Indians,[35] and Providence, despite later becoming the central mart for the sale of Indian war refugees, ordered in August 1676 that Indian "Men Women & Children should be sent out of Town." It was subsequently noted in the town record that a designated ship's captain "cleard the Towne by his vessel of all the Indians to the great peace and Content of all the Inhabitants."[36]

In 1704, during Queen Anne's War, when the French with their Indian allies were harassing the northern borders of New England, the Rhode Island Assembly forbade the import of "Eastern Indians . . . lately taken in . . . Massachusetts" on the grounds that they provoked "other Indians in . . . [the] Collony, to do mischief." The most strenuous attempt to curb the flow of Indians to Rhode Island came toward, and after, the end of that war. In 1712, a tax was imposed on imported slaves: £3 for blacks and £2 for Indians. Three years later, additional legislation was passed which, if rigidly applied, must have curtailed the import of Indians, while leaving the trade in African slaves unaffected: it was resolved that all Indians brought into Rhode Island should be forfeited to the government, unless the importer gave security of £50 to transport them out again within a month. According to the preamble of the act:

> Divers conspiracies, insurrections, rapes, thefts and other execrable crimes, have been lately perpetrated in this and the [adjoining] governments, by Indian slaves and the increase of them in the colony daily discourages the importing of white servants from Great Britain.

Exemption from the 1712 and 1715 acts was allowed in the case of some ladies from South Carolina, who were forced to leave their southern colony because of the Indian wars, and who were permitted to bring with them their Indian slaves free of duty. Despite such charitable gestures, however, the legislation against the import of Indians—though, crucially, it did nothing to inhibit the enslavement of the offspring of previously imported Indians—was one of the reasons why Native American slavery never reached the proportions of African slavery in Rhode Island.[37]

In addition to these enactments controlling their entry, Indian servants and slaves, together with blacks, were subject within the colony to restrictive legislation. An act of 1704 imposed a 9:00 P.M. curfew on "any Negroes or Indians, Freemen or Slaves." The act was repeated in 1751 with the exclusion of free blacks and free Indians. This 1751 law banned liquor or "dancing, gaming or diversion of any kind" for non-white servants and slaves. Significantly, the punishment of offering such entertainment was a £50 fine or a one-month imprisonment for whites, while non-whites faced loss of property and being put out to service.[38] Indian slaves were also subject to discriminatory jurisdictional treatment. An act of 1718 authorized that black and Indian slaves found stealing be summarily tried without jury before any two Assistants, justices of the peace, or wardens in the town where the offense was committed.[39]

While the legal status of Indians in Rhode Island can be fairly readily ascertained, there is less certainty about the actual occupations in which Indians, bound or free, engaged. However, regional variations in the distribution of Indian labor, together with fragments of other information, yield some evidence about Native American employment. The disproportionate number of female Indians living with white families in Newport, for example, suggests that the demand for female household servants was not satisfied by the available supply of black slaves. In the area of Narragansett (particularly South Kingstown), the emergence of a prosperous agriculture, dairying, and raising sheep and horses produced a demand for bound farm labor, both Indian and African, an unusual condition for New England.[40] Indians included in estate inventories in South Kingstown are usually listed alongside other entries associated with large-scale farming operations.

Free Indians, as well as contracting themselves for construction work, commonly engaged in military service in wars against the French, and they were also among the first volunteers for the Revolutionary battalions. A census conducted in 1776 to identify those able to bear arms shows that in Charlestown, out of twenty-nine individuals who had already volunteered for service, seventeen were Indians. The incentive to volunteer was increased by an act of 1778 offering freedom to African and Indian slaves prepared to enlist in the Rhode Island battalions. There is also evidence that Rhode Island Indians (like other New England natives) became sailors, though perhaps not enthusiastically. In 1746, James Browne of Providence offered for sale or monthly lease an Indian, who he claimed was "a very good Sailor," except for his habit of running away.[41]

Despite the fact that Indians became associated with white society in a number of ways, their labor was not highly coveted. The 1715 legislation showed the Rhode Island government hostile to the expansion of Indian labor in the colony, while it maintained a neutral attitude to African slavery and a bias in favor of white indentured servitude. Indian slaves in Rhode Island were generally valued at a lower rate than black slaves in estate inventories,[42] and there is little evidence that the labor of bound Indians was anything other than unskilled. African American slaves, by contrast, were employed in a wide range of skilled occupations. Contracted labor apart, it seems that a sustained demand for Indian service came only from areas such as Narragansett, where there was an unusually high demand for unskilled labor, and from individuals (like Thomas Thornton, constable of Providence) who could not afford the expense of a black slave or white indentured servant. It is conceivable that the psychological resistance displayed by New England Indians against permanent, as distinct from occasional, labor for whites, attested to by early commentators,[43] survived to some degree throughout the colonial period—the result perhaps of the Indians being a displaced group rather than a transplanted one like African slaves.[44] In addition, the survival of remnant tribal structures provided Indian runaway servants with a sanctuary, which must have made the employment of Indians something of a hazard.[45] With some exceptions, Indian employment by white colonists in Rhode Island was the result not of economic conditions providing a general market exclusively for such labor, nor of an enthusiastic Indian adjustment to white society, but rather of Indian tribal disintegration severely constraining alternative options for autonomous Indian development.

Author's Postscript

At the time this article was first published, little scholarly work had been done on the history of New England's Indians in the period after Metacom's War of 1675–76. As the original article implied, it was as if historians' interest tended to dissipate at the point at which the New England tribes no longer seriously challenged English security. A lot has changed in the last twenty years. During that time, some important work has appeared on the post-1776 history of the Narragansetts and affiliated tribes. (See, for example, Ethel Boissevain, *The Narragansett People* [Phoenix: Indian Tribal Series, 1975]; Campbell and LaFantasie, "'Scattered to the Winds of Heaven'" [see n. 3]; and William S. Simmons, "Narragansett," in *Handbook of North American Indians: Northeast,* ed. Bruce Trigger [Washington: Smithsonian Institution, 1978], pp. 190–97).

Much of this scholarship—for instance, detailed accounts of Indian land disposal—sheds additional light on the processes that led to Indian servitude for whites. We also know a great deal more about the phases of Indian acculturation to white society following the breakdown of traditional tribal structures. Narragansett Indians, once resistant to Christianity, embraced "New Light" religion in ways that, at one level, represented an identification with European values while at the same time reviving possibilities of autonomous spiritual development (see William S. Simmons, "Red Yankees: Narragansett Conversion in the Great Awakening," *American Ethnologist* 10 [1983]: 253–71; *Old Light on Separate Ways: The Narragansett Diary of Joseph Fish, 1765–1776,* ed. William S. Simmons and Cheryl L. Simmons [Hanover and London: University Press of New England, 1982]). This work raises some tantalizing questions with respect to Indian labor. Did the belated conversion of the Narragansetts render them more pliable servants? Or did it, by contrast, help provide them with the psychological wherewithal to break the spiral of indebtedness and poverty that led to servitude in the first instance?

Beyond work with specific relevance to the post-seventeenth-century history of Rhode Island Indians, the recent thrust of ethnohistory as a discipline carries important general implications for the ways in which the history of Indian labor is most appropriately studied. The article, in that respect (despite some amendments to the original), remains somewhat dated. It gives heavy priority to the institutional aspects of Indian servitude and to the needs and preoccupations of governments and white employers and too readily assumes that Indians were merely passive victims in a process that deprived them of individual or collective agency. Though the general conclusion—that Indian labor for whites reflected the closure of other options—will likely withstand further research, the character of Indian identity within the harsh constraints of a settler-imposed labor regimen needs to be recovered. That undertaking requires careful, subtle, and sometimes speculative interpretation of fragmentary evidence. What are we to make, for example, of the eighteenth-century Narragansett woman whose only English word was "broom"? (Simmons, "Red Yankees," p. 262). Was she perhaps making a pragmatic adjustment to the requirements of domestic service while resisting the broader hegemonic impulses of the dominant culture?

Though many of the intellectual tools for the study of Indian labor in New England are now in place, it curiously remains a neglected field. There are, however, some laudable exceptions to that generalization—for example, Daniel Vickers's account of the Indian whalemen of Nantucket ("The First Whalemen of Nantucket," *William and Mary Quarterly,* 3d ser. 40 [1983]: 560–83)—which provide excellent models for future research.

Notes

1. A useful statement of this kind of approach, and guide to its literature, is James H. Merrell's "'The Customes of Our Countrey': Indians and Colonists in Early America," in *Strangers within the Realm: Cultural Margins of the First British Empire,* ed. Bernard Bailyn and Philip D. Morgan (Chapel Hill: University of North Carolina Press, 1991), pp. 117–56.

2. Berkeley, quoted by Wilkins Updike, in *A History of the Episcopal Church in Narragansett, Rhode Island,* 2d ed., 3 vols. (Boston: D. B. Updike, 1907), 1:211; John Callender, "An Historical Discourse, on the Civil and Religious Affairs of the Colony of Rhode Island," *Collections of the Rhode Island Historical Society* 4 (1838): 132–33; *Gentleman's Progress: The Itinerarium of Dr. Alexander Hamilton, 1744,* ed. Carl Bridenbaugh (Chapel Hill: University of North Carolina Press, 1948), p. 168.

3. Paul Campbell and Glenn LaFantasie, "'Scattered to the Winds of Heaven'—Narragansett Indians, 1676–1880," *Rhode Island History* 47 (1978): 66–83; *Narragansett Tribe of Indians, Report of the Committee of Investigation* (Providence, 1880), pp. 10–11; Henry C. Dorr, "The Narragansetts," *Collections of the Rhode Island Historical Society* 7 (1885): 226–28; Mss. Narragansett Indians, 1735–1842, nos. 3, 6, 10, 11, Rhode Island Archives, State House, Providence; *A Statement of the Case of the Narragansett Tribe of Indians, as shown in the Manuscript Collection of Sir William Johnson,* comp. James N. Arnold (Newport, 1896), pp. 3–60; William F. Tucker, *Historical Sketch of the Town of Charlestown* (Westerly, 1877), pp. 50–51.

4. Almon Wheeler Lauber, "Indian Slavery in Colonial Times within the Present Limits of the United States," *Columbia University Studies in History, Economics and Public Law* 54 (1913): 122, 164, 170–80, 187–93; Verner W. Crane, *The Southern Frontier, 1670–1732* (Ann Arbor: University of Michigan Press, 1956), pp. 113–14.

5. The claim that marriages between Indians and whites did occur in New England (see William B. Weeden, *Economic and Social History of New England, 1620–1789,* 2 vols. [Boston and New York, 1890], 1:403) cannot be substantiated for Rhode Island. The vital records of Rhode Island towns reveal no instances of marriages between Indians and whites in those areas where analysis of the 1774 census suggests that they might conceivably have taken place.

6. Such a category might have been expected in Newport because of the possible presence of temporarily landed Indian sailors. The 1774 census returns, however, list only four adult male Indians living with white families in the town.

7. *The Complete Writings of Roger Williams,* 7 vols. (New York: Russell and Russell, 1963), 6:35, 54–55.

8. Daniel Gookin, "Historical Collections of the Indians in New England," *Collections of the Massachusetts Historical Society,* 1st ser. 1 (1792): 210.

9. *The Early Records of the Town of Warwick,* ed. Howard M. Chapin (Providence: E. A. Johnson Company, 1926), pp. 80–81.

10. *The Early Records of the Town of Providence,* 21 vols. (Providence, 1892–1915), 16:154, 244; Record of Wills, Warwick, vol. 1 (1703–45), p. 265, vol. 3 (1761–81), pp.

249, 308, Warwick Town Hall; Town of South Kingstown: Probate and Council Records, vol. 2 (1723–35), p. 114, 261, vol. 3 (1735–43), p. 75, vol. 4 (1743–54), pp. 85, 349.

11. Merrell, "'Customes of Our Countrey,'" p. 137.

12. Providence Town Records, ms. no. 01106, Rhode Island Historical Society Library, Providence. Other material relating to the case is in *Early Records of the Town of Providence*, 15:22–25.

13. Petitions to the Rhode Island General Assembly, vol. 1 (1725–29), p. 4, Rhode Island Archives; S. T. Livermore, *A History of Block Island* (Hartford, 1877), p. 160.

14. *Records of the Colony of Rhode Island and Providence Plantations, in New England*, ed. John R. Bartlett, 10 vols. (Providence, 1856–65), 1:412–13 [hereafter cited as *Rhode Island Records*]; *Newport Historical Magazine* 4 (1883): 114–15. The 1676 legislation banning Indian slavery did not extend to Indians sent out of the colony.

15. Ringleaders in attacks on the English were executed: *Early Records of the Town of Providence*, 17:152.

16. Connecticut disposed of its Indian captives in a manner similar to Rhode Island's. The treatment of defeated Indians by other New England colonies is discussed in detail in Lauber's "Indian Slavery," pp. 125–49.

17. *Rhode Island Records*, 1:535; Lauber, "Indian Slavery," pp. 304–5.

18. *Rhode Island Records*, 1:549; *Early Records of the Town of Providence*, 17:154–55.

19. *Rhode Island Records*, 1:540; *Early Records of the Town of Providence*, 17:151–53.

20. Providence Town Records, ms. nos. 01807, 01282. For additional material concerning the sale of the Indians, see *Rhode Island Historical Society Publications* 1 (1893): 234–40; *Early Records of the Town of Providence*, 17:156–58, 161–62.

21. *The Early Records of the Town of Portsmouth*, ed. Clarence S. Brigham (Providence, 1901), pp. 430–32.

22. Minutes of Town Council Meeting, 12 February 1759, Town of South Kingstown: Probate and Council Records, vol. 5 (1754–62). Paupers and orphans of other races were similarly disposed of: see advertisements in *Providence Gazette and Country Journal*, 2 January 1765, and *Newport Mercury*, 12 December 1763. In 1770, an act was passed that permitted town councils to bind out manumitted slaves (Indian and black) if they threatened to become a charge on the town: *Acts and Laws of the English Colony of Rhode Island* (Newport, 1772), p. 36.

23. Mss. Narragansett Indians, 1735–1842, ms. A.

24. Acts and Laws of Rhode Island, 1730–60, facsimile in Rhode Island Historical Society Library, p. 219.

25. Lauber, "Indian Slavery," pp. 199–200; Livermore, *Block Island*, p. 60.

26. Petitions to the Rhode Island General Assembly, vol. 2 (1730–33), pp. 69, 72.

27. *Early Records of the Town of Portsmouth*, pp. 433–34. A curious feature of this transaction is that the Indian woman signed a document to approve her own committal to perpetual servitude.

28. *Early Records of the Town of Portsmouth*, p. 188.

29. *Acts and Laws of his Majesty's Colony of Rhode Island and Providence Plantations* (Newport, 1730), pp. 50, 104; Rhode Island Acts and Resolves, 1747–52, facsimile at

the Rhode Island Historical Society Library, Providence, pp. 85–86; *Rhode Island Records*, 4:133–35, 193; 5:340; 8:359–61.

30. *Boston News-Letter*, 22 July 1706. Other notices for runaway Indian slaves can be found in *Newport Mercury*, 4 July 1768 and 11 November 1765. There are frequent notices for Indian runaways whose precise status is not given; for example, in *Newport Mercury*, 4 September 1759 and 26 October 1762, and *Boston Gazette*, 28 October 1728. One intriguing notice is for an Indian boy, who had run away from his master, Thomas Ninigret, the sachem of the Narragansett/Niantic tribe: *Newport Mercury*, 10 May 1766.

31. Town of South Kingstown: Probate and Council Records, vol. 2 (1723–35), pp. 27, 101, 228; Record of Wills: Warwick, vol. 1 (1703–45), pp. 78, 144, 165, vol. 2 (1745–61), p. 156.

32. Lorenzo J. Greene, *The Negro in Colonial New England, 1620–1776* (New York: Columbia University Press, 1942), pp. 74–75.

33. S. G. Arnold, *History of the State of Rhode Island and Providence Plantations*, 2 vols. (New York, 1874), 1:505.

34. *Rhode Island Records*, 1:550. The assembly had earlier enacted that any owner of an Indian above twelve years of age was to provide him with a keeper during the day and lock him up at night (p. 549).

35. *Early Records of the Town of Portsmouth*, p. 188.

36. *Early Records of the Town of Providence*, 17:152. The Providence order obliged those who had purchased Indians to find people out of town who were willing to keep them until the restriction was lifted. See Letter from Thomas Field to Thomas Harris, [1676?], Providence Town Records, ms. no. 01087.

37. *Rhode Island Records*, 3:482–83, 4:133–35, 185–86, 193, 196–98.

38. *Acts and Laws . . . of Rhode Island* (1730), p. 50; Rhode Island Acts and Resolves, 1747–52, pp. 85–86. Occasionally laws were passed that discriminated in favor of bound Indians as opposed to free ones. For example, Providence town council ordered in 1683 that "no Indian . . . shall come within our towneshipp (that have not served theire time in our towne) to hunt or fish, or to inhabitt." *Early Records of the Town of Providence*, 8:130.

39. *Acts and Laws . . . of Rhode Island* (1730), p. 104. Cf. Yasuhide Kawashima, *Puritan Justice and The Indian: White Man's Law in Massachusetts, 1630–1763* (Middletown, Conn.: Wesleyan University Press, 1986), p. 35.

40. Edward Channing, "The Narragansett Planters: A Study of Causes," *Johns Hopkins University Studies*, 4th ser. 3 (1886): passim.

41. Petitions to the Rhode Island General Assembly, vol. 6 (1743–48), p. 165, vol. 9 (1755–57), p. 106, vol. 11 (1762–65), p. 201; Charlestown Listings, 1776 Census, Rhode Island Archives; *Rhode Island Records*, 8:359–61; *The Letter Book of James Browne, of Providence, Merchant* (Providence: Rhode Island Historical Society, 1929), p. 33. Another reluctant sailor is described in the *Newport Mercury*, 2 October 1760. Further references to Indian sailors are made in *Newport Mercury*, 23 June 1761, and *Providence Gazette and Country Journal*, 17 October 1767.

42. Dorr, "The Narragansetts," p. 238, makes an (undocumented) estimate that

black slaves were generally appraised at five or six times the value of Indian slaves in Rhode Island. A precise estimate is almost impossible to make because of variations in price owing to differences in age and sex, and to complications induced by currency fluctuations. Also it is sometimes difficult to distinguish between highly valued indentured servants and lowly valued slaves in estate inventories where precise status is not specified.

43. For example, William Wood, *New England's Prospect* (Boston, 1865), p. 73.

44. Winthrop D. Jordan, *White Over Black: American Attitudes Toward the Negro, 1550–1812* (Chapel Hill: University of North Carolina Press for the Institute of Early American History and Culture, 1968), pp. 89–91.

45. Elisha Potter, "The Early History of Narragansett," *Collections of the Rhode Island Historical Society* 3 (1835): 71; "Wyllys Papers, 1590–1796," *Connecticut Historical Society Collections* 21 (1924): 252.

APPENDIX: Indians in Rhode Island, 1774

| | Indians living with white families | | | | Indians living independently | | | | | |
| | Males | | Females | | Males | | Females | | | % of Indians living with white families |
	Over 16	Under 16	Over 16	Under 16	Over 16	Under 16	Over 16	Under 16	Totals	
Newport	4	8	30	3	–	–	1	–	46	98
Providence	4	6	14	10	6	10	9	9	68	50
Portsmouth	2	8	6	5	–	–	–	–	21	100
Warwick	8	19	15	9	7	14	10	6	88	58
Westerly	6	8	9	7	–	2	3	2	37	81
New Shoreham	4	6	9	7	1	6	11	11	51	43
East Greenwich	3	6	8	7	2	1	3	1	31	77
North Kingstown	4	8	8	3	6	15	19	16	79	29
South Kingstown	27	23	31	18	13	25	38	35	210	47
Jamestown	2	1	7	2	4	3	7	6	32	37.5
Smithfield	4	1	–	–	4	6	4	4	23	22
Scituate	1	3	2	–	–	–	1	–	7	86
Glocester	–	–	–	–	–	–	–	–	–	
West Greenwich	–	–	–	–	–	–	–	–	–	
Charlestown	16	8	7	5	108	132	154	98	528	7
Coventry	2	–	1	1	2	1	3	2	12	33

Exeter	3	5	6	3	—	—	—	—	17	100
Middletown	4	1	4	1	1	—	1	1	13	76
Bristol	3	4	2	—	1	3	1	2	16	56
Tiverton	1	11	1	3	5	15	24	12	72	22
Warren	1	—	1	1	—	—	2	2	7	43
Little Compton	1	4	6	4	1	1	7	2	25	60
Richmond	—	8	—	3	1	2	3	2	20	55
Cumberland	—	—	2	1	—	—	3	3	3	100
Cranston	4	2	2	4	4	2	1	1	20	60
Hopkintown	5	5	—	3	2	3	2	1	21	62
Johnston	1	1	—	1	2	1	3	—	9	33
North Providence	—	2	—	—	1	1	1	2	7	29
Barrington	—	1	2	7	2	2	3	1	18	55
	110	149	173	104	172	245	311	217	1481	35.5

NOTE: The table is based on the Rhode Island Census of 1774, Rhode Island Archives. The figures indicate an apparent rise in the Indian population from earlier estimates (see *Extracts from the Itineraries and Other Miscellanies of Ezra Stiles, D.D., LL.D., 1755–1794, with a Selection from his Correspondence,* ed. Franklin B. Dexter [New Haven: Yale University Press, 1916], pp. 54, 114; Elisha Potter, "The Early History of Narragansett," *Collections of the Rhode Island Historical Society* 3 [1835]: 114, which contains John Callender's 1730 estimate) despite the existence of factors assumed to be producing a population decline. There are a couple of reasons for this apparent contradiction: (1) Rhode Island's boundaries were extended in the eighteenth century to enclose areas of significant Indian population, and (2) the 1774 census did not include a separate category for mulattoes, many of whom were probably designated as Indian.

II

The Red Man Dispossessed
The Williams Family and the Alienation of Indian Land in Stockbridge, Massachusetts, 1736–1818

LION G. MILES

Stockbridge, Massachusetts, dramatically illustrates two Euroamerican approaches to New England's natives. Some colonists were cultural paternalists: Indians, they believed, needed to adopt Christianity and English customs, which inspired the paternalists to create missionary villages to inculcate those cultural attributes and shield the neophytes from unsavory Euroamericans. Other colonists were appropriators: Indians, they knew, possessed valuable goods, especially land, which motivated the appropriators to acquire Indian territory by fair means or foul. Stockbridge was founded by the former type of colonist but within half a century succumbed to the latter.

Many Indians distrusted both types of colonists, seeing little difference between (to use modern terminology) cultural imperialists and territorial imperialists. But for some Indians, the paternalists offered acceptable, even desirable, ways to build new lives in a fast-changing world. No Indian, in all probability, thought kindly of the appropriators. Stockbridge, as Lion G. Miles's article sadly demonstrates, began as a cooperative venture between paternalistic missionaries and a portion of the Housatonic band; half a century later, the Algonquians and their few Euroamerican friends had been displaced by land grabbers and their political henchmen.

How representative is the Stockbridge paradigm? In its particulars, of course, it is unusual, but in its broad scope—of Praying Towns becoming predominantly Euroamerican communities, of Algonquians losing their land through debt foreclosure, of English squatters commandeering Algonquian lands, of courts and legislatures ignoring Algonquian interests—the encounters at Stockbridge were all too common in eighteenth-century New England. By the dawn of the nineteenth century, Indian landholdings in southern New England were minuscule and were shrinking rapidly even in the region's relatively remote northeastern and northwestern areas.

THE QUINCENTENNIAL CELEBRATION of Columbus's first voyage to the Americas has occasioned much discussion about "first contact." In colonial New England, no less than in Central America, disruptions were more common than accommodations as two quite different cultures collided. The English settlers' established rules regarding law, religion, and ownership of property did not mesh with the Indians' complex patterns of tradition. Nowhere is this cultural discrepancy more evident than in the attempts Indians made to reconcile their needs with the settlers' ever growing demands for land. Scarcity of documentation revealing the Indian point of view complicates study of the matter.[1] The experimental Indian community at Stockbridge, Massachusetts, active in the second half of the eighteenth century, therefore provides an exceptional opportunity to examine the divergent attitudes of the two groups.

Forming the Town of Stockbridge (1736–39)

In the seventeenth century, the General Court of Massachusetts Bay established fourteen communities for Indians who had been converted to Christianity. These "Praying Towns" were designed to separate their inhabitants from whites as well as from other Indians. King Philip's War (1675–76) so disrupted the New England tribes that by 1684 only four Praying Towns remained, all of them in decline.[2] In 1736 the General Court authorized a new arrangement, an experiment in Indian-white cooperation at Stockbridge, a town in the westernmost county of Berkshire.

Near Stockbridge, and extending north to Lake Champlain, west to Albany, and south into Connecticut, lived the scattered remnants of the once great Mahican confederacy of Algonquian-speaking peoples. Known as the Hudson "River Indians," they had dwindled to about five hundred individuals by the turn of the eighteenth century. Some had moved east from the Hudson and merged with a related band of Indians living in four small settlements along the Housatonic River.[3] In 1724 these Housatunnuck Mahicans sold a tract of land to the General Court so that two towns could be settled in an area that today encompasses Sheffield, Great Barrington, and the southern half of Stockbridge.[4] The Mahicans reserved for themselves a small tract at Skatekook, in Sheffield, while another group settled further up the Housatonic at Wnahktakook ("the great meadow") in Stockbridge. The first white settlers arrived in the area the following year. In 1734 the chief sachem of the Housatunnucks, John Konkapot, suggested to the Reverend Samuel Hopkins of Springfield that a missionary would be welcome among his people to teach them the principles of Christianity and instruct them in reading and writing English.[5]

Governor Jonathan Belcher demonstrated the colony's good faith by bestowing a captaincy on Konkapot and a lieutenancy on the chief at Skatekook, Aaron Umpachene. Shortly thereafter, the Commissioners for Indian Affairs at Boston appointed John Sergeant, a tutor at Yale College, to be missionary to the Housatunnuck Indians. Sergeant, with the assistance of a Springfield schoolmaster, Timothy Woodbridge, preached through the scattered Indian villages for the next year and a half. Fully aware that by concentrating the Indians in one location it could control them more effectively and free more land for English settlement, the provincial government now proposed to reserve the land at Stockbridge for the Indians so that they could live together and have a school. At Sergeant's suggestion, Belcher agreed that "some English families . . . be interspers'd and settled among the Indians; for to *civilize* will be the readiest way to *Christianize* them."[6]

The tribe did not receive the governor's proposal with universal enthusiasm. According to Sergeant, some members viewed the "design" as a means "only to get the greater advantage of them, and bring them more into our power that we may enslave them and their children," but the young missionary was finally able to persuade the Indians that the new arrangement was for their own good.[7]

In March 1736 the General Court granted a riverfront township six miles square (23,040 acres) to the Housatunnucks, comprising the northern portion of Sheffield along with a tract north of Sheffield known as Upper Housatunnuck. The four Dutch settlers already in the town received equivalent land elsewhere. Sergeant and Woodbridge obtained the rights to 400 acres each. An additional four English families would be permitted to settle there, each to receive 400 acres as well.[8] The Indians retained ownership of all the remaining land in "Indian Town," soon to be called Stockbridge. When Colonel John Stoddard and his party arrived to survey the township, Lieutenant Umpachene asked them some hard questions. He expressed gratitude for "the great favour" shown his people but enquired why they had been neglected so long. He wondered if there was some hidden motive in this fresh interest and asked why so many Christians lived "such vicious lives." Stoddard assured him that the government sought only the good of the Indians, but Umpachene suggested that, since most of the land would belong to the tribe, "some contention" might in future arise between them and the English. Stoddard replied that the Indians would have land titles and the protection of law in the same manner as all other citizens.[9]

A survey of the town in 1739 laid out for the Indians thirty-two "inter-vale," or meadow, lots of the most desirable land, two to ten acres each, north and south of the river.[10] The six English proprietors—Sergeant, Timothy Woodbridge and his brother Joseph, Ephraim Williams of Newton, Ephraim Brown of Watertown, and Josiah Jones of Weston—were not granted intervale lands and had to settle on the hill above the meadow. Each received the right to lay out "settling lots" of seventy-five to one hundred acres. These they tried to place close to the center of town, much to the Indians' annoyance.

Conflicts Multiply (1739–59)

The division of lands in 1739 had been imprecise, and during the next ten years conflicts arose and intensified as the English encroached on Indian land. In 1740 Timothy Woodbridge purchased a square mile of timber land, plus an additional 150-acre parcel, from members of the tribe without first securing the required approval from the General Court. When other Indians complained that they had not agreed to the sale, the court sanctioned the transaction because Woodbridge had "spent the Prime of his Life" serving the Indians. The tribe lost 790 acres with this stroke of the pen. Two years later, in 1742, several Indians began to clear and fence a 70-acre tract with Sergeant's encouragement. Ephraim Williams claimed this land for himself and ordered that the work be stopped. When the tribe protested, the General Court permitted Williams to keep the land, provided he pay the Indians £10 for their labor. Samuel Brown built his house on Indian land and then admitted to having made a 19-acre error in measurement. Faced with a house already completed, the tribe accepted payment for the land and the court approved the transaction.[11]

These and similar incidents raised tensions, only temporarily eased by the outbreak of war between England and France in 1744 (King George's War). Exposed to French attack, Stockbridge became a garrison town, and the young men of the tribe went off to war as scouts under Major Ephraim Williams, the powerful proprietor who had already displayed his designs on Indian land. For the duration of the war, the Stockbridge Indians remained loyal to the English.[12] With the cessation of French hostilities in 1748, however, conflicts reemerged in the town.

By 1747, eleven years after its establishment, Stockbridge had grown from fewer than ten Indian families to nearly fifty with the addition of members from other Mahican bands in New York and Connecticut. By 1749 the Indian population numbered 218 persons, who were living in twenty English-style timber houses as well as traditional bark wigwams.[13] The number of English families had also increased, from the first six to twelve or thirteen, totaling 60 persons. Whereas Ephraim Williams had 7 living children, Timothy Woodbridge and Joseph Woodbridge, 8 each, and Josiah Jones, 5, Indian families averaged only 2 children.[14] If that rate of growth were sustained, the English would soon overwhelm the Indians by weight of numbers, a danger that soon became apparent to the tribe. The Indians reported after King George's War that "they were told at first That but few Families, besides the Minister & School master should settle with them; But now there are many Families settled in the Place." The settlers responded that "it must be allowed that it was reasonable that as the English increased, they should settle their Children on their Lands." The Indians "allowed it was reasonable but said they were not told so at first."[15]

Five of the original English settlers and a cousin of the sixth, Samuel Brown, petitioned the court in 1748 to resolve the difficulties that had arisen over Indian lands by identifying the Indian proprietors and determining what powers they had to dispose of their lands. Citing the increasing population of the town, the petitioners stressed their need to claim the balance of their original 400-acre grants. They added that Indians were quarreling over individual parcels of land, and they urged the court to act swiftly "for the peaceable & quiet Settlement of the Indian Affairs & Controversies respecting their Lands." The court dispatched a committee, led by Oliver Partridge of Hatfield, to investigate the situation in Stockbridge.[16]

The Indians informed the committee that "the English layout Lands they know not how much," that "no Indian was with them," and "they did not lay out Swamps & Ponds." The tribe had supposed that "when we came to an agreement with the English . . . they Should have or Lay out their Lands any where East of the Dividing Line we agreed upon." However, the Indians found that "the English are not content with that, but Lay out Lands Elsewhere which we Supposed Contained two mile and [a] half one way and three miles the other." In other words, the Indians charged that the English had claimed lands amounting to seven and a half square miles, or 4,800 acres, twice the 2,400 originally allocated. The English denied the allegation and produced a plan showing that they were entitled to yet another 485 acres.[17]

The committee settled the dispute by declaring that the English should "go off at some distance" to lay claim to the rest of their lands. The north-south line in the "Out Lands" earlier agreed upon verbally was now set down on paper. East of the line the English could lay out lots wherever they pleased, and the Indians could do the same to the west. The remaining land in the township, approximately 20,000 acres, was reserved to the Stockbridge Indians "to their Use & Behoof forever." To forestall any future land disputes, the committee recommended to the General Court that the land be surveyed once again.[18]

The resulting "second division" did indeed eliminate much of the confusion over land claims. By a resolve of 30 December 1749, the Massachusetts Council declared that the Housatunnuck Indians were "a distinct propriety" and ordered Colonel Timothy Dwight of Northampton to travel to Stockbridge and call a meeting of the Indian proprietors to ascertain their number, determine the proportion of land each would receive, and appoint officers for regulating their affairs, including the disposition of common or undivided land among themselves. The Indian proprietors were to maintain a book listing all grants made.[19]

When the proprietors met on 11 June 1750, fifty-five members of the tribe received shares ranging from 10 to 80 acres, and three Indians from outside Stockbridge were permitted "a suitable quantity of Land for present improvement," for a total of 2,990 acres. The proprietors voted to set aside half of the remaining land for distribution to Indians of other tribes who might choose to live with them. Dwight then laid out twenty house lots for Indians only along the main street of the settlement and sixteen Indian meadow lots north and south of the Housatonic River.[20]

The surveys gave the force of law to some of the divisions orally agreed upon between the Indians and the English. But still there was trouble regarding Ephraim Williams's self-appropriated land. Eight Indian proprietors complained to the General Court that "by the disposition and conduct of Coll Williams [they] have been and still are disturbed and wrong'd in Several instances respecting their lands." Williams asked his friend Timothy Dwight to survey a tract behind his house lot, including the disputed land previously cleared by the Indians. Dwight also surveyed a 30-acre tract for Williams near the meetinghouse, land the Indians claimed had been taken from them to serve as the site for a mill. Finally, Williams had coopted 240 additional acres to which he was not entitled under the terms of his initial grant. According to the Indians, Williams had seized land without consulting them, offering any compensation, or obtaining the General Court's approval. "Such a piece of unreasonable and unjust conduct" should be discountenanced by the General Court, they urged. Williams argued that he had developed the mill at his own expense and that it had benefited the Indians, that he and Timothy Woodbridge had purchased the 240 acres, and that there had been no "uneasiness" about the transaction until the present time. He added that he believed the matter had been "Stirred up" by "some Evil minded persons" who were intimate with the Indians, "partly to Vex your Respondent but principally for their own Self interest & views."[21]

A committee of the Court, after hearing Williams's side of the story, decided that the disputed land behind his home lot was part of the second division among the English lots and that therefore "it would be inconvenient for said Williams not to have it." The committee recommended that he convey 8 acres of meadow land to the Indians in return for their trouble. As for the other lands taken by Williams, when neither side showed any willingness to yield, the Court ordered that the parties work out "an Accommodation" and transmit it to the Court's next session.[22] There is no complete record of the terms of the compromise that resulted, but, judging from accounts of later transactions, Williams kept much of the land in question. Recorded in the registry at Springfield is a deed showing that in 1751 he sold the 240-acre tract to his son Josiah for £160.[23] A pair of deeds indicates that he also retained land not specifically disputed by the Indians but nonetheless falling outside the area reserved for the English. In 1748 he sold 200 acres in the northeast corner of the township to Josiah for £150, but in 1752 he again sold the same piece of property to Josiah for the same amount.[24] Whether this double deeding reflects a compromise with the Indians or some double dealing by Williams has not been determined.

John Sergeant died in 1749. Late in 1750 the Stockbridge congregation invited the Reverend Jonathan Edwards of Northampton to be his replacement. Edwards's congregation had recently ousted him, so he was free to accept the invitation. Edwards blamed his dismissal on the powerful Williams clan, influential not only in Northampton but throughout the Connecticut Valley.[25] Indeed, there is ample evidence that Ephraim Williams did his best to block Edwards's appointment in Stockbridge.[26]

Soon after Edwards's arrival, Williams attempted to buy up the land owned by the English inhabitants of the town, offering "very high prices, and cash in hand," but the settlers refused to sell.[27] The Indians also refrained from further dealings with Williams, and the proprietors independently conducted their affairs under the guidance of Timothy Woodbridge. The Woodbridge brothers, Timothy and Joseph, Josiah Jones, and a few other early settlers were concerned for the well-being of the Indians. In most matters, they were opposed by Ephraim Williams, his son Elijah, and the new resident agent for Indian affairs, Colonel Joseph Dwight, who had arrived in Stockbridge in 1752 and had powerful connections in government.

Although tensions had escalated in 1753–54 over the apparently unprovoked murder of an Indian by two white men, who were then treated leniently by the Springfield court, the outbreak of the French and Indian War in 1755 unified the town.[28] In the interest of self-defense, Stockbridge became a garrison town for the second time. Over the next five years, nearly all the able-bodied male Stockbridge Indians, numbering about fifty, went to war as a company of rangers under Major Robert Rogers.[29]

The Great Land Grab (1759–74)

The government of Massachusetts had long pursued a policy of cultivating the friendship of the Indians on the province's western frontiers as a defense against the French threat. During King George's War the wisdom of that policy had been evident at Stockbridge. The Reverend Samuel Hopkins observed in 1753 that "Stockbridge is in the very road of, and more expos'd to, the Indians from Canada, than any other place whatever; yet we see that the enemy turn'd off east to Connecticut River and west to the Dutch settlements, where they did much mischief; while Stockbridge, Sheffield, New Marlborough and Number One [Tyringham], tho' more expos'd, were not molested. This, so far as we can discern, was owing to a small number of Indians dwelling at Stockbridge, who are our hearty and fast friends."[30]

When the threat of French invasion was removed after Quebec fell in 1759, however, English settlers poured into western Massachusetts looking for cheap land. By the end of 1759, more than one thousand English families had migrated into the northern part of Berkshire County without making payment to the tribe for the lands on which they had settled. When the Indians complained to the General Court, that body appointed a committee to lease any unappropriated lands west of the Connecticut River "as they shall think best for the interest of the province," an interest that no longer needed to recognize the concerns of the Indians.[31]

As had happened elsewhere in New England, government land grants in Berkshire County soon eclipsed direct purchases of land from the Indians.[32] By 1762 the General Court had granted so much tribal land to English settlers that the Indian leaders of Stockbridge—including Chief Nimham, who had moved his Algonquian tribe, the Wappingers, from Dutchess County, New York, to Stockbridge—petitioned Boston for some "purchase Consideration." The committee appointed to review the matter recommended that, although the tribe had received frequent payments for its land, the province should pay it a "gratuity" of £1,000 "to have the Indians quiet & in good temper."[33] The Indians refused to accept the payment and appealed directly to the king. In response, Massachusetts increased the gratuity to £1,500, then to £1,700, in exchange for an Indian release of "all Claims to any of the Lands of this province."[34] On 12 January 1763, twenty Stockbridge Indian leaders deeded to the province all unsold tribal lands in Berkshire County west of the Westfield River, except the township of Stockbridge and portions of Lenox and Richmond; just a month later the General Court ordered a release of the Lenox and Richmond claims as well.[35]

The Stockbridge Indians now controlled only a small island in the midst of an English sea. The town of Stockbridge was all that remained to them in Massachusetts, and within the township the English had already acquired about 5,000 acres, more than double their original grant of 2,400.[36] This acreage included the mile-square purchase made by Timothy Woodbridge plus 150 acres, nearly 740 acres in the southeast, and approximately 500 acres in the northeast section that were in excess of the original English grant. Finally, from 1750 through 1763 about 600 acres were legally deeded by Indians to non-Indians and approved by the General Court. Jonathan Edwards obtained 60 acres, and his successor, the Reverend Stephen West, received 50; Stephen Nash received 50 acres to carry on his trade as blacksmith; the General Court had allowed a disabled Indian to sell 50 acres of woodland to a free Negro; Timothy Woodbridge received 30 acres for his services; Joseph Woodbridge obtained land for the construction of a saw and grist mill; the estate of a deceased Indian was sold to pay his debts; Jacob Cheeksonkun sold 12 acres to Isaac Brown for a trading house "to the publick benefit"; and "an aged Indian Woman" was allowed to sell 37 acres to support herself—all legitimate transactions.[37]

But now a new English entrepreneur had decided to strike his fortune in Stockbridge. Elijah Williams, the youngest son of Ephraim, had purchased his father's Stockbridge properties in 1752, the year before Ephraim left town and just two before he died in Deerfield. Elijah had graduated from the College of New Jersey at Princeton in 1753, and after attaining the rank of major in the French and Indian War, he had studied the law.[38] As an entrepreneur and as sheriff of Berkshire County from 1761 to 1775, he used his expertise to unburden the Indians of their remaining land.

Control of the annual town meeting was the vehicle Williams used to extend his power. The first Stockbridge town meeting in 1739 had chosen as selectmen one Englishman and two Indians, John Konkapot and Aaron Umpachene. The next year, three Indians served in that office, but in 1745 the ratio shifted three to one in favor of the English. Members of the tribe also acted as tithingmen, surveyors of highways, and hogreeves. From 1747 the town elected two constables, one for the English and one for the Indians.[39] The tribe, of course, did not fully comprehend the town meeting form of government, a system foreign to its powwows and councils. When the town was to be notified of the meeting of 1747, the constable was absent and the Indian selectmen, "being ignorant of the Law," announced the meeting themselves. They then met and elected selectmen. The English informed them that the procedure was illegal and had the constable call another meeting. But the tribe, as the English proprietors reported, "refused to act on any thing (being Indians could not be convinced that the first Meeting was illegal), upon which the Meeting drop'd" and the town was without officers. Seeking to resolve the matter, the English inhabitants petitioned the General Court, which ordered that the selectmen chosen by the Indians should convene the inhabitants and elect the necessary officers.[40]

Indians attended town meetings and occasionally held some nominal offices, even though they did not pay taxes to support town expenses, including those for maintaining the Christian ministry. The English inhabitants thus found themselves in a peculiar position, and in 1751 they petitioned the General Court. Granting their petition, the Court allowed the English, "exclusive of the Indian Inhabitants," to exercise the powers of a precinct and to collect taxes.[41] The precinct provided a means for the English to formulate a separate course of action regarding town matters and dealings with the Indians. On many occasions the precinct convened at the home of an English inhabitant in the morning of the day of the town meeting, which usually met in the afternoon at the meetinghouse or schoolhouse. The same man, always a settler and never an Indian, acted as moderator at both meetings, so that an English inhabitant invariably decided all parliamentary questions. Frequently, the moderator was Timothy Woodbridge, whom the Indians regarded as their "patron" and who guided them through the intricacies of town meeting procedure and translated the proceedings for them. When he was absent, the Indians were at a loss.

The Williams group, now controlled by Elijah Williams, was dissatisfied with the organization of the Indian town. Representing himself as the spokesman for the English inhabitants, Williams appealed to the General Court in 1761. He declared that the Indian "manner of living" was so different that the English labored "under many inconveniences." The Indians, he said, had little use for schools, roads, or fences, and paid no taxes. He urged the Court to allow the English to transact all town matters among themselves, without the Indians. The Council sent a copy of Williams's petition to the Indians so that they could show cause on the matter, "if any they have." The records do not reveal whether the Indians responded, but they do document that someone, name not recorded, introduced an act in the legislature to enable the English inhabitants to transact certain matters "separate and distinct from the Indian Inhabitants." The House of Representatives passed the bill, but the Council voted to give it more study, and it went no further.[42] The Indians gained another victory the next month when the House exempted them from paying town taxes and assessed the English inhabitants for the entire sum of £93 6s. 4d.[43]

Momentarily blocked, Williams and his supporters decided on a more direct approach. In 1763 Elijah Brown, an English inhabitant who had no official authority, notified the Indian constable that town meeting would be held on 21 March; he did so, according to the Indians, only the evening before, whereas the English had been notified eleven days earlier. At the time of the meeting, Timothy Woodbridge was in New York on business, and most of the Indians were working in their maple-sugar houses several miles from town center. Only a few Indians were able to attend the meeting. An aging Chief Konkapot described the strategy used to defeat them. When the time came to choose selectmen, he claimed, the English introduced written ballots. "We Indians," he said, "did not know what it was and nobody would Let us understand it for we allways voted before by lifting up the hand. . . . Then the people brought in their papers and we did not know what they were doing but they said Mr Williams was chosen a Selectman. Then we desired that Mr Woodbridge might be chosen . . . but they would not hear us." Thereupon the Indians walked out of the meeting and refused to serve in any town offices. To support them, the English constable, Elihu Parsons, and the town treasurer, Joseph Woodbridge, also refused to serve.[44]

Without officers to conduct the town's daily business, four selectmen from the previous year, two English and two Indians, signed a warrant for a second meeting. Only Elijah Williams refused to sign, objecting that new selectmen (including himself) were already seated and that they had sole authority to call a new meeting. Nonetheless, another meeting did convene on 30 March, and a majority of the English and Indian inhabitants elected a full slate of officers, the identities of whom are not recorded except for Timothy Woodbridge, selectman. The selectmen chosen at the first meeting, however, refused to be turned out. Upon the recommendation of an investigating committee, the General Court permitted them to remain in office and simply ordered them to call a third meeting to elect a replacement for the constable who had refused to serve.[45]

Having forced his reelection as selectman and squeezed out Woodbridge, the Indians' candidate, Williams next tried by equally devious means to obtain the town's seat in the House of Representatives. In May, the Indians again received notice of a meeting only the night before, Williams's excuse being "that the Indians who paid nothing towards a Representative might not be tampered with to choose a Person for the English, who paid the whole Charge." At the meeting, Konkapot and the Indian freeholders noted that "the voters till now never was forty in number at the choice of a representative, But now all at once more than Sixty." Williams received thirty-two votes to Timothy Woodbridge's twenty-nine, and the Indians felt cheated. They claimed that many voted for Williams who "were poor fellows that we never heard had any business in this Town only as they were hired To work and we have reason To believe to vote."[46]

The laws of Massachusetts required an annual income of at least 40 s., or other estate valued at £40, plus three months' residence in a town, for a man to qualify as an elector. Williams had introduced nine young men as voters who possessed doubtful qualifications. Three of them did not live in Stockbridge; three were sons of Williams's supporters who claimed freeholds of £100 in "wild or unimproved Lands"; one was a transient granted "parole admission as an Inhabitant" by the selectmen chosen at the 21 March meeting; and one was a laborer hired by Williams who swore his estate was worth £40. Though the General Court's investigating committee declared the election illegal, Williams represented Stockbridge in the House the next year, the only time he ever held that office.[47]

Joseph Woodbridge, Timothy's brother, was so upset by what he called Williams's "legerdemain practice" that he wrote the investigating committee that "the Town as such do not own him as their representative, his crouding inn, in the manner he did and his unconstitutional Treatment of those that had a better right than many of those that voted him in." He added, "I know so much of the violent and inconsiderate disposition of many of the english that I am unwilling to be controled by them if I can avoid it." Timothy Woodbridge wrote the governor and Council that some of the English were trying to "worm [the Indians] out of their priviledges" and complained that "it appears very injurious . . . for the people by all ways and means to croud into the Town to get estates and then to cry out that they cannot bear to be a Society with Indians nor to be controld by their votes." To resolve this nasty situation, the investigating committee recommended separating the English and Indians into "distinct Societys," each with its own representative, but an act for that purpose failed to pass the General Court.[48]

Among the complaints lodged by the Stockbridge Indians during the crisis of 1763 was that "Williams and a party he has made in the Town are endeavouring not only To get all the power but our Lands too into their hands." Williams denied the charge, claiming only that he had leased 140 acres from Konkapot's son and had made no other purchase of the Indians, a statement true to the letter, although not the spirit, of the law.[49] Because Massachusetts required legislative approval of any purchase or lease from an Indian, Williams and his supporters had devised other, less direct means for acquiring land. The instrument initially employed was called a "security." An English settler would pay an Indian landowner a certain amount of money for "the Possession and Improvement" of a piece of land. The Indian would agree to repay the security at the end of the stated term, either three or seven years; he also agreed that if he failed to do so, he was obligated "whenever the way may or can be made Lawful, To Execute a good Deed of Sale" to the English party.[50]

A second tool was the five-hundred-year lease, a transaction requiring legislative approval but one not always enforced by the General Court. Three leases are recorded in the Berkshire Middle Registry and the Dwight Collection, all in 1763 to Elijah Williams—50 acres from Hendrick Waumpunkeet and Jacob Hunkamugg, 50 from Abraham Wnupas, and 140 from Robert Nungkauwaut (alias Konkapot). The usual terms required a one-time payment of cash by the lessee and a token rent of "one peppercorn" per year.[51] Here was an easy way to have land without actually buying it. Although the committee sent by the General Court to investigate the town meeting dispute held that the lease made by Nungkauwaut "cannot be justified by the Laws of this Government," Williams had sought protection for himself by obtaining a license for the lease from the Court of General Sessions of the Peace in Great Barrington.[52] Apparently, the lease was allowed to stand.

Another device Williams used was the conditional loan, of which there is one record extant. On 1 December 1762, he lent Ephraim Paumpkhaunhaun £300 provided the Indian would "during the Course of one Year . . . use his faithfull Endeavours by his Petition and Petitions if Need shall be to the Gen¹ Court of the Province . . . to obtain Leave of the said Gen¹ Court for his Selling Twenty five Acres of Land belonging to him . . . in the Northwest Corner of the said Town of Stockbridge at a Place Called Quabauguk [now West Stockbridge], . . . and Execute a good Deed of Sale and Conveyance of the said Twenty five Acres of Land to the said Williams." No petitions from Paumpkhaunhaun are found in the archives, but there is a 1766 deed of seventy-five acres in the northwest part of the town made over from him to Elijah Williams. In 1773 Williams sold this land to his cousin William Williams for a profit of nearly 17,000 percent.[53]

Williams was also able to seize Indian lands used as collateral for loans gone sour. In 1767 Jehoiakim Mohkhowwauweet could not repay Williams for a loan of £16 New York currency. The Indian had put up 120 acres in western Stockbridge as collateral and had signed an agreement offering to deed the land to Williams if he defaulted on the loan and if Williams would pay him an additional £34.[54]

By far the most common device the English used against the Indians was the manipulation of debt. Traditionally, the Mahicans had been hunter-gatherers; their farming, usually performed by the women, was restricted to raising corn and beans.[55] They had no farm implements and at Stockbridge became dependent upon European traders and settlers for such items. In many cases, the English inhabitants plowed the Indians' fields for them.[56] By 1763, their cultivated lands were so overworked and so little fertilized that they produced "very thin Crops."[57] Trading with the Dutch in New York province was an important activity, and members of the tribe camped periodically at Kinderhook, a transfer point for goods coming up the Hudson River. One notable item the Indians had to offer was the ginseng root, which they gathered for the European market.[58]

The most prominent of the Dutch traders was Cornelius Van Schaack, a wealthy merchant and landowner; his sons, Cornelius Jr. and David, also traders, owned land in Stockbridge. In 1762 David wrote Elijah Williams, whom he supplied, that he was "extreamly obliged to [Williams] for the information you give me about the Savage Tribe, Shall make a proper use of the Kind hints you give me." In 1764 he wrote again concerning Indian debts, asking Williams "for some Information on that head, and it would Give me pleasure to Rec^e[ive] an answer Suitable to my Wishes as I have Still a large Demand on the Tribe."[59] Between 1765 and 1774 the Van Schaack brothers took five Indians to court in Berkshire County for neglecting their accounts. With their father, they accumulated a total of 822 acres of Indian land in Stockbridge, 491 acres in payment of debts.[60]

Until 1765 it was illegal in Massachusetts for Europeans to seize or purchase Indian lands to satisfy debts without first securing General Court approval. The Stockbridge investigating committee of 1763 had reported the effects of that policy: "The Indians are constantly running in debt either to the Inhabitants of New York Government or to some of our own People. Some of the Indians have been put to Goal [Jail] in Albany for debt, and Others are sued for debts in this Government, and have no means of discharging their debts, but by sale of their Lands." Some of the Indians were so reduced financially that they pleaded with Williams to take their land. Abram Aukomock wrote from Albany in 1762: "Mr Elijah Williams Please to Let Me have Som Money for Which I Desire that You take 50 Eacors of Land for Which I Will Give Good deed. I Am Almost ded for Want of Provetion and I Preay Let Me have fore Pounds of Money Out [of] My Land."[61] Ever careful to stay within the limits of the law, Williams declined Aukomock's deed.

TABLE 1. Indian Land Sales to Non-Indians in Stockbridge, 1751–1818

Year	No.	Acreage	Avg. Acres/ Sale	Total Paid (£.s)	Avg. Price/ Acre
1751	2	11	5.5	84.0	£7.13s.[a]
1752	2	40	20	50.0	1.5s.
1753	1	14	14	50.0	3.10s.
1754	1	70	70	40.0	11s.
1755	2	55	27.5	23.8	9s.
1757	2	3	1.5	0.0	0
1758	1	70	70	20.0	6s.
1759	5	192.75	38.5	134.5	14s.
1761	2	55	27.5	10.0	4s.
1762	2	97[b]	48.5	45.0	9s.
1763	1	60[b,c]	60	40.0	13s.
Unknown[d]	1	6	6	?	?
1764	2	73	36.5	31.4	9s.
1765	8	409[a]	51	148.10	7s.
1766	30	3,399.5	113.33	1,161.13	7s.
1767	15	1,168.25	78	459.8	8s.
1768	20	1,192.25	59.67	708.15	12s.
1769	10	319.5	32	99.0	6s.
1770	7	236	33.75	113.5	10s.
1771	19	624.75	33	211.5	7s.
1772	13	2,363	181.75	367.0	3s.
1773	9	200	22.25	165.6	16s.
1774	11	256.5	23.33	249.10	19s.
1777	3	294	98	352.0	1.4s.
1778	4	22	5.5	195.0	8.17s.
1779	2	40.5	20.25	390.0	9.15s.
1780	5	95.5	19	168.0	1.15s.
1781	8	353	44	379.0	1.1s.
1782	1	.5	.5	17.0	34.0s.
1783	8	97	12.125	387.0	4.0s.
1784	8	124.33	15.5	408.0	3.6s.
1785	14	292.5	21	419.10	1.9s.
1786	7	25.5	3.5	142.8	5.14s.
1788	3	2.5	1	27.10	13.10s.
1794	2	40	20	85.0	2.3s.
1797	1	4	4	$10.00	$ 2.50
1809	1	Burial Gr.	—	0.00	0
1810	2	.75	.33	$25.00	$33.33
1818	1	4	4	$10.00	2.50
	236[e]	12,311.5		£7,181.17s. (plus $45)	

SOURCES: Books 1–26, 28–30, 36–38, 46, 49–50, 52, 56, 60, Berkshire County Middle Registry; books M, 1, Hampden County Registry; Indian Deeds, Stockbridge Library; Indian

Documents, Scheide Collection, Firestone Library, Princeton University; folder 51, box 1,
Van Schaack Papers, Ayer Manuscripts, Newberry Library, Chicago, Ill.

NOTES: All figures are reasonable approximations. Monetary values are rounded to the nearest shilling in Massachusetts currency. New York currency is converted to Massachusetts at £1 N.Y. to 12s. Mass.

Much acreage is unaccounted for and many sales went unrecorded. The disruption in normal record keeping during the Revolution may explain some of the missing sales. No deeds were recorded in the Berkshire Registry in 1777 because Mark Hopkins, the registrar, died in 1776 while serving with the army in New York. His successor did not take office until January 1778. An advertisement by the registrar's widow in the *Connecticut Courant* of 10 February 1778 indicates that fees had not been paid on a number of deeds, which normally would preclude their recording.

ªOne pound equals 20 shillings.

ᵇDoes not include 59.5 acres in 4 securities (1762, 1763, 1765).

ᶜDoes not include 240 acres in 3 leases (1763).

ᵈA sale mentioned in a deed recorded in the Berkshire Middle Registry, book 6, p. 42, but not itself recorded.

ᵉTotals include 3 leases and 4 securities.

The problem of Indian debt became so acute that in January 1765 Captain Jacob Cheeksonkun and nine other leaders of the tribe petitioned the General Court for relief. In essence they wanted to be freed of any restrictions on their ability to dispose of their own property. They requested the same rights as Englishmen to "exercise Their own reason and use Their own Estates and Take the consequences of their own doings." In addition, they requested permission to sell the "out lands" they held in common in the western part of the town. "As the case now stands," they added, "the Stockbridge Indians can neither keep out of prison nor get out when they are in." In another petition, a few months later, Timothy Woodbridge explained that the Indians, holding land they were forbidden to sell, were threatened with financial ruin and would soon be forced to leave Stockbridge. The General Court responded in November by empowering the tribe "to make Sale of so much of their Lands lying in the Town of Stockbridge . . . as will be sufficient to discharge their just debts." It limited leases to a term of one year and appointed Timothy Woodbridge and John Ashley to review all sales to assure that the Indians were not cheated.⁶²

This landmark decision was the final death blow. As Table 1 shows, in 1766 land sales to non-Indians increased dramatically. Thirty sales transpired that year, accounting for more than 3,000 acres. In the next two years, thirty-five sales involving 2,300 acres compensated creditors for notes in default. Of the deeds recorded in the Berkshire County Middle Registry for those years, forty-five, or 69 percent, are certified by Timothy Woodbridge as approved "for the payment of . . . just debts." The largest single sale was an area of 1,023 acres in the northeast known as the Rattle-snake Mountain Division. Five Englishmen, including Elijah Williams, purchased this hilly tract for only £150. They then divided it into ten lots and sold some of these at considerable profit.[63]

Prices varied by location and degree of improvement. Generally, in the years before the Revolution, cleared meadow land and house lots brought one pound per acre for an Indian but double that for a European. Unim-proved or mountainous land, as in the western part of town, brought much less, sometimes as little as two or three shillings per acre. When the last parcel of common land in present-day West Stockbridge (about 1,700 acres) was sold to Samuel Brown, Jr., and William Goodrich in 1772, the Indians received only about ten pence per acre.[64]

Although the tribe now had the means of satisfying its creditors, debt continued to plague it. Men like Major (now styled "Colonel") Williams encouraged the Indians to increase their dependency on the English. The land leased from Nungkauwaut in 1763 and then purchased in 1765 became the site of a mill, ironworks, and store owned and operated by Williams. He built a home there in 1766, and the present village of West Stockbridge sprang up around it. At his store Williams offered a wide variety of goods and was quite willing to accept the Indians' credit. His papers contain many notes signed by members of the tribe. One reads, "Please to let Da-vid Naunaunukannuck have a Shirt and Hat and a pair of Stockings, and charge the same to the Indian Proprietors." Another allows Timothy Yo-kun to charge a hat, a pair of buckles, stockings, and shoes to the proprie-tors. Indian land often served as collateral, eliciting Timothy Wood-bridge's implicit censure that Williams must "Judge the propriety" of giving goods for land.[65]

Williams allowed the Indian proprietors twelve-month's credit for goods and accepted numerous demand notes from individual Indians, usu-ally bearing 6 percent interest. One note signed by Josiah Mauhautauweh in 1771 for a loan of £2 12s. 6d. shows interest calculated for the next three years, bringing the Indian's debt to £3 3s. 5d. in 1774. As the tribe's indebt-edness mounted, so did the number of court cases brought against its members. Between 1761 and 1765 there were only eight actions for debt against Stockbridge Indians in the Berkshire County Inferior Court of Common Pleas. From 1766 to 1774 the number rose to thirty-seven, and the tribe complained that "we greatly suffered in being sued by almost every one to whom we owed so much as a few shillings." In every case the Indian defaulted by not appearing, so the court awarded damages and costs to the English plaintiff. As sheriff of Berkshire County, Elijah Williams was responsible for enforcing the court's execution orders. In so doing, he frequently advanced the money required and presented the Indian proprietors with the bill.[66]

The single largest purchaser of Indian land and the largest taxpayer in West Stockbridge, Williams became a very wealthy man. By 1781 he owned several houses, a forge, a sawmill, 35 acres of improved land, and 546 acres of unimproved land. In 1795 his farm covered 1,000 acres, with five houses and three barns. From 1763 he had purchased or leased 1,288 acres from the Indians, all apparently transferred in discharge of debts. It should be remarked that not one of his Indian deeds bears Timothy Woodbridge's certification that the transaction was approved for debt payment, as required by the General Court's resolve of 1765. Indeed, none of his Indian deeds on file at the Berkshire Middle Registry was recorded until 1785; his papers contain a document listing them all under the heading "Acc^t of Deeds put to Reg[istry] to record July 28. 1785."[67] By this date Woodbridge was dead, and nearly all the Indians had left Stockbridge. The late recording seems to indicate that Williams did not wish his land transactions with the Indians to be subject to the scrutiny and veto of his old adversary, Timothy Woodbridge.

In 1773 the Indians complained again to the General Court that "their Tribe are brough[t] into the Utmost Dificulty & Distress by Reason of the Traders who have Setled Among & Near us as well as other Designing People who Aim At Getting Away all That The Indians are Possessed of." These creditors, they said, were putting their debts in suit against them and "very often Takeing Notes beyond their Just Demands & Then Puting the Indians in Prison if they Wont Part with their Land At an Undervalue." The Indians called on the Court to empower Woodbridge to take charge of their affairs so that justice might prevail in their dealings over lands sold for debt "& also those Lands that Several People have got Possess^d of & not Paid for." The Court ordered that after 31 March 1773 no person would be permitted to take action in law against the Stockbridge Indians for any debt or contract of more than thirty-five shillings. In June the House of Representatives authorized Woodbridge to examine all Indian sales for debt and signify his approval "on the Back of the Deeds."[68]

These measures, of course, came too late. By the end of 1774, the Stockbridge Indians had already given up most of their lands. Only about 1,200 acres remained in their hands, and virtually all of the western part of the township was owned by non-Indians. That same year, the district of West Stockbridge was separated from Stockbridge and incorporated. That year, too, the tribe's greatest English friend, Timothy Woodbridge, died.

TABLE 2. Leading Purchasers of Indian Land in Stockbridge, 1763–1786, Buyers of More Than 200 Acres

Name	No. of Purchases	Total Acreage	Amt. Spent (Mass. Currency)
Elijah Williams (sheriff & trader)	13[a]	1,048[b]	£294.17s.
Samuel Brown Jr. (deputy sheriff & gentleman)	8	1,100	157.15s.
William Goodrich (yeoman & innkeeper)	13	1,011	329.15s.
Elias Willard (innkeeper)	6	547.33	215.7s.
David Van Schaack (Kinderhook trader)	8	447	165.0s.
John Minkler (New York yeoman)	2	440	105.0s.
Benjamin Willard (yeoman)	11[c]	356.33	197.7s.
Timothy Edwards (merchant)	11	325.25	247.17s.
Cornelius Van Schaack (Kinderhook trader)	9	259	173.10s.

SOURCES: Books 2, 4–6, 9–10, 13–14, 16, 19, 21–22, 25, 29, Berkshire County Middle Registry; Indian Deeds, Stockbridge Library; Indian Documents, Scheide Collection; folder 51, box 1, Van Schaack Papers.

[a]Plus 3 leases.
[b]Lease adds 240 acres.
[c]Plus 3 securities.
[d]Security adds 53.66 acres.

The Final Years (1774–1818)

Elijah Williams lived out his life in luxury, but his coarse and avaricious conduct cost him the respect of both his Indian and his English neighbors. In 1764 one Mary Willson, a single woman of Stockbridge, took him to court, declaring that "she was delivered of a Bastard male child begotten by said Elijah who refuses to contribute toward support." He pleaded not guilty and the case dragged on until the court judged him the "reputed father" and ordered him "to pay toward maintenance." In 1773 Williams became embroiled in a legal dispute with Timothy Woodbridge, then a justice of the peace. Exceeding his authority as sheriff, Williams had arrested several inhabitants of Great Barrington and other Berkshire County towns and committed them to jail in Albany without a proper warrant. Called before the General Court in Boston, Williams was cautioned to observe the law strictly in future.[69]

During the Revolution, the Pittsfield Committee of Inspection received certain allegations concerning Williams's loyalty and decided that he was "possess'd of principles contrary to those of his Country." Accused by many in Berkshire County of being a Tory, he was arrested in May 1777, sent to the Northampton jail and later to Boston, where he spent at least a month in confinement. Released to Hatfield in 1779, he appealed to the people of the county to "suspend their resentment, and again receive into favor, their real Friend." He was back at West Stockbridge in 1781 accepting notes from the Indians.[70]

The Stockbridge tribe loyally served the American cause throughout the war. A company of their warriors participated in the siege of Boston, acted as scouts with the army of General Gates before the battles of Saratoga, and marched with the main army in 1780. At the Bronx, New York, in August 1778, British troops killed nearly twenty members of the tribe during a bloody, pitched battle. The old Wappinger Captain Daniel Nimham and his son fell in that engagement.[71]

In 1774 the Oneidas of New York offered a tract of land to various New England tribes that had been reduced to a "Small Pittance of Land." During the Revolution, British Indians forced the Oneidas from their homes, and forty-four of them fled to West Stockbridge. After the war they extended their invitation to the Stockbridge Indians, who decided in 1784 to leave the town that now offered them so little. In 1785 the main body of the tribe moved to New Stockbridge in Madison County, New York, after looking in vain for land in Vermont. Only a handful of widows and elderly remained. The last Indian land in West Stockbridge was sold in 1783, and the last Indian proprietors' meeting was held in Stockbridge on 7 February 1785. At that meeting the proprietors appointed two Indians to execute deeds for all their lands not previously deeded. In 1809 they granted to Dr. Oliver Partridge, for $10 in services rendered the tribe, the Indian burial ground on condition that "the bones of our Ancestors may there lie undisturbed." Partridge could fence the property, plant trees, and improve the land in any way "except tilling or breaking up the Soil." The last piece of Indian land in the town was a narrow strip laid out for a road that was never built. The Indians sold it in 1818.[72]

Conclusion

Almost from its beginnings in 1736, Stockbridge was torn by conflict between the few English allowed to settle there and the Indians whose property the town was intended to be. Supposedly established on an equal footing with the English, the Indians lost their advantage to the ever-expanding numbers and influence of the colonials. At first, the English

TABLE 3. Estimated Population of Stockbridge, 1736–1790

	Indians	Whites
1736	90	10
1740	120	25
1749	218	60
1751	220 (58 proprietors)	70 (14 proprietors)
1763	206 (20 voters)	160 (45 voters)
1776	300	970[a]
1790	5	2,449[a]

SOURCES: *Mass. Archives*, 13:252; 33:287; 322:99; Hopkins, *Historical Memoirs*, pp. 65, 92, 153; Ted J. Brasser, *Riding on the Frontier's Crest: Mahican Indian Culture and Culture Change* (Ottawa: National Museums of Canada, 1974), pp. 35–36; U.S. Federal Census of 1790.

[a]These figures include the present town of West Stockbridge, which separated from the original township and was incorporated in 1774.

simply grabbed land illegally. Led by the intimidating Ephraim Williams, they took what they wanted and the General Court acquiesced. Men who tried to protect the tribe—John Sergeant, Jonathan Edwards, and especially Timothy Woodbridge—were all but powerless against the aggressive Williams and his supporters. Indeed, it may be argued that in assuming they could instill the Indians with English values and in failing fully to appreciate the Indians' cultural integrity, they simply strengthened a system that was inevitably in conflict with a population it must, for its very survival, seek to control.[73]

Elijah Williams used that system to consolidate political control at the town meeting of 1763. Employing such questionable practices as long-term leases, concealed bribes, and land pledged as security or collateral, he operated on the very fringe of the law to enhance his land holdings at the expense of Indians ever more desperate for cash. In this effort he was joined by and conspired with unscrupulous traders in Berkshire County and neighboring New York who were pursuing the same end, as were other merchant-entrepreneurs throughout New England, who dominated the diverse, acquisitive societies the colonists had formed.[74] When, in 1765, the General Court released the Stockbridge Indians from restrictions on using their lands for debt payment, the English were well positioned to increase their properties dramatically. By 1774 the Stockbridge Indians' holdings were reduced to a mere fraction of the original grant, and they could no longer sustain themselves in the town.

There was little Indian political participation in Stockbridge, and virtually every important decision affecting the town as a whole, from taxation to land sales, had to be made by the General Court in Boston, upon petition from one side or the other. There was never unanimity in the town meeting, and the majority did not rule. From 1752, the division between the two societies was formalized in two contesting bodies, the English precinct and the Indian proprietors. The differences between colonists and Indians were irreconcilable, and it is to the credit of the tribe and men like Timothy Woodbridge that open violence did not break out between the two groups.

Ephraim Williams, his son Elijah, and designing European traders cheated the Indians out of their land and drove them from their town. Though the Indians were not passive victims, their efforts to protect their rights proved ineffectual, partly because pressure from the entrepreneurs was unrelenting and partly because their leaders were not always sufficiently skillful. Eventually, the General Court lost interest in the tribe. After the French and Indian War, supporting a small band of friendly Indians in Berkshire County no longer served a military purpose. The failure of the Stockbridge Indian experiment was from that point inevitable; all that was required to complete the process was the rapacity of a few daring and unprincipled men.

Notes

1. William N. Fenton, *American Indian and White Relations to 1830: Needs and Opportunities for Study* (Chapel Hill: University of North Carolina Press, 1957), p. 17; Douglas Edward Leach, *Flintlock and Tomahawk: New England in King Philip's War* (New York: Macmillan, 1958), pp. 4, 16; William Cronon, *Changes in the Land: Indians, Colonists, and the Ecology of New England* (New York: Hill and Wang, 1983), p. 67.

2. Leach, *Flintlock and Tomahawk*, pp. 245–46; Neal Salisbury, "Red Puritans: The 'Praying Indians' of Massachusetts Bay and John Eliot," *William and Mary Quarterly*, 3d ser. 31 (1974): 54.

3. *Northeast*, ed. Bruce G. Trigger, vol. 15 of *Handbook of North American Indians* (Washington: Smithsonian Institution, 1978), pp. 204–7.

4. Harry Andrew Wright, ed., *Indian Deeds of Hampden County* (Springfield, Mass., 1905), pp. 116–18.

5. Samuel Hopkins, *Historical Memoirs Relating to the Housatunnuk Indians* (Boston, 1753; reprinted as a supplement to *Magazine of History* 17 [1911]: 15–16).

6. Hopkins, *Historical Memoirs*, pp. 54, 55.

7. Hopkins, *Historical Memoirs*, pp. 55–56.

8. Order of 25 March 1736, *The Acts and Resolves, Public and Private, of the Province of the Massachusetts Bay*, 21 vols. (Boston: Wright & Potter, 1869–1922), 12:245–46. The order allowed one-sixtieth part of the township each to Sergeant and Wood-

bridge, which is 384 acres; however, in practice, each right was calculated at 400 acres. See deed dated 1747, book R, p. 116, Hampden County Registry of Deeds, Springfield, Mass.; and Ephraim Williams to General Court, October 1750, *Massachusetts Archives*, 32:72. James Axtell and others examining the early history of Stockbridge have labored under the impression that the township contained only six square miles when in fact it was six miles square or thirty-six square miles. See Axtell, "The Rise and Fall of the Stockbridge Indian Schools," *Massachusetts Review* 27 (1986): 368.

9. Hopkins, *Historical Memoirs*, pp. 59–60.

10. Plat of the Intervale Lands, November 1739, Stockbridge Proprietors Book, Berkshire County Middle Registry of Deeds, Pittsfield, Mass., p. 412.

11. All of the Indians' complaints were lodged and addressed many years later, after a committee appointed by the General Court had arrived in Stockbridge to investigate land disputes. See Indian Petition, 11 November 1749, *Mass. Archives*, 31:653–54, and Order of Council, 30 December 1749, *Acts and Resolves*, 14:326–27. I have been able to establish dates by correlating internal evidence in the petition with other, dated documents. A law of 1702 required General Court approval of all sales, leases, or other conveyances obtained from Indians by any person or town (see *Acts and Resolves*, 1:471–72).

12. For the Indians' war service, see Wyllis E. Wright, *Colonel Ephraim Williams: A Documentary Life* (Pittsfield, Mass.: Berkshire County Historical Society, 1970), pp. 23–24.

13. Hopkins, *Historical Memoirs*, pp. 137, 153.

14. Wright, *Ephraim Williams*, p. 3; Electa Jones, *Stockbridge: Past and Present* (Springfield, Mass.: Samuel Bowles & Co., 1854), pp. 135–38, 143, 149.

15. Settling Committee Report, 10 November 1749, *Acts and Resolves*, 14:328.

16. Petition of Stockbridge Inhabitants, 26 October 1748, *Mass. Archives*, 31:604–5; Order of Council, 19 June 1749, *Acts and Resolves*, 14:272.

17. Settling Committee Report, 10 November 1749, *Acts and Resolves*, 14:327–28; Indian Petition, 11 November 1749, *Mass. Archives*, 31:654.

18. Settling Committee Report, 10 November 1749, *Acts and Resolves*, 14:328.

19. Settling Committee Report, 10 November 1749, *Acts and Resolves*, 14:328–30. The Indian Proprietors Book, currently at the Stockbridge Town Hall, covers the period from 1749 to 1780, despite its label of "1749–1790." Many meetings of the proprietors and their land grants are not recorded.

20. Stockbridge Indian Proprietors Book, pp. 4–5; Stockbridge Proprietors Book, p. 400.

21. Indian Petition, 26 September 1750, Richard H. W. Dwight Collection, 37:7 (reel 5, frames 2986–88), Stockbridge Library Historical Room Collections, Stockbridge, Mass.; A Plat of one Hundred & twenty five Acres . . . laying between the Rear of Ephraim Browns & Col Williams's House lots, June 1750, Dwight Collection, 37:4 (reel 5, frame 2973); Response of Ephraim Williams, October 1750, *Mass. Archives*, 32:72–73. The Indians finally agreed to give Williams 155 acres in the western part of town in exchange for his claim to the mill. See Stockbridge Proprietors

Book, p. 406. The original documents in the Dwight Collection are the property of the Norman Rockwell Museum, Stockbridge, Mass., from which I have permission to quote.

22. Order of Council, 11 October 1750, *Acts and Resolves,* 14:454–55.

23. The original of this deed is in the Dwight Collection, 8:9 (reel 2, frames 1231–32). It is recorded in book V, p. 270, Hampden County Registry of Deeds.

24. The originals are in the Dwight Collection, 7:2 (reel 2, frames 1233–34), recorded at Springfield in, respectively, book P, p. 504, and book X, p. 219.

25. Patricia J. Tracy, *Jonathan Edwards, Pastor* (New York: Hill and Wang, 1979), pp. 183–85.

26. Ephraim Williams, Jr., charged that Edwards was "a very great Bigot" and too old at age forty-seven to learn the Indian language. Ephraim Williams, Jr., to Rev. Jonathan Ashley, 2 May 1751, quoted by Arthur L. Perry, in *Origins in Williamstown,* 2d ed. (New York: Charles Scribner's Sons, 1896), pp. 639–40. Edwards himself acknowledged this opposition three years later when he wrote, "I have good reason to think there are some in the town would do their utmost to alienate the Indians from me" (Jonathan Edwards to Rev. Thomas Prince, 10 May 1754, in *A Jonathan Edwards Reader,* ed. John E. Smith et al. [New Haven: Yale University Press, 1995], p. 316).

27. Jonathan Edwards to Andrew Oliver, October 1752, quoted by S. E. Dwight, in *The Life of President Edwards* (New York: G. & C. & H. Carvill, 1830), pp. 504–5.

28. Events surrounding the murder of Waumpaumcorse are revealed in the *Mass. Archives;* see esp. 32:431, 482, 521.

29. Dwight, *President Edwards,* pp. 544–45; for the Indians' war services, see Account Book of General Jeffrey Amherst, 1759–62, Peter Force Collection, Library of Congress, ser. 8D, item 1, reel 31, frames 14, 19, 68; English Petition, April 1757, *Mass Archives,* 117:286; Timothy Woodbridge to Governor and Council, 20 April 1759, *Mass. Archives,* 117:471; *Journals of Major Robert Rogers,* ed. Howard Peckham (London, 1765; reprinted, New York: Corinth Books, 1961), pp. 98, 107, 121; *The Papers of Sir William Johnson,* ed. Milton W. Hamilton, 14 vols. (Albany: University of the State of New York, 1921–65), 13:113; and Patrick Frazier, *The Mohicans of Stockbridge* (Lincoln: University of Nebraska Press, 1992), pp. 111–45.

30. Hopkins, *Historical Memoirs,* pp. 179–80.

31. Indian Petition, 5 December 1759, *Mass. Archives,* 33:115–17; Act of 23 June 1760, *Acts and Resolves,* 4:369.

32. For a discussion of the basis for colonial claims to land ownership, see Cronon, *Changes in the Land.*

33. Indian Memorial, 27 May 1762, and Committee Report, 1 June 1762, *Mass. Archives,* 33:210–12, 214–16. I have found no evidence of government payment for Stockbridge Indian land before 1763, and a study made by Massachusetts in 1870 failed to produce any conclusive documentation. See Charles Allen, Attorney General of Massachusetts, *Report on the Stockbridge Indians, to the Legislature* (Boston: Wright & Potter, 1870), pp. 8–10.

34. *Extracts from the Itineraries and Other Miscellanies of Ezra Stiles, D.D., LL.D.,*

1755–1794, ed. Franklin B. Dexter (New Haven: Yale University Press, 1916), p. 165; Order of Council, 11 June 1762, and Resolves of 17 February 1763, *Acts and Resolves*, 17:244, 354–55.

35. Wright, *Indian Deeds of Hampden County*, pp. 184–87; Berkshire County Middle Registry, book 2, pp. 172–75; Resolve of 17 February 1763, *Acts and Resolves*, 17:354–55; David H. Wood, *Lenox, Massachusetts Shire Town* (Lenox: Published by the Town, 1969), pp. 7–8.

36. Committee Report, 1764, *Mass. Archives*, 117:286–87.

37. Berkshire County Middle Registry, book 1, pp. 40, 306, book 2, pp. 234, 238, and book 6, p. 346; Wright, *Indian Deeds of Hampden County*, pp. 151–52; *Acts and Resolves*, 15:123, 556, 745, and 16:92; *Mass. Archives*, 32:435, 718–19, 765–66, and 33:21, 154–55, 167–68; Stockbridge Proprietors Book, pp. 406, 408.

38. Wright, *Ephraim Williams*, p. 65; James McLachlan, *Princetonians, 1748–1768: A Biographical Dictionary* (Princeton: Princeton University Press, 1976), pp. 87–88; Dwight Collection, 1:18 (reel 1, frame 46), and Berkshire County Probate Records, book 20, p. 3 (microfilm reel 150), Berkshire Athenaeum, Pittsfield, Mass. The Elijah Williams of Stockbridge (1732–1815) is not to be confused with his cousin of the same name in Deerfield (1712–71).

39. Stockbridge Town Book, 1739–1759, pp. 1–9.

40. Stockbridge Town Book, 1739–1759, p. 12; English Petition, 26 October 1748, *Mass. Archives*, 31:604; Order of House of Representatives, 17 June 1749, *Acts and Resolves*, 14:272.

41. English Petition, 3 December 1751, and Order of Council, 14 January 1752, *Mass. Archives*, 116:151–52.

42. Petition of Elijah Williams, May 1761, *Mass. Archives*, 117:690; Order of Council, 17 June 1761, *Mass. Archives*, 117:691; An Act to Enable the English Inhabitants . . . to Call town Meetings & transact Certain Matters Separately from the Indian Inhabitants, June 1761; Order of Council, 16 June 1761, *Mass. Archives*, 177: 733–34.

43. House Resolve, 11 July 1761, *Mass. Archives*, 33:174; *Acts and Resolves*, 17:46.

44. Memorial of Timothy Woodbridge et al., 28 December 1763, *Mass. Archives*, 33:251; Committee Report, 1764, *Mass. Archives*, 33:277; Petition of John Konkapot et al., 31 May 1763, *Mass. Archives*, 33:265–66. Curiously, the record of the town meeting in the Stockbridge Town Book makes no mention of a dispute.

45. Committee Report, 1764, *Mass. Archives*, 33:280–81; Resolve of 3 February 1764, *Mass. Archives*, 33:256–58; *Acts and Resolves*, 17:500.

46. Committee Report, 1764, *Mass. Archives*, 33:282; Indian Petition, 31 May 1763, *Mass. Archives*, 33:267.

47. Province Charter of 1691 and Act for Regulating of Townships, 16 November 1692, *Acts and Resolves*, 1:11–12, 67; Committee Report, 1764, *Mass. Archives*, 33:284–85; *Journals of the House of Representatives of Massachusetts*, 55 vols. to date (Boston: Massachusetts Historical Society, 1919–1990), 40:4, 66, 255, 257.

48. Joseph Woodbridge to Andrew Oliver, 3 February 1764, *Mass. Archives*, 33:260–61; Memorial of Timothy Woodbridge et al., 28 December 1763, *Mass. Ar-*

chives, 33:250; An Act for regulating the choice of Representatives in the Town of Stockbridge for the year 1764, *Mass. Archives,* 33:256–59.

49. Petition of John Konkapot et al., 31 May 1763, *Mass. Archives,* 33:267; Committee Report, 1764, *Mass. Archives,* 33:285.

50. Four of these agreements, dated between 1762 and 1765, are in box 33.7.1 (Indian Documents), Scheide Collection, Princeton University Library, Princeton, N.J. I am indebted to Neal Salisbury of Smith College for informing me of these papers and to the Scheide Library for permission to quote and make use of materials in the Indian Documents.

51. Berkshire County Middle Registry, book 2, pp. 143–44; book 22, p. 195; Dwight Collection, 6:11 (reel 2, frame 1038). A precedent for these long-term leases was established in 1737 when three Stockbridge Indians signed a 990-year lease for land in what is now Pittsfield. See the William Williams Collection, bound typescript, Berkshire Athenaeum, p. 66. I have permission from the Berkshire Athenaeum to quote from documents in the William Williams Collection.

52. *Acts and Resolves,* 1:472, 17:500; Dwight Collection, 7:12 (reel 2, frame 1040).

53. Dwight Collection, 7:10 (reel 2, frame 1036); Berkshire County Middle Registry, book 5, pp. 121–22; William Williams Collection, p. 337.

54. Berkshire County Middle Registry, book 22, pp. 181–82.

55. Hopkins, *Historical Memoirs,* p. 40.

56. John Sergeant agreed to plow for the Indians in 1742, and Timothy Woodbridge paid to have several Indian lands plowed in 1765. See Dwight Collection, 37:7 (reel 5, frame 2986); and Account of Money Paid for the Indians, November 1765, *Mass. Archives,* 33:352. Axtell, *European and Indian,* p. 51, says Indians preferred their own methods to the use of "heavy technology" like the plow.

57. Committee Report, 1764, *Mass. Archives,* 33:288.

58. "Letter from Gideon Hawley," *Collections of the Massachusetts Historical Society* 4 (1795): 51–53; Hopkins, *Historical Memoirs,* p. 153n.

59. Edward A. Collier, *A History of Old Kinderhook* (New York: G. P. Putnam's Sons, 1914), pp. 159, 367–70; David Van Schaack to Elijah Williams, 21 November 1762, and 1 March 1764, Dwight Collection, 1:28 (reel 1, frame 65) and 1:31 (reel 1, frame 72).

60. Writs of Berkshire Inferior Court of Common Pleas, Superior Court of Berkshire County, Pittsfield, Mass., vol. 2 (1765–67), p. 93; vol. 1B (1767–70), p. 459; vol. 2A (1770–72), pp. 145–46, 241; vol. 3A (1773–74), p. 190. Van Schaack lands in Stockbridge are calculated from deeds at the Berkshire County Middle Registry. The sales were made between 1764 and 1768.

61. Committee Report, 1764, *Mass. Archives,* 33:287; Abram Aukomock to Elijah Williams, 12 August 1762, Dwight Collection, 7:9 (reel 2, frame 1035).

62. Indian Petition, January 1765, *Mass. Archives,* 33:311–12; Petition of Timothy Woodbridge, April 1765, *Mass. Archives,* 33:36–57; Resolve of 7 November 1765, *Acts and Resolves,* 18:71.

63. Berkshire County Middle Registry, book 4, p. 528; book 6, p. 20.

64. Berkshire County Middle Registry, book 14, pp. 13–14. In 1752 Rev. Jonathan

Edwards purchased twenty acres near the center of town from Robert Konkapot for £20. The deed stated that "about Twelve Acres of it, being the more improveable part [sold] for the Sum of one pound Six Shillings & Eight pence pʳ Acre and the remainder being Rocky and mountainous for two Shillings & Eight pence pʳ Acre." See Berkshire County Middle Registry, book 2, p. 239.

65. Edna Bailey Garnett, *West Stockbridge, Massachusetts, 1774–1974* (Great Barrington, Mass.: Berkshire Courier, 1976), p. 54; Dwight Collection, 7:13 (reel 2, frame 1043); notes of 30 March and 5 April 1773, Dwight Collection, 7:32–33 (reel 2, frames 1079, 1081); Timothy Woodbridge to Elijah Williams, 8 April 1773, Dwight Collection, 7:33 (reel 2, frame 1081).

66. Dwight Collection, 7:22, 26, 37 (reel 2, frames 1060, 1068, 1088); Indian Petition, January 1776, *Mass. Archives*, 180:156. Writs of Berkshire Inferior Court of Common Pleas, vols. 1–5; Sundry Account allowed by the Proprietors, 1773, Dwight Collection, 7:30 (reel 2, frame 1076).

67. West Stockbridge Poll Tax List, c. 1780, Dwight Collection, 7:37 (reel 1, frame 95); List of Elijah Williams's Property, November 1781, Dwight Collection, 10:34 (reel 3, frames 1595–96); *Stockbridge Western Star*, 17 March 1795; Account of Deeds, Dwight Collection, 2:50 (reel 1, frame 367).

68. Indian Petition, n.d. (c. 1773), *Mass. Archives*, 33:591; Act of 6 March 1773, *Acts and Resolves*, 5:238; House Resolve, 2 June 1773, *Mass. Archives*, 33:592.

69. Dwight Collection, 7:11 (reel 2, frame 1040); *Journals of the House of Representatives*, 49:221–23, 226–28, 242–43.

70. Dwight Collection, 2:35–41 (reel 1, frames 273–84), and 7:12 (reel 2, frames 1041–42); Dwight Collection, 7:37 (reel 2, frame 1088). See Sarah Cabot Sedgwick and Christina Sedgwick Marquand, *Stockbridge, 1739–1939, A Chronicle* (Great Barrington, Mass.: Berkshire Courier, 1939), pp. 141–42.

71. Timothy Pickering Papers, Massachusetts Historical Society, 62:167–68 (microfilm).

72. Berkshire County Middle Registry, book 18, pp. 41–44; Indian Petition, 25 March 1782, Papers of the Continental Congress, Library of Congress, item 41, vol. 4, p. 435 (microfilm M247, reel 50); Berkshire County Middle Registry, book 15, p. 149, book 19, p. 400, book 50, p. 47, and book 60, p. 255; Memorial of Oneida Brotherton Indians, 28 January 1782, *Mass. Archives*, 187:378–79.

73. See Salisbury, "Red Puritans," pp. 27–28; Axtell, *European and Indian*, pp. 84–86.

74. Stephen Innes, *Labor in a New Land: Economy and Society in Seventeenth-Century Springfield* (Princeton: Princeton University Press, 1983), pp. 171–79.

PART FIVE

Indians in the New Nation

12

Indians and the Literature
of the Federalist Era
The Case of James Elliot

EUGENE L. HUDDLESTON

As New England's Indian population declined precipitously in the eighteenth century, fewer and fewer Euroamericans encountered Native Americans in person. Yet the more separate Indians and Euroamericans became in fact, the more integrated they became in some literary genres, as New England writers increasingly addressed Indian themes or, more often, incorporated Indians into the emerging national literature. James Elliot's writings are illustrative.

He was not, of course, the first New England author to write about Indians or Indian-white relations. From the earliest days of English contact with the region, English explorers and their successors in the colonial enterprise frequently wrote about the natives they encountered, and readers back home, for their part, were fascinated by descriptions of people so different from themselves. That interest did not abate once colonization was well underway. The stay-at-homes in Europe wanted to know how newcomers and natives got along (English readers craved evidence that the Indians were docile converts to everything English); colonists wanted reliable information about their new neighbors. Authors of promotional tracts were accordingly prone to produce happy versions of Indian-white relations, present and predicted. When, instead, war between natives and newcomers became the awful reality, New England writers turned almost univocally pessimistic. The tremendously popular narratives of "Indian wars" and of captivities among the Indians are cases in point. The only substantial body of colonial writing that clung to hopeful views of New England's natives (not as they were but as, in the writers' eyes, they ought to be) came from the missionaries and their secular allies.

By the late-eighteenth century, new belletrist genres were in vogue: novels, poetry, and philosophical essays. In these works, New England writers such as James Elliot of Vermont voiced the era's ambivalence about the people who were no longer a military power in the region but who on the national stage posed a major obstacle to America's expansionist aims. And like many of his contemporaries, Elliot drew for his observations not only on the Algonquians of New England, with whom he had some acquaintance, but also on Indians of the West, whom he encountered on his travels. The resulting composite notions inevitably distorted the reality of any single Indian nation.

*U*NLESS ONE has tastes for the likes of Sarah Wentworth Morton's *Ouâbi* or Charles Brockden Brown's novel *Edgar Huntly,* he will not likely look to the Federalist period for literature on the American Indian. The scarcity of good writing, belletristic and otherwise, is unfortunate, for the Federalist years, 1789–1801, are significant in Indian history. Early in the decade President George Washington and Secretary Henry Knox were unwittingly initiating policies that soon would dispossess most of the tribes east of the Mississippi of their "happy hunting grounds," and the period saw the commencement of a series of wars that made coexistence on any but the white man's terms virtually impossible. James Elliot (1775–1839), ordinarily dismissed as a poet and essayist, deserves a modicum of fame for demonstrating some of the difficulties that writers of the young republic faced in giving Indians their due.

Elliot, a "poor but independent" New Englander, had ample credentials for writing about Indians.[1] At eighteen he had enlisted as a sergeant in the Second United States Sub-Legion in order, as he put it, to "claim the glorious meed of martial praise" (p. 23)[2] and to view for himself the "western regions," descriptions of which "enamoured him" (p. 116). Although he had little opportunity for glory, there was much to see. After a march across the Alleghenies, his group joined forces at Washington, Pennsylvania, with other militia, who had already completely squelched the Whisky Rebellion; following a slow trip from Pittsburgh down the Ohio, he landed at Cincinnati and arrived at Greenville on 11 March 1795, just in time to witness the treaty negotiations that were getting underway. Upon his discharge from the army some fifteen months later, he returned to Vermont, and his career in Guilford and Brattleboro as a "respected and useful citizen" included three terms in Congress (1803–9).

Although his literary ventures included participation for a time in the Colon and Spondee literary coterie of his friend Royall Tyler, some contributions to the *Farmer's Museum* and *Port Folio,* and a short term as editor of the *Freeman's Journal* in Philadelphia, his most ambitious belletristic effort was his *Works* (1798), published by subscription two years after his return home from the Northwest and containing 282 pages of poems, essays, and journal sketches, many of which focus on Indians. Largely self-taught, Elliot attained a remarkable degree of literary sophistication for a youth of twenty-three brought up fatherless and in poverty. In the *Works* he quotes maxims from Virgil's *Eclogues,* cites Lord Kames on ethics, and alludes to authors as diverse as Ann Radcliffe and Phillis Wheatley.[3] The imitativeness of the book is, of course, its downfall. Yet the fact that much in it records the author's experiences on the wilderness frontier raises it in interest above other miscellanies in which American literati were showing that they too had read Addison and Steele and could write poems on the seasons as felicitously as James Thomson.

The comparative vigor of Elliot's journal entries, contrasted with his stilted poetry and pretentious essays, demonstrates anew the inability of American writers to assimilate the frontier into a literary tradition that emphasized uniformity in tastes, genteel sensibilities, and strict morality. His handling of Indians illustrates this conflict between experience and tradition. On one hand, as Roy Harvey Pearce discovered, the poetry of Elliot, and of a great many of his contemporaries, melodramatically depicts Indians as savages reveling in "bloody glory in victory over Americans sent to punish them."[4] On the other hand, his biographer in the *Dictionary of American Biography,* undoubtedly referring to Elliot's journal entries, says that he is "just and rational in his observations on the Indians."[5] On neither hand do his delineations have the vividness or penetration to give them lasting literary value, but they do provide a case history of unresolved conflicts—specifically between the freedom he felt as a professed democrat to interpret his own experiences and the authority implicitly imposed by the "Republic of Letters."[6] Elliot, evidently unaware of this conflict, saw himself as rebelling against unjust and despotic authority as much in belles lettres as in his politics, which were "democratic republican" (p. vi). In the *Works* he defends the "natural expression" of his poetry against possible charges of stylistic impropriety by "severe and illiberal" critics. Addressing the "learned reader," he claims that he has never sacrificed "the natural sense of his ideas" to rules, whether of rhyme, rhythm, or syntax (p. 10). Notwithstanding his opinion of himself as a writer not held in bondage to rules, Elliot was never able to resolve the conflicts that sent his writings into deserved obscurity.

The deadening influence of a literary tradition irrelevant to pioneer life is plainly seen in the three poems from the *Works* in which Indians figure prominently. One commemorates the defeat of General Harmar on the upper Maumee; a second, the rout of St. Clair at Ft. Recovery; and the third, the victory of Wayne at Fallen Timbers. These pieces thoroughly stereotype the Indian, and Pearce uses them to substantiate his findings on polarities of theme so often in evidence—the Indian as "nature's nobleman," "subhuman" savage, and sometimes both.[7] He is usually subhuman in Elliot's battle descriptions; as the opening of the Harmar "elegy" attests, cliché is piled on cliché to create the proper sublime effect:

> Melpomene, this painful task is thine!
>   'Tis thine the *Indian* triumphs to rehearse,
> Around the sufferers pity's wreath intwine,
>   And sooth [*sic*] their sorrows with the charms of verse!
>
> To sing of fair *Miami's* fated soil,
>   And strive to paint its people's varied woes,
> While the rich product of their arduous toil
>   Becomes a prey to ruthless savage foes. [P. 63][8]

In describing the battle in which St. Clair's army suffered almost one thousand casualties, the author marshals "ruin" imagery of the type with which eighteenth-century poets inspired terror in their readers:

> The ruffian race in horrid pomp advances,
>   With gloomy aspect and terrific mien;
> The thrilling yell, and the infernal dance,
>   Increase the horrors of the dreadful scene. [P. 72][9]

Even when he tries to give the Indian his due, Elliot cannot transcend convention, and he moves easily from ignoble savage to noble savage:

> With haggard fury and indignant pride,
>   Fiercely vindictive, barbarously brave,
> The savage warrior stems the adverse tide,
>   Or scorns to fly, and seeks a glorious grave. [P. 75][10]

Consistent with his depictions of the Indian's character, Elliot polarizes the ethics of Indian warfare into "outrag'd virtue" vs. the "destructive hand" of the "rude barbarian." The only issue, apparently, is whether "the just and good" will "espouse the cause of suffering innocence" and swear "revenge upon the barb'rous race" (pp. 64–65). For a writer as politically minded as Elliot, there was ample material for at least one indignant poem: by all accounts, General Harmar was incompetent.[11] But Elliot, despite strong republican antipathies to the British and their ways, was evidently trying to compose his battle pieces the way a periwigged Augustan might compose an epic on some forgotten war. Hence, both Harmar and St. Clair appear in properly heroic guises: Harmar is simply "Brave," and St. Clair is the "Brave chief, for valor and misfortune fam'd" (pp. 65, 73).

Because Elliot and most of his contemporaries held almost identical ideas on what constitutes good poetry, one can isolate particular influences and sources rather easily. Among those that color Elliot's attitudes toward Indians most strongly are the Della Cruscan fad and Hugh Blair's highly regarded lectures on the sublime. In 1790 "Philenia" (Sarah Wentworth Morton) launched the Della Cruscan craze in America, and in his General Harmar "elegy" Elliot singled her out as more suited than himself ("th' inferior bard") to describe the "varied woes" he must relate:

Such scenes as these, with more than mortal grief,
    Might a *Philenia's* matchless muse inspire;
And to afford the troubl'd heart relief,
    Demands a *Della Crusca's* peerless lyre. [P. 64][12]

Unlike his friend Royall Tyler, who in 1797 composed a satirical "Address to Della Crusca," Elliot could not view this debased manifestation of sensibility with detachment but readily succumbed to its affectations and eccentricities.[13] As his "Lines to Philenia" reveals, it is her "power to *set the soul on fire*" and to "ease the mind that's tortur'd with Despair" that so captivates him and that leads him to imitate what Tyler mockingly calls her "sublime style," graced by "cerulean tomahawks" and "blue ey'd wampum" (p. 28).

The sublime, a key term in eighteenth-century aesthetics, is also a key to understanding Elliot's highly stereotyped descriptions of Indians and warfare. From Blair's *Lectures on Rhetoric and Belles Lettres*, with which he was familiar, Elliot would have learned that terror can inspire sublimity and that "the Works of Ossian," primitive and terrifying, "abound with examples of the Sublime."[14] If Elliot's more passionate descriptions aim at the "sublimity" of Macpherson's *The Poems of Ossian*, it is not surprising; for Blair quotes from *Fingal* a passage of melodramatic horrifics ("Helmets are cleft on high; blood bursts . . .") with the comment that "never were images of more awful Sublimity employed to heighten the terror of battle," and Elliot himself classed Ossian as one of the four greatest poets of all time (p. 245).[15]

With attitudes toward poetic style and subject matter formed so bookishly, it is no wonder that Elliot—even after firsthand observations of Indians and their battlegrounds—treats them as stage properties of melodrama. In sizing up himself at the end of the *Works*, Elliot claimed that he possessed "a soul of exquisite sensibility" (p. 239), and sensibility—that is, keen sensitiveness to moral and aesthetic beauty—proves his undoing as an artist. For all his intense interest in politics, he never wrote a satire, and for all his exposure as a soldier to varied men and manners, he never wrote a line that could offend the most demure among his lady readers. By separating everyday life from his literary life, he confused sentimentality with deep feeling and emotional titillation with sublimity. The consistent irrelevancy of his poetry to his emotional and intellectual life suggests the "two mentalities" that George Santayana saw underlying the Genteel Tradition in American life.[16]

Wherever Elliot treats Indians in poetry, one can be sure of patently secondhand views; wherever he treats them in prose, one can assume attitudes that, while derived from reading, are strongly reinforced by personal experience. His accounts fall into two categories: informal sketches from his journal and a formal essay on "Aboriginal Inhabitants." In general, the journal entries are favorable. Whether noting the "alacrity and harmony" of the treaty negotiations in progress or the "honesty and sobriety" of a particular Indian chief, Elliot sees peace ahead in Indian relations (pp. 142, 158). Where he cannot be favorable, he scrupulously avoids making judgments. For example, he adds no comment in reporting that on 6 March 1795 "the Indians killed a man in the village of Northbend, and on the following evening stole 8 horses from that place" (p. 138). The same dispassion marks a later observation that "2 Indians came into camp . . . , bringing with them 6 of our people, 2 of them young women, whom they had taken prisoners in . . . the war" (p. 139). Another incident, which might have provoked condescension or cutting humor, was reported neutrally. On 24 June 1795, when the powder magazine at Fort Greenville exploded, hundreds of Indians were in camp for the treaty: "The Indians, on their part, were not less alarmed than we were," wrote Elliot. "They left the camp in confusion. Many of them hid themselves in the woods, and were not easily persuaded to return" (p. 140).

Elliot refrains from condemning even the most serious of Indian depredations. He records that on 9 September "about 70 Indians and Squaws, of the Shawanese nation, came into camp" with four prisoners captured in Virginia several months before. One of the four, a woman, had seen her house "plundered and destroyed" and her two daughters killed during the attack. "Her husband," Elliot adds, "was not taken, being absent at work." Making no comment whatsoever on the savagism of the Indians, he concludes that their surrender "may be considered as a fresh proof of the sincerity of the Shawanese" and that "there is not the least doubt but that the present peace will be permanent" (p. 146). Likewise, referring to murders "lately . . . committed by the Señaca Indians, on the head waters of the Allegany [sic]," he blames the hostilities that he thinks are likely to result on "the imprudent and barbarous conduct of some frontier citizens," who in firing on a canoe, "killed or wounded" an Indian and his Squaw. "No wonder," says Elliot, "that the Senecas retaliate" (p. 142).

Elliot's formal essay on aborigines attempts an "epitome of the Indian character" based on his "own observations" and the "remarks" of contemporary historians, travelers, and statesmen, such as Jedidiah Morse, John Filson, and Thomas Jefferson. The virtues, catalogued hardly without comment, are wholly those of the Noble Savage: a "natural genius," which makes him equal, if not "generally superior," to more civilized peoples; a "high sense of religion," both as professed and practiced; a love of liberty, with distinctions in rank based on "age, and its general concomitants, experience and wisdom"; probity of character; faithfulness to engagements, more so than white men; an "exalted degree of benevolence and beneficence"; eloquence in speech; and the "best marksmen in the world" (pp. 175–77). Although he seldom elucidates these virtues, Elliot refers once to his own experiences in an anecdote illustrating the native religious sense of Indians: "An Indian, at Greenville, observing some soldiers earnestly engaged in conversation, and not being able to understand them, found means to enquire the subject, and on being informed that their converse had reference to the Supreme Being, he expressed the utmost degree of reverence, and appeared to be at once engaged in the most profound contemplation" (pp. 176–77).[17]

Whatever vices Indians possess are usually balanced by compensating virtues. Although the youth of both sexes exhibit "unrestrained indulgence" of their sexual appetites, "their chastity after marriage is remarkable," except when they are "in a state of intoxication." And even though they are "violently addicted" to drunkenness, which turns them into brutes, they abstain from violence and even the "least indecency" in treating "white women whom the fortune of war places in their possession." While their cruel manner of warfare "cannot be justified," balancing "the account in their favor" are the "influence of education and habit," and "their tenderness and hospitality to those whom they consider as their friends." Also, the Indians' government, "though in some instances nominally regal, is really republican, and they are extremely tenacious of liberty" (pp. 178, 177).

Clearly Elliot's opinions of the American Indian owe more to books than to direct experience, and his tendency to discover the best in the "aboriginal inhabitants" accords with his "soul of exquisite sensibility"; indeed, his benevolence, moralism, and sentimentality persist throughout the *Works*, and if they hindered objective portrayals of Indians, they at least made him responsive to social change. Notwithstanding his lack of wit and even a sense of humor, his capacity for deep and serious feeling made him espouse causes linked with the burgeoning liberalism of the American Enlightenment. Freedom from tyranny and equality for all form the basis of his views on slavery, female education, war, and politics. Unreservedly condemning Negro slavery, which exerts its "pernicious influence" even in the Ohio country, he "ardently" anticipates its eventual "extirpation" nationwide (p. 182). To support his pleas for female education, he cites William Godwin's belief that knowledge, "the only remedy for the evils which afflict mankind" (p. 220), should be generally diffused. And he lists several female authors, English and American, whose writings, by their display of "piety, taste, sensibility, fancy, feeling, and moral sentiment," answer those who ridicule "the pretensions of the fair sex to any eminent degree of genius" (p. 222). Two essays in the *Works* argue against militarism. In "On Standing Armies and their Political Consequences" he writes that military forces in despotic governments serve "the double purpose of extending foreign conquests and enslaving the people at home" (p. 190); in "On the Moral Consequences of Standing Armies," he asserts that "to suppose a man whose occupation is war . . . governed by principles of justice . . . is almost paradoxical" (p. 201). And he concludes his case against military establishments with an appropriate quotation from William Cowper's *The Task:*

> The field of glory, as the world
> Misdeems it, dazzled by its bright array,
> With all the [its] majesty of thund'ring pomp,
> Enchanting music, and immortal wreaths,
> Is but a school where thoughtlessness is taught
> On principle, where foppery atones
> For folly, gallantry for every vice. [P. 207][18]

Throughout the *Works* Elliot is consistently anti-British and anti-Federalist. Although the Treaty of Greenville, which he witnessed, portends the "happiest consequences . . . to posterity," the Jay Treaty, ratified the same year, is "calamitous in the highest degree" (pp. 145, 150). And he believes that the mercantile interests "in the principal commercial towns of the Union" applied "improper influence" on the House to assure its reluctant support of the treaty (pp. 156–57). In this and similar affairs the position of James Madison, then a Congressman from Virginia, is "candid, moderate, dispassionate, yet determined," and even his enemies "must allow him the applause which is due to genius, eloquence, and erudition" (p. 212). Hamilton and Jay, on the other hand, are apostates from the cause of liberty, and Elliot attributes their fall not to "depravity of heart" or "British bribery" but to a "love of power and a natural inclination to aristocracy" among those "whose superior attainments induce them to exaggerate their own merits, and consequently to look down upon the more ignorant and less favored part of mankind with unmerited contempt" (p. 151). Consistent with his republican principles, he upbraids Joseph Dennie, a rabid Federalist, for holding beliefs "rigidly aristocratical and probably monarchical" (p. 230). And he maintains that if the Federalists continue unchecked, the rapid drift of the country toward monarchy will force "Liberty, hunted and exiled from the Eastern States," to seek "lasting asylum beyond the Allegany [*sic*]."[19]

Elliot's liberalism, conditioned as it is by an acute sensibility, does not extend to religion and ethics. Although professing no denomination, he calls himself a Christian and labels his early attachment to the Bible, "that sublime book," as "the most fortunate occurrence" of his life (p. 113). His moral imperatives ring with the assurance of a true believer: "Prayer in private families ought to be revived"; and "public worship ought to be constantly attended" (pp. 244, 245). An uncompromising morality leads him to commend Thomas Paine as a politician but to censure him for his "impious witticisms" (pp. 190, 236). And the future glory that he envisions for the West at the conclusion of his poem commemorating General Wayne's victory at Fallen Timbers is in part dependent on keeping the presumably virgin land free of moral pollution: "And banish from hence, Great Source of Good, / The lewd licentious manners of the stage" (p. 77).

The "soul of exquisite sensibility" that encouraged Elliot to support benevolent and humanitarian causes also refined his perceptions of natural beauty to the point where he became aware of the power of scenery to elevate the soul. This heightened awareness shows most strongly in his prose, for hackneyed conventions associated with the cult of rural simplicity thoroughly deaden his poetry.[20] His prose, however, is specific enough to warrant attention, even if it too apes English fashions, such as Addison's Pleasures of the Imagination—the delights in greatness, novelty, and beauty that derive from viewing landscapes with a practiced eye.[21] A neoclassic literary heritage, coupled with the Edenic purity of the American scene, conditioned Elliot to think of American landscapes in association with classical Arcadia. He called the Western country "the Garden of North America" (p. 170), and if in the right mood he could enjoy the solitary wilderness surrounding Greenville:

This afternoon I took a walk, accompanied by two of my fellow soldiers, into the woods west of the cantonment. . . . If a person could be removed in his sleep from the populous shores of the Atlantic to the western wilderness, at this blooming season, he would, on waking, almost fancy himself in the midst of a terrestrial paradise. Murmuring rills, and gentle cascades; an exuberant variety of herbs, plants, and flowers, all . . . conspire to render the scene delightfully enchanting. In these sweet retreats and *philosophic* shades, a contemplative and poetic genius might almost realize another golden age. [P. 139][22]

Elliot's discernment of Edenic qualities in the American wilderness accords with his progressivism and recommends him as a man of taste, but it hardly qualifies him as a significant interpreter of nature. Although he admired—and quoted from—the poetry of Thomas Odiorne, called an American predecessor of Wordsworth, he had little in common with the author of the *Progress of Refinement,* for he lacked Odiorne's relatively mature insights into nature as a source of knowledge.[23] Nature neither elicited from him Wordsworthian epiphanies nor supplied him with images that he could relate to his own consciousness. While confined to the field hospital at Ft. Hamilton (Ohio) with a severe fever and "paroxysms of the ague," he composed an "elegy" on his illness featuring a tribute to rural contentment complete with epithets such as "fruitful fields," "sweet retreat," and "unletter'd swain" (pp. 67–69).[24] He responds to his immediate environment only with a wish to escape it—"T' indulge a retrospect of happier days." In ill health at a frontier outpost and lacking in companions to share his particular tastes, he undoubtedly had complex states of consciousness wanting expression; yet his imagination, furnished with no images from present experience to give them substance, finds release only in sentimental self-pity:

In these lone walls, where gloomy silence reigns,
    While whistling winds through every opening creep,
Worn with disease, and rack'd by tort'ring pains,
    In vain I court the soothing smiles of sleep.

In vain I strive to dissipate my fears,
    And stop the swelling cataract of woe;
Relentless fate, regardless of my tears,
    Bids the o'erwhelming tide of misery flow!

A discrepancy between his formal literary expression and the intellectual and emotional experience that lay back of it underlies Elliot's failures both with nature and with Indians. In the poetry—his formal literary attempts, that is—form and content are so derivative and stereotyped as to suggest artificiality and insincerity. The journal entries, however, belie such an interpretation, for he keenly appreciated nature and desired fairness in Indian relations. Most likely, in his formal expression, he thought that he was venting his own distinct self, as a good democrat should, and not aping British ways, which he detested. If he esteemed British writers, it was for their eminence in the Republic of Letters, which for Elliot at least commanded loyalties transcending ordinary political boundaries.

Because his formal compositions are so derivative and his journal entries largely limited to observations on his travels, it is difficult to learn much about the actual intellectual and emotional experiences underlying his formal writings. For example, the illness that inspired his "elegy" at Ft. Hamilton and the comment in his journal eleven months later that "during the whole of the last year" contentment had eluded him hints at a significant psychological disturbance but one about which he had little to say (p. 149). Elliot's politics further illustrate the difficulty of getting to know the real man. Because of his seemingly consistent liberalism, one might readily categorize him as a Jeffersonian democrat. But this discounts his religious orthodoxy, his strict morality, and most interestingly his defense of law and order. On his way to Pittsburgh in 1794 to participate in suppressing the Whisky Rebellion, he observed: "All ranks and conditions of men were united in one common bond of citizen soldiers and appeared to be irresistibly determined to vindicate and maintain the violated majesty of the laws" (p. 126). Once encamped in the "very centre of the territory of sedition," he sounds like a martinet: "The country trembled around us, and the late insurgent inhabitants were as humble and submissive as they had been insolent and daring before the army appeared" (p. 129).

If attitudes of the "real" James Elliot are so difficult to ascertain, then the question of the effect of the frontier on his *Works* becomes too complex to answer without an investigation of his life and intellectual milieu, which is beyond the scope of this essay.[25] One can speculate, however, that his attitudes toward Indians were formed before he journeyed West and that experience confirmed his predispositions. Undoubtedly the poverty and insecurity of his childhood greatly affected the shaping of his opinions. Generally he had strong emotional reactions against entrenched authority; hence his antipathies to standing armies, the British, Federalists, and aristocrats in general, and his sympathies for underdogs like women, slaves, and Indians. His attitudes toward Indians were formed mostly in his viscera, and his preconceptions could never stand up to flesh-and-blood encounters. Even in his journal extracts, he seldom wrote of Indians except as abstractions; no individual profiles or character sketches enliven his genteel and dully picturesque accounts.

Elliot's progressivism, his pro-Western bias, and his heightened sensibility should have freed him of the need for dependence on tradition and have enabled him to write forthrightly of the world as he saw it. Yet except for the extracts of his journal entries, which are all too scant and which deal often in trivia, his *Works* abound with moribund conventions and ideas. In his topical essays and sketches on politics, however, he could rise above his usually vague, sentimental, and derivative amateurism and cogently marshal his ideas. He perhaps owed this ability to the absence of inhibitions imposed by his Puritanical and quite moralistic religious heritage, which had little bearing on his writings about current affairs, but which had a marked influence wherever his aim was to practice "conscious rectitude of heart" (p. 69). Whether or not his religious heritage was responsible, Elliot clearly displayed side by side a female intellect—one introverted, sensitive, and easily molded by authority—and a male will—one assertive, committed to social action, and manifesting self-confidence. This duality, which is at the heart of the conflict between tradition and experience displayed in his writings, suggests, of course, that Elliot's plight was an early manifestation of that infamous malady of American intellectual life—the Genteel Tradition.

Elliot himself failed to perceive the conflict; with his sentimental temperament and his adherence to literary formalities he found it impossible to confront the realities of the West. For the Republic of Letters he had to create Indians who were subhuman, terrifying savages, or if not bowing to this stereotype, as he did in his poetry, and attempting more direct appraisals, as he did in his prose, his "exquisite sensibility" forced creation of another stereotype—the noble and virtuous child of nature, whom he tried to accommodate in a Utopian landscape consistent with his progressivist mentality and pro-Western bias. Like many of his contemporaries, he thought that the Indian, primeval inhabitant of the "Garden of North America," could be perfected as easily as the land.[26] The reality was that the aborigines inhabiting the Garden were no more noble than the land was Edenic, but Elliot could not face this fact because it would have destroyed his progressivist dream of the West. Unlike his distant cousin T. S. Eliot, he could not overcome the force of convention by pioneering new forms and hence could not confront the Indian freed of the accretions of sentiment and authority that his intellectual milieu so plentifully supplied. Instead, he finally abandoned belles lettres for politics, where his progressivism found a viable outlet.

Author's Postscript

To test how my article holds up twenty-five years later, I (1) reexamined the text of Elliot's *Works* to see if my published analysis accurately represented what Elliot wrote, (2) reviewed trends in literary theory and historiography since 1970 to determine their effect on the analysis, and (3) compiled a bibliography of significant scholarship since 1970 to decide if the information in the sources was supplemental or required textual revision or commentary.

Scrutinizing Elliot's *Poetic and Miscellaneous Works,* I found nothing new or startling. However, I believe Elliot's poetry has more substance than my analysis originally indicated. In particular, his poems on Indian warfare show that Elliot had a keen grasp of his subject. His two elegies bemoan the fates of fallen or otherwise ill-starred Americans, among the most prominent Major General Richard Butler, Major John P. Wyllys, and Major John F. Hamtramck. In light of Elliot's demonstrated involvement in his frontier and military environment, I decided it was not indifference to realities that accounts for his failure to write (in my original words) an "indignant" poem on General Harmar's defeat in 1790 or to be critical of St. Clair's debacle a year later. Rather, his "failure" was in conforming so well to the conventions of the poetical genre he was attempting. Working within a well-established tradition required commemorating the dead, not analyzing the causes of deaths.

And eighteenth-century elegies also demanded (as my article notes) "ruin" imagery—imagery that "savages" (Elliot's term) lurking in darkened woods well supplied. My article cited the St. Clair elegy as illustrating such "ruin" imagery; but I could probably have more aptly cited the Harmar elegy (*Works,* p. 65) for its skillful mixing of theatricality with topographical exactitude:

On wild St. Joseph's distant, dreary shore,
    Near where majestic Wabash rolls his flood;
Where prowling savages the groves explore,
    Or scour the plain, to glut themselves with blood.

In summary, my original analysis of Elliot's poetic treatment of the Indian is still valid. Re-reading his poems after twenty-five years makes me realize, however, that the youthful Elliot was more in control of his frontier material than I gave him credit for. He was adroitly manipulating the Indian and the dead (or victorious) Americans in order to create moving poems within conventions that the audience he was addressing expected.

A new way of looking at old material—whether it amounts to a meaningful trend or temporary fad—is in the purview of historiographers and literary critics. A recent trend in literary textual analysis, deconstruction, though applicable to Elliot's poems, essays, and journal in the *Works,* seems, with its structural bias, of unlikely relevance in analyzing Elliot's attitudes toward frontier Indians in the 1790s. The combined cultural, historical, and literary analysis followed in the original article still holds as the best approach to the *Works*. More germane is a trend in historiography-ethnicity, an awareness that all ethnic groups in America have contributed to the country's history and literature and that therefore no one group should dominate the study of its history and literature. When I wrote the original article, "ethnicity" was not in most dictionaries. But as I write this postscript, "ethnicity" has so permeated American culture at all levels that the Disney film "Pocahontas" (1995) could celebrate diversity and reject domination by white Americans with a directness that most Americans heartily assented to.

As for specific effects on the article of the "new scholarship of ethnicity" (Frank Shuffelton in *A Mixed Race: Ethnicity in Early America,* ed. Shuffelton [New York: Oxford University Press, 1993]), none has much impact because the article is not focused on ethnic domination or diversity or authorship by native Americans. One effect might be to encourage in the article the substitution of "Native American" for "Indian." But to many this is more a stylistic than a substantive decision. The fact that this article is being reprinted effectively demonstrates how ethnicity has influenced the direction of scholarly pursuits. Also, the new scholarship adds richness to this article by letting the reader see not only Elliot's side of the conflict but the Indians' as well. Typical is the review of white Americans' twenty years of warfare against the Shawnee from 1775 to the Treaty of Greenville in Colin G. Calloway's "'We Have Always Been the Frontier': The American Revolution in Shawnee Country," *American Indian Quarterly* 16 (Winter 1992): 39–52.

Conducted in the summer of 1995, my survey of publications (since 1970) on white-Indian relations in the early national period has uncovered no data requiring outright revision of my article. In existing footnotes, I have tried to acknowledge work supplementing or reinforcing my coverage of particular points. One book, though, requires commentary: Bernard W. Sheehan's *Seeds of Extinction: Jeffersonian Philanthropy and the American Indian* (Chapel Hill: University of North Carolina Press for the Institute of Early American History and Culture, 1973). Its categories of analysis include many of the same topics that I culled from Elliot's *Works,* including the concept of the Noble Savage, savagery, sexuality, intoxication, and eloquence. Possibly Sheehan derived these topics, in part, from reading Elliot's *Works.* But even though Sheehan lists the *Works* in his bibliography, he neither cites Elliot in his text nor acknowledges the *Works* in a footnote. Nor does he state whether his bibliography (which follows an unhelpful "Notes on Sources") is comprehensive or covers only works actually drawn from.

Not all our topics are perfectly correlated; one with a complex correlation is Sheehan's major emphasis on Jeffersonian philanthropy as a source of eventual mischief in Indian relations, a point which at first seems to have no linkage with Elliot's mind set. Pinning ideological labels like philanthropy on Elliot is difficult because in the *Works* he feels more than he thinks. However, his confessed "soul of exquisite sensibility" and his desire to see social justice prevail do have a connection, albeit loose, with Jeffersonian philanthropy. The problem is Elliot's political orientation, and reading Sheehan offers no help. Elliot's prose allusions to and poems on domestic and European political events, contemporary and historical, find no correspondence in Sheehan's discussion of Jeffersonian philanthropy. Sheehan's failure to discuss political currents, polarities, and precedents seems a weakness in the book, for politics strongly influenced Elliot's views. Especially puzzling is that Sheehan's coverage of religious and secular sources of philanthropy neglects to take into account Elliot's strongly orthodox Christian professions in the *Works.*

These problems aside, I decided that Elliot's writings conformed so well with Sheehan's analysis that I started looking to him for categories of white-Indian relations that I might have overlooked in the *Works.* Soon I knew what my chief omission had been. I had not dealt with what Elliot thought about future Indian-white relations, unlike Sheehan, who firmly grapples with the disintegration of Indian culture, brought on by attempts at acculturation, and with the failure of removal as a solution. The omission was easy enough, for Elliot makes no substantive predictions on the Indians' future, even though (as originally cited) he sees the "happiest consequences . . . to posterity" of the Treaty of Greenville and "peace ahead in Indian relations" (my words). One can infer that he intended Indians to be treated justly by his stands on human rights in the *Works;* namely, against the evils of slavery, the low status of women, and the tyranny of the military.

Close examination of the *Works* reveals only fuzziness on what constitutes just treatment. Elliot's most important pronouncement (*Works,* p. 176) on future Indian-white relations follows his praise of the Indians' "natural genius": "Education only is wanting to produce, among the aborigines of America, painters, poets, mathematicians, philosophers, etc., to rival those of antiquity." One gathers from this statement that book learning will eventually civilize the Indian.

However, from a statement elsewhere, one infers that education will be hard for Indians to acquire because of their alleged laziness. In passing through Marietta, Ohio, enroute to Fort Greenville, Elliot recorded in his journal the presence of an "artificial mound" and ruins of an "ancient fortification" (*Works,* p. 173). He added: "Many serious attempts have been made to account for the origin of these stupendous ruins. . . . It is sufficient to know . . . that the Indians, in their present state of society, and with that aversion to labor which at present seems natural to them, could never have been the authors of works of such magnitude." Apparently Elliot failed to see that the conflict in his assessment of Indian capabilities would increasingly complicate the question of fairness to the Indian.

The pressure of population growth west of the Appalachians is another issue affecting fairness to Indians that Elliot could not comprehend. He failed to see problems arising from his acknowledgment that Indians want hunting grounds and his prediction that the West will fill with whites. On the one hand, his journal recorded, "The treaty goes on with alacrity and harmony. . . . It is said the Indians have insisted on the privilege of hunting on all the lands which they are to cede to the United States, which has been granted them" (*Works*, p. 142). On the other hand, just after the treaty signing, he noted with approval that the "Great Miami Valley is filling with settlers" (p. 153). Further in his journal he confidently estimated that "the next census, which is to be taken in 1800, will return one million of American citizens, west of Apalachian [*sic*] Mountains" (p. 180). Although he said nothing about assimilating the Indians or managing their presence otherwise, he concluded his journal with a paean on the future glory of America. For Elliot (p. 181) there will be "a degree of glory to those western regions which has never yet been equalled by any nation upon earth." This is, of course, a prose version of the poetic paean he had written for the conclusion of his poem celebrating Wayne's victory at Fallen Timbers. Interestingly, the settlers in prose will be "an agricultural people" in contrast to those in poetry, who will inhabit "the lofty spire, the sumptuous dome."

If Indians are to share in this future glory, Elliot does not say. About all that one can safely assume is that Elliot would be against coercing Indians into accepting what whites thought best for them, for he was strongly against a "standing military force" (*Works*, p. 199) as destructive of freedom, and he believed that (p. 182) "the government of our country is verging . . . towards monarchy," so that "it is not improbable that Liberty, hunted and exiled from the Eastern States, may seek and obtain a lasting asylum beyond the Allegany [*sic*]."

It is difficult to understand why Elliot is so assertive about the loss of freedoms that Americans face from political developments in the "Eastern States" and yet is so complacent about the future of the Indians of the Old Northwest, who had just been tyrannized into surrendering to an invader. I suggested in the conclusion of my article that Elliot could not confront the realities of the West because "his 'exquisite sensibility' forced creation of . . . the noble and virtuous child of nature, whom he tried to accommodate in a Utopian landscape consistent with his progressivist mentality and pro-Western bias." His "Gentility" perhaps explains his complacency about the Indians' future. Certainly, he was well meaning toward Indians but was overly optimistic about the possibilities of the West as a "New Eden" which would support liberty, absorb everyone who moved there, and assimilate both natives and invaders. But he was not alone. Few were around then who could (or had the will to) foresee the trail of tears and the bloodshed ahead in Indian relations.

Notes

1. Elliot describes himself as "poor but independent, unfortunate but honest" in his *Poetical and Miscellaneous Works* (Greenfield, Mass., 1798), p. 239. Hereafter the *Works* will be cited parenthetically in the text.

2. "Lines, Written at the Age of Eighteen, on the Author's Enlisting Himself as a Soldier in the Army of the United States, August, 1793."

3. In a "Rural Wanderer" essay in the *Port Folio* for 14 February 1801, p. 50, Elliot says, with undoubted justification, that he has read "the British poets, from Chaucer and Sackville, to Cowper and Campbell" and that his "stock of historical and classical information is by no means contemptible." While in Congress he diligently pursued intellectual interests. In a speech in the House in 1803 in favor of the Louisiana Treaty, he quoted Emerich de Vattel, Hugo Grotius, Samuel Pufendorf, "and other eminent writers on the law of nature and nations." See *Abridgment of the Debates of Congress, from 1789 to 1856*, 16 vols. (1857), 3:66.

4. Roy Harvey Pearce, *The Savages of America: A Study of the Indian and the Idea of Civilization* (1953; reprinted, Baltimore: Johns Hopkins University Press, 1965), p. 179.

5. *Dictionary of American Biography*, s. v. "Elliot, James." See also Paul Lehmberg's sketch of Elliot in *American Writers Before 1800: A Biographical and Critical Dictionary*, ed. J. A. Levernier and D. R. Wilmes, 3 vols. (Westport, Conn.: Greenwood Press, 1983).

6. Faithful Federalists, supporting the "concept of a stable, authoritarian republic," saw an analogy "between such a conception of political order and the nature of literary order." See Lewis P. Simpson, "Federalism and the Crisis of Literary Order," *American Literature* 23 (1960): 253–66. Elliot himself uses the phrase in explaining the low estate of literature in Vermont: "The State in which the author lives has not attained a high rank in the republic of letters" (*Works*, p. 223).

7. Pearce, *Savages of America*, p. 179. In the footnote citing these poems, Pearce incorrectly identifies Elliot as "James Lewis."

8. "Elegy, Commemorative of the Expedition of Brigadier General Harmar, into the Indian Country Northwest of the Ohio, in the Autumn of 1790; and the Defeat of a Detachment from his Army, Commanded by Major Wyllys, of the 1st U.S.

Regiment." Similar poetic conventions and Indian stereotypes are in Matilda [pseud.], "Elegy Supposed to be Written on the Banks of Detroit River," *New York Magazine,* new ser. 2 (1797): 217–18.

9. "Elegy, Descriptive of the Defeat of the American Army, under General St. Clair, by the Indians, on the 4th of November, 1791. Written near the Fatal Spot."

10. "Lines, Commemorative of the Victory Obtained by General Wayne, and his Gallant Army, over the Whole Hostile Force of the United *Indian* Nations . . . on the 20th of August, 1794. . . ."

11. Washington wrote Knox privately on 19 November 1790: "I . . . will declare to you without reserve, that my forebodings with respect to the Expedition against the Wabash Indians are of disappointment; and a disgraceful termination under the conduct of B. Genl. Harmar." See *The Writings of George Washington from the Original Manuscript Sources, 1745–1799,* ed. John C. Fitzpatrick, 39 vols. (Washington, D.C.: U.S. Government Printing Office, 1931–44), 31:156. For incisive, modern perspectives on Harmar's and St. Clair's defeats, see back-to-back articles in *The Northwest Ohio Quarterly* 65 (Spring 1993). Both Leroy V. Eid's "'The Slaughter Was Reciprocal': Josiah Harmar's Two Defeats, 1790" (pp. 51–67) and William O. Odom's "Destined for Defeat: An Analysis of the St. Clair Expedition of 1791" (pp. 68–73) emphasize the brilliant battlefield leadership of Little Turtle, the Miami leader.

12. Beginning in the *London World* in 1787, Robert Merry ("Della Crusca") and Mrs. Hannah Cowley ("Anna Matilda") engaged in a poetic epistolary flirtation which proved enormously popular and which inspired numerous American imitations throughout the 1790s.

13. For the text of this satire, see *The Verse of Royall Tyler,* ed. Marius B. Péladeau (Charlottesville: University Press of Virginia, 1968), pp. 59–61.

14. Hugh Blair, *Lectures on Rhetoric and Belles Lettres,* ed. Harold F. Harding, 2 vols. (Carbondale, Ill.: Southern Illinois University Press, 1965), 1:65.

15. Blair, *Lectures,* 1:65–66. The other three were Homer, Virgil, and Milton. See *Works,* p. 245.

16. Santayana metaphorically described the split in consciousness as a female Intellect vs. a male Will or a Sunday conscience vs. a weekday conscience. See *The Genteel Tradition: Nine Essays by George Santayana,* ed. Douglas L. Wilson (Cambridge: Harvard University Press, 1967), pp. 9, 40, 82.

17. *Works,* pp. 176–77. Elliot also quotes from Freneau's "The Indian Burying Ground" to illustrate that "they believe in the immortality of the soul" and that they "carry their belief . . . to a ridiculous though laudable absurdity."

18. Apparently Elliot had modified his opinions of the military by the time he wrote these essays. In his enlistment poem, dated 1793 (cited in n. 2), he holds up military life as a means of winning fame and fulfilling his duty to his country. Jingoism mixed with sentimentality makes it one of his worst efforts. On his discharge he felt poetically released "from military chains" ("Lines, Written at the City of Marietta . . . July, 1796," *Works,* p. 79).

19. Even though he customarily regarded "Federalist" as an "invidious appellation," he thought that Adams acted with "prudence and dignity" during the "crisis"

with France over the XYZ Affair (*Works*, p. 270). *The Biographical Directory of the American Congress, 1774–1961* (p. 855) states that Elliot was elected to the House as a Federalist, a fact that his biographer in the *DAB* sees as "the one mystery of his life" because "he was a Democrat in his principles." Other chroniclers disagree on his official party affiliation. Mary R. Cabot in *Annals of Brattleboro, 1681–1895*, 2 vols. (Brattleboro, 1921), 1:215, confirms the assertion in *The Biographical Directory*. But in an essay on Windham County politics in Cabot's *Annals* (2:907), Kittredge Haskins, prominent Windham County attorney, says that by 1803 Elliot had "by the force of his intellect . . . become a Democratic leader in the southeastern part of the State." And a basic history by Henry Burnham (*Brattleboro, Windham County, Vermont* [Brattleboro, 1880], p. 79) records: "In politics, Mr. Elliot was a Jeffersonian democrat and, to some extent, a party man: but he estimated character and ability far above party lines." Elliot himself wrote in the preface (p. vi) to the *Works:* "In politics, the author will not hesitate a moment to declare himself a democratic republican." The confusion is compounded by Elliot's remark in a speech in the House in 1804 (*Abridgment of the Debates of Congress from 1789 to 1856*, 3:108) that he had passed a "political ordeal . . . under circumstances of gloom and depression which have fallen to the lot of but few young men of this country."

20. A typical statement of the rural retirement theme is in "Invocation to Memory. Written at Greenville . . . November, 1795" (*Works*, pp. 32–34): "Lead me to the retreats of early youth, / The seats of pleasure, and the bowers of ease / Where, cloth'd with native innocence and truth . . . / I listen'd to the sound of the soft gale."

21. See *Spectator*, no. 412, for the formulation of these concepts so influential in eighteenth-century aesthetics.

22. *Works*, p. 139, journal entry dated June 1795. Elliot's mood shifts toward frontier nature are covered in my "James Elliot and 'The Garden of North America': A New Englander's Impression of the Old Northwest," *Northwest Ohio Quarterly* 42 (1970): 64–73.

23. Elliot places Odiorne in a catalogue of prominent American poets (*Works*, p. 105) capable of competing with "Britannia's Genius." For Odiorne's significance, see Leon Howard, "Thomas Odiorne: an American Predecessor of Wordsworth," *American Literature* 10 (1939): 417–36.

24. "Elegy, Written at Fort Hamilton, on the Great Miami River, during an Indisposition—February, 1795," *Works*, pp. 67–69.

25. Leon Howard dealt with the effect of the frontier on a writer's mode of expression in "Literature and the Frontier: The Case of Sally Hastings," *ELH: A Journal of English Literary History* 7 (1940): 68–82. Hastings's frontier poems and journal, free from cant in ideas, nevertheless are traditional and conventional in style.

26. The difficulties of conforming the image of the Noble Savage to the exigencies of change are discussed in Bernard W. Sheehan's "Paradise and the Noble Savage in Jeffersonian Thought," *William and Mary Quarterly* 26 (1969): 327–59. Essentially the same discussion is in chap. 4 of Sheehan's *Seeds of Extinction: Jeffersonian Philanthropy and the American Indian* (Chapel Hill: University of North Carolina Press for the Institute of Early American History and Culture, 1973), pp. 89–116.

13

"A Perpetual Harrow upon My Feelings"
John Quincy Adams and the American Indian

LYNN HUDSON PARSONS

*As the United States grew in population, territory, and international impor-
tance during the late eighteenth and early nineteenth centuries, several New
Englanders rose from the regional to the national stage. Foremost among them
were two members of the Adams family—the new nation's second president and
its sixth. Both John and John Quincy Adams were born and bred in Massachusetts; the ideas they carried to Washington, D.C.—whether about Indians,
slavery, commerce, nationalism, or almost anything else—were accordingly to
a large extent New England–based. This is not to say that the Adamses did
not modify their earlier judgments as they moved from New England's relative
insularity to the wider world of national and international politics; often they
did. Still, the Adamses' perspectives on Indians and many other matters had a
decidedly New England cast, which they applied to issues concerning Indians
beyond the region's borders, and their ingrained views of Indians had important
ramifications for national debates and policies.*

*In John Quincy Adams's case, as Lynn H. Parsons's article insightfully dem-
onstrates, the assumptions about Indian territorial rights that Adams presumably absorbed during his youth and that he vigorously advocated in his Plymouth Oration of 1802 underwent profound changes during and especially after
his presidency. Adams did not alter all of his attitudes toward Indians; like most
Euroamerican New Englanders, he believed throughout his life that they should
shed their "savage" customs and beliefs. Only then would their title to ancestral
lands be wholly legitimate and justify the federal government's active support.
Indeed, when the South's "Five Civilized Tribes" met that requirement, Adams
championed their cause during his long tenure in the House of Representatives.
The ex-president took a stand that he had earlier, as secretary of state and president, publicly repudiated.*

*Adams's evolving stance on Indian rights sheds light on not only the national
crisis over Indian removal but also its intersection with the emerging antislav-*

ery debate. *To the former president's political supporters and especially to his opponents, the Cherokee issue, as it played out in the halls of Congress, was as much about the South's "peculiar institution" as it was about states rights and Indian rights. That hardly dissuaded Adams from fighting on.*

*T*HE YEAR 1841 saw the Whig Party in control of the presidency and both houses of the United States Congress for the first—and, as it turned out, the only—time. The takeover insured that all congressional committee chairmanships could go to loyal party members, and so eyebrows were raised when it was announced that John Quincy Adams, a maverick Whig at best, had been appointed chairman of the House Committee on Indian Affairs. A few days later Adams rejected the appointment. When some of his colleagues attempted to extract from him the reasons for his action, they were shouted down.[1] As is so often the case with an Adams, his diary reveals the private reason behind the public act. On 30 June 1841, he wrote of his appointment, "I was excused from that service at my own request, from a full conviction that its only result would be to keep a perpetual harrow upon my feelings, with a total impotence to render any useful service." Of United States Indian policy, he added, "It is among the heinous sins of this nation, for which I believe God will one day bring them to judgment—but at His own time and by His own means. I turned my eyes away from this sickening mass of putrefaction."[2]

The outburst is remarkable in itself, but even more so when compared with Adams's earlier career, which saw him professing quite dissimilar views. In 1814, when at Ghent he chaired the American delegation charged with negotiating an end of the War of 1812, Adams claimed the extinction of all Indian rights as a national duty. "I had till I came here," wrote one of Adams's English counterparts, "no idea of the fixed determination which prevails in the breast of every American to extirpate the Indians and appropriate their territory; but I am now sure that there is nothing which the people of America would so reluctantly abandon as what they are pleased to call their natural right to do so."[3] Four years later, as secretary of state, Adams defended not only Andrew Jackson's invasion of Spanish Florida but also his execution of Indian prisoners without trial. "It is thus only," he wrote in a widely publicized diplomatic dispatch, "that the barbarities of the Indians can successfully be encountered."[4]

In 1814, the views of John Quincy Adams and those of Andrew Jackson regarding Indians differed very little. But twenty-seven years later, Adams regarded United States Indian policy as "among the heinous sins of this nation." It would be tempting to explain this reversal in terms of Adams's

326 ~ LYNN HUDSON PARSONS

resentment against Jackson himself, for it is certain that the guiding spirit behind federal Indian policy since 1829 was the same man who had defeated Adams for reelection to the presidency. For Adams and his heirs, Jackson became the symbol for the decline of the Republic of the Founding Fathers, the catalyst that precipitated the forces of demagoguery, hypocrisy, and greed which were to characterize so much of nineteenth-century America.[5] Yet, as the congressman from the Plymouth District of Massachusetts, Adams did not hesitate to support Jackson when he thought he was right, as on the Nullification issue in 1833 and the confrontation with France over spoliation claims in 1835–36. (The latter stand probably cost Adams a seat in the Senate).[6] Neither partisanship nor personalities had much to do with Adams's views on the American Indian or on any other public question.

In some respects, Adams remained consistent in his opinions about the Native American. At no time did he doubt the superiority of white Christian civilization over that of the "pagan" or "savage" Indian. At no time did he question seriously the right of the European settler in the New World. But within the range of these views—held by nearly all white Americans of his time—John Quincy Adams progressed from an attitude of hostility to one of curiosity and from curiosity to the sense of outrage indicated by his denunciation of 1841. This essay will explore Adams's changing perspective on the aboriginal Americans within the context of the events of his diplomatic, presidential, and congressional careers. It will also try to shed some additional light upon the role the American Indian played in the emergence of the Democratic and Whig Parties of the 1830s. The focus, however, will remain on John Quincy Adams and the way in which the American Indian came to affect his perception of his fellow countrymen and that of the future of the United States.

I

On 22 December 1802, the anniversary of the landing of the Pilgrims, the citizens of Plymouth, Massachusetts, invited John Quincy Adams—formerly a successful young diplomat but at that time a none-too-successful Boston attorney—to deliver a suitable oration. As was to be expected, the discourse proved to be full of self-indulgent praise for the Fathers of the Plymouth Colony and of New England generally. Unlike the Europeans, Adams told his audience, New Englanders were able to trace their origins within the confines of recorded memory rather than into the recesses of a shadowy antiquity:

The founders of your race are not handed down to you, like the father of the Roman people, as the sucklings of a wolf. The great actors of the day we now solemnize were illustrious by their intrepid valor, no less than by their christian graces; but the clarion of conquest has not blazon'd forth their names to all the winds of Heaven. Their glory has not been wafted over oceans of blood to the remotest regions of the earth. They have not erected to themselves, colossal statues upon pedestals of human bones, to provoke and insult the tardy hand of heavenly retribution.[7]

Such a roseate view required an explanation of the Pilgrims' right to settle upon land previously inhabited by the aboriginal Americans, a task to which Adams devoted some time. Historically, the issue had been largely resolved by the devastation of the Indian tribes by plague in the early seventeenth century, but Adams was interested in propounding a more acceptable rationalization.[8] That the Fathers of Plymouth had in fact purchased their original settlement did not really resolve the issue either, for many who came later had not. In the background lay the more fundamental question of the right of Europeans to intrude upon America in the first place.[9]

Noting that "moralists" and "philanthropists" had raised the issue, Adams defended the European right of settlement through the standard arguments derived from Vattel and Locke, that intensive agrarian communities have stronger claims to the same land than do extensive hunting or nomadic groups. The Indians, less numerous than the Europeans, had no right to stand in the way of those who would use the land to sustain several times the number of human beings:

What is the right of a huntsman to the forest of a thousand miles over which he has accidentally ranged in quest of prey? Shall the fields and the vallies, which a beneficent God has formed to teem with the life of innumerable multitudes, be condemned to everlasting barrenness? Shall the mighty rivers poured out by the hands of nature, as channels of communication between numerous nations, roll their waters in sullen silence and eternal solitude to the deep? Have hundreds of commodious harbours, a thousand leagues of coast, and a boundless ocean been spread in the front of this land, and shall every purpose of utility to which they could apply be prohibited by the tenant of the woods? No, generous philanthropists! Heaven has not been thus inconsistent in the works of its hands![10]

Although in time the Plymouth Oration would be used in support of programs and policies that he abhorred, Adams never repudiated nor questioned the fundamental right of the European to settle in America.[11] And if anything, his views on this matter hardened over the next eighteen years. He remarked in 1824 that the arguments of the Plymouth Oration proved of great assistance against British attempts in 1814 to negotiate the creation of an independent Indian state in the upper Ohio River Valley.[12] Adams, writing in 1814 from Ghent to Secretary of State James Monroe, saw the British proposal as proof of "no other than a profound and rankling jealousy at the rapid increase of population and of settlements in the United States, [and] an impotent longing to thwart their progress and to stunt their growth."[13]

Adams was prepared to go further than any of his colleagues in asserting white power over the natives as well as in proclaiming the manifest destiny of Anglo-Saxon civilization. In his proposed draft of an American reply to the British Indian proposal he reiterated the Plymouth arguments:

It cannot be unknown to the British government that the principal if not the only value of lands to the Indian state of society is their property as hunting grounds. That in the unavoidable, and surely not to be regretted, progress of a population increasing with unexampled rapidity, and of the civilized settlements consequent upon it, the mere approximation of cultivated fields, of villages and of cities, necessarily diminishes and by degrees annihilates the only quality of the adjoining deserts, which makes them subject of Indian occupancy.[14]

Therefore, concluded Adams, it was in the Indians' own best interest to make way for the white man and to sell the lands that the latter's encroachments had made worthless. Any idea of an independent Indian state was not only contrary to the interests of all concerned but in defiance of the flow of history. Even if Great Britain were successful in extracting "a concession so pernicious and degrading" from the Americans,

Can she believe that the swarming myriads of her own children, in the process of converting the western wilderness to a powerful empire could be long cramped or arrested by a treaty stipulation confining whole regions of territory to a few scattered hordes of savages, whose numbers to the end of ages would not amount to the population of one considerable city?[15]

To Adams's disgust, his proposed reply received a tepid response from his colleagues. "It was considered by all the gentlemen that what I had written was too long, and with too much argument about the Indians." A few days later Adams noted that almost all he had written on the Indian matter had been struck out of the final draft.[16]

Not content with leaving matters at this point, Adams sought out Henry Goulburn, a member of the British delegation, in order to underscore his personal view. It was American policy, he said, to respect the possessions of Indian tribes, who, like the Cherokees, had adopted agricultural ways. "But," Adams went on, "the greater part of the Indians could never be prevailed upon to adopt this mode of life. . . . It was impossible for such people ever to be said to have possessions." He defended the United States policy of purchase and removal, insisting it was better than the theft and extermination he alleged other nations had practiced. He concluded with a baleful warning. "If Great Britain meant to preclude forever the people of the United States from settling and cultivating those territories, she must not think of doing it by a treaty. She must formally undertake, and accomplish, their utter extermination."[17]

Goulburn was not intimidated: "All that I think I have learnt from them is this: that Mr. Adams is a very bad arguer," he told his superiors in London.[18] A few weeks later, Adams was still demanding a more militant stance on the Indian question. He proposed that his colleagues insist on "the moral and religious duty of the American nation to cultivate their territory, though to the necessary extinction of all the rights of savage tribes by fair and amicable means." Albert Gallatin and the other members of the American delegation were willing to acknowledge this "duty" but preferred to leave religion and morality out of the equation.[19] Even after the British abandoned the demand for an independent Indian state, Adams opposed any settlement that did not explicitly recognize total white American control over the natives. He would have been prepared to break off negotiations over the issue, he told his wife, but his colleagues talked him out of it.[20] In 1814 the American Indian was, to Adams, anything but "a perpetual harrow" upon his feelings.

Nor had matters changed much by 1818, the year of Andrew Jackson's war against the Seminoles in Spanish Florida. Now secretary of state under President James Monroe, Adams was once more alone among his associates. Monroe's cabinet, including Secretary of War John Calhoun, favored disciplinary action against Jackson.[21] Adams's view, which eventually prevailed, was that the general's apparent violation of his orders and his execution of prisoners without trial should not be allowed to obscure the fact that European powers—in this case Spain and possibly Britain—were using the Seminoles and their runaway slave allies to threaten the security of the United States, and all other considerations should be subordinated to that state of affairs.[22]

Adams was well aware of the weaknesses of Jackson's—and his own—case. He noted that the general's actions toward the Indian prisoners were "without due regard to humanity," and he told a colleague that he was "not prepared for such a mode of warfare."[23] There was no doubt about Jackson's violation of orders not to attack or occupy Spanish forts. Whether Adams was also aware that the war was the result of white attempts to deny sanctuary to escaped Georgia slaves, as demonstrated many years later by William Jay and Joshua Giddings, is not clear.[24] In any event, Adams's official defense of the Seminole War to the Spanish and British ministers was a model of its kind, illustrating, as George Dangerfield put it, the principle that "when one's position is morally unsound it is better to attack than to defend."[25] Placing the blame for the affair on Spanish inability or unwillingness to control the Seminoles and the "banditti of negroes" who were their allies, Adams presented a highly inaccurate picture of the events that led to Jackson's invasion of Florida. He concentrated on the "barbarous, unrelenting, and exterminating character of Indian hostilities" and abandoned his reservations over the execution of the Indian prisoners. "Contending with such enemies," he told the American minister at Madrid, "although humanity revolts at entire retaliation upon them, . . . yet mercy herself surrenders to retributive justice the lives of their leading warriors taken in arms."[26] In a more restrained mood, Adams wrote that the deterrent effects of the invasion "will be the greatest benefit ever conferred by a white man upon their tribes, since it will be the only possible means of redeeming them from the alternative otherwise unavoidable of their utter extermination."[27]

In later years, when the temptation must have been very great, Adams never wavered from his earlier support of the First Seminole War and of Andrew Jackson. In 1830 a pamphlet appeared that attacked both Adams and Jackson over the Seminole affair and suggested that Adams's defeat for reelection as president in 1828 by the very man he had defended was a form of divine punishment. Written by the Virginian Benjamin Watkins Leigh, the pamphlet also demonstrated that Adams had played fast and loose with certain passages from Vattel which he had used to justify the execution of the Indians.[28] Adams dismissed Leigh's contentions as "lawyer's arguments." "Scruples of law and constitution with such enemies," he continued, "are like the scruples of the Jews butchered by their enemies rather than violate the Sabbath by self-defense." To his son, Adams melodramatically proclaimed that "were it to go over again, I would do the same, should the retribution reserved for me, instead of that which I endure, be crucifixion."[29]

Adams never abandoned his position that since the Seminoles in 1818 were covertly supported by the Spanish and possibly the British, military action against them was justified by the principle of self-defense.[30] Owing to the combination of Jackson's exploits and Adams's diplomacy, the United States acquired Florida, and Spain renounced any interests north of the Adams-Onis Treaty Line of 1819.[31] Spain was a crumbling power. As for the British, their newfound interest in manufacturing for a world market led to a "diplomacy of coal and iron"; thus diverted, they abandoned their hostility toward American expansion.[32] Under such conditions, the dwindling number of Indians who menaced the borders of the United States could scarcely be seen as either the obstacle or the threat to the progress of Anglo-Saxon civilization that Adams had once proclaimed them to be. Not surprisingly, then, the years following 1820 saw Adams's earlier hostility begin to recede.

At about the same time, the other main support for Adams's anti-Indian prejudice was also weakening. The simplistic dichotomy between the Euroamerican's agrarian culture and the Native American's hunting and nomadic civilization, whatever basis in fact it may have had in the days of Vattel and Locke, could no longer be accurately applied to most of the Indians east of the Mississippi in the early nineteenth century. Not only the "Five Civilized Tribes" of the South (Cherokees, Creeks, Choctaws, Chickasaws, and Seminoles) but the tribes composing the Iroquois Nation in the North, as well as most other remaining tribes in the East, had developed agrarian ways, either because they wished to or because they thought it strategically wise.[33] Although hunting was still a large part of their existence, this was true also of white frontiersmen. A close look at Indian society east of the Mississippi seriously undermines the standard arguments against Indian rights to the land. Needless to say, few whites were willing to take that look.

Adams's first recorded contact with Indians had been back in 1794, when on the eve of his departure as American minister to the Netherlands, President Washington invited Adams to witness a ceremonial session with a group of Chickasaw chiefs. The twenty-seven-year-old Adams was not impressed. Their speech, he reported, "more than once reminded me of the Houynhms [*sic*]."[34] As secretary of state from 1817 to 1825, Adams had the opportunity to observe delegations of Indians from time to time, and what he saw rarely fit the stereotypes of Plymouth and Ghent. Not long after his return to Washington in 1817, Adams witnessed a meeting between President Monroe and a delegation of "northern" Indians—Senecas, Wyandots, and Delawares. He noted approvingly that "they said they had all become cultivators of the land, and had altogether abandoned the life of huntsmen."[35] Adams was even more enthusiastic after meeting with some Cherokees in 1824. Not only were they farmers, but they "were dressed entirely according to our manner. Two of them spoke English with good pronunciation, and one with grammatical accuracy. They gave me some account of their institutions, which are incipient."[36] Five months later, Adams added

> The manners and deportment of these men have in no respect differed from those of well-bred country gentlemen. They have frequented all the societies, where they have been invited at evening parties, attended several drawing-rooms, and most of Mrs Adams's Tuesday evenings. They dress like ourselves, except that Hicks, a young and very handsome man, wore habitually a purfled scarf. . . .[37]

Yet Adams still distinguished between "savage" and "civilized" Indians, as is shown by a different account, given at about the same time, of a meeting with some "Plains Indians"—Sauks, Fox, Iowa, Menomonee, Chippewa, and Sioux. These, he said, were "among the most savage of the desert," and some of them "all but naked."[38]

Many years later, when he was attracting attention as a friend of the Indians, Adams still maintained that what "civilization" they had acquired was a result of contact with whites. Before the arrival of the European, he wrote in 1837, they were "Savages and Idolators."[39] But there was no denying that many of the Indians under pressure from the whites in the nineteenth century were no longer "Savages and Idolators." This was a result not only of their proximity to white men but of the efforts of several generations of white missionaries. The new circumstances were reflected in Adams's changed attitude toward Indian claims in the 1820s, both as secretary of state and as president.

II

The roots of the southern Indian controversies of the 1820s were sunk deep in the Jeffersonian past. In an agreement with Georgia in 1802, the federal government had pledged to extinguish by peaceful and reasonable means the rights of all Indians in that state but had since failed to do so, primarily because of the refusal of the Creeks and Cherokees to leave their ancestral lands.[40] When the subject first arose in Monroe's cabinet in 1820, Adams, still functioning in the charged atmosphere of the Seminole War, urged the president to accommodate the increasingly militant Georgians by persuading the Indians to emigrate.[41] By 1824, however, his contacts with the

Cherokees and Creeks, the removal of the danger of foreign intrigue with the Indians, and the affair's implications for federal-state relations caused Adams to reverse himself. Albeit in the privacy of Monroe's cabinet, Adams for the first time took the side of the Indian against the white man.

As the Georgia governor and legislature became more and more threatening in their insistence upon the removal of the Creeks and Cherokees, Monroe was inclined to throw the matter into the lap of Congress. Adams (supported by John C. Calhoun, who was in trouble with the Georgia congressional delegation because he had inadvertently addressed the Cherokee leaders as "gentlemen") objected. If Congress were to be invited to resolve the issue, it at least should be reminded that the agreement of 1802 called for a peaceful solution. "The Indians," said Adams, "had perfect right on their side in refusing to remove."[42] Monroe proceeded to revise his message to Congress to include the reminder urged by Adams and Calhoun.[43] When Georgia threatened to remove the Indians on her own authority, Adams recorded his conviction that "this bursting forth of Georgia upon the Government of the United States was ominous of other events."[44]

By 1825, when Adams became president, the Georgia controversy was reaching a boiling point. By then the constitutional implications of the affair gave it particular significance. For Adams, whose constitutional nationalism was more thoroughgoing than that of any other president of his generation, the integrity of the federal government was closely tied to the protection of the Indians—and vice versa. Even before he took the oath of office, John Quincy Adams was headed on a collision course with two of the more basic precepts of what later would be called "Jacksonian democracy": the rights of the states over the federal government, and the rights of white men over Indians.

On 12 February 1825, three days after the House of Representatives selected Adams as president over Andrew Jackson and William Crawford, a treaty was concluded between commissioners of the federal government and certain chiefs of the Georgia Creeks.[45] The Treaty of Indian Springs provided for the voluntary removal of the entire Creek nation from Georgia and liberal *douceurs* for those Creek leaders who had signed the document—a standard feature of such agreements. Since the treaty was approved by the Senate on 3 March 1825, less than twenty-four hours before Adams was to take office, it became virtually the first order of business of the new administration. Since the treaty had been duly negotiated by authorized federal commissioners, approved by two-thirds of the Senate, and offered the possible resolution of a particularly volatile issue, Adams proceeded to ratify it.

Two months later he learned that the two federal commissioners had worked in collusion with certain Georgia officials, that those Creeks who signed the treaty were unrepresentative of the nation, that their leader, McIntosh, was a distant relative of the governor of Georgia, and that in reprisal for negotiating the treaty, McIntosh had later been slain by his fellow Creeks.[46] The majority Creek faction rejected the Treaty of Indian Springs and refused to leave their lands.

This rejection, Adams told Congress the following year, released the government from the terms of the treaty. There were two options open: the government could forcibly eject the Creeks from their land, or it could attempt to negotiate a new treaty to obtain the same result peacefully and in accord with the agreement of 1802. "The preference dictated by the nature of our institutions and by the sentiments of justice" required the government to seek the second solution, said Adams.[47] His secretary of war, James Barbour, accordingly produced a second treaty providing for the peaceful removal of the Creeks from all but a small portion of Georgia.[48]

The governor of Georgia, George McIntosh Troup, insisted upon the original treaty. Land surveys, he announced, would proceed, regardless of what the Adams administration did. Troup's surveyors entered Creek and Cherokee territory in the summer of 1826 and complained loudly of Indian treachery when they met resistance. On 5 February 1827, Adams placed the matter before Congress, asserting that the actions of Georgia were "in direct violation of the supreme law of this land, set forth in a treaty which has received all the sanctions provided for by the Constitution which we have been sworn to support and maintain."[49] But by this time, Adams's presidency was entangled in the thicket of partisanship that would ultimately bring it down. Congress showed no disposition to act. Governor Troup threatened resistance should federal force be used on behalf of the Indians. Here matters stood until later in the same year, when Adams was none too gracefully let off the hook by the conclusion of a third treaty which ceded the remaining portion of Georgia to the whites.[50]

Parallel with the Creek controversy was a dispute between Georgia and the Cherokees. The story is well known.[51] Showing more unity than the Creeks, the Cherokees adamantly refused even to discuss removal. More than any other tribe, they confounded the standard white arguments for Indian removal. Not only did the Cherokees take up farming, they raised livestock, ground grain, and manufactured textiles. An 1826 census showed them owning 22,000 cattle, 7,600 horses, 46,000 swine, 726 looms, 2,488 spinning wheels, 31 gristmills, 10 sawmills, and 62 blacksmith shops. They had even progressed so far in white "civilization" as to own 1,277 slaves.[52] They established an alphabet, printed a newspaper, and, in true Lockean

style, called a convention and adopted a constitution, which they proclaimed as supreme law for all Cherokees. Under the leadership of John
Ross, the remarkable chief who was to lead them through all their tragic
vicissitudes until his death in 1866, the Cherokees lobbied in Congress on
behalf of their rights for more than twenty years. "They have sustained a
written controversy against the Georgia delegation with great advantage,"
Adams wrote admiringly in 1824.[53] The Georgians were less enchanted,
and they pressed for Cherokee removal. They finally attained their goal in
1838, with the help of President Martin Van Buren and the United States
Army.

From the adoption of the Constitution to Monroe's administration, the
federal Indian policy had been primarily assimilationist. Thomas Jefferson
and his successors hoped that as many Indians as possible could be converted to Anglo-Saxon ways.[54] But by the early 1820s, the policy was suc-
cumbing to the resistance of many Indians who refused to become Anglo-
Saxon and of whites who wanted more land, no matter what the Indians
did. Impressed by the intransigence of the Georgians, Monroe, in his last
message to Congress, had suggested peaceful removal and the creation of
a federally guaranteed Indian Territory west of the Mississippi as a means
of protecting both races.[55] However, John Quincy Adams's inaugural address as well as his diary indicates that he still believed in assimilation.
Thus he ignored his predecessor's last-minute switch to removal and
praised the progress the previous administration had made in "alluring the
aboriginal hunters of our land to the cultivation of the soil and of the
mind."[56]

Apart from its effect upon the Indians themselves, the most serious
practical defect in the assimilationist approach was the fact that most frontier politicians were dead set against it. As Adams and Barbour, even more
of an assimilationist than his chief, eventually came to realize, what was
wanted was not the conversion of the native to the white man's ways; what
was wanted was the native's land—nothing more, nothing less. Furthermore, assimilation could result in such embarrassments as the Cherokee
constitution, which, if it had been successful, would have deprived white
speculators of several hundred thousand acres of land. Finally, there was
the pessimistic belief of men like Henry Clay—a westerner and Adams's
secretary of state—who doubted the efficacy of assimilation on racial and
cultural grounds. As Adams reported late in 1825:

Mr Clay said he thought . . . that it was impossible to civilize Indians;
that there never was a full-blooded Indian who took to civilization. It was

not in their nature. He believed they were destined to extinction, and, although he would never use or countenance inhumanity towards them, he did not think them, as a race, worth preserving. He considered them as essentially inferior to the Anglo-Saxon race, which were now taking their place on this continent. They were not an improvable breed, and their disappearance from the human family will be no great loss to the world. In point of fact they were rapidly disappearing, and he did not believe that in fifty years from this time there would be any of them left.

"Governor Barbour was somewhat shocked at these opinions," noted Adams, "for which I fear there is too much foundation."[57] Although Adams may not have agreed with Clay's racial notions, it is more than probable that he was increasingly pessimistic about the Indian's chances for survival in the face of the land-hungry white man and the impotence of the federal government to control the situation.[58]

Even Secretary Barbour eventually gave up on assimilation and joined the voluntary removalists out of sympathy for the Indian. His report in 1826 is one of the few official documents of that era that points out the hypocrisy of the prevailing policies toward the Indians:

They have been persuaded to abandon the chase—to locate themselves, and become cultivators of the soil—implements of husbandry and domestic animals have been presented them, and all these things have been done, accompanied with professions of a disinterested solicitude for their happiness. Yielding to these temptations, some of them have reclaimed the forest, planted their orchards, and erected houses, not only for their abode, but for the administration of justice, and for religious worship. And when they have so done, *you* send *your* Agent to tell them they must surrender their country to the white man, and re-commit themselves to some new desert, and substitute as the means of their subsistence the precarious chase for the certainty of cultivation. . . . They see that our professions are insincere—that our promises have been broken; that the happiness of the Indian is a cheap sacrifice to the acquisition of new lands.[59]

Adams, while admiring Barbour's "benevolence and humanity," remained skeptical about removal. The problem was, he told Isaac McCoy, a Baptist missionary and philanthropist,

We have scarcely given them time to build their wigwams before we are called upon by our own people to drive them out again. My own opinion is that the most benevolent course towards them would be to give them the rights and subject them to the duties of citizens, as part of our own people. But even this the people of the States within which they are situated will not permit.[60]

Thus, to Adams, neither proposal seemed to promise a solution. Removal—apart from the basic injustice involved—was only a stopgap policy leading to further aggression. Assimilation, even if feasible, collided with the rapaciousness of the frontier. The hunters, Adams told McCoy, were now "themselves hunted by us like a partridge upon the mountains."[61] His position now was close to that of the British commissioners in 1814, confronted by the determination of the white American to appropriate the West for his own use regardless of the consequences. The matter caused him to stay up until midnight one winter's eve in 1827, reading old statutes and presidential messages. "This examination," he wrote, "like many others, leads me deeper and deeper into research, till I am compelled to stay my inquiries for want of time to pursue them."[62]

In the last weeks of his presidential term, Adams showed signs of acceding to the white demands. In his last annual message, he alluded to the Cherokee constitution as one of the "unexpected" results of the "civilizing" policies of the past. The claim of the Cherokees for independent status had set at odds the otherwise consistent principles of national supremacy and Indian rights. A solution had to be found, he told Congress, "which, while it shall do justice to those unfortunate children of nature, may secure to the members of our confederation their rights of sovereignty and of soil."[63] He then called attention to the recommendations of his new secretary of war, Peter B. Porter, whose ideas differed from Barbour's. Not only did Porter oppose assimilation, he favored withdrawing federal support from missionaries in the East and transferring it to the trans-Mississippi West, a suggestion that provided what one authority has called "a bridge between the voluntary removals of Monroe and Adams and the coercive [removals] of Jackson."[64] At about the same time, Adams was advising a group of Winnebagoes who were under white pressure to move that "they had better let us have the land where the land was of no use to them."[65]

The tenor of Adams's remarks indicates that his image of the American Indian as a huntsman-nomad was slow to die, that the 1820s were transitional in his thinking, and that the fruits of that transition had yet to be borne. As for federal Indian policy itself, like so much else in Adams's presidency, it seemed to be marking time, awaiting the momentous changes that the Jackson era would bring.

III

There was no ambivalence in Andrew Jackson's position on Indian affairs from the moment of his inaugural address to the end of his life.[66] The initial focal point of Jacksonian Indian policy became the Removal Bill of 1830. Although the use of force was not provided for, the bill, when enacted, threw the federal government for the first time in support of removal rather than assimilation. Regardless of past promises, guarantees, or treaties, all Indians east of the Mississippi were to be encouraged to give up their lands and move west. Sympathetic whites were divided over the issue. The majority opposed the Removal Bill, citing its betrayal of past promises as well as the determined opposition of the Indians themselves. A minority, however, sided with the Jacksonians, claiming that the "corrupting" influence of white civilization made removal desirable from the Indian standpoint as well.[67] The removalists stuck doggedly to the hunter-farmer dichotomy in spite of its inapplicability in most instances.[68]

John Quincy Adams did not enter the House of Representatives until December 1831 and therefore did not have the opportunity to vote against the Removal Bill, which he certainly would have done. During the interim between his presidential and congressional careers, Adams had had ample time to reflect on the forces that had destroyed his presidency. Among them had certainly been his ambivalent Indian policies.[69] Secretary Barbour's humanitarianism excited only contempt in the West, while the constitutional nationalism of Adams's messages to Congress alienated the entire South. There can be no doubt that those who were interested in the most rapid settlement of the land in the West or South had more to gain from Jackson's election than from his defeat. Before those lands could be developed, the Indians had to be removed. To the ex-president, Indian removal was a part of the Jacksonian conspiracy to bankrupt the nation of its public lands, dissipate its economic strength, and destroy its political integrity.[70]

Recognizing that the victimization of the Indians would add to, rather than detract from, Jackson's popularity as president, Adams was convinced that the Removal Bill would ultimately pass.[71] Early in 1830 he was visited by Edward Everett, one of its leading congressional opponents. "I said there was nothing left for the minority to do but to record the perfidy and tyranny of which the Indians are to be made the victims, and leave the punishment of it to Heaven."[72] Two months after delivering this unhelpful advice, Adams saw the Indians as "already sacrificed." On the day of the vote, he wrote to Alexander H. Everett, brother of the congressman. "I have heard much of a speech of your brother's," he said, "but that was perhaps on the Indian Question which is prejudged."[73]

Yet the vote in favor of the bill was close, 102 to 97. The pattern of opposition indicates that the Removal Bill of 1830—not the Bank Veto of 1832—provided the first major confrontation between those forces that would later comprise the Democratic Party and its opposition. Votes against the bill came from the same areas that had supported Adams in 1828, would support the Bank of the United States in 1832, and would later form the nucleus of the Whig Party. The New England delegation in the House voted 9 to 28 against the bill, and the entire North opposed it, 42 to 79. The South voted 60 to 15 in favor, while the West favored it 23 to 17.[74]

Adams saw too that the doctrine of Nullification was first applied not by the state of South Carolina against federal tariff laws but by the state of Georgia against the Indians. In 1830, two years before the crisis in South Carolina, Adams noted that "a discovery has been made of a new attribute of State sovereignty."

> It is convenient to three or four Southern States to extrude or exterminate all the Indians within their borders. They have suddenly discovered that all the Acts of Congress and all the Indian Treaties made for the last forty years are *palpably unconstitutional.* So their Legislatures have nullified them all. [They] have extended the State Laws over the persons and property of the Indians and determined that they shall be *deported* west of the Mississippi at the expence of the United States. The President of the United States tells us and tells the Indians that this is all right—and so it shall be.[75]

The idea of Nullification had once thrived in New England, Adams told a New Hampshire correspondent, but it had since become extinct there. "It now rages in the South, with much more favorable prospects of success. Georgia has effected it so far as respects the Indians. So have Alabama and Mississippi. South Carolina is attempting it with regard to the Tariff, and I think will succeed."[76]

In 1830 and 1831 the Cherokees transferred their battle for survival in Georgia to the Supreme Court. Although he doubted their claim of independent status, Adams was interested enough in the case of *Cherokee Nation v. Georgia* to attend the summations of the attorneys for the Cherokees, William Wirt and John Sergeant.[77] Wirt had been Adams's attorney general, and the former president had the highest regard for both men. The Cherokees contended that their "independent" status precluded the authority of the states over them. This argument might have appealed to his constitutional nationalism, but Adams was not surprised when Chief Justice Marshall, with Justices Story and Thompson dissenting, denied the Indians' right to sue in the federal courts. After all, the Cherokee argument came close to challenging the rights of the first white settlers in the New World, something Adams never conceded. "As to a primitive abstract right of soil, owned by the Indians when the European settlers first came here," he told Judge Ambrose Spencer of New York, "I did not believe in any such right."[78]

But the Cherokees were more successful a year later when the Marshall Court struck down Georgia's laws concerning Indians, implying that only federal and not state authority could deal with them. But Jackson defied the Court in 1831 by refusing to enforce its decision in *Worcester v. Georgia*. Adams had foreseen the outcome:

> The old vice of confederacies is pressing upon us—anarchy in the members. Whenever a State does set itself in defiance against the laws or power of the Union, they are prostrated. This is what the States having Indian tribes within their limits are now doing with impunity, and all the powers of the General Government for protection of the Indians, or the execution of the treaties with them, are nullified.[79]

In the 1830s the question was not whether the Indians had sovereign rights to the soil, which was denied by nearly all whites, Adams included, but whether they had any rights that white men were required by law to respect. For John Quincy Adams, as well as for most of those who would later comprise the Whig Party, their constitutional nationalism combined with humanitarian sentiment and partisan opposition to produce an affirmative answer.

Adams had been in Congress only a few months when he touched off a day-long House debate by presenting petitions in favor of the Cherokees and in opposition to the state of Georgia. One of the petitions was from New York City and, in the tradition of the day, was forty-seven yards long. (Not only did Adams offend the Jacksonians, but he also violated one of the courtesies of the House by presenting petitions from another state.) A motion to table the petitions was narrowly defeated, 91–92, and they were ultimately referred to the Committee of the Whole. The roll call on tabling showed the same pattern as the vote on removal two years before and prefigured the vote on the recharter of the Second Bank of the United States four months later.[80] Adams was at first reluctant to present the petitions, "well assured that it will be of no avail," but eventually relented.

Afterward, foreseeing the defeat for the Cherokees and the Union in the *Worcester* case, he declared that "convinced that I can effect nothing, my own course will be to withhold myself from all action concerning it."[81] For the next ten years, tension would build between Adams's sense of outrage and his reading of political realities.

IV

The Jacksonian removal policy provoked violence in Georgia, Alabama, and Florida. While the administration was relatively successful in deporting the less numerous Chickasaws and Choctaws, the Creeks, Cherokees, and Seminoles either refused to negotiate treaties for "voluntary" removal or, claiming fraud and bad faith, refused to leave once the instruments were signed. In the case of the Alabama Creeks, the provisions of the removal treaty signed in 1832 allowed those who desired to remain in Alabama to be given small farms, guaranteed free from white intrusion by the federal government. Yet as soon as the word of the treaty reached Alabama, the Creek lands were overrun by white adventurers, speculators, horse thieves, and looters, eventually numbering some ten thousand. The Jackson administration was either unwilling or unable to stop the invasion. Inevitably, the Indians retaliated, providing the excuse for federal troops to move into Alabama and eventually force the total removal of the Creeks, contrary to the terms of the treaty of 1832.[82]

At the same time, a split had developed among the Cherokees. A minority faction now favored removal, but the majority, led by John Ross, stood firm, refused to leave Georgia, and cited innumerable solemn treaties and compacts. As part of an emerging pattern in such situations, members of the minority faction were hailed as the "true" representatives of the tribe, and negotiations were held with them. After some difficulty, the Treaty of New Echota (1835), committing the Cherokees to removal, was extracted from the minority. Only about 400 of the 17,000 eligible Cherokees signed the treaty. The fraud was so obvious that even the usually docile United States Senate nearly rejected the agreement.

By this time Indian removal had become a clear issue between the Democratic and Whig Parties. In 1836, an election year, the Treaty of New Echota was attacked by Webster, Clay, Calhoun, and most other opponents of Jackson and Van Buren, including of course John Quincy Adams. It was approved by the Senate with only one vote to spare. Still later, a national attack was mounted against the treaty, culminating with a petition signed by John Ross and 15,664 other Cherokees, but to no avail. In 1838, the army was ordered into Georgia by President Van Buren, and the "Trail of Tears" began.[83]

The Seminoles were already condemned to the Florida swamplands when they were told to prepare to move west. The government construed a cautious agreement by certain Seminole leaders to an investigatory tour of western territories as an all-out commitment to removal. Again, by rounding up a minority faction and proclaiming it representative of the entire tribe, a treaty was produced and approved by the Senate in 1834. Predictably, violence broke out the following year, and eventually developed into the Second Seminole War. Ultimately, it accounted for more white combat deaths than either the Mexican or Spanish-American Wars.[84]

Congressional and administration reaction to the Indian hostilities of the 1830s formed a pattern familiar to many Americans in later years. White casualties would be reported in gory detail and Indian treachery denounced. Those naive enough to seek more information or question the causes of the conflict were denounced as sickly sentimentalists and soft on Indians.[85] In any event (so the argument ran) blood had been shed and it was too late to look back. By then, few congressmen could resist such pressure and withhold support for the military.

It also became evident that something other than removal of the Indians was at stake. Creeks, Cherokees, and Seminoles all owned slaves, though the ownership seems to have been much more lenient and informal than that practiced by the whites.[86] With the departure of the Indians, not only real estate but other forms of "property" might become available to whites. In 1837 an agreement providing for the peaceful removal of the Seminoles was reached with the army but was sabotaged by Florida whites eager to obtain alleged runaway slaves thought to be living with the Indians.[87] The war was renewed for another five years. In the North, the conviction grew in abolitionist circles that the Indian conflicts of the 1830s involved slavery as well. John Quincy Adams referred to "the Indian and Negro war, already raging within our borders."[88]

Adams's perspective on the American Indian was undergoing a second shift. He no longer regarded them as threats to the survival and security of the Union; on the contrary, he was beginning to see them, and their preservation, as one of the means by which the Union could be strengthened and maintained. "The Indians, the Public Lands, the Public Debt, the Bank, have been ties, to hold the Union together," he told his former navy secretary, Samuel Southard.[89] It did not surprise him that the Jacksonians were undermining each one. He therefore came to defend the Indians in the same way that he defended the Bank of the United States and the preservation of the nation's landed resources.

Not only Adams's view of the Indians was changing; his characterization of the Anglo-Saxon American was also shifting as well. Before, at Plymouth and at Ghent, he confidently trumpeted the virtues of an ever-expanding white civilization. By 1836 it appeared that a substantial portion of that civilization was committed to the expansion of slavery. As his opposition both to the annexation of Texas and later to the Mexican War attested, he no longer believed that an expanding America automatically meant an extension of the "area of freedom." If the Indians were to be the immediate victims of American expansion, the eventual victim was to be liberty itself. So long as the Indians were preserved, their lands would be free from the white slaveholder. For John Quincy Adams, the cause of the American Indian and the cause of antislavery were becoming one and the same.

On 25 May 1836, Adams delivered, without notes and with little preparation, a speech that he later characterized as "one of the most hazardous that I ever made."[90] It was also one of his greatest. In the space of one hour, and over the shouted interruptions of many of his colleagues, the sixty-eight-year-old ex-president tied together in one unpleasant package the issues of Indian removal, the congressional "Gag Rule" on antislavery petitions, and the drive toward Texas annexation. He addressed the dangers of a war against Mexico, predicted that civil war over slavery would open the door to emancipation under martial law, and closed with a bitter excoriation of Jacksonian Indian policy.[91]

How tragic and ironic it was, he said, that the noble Anglo-Saxon race, of which he and most members of Congress were a part, had ceased to carry the burden of freedom in the world and was now plotting to carry slavery into a land where it had been legally abolished. Already he had been told that Anglo-Saxons should rejoice at the rumored execution without trial of the hated Santa Anna. (Long before, he had defended an American general who had also executed prisoners without trial, with lasting repercussions for the nation and for himself. He would not follow that road again.) Such rejoicings were "no inconsiderable evidence of the spirit which is spurring us into this war of aggression, of conquest, and of slave-making."[92] He then laid bare the racial basis of the coming struggle for the continent.

What is the temper of feeling between the component parts of your own Southern population, between your Anglo-Saxon, Norman French, and Moorish Spanish inhabitants of Louisiana, Mississippi, Arkansas, and Missouri? Between them all and the Indian savage, the original possessor of the land from which you are scourging him already back to the foot of the Rocky Mountains? What between them all and the native American negro, of African origin, whom they are holding in cruel bondage? Do you not, an Anglo-Saxon, slaveholding exterminator of the Indians, from the bottom of your soul, hate the Mexican-Spaniard-Indian, emancipator of slaves and abolisher of slavery?[93]

At Plymouth in 1802 he had spoken buoyantly of making the wilderness blossom like the rose, of mighty rivers as channels of communication between thriving cities, of hundreds of commodious harbors. At Ghent in 1814 he had lectured to Great Britain concerning "the unavoidable, and surely not to be regretted, progress of a population increasing with unexampled rapidity," and of "the swarming myriads of her own children, in the process of converting the western wilderness to a powerful empire."[94] Now, in Washington in 1836, he had his doubts not only about the children of Great Britain but about powerful empires as well:

> As to the annexation of Texas to your confederation, for what do you want it? Are you not large and unwieldy enough already? Do not two millions of square miles cover surface enough for the insatiate rapacity of your land-jobbers? Have you not Indians enough to expel from the land of their fathers' sepulchres, and to exterminate?[95]

Though the remarkable indictment has been remembered primarily within the context of Adams's enunciation of the doctrine of emancipation under martial law—later said to be utilized by Abraham Lincoln in 1862— it was in fact sparked by a resolution calling for the distribution of army rations to white victims of Indian attacks in Alabama. Adams used his address to unburden himself of his forebodings concerning the future of American expansion, but he did not forget the origin of his comments. Like most Americans, he favored aiding the victims of the Indian wars, but he blamed both Congress and the citizens of Alabama and Georgia for the current state of affairs, the result of their defiance of federal treaties, laws, and court decisions:

> You have sanctioned all these outrages upon justice, law, and humanity, by succumbing to the power and policy of Georgia; by accommodating your legislation to her arbitrary will; by tearing to tatters your old treaties with the Indians, and by constraining them, under *peine forte et dure,* to the mockery of signing other treaties with you, which, at the first moment when it shall suit your purpose, you will again tear to tatters and scatter to the four winds of heaven, till the Indian race shall be extinct upon this

continent, and it shall become a problem beyond the solution of antiquaries and historical societies what the red man of the forest was.[96]

Once the goal had been to assimilate as many Indians as possible, but it had been abandoned amidst the rise of Jacksonianism. The reaction was only to be expected:

> you have met with all the resistance which men in so helpless a condition as that of the Indian tribes could make. Of the immediate causes of the war we are not yet fully informed; but I fear you will find them, like the remoter causes, all attributable to yourselves. It is in the last agonies of a people, forcibly torn and driven from the soil which they had inherited from their fathers, and which your own example, and exhortations, and instructions, and treaties, had riveted more closely to their hearts; it is in the last convulsive struggles of their despair that this war has originated; and if it brings with it some portion of the retributive justice of Heaven upon our own people, it is our melancholy duty to mitigate, as far as the public resources of the national Treasury will permit, the distresses of the innocent of our own kindred and blood, suffering under the necessary consequences of our own wrong.[97]

Adams noted in his diary that "the greatest excitement" grew not out of the doctrine of emancipation under martial law, but out of his indictment of federal Indian policy and the states of Georgia and Alabama.[98] Although the speech seemed to suggest that Adams was abandoning his long-held belief in the primacy of the white man's claim to America, such was not the case. The issue simply remained what it had been for some time, a question of whether the Indians had the rights not of soil but of preservation. Adams hoped that the speech might in some way alter the fate of "that hapless race of native Americans, which we are exterminating with such merciless and perfidious cruelty."[99] The favorable reaction that the speech received among antislavery elements undoubtedly played a role in the administration's decision to postpone Texas annexation until another day, but it did not have any visible effect on Indian policy.[100] The refusal of Congress to reconsider the odious Treaty of New Echota reconvinced Adams that "it is vain to plead for justice in any case concerning Indians."[101]

The removalists came to see in John Quincy Adams one of their most formidable enemies, and they treated him accordingly. They also saw in him the canting hypocrisy typical of many New Englanders, who, having profited from slavery and exterminated their Indians in years gone by, were now sitting in judgment upon others. It was a powerful and not entirely answerable argument. Georgia congressmen were particularly piqued. Congressman Charles Haynes of that state soon rebutted the New Englander in an able speech that quoted at length from the Plymouth Oration and suggested that the old man's animus against Georgia arose from that state's consistent opposition to the presidencies of both John and John Quincy Adams. Haynes was called to order before much of the speech was read, and Adams took little notice of it, but in its printed version it remains as one of the most thorough defenses of Jacksonian Indian policy.[102] Two years later, Adams noted that the Plymouth Oration had again been used against him by another Georgian, but the *Congressional Globe* gives no indication of what was said.[103]

Adams's denunciations of federal Indian policy now brought him a following second only to that which he acquired through his defense of the right of petition in the cause of abolition. Correspondents, both Native American and white, hoped Adams would assert even more leadership than he already had. He received a seventeen-page letter from Chief Big Kettle and twenty-three other New York Senecas who claimed fraud concerning a removal treaty negotiated in 1837.[104] An outraged New Yorker sent him a petition requesting release from United States citizenship as his response to the nation's treatment of Indians. (Adams submitted the petition but was unsympathetic to the tactic.)[105] He went out of his way three times in one day to be part of the audience witnessing a treaty between certain Plains Indians and the Van Buren administration.[106] As events moved toward the inevitable denouement with the Cherokees in 1838, Adams received several dozen petitions on their behalf. Increasingly the pleas invoked notions of divine retribution. "Sir, if in this thing, you will be our Moses," wrote a woman from New Hampshire, "we promise you that we, like his two sons, will hold up your arms by our united prayers, until we save the poor Indians from this dreadful fate, and this nation from the tremendous curse [that] will otherwise come upon her. . . ."[107] On 21 May 1838, Adams presented some twenty-four petitions on behalf of the Cherokees, as did several Whigs, all to no avail.[108] The petitions were tabled, and General Winfield Scott moved into Georgia.

While he continued to submit pro-Indian petitions, Adams still voted funds to suppress Indian hostilities. He maintained that the government was obligated to aid the innocent victims of its policies, and thus he lagged behind a small number of Whigs who by 1838 refused to vote for such appropriations.[109] But by 1840 Adams began to waver even on this matter. He became increasingly disturbed over the seemingly endless Second Seminole War and its fruitless results. A careful reading of a speech by the

Vermont Whig Horace Everett convinced him that in this case, as in so many others before, the whites were entirely to blame:

> It depresses the spirits and humiliates the soul to think that this war is now running into its fifth year, has cost thirty millions of dollars, has successfully baffled all our chief military generals. . . . Sixteen millions of Anglo-Saxons unable to subdue in five years, by force and by fraud, by secret treachery and by open war, sixteen hundred savage warriors. . . . There is a disregard of all appearance of right in all our transactions with the Indians, which I feel is a cruel disparagement of the honor of my country.[110]

(Nowhere did he comment on the equally dubious origins of the *First* Seminole War of 1817–18.)

In this mood, Adams released a volley of his vaunted sarcasm when he learned that the government of the United States had purchased, at a cost to the taxpayers of $151.72 each, a number of bloodhounds from Cuba (plus five Spanish interpreters since the dogs were monolingual) to pursue Indians and runaway slaves across the Florida swamps.[111] On 9 March 1840, he presented the following resolution to the House of Representatives:

> Resolved, That the Secretary of War be directed to report to this House the natural, political, and martial history of the bloodhounds, showing the peculiar fitness of that class of warriors to be the associates of the gallant army of the United States, specifying the nice discrimination of his scent between the blood of the freeman and the blood of the slave—between the blood of the armed warrior and that of women or children—between the blood of the black, white, and colored men—between the blood of the savage Seminoles and that of the Anglo-Saxon pious Christian. Also, a statement of the number of bloodhounds and their conductors, imported by this government, or by the authorities of Florida, from the island of Cuba, and the cost of that importation. Also, whether a further importation of the same heroic race into the State of Maine, to await the contingency of a contested Northeastern boundary question, is contemplated, or to set an example to be followed by our possible adversary in the event of a conflict. Whether measures have been taken to secure exclusively to ourselves the employment of this extraordinary force, and whether he deems it expedient to extend to the said bloodhounds and their posterity the benefits of the pension laws.[112]

The introduction of the bloodhounds was too much for Adams. The following July, he spoke for more than five hours in 90-degree heat in unsuccessful opposition to further expenditures on the Second Seminole War.[113] It was to continue until 1842, when all but a few Seminoles were rounded up and shipped westward.

This, then, was the background to the appointment of John Quincy Adams as chairman of the House Indian Affairs Committee following the Whig takeover of Congress in 1841. Under the circumstances, it was unexpected and unwanted. His sense of futility and frustration led him to reject not only the chairmanship of the committee but membership on it. A meeting with John Ross and a group of Cherokees—who by that time had been deported to Arkansas and were seeking Adams's help in redressing frauds that had arisen out of their removal—caused him to confess to the "harrow upon my feelings" that the Indian tragedy created for him.[114]

V

Adams had little to say about the Indians after 1841. His remaining years were caught up in his spectacular "trial" for censure before the House of Representatives and his successful fight against the congressional Gag Rule. Moreover, Indian removal had become a reality by the 1840s, and there was nothing left to be done.

In 1843, Adams made what became a triumphal tour through western New York, the one region that, outside of the Plymouth district, had always remained faithful to him. One Sunday in July in Niagara Falls, he inquired for the nearest church. Upon being told that it was "not fashionable" for resort guests to go to church, Adams joined a group headed for divine services at the Tuscarora Indian reservation seven miles away. As he later recalled, following the sermon it was announced to the Indians that "John Quincy Adams, once President of the United States was present; whereupon I made to them a short address."[115] He did not record what he said, but an anonymous observer reported:

> Mr. Adams alluded to his advanced age, and said that this was the first time he had ever looked upon their beautiful fields and forests—that he was truly happy to meet them there and join with them in the worship of our common Parent—reminded them that in years past he had addressed them from the position which he then occupied, in language, at once that of his station and his heart, as "his children"—and that now, as a private citizen, he hailed them in terms of equal warmth and endearment, as his "brethren and sisters." He alluded, with a simple eloquence which seemed to move the Indians much, to the equal care and love with which God regards all his children, whether savage or civilized, and to the common destiny

which awaits them hereafter, however various their lot here. He touched briefly and forcibly on the topics of the sermon which they had heard, and concluded with a beautiful and touching benediction upon them.[116]

In his Plymouth Oration of nearly two generations before, Adams had complimented his listeners on the fact that their Pilgrim ancestors had not erected "colossal statues upon pedestals of human bones, to provoke and insult the tardy hand of heavenly retribution."[117] But the anti-Texas speech of 1836, and his outburst to his diary in 1841, indicate that in Adams's mind the "land-robbing" Anglo-Saxon American no longer merited such indulgence. The lands to the west were to be used in a different manner. "I had long entertained and cherished the hope," he told his constituents,

> that these public lands were among the chosen instruments of Almighty power, not only of promoting the virtue, welfare and happiness of millions upon millions of individuals and families of the human race, but of improving the condition of man, by establishing the practical, self-evident truth of the natural equality and brotherhood and all mankind, as the foundation of all human government, and by banishing Slavery and War from the earth. . . . Was all this an Utopian daydream? Is the one talent, entrusted by the Lord of the harvest, for the improvement of the condition of man, to be hidden under a bushel? Is the lamp, destined to enlighten the world, to be extinguished by the blasting breath of Slavery?[118]

His southern critics were correct: there was a double standard in Adams's views of white expansion and Indian rights. When in 1846 it was proposed to extend the northwest border of the United States to 54°, 40′, Adams supported it. But the plantation-oriented civilization that Adams saw as the cornerstone to Jacksonian "democracy" was not what he had in mind. Better to let the Indians remain than to allow the once-free lands to be tilled by the slave or to fall under the land speculator's auction hammer. The land speculator was no better than the savage; in fact, he was worse, for all knew that the Indian loved the land for its own sake, and not for profit in the marketplace. Thus Adams could reconcile his support of white expansion in 1802 with his opposition in 1836.

It is tempting to read more than simple dismay and frustration into Adams's rejection of his appointment in 1841. After all, if the Indian were to be exterminated as a result of the white man's territorial expansion, if indeed it was to be a question for future learned societies as to what the red man was like, then whose diplomacy was responsible for making that expansion and extermination possible? If the Second Seminole War was part of a "sickening mass of putrefaction," then who had arranged for the incorporation of Florida and the Seminoles into the United States in the first place? If Andrew Jackson, his administration, and its successors were responsible for the policy that was "among the heinous sins of this nation," who was it that had rushed to Jackson's defense on a matter concerning those same Seminoles when the general had needed it most?

As was the case with the cause of antislavery, Adams's sympathy with the American Indian came late in his life. Both causes he came to see as involved with the maintenance of the Union, yet here the resemblance ends. As early as 1820 Adams was convinced that a life devoted to the cause of emancipation "would be nobly spent or sacrificed." By 1838 he was able to write, "that the fall of slavery is predetermined in the counsels of Omnipotence I cannot doubt; it is a part of the great moral improvement in the condition of man, attested by all the records of history."[119] Yet Adams had also written of the extinction of the American Indian as being equally "prejudged." By whom? By God? Or Andrew Jackson? Or both? Such an alliance was beyond Adams's comprehension. And what if the same "great moral improvement" that Adams professed to see in the nineteenth century doomed the Indian at the same time as it doomed slavery? Small wonder that he shrank from the dilemma and fell back upon the comforting notion of divine retribution.

Author's Postscript

In the quarter-century that has elapsed since this article was published, the area of Indian (or Native American)-white (or Euroamerican) relations has been the subject of scrutiny by a new generation of historians utilizing the insights of anthropology, ethnography, and psychology. Of particular interest to students of the early nineteenth century are Bernard Sheehan's *Seeds of Extinction* (Chapel Hill: University of North Carolina Press for the Institute of Early American History and Culture, 1973), which explores the nature of Jeffersonian assimilationism, and Michael Paul Rogin's *Fathers and Children* (New York: Knopf, 1975), which attempts an intriguing if controversial analysis of Jackson's Indian policy, utilizing Freudian terminology and assumptions. Linda Kerber, "The Abolitionist Perception of the Indian," *Journal of American History* 62 (1975): 271–95, elaborates on the generally sympathetic stance taken by most abolitionists toward the Indian. Ronald N. Satz's *American Indian Policy in the Jacksonian Era* (Lincoln: University of Nebraska Press, 1975) and Anthony F. C. Wallace's *The Long, Bitter Trail: Andrew Jackson and the Indians* (New York: Hill and Wang, 1993) are far more hostile to Jackson than Prucha's earlier work, cited in the article.

Robert V. Remini's massive biography of Andrew Jackson, *Andrew Jackson and the Course of American Empire* (New York: Harper and Row, 1977), *Andrew Jackson and the Course of American Freedom* (New York: Harper and Row, 1981), and *Andrew Jackson and the Course of American Democracy* (New York: Harper and Row, 1985), while predictably sympathetic to the subject, is sensitive to the complexities involved. The third volume gives a good account of Jackson's vehement hostility towards Adams, and vice versa. A more recent study of Martin Van Buren and his administration is John Niven's *Martin Van Buren: The Romantic Age of American Politics* (New York: Oxford University Press, 1983).

As for John Quincy Adams himself, two full-length biographies have appeared since this essay was first published: Paul Nagel's *John Quincy Adams: A Public Life, A Private Life* (New York: Knopf, 1997), and my *John Quincy Adams* (Madison, Wisc.: Madison House, 1998). His diplomacy as secretary of state is examined in William Earl Weeks's *John Quincy Adams and American Global Empire* (Lexington: University Press of Kentucky, 1993), and his presidency is fully explored in Mary W. M. Hargreaves's *The Presidency of John Quincy Adams* (Lawrence: University Press of Kansas, 1985). Leonard Richards deals admirably with Adams's congressional years in *The Life and Times of Congressman John Quincy Adams* (New York: Oxford University Press, 1986), and Adams is the subject of chap. 3 of Daniel Walker Howe's *The Political Culture of the American Whigs* (Chicago: University of Chicago Press, 1979). Those seeking a full Adams bibliography as of 1993 are directed to my *John Quincy Adams: A Bibliography of* (New York: Greenwood Press, 1993).

Subsequent study has persuaded me that another reason for Adams's rejection of the chairmanship of the Indian Affairs Committee was his pique at not being appointed chairman of the House Foreign Relations Committee. He had expected this plum but was denied it, probably through the influence of Secretary of State Daniel Webster. He later received the appointment but immediately became the subject of southern and proslavery attack. See my "Censuring Old Man Eloquent," *Capitol Studies* 3 (Fall 1973): 89–106.

Notes

1. *Congressional Globe*, 18 June 1841, p. 72.

2. John Quincy Adams, *Memoirs of John Quincy Adams*, ed. C. F. Adams, 12 vols. (Philadelphia, 1874–77), 10:491–92 (30 June 1841).

3. Henry Goulburn to Earl Bathurst, 25 November 1814, quoted by Arthur Wellesley, Duke of Wellington, in *Supplementary Despatches, Correspondence, and*

Memoranda, 15 vols. (London, 1858–72), 9:452, 454. For the background to this statement, see Samuel Flagg Bemis, *John Quincy Adams and the Foundations of American Foreign Policy* (New York: Knopf, 1949), pp. 200–208, George Dangerfield, *The Era of Good Feelings* (London: Methuen, 1953), pp. 64–70, and Bradford Perkins, *Castlereagh and Adams* (Berkeley: University of California Press, 1964), pp. 68–101.

4. Adams to George William Erving, 28 November 1818, *Writings of John Quincy Adams,* ed. W. C. Ford, 7 vols. (New York, 1913–17), 6:498–99. See also Dangerfield, *Era of Good Feelings,* pp. 137–40; Bemis, *Adams and Foreign Policy,* pp. 315–16; Robert V. Remini, *Andrew Jackson and the Course of American Empire* (New York: Harper and Row, 1977), p. 369; William Earl Weeks, *John Quincy Adams and American Global Empire* (Lexington: University Press of Kentucky, 1993), pp. 139–46.

5. For the best example of this attitude, see Brooks Adams's introduction to Henry Adams's *The Degradation of the Democratic Dogma* (New York: Harper Torchbook, 1969), pp. 27–28, 77–86.

6. See Samuel Flagg Bemis, *John Quincy Adams and the Union* (New York: Knopf, 1956), pp. 263–69, 305–25. On Adams's rejection of partisanship, see his letter to Nicholas Biddle, 10 June 1836, quoted by Charles Francis Adams, Jr., in *Emancipation Under Martial Law (1819–1842)* (Cambridge: J. Wilson and Son, 1902), pp. 88–89.

7. John Quincy Adams, *An Oration, Delivered at Plymouth, December 22, 1802, at the Anniversary Commemoration of the First Landing of Our Ancestors* (Boston, 1802), pp. 8–9.

8. Alden T. Vaughan, *The New England Frontier: Puritans and Indians, 1620–1675* (Boston: Little, Brown, 1965), pp. 21–22.

9. For an introduction to the literature on this subject, see Albert K. Weinberg, *Manifest Destiny* (Chicago: Quadrangle, 1963), chap. 3, and Wilcomb E. Washburn, "The Moral and Legal Justifications for Dispossessing the Indians," in *Seventeenth-Century America: Essays in Colonial History,* ed. James Morton Smith (Chapel Hill: University of North Carolina Press, 1959), pp. 15–32.

10. Adams, *Oration at Plymouth,* pp. 22–25.

11. Adams, *Memoirs,* 8:205 (22 March 1830).

12. Adams, *Writings,* 3:10–11. For a later statement of the same theme, though without any references to the American Indian, see Adams, "The Progress of Society from Hunter State to that of Civilization," *American Whig Review* 2 (1845): 80–89. For an amusing commentary on the latter essay, see Wendell Glick, "The Best Possible World of John Quincy Adams," *New England Quarterly* 37 (1964): 3–17. See also Adams's lecture *The New England Confederacy of MDCXLIII* (Boston, 1843), pp. 12–15.

13. Adams to James Monroe, 5 September 1814, *Writings,* 5:119–20.

14. Adams, Draft of reply to British Commissioners, 21 August 1814 *Writings,* 5:96.

15. Adams, *Writings,* 5:98–99.

16. Adams, *Memoirs,* 3:21–23 (21 and 23 August 1814).

17. Adams, *Memoirs,* 3:27–29 (1 September 1814).

18. Goulburn to Earl Bathurst, 2 September 1814, in Wellington, *Supplementary Despatches*, 9:217.

19. Adams, *Memoirs*, 3:39–40 (23 and 25 September 1814); Bemis, *Adams and American Foreign Policy*, pp. 207–8; Weinberg, *Manifest Destiny*, p. 76.

20. Adams to Louisa Catherine Adams, 14 October 1814, *Writings*, 5:158; Perkins, *Castlereagh and Adams*, pp. 88–91.

21. Dangerfield, *Era of Good Feelings*, pp. 137–38; Bemis, *Adams and American Foreign Policy*, pp. 315–16; James, *The Border Captain*, pp. 318–20.

22. Adams, *Memoirs*, 4:107–14 (15–21 July 1818).

23. Adams, *Memoirs*, 4:87 (4 May 1818).

24. William Jay, *Miscellaneous Writings on Slavery* (New York, 1853), pp. 247–49; Joshua Giddings, *The Exiles of Florida* (Gainesville: University of Florida Press, 1964), pp. 35–56; Edwin C. McReynolds, *The Seminoles* (Norman: University of Oklahoma Press, 1957), pp. 73–80. Neither Bemis, *Adams and American Foreign Policy*, p. 313, nor Dangerfield, *Era of Good Feelings*, mentions the proslavery origins of the First Seminole War.

25. Dangerfield, *Era of Good Feelings*, p. 148; Bemis, *Adams and American Foreign Policy*, pp. 325–27.

26. Adams to Don Luis de Onis, 23 July 1818, and to George William Erving, 28 November 1818, *Writings*, 6:386–94, 498–99.

27. Adams to Gallatin, 30 November 1818, *Writings*, 6:513.

28. "Algernon Sydney" [Benjamin Watkins Leigh], *The Letters of Algernon Sydney in Defense of Civil Liberty and Against the Encroachments of Military Despotism* (Richmond, Va., 1830), pp. viii, 22–26. These letters originally appeared in the *Richmond Enquirer* in 1818 and 1819. See Adams to his father, John Adams, 14 February 1819, *Writings*, 6:528–32.

29. Adams, *Memoirs*, 7:223 (29 April 1830); Adams to Charles Francis Adams, 28 April 1830, Adams Family Manuscript Trust, microfilm reel 150. Hereafter cited as Adams MSS Trust, with reel number.

30. Adams to William H. Crawford, 30 July 1830, Adams MSS Trust, reel 150.

31. Bemis, *Adams and American Foreign Policy*, pp. 329–40; Philip C. Brooks, *Diplomacy and the Borderlands: The Adams-Onis Treaty of 1819* (Berkeley: University of California Press, 1939); C. C. Griffin, "The U.S. and the Disruption of the Spanish Empire," *Columbia University Studies, No. 429* (New York: Columbia University Press, 1937).

32. Dangerfield, *Era of Good Feelings*, pp. 283–92; Bemis, *Adams and American Foreign Policy*, pp. 293–99.

33. See Weinberg, *Manifest Destiny*, chap. 3; Washburn, "The Moral and Legal Justification for Dispossessing the Indians"; Roy Harvey Pearce, *The Savages of America* (Baltimore: Johns Hopkins University Press, 1965), pp. 66–73, 123.

34. Adams, *Memoirs*, 1:34–36 (11 July 1794).

35. Adams, *Memoirs*, 4:20 (10 November 1817).

36. Adams, *Memoirs*, 6:229 (8 January 1824).

37. Adams, *Memoirs*, 6:373 (3 June 1824).

38. Adams, *Memoirs*, 6:402, 406 (31 July and 4 August 1824).

39. Adams to Sherlock S. Gregory, 23 November 1837, Adams MSS Trust, reel 153.

40. Ulrich B. Phillips, *Georgia and States' Rights* (Yellow Springs, Ohio: Antioch Press, 1968), pp. 39–65; Annie H. Abel, *History of Events Resulting in Indian Consolidation West of the Mississippi River* (Washington, D.C.: Government Printing Office, 1908), pp. 322–26; Francis Paul Prucha, *American Indian Policy* (Cambridge: Harvard University Press, 1962), pp. 227–33. See also Reginald Horsman, "American Indian Policy in the Old Northwest," *William and Mary Quarterly*, 3d ser. 18 (1961): 35–53.

41. Adams, *Memoirs*, 5:21–22 (13 March 1820). As late as July 1820, Adams supported the appointment of Andrew Jackson as a federal commissioner to negotiate with the Indians. See his letter to Governor Clark of Georgia, 24 July 1820, in *Writings*, 7:54–56.

42. Adams, *Memoirs*, 6:267–68, 271–72 (26 and 29 March 1824).

43. Monroe to Congress, 30 March 1824, *Messages and Papers of the Presidents*, ed. James D. Richardson, 10 vols. (Washington, 1899) 2:234–37.

44. Adams, *Memoirs*, 6:255–56 (12 March 1824).

45. The details of the Georgia-Creek controversy can be found in Phillips, *Georgia and States' Rights*, pp. 15–66; Abel, *Indian Consolidation*, pp. 335–46; and Bemis, *Adams and the Union*, pp. 79–87.

46. Adams, *Memoirs*, 7:3–11 (15–20 May 1825).

47. Adams, First Annual Message, 6 December 1825, Richardson's *Messages*, 2:306; Adams to Senate, 31 January and 25 April 1826, *Messages*, 2:324–26, 345.

48. Richard J. Hryniewicki, "The Creek Treaty of Washington, 1826," *Georgia Historical Quarterly* 48 (1964): 425–41. Also, Adams, *Memoirs*, 7:61–62 (26 November 1825). The progress of negotiations with the Creeks is touched upon intermittently in Adams's diary from 1825 to 1827.

49. Adams to Senate, 5 February 1827; Richardson's *Messages*, 2:370–73; Bemis, *Adams and the Union*, pp. 85–87; Abel, *Indian Consolidation*, pp. 349–55.

50. Richard J. Hryniewicki, "The Creek Treaty of November 5, 1827," *Georgia Historical Quarterly* 52 (1968): 1–15; Adams, *Memoirs*, 7:370–71 (6 December 1827).

51. Grant Foreman, *Indian Removal* (Norman: University of Oklahoma Press, 1953), pp. 229–312; Dale Van Every, *Disinherited: The Lost Birthright of the American Indian* (New York: Morrow, 1966), pp. 43–74, 198–235; George D. Harmon, *Sixty Years of Indian Affairs* (Chapel Hill: University of North Carolina Press, 1941), pp. 192–96; Prucha, *Indian Policy*, pp. 231–49; Grace Steel Woodward, *The Cherokees* (Norman: University of Oklahoma Press, 1963).

52. Van Every, *Disinherited*, pp. 44–45, 74.

53. Adams, *Memoirs*, 6:373 (3 June 1824).

54. Prucha, *Indian Policy*, pp. 213–24; Horsman, "Indian Policy in the Old Northwest," pp. 35–53; Harmon, *Sixty Years of Indian Affairs*, pp. 157–66.

55. James Monroe, Eighth Annual Message, 7 December 1824, in Richardson's *Messages*, 2:261; Abel, *Indian Consolidation*, p. 341.

56. Adams, Inaugural Address, 4 March 1825, in Richardson's *Messages*, 2:298.

57. Adams, *Memoirs*, 7:89–90 (22 December 1825).

58. Bemis, *Adams and the Union*, pp. 83–84.

59. Quoted by Abel, in *Indian Consolidation*, p. 366.

60. Adams, *Memoirs*, 7:113, 119, 410–11 (7 February and 3 July 1826, 23 January 1828).

61. Adams, *Memoirs*, 7:410 (23 January 1828).

62. Adams, *Memoirs*, 7:231–32 (25 February 1827). For the problems arising from alleged fraud by white government agents upon the New York Senecas during Adams's presidency, see letters from the Seneca Chiefs to Adams, 27 September and 25 October 1826 and 15 March 1827, Adams MSS Trust, reels 477–79. Also *Memoirs*, 7:465 (7 March 1828).

63. Adams, Fourth Annual Message, 2 December 1828, Richardson's *Messages*, 2:415–16. See also *Memoirs*, 7:426–27 (8 February 1828).

64. Abel, *Indian Consolidation*, pp. 368–69.

65. Adams Diary, 29 November 1828, Adams MSS Trust, reel 39; *Memoirs*, 7:82 (14 December 1828).

66. Prucha, *Indian Policy*, pp. 233–40.

67. Prucha, *Indian Policy*, p. 225; Abel, *Indian Consolidation*, pp. 377–79.

68. Weinberg, *Manifest Destiny*, chap. 3; Pearce, *Savages of America*, pp. 63–75.

69. Robert V. Remini, *The Election of Andrew Jackson* (Philadelphia: Lippincott, 1963), pp. 75–76.

70. Adams to Alexander H. Everett, 15 April 1830, Adams MSS Trust, reel 150. See also *Memoirs*, 9:485 (3 February 1838), and Adams's address to his constituents in 1842, quoted in Henry Adams's *Degradation of the Democratic Dogma*, pp. 27–28.

71. Adams, *Memoirs*, 8:232–33 (22 and 25 June 1830).

72. Adams, *Memoirs*, 8:206 (22 March 1830). At this time, Adams's son, Charles Francis, was taking a more conservative position on Indian affairs. See C. F. Adams to J. Q. Adams, 24 January and 14 February 1830, Adams MSS Trust, reel 492, and J. Q. Adams to C. F. Adams, 5 and 21 February 1830, reel 150.

73. Adams *Memoirs*, 8:229 (22 May 1830); Adams to Alexander H. Everett, 24 May 1830, Adams MSS Trust, reel 150.

74. Van Every, *Disinherited*, p. 120; Abel, *Indian Consolidation*, pp. 377–78. Compare the House vote on Indian removal, 24 May 1830 (*Register of Debates*, vol. 6, pt. 2, p. 1133) with the vote on Bank recharter two years later, 3 July 1832 (vol. 8, pt. 3, p. 3852). Of the 30 Senators who voted on both issues, 28 were "consistent," i.e., for removal and opposed to the Bank, or vice versa. Of the 14 Senators who opposed removal, 13 later became Whigs. Of the 16 who favored it, 12 became Democrats, plus John Tyler and Robert Y. Hayne. The major speeches in opposition to removal were collected in *Speeches on the Passage of the Bill for the Removal of the Indians*, ed. Jeremiah Evarts (Boston, 1830).

75. Adams to Peter B. Porter, 4 April 1830, Adams MSS Trust, reel 150. See also William W. Freehling, *Prelude to Civil War* (New York: Harper and Row, 1966), p. 232, and Charles S. Sydnor, *The Development of Southern Sectionalism* (Baton Rouge: Louisiana State University Press, 1948), pp. 182–86.

76. Adams to William Plumer, 24 September 1830, Adams MSS Trust, reel 150. See also his letters to Alexander H. Everett, 15 April 1830, to Samuel Southard, 6 June 1830, and to Joseph Story, 23 October 1830, all of which list the Indian question ahead of all other political issues.

77. Adams, *Memoirs*, 8:343–45 (12 and 14 March 1831). For the Cherokee case, see Phillips, *Georgia and States' Rights*, pp. 74–83; John P. Kennedy, *Memoirs of the Life of William Wirt*, 2 vols. (Philadelphia, 1849), 2:277–303, 334–43, 370–73; Abel, *Indian Consolidation*, pp. 381–87.

78. Adams, *Memoirs*, 8:205 (22 March 1830). For a brief period in 1831–32, Adams gave editorial assistance to his former superintendent of Indian Affairs, Thomas L. McKenney, in the latter's projected history of the American Indian. Adams was forced to give up this activity because of the press of congressional and other business. See Adams to McKenney, 12 and 27 September, 14 October, 5 and 17 December 1831, and 2 January 1832, Adams MSS Trust, reel 150; *Memoirs*, 8:457 (15 January 1832). McKenney's book was published as *The History of the Indian Tribes of North America*, 3 vols. (Philadelphia, 1837–44).

79. Adams, *Memoirs*, 8:343–44 (12 March 1831). See also Freehling, *Prelude to Civil War*, pp. 233–34.

80. Joseph Blunt to Adams, 17 February and 2 March 1832, Adams MSS Trust, reel 495. For the debate and vote on tabling the petition, see *Register of Debates*, vol. 8, pt. 2, pp. 2010–36 (5 March 1832). Compare vote on tabling (pp. 2015–16) with vote on Bank, cited in n. 75 above.

81. Adams, *Memoirs*, 8:486–89, 492 (3–5 and 11 March 1832). See also letters from Joseph Hopkinson, 12 February 1832, and Caleb Cushing, 24 March 1832, to Adams, Adams MSS Trust, reel 495.

82. Foreman, *Indian Removal*, pp. 107–90; Van Every, *Disinherited*, pp. 160–73; Mary E. Young, "Indian Removal and Land Allotment: The Civilized Tribes and Jacksonian Justice," *American Historical Review* 44 (1958): 31–45.

83. Foreman, *Indian Removal*, pp. 238–312; Van Every, *Disinherited*, pp. 198–235.

84. Giddings, *Exiles of Florida*, pp. 127–310; Van Every, *Disinherited*, pp. 11, 178–93, 232–33; Foreman, *Indian Removal*, pp. 324–31. See also John K. Mahon, *History of the Second Seminole War* (Gainesville: University of Florida Press, 1967) and Arthur W. Thompson's introduction to Giddings, *Exiles of Florida*. Giddings listed white casualties at 1,500.

85. Van Every, *Disinherited*, pp. 184–85. For an example of the tactics of the pro-war faction, see the speeches of Congressmen Speight and Mann, *Register of Debates*, vol. 12, pt. 3, pp. 3168–771 (18 May 1836).

86. Giddings, *Exiles of Florida*, pp. 79, 153–54; Edwin L. Williams, Jr., "Negro Slavery in Florida," *Florida Historical Quarterly* 38 (1949): 104; Kenneth W. Porter, "Florida Slaves and Free Negroes in the Seminole War, 1835–1842," *Journal of Negro History* 48 (1943): 390–421.

87. Giddings, *Exiles of Florida*, p. 140; Mahon, *Second Seminole War*, pp. 200–201. See also the speech of Congressman Horace Everett, 3 June 1836, *Congressional Globe*, app., 24th Cong., 1st sess., 573–78.

88. Adams to S. Sampson, 21 May 1836, quoted by Charles Francis Adams, Jr., in *Emancipation Under Martial Law*, p. 84; Adams, *Memoirs*, 9:286–87 (25 May 1836); Bemis, *Adams and the Union*, p. 417.

89. Adams to Southard, 6 June 1830, Adams MSS Trust, reel 150.

90. Adams, *Memoirs*, 9:289 (29 May 1836).

91. The speech, revised by Adams for publication, may be found in *Register of Debates*, vol. 12, pt. 4, pp. 4036–49. It is discussed in Bemis, *Adams and the Union*, pp. 338–39, and C. F. Adams, Jr., *Emancipation Under Martial Law*, pp. 81–99.

92. *Register of Debates*, vol. 12, pt. 4, p. 4041.

93. *Register of Debates*, vol. 12, pt. 4, p. 4041.

94. Adams, *Oration at Plymouth*, pp. 23–34; *Writings*, 5:93, 98–99. For an unconvincing argument that Adams reversed himself on Texas annexation in order to keep up with opinion in his Congressional district, see R. R. Stenberg, "J. Q. Adams: Imperialist and Apostate," *Southwestern Social Science Quarterly* 16:37–49 (1936).

95. *Register of Debates*, vol. 12, pt. 4, p. 4044.

96. *Register of Debates*, vol. 12, pt. 4, p. 4048.

97. *Register of Debates*, vol. 12, pt. 4, p. 4049. Adams on "kindred and blood" was indirectly struck down by the Second Seminole War, when, in December 1837, his nephew Thomas Boylston Adams, Jr., died of typhoid fever while stationed in Florida. In her reaction to young Adams's death, Mrs. John Quincy Adams exceeded her husband in her denunciation of this war and U.S. Indian policy in general. See her letters to her son, Charles Francis Adams, 2–5, 6–22, 30–31 January, 1–3 and 4–14 February 1838, Adams MSS Trust, reel 508.

98. Adams to Robert Walsh, 3 June 1836, quoted by C. F. Adams, Jr., in *Emancipation Under Martial Law*, p. 86.

99. Adams to George Parkman, 22 June 1836, quoted in C. F. Adams, Jr., *Emancipation Under Martial Law*, 90.

100. Jackson himself blamed Adams for the frustration of Texas annexation in 1836. See his letter to William B. Lewis, 18 September 1843, *The Correspondence of Andrew Jackson*, ed. John Spencer Bassett, 7 vols. (Washington, D.C.: Carnegie Institution, 1926), 6:229.

101. Adams, *Memoirs*, 9:518 (28 March 1838). For the politics of Texas annexation at this time, see Glyndon G. Van Deusen, *The Jacksonian Era* (New York: Harper and Row, 1959), pp. 109–10, and Justin H. Smith, *The Annexation of Texas* (New York: Barnes and Noble, 1941), pp. 54–57, 60–62.

102. The full text of Haynes's intended reply to Adams and other critics of Jacksonian Indian policy is in the *Congressional Globe*, app., 24th Cong., 1st sess., 474–82, dated 27 June 1836. Adams mentions Haynes briefly in *Memoirs*, 9:299 (27 June 1836).

103. Adams, *Memoirs*, 9:548–49 (30 May 1838).

104. Big Kettle et al., to Adams, 28 February 1838, Adams MSS Trust, reel 508.

105. Adams to Sherlock S. Gregory, 23 November 1837, Adams MSS Trust, reel 153. Also *Memoirs*, 9:460 (29 December 1837).

106. Adams, *Memoirs*, 9:415–16 (21 October 1837).

107. M. M. Brooks to Adams, 23 April 1838, Adams MSS Trust, reel 509. See

also petitions of A. Johnson and J. R. Hayes, 26 April; A. B. Allen and H. P. Pratt, 1 May; Horace Hall, 2 May; Joseph Battel [?], 4 May; unsigned, 7 May; I. M. Carr, 10 May; and Francis H. Case, 12 May 1838.

108. Adams, *Memoirs*, 9:536 (21 May 1838).

109. Adams, *Memoirs*, 9:477 (24 January 1838); 9:9–10 (4 June 1838).

110. Adams, *Memoirs*, 9:256 (7 April 1840).

111. Giddings, *Exiles of Florida*, p. 266.

112. *Congressional Globe*, 17 March 1840, p. 252; Adams, *Memoirs*, 10:233 (9 March 1840).

113. *Congressional Globe*, 14 July 1840, pp. 527–28; Adams, *Memoirs*, 10:333–35 (14 and 15 July 1840). The *Globe* listed 23 opponents of the appropriation, but only 20 names were given.

114. Adams, *Memoirs*, 10:491–92 (30 June 1841); Ross to Adams, 16 June 1841, Adams MSS Trust, reel 518; Adams to Ross, 29 June 1841, reel 154. Also Seneca White et al. to Adams, 18 June 1841, and Joseph Smith to Adams, June 1841, reel 518.

115. Adams, Diary, 23 July 1843, Adams MSS Trust, reel 47. See also Bemis, *Adams and the Union*, pp. 466–68.

116. Quoted by William H. Seward, in *Life and Public Services of John Quincy Adams* (Auburn, N.Y., 1849), pp. 312–13.

117. Adams, *Oration at Plymouth*, pp. 8–9.

118. John Quincy Adams, *Address of John Quincy Adams to his Constituents . . . September 17th, 1842* (Boston, 1842), pp. 51–52; Henry Adams, *Degradation of the Democratic Dogma*, pp. 27–31.

119. Adams, *Memoirs*, 4:531 (24 February 1820); 10:63 (13 December 1838).

14

The Mashpee Indian Revolt of 1833

DONALD M. NIELSEN

While John Quincy Adams was fretting about the federal government's treat-ment of the Cherokees and other Indian peoples in the American South and West, his home state was setting a poor example. True, the surviving Algonqui-ans of Massachusetts now numbered, by some counts, fewer than two thousand, and they inhabited lands that—in theory at least—could not be taken from them by acquisitive neighbors, but Indians had little say in the management of their reservations or even their religious congregations. State and local govern-ments paid little attention to Native Americans, individually or collectively.

Had the remnants of the Pequots, Wampanoags, Narragansetts, and the other major Indian nations of the seventeenth century been numerous and moderately prosperous in the mid–nineteenth century, they might have found the political clout to ameliorate their condition. Under the existing circumstances, a successful pan-Indian movement in New England was improbable at best. Most of New England's Indians were impoverished, and most lived in communities of only a few hundred persons. Few of those residents were of exclusively Indian ances-try; some were not ethnically Indian at all; and most reservations encompassed a variety of tribal heritages. Those characteristics were especially true of reserva-tions in the former Plymouth Colony (after 1691 a part of Massachusetts) and Connecticut. Any concerted action by reservation Indians was unlikely.

Donald M. Nielsen narrates the remarkable "revolt" of the Mashpee Wampa-noags against local and state authorities. The movement was partly political, partly economic, and partly religious, for in all three realms of public life, the Mashpees' rights and opinions had long been ignored. The Euroamericans who were supposed to ensure the Mashpees' welfare were either indifferent or unsym-pathetic. With a notable assist from the Pequot William Apes, the Mashpees took matters into their own hands.

*I*N THE FIRST HALF of the nineteenth century, an age of repeated set-
backs for the American Indian, the Mashpee tribe's struggle for self-
government resulted in a unique, if incomplete, victory for Indian rights.[1]
Given the mood of Massachusetts in the 1830s, the tribe wisely spoke the
language of reform, and their cause was in turn taken up by reformers.
From civil rights, to temperance, to revivalism, the Indians at Mashpee
reflected the concerns of the time, yet their outlook was different from
that of most reformers. Unpolished but earnest, and often eloquent, the
Mashpees addressed the problem of the Indian's place in a white man's
world, and for a brief period around 1833 Indian values and pride inter-
sected with reform and revivalism to revitalize Mashpee as an Indian community.

In the 1830s, about 1,500 Indians from a variety of tribes lived on reservations scattered throughout Massachusetts; the most extensive were located in southeastern coastal Massachusetts, on Cape Cod or the outlying
islands.[2] The largest single group of Indians in Massachusetts lived at
Mashpee, where conditions were similar to those of the neighboring reservations at Chappequiddick, Christiantown, Gay Head, and Herring Pond.
Although reservations were within local municipalities, Indians living
there were not subject to local jurisdiction; instead, they were bound by
state laws but had no political representation to affect those laws. In the
1816 Massachusetts Supreme Court case of *Andover v. Canton,* the state
declared Indians the "unfortunate children of the public, entitled to protection and support" even if "incapable of civilization."[3] Massachusetts'
legislators, although the source of some of the most wide-ranging reforms
of the period, also seemed unable to protect the Indians without restricting
them. In attempting to preserve reservation lands for use by Indians, for
example, the state required that such lands not be sold to non-Indians. In
this, as well as many other particulars, the state thus denied the individual
Indian the opportunity to learn how to conduct his own affairs.

Massachusetts' reservations, like those in other New England states,
were rural slums. Alcoholism, high mortality rates, and transience were
both cause and effect of low self-esteem, dependency, and apathy. Although few characteristics of their original way of life remained, Indians
were still able to sustain a particular identity by subtle means, from small
memorials to a manner of speech,[4] but in fact, despite white protestations
that assimilation was the end desired, white-imposed restrictions were the
most powerful influence reinforcing Indian identity. Indians could never
forget that they were different, that they were the country's deposed rulers.

The Mashpee plantation dated from 1660 when Richard Bourne, a follower of Indian missionary John Eliot, secured a grant of 10,500 acres on

the south shore of Cape Cod for the exclusive use of the Indians of Mashpee and their descendants. Over the years the plantation's relation-ship to Massachusetts changed several times. Then in 1788, revoking an attempt at limited self-government, the state legislature mandated that three men, to be appointed by the governor and his executive council, form a board of overseers and be given broad powers to regulate and improve the plantation. As Massachusetts governor Levi Lincoln pointed out, the overseers were to assure that Indians were protected "against the frauds and wicked devices of unprincipled and profligate white men."[5]

The plantation entrusted to the overseers supported a population of 315 Indians in 1832, of whom 229 were proprietors, those entitled to economic and legal rights in the plantation through inheritance or adoption into the tribe.[6] As with other Massachusetts tribes, over the years many had inter-married with other racial groups. A report in 1835 revealed that only two men and six women at Mashpee claimed to be of "pure blood."[7] Some were sons and daughters of Hessians who had remained after the Revolu-tion, but most intermarriage had been with blacks.[8] Lorenzo Greene has argued that "the scarcity of Negro women in Massachusetts, on the one hand, and of Indian men on the other, was undoubtedly a factor in the steady amalgamation of the two races."[9]

Although Mashpees had intermarried for many years, the rate had steadily accelerated as the male population dwindled. Many Indians adopting the seafaring life, a popular choice during the late eighteenth and early nineteenth centuries, either died at sea or found new homes and families. During the Revolution twenty-one of twenty-two Mashpee men in the same Continental regiment were said to have died, and there were reported to be "no less than seventy widows" at Mashpee in 1783.[10] The continued influx of non-native males, who were allowed to live on reserva-tion land, and the exodus of native males greatly reduced the number of Indian names. Indian women often found husbands while serving white families, where black men filled similar roles.

The Mashpee population, scattered throughout the entire area of the plantation, met their economic needs through fishing and whaling, agri-culture, hunting, and selling plantation wood. Although the Mashpee ac-quired a reputation as "dextrous whalemen," it was the heavy demand for their timber, streams, and land that would bring them most directly into conflict with their white neighbors. The overseers rented land to whites for grazing, auctioned wood shares to outsiders, and allowed them to fish Mashpee streams. The guardians believed there was plenty for all.

Religious life at Mashpee was subject to the same control as the eco-nomic and political life. Founded as a Christian plantation, Mashpee remained in the faith, but by the nineteenth century its inhabitants had lost the privilege of selecting their own minister. Phineas Fish, the official missionary at Mashpee and a Congregationalist, was supported independently by the Williams Fund, established in 1711 by Daniel Williams and entrusted to the Corporation of Cambridge College (Harvard) to serve the Indians of New England. An 1807 Harvard graduate, Fish began missionary work at Mashpee in 1809 and received an official appointment from Harvard and the overseers in 1811.[11] The initial contract called for an annual salary of $520, a $250 settlement fee, and "so much Meadow & Pasture Land, as shall be necessary to winter and summer." The sale of wood from the parsonage woodlot brought him several hundred dollars more per year. Fish was assured a comfortable living on Mashpee land with money designated to help the Indians, yet he was in no way accountable to his Indian flock. His economic and religious rights gave him sole control of his own church, but he expressed no great feelings of responsibility either to Harvard or the Indians. In 1824, thirteen years after his original settlement, Fish wrote Harvard President John Kirkland, "It has been a long time indeed since I have made a statement of affairs in this place. Had I known that any thing of the kind had been particularly expected, I should have done it, though there is seldom any thing of an interesting nature to be mentioned, & my letters might be tiresome."[12] In the same letter he described the course of the Indians as "retrograde" and admitted there had been no "coloured" additions to his church for several years.

Mashpee had been strongly Congregationalist until the death of its popular Indian pastor Solomon Briant in 1775. From that point the Baptists, as well as other denominations, continually challenged Mashpee orthodoxy. Explaining in 1833 that he had "*survived as many as 7 different* sectarian preachers," Fish spoke of the "pain of seeing these good houses used for the purposes of *Baptist* & *Methodist* meetings. . . . The *sectarian busy-bodies* . . . now feel quite sure of demolishing the remnant of Congregationalism."[13] Fish, who began his career as a Unitarian before becoming an orthodox Congregationalist, hoped the Indians would be "contented with becoming religious in a rational way."[14] Religion, he believed, should be respectable and orderly. The Indians, however, were given to excitement and revivalism. Fish considered it unlawful to allow non-Congregational services to be conducted in the Mashpee meetinghouse, a meetinghouse built entirely with Indian funds; instead, he used the building to preach to the local white community and a handful of Indians, usually no more than ten or twelve from Mashpee.[15] It is not surprising, then, that an itinerant Indian preacher, a Pequot from Connecticut who had experienced much the same treatment as the Mashpee and was inspired by reform ideals and

Christianity, would enflame the native population and spark the protest at Mashpee.

Born at Colrain, in northwestern Massachusetts, in 1798, William Apes was the son of a "half-breed" father and an Indian mother. Within a year the family moved to Connecticut near two small Pequot reservations. Before he was five, Apes's family had broken apart. He was left in the care of alcoholic grandparents, who beat him, then bound him out to several white families in succession. As he grew older, he turned increasingly to emotional religion for comfort and consolation and, perhaps, as a form of rebellion against his respectable white foster parents. He was particularly attracted to Methodist revivals, where, according to his autobiography, he learned that Christ had died for all men, including Indians. Apes identified Christ as the leader of all subjugated peoples and applied this vision to the experiences of his own people.[16]

As a teenager Apes was an unwilling army recruit serving at the New York–Canada border during the War of 1812. At the end of the war he lived for a short time with the Indians of northern New York, where he suffered from alcohol abuse and was unable to hold a job. He returned to the Pequot reservation in Connecticut, where he was able to settle down, work for local farmers, and attend revivals. The Pequot situation, however, was similar to that at Mashpee; intemperance, disorganization, and poverty thrived where no institutions were present to foster social cohesiveness.

In the early 1820s Apes was reunited with his parents. He experienced new feelings of dignity and pride and decided that he had been called to preach. He began speaking to mixed crowds with whom neither his brand of religion nor his color were always popular. Although he believed himself an outcast, Apes persevered and remained convinced of his calling. In 1824 he moved to Providence, where he became a leader in a Methodist church and began abstaining from liquor. From 1826 to 1829 he traveled through New York and New England preaching to all and making contacts with various reformers. In 1829, the year he was ordained a Methodist minister, Apes's autobiography was published. Entitled *A Son of the Forest: The Experience of William Apes, A Native of the Forest,* it emphasized racial pride and evangelical Christianity. By this time Apes was well known, and his publications began to reflect certain views of the reform-minded whites who funded his book and pamphlets.

In his revivalist, egalitarian rhetoric, Apes revealed a vision of society adapted to the circumstances of the Indians. While he acknowledged that his people, unlike western tribes, had experienced white rule for two hundred years, Apes offered no prophecy of a return to pre-European days of Indian glory and religion. Indians, he argued, were really descendants of the lost tribes of Israel, and therefore conversion was an important ful-fillment of their biblical heritage. The final kingdom would bring the tri-umph of evangelical social Christianity for all races. Curiously, however, Apes believed in the vanishing race theory so common at that time. Indi-ans would retreat before the white man and vanish for the greater glory of God and America in a society where racial differences no longer mattered; Indians would transcend their past for the greater good while still striving for equality, respect, and an end to exploitation.[17]

An active preacher and author, Apes had yet to transform his ideas into action. While visiting a Pequot reservation in Connecticut, he heard that relations between Indians and whites were deteriorating at Mashpee, and in May 1833 he left for Cape Cod.

Apes first attended one of Fish's services at the Indian meetinghouse. He was taken aback by the sight of Fish preaching to a predominately white congregation. Upset, Apes questioned Fish about his duties and re-sponsibilities. When Fish responded that the Indians had trouble handling the liberty they already had and questioned their capacity for improve-ment, Apes called a public meeting.[18] According to his own account, Apes read from his "sketch of the history of the Indians of New England." A listener responded with cries of "Truth, truth!" and a general discussion of Indian grievances followed. Apes recounted that "it was truly heart-rending to me to hear what my kindred people had suffered at the hands of whites."[19]

Here was Apes's chance to apply his ideas, so he organized the Indians and helped them list their grievances. Not long after, the proprietors voted to adopt Apes into the tribe. On 21 May 1833, only days after Apes's arrival, the Mashpee sent a memorial to the governor and council of Massachu-setts expressing the Indians' hopes and concerns. There was no doubt in the minds of interested whites that Apes was behind it. It is worth quoting at length:

> Permit us poor Indians who for the space of two hundred & ten years or ever since this country has been setled. Who ever have been degraded or imposed upon more or less—by the White man, to address you thus. & as we the Marshpee Tribe speake as the voice of one man we would wish to be heard, & as former attemps has been fruitless. and over ruled by de-sign men that cared not for the Indians any thing further than what they could cheat or rob them out of we trust we shall be heard by your hon-ors—We say as the voice of one man that we are distressed and degraded daily. By those men, who we under stand were appointed by your honor

that they have the rule of every thing. that we are not consulted, is true, and If wee are, they do as they please, and If we say one word we are then called poor drunken Indians, when in fact we are not, that we have joined the temperance cause and wish to be counted so and heard to by your honors.

The memorial went on to list grievances concerning the use of Mashpee meadows and streams by whites and the belief that the treasurer and over-seers were mismanaging Indian funds. The treasurer, Obed Goodspeed, was judged a man of no religious principle "as he says that he does not believe that a man is capable of commiting a crime where by he is made accountable here after." The Mashpee believed that "if we were whites one half [the complaints] would be enough for redress." The document concluded with three resolutions:

RESOLVED
That we as a tribe will rule our selves, and have the right so to do for all men are born free and Equal says the Constitution of the Country

RESOLVED
That we will not permit any white man to come upon our plantation to cut or carry of [*sic*] wood or hay any other artickle with out our permis-sion after the first of July next

RESOLVED
That we will put said resolutions in force after that date July next with the penalty of binding and throwing them from the plantation If they will not stay a way with out

The memorial was signed by 102 persons.[20]

These were strong and eloquent words from a "degraded" people. Couched in the rhetoric of reform, they reflected issues of equality, tem-perance, civil rights, the Constitution, and religion. Though the Mashpee threatened forcible eviction of whites, they proposed first to go through the governor and obtain his consent. In June a delegation including Apes was sent to Boston to present the memorial directly to the governor. While it is not clear exactly what took place, the Indians left Boston mistakenly supposing that Governor Levi Lincoln approved of their reforms. They returned home to implement their resolutions.

On 22 June the tribe notified Obed Goodspeed that he was to turn over the plantation books and papers so that "harmony & peace may prevail amongst us. The governor has been notifyed and it would be agreeable to him, to hear that there was peace."[21] They elected their own tribal council and on 25 June sent out public notices that "said Resolutions be inforced."[22] The next day Phineas Fish was told to "be on the Lookout for another home." Because the Indians desired to "be men in this business and not savages altogether," they provided Fish a detailed list of their complaints. Familiar issues were aired with confidence and pride. They argued that as a people they had not benefited by his preaching and added that "we no [*sic*] of no Indian that has been Converted under your preaching and from 8 to 12 only are your Constant Attenders." Twenty years was "Long Enough for one trial." Most significant was their statement on race.

> We do not be Lieve in your trying to Make us be Lieve that we have not as good Rights to the table of the Lord as others that we are kept back merely because our skin is of A Different Complexion and we find nothing in so doing to Justify you in the scripture

The Indians concluded, "We are for peace rather than any thing else but we are satisfied that we shall never injoy it until we have our Rights." They then threatened to publish their complaints against Fish "to the world" if their requests were not granted and their resolutions not obeyed.[23]

On 25 June the Governor's Committee on the Mashpee Memorial recommended that some discreet person be delegated to visit Mashpee and assess conditions. Lincoln appointed Josiah Fiske, a member of the governor's council, to represent to the Indians "the parental feelings and regard of the Government of the Commonwealth towards them, and especially, the obligation in which the Executive is placed, *under the Laws,* to see that their property is preserved, and that order and quiet are maintained." He offered to replace the guardians only if they were found unjust or unkind; moreover, the governor and council could alter the guardianship system only with the approval of the legislature.[24]

As 1 July approached, the date specified for enforcement of the resolutions, matters became more heated. The guardians and white neighbors of Mashpee were alarmed. Phineas Fish wrote the governor that "a large proportion of the Indians of this place are in a state of insurrection," and he placed the blame squarely on Apes: "All how ever was apparently quiet till a little over a month since a wandering Indian by the name of Apes came along, . . . certainly from the moment of his coming among them, there has been a marked change in the temper & conduct of a large number of the Indians." The new Indian officers of Mashpee were members of the

Baptist faction long opposed to Fish. Fish sensed danger and notified the governor that he was in "no very pleasant, perhaps in a perilous condition" and that "several of the blacks are hostile to the proceedings of their Brethren & that others are kept back from expressing their feelings by terror." On 30 June Lincoln wrote Fiske to delay not *"for an hour more"* in visiting Mashpee.[25] Overseer Gideon Hawley, son of former Mashpee missionary Gideon Hawley, traveled to Worcester to impress upon Lincoln the seriousness of the situation.

The first full attempt to enforce the resolutions came on the scheduled day, 1 July. The Indians trusted that overseer Charles Marston would be "wise and manly enough" to deliver the meetinghouse key to them. More important, a group of nine Indians, including Apes, forcibly prevented two white men from removing wood from reservation land. One of the whites, William Sampson, formally complained that the Indians unlawfully, riotously, and violently assaulted him "to the terror of the people & against the Peace & dignity of the Commonwealth."[26]

The Indians were exhilarated with their new freedom, their boldness fed by the mistaken impression that the governor supported them. Josiah Fiske arrived 2 July at Mashpee and talked with "squaws" but no men or leaders. The women, however, were "in full glee" at the prospect of controlling their own affairs. The rest of the "Indian combatants," as Fiske called them, appeared to be hiding, "concentrated in secret places ready to operate in little squads as occasion may require." Both sides were deadly serious. Fiske wrote Lincoln:

It is thought by the best judges that these insurgents will not be made to submit without arrest or bloodshed—Apes has got the entire control and confidence of nearly all the tribe & they suppose that the Government is fully with him in all his movements. He is a very deceptive imposter—

On 3 July Gideon Hawley and other whites returned to the plantation, to the surprise of both Fiske and the Indians, and hauled away several loads of wood. Though the whites were advised not to proceed, the Indians finally relented but insisted that there would be "serious work" if the whites returned the next day. Fiske could not determine whether the Indians had yielded or whether they were merely taken off guard. One rumor, which Fiske discounted, had Apes riding to Sandwich immediately after the incident for assistance. Fiske learned that several whites intended to return the next day, and he looked forward, as he put it, to "warm work" on the fourth.[27]

A warlike posture, or at least the language of war, was adopted by newspapers, white neighbors, and even the governor. The 4 July *Boston Daily Advocate*, a pro-Mashpee paper, ran a headline "Hostilities Commenced in Marshpee." The *Daily Advocate* of 9 July reported, in the words of an "informant," that Apes "is going about the plantation in full command of all its disposable force and treasure, ordering every white man he meets, to quit the territory of his new Republic." Further, "about thirty of the most able men of the military forces of Cape Cod . . . were to appear on the 3rd, upon the plantation armed and equipped . . . to apprehend the Rev. Mr. Apes and six of his principal counsellors and abbettors." Fortunately, "the commencement of hostilities was postponed for a day or two." Governor Lincoln granted Fiske and the Barnstable sheriff power to call out a posse, and if that should prove insufficient, he promised to "be present personally, to direct any military requisition."[28]

Both the newspapers and Lincoln were several days behind in reporting events, and rumors seem to have swelled as distance from the plantation increased. The climax of the Mashpee "revolution" came, appropriately, on 4 July 1833. A meeting, which began at 9 A.M., at first involved only Fiske and between eighty and one hundred Indians, many armed with muskets. Fiske had advised the overseers not to appear so that the Indians might speak freely. The confident Mashpee stated that they had no complaints that they did not care to make in front of the overseers, who were then summoned and arrived about 10 A.M. in the company of the sheriff and a few deputies. The meeting, which all agreed was orderly, went on until nearly sunset.[29]

Referring to Apes as "the principal manager for the complainants," Fiske thought that "the natives would be yielding enough . . . were it not for Apes their leader." Fiske made little headway, even though it was "very evident" to him that many of the Indians had no idea what had appeared in their memorials. Apes refused to withdraw the resolutions and, in a manner Fiske thought "peremptory," demanded assurances that the plantation would be totally independent.[30] Borrowing from Thomas Jefferson the idea that each generation had a right to act for itself, Apes argued that guardianship laws which had been imposed by the consent of one generation could not be enforced against the will of another.

A member of the governor's council was not about to endorse the idea of a revolution in each generation. Fearing that such an attitude might lead to bloodshed, Fiske had Apes arrested on a warrant secured after the incident on 1 July when two white men were prevented from carrying off some wood from Mashpee lands. The arrest, both sides agreed, was calm, but the reason for its orderliness was a matter of disagreement. Fiske thought the Indians stunned:

> The Indians seemed to have forgotten for a moment that they had muskets with them and looked with perfect amazement at the Sheriff when he was taking their Champion from the Moderator's seat in the meeting house and conducting him with great dignity to a seat in his carriage at the door.

Apes's version, on the contrary, reflected confidence and the belief that the arrest could have been resisted if he had chosen to do so:

> It is admitted by all that nothing was done contrary to good order, though I admit, that if I had refused to obey the warrant, the Sheriff would not have been able to enforce it. The fact is I was in no wise unwilling to go with him, or to have my conduct brought to the test of investigation, or to give all the satisfaction that might be required, had it appeared that I had done wrong.[31]

The arrest quickly subdued the Indians. Apes, however, was released that night on bail, the two hundred dollars supplied by former Mashpee treasurer Lemuel Ewer, a white man. Fiske thought "it was hardly to be believed that any white man whatever would be bail for him." Whites were not pleased to have Apes "at large," but the sheriff was convinced that if bail had been set so high that it could not have been met, the Indians would have been driven to "greater acts of discontent and violence." Rumors persisted that Apes was trying to convince the Indians to hold on to the meetinghouse, but Fiske did not know if they were true, as Apes had acknowledged to Fiske personally "that he has done wrong and promises to desist from any further operations."[32]

The Indians decided to take no further action until the legislature met. Mashpee leader Daniel Amos wrote Fish on 5 July that they were willing to live in peace until the "Law shall Decide." On 8 July the Indians revoked the resolutions pending a decision by the General Court.[33] While the Indians still believed strongly in equality and their right to govern themselves, Fiske was nonetheless pleased with the revocation; after concluding his investigation, he issued a favorable report.

Echoing the language of reform rather than revolution, Fiske explained how he had continually stressed to the Indians the importance of submission to authority and law. If radical tactics had brought their situation to the attention of the authorities and the press, only in retreating from radicalism would the Mashpees achieve a modicum of success. Viewing the Indians almost as sinners redeemed, Fiske ended with praise for them:

> It is but an act of justice to the natives to acknowledge that, in all his interviews with them, the commissioner never received any other than the kindest and most respectful treatment from them. That they had placed themselves in the wrong by their precipitate movements, they at last admitted. They, however, never abandoned the ground, that all men were born free and equal, and that they ought to have the rights to rule and govern themselves.[34]

The Indians continued their campaign into the fall and winter, demanding change yet mindful of the consequences of excess. Their impassioned, but to the modern ear increasingly melodramatic, memorials caused many in the legislature to view their cause favorably. In one memorial, for example, the Mashpees tried to capitalize on support for the Cherokees: "While ye are filled with the fat of our father's land, and enjoy your liberties without molestation, will not this Honorable Body be as benevolent to us, poor Mashpee Indians, who are sighing and weeping under bondage, as ye are to the poor Cherokees?"[35] The Mashpee cause was also pleaded in the Boston press, their principal defender and outlet being Benjamin Hallett's *Daily Advocate*. Engaged as legal counsel for the Mashpees, Hallett published his legal opinion in pamphlet form, *The Rights of the Mashpee Indians*. He was quick to notice a difference between the way Massachusetts reformers talked about the Cherokees and the way the Mashpees were treated:

> We have had an overflow of sensibility in this quarter toward the Cherokees, and there is now an opportunity of showing to the world whether the people of Massachusetts can exercise more justice and less cupidity toward their own Indians than the Georgians have toward the Cherokees.

William Lloyd Garrison's *Liberator* condemned the overseer system and praised the Indians. Eventually even the national press took notice. Apes, however, was continually attacked by the opposition press for inciting the otherwise peaceful Indians to revolt. Finally, in December 1833, Daniel Amos and other Mashpee Indians signed a letter to the *Daily Advocate* stressing that "we know something of our own rights without being told by Mr. Apes or any one."[36] Indeed, Apes's star seemed about to fade.

In March 1834 the Legislative Joint Special Committee on the Mashpee

Indians noted that "the becoming manner in which the Indians have presented their grievances . . . has gone far to atone for the irregularities with which they were doubtless chargeable, last summer" and that the object of "advancing their civility" had been "in a measure attained." Mashpee reacquired the status of a district, and the Indians were granted the right to elect selectmen who would exercise their duties as overseers of the poor, highway surveyors, and school committeemen under the supervision of a single commissioner and a treasurer appointed by the governor. Charles Marston, a former overseer, was appointed commissioner and made himself not only acceptable but even popular by the role he played in easing the transition to self-government.[37]

The Indians' rapid, even surprising, success in changing their form of government was in sharp contrast with their efforts to remove the stubborn Reverend Fish. As early as July 1833, Josiah Fiske had wondered if Fish had outlived his usefulness at Mashpee. In August of the same year, the Mashpee had again written to Harvard asking that Fish be removed.

> The longer he stays the more irritated we are. And now sir if you think that the Indians are worthy of your notice we wish that you would please to communicate to us and let us no [*sic*] what to depend upon—for we think it is time to no [*sic*]—and we say to you and all the world as we have before that we will not hear Mr. Fish preach.[38]

Fish, however, was determined to hold on to his position. He wrote long defenses to Harvard President Josiah Quincy and was able to obtain fifty signatures on a petition of support; he even sent an Indian backer, Nathan Pocknet, to Boston as a supposed representative of the Indians' true feelings. An unreliable emissary, Pocknet "was incapable of attending to his Meals some part of the time being intoxicated and when he was not Able to leave his Bed he would call for Rum . . . and other things in the Way of Conversation that was very much against any Gentlemans Characture."[39]

Harvard was slow to abandon Fish even though embarrassed by his "pastoral failure." Although his salary was cut in half in 1836, little else was done. The years passed, and the Mashpee once more became impatient. In 1840 the Mashpee again forcibly removed Fish from the meetinghouse and changed the lock. In their 1841 "Report of the Committee on the Claims of Mr. Fish & the Mashpee Indians," Harvard's representatives recommended that Fish be cut off entirely from university-controlled funds. Fish made other appeals, even applying to the Society for the Propagation of the Gospel among the Indians and Others in North America for aid to preach to the local poor white population in the Mashpee area who, he argued, had no other minister. Not until 1846 could the Indians write to the president of Harvard that Fish "released all claim to be our Minister and that matter which caused so much trouble is now all settled to mutual Satisfaction. Mr. Fish has sold his house on Marshpee and as we understand, he has no further connexion with Marshpee."[40]

Apes too was eclipsed, although exactly why is unclear. Many whites thought he had been dishonest with the Mashpee, and this suspicion may have spread among the Indians. Perhaps the initial "misunderstanding" over the governor's approval of the Mashpees' first memorial was orchestrated by Apes so that he might implement his reforms more readily. After the meeting with Fiske and Apes's arrest, however, the Indians wanted to consolidate their gains, and they made it clear to the press that Apes was not sole spokesman for the tribe. Having brought recognition, Apes had also courted disaster. As early as 1833, Fish, while obviously looking after his own interests, wrote that "what was once [Apes's] party are now divided & separated. His *followers* are now reduced (comparatively speaking) to a handful." This belief was confirmed by James Walker in his 1835 report to Harvard: Apes "was popular among the Indians for a while but is now understood to be rapidly loosing [*sic*] this confidence, & not without good reason." Benjamin Hallett, a strong defender of the Indians, agreed that the Indians were "dissatisfied with Apes" but gave no explanation.[41] Apes's influence diminished in part due to the increasing popularity of Blind Jo Amos, a native Baptist preacher. More important, the Indians were mollified by the government and pleased with their new freedoms. The time for agitation seemed over.

By 1833–34 the Mashpee had again, after years of disarray, begun to consider themselves a tribe, and outsiders testified to observing signs of a new self-respect. By 1849 the state report on the condition of the Indians gave glowing testimony to the "wonderful improvement which has taken place at Mashpee, since the passage of the act of 1834":

> Previous to that time, they were indolent, ignorant, improvident, intemperate, and licentious. It is not strange that so general a distrust was entertained, at that time, of their ability to manage their internal affairs. But we believe it is admitted now, even by those who most earnestly opposed that law, that the experiment has succeeded; and, though the result may not be all that the most sanguine dreamed, yet, all circumstances considered, it has been all that could rationally be expected.[42]

The Mashpee revolt was a rare success story in a period of continual reversals for American Indians. There is no evidence that the excitement at Mashpee aroused the interest of other Massachusetts Indians, even though, given the proximity of Massachusetts tribes and their frequent intermingling, they must have been aware of the situation. Such open defiance of authority occurred among no other tribes in nineteenth-century Massachusetts, in part simply because they lacked numbers. Mashpee had the largest Indian population in the state, and, with the exception of Gay Head, no other tribe had more than one hundred members. Such small groups were less likely to challenge authority or develop strong group consciousness.

Mashpee, of course, did not become an Indian paradise. Prejudice, poverty, lack of full civil rights, and the obstinate Phineas Fish would remain, but the revolt of 1833 and subsequent events indicate how Indians dealt with themselves and the outside world, how they were able to make use of the rhetoric and techniques of the white man's reform movement, and how, in this instance, they were able to revitalize their community and achieve a measure of self-government.

Author's Postscript

In *On Our Own Ground: The Complete Writings of William Apess, A Pequot* (Amherst: University of Massachusetts Press, 1992), p. xv, Barry O'Connell has written that, with the exception of the Mashpee revolt, historians record no expressions of Indian rights or significant organizations, cultural, political, or otherwise, among Native Americans in New England in the nineteenth century. Although the revolt itself has not spawned an abundance of scholarship, its central place in the history of the Mashpees and the life of William Apes ensures continued reconsiderations. Most recent work on the Mashpees arises out of and reflects the relatively recent legal and political battles waged by the Mashpees to gain recognition as a tribe and recover land. The key event was a forty-day federal trial in which the jury concluded that the Mashpees did not constitute a tribe at crucial points in their history. The district court upheld the jury's verdict and was affirmed by the First Circuit Court of Appeals. 447 F. Supp. 940 (D. Mass. 1978), *aff'd* 592 F.2d 575 (1st Cir.), *cert. denied,* 444 U.S. 866 (1979).

The jury concluded that the Mashpees were a tribe in 1834 and 1842, shortly after the revolt, but not thereafter (or before). Exactly how the jury arrived at its verdict is unclear, but sufficient evidence existed to find that the intense political activity at Mashpee between 1833 and 1842 was novel for the group and limited in time and scope of objective. The goal of becoming a district with certain rights of self-government was achieved in

1834, and that of being permitted to divide common land among Indian members of the community was achieved in 1842. The jury could have found that the tribal organization, having accomplished its purposes, became less important to the community, and indeed the Mashpees' opponents presented evidence that the tribe had assimilated into general non-Indian society, that assimilation was voluntary, and that the Indian residents focused more on the ability of individuals to compete as members of the larger society than of the tribe to resist that society. It is not obvious that the Indians of 1833, inspired by the rhetoric of reform, evangelical Christianity, and republican rights, would have disapproved of such a result.

Contemporary Mashpee partisans, seeking tribal recognition and the rewards that go with it, have expended considerable effort trying to explain their failure. The most compelling of these efforts is Jack Campisi's *The Mashpee Indians: Tribe on Trial* (Syracuse: Syracuse University Press, 1991). Campisi, an anthropologist and expert witness for the Mashpees, does not hide his sympathies for the Indians or his frustration with the legal system. In addition to his discussion of the trial, Campisi presents a valuable ethnohistory of the Mashpees, including a short section on the 1833 revolt and the events surrounding it. As an advocate, and understandably in light of the jury verdict, Campisi treats the 1833 revolt not as a unique expression of rights and identity by the Mashpees but as one of many important events in a historical continuum revealing the Mashpees' essential character and tribal attributes.

Campisi, along with other advocates for the Mashpees, provides some evidence for the principle that a culture is most stridently defended when it is irretrievably lost. In *Restitution: The Land Claims of the Mashpee, Passamaquoddy, and Penobscot Indians of New England* (Boston: Northeastern University Press, 1985), journalist and long-time friend of the Mashpees Paul Brodeur focuses on contemporary Mashpees and blames their court defeat on political factors. Russell M. Peters, a Mashpee Indian leader and witness in the trial, wrote *The Wampanoags of Mashpee: An Indian Perspective* (n.p., n.d.) in an effort to show how the Mashpees maintain a spiritual and cultural identity. James Clifford, "Identity in Mashpee," in *The Predicament of Culture: Twentieth-Century Ethnography, Literature, and Art* (Cambridge: Harvard University Press, 1988), provides further perspective on the trial and contemporary Mashpees without delving into the historical record.

Barry O'Connell's lengthy introduction to *On Our Own Ground* is a thorough and scholarly analysis of Apes and his writing which provides new information and helps to fill out the relative scarcity of books and articles on New England Indians in the nineteenth century. In contrast to Campisi, who was attempting to show historical continuity among the Mashpees, O'Connell emphasizes Apes's (a Pequot) role in initiating and leading the Mashpee revolt. O'Connell at times appears to overstate his case and romanticize Apes (who is set against generic "Euroamerican" racist aggressors), and his literary criticism is beyond the scope of this postscript, but O'Connell's work is clearly a vital contribution to understanding Apes as an historical and literary figure in nineteenth-century New England.

Notes

1. Although the nomenclature "Mashpee" is uniformly used today, "Marshpee" was more common in the nineteenth century. In this article "Mashpee" will be used except in direct quotations.

2. The only complete census of Massachusetts Indians, conducted by John Milton Earle and published in 1861, lists 1,438 Indians in 376 families across the state. *Report to the Governor and Council, Concerning the Indians of the Commonwealth, Under the Act of April 6, 1859,* Massachusetts Senate Document No. 96 (Boston: William White, 1861).

3. *Reports of Cases Argued and Determined in the Supreme Judicial Court of the Commonwealth of Massachusetts,* vol. 13 (Philadelphia, 1823), November 1816, "The Inhabitants of Andover *versus* The Inhabitants of Canton."

4. Frank G. Speck, "Reflections upon the Past and Present of the Massachusetts Indians," *Massachusetts Archaeological Society Bulletin* 4 (April 1943): 36.

5. Levi Lincoln to Josiah Fiske, 27 June 1833, Guardians of Indian Plantations and Related Records, 1788–1865/Secretary of State, Archives of the Commonwealth, Boston, Mass. All quotations by permission.

6. Enumeration of Proprietors and Non Proprietors of Mashpee. November 1832, Guardians of Indian Plantations.

7. James Walker, "Facts in Regard to the Difficulties at Marshpee," 17 October 1835, Marshpee Indians 1811 to 1841, Harvard University Archives, Cambridge, Mass. All quotations by permission of the Harvard University Archives.

8. For debate over the effects of racial mixing between Indians and blacks in Massachusetts, see, e.g., Report of the Select Committee, 4 November 1841, Society for the Propagation of the Gospel among the Indians and Others in North America, Massachusetts Historical Society (MHS), Boston, Mass.; Report of F. Parkman on the Schools etc. among the Indians, 29 October 1835, MHS, and *Report of the Commissioners Relating to the Condition of the Indians of Massachusetts* (Boston, 1849). Gideon Hawley, missionary at Mashpee from 1758 to 1807, considered blacks inferior to Indians and feared that Mashpee would be taken over by blacks and foreigners. Hawley to James Freeman, 2 November 1802, Hawley Papers, MHS.

9. Lorenzo Greene, *The Negro in Colonial New England, 1620–1776* (New York: Columbia University Press, 1942), pp. 95–96.

10. Frederick Freeman, *The History of Cape Cod: The Annals of Barnstable County, including the District of Mashpee,* 2 vols. (Boston: The Author, 1858–62), 1:692; *Boston Daily Advocate,* 3 March 1834.

11. "Contract between the Marshpee Overseers and Phineas Fish," 23 August 1811; "Contract of the Corporation of Harvard with Phineas Fish," 18 September 1811, Marshpee Indians 1811 to 1841.

12. Phineas Fish to John Thornton Kirkland, 1 May 1824, Marshpee Indians 1811 to 1841.

13. Fish to Josiah Quincy, 25 November 1833, Marshpee Indians 1811 to 1841.

14. Fish to John Davis, 11 August 1810, Harvard College Papers, vol. 6, 1809–11, Harvard University Archives.

15. Josiah Fiske, sent by Governor Levi Lincoln to investigate the revolt at Mashpee in 1833, estimated the number of natives hearing Fish on 7 July 1833 at 18. In 1834 Fish's rival, William Apes, estimated that Fish spoke to between 5 and 20 natives with not one male among them. Apes estimated his own audience at 50 to 70 and that of another Indian preacher (Blind Jo Amos) at 30 to 50. Fiske to Lincoln, 6 and 7 July 1833, Guardians of Indian Plantations, and William Apes, 30 July 1834, Marshpee Indians 1811 to 1841.

16. Apes's autobiography, *A Son of the Forest: The Experience of William Apes, a Native of the Forest* (New York, 1831), is the source used for most biographical material about him. Barry O'Connell's thorough introduction to *On Our Own Ground: The Complete Writings of William Apess, A Pequot* (Amherst: University of Massachusetts Press, 1992) is also quite valuable. The spelling of Apes's name cannot be definitively given, and O'Connell, for valid reasons, uses "Apess," although "Apes" is the more common version. Kim McQuaid's "William Apes, Pequot: An Indian Reformer in the Jackson Era," *New England Quarterly* 50 (December 1977): 605–25 (chap. 15 of *New England Encounters*), should also be consulted.

17. McQuaid, "William Apes," p. 613.

18. Fish had expressed such opinions before. In 1826 he had cited the Indians' instability of character as a reason for protectionism. While they often set out with "great ardour," he explained, Indians soon returned to "habits of profligacy." The Indians themselves, he continued, were aware of this tendency and feared to take the first steps toward civilization. See Fish to Kirkland, 25 June 1826, Marshpee Indians 1811 to 1841. The situation at Mashpee in some ways parallels the model set forth by Anthony F. C. Wallace in *The Death and Rebirth of the Seneca* (New York: Random House, 1969) and William G. McLoughlin in *Revivals, Awakenings, and Reform* (Chicago: University of Chicago Press, 1978).

19. William Apes, *Indian Nullification of the Unconstitutional Laws of Massachusetts Relative to the Marshpee Tribe; or, The Pretended Riot Explained* (Boston, 1835), p. 17. Much of the background for the revolt is taken from this source and the reports of Josiah Fiske, in Guardians of Indian Plantations.

20. Memorial of the Marshpee Indians, 21 May 1833, Guardians of Indian Plantations.

21. The Marshpee Tribe to Obed Goodspeed, 22 June 1833, Guardians of Indian Plantations.

22. Public Notice of the Marshpee Tribe, 25 June 1833, Guardians of Indian Plantations.

23. Daniel Amos to Fish, 26 June 1833, Guardians of Indian Plantations.

24. Report of the Governor's Committee on the Memorials of the Marshpee Indians, 25 June 1833, and Levi Lincoln to Josiah Fiske, 27 June 1833, Guardians of Indian Plantations.

25. Fish to Lincoln, 28 June 1833, and Lincoln to Fiske, 30 June 1833, Guardians of Indian Plantations.

26. Daniel Amos to Charles Marston, 1 July 1833, and Complaint of William Sampson, [1–4?] July 1833, Guardians of Indian Plantations.

27. Fiske to Lincoln, 3 July 1833, noon and 6 P.M., Guardians of Indian Plantations.

28. Boston *Daily Advocate,* 4 and 9 July 1833; Lincoln to Fiske, 5 July 1833, Guardians of Indian Plantations.

29. For descriptions of the meeting by the participants, see Fiske to Lincoln, 4 July 1833, Guardians of Indian Plantations; Commissioners Report, *Documents Printed by Order of the Senate of the Commonwealth of Massachusetts During the Session of the General Court,* A.D. *1834* (Boston: Dutton & Wentworth, 1834), 14: 24–25, and Apes, *Nullification.*

30. Fiske to Lincoln, 4 July 1833, Guardians of Indian Plantations; Commissioners Report, *Massachusetts Senate Documents, 1834,* 14:23–24.

31. Fiske to Lincoln, 4 July 1833, Guardians of Indian Plantations; Apes, *Nullification,* p. 36.

32. Apes had said of Ewer, "Lemuel Ewer, Esq. of South Sandwich, who had, in former times, been treasurer of the tribe, knew their wrongs, and was their friend. It was well for me that there was one man who knew on which side the right lay, and had the courage to support it, for I verily believe that no other person would have dared to become my bondsman" (*Nullification,* p. 38). Fiske to Lincoln, 5 July 1833, Guardians of Indian Plantations.

33. Daniel Amos to Fish, 5 July 1833, and Public Notice of the Marshpee Tribe, 8 July 1833, Guardians of Indian Plantations.

34. Commissioners Report, *Massachusetts Senate Documents, 1834,* 14:33.

35. "Memorial of the Mashpee Indians," January 1834, *Massachusetts Senate Documents, 1834,* 11:11–14.

36. Boston *Daily Advocate,* 10 August 1833; *Liberator,* 25 January 1834; e.g., *Niles' Weekly Register,* 29 November 1834; *Boston Daily Advocate,* 27 December 1833.

37. "Report of the Joint Special Committee Relative to the Marshpee Indians," and "An Act to Establish the District of Marshpee," *Massachusetts Senate Documents, 1834,* 65:1–13.

38. Marshpee Indians to Harvard College, 5 August 1833, Harvard College Papers, 2d ser., vol. 6, Harvard University Archives.

39. Josiah Fiske to Levi Lincoln, 6 July 1833, Guardians of Indian Plantations; Fish to Josiah Quincy, 5 December 1833, 7 December 1833, and 29 January 1834, and "Mrs. Wallace certificate respecting Nathan Pocknet and Wm. Amos," 3 February 1834, Marshpee Indians 1811 to 1841. In spite of the image presented by Pocknet, a temperance society had been formed at Mashpee in October 1833; Apes was president.

40. Harvard Corporation Records, 1827–36, vol. 7, pp. 430–35, 21 July 1836, Harvard University Archives; Francis Hutchens, *Mashpee: The Story of Cape Cod's Indian Town* (West Franklin, N.H.: Amarta Press, 1979); "Report of the Committee on the Claims of Mr. Fish & the Marshpee Indians," July 1841, Harvard University Archives; "Petition to the President and Fellows of Harvard University," July 1846, Harvard College Papers, 2d ser., vol. 8.

41. Fish to Quincy, 7 December 1833, Marshpee Indians 1811 to 1841, and James Walker, 17 October 1835, "Facts in Regard to the Difficulties at Marshpee," and Hallett to Walker, 11 September 1835, Marshpee Indians 1811 to 1841.

42. *Report of the Commissioners*, p. 37.

15

William Apes, Pequot
An Indian Reformer in the Jacksonian Era

KIM MCQUAID

Writings about Indian-white relations in New England, as elsewhere, have focused overwhelmingly on the white participants, such as Roger Williams, John Eliot, or John Quincy Adams. Occasionally a book or article gives center stage to an Indian leader whose resistance or accommodation was exceptional—King Philip, for example, or Squanto, or Samson Occom—but they are notable exceptions. Most other Native Americans in early New England remain anonymous, partly because of historians' conscious or unconscious choices, partly because of the surviving sources' frustrating selectivity. Even with the best of intentions, scholars often cannot reconstruct the lives of historically significant Indians.

That, fortunately, is not the case with William Apes (his preference for "Apes" suggests the correct pronunciation). The previous essay (see chapter 14) documents Apes's important contribution to the Mashpee revolt of 1833 and, in the process, gives a glimpse of his life before that important event. In this chapter, Kim McQuaid looks closely at Apes's full career and at his several publications, both before and after his involvement at Mashpee.

Apes's response to the prejudices of his time combined resistance and accommodation. As a Christian preacher and a believer in the Indians as a "vanishing race," he was a spokesman for Euroamerican culture; as an advocate of Indian (and black) equality, on the other hand, he fought against the prevailing American notions of racial hierarchy, in which Indians and African Americans were assigned to the bottom level. For most of his adult life, Apes struggled against institutionalized racism through his temporary leadership of the Mashpee revolt and, of more lasting importance, through his preaching and writing.

McQuaid's insightful account of William Apes offers a fitting conclusion to this volume. Apes was a son of New England: born in Massachusetts, raised mostly in Connecticut, resident for a time in Rhode Island, and an itinerant preacher throughout the region. He embodied both Indian and Euroamerican ancestry and perhaps (judging from dominant patterns of miscegenation in nineteenth-century eastern Indian communities) African American as well, and he preached to all races. Apes also symbolizes the reemergence in the nineteenth century of Native Americans as significant players on the New England socio-political scene. Finally, his Pequot ancestry and his authorship of a sympathetic reassessment of the Wampanoag sachem King Philip link the 1830s thematically to the 1630s and 1670s. The life of William Apes, Pequot, brings this collection of essays full circle.

$\mathcal{D}$URING THE first half-century of the United States' national existence, the pattern of Indian-white relations changed markedly. Since early colonial days, few citizens had ever believed that tribal folkways and collective land tenure systems could long survive in an ambitious, expansionary society operating according to European legal precepts, property rights, and governance. Indians must cede their lands when required—or face wars that would, in time, decimate their numbers. Yet, within this broad pattern of consensus, there existed a subsidiary desire to "civilize" aboriginal tribes rather than to drive them beyond the boundaries of white settlements. Missionaries, Quaker philanthropists, and a handful of influential politicians (notably Thomas Jefferson) sought to instill an appreciation for Christianity, private property, and agricultural technique in the minds of their Indian brethren. Thereby, they reasoned, Native Americans could gradually amalgamate themselves into the social and pecuniary customs of a growing nation state. Government and religious officials both urged tribes like the Chickasaw, Choctaw, Creek, Seminole, Tuscarora, Oneida, and Delaware along the "White Man's Road." Seneca and Cherokee leaders, Chiefs John Ross and Handsome Lake among them, sought more ambitious translations of white institutions within traditionalist social and religious frameworks. In western Massachusetts and northern New York, Eastern Algonquin remnants in the Stockbridge and Brothertown tribes were effectively reorganized by leaders like the Mohegan Indian preacher Samson Occom. Throughout much of the rest of New England, missionary attentions were finally being drawn towards small and impoverished tribes like the Penobscot, Passamaquoddy, and Montauk.[1]

The triumph of Andrew Jackson in the 1828 presidential elections, however, spelled disaster for nascent amalgamationist efforts. Speaking for the land-hungry settlers of the western frontiers, Jackson proposed a forthright policy of "Indian Removal" beyond the Mississippi River. Rather than being acculturated within American society, Indians should be relocated beyond its boundaries where, presumably, they might obtain a relative geographic and temporal freedom to work out their own cultural destiny separated from the degenerative effects of customary white-Indian contacts. Jackson's mixture of expediency and power politics elicited a generally enthusiastic response from political leaders like ex-president James Monroe, John Calhoun, and Lewis Cass. Only a handful of northeastern congressmen, joined by Tennessee Whig and frontiersman David Crockett, opposed the Jacksonian program. Accordingly, after suitable pietistic verbalisms, Congress passed the so-called "Indian Removal Act" in May 1830. In the succeeding decade, despite protests from Indians and ill-organized reform elements alike, the vast majority of Indians were cleared from the states and territories east of the Mississippi. In 1832, when Chief Black Hawk led a forlorn attempt to reoccupy Sauk-Fox lands in western Illinois, Jackson appointed a commissioner of Indian Affairs within the war department to administer the relocation campaign.[2]

It was plainly not a period for optimistic assumptions on the part of Indians residing in or near the white settlements. The preservation of remaining property rights and cultural patterns would be difficult, at best. Among southern New England's tribal remnants, the situation was particularly dire. Exposed to the corroding influences of white culture for almost two centuries, scattered bands of Mohegans, Pequots, Narragansetts, and Wampanoags were socially degraded, culturally disorganized, economically exploited, and politically disfranchised. Yet, even among these Indian populations, reformers attempted to regain some small part of the rights and dignities that New England's aborigines had so emphatically lost. Perhaps the best-known of these early native Indian rights advocates was William Apes, of the Pequot (or Pequod) tribe.[3]

Born in a woods encampment near Colrain, Massachusetts, in 1798, William Apes was one of three children born to a "half-breed" father and an Indian mother. For a year after William's birth, the Apes family lived in sparsely settled areas making and selling baskets. They then moved to Colchester, Connecticut—within convenient distance of the two tiny reservations still held by the Pequot tribe. After three years of "comparative comfort," the family disintegrated. William and his siblings were abandoned by their mother and father and left in the care of alcoholic maternal grandparents. Intemperance soon exacted a personal toll. At the age of five, young William had been so badly beaten by his Indian grandmother that he required the service of two physicians and a year's support from town charity funds to ensure his recovery. At age six, he was "bound out" as a pauper by town officials until he should reach the age of twenty-one. Apes's sympathetic white foster parents were devout Baptists who introduced him to religious observances and allowed him the six years of winter school sessions that constituted his entire formal education. Absorbing his foster parents' attitudes towards Indians—and remembering his own wretched childhood—young William feared the possibility of any eventual return to his native society.

For several years, Apes's childhood was relatively free from stress. But, by the age of eleven, whippings, slurs upon his Indian ancestry, and precocious non-Baptist religious interests had alienated him from his white guardians. After he made a halfhearted attempt to abscond, Apes learned that his indenture was sold to an affluent New London Presbyterian for twenty dollars. Within a year following his arrival at his new home, William ran off again, visited his Indian father for a week, then returned to his white master. In short order, his disputatious behavior caused him to be sold to another Presbyterian family in the city. Until the age of fifteen, young Apes suffered only occasional indignities in his new home, but thereafter, his penchant for attending Methodist revival meetings stirred up new problems. Energized by the Christian ideal that Christ had died for *all* men, including Indians, William refused to cease his desperate religious strivings. As Apes later recounted:

> I had no character to lose in the estimation of those who were accounted great. For what cared they for me? They had possession of the red man's inheritance, and had deprived me of liberty; with this they were satisfied, and could do as they pleased; therefore, I thought I could do as I pleased, measurably.[4]

In March 1813, the young Indian boy, confused about his own cultural background and individual worth, underwent a religious awakening that affected the remainder of his life. Shortly thereafter, the family to whom he was indentured forbade him to attend any more Methodist revivals. Within months, he ran away from his third foster home—never to return. After a series of wanderings which took him to New York City, Apes obtained a job paying sixty-two cents a day and began achieving some stability. His respite, however, proved ephemeral. When his foster parents offered a reward of $15.00 for his return to New London, Apes, fearful of discovery, fled from his new abode. On his way to Philadelphia, he fell in with a United States Army recruiting party, got drunk, and enlisted as a drummer boy. After the hangover wore off, Apes found himself in an uncongenial environment. Following several dissolute months in an encampment near New York, his unit moved north to Plattsburgh in preparation for an invasion of the Canadas. Along the route, Apes was arbitrarily reclassified as a combat infantryman. Believing that the terms of his enlistment had been violated, Apes soon deserted. While trying to reach his Indian father's home, he was apprehended, threatened with "Indian tortures" by irate officers, then made a driver for an artillery team. During the next two years, he served honorably in several halfhearted American invasions of Canadian territory and engaged in the spirited defense of Plattsburgh which formed part of the Battle of Lake Champlain. After the armistice, Apes, like hundreds of other Indian recruits in the American forces, was released without the back pay, recruitment bounties, or 160-acre homesteading options tendered to enfranchised veterans.

Embittered, Apes lived with fellow Indians in northern New York and then, seeking work, emigrated to Canada. Intemperance hampered his ability to find or retain jobs, but during the next two years, he worked as a baker, farmhand, sailor, and store clerk from Montreal westwards to the Bay of Quinte. Along with other disorganized Indian groups in the Canadas, Apes responded to the ambitious missionary efforts of the Methodist Church. Late in 1817, the itinerant Pequot, then nineteen years old, decided to return to his tribe's homeland. Economic hardships, prodigalities, and occasional exposure to anti-Indian prejudice marked his six-to-nine-month journey. After being reunited with a pious aunt and other relations living on or near the Pequot reservation in Groton, Connecticut, young Apes sought a more secure foundation for his life.[5]

His task was hardly easy. Since his tribe's decimation during the so-called Pequot War of 1637, its numbers had dwindled until, by 1740, only about 250 remained on two tiny reserves. The most feared tribe in early colonial New England (whose name meant "destroyers of men" in the Narragansett tongue), the Pequots were subjected to a series of injustices. In the seventeenth century, many tribesmen were sold into slavery in the West Indies. Throughout the eighteenth and early nineteenth centuries, little or nothing was done to preserve tribal lands and rights against white encroachments. Institutions of intellectual, religious, and agricultural instruction were nonexistent. Drunkenness, social disorganization, and poverty took their toll. About a third of the tribe's population eked out an existence as agricultural laborers, while the remainder engaged in subsistence farming, basket weaving, occasional seafaring, and other irregular employments. "The whole body of these Indians," Yale College President Timothy Dwight imperiously remarked after a visit in the autumn of 1800,

> are a poor, degraded and miserable race of beings . . . shrunk into the tameness and torpor of reasoning brutism. All the vice of the original [Pequot racial stock] is left. All its energy has vanished. . . . Their chil-

dren, when young, they place in English families as servants. In the earlier parts of life these children frequently behave well; but when grown
up throw off all that is respectable in their character and sink to the [de-
graded] level of their relatives.[6]

More sympathetic observers, like young Harvard graduate Henry David
Thoreau, agreed that the remnants of the Pequot and other New England
tribes were vanishing before the march of white civilization like dew in a
summer sun. Pequot cruelty and barbarism became a staple subject in New
England juvenile literature. Latter-day classics like *Moby Dick* (1851) also
mirrored the climate of opinion, when, for example, Herman Melville had
Captain Ahab set off upon his merciless search for the white whale in the
Pequod.[7]

By 1818, William Apes had survived a broken family, difficult appren-
ticeships, war, liquor, and poverty. His future hardly appeared bright, but
within the next five years the tenor of his life and purposes began to
change. Shortly after his return to the Groton reservation, Apes, like many
of his fellow tribesmen, hired himself to a local farmer. At the conclusion
of the harvest, problems developed. "[W]hen I wanted my pay," Apes later
recalled, the farmer

> undertook to treat me as he would a degraded African slave, [and] he
> took a cart-stake in order to pay me; but he soon found out his mistake,
> as I made him put it down as quick as he had taken it up. I had been
> cheated so often that I determined to have my rights this time, and for-
> ever after.[8]

Apes's life patterns became "quite steady" after this event. The twenty-
year-old Indian continued to work for local farmers, attended Methodist
meetings, and took part in occasional revivals. After several years at Groton, Apes decided to visit his parents near Colrain, Massachusetts, where
some small improvement in family fortunes had taken place. His father
was now a practicing Baptist and a shoemaker. Glad to be reunited with
parents he had not known since infancy, Apes agreed to spend the winter
of 1821–22 at Colrain to learn the trade of shoemaking. Seemingly, the
young Indian's sense of his own dignity grew steadily during this period.[9]
After holding religious discussions with his father, William decided that
he had been "called" to preach the gospel. Despite his fears that whites
would not hear a "poor ignorant Indian," Apes began speaking to mixed
audiences. Large crowds came to "see the Indian preach," but not all were
friendly. Apes was pelted with missiles and epithets by whites who admired neither his theology nor his complexion. But the twenty-three-year-

old Indian continued to "exercise his gift." By early 1822, however, Apes's father had joined the ranks of those who demanded that his lay sermonizings cease. The local Methodist circuit rider, angered by Apes's lack of a ministerial license, finally forbade him to preach.[10]

This setback almost ruined Apes. Not only had his right to exercise his calling been denied by religious authorities, but his own father had joined the ranks of his opponents. For some months Apes believed himself to be an "outcast from society" and reacted accordingly. Finally, however, he returned to the Groton reservation to be near his beloved aunt, Sally George, who assisted him in gathering together small congregations of Pequots to hear his words. Apes also occasionally traveled to nearby Saybrook, Connecticut, to meet in worship with a group of African Americans. By the time William's aunt died in 1826, his position had again improved. Between 1823 and 1824, Apes married a thirty-six-year-old woman of "nearly the same color" as himself.[11] While fathering several children, Apes supported his wife and family by farming, day labor, and a short career as a tavern keeper. In 1824, he removed to Providence, Rhode Island, to visit his sister where, shortly thereafter, he became a "class leader" in a Methodist church for two years. Though often absent from home, Apes saved money and began abstaining from liquor. During the next three years, Apes began traveling about New England and New York preaching to white, Indian, and black congregations and selling religious tracts. Finally, in 1829, he was regularly ordained as a minister by the Methodist Society.[12]

Slowly, Apes gained repute as an "Indian preacher." In 1829, he published a short autobiography, *A Son of the Forest*. Two years later a second, enlarged edition of the work appeared— funded by various "respectable persons" whom he had met in his travels. In this work, and in several tracts published soon after, the author's religious and social concerns were clearly set forth. William Apes's evangelical Christianity was of a highly "muscular" and egalitarian variety. Christ, the "suffering and risen Saviour," had died for *all* men—including Indians. Whites must repent the errors of their ways, cease enslaving and warring against the colored races, and civilize them through missionary activity, education, and expanded sociopolitical rights. "If black or red skins, or any other skin of color is disgraceful to God," Apes remarked,

> it appears that [God] has disgraced himself a great deal—for he has made fifteen colored people to one white, and placed them here upon this earth.

God was no respecter of persons. He had chosen his apostles "not from the noble and mighty . . . but from the walks of obscurity." So, his latter-day servants might well come from among even the most degraded populations of Indians and blacks.[13]

Like most educated men of his time, Apes believed that Indians were a "vanishing race," but this did not imply that Native Americans could be ignored by white society. John the Baptist had been born a Jew. He and his co-religionists had seen Hebrew society conquered, enslaved, and scattered to the ends of the earth. But he had chosen to transcend his past to preach God's Word: to subsume Judaism into the greater glory of Christianity. So, too, Apes would assist Indians, whites, and blacks to sink their racial differences under the banner of evangelical social Christianity. Indians might, indeed, vanish. But they would do so for the greater glory of God and American society.

Williams Apes's effort to create a secure place for the Indian within a white world also predisposed him to accept a notably inaccurate theory of Indian evolution. Since about 1815, assorted religious publicists had argued that American "Indians" were really descendants of the Ten Lost Tribes of Israel. Discovery of the mysterious but impressive remains of the so-called "Mound Builder" civilization in the midwestern states lent credence to the idea. If, indeed, Indians were really strayed Hebrews, it was even more incumbent upon a Christian civilization peacefully to convert the "sons of the forest" rather than exterminate them. As "unshackled, free-born men" in whom "the blood of Israel" flowed, Indians deserved freedom from exploitation and enhanced respect in the eyes of their fellow men.[14]

Apes's religious approach was clearly nonconformist. He stood forth as one of the relatively few spokesmen arguing for equality of whites, blacks, and Indians in an era when "Indian Removal" had become a popular national policy. But such views had, as yet, not led him into reform activity. He had done little to better the economic and political position of Indians living on or near the small reservations scattered throughout New England—people whom he judged (with some accuracy) as being "the most mean, abject, miserable race of beings in the world."[15]

In May 1833, however, this situation changed dramatically. While visiting the Groton Pequot reservation, Apes was advised to visit the Wampanoags in Mashpee, Massachusetts, on the south shore of Cape Cod. Relations between the tribe and their resident white minister, Reverend Phineas Fish, were deteriorating, and moves were afoot to gain expanded political and economic rights. Shortly after Apes arrived in Mashpee, his fears about the gravity of the situation were confirmed.

The problems at Mashpee had been developing for almost two centuries. In 1660, Reverend Richard Bourne had obtained a grant of 10,500 acres near Barnstable, Massachusetts, upon which to settle and proselytize scattered Indian groups. Before his death in 1667, Bourne, a spiritual follower of the famous Indian missionary John Eliot, had set up a nonalienable reserve for his "Praying Indians." Though almost all other such "Praying Towns" were destroyed by enraged colonists during King Philip's War of 1675–76, Mashpee survived. In the following century, five ministers (three whites and two Indians) preserved the settlement. They did not do so without cost. In 1760, the Mashpee tribe had sent a representative to the court of King George III complaining about their lack of civil and political rights. Following the issuance of a royal decree, the Massachusetts colonial legislature granted the inhabitants the right to elect officers for the territory. With the outbreak of the Revolutionary War, however, Massachusetts legislators rescinded Mashpee's right to self-government despite the fact that the tribe had sent a higher percentage of its total male population to serve in the Continental forces than any other town on Cape Cod. By 1783, several score Indians had been killed in action or died of disease. But, for all that, "[a]fter helping America to win her freedom, the tribe lost its own." A board of three nonresident white overseers was appointed by the governor and council of Massachusetts to rule over the Mashpees. These overseers possessed broadly defined powers. They could, as one journalist summarized,

> regulate the police of the plantation . . . establish rules for managing the affairs, interests, and concerns of the Indians and inhabitants . . . improve and lease the lands of the Indians and their *tenements*, regulate their streams, ponds, and fisheries,—mete out lots for their particular improvement—control and regulate their bargains, contracts, wages, and other dealings, take care of their poor, and bind out their children to suitable persons.[16]

Such absolute powers were bound to create abuses. The absentee overseers were made the judges of the "just debts" of their Indian wards, and could, if they deemed it necessary, bind out "idle" or drunken Indians for recurrent three-year periods until they mended their ways. Inhabitants of Mashpee could not even cut wood on their own lands until they had received permission from, and paid charges to, the overseers. Lacking any voice in their government, the Mashpees were sometimes defrauded of wages, lacked legal or police protection, and saw white contractors purchase rights to cut down large areas of their timber. Even in the religious sphere, they had little or no control over their destinies. An Indian mission church had functioned at Mashpee since late in the seventeenth century.

By the late eighteenth century, however, ministers were established at Mashpee without the wishes of the Native Americans having been consulted.[17]

Such political and economic subjection seemingly did not bother most of the citizens of Massachusetts. Few, indeed, even knew of the continued existence of Indian reservations in the state. For those who did know, the "degenerate and degraded" condition of the Mashpee tribe seemed to rule out democratic procedures. In large part, the problem was race. Over several centuries, Portuguese, Cape Verdeans, Hessian prisoners of war, and free blacks had intermarried with the Wampanoag Indians at Mashpee. In a nation that lacked mulatto or *mestizo* racial-ethnic classifications, the Mashpees were stigmatized as "half breeds" or "mongrels." The fact that the Mashpees had a relatively larger infusion of "Negro blood" than nearby tribes such as the Gay Head Indians on Martha's Vineyard further prejudiced white opinion. In 1815, for example, an anonymous author in the *North American Review* compared Mashpee to

> a pasture, which is capable of feeding fifteen to sixteen hundred sheep; but into which several good-natured and visionary gentlemen have put three or four hundred wolves, foxes, and skunks, by way of experiment, with the hope that they might in time be tamed. . . . But the attempt has been in vain. . . . [I]t is surely time [the reviewer concluded] that the State should cease to maintain a depot for vagabonds of all colours; from all parts of the country; or keep up an establishment for producing every possible variety of *cross*, between Indians and Negroes.[18]

When William Apes came to Mashpee in May 1833, he soon became an enthusiastic social reformer. Reverend Mr. Fish, the incumbent minister, was devoting almost no attention to the spiritual welfare of the Indians; he preferred instead to preach to congregations of neighboring whites. When Apes suggested that Fish help the Mashpees obtain expanded economic and political rights, Fish replied that the tribe had "quite liberty enough." If given more, they would only sell all of their lands to gratify the desires of the moment. Though Fish advised against stirring up discontents, Apes held several public meetings. When the Indians began detailing long-standing complaints, further discussion ensued, and Apes organized a council to draw up grievances. One hundred of the adult tribesmen voted to adopt Apes and his family into the Mashpee tribe so that he might serve as a spokesman in negotiations with the overseers and the Massachusetts state government. Shortly thereafter, Apes moved his family to Mashpee. On 21 May 1833, a large majority of the tribe assembled in council and passed the following resolutions:

1. RESOLVED, that we, as a tribe, will rule overselves, and have a right to do so; for all men are born free and equal, says the Constitution [*sic*] of the country.

2. RESOLVED, that we will not permit any white man to come upon our plantations, to cut or carry off wood or hay, or any other article, without our permission, after the 1st of July next.

3. Resolved that we will put said resolutions in force after that date [1 July 1833] with the penalty of binding and throwing [white trespassers] from the plantation, if they will not stay away without.

A companion resolution was also sent to Harvard College. The executor of a will from whose resources ministers at Mashpee were largely paid advised that the Mashpees intended to discharge Fish and choose their own ministers.[19]

Such actions aroused interest and opposition throughout the surrounding white communities. About a week after the Mashpee tribe's resolutions were adopted, William Apes journeyed to New Bedford to defend them. "Strong excitement" took place among members of the audience fearful that Apes's advocacy of Indian rights would provoke African American insurrections. Though Quaker spokesmen supported the Mashpees' position, local papers branded Apes as an impostor or outside agitator. In June 1833, Apes was part of a small Mashpee delegation that presented a petition to Massachusetts' lieutenant governor asking to be allowed to abolish the overseer system; manage their own property; incorporate their reserve as a township; and formulate municipal regulations under which to govern themselves. After mistakenly assuming that the governor and secretary of state had sanctioned their actions, the Mashpees elected a twelve-man tribal council; discharged the overseers; and relieved Fish of his pastoral duties. On 1 July, in line with the tribe's public resolutions, Apes and a small group of Indians forcibly stopped two white men from hauling a load of wood off reservation lands.[20]

At this point, the overseers, Fish, and disgruntled spokesmen in nearby towns raised a cry of Indian rebellion. Governor Levi Lincoln sent a commissioner, J. J. Fiske, to meet with the tribe and attempt to calm agitated local feelings. On 4 July, Fiske met with the one hundred Indians most concerned with ending the overseer system and strongly urged the Mashpees to cease their efforts to nullify the laws of Massachusetts. Apes, whom Fiske referred to as "the principal manager for the complainants," argued that Mashpee demands must be immediately met. How could the governor ask Indians to be "good citizens" when they enjoyed none of the rights of citizenship? Fiske, no enemy of the overseer system, believed Apes to be a potentially dangerous agitator. Near the close of the orderly meeting, Apes was arrested on a charge of assault and inciting to riot. A white man who had formerly served as a treasurer for the tribe promptly supplied bail. But, several months later, Apes and six other Indians were convicted and sentenced to serve thirty days in the Barnstable County jail.[21]

Following William Apes's arrest, the Mashpee tribal council revoked its resolutions of 21 May 1833 without surrendering their belief that they should have the right to govern themselves and to control the sale of increasingly valuable timber from their own lands. Plans were made to petition the state legislature for a redress of grievances after it began its session in September. In the interim, Apes and his supporters were harassed by local opponents. Increasingly, Apes publicized the Mashpees' case in the Boston press. Among his strongest supporters was Benjamin Franklin Hallett, editor of the anti-Masonic *Boston Daily Advocate*. Born in Barnstable County, Hallett had begun his career in reform journalism by supporting, in turn, movements for expanded suffrage, anti-monopoly, anti-Masonry, and Jacksonian democracy. An early acquaintance with the Mashpee region led Hallett to open his columns to Apes. Couching his arguments in more diplomatic idioms, Apes tried to broaden the issue of Mashpee rights. Many of the Massachusetts electorate, he remarked, were critical of the state of Georgia's contemporary attempts to eject the Cherokees from their lands. Would they, then, support Massachusetts Indians in their attempts to gain expanded civil rights within a white society? Since the early seventeenth century, "the conduct of the whites toward the Indians has been one continued system of robbery."[22]

By January 1834 Apes's journalistic campaign was beginning to enjoy some success. Abolitionist editor William Lloyd Garrison carried news of the Mashpees' efforts in *The Liberator*. And, more important, the Massachusetts state legislature granted a tribal delegation the right to state their case in the house of representatives in Boston. After addresses by Isaac Coombs and Daniel Amos, organizers of the Mashpees' resistance, Apes addressed a large audience. Without criticizing the overseers as individuals, he made "dexterous and pointed" arguments against the absolutist system of government under which the Mashpees lived. Indians, he argued, must be granted political rights to vote and hold public office, rights exercised by the white and black citizens of Massachusetts. The overseer system must be abolished. The Mashpees should be allowed to incorporate themselves as a town; set up municipal regulations; hire an attorney; and be supplied with magistrates to enforce the laws. Collective land-tenure customs should be protected until the time the tribe was able to educate its ignorant members.

The reception accorded Apes's speech was enthusiastic. Garrison's *Liberator* charged that:

In the [Mashpee] case, this State is guilty of a series of petty impositions upon a feeble band, which excite not so much indignation as disgust. . . . Fearing, in the plenitude of its benevolence, that the Indians would never rise to be men, the Commonwealth has, in the perfection of its wisdom, given them over to absolute pauperism. Believing they were incapable of self-government as free citizens, it has placed them under . . . a servile dependence. Deprecating partial and occasional injustice to them on the part of individuals, it has shrewdly deemed it lawful to plunder them by wholesale, continually. . . . Dreading lest they should run too fast and too far, in an unfettered state, it has loaded them with chains so effectually as to prevent their running at all.[23]

Garrison overstated the case. But even his most fervid prose could not obscure the fact that Indians enjoyed fewer civil and political rights than any other segment of Massachusetts' population. In the several months following the Mashpee memorial to the legislature, Apes was virulently attacked by papers like the *Boston Courier* and the *Barnstable Patriot*—and just as warmly defended by the *Boston Advocate*. Editor B. F. Hallett's legal skills were soon joined to the Mashpee cause. Early in March 1834, Hallett argued the Indians' case before a joint committee of the Massachusetts legislature. Soon thereafter, he printed a pamphlet summarizing his arguments. Apes's journalistic efforts also continued, and the publicity had an increasing effect. The Mashpees soon received editorial notice in national journals like *Niles' Weekly Register*.[24] But opposition grew. Although Fish and the overseers obtained fifty Mashpee signatures on a counter-petition against Apes and his supporters late in March, the state senate finally ratified an act that allowed the Mashpees to incorporate their territories, elect selectmen, and manage their own financial, educational, political, and judicial affairs. The act did not, however, gain all that Apes had hoped. A "guardian" with advisory powers was appointed to replace the three overseers. Reverend Mr. Fish continued to occupy 500 acres of land on the Mashpee territories. And, despite protections against land alienation, the legislature reserved the right to repeal the so-called "Marshpee Act" at any time.[25]

In the wake of this partial political victory, the Mashpee tribe elected three selectmen, a town clerk, and several constables. But party divisions arose over the issues of the state-appointed guardian and the perquisites still enjoyed by Fish. In the following decade, the guardian, Charles Marston (a former overseer) made himself acceptable to the tribal majority, and, after a lengthy fight, Fish finally left Mashpee. By 1843, the Mashpees had obtained the right to elect their own ministers. For a short time, Apes continued active on the reserve by organizing a temperance society and recruiting a small congregation for his nonsectarian "Free and United Church." Early in 1835, the Pequot minister published a documented summary of the Mashpee affair. In the preface to the book, Benjamin Hallett and the three selectmen of the Mashpee tribe defended Apes's character from the aspersions being cast upon it by his still active enemies. Yet, even as the work appeared, Apes's influence in Mashpee councils declined. A native Baptist preacher enjoyed increasing ascendancy in spiritual matters. And tribal leaders, forswearing further ambitious reform agitations, settled down to make the best of the situation. Apes's work at Mashpee was done.[26]

The Mashpees' successful struggle for added measures of self-government stood as one of the very few substantial victories for Indian rights in the 1830s. Indian groups hung on to tribal territories in New England and New York, but, in the remainder of the nation, removal followed removal. The growing debate over the abolition of slavery relegated the plight of the American Indian to a secondary place in reform thinking. A hazy sentimentality had begun to characterize novels and histories of the Indian being produced in the Northeast. But writers like James Fenimore Cooper were glorifying the image of a "vanished race," not quarreling with the frontier mores of an expansionary society. Throughout these troubled years, William Apes's opposition to the cruder forms of Manifest Destiny and racialist theories steadily increased. He began an ambitious study of white-Indian relations in seventeenth- and eighteenth-century New England. Finally, in 1836, he organized such materials into his most broadly conceived work on Indian rights. Mincing no words, Apes entitled his book *Eulogy on King Philip.*

His choice of title required courage. Of all the famous Indians then known in the nation's history, few had a worse reputation than King Philip (or Metacomet), sachem of the Wampanoags. In June 1675, relations between Philip, the grandson of Massasoit, and the government of the Massachusetts Bay Colony had deteriorated to a point where attacks were launched upon English towns around the Narragansett Bay. Philip, fearful that land cessions and religious and cultural conflict would, in time, destroy his people, called for a coalition of Indian tribes to drive the whites from New England. In the following year, loosely coordinated attacks were launched on settlements from Maine to Connecticut. In this, the most destructive Indian war in New England's history, thousands of whites died, a score of towns were destroyed, and frontier regions were largely depopulated. Indians, too, experienced great losses of lives and property. After Philip's death in August 1676, hostilities largely ceased. But enslavement, starvation, and executions were suffered by the Indians who had survived. The terrors of the war caused whites to destroy or scatter the inhabitants of almost all the communities of christianized Indians throughout the Massachusetts Bay Colony, sounding the death knell of ambitious civilizing missions among the New England tribes.[27]

In his survey of King Philip's career (originally delivered as public lectures at the Odeon theater in Boston), Apes attacked a Puritan theocracy of the "pretended pious" for denying justice to New England's Indians. As it was in Philip's day, so it remained. The "prayers, preaching, and examples" of Puritan divines like Cotton Mather had been "the foundation of all the slavery and degradation in the American colonies towards colored people." The Puritans had sold King Philip's son into slavery with the same unctuous hypocrisy earlier enunciated when, in the late 1630s, large numbers of Pequots were sold into bondage in the West Indies. The founders of New England had destroyed traditional Indian social and economic systems and had then proved unwilling to civilize the Native American within a white society. Such policies had not produced men—nor Christians. Instead, scattered fragments like the Mashpees lived in virtual slavery. If civilizing efforts were to succeed, the "ministers and people [must] use the colored people they have already about them, like human beings, before they go to convert any more." Such uplift efforts should begin in New England where improvement was most possible. King Philip should be esteemed as "the greatest man that ever was in America . . . to the everlasting disgrace of the pilgrim fathers." The national rights of all Indian tribes should be respected within a white society, thus avoiding the necessity of removing Indians beyond the pale of civilization and settlement. Once mindless prejudices against Indians—and Indian cultures— were removed, the white man and the red could "bury the hatchet and those unjust laws, and Plymouth Rock together, and become friends."[28]

In this, his final work, William Apes highlighted ideas that he had enunciated many times, but he did so in a fashion that was more overtly critical of white actions—and the conceptual frameworks that underlay them—than in his earlier books. The symbol of Plymouth Rock held no cherished place for the Native or the African American. If colored peoples were to occupy an honorable place in New England society, more ambitious and egalitarian social formulations were required.

After the publication of his *Eulogy on King Philip*, Apes's career faded from public notice. Slowly, Massachusetts' Indian populations gained expanded civil and political rights until, in 1870, the Indian reserves at

Mashpee and Gay Head were incorporated as townships, the common lands divided among the proprietors, and full responsibilities of citizenship granted to the populations. In Connecticut, however, the Pequot, Mohegan, and Nipmuck tribes preserved a considerably more tenuous existence on their few tiny reserves. Whether William Apes perished or returned to the Pequot territories is unknown. If any wondered, they perhaps contented themselves with the thought that men who attempted to comprehend the necessities of a "vanishing race" were engaged in a quixotic exercise. New England's Indians, however, did not disappear from the social and cultural scene. This fact is not a historic accident. Instead, it is due, in large part, to the efforts of little-known reformers like William Apes: crusaders for human dignity in a period when the future of the Indian within American society seemed nonexistent.[29]

Author's Postscript

When I wrote this essay in 1975 and it was published in 1977, New England's post-colonial native inhabitants counted for little politically or economically. They were also invisible as an academic specialty.

Now both conditions are very significantly changed. Some of the indications of the recent upsurge in academic interest are treated in the footnotes. More important is a summary of some of the real world events of the past two decades that mix continued frustrations with a Cinderella story.

To begin with the Cinderella story, the Mashantucket Pequots of southern Connecticut (though not, be it noted, the nearby Eastern Pequots) have won federal recognition as a tribe. The Mashantucket Pequots have also gone from being one of the tiniest and least affluent Native American groups in the United States to being one of the best known and most affluent.

Improvements in Pequot political status began after high-profile Indian land claims in New England, Alaska, and elsewhere helped give birth to an American Indian Policy Review Commission during the presidencies of Gerald R. Ford and James Earl Carter. This commission, led by ex–U.S. Senator James Abourezk of South Dakota (whose ancestry mixed both Lakota/Sioux and Lebanese strains) proposed changes in law and politics that soon addressed the peculiar difficulties of tribal groups remaining in the eastern half of the United States, many of which had never enjoyed any federal protection and most of which existed under a mélange of state and local rules—or under none at all. The Mashpee Wampanoags of Massachusetts were, as we shall later see, one major factor in energizing Abourezk's commission, changing laws, and improving Pequot political fortunes as a tribe for the first time in three hundred years.

Pequot economic fortunes, meanwhile, also improved. And, again, they did so as a result of changes in national policy prodded by grassroots Indian efforts. In 1988, most significantly, Congress passed an Indian Gaming Regulatory Act which requires states to negotiate agreements with Indian tribes interested in setting up gambling casinos on tribal lands. So long, for instance, as a state allowed any kind of gambling in, say, a "private club," it could not restrict Native Americans from encouraging such wagers on their reservations.

Two years after this federal law was passed, the Mashantucket Pequots, after attempting various other economic ventures, opened a high-stakes casino that quickly became the most profitable gambling operation in the western hemisphere. That casino now employs between 6,000 and 10,000 people and rakes in profits of between $100 million and $600 million every year. Flush with revenue, the tribe began diversifying its economic holdings into pharmaceuticals by 1994. Nor did its leaders forget the value of good public relations. Reported amounts of between $100 million and $200 million in annual tribal profits were allocated as political protection money to Connecticut in the form of voluntary contributions to the state's budget. Funds were also allocated to strengthen tribal identity and structure—from recovering the tribal past through archaeological digs, to buying land to expand the tiny Mashantucket reservation, to creating, for the first time in Pequot history, a written legal code to govern the tribe's civil affairs. The Pequots branched out into party politics in 1993 and 1994 by contributing an estimated $815,000 to varied state and national Democratic Party organizations. And, in 1995, they gave $10 million to the Smithsonian Institution in Washington to help establish a National Museum of the American Indian in the nation's capital. This last donation alone, one of the largest cash contributions in Smithsonian history, demonstrates how scholarly concern and economic clout often intersect. It also shows how historical truth is often far stranger than historical fiction. Whisky, beads, gunpowder, and artillery might have denied Pequots like William Apes much of a tribal patrimony by the nineteenth century. But, by the late twentieth century, gambling revenues were gradually buying parts of that patrimony back.[30]

The Mashpee Wampanoag of Massachusetts, the other half of the history of Indian survival that I treated, have fared less well. In the early 1970s, as previously stated, New England's Native Americans launched legal counterattacks to gain federal recognition as tribes and to regain portions of lands earlier ceded to state or local authorities without federal agreement or oversight. This legal process began among the Passamaquoddy and Penobscot Indians of the author's native state of Maine by 1972. It was well under way among the Mashpee Wampanoags as well by 1975.

Few initially noticed or cared about such legalities. But Passamaquoddy, Penobscot, and Mashpee claims, as presented by their determined, non-Indian lawyers, were strong—strong enough that all the standard forms of political demagoguery Apes experienced in the 1830s were re-deployed in Maine in 1975 and 1976 and in Massachusetts shortly thereafter.

To make a long story that has been well told elsewhere short, the Passamaquoddy and Penobscot of Maine finally achieved a partial victory after the U.S. Congress passed a Maine Indian Land Claims Act in September 1980. They won federal recognition and received 81 million federal dollars to buy back lands and to establish an economic base for the tribes in return for extinguishing all of their damage claims against the state and federal governments.

The Mashpee Wampanoag, meanwhile, lost. In an equally complicated, dramatic, and politics-prone legal procedure, they were denied land restitutions or status as a federally recognized tribe in a decision of the U.S. Court of Appeals. Subsequent and varied legal efforts to overturn this verdict in whole or in part also failed.[31]

That judicial result wrote into history another, and furiously ironic, chapter in the relations between the Pequot and Wampanoag tribes of New England. In the 1830s, the darkest hour for Native Americans east of the Mississippi—the decade of Indian Removal and the Cherokee Trail of Tears—a young Pequot came to Wampanoag country to serve as an agent of tribal revival and growth. William Apes did not gain economically from his reform successes; indeed, soon bankrupt, he disappeared from the historical record. One hundred and fifty years later, the Mashpee Wampanoags whom Apes had helped paid back their debt by initiating one of the land claims cases that created the political and economic environment that paved the way for the Mashantucket Pequots' spectacular success. Just like Apes, though, the Mashpees reaped no profits from their experience. The calculus of reform success and failure was reversed in the 1970s and 1980s.

Both the Pequots and the Wampanoags, however, survived. And they did so on the basis of inter-relationships that sometimes sufficiently bound them together to gain hearings in the broader, non-Indian world. This enduring fact, more than any other, is the still ongoing lesson to be learned from the life of one of the very small handful of pioneering pan-Indian spokesmen who existed during the first three centuries of settler–indigenous contact in North America.

Notes

1. Francis Paul Prucha, *American Indian Policy in the Formative Years . . . 1790–1834* (Cambridge: Harvard University Press, 1962), pp. 214–23; Timothy Dwight, *Travels in New England and New York,* 4 vols. (New Haven: Published by the author, 1823), 3:103–7; Anthony F. J. Wallace, *The Death and Rebirth of the Seneca* (New York: Random House/Vintage, 1970), pp. 318–52; William DeLoss Love, *Samson Occum and the Christian Indians of New England* (Boston and Chicago, 1899), pp. 196–282; James Axtell, *The Invasion Within: The Contest of Cultures in Colonial North America* (New York: Oxford University Press, 1985); Roy Harvey Pearce, *Savagism and Civilization: A Study of the Indian and the American Mind,* rev. ed. (Berkeley: University of California Press, 1988).

2. D'Arcy McNickle, *The Indian Tribes of the United States: Ethnic and Cultural Survival* (London: Oxford University Press, 1962), p. 40; *Speeches on the Passage of the Bill for the Removal of the Indians delivered in the Congress of the United States, April and May 1830* (Boston, 1830), passim; Prucha, *American Indian Policy,* pp. 225–47; Dee Brown, *Bury My Heart at Wounded Knee* (New York: Holt, Rinehart & Winston, 1971), pp. 5–8.

3. McNickle, *Indian Tribes,* p. 53. For the prevalence of "vanishing race" concepts of American Indians, see, for example, Samuel Drake, *Biography and History of the Indians of North America* (Boston, 1837); Laurence M. Hauptman and James D. Wherry, eds., *The Pequots of Southern New England: The Fall and Rise of an American Indian Nation* (Norman: University of Oklahoma Press, 1990) provides by far the best interdisciplinary overview of Pequot tribal survival during and after the colonial period. Barry O'Connell, ed., *On Our Own Ground: The Complete Writings of William Apess, A Pequot* (Amherst: University of Massachusetts Press, 1992), finally gathers together Apes's writings in one convenient and affordable place. O'Connell's textual notes make a heroic effort to expand upon the details of Apes's life and career. O'Connell's bibliographic essay on pp. 325–29 is a very useful introduction to current scholarship, as is Neal Salisbury's *The Indians of New England: A Critical Bibliography* (Bloomington: Indiana University Press, 1982).

4. William Apes, *A Son of the Forest, The Experience of William Apes, A Native of the Forest, written by himself,* 2d ed. (New York, 1831), pp. 7–41, esp. p. 38.

5. Apes, *A Son of the Forest,* pp. 41–47. (For the effect of Methodism among Indian tribes in the Canadas during the first several decades of the nineteenth century, see Peter Jones, [Kah-ke-wa-quo-na-by], *History of the Ojebway Indians: with especial reference to their conversion to Christianity* [London, 1864], and Alvin Torry, *Autobiog-*

raphy of the Rev. Alvin Torry, First Missionary to the Six Nations . . . of British North America [Auburn, N. Y., 1861]).

6. John DeForest, *History of the Indians of Connecticut from the Earliest Known Period to 1850* (Hartford, 1852), pp. 421–45; Mathias Spiess, *The Indians of Connecticut* (New Haven: Connecticut Historical Society, 1933), pp. 4–6; Timothy Dwight, *Travels in New York and New England,* 4 vols. (Cambridge: Harvard University Press, 1969), 3:13–14, 18.

7. *The Journal of Henry D. Thoreau,* ed. Bradford Torrey and Francis Allen, 14 vols. (New York: Dover, 1962), 1:443–44; 2:42; [anon.], *William Weston: Or, The Reward of Perseverance* (Hingham, Mass., 1832), pp. 27–41, 112–14; Herman Melville, *Moby Dick* (Garden City, N.Y.: Doubleday, 1937), p. 100.

8. Apes, *A Son of the Forest,* p. 79.

9. Apparently, Apes's father and mother had been reunited by 1821, as Apes mentions visiting his mother at approximately the same period as he visited his father. However, his mother occupied none of his attention in his few writings about his family.

10. Apes, *A Son of the Forest,* pp. 80–97.

11. William's wife, Mary, was, like her husband, "bound out" by her widowed mother. From the age of six to eighteen she worked as a servant in a white home. She described her mother as being "of English descent" and her father as coming from Spain or "one of the Spanish islands." Thus, in one sense, she was "white." However, from Apes's autobiographical comment, it appears likely that his wife was a *mestizo* or mulatto.

12. Apes, *A Son of the Forest,* pp. 98–108; William Apes, *The Experiences of Five Christian Indians: Or, The Indians' Looking Glass for the White Man* (Boston, 1833), pp. 22ff.; *Dictionary of American Biography,* s.v. "Apes, William."

13. William Apes, "The Increase in the Kingdom of Christ: A Sermon" (New York, 1831), pp. 6, 21–23, 3–5; William Apes, *The Experiences of Five Christian Indians,* p. 55. To the author's knowledge, Apes's autobiography was the first such narrative published in book form by an American Indian, preceding the much better-known narrative of Chief Black Hawk by four years.

14. Roy Harvey Pearce, *The Savages of America: A Study of the Indian and the Idea of Civilization* (Baltimore: Johns Hopkins University Press, 1953), pp. 61–62; Josiah Priest, *American Antiquities and Discoveries in the West* (Albany, N.Y., 1838), passim; Apes, "The Increase of the Kingdom of Christ," pp. 12ff.; Apes, *A Son of the Forest,* pp. 149ff.

15. Apes, *The Experiences of Five Christian Indians,* pp. 53, 56.

16. Gideon Hawley, "Biographical and Topographical Anecdotes respecting Sandwich and Mashpee, Jan. 1797," *Massachusetts Historical Society Collections,* 1st ser. 3 (1794): 188–93; "Rev. Gideon Hawley's account of his service at Mashpee," *Massachusetts Historical Society Collections,* 1st ser. 4 (1795): 50–67; Federal Writers' Project, *Massachusetts: A Guide to Its Places and People* (Boston, 1937), pp. 593–94; Dwight, *Travels,* 1823 ed., 3:103–7; Jeremiah Digges and the Federal Writers' Project, *Cape Cod Pilot* (Provincetown, Mass.: Modern Pilgrim Press, and New York: Viking

Press, 1937), pp. 349–50; "The Mashpee Indians," *Boston Daily Advocate*, 18 January 1834.

17. *Boston Daily Advocate*, 27 December 1833; William Apes, *Indian Nullification of the Unconstitutional Laws of Massachusetts relative to the Mashpee Tribe; or, the pretended riot explained* (Boston, 1835), pp. 55–62, 117–18; Simeon L. Deyo, ed., *History of Barnstable County, Massachusetts* (New York, 1890), p. 712.

18. Digges, *Cape Cod Pilot*, pp. 350–51; Jedidiah Morse, *A Report to the Secretary of War of the United States on Indian Affairs* (New Haven, 1822), pp. 68–73; Carter G. Woodson, "The Relation of Negroes and Indians in Massachusetts," *Journal of Negro History* 5 (1920): 45–50; *North American Review*, November 1815, pp. 113–14, 118–19. Mixed black-white-Indian tribal groupings in the Eastern states continue to suffer from simplistic social classifications regarding racial/ethnic identity. See Brewton Berry, *Almost White* (New York: Collier Publishers, 1963).

19. Frederick Freeman, *History of Cape Cod: The Annals of Barnstable County, including the District of Mashpee*, 2 vols. (Boston, 1858), 1:705ff.; Apes, *Indian Nullification*, pp. 16–20, 21.

20. Freeman, *History of Cape Cod*, p. 708; Apes, *Indian Nullification*, pp. 25–32. Donald M. Nielsen, "The Mashpee Indian Revolt of 1833," *New England Quarterly* 58 (1985): 400–420 (chap. 14 of *New England Encounters*) uses state and local legislative and judicial documents not available to the author in 1977.

21. Apes, *Indian Nullification*, pp. 32–43; [J. J. Fiske], "Commissioner's Report," in "Documents Relative to the Mashpee Indians," *State of Massachusetts—Senate—Legislative Documents—1834* (n.p., n.d), pp. 17–25; *Dictionary of American Biography*, s.v. "Apes, William." (The lack of civil and political rights enjoyed by Massachusetts Indians is demonstrated by the fact that free blacks, who were taxed, were enfranchised and legally eligible for the highest offices in the state government. For an example of punitive legislation directed against the Gay Head Indians in 1828, see Woodson, "Negroes and Indians," pp. 48–51.

22. "The Marshpee Indians," *Boston Daily Advocate*, 10 August 1833; *Dictionary of American Biography*, s.v. "Hallett, Benjamin F."; Freeman, *History of Cape Cod*, pp. 706–7; Apes, *Indian Nullification*, pp. 50–55, 80, 86–87.

23. Apes, *Indian Nullification*, p. 96; *Liberator*, 25 January 1834, p. 15; "Memorial of the Mashpee Indians . . . Jan. 1834," *Massachusetts, House of Representatives, Legislative Documents, 1834* (n.p., n.d.), passim. (This Mashpee memorial is also printed in the *Liberator*, 1 February 1834).

24. "The Mashpee Indians," *Liberator*, 22 February 1834, p. 32; Benjamin Franklin Hallett, "Rights of the Mashpee Indians: Argument of Benj. F. Hallett, counsel . . . before a joint committee of the legislature of Massachusetts . . . March, 1834" (Boston, 1834), passim; *Niles' Weekly Register*, 29 November 1834, p. 205; Freeman, *History of Cape Cod*, pp. 707–8.

25. "The Marshpee Act," *Boston Daily Advocate*, 25 March 1834; "The Mashpee Indians," *Boston Daily Advocate*, 26 March 1834; *Boston Daily Advocate*, 5 May 1834.

26. "The Indian Proprietors of Marshpee," *Boston Daily Advocate*, 5 May 1834; Deyo, *History of Barnstable County*, pp. 711–13; Freeman, *History of Cape Cod*, pp.

710–11; Apes, *Indian Nullification,* pp. 117–18. Nielsen, "Mashpee Indian Revolt," pp. 418–19, adds details regarding Apes's fall from grace among the Mashpee; O'Connell, *On Our Own Ground,* p. lxxxi, adds the key detail that Apes's estate and household goods were attached for debt by the Barnstable Court of Common Pleas in 1838. O'Connell, like the author, was able to uncover no data about William Apes after this time.

27. Contemporary English opinion on the causes and results of the war are collected in *King Philip's War Narratives* (Ann Arbor, Mich.: University Microfilms, 1966), and *Narratives of the Indian Wars, 1675–1699,* ed. Charles H. Lincoln (New York: Scribner, 1952). King Philip's stature as a historical rogue is demonstrated in the classic novelette *The Devil and Daniel Webster,* by Stephen Vincent Benét [1937]. The devil-picked jury before whom Webster must plead for the soul of a strayed farmer is composed of the most terrible figures in the colonial history of the New England and Middle Atlantic colonies. King Philip, pirate Edward Teach, loyalist Walter Butler, and pro-Indian renegade Simon Gurty are among them.

28. William Apes, *Eulogy on King Philip: as pronounced at the Odeon, in Federal Street, Boston . . . (etc.)* (Boston, 1836), esp. pp. 22, 28, 50–51, 54, 56–59. This book went through at least two printings.

29. Deyo, *History of Barnstable County,* p. 709; *State of Massachusetts, House of Representatives, Legislative Documents, 1839,* document no. 72, passim; [1882], document no. 226, passim; *State of Massachusetts, Senate, Legislative Documents, 1878,* document no. 238, passim; Freeman, *History of Cape Cod,* p. 713; Frank Speck, "Native Tribes and Dialects of Connecticut: A Mohegan-Pequot Diary," *43rd Annual Report of the Bureau of American Ethnology, 1925–1926* (Washington, D.C., 1928), passim. Speck does not list Apes as an existent Pequot or Mohegan family name as of 1925. C. P. Thresher, "Homes and Haunts of the Pequots," *New England Magazine,* February 1902, pp. 753–54; "Report of the Connecticut Indian Affairs Council—1974" (New Haven: Connecticut Indian Affairs Council, 1975), passim.

A major new academic sub-specialty of "Native American Literature" has arisen since the proliferation of novels, short stories, and autobiographies by American Indian authors began in the 1970s. Various techniques of literary analysis are used to try to explain the mind-sets of authors and audiences alike. Given the comparative rarity of Native American writers before the early twentieth century, William Apes's works are covered in studies such as Arnold Krupat's *The Voice on the Margin: Native American Literature and the Canon* (Berkeley: University of California Press, 1989); David Murray's *Forked Tongues: Speech, Writing and Representation in North American Indian Texts* (Bloomington: Indiana University Press, 1991); and H. David Brumble III, *American Indian Autobiography* (Berkeley: University of California Press, 1988).

Another academic effort that growing concern with Native American writers has called forth is biographical. O'Connell's edited volume of Apes(s)'s work has already been mentioned. Others include: Raymond Wilson's *Ohiyesa: Charles Eastman, Santee Sioux* (Urbana: University of Illinois Press, 1983); Dorothy R. Parker's *Singing an Indian Song: A Biography of D'Arcy McNickle* (Lincoln: University of Nebraska Press, 1992); and reprints of long hard-to-find books by twentieth-century Indian writers such as Thomas Wildcat Alford's *Civilization and the Story of the Absentee Shawnees* ([1936]; reprinted, Norman: University of Oklahoma Press, 1979) and John Rogers's (Chief Snow Cloud) *Red World and White: Memories of a Chippewa Boyhood* ([1957]; reprinted, Norman: University of Oklahoma Press, 1974). Every Indian author newly familiar to scholars is being anthologized, analyzed, and reprinted, though several nineteenth-century Indian authors who deserve such attentions have, thus far, eluded the net.

30. No history of Pequot tribal survival after early colonial times has ever been written, although a one-hundred-million-dollar tribal museum opened in 1998. But contemporary Pequot resurgence has become a staple rags-to-riches theme in contemporary journalism. See, e.g., Francis X. Clines, "The Pequots: It's One Thing for Tribal Casinos to Strike It Rich, But When a Tiny Band of Nearly Extinct Indians Beats the Industry at Its Own Game, They Strike a Nerve," *New York Times Magazine*, 27 February 1994, pp. 49–52; Neil Asher Silberman, "Pequot Country," *Archaeology Magazine*, July–August 1991, pp. 35–39; Carol Bogert, "Casino Clout for Native Americans," *Newsweek*, 28 March 1994, p. 24; Kirk Johnson, "Pequots Invest Casino Wealth in a New Game: Party Politics," *New York Times*, 30 August 1994, pp. A-1, A-9.

Other recent journalistic treatments I've enjoyed include: "Tribal Dance," *The Economist*, 18 September 1993, p. 31; "How a Law Is Born," *The Economist*, 15 April 1995, pp. 27–28; and Strat Douthat, "Indians Win Battle, Statue Will Go: Figure of Massacre Leader Inflammatory," an Associated Press wire service story printed in the *Seattle Times*, 16 January 1994, p. A–8, regarding the often unremarked-upon Eastern Pequots.

31. The best single source for New England Indian land claims cases is Paul Brodeur's *Restitution: The Land Claims of the Mashpee, Passamaquoddy, and Penobscot Indians of New England* (Boston: Northeastern University Press, 1985). Brodeur knew and cared about these people as human beings before they became anyone's academic subject, and his prose shows it.

A sympathetic academic treatment of Mashpee legal difficulties is Jack Campisi's *The Mashpee Indians: Tribe on Trial* (Syracuse: Syracuse University Press, 1991). For an academic voice from the other side of the legal debates, see Francis G. Hutchins's *Mashpee: The Story of Cape Cod's Indian Town* (West Franklin, N.H.: Amarta Press, 1979).

Note on Contributors

DAVID BUSHNELL, a specialist in Latin American history, is Professor Emeritus at the University of Florida. He is the author of *The Santander Regime in Gran Colombia* (1954) and *The Making of Modern Colombia: A Nation in Spite of Itself* (1993), coauthor of *The Emergence of Latin America in the Nineteenth Century* (1988), and editor of *The Liberator Simon Bolivar: Man and Image* (1970). "The Treatment of the Indians in Plymouth Colony" appeared in the June 1953 issue of *NEQ*.

ALFRED A. CAVE is a Professor of History at the University of Toledo. He is the author of *Jacksonian Democracy and the Historians* (1964), *An American Conservative in the Age of Jackson: The Political and Social Thought of Calvin Colton* (1969), and *The Pequot War* (1996). Cave's articles on early American ethnohistory have appeared in several scholarly journals. "Why Was the Sagadahoc Colony Abandoned? An Evaluation of the Evidence" appeared in the December 1995 issue of *NEQ*.

EUGENE L. HUDDLESTON, until his retirement in 1993, taught in the Department of American Thought and Language at Michigan State University. He is the author or coauthor of *The Relationship of Literature and Painting: A Reference Guide* (1978), *Thomas Jefferson: A Reference Guide* (1982), *The Allegheny: Lima's Finest [Locomotive]* (1987), *Riding That New River Train* (1989), and *Appalachian Crossing: The Pocahontas Roads* (1989). His article "Topographical Poetry of the Early National Period," *American Literature* (1966), won the Norman Foerster Prize. "Indians and the Literature of the Federalist Era: The Case of James Elliot" appeared in the June 1971 issue of *NEQ*.

STEVEN T. KATZ is Professor of Religion and Director of the Center for Judaic Studies at Boston University. His publications include *Jewish Philosophers* (1975), *Jewish Ideas and Concepts* (1977), *Post-Holocaust Dialogues* (1984; National Jewish Book Award), and *Historicism, the Holocaust, and Zionism* (1992). He is currently writing a multivolume study, *The Holocaust in Historical Context,* of which the first (prize-winning) volume was published in 1994. Katz has also edited and contributed to four volumes of essays on mysticism and is the editor of the journal *Modern Judaism.* "The Pequot War Reconsidered" appeared in the June 1991 issue of *NEQ.*

KIM MCQUAID, Professor of History at Lake Erie College, Painesville, Ohio, has published widely on history, business, economics, geography, and law. He is the author of *Big Business and Presidential Power: From FDR to Reagan* (1982), *The Anxious Years: America in the Vietnam-Watergate Era* (1989), and *Uneasy Partners: Big Business in American Politics, 1945–1990* (1994); he is coauthor of *Creating the Welfare State: The Political Economy of Twentieth Century Reform* (1980; revised edition, 1988). In 1985–86, McQuaid was the Mary Ball Washington Visiting Professor of American History at the University College Dublin. "William Apes, Pequot: An Indian Reformer in the Jacksonian Era" appeared in the September 1977 *NEQ.*

JOHN MCWILLIAMS is Abernethy Professor of American Literature at Middlebury College. His books include *Political Justice in a Republic: Fenimore Cooper's America* (1972), *Hawthorne, Melville and the American Character: A Looking-Glass Business* (1984), *The American Epic: Transforming a Genre, 1770–1860* (1989), and *The Last of the Mohicans: Civil Savagery and Savage Civility* (1995). He is on the Editorial Board of *Early American Literature* and *Nineteenth-Century Literature* and is presently working on a book on New England historiography. "Indian John and the Northern Tawnies" appeared in the December 1996 issue of *NEQ.*

JOSHUA MICAH MARSHALL, a doctoral candidate in Early American History at Brown University, is currently writing his dissertation on late seventeenth-century New England and the social and cultural repercussions of King Philip's War. "'A Melancholy People': Anglo-Indian Relations in Early Warwick, Rhode Island, 1642–1675" appeared in the September 1995 issue of *NEQ.*

LION G. MILES, a freelance historical researcher who specializes in eighteenth-century America, is currently writing a book on the battle of

Bennington in 1777 and compiling a dictionary of the Mahican Indian language. He is a board member of the new Native American Institute at Columbia–Greene County Community College in Hudson, New York. "The Red Man Dispossessed: The Williams Family and the Alienation of Indian Land in Stockbridge, Massachusetts, 1763–1818" appeared in the March 1994 issue of *NEQ*.

DONALD M. NIELSEN is an attorney in Winston-Salem, North Carolina, and formerly the Associate Editor of Publications at the New England Historic Genealogical Society. "The Mashpee Indian Revolt of 1833" appeared in the September 1985 issue of *NEQ*.

LYNN H. PARSONS is a Professor of History at the State University of New York at Brockport. He is the compiler of *John Quincy Adams: A Bibliography* (1993) and the author of *John Quincy Adams: A Biography (1998)*. "'A Perpetual Harrow upon My Feelings': John Quincy Adams and the American Indian" appeared in the September 1973 issue of *NEQ*.

RICHARD W. POINTER, Professor of History at Westmont College, Santa Barbara, California, is working on a book about the Indian impact on European colonial religion. "'Poor Indians' and the 'Poor in Spirit': The Indian Impact on David Brainerd" appeared in the September 1994 issue of *NEQ*.

PHILIP RANLET is the author of *Enemies of the Bay Colony* (1995), which discusses Indian relations in New England both before and after King Philip's War. He has also written *The New York Loyalists* (1986) and scholarly articles on a broad array of historical subjects. He is presently an Adjunct Assistant Professor of History at Hunter College of the City University of New York. "Another Look at the Causes of King Philip's War" appeared in the March 1988 issue of *NEQ*.

JOHN SAINSBURY is Chair of the Department of History at Brock University, St. Catharines, Ontario. His publications in the field of Angloamerican history include *Disaffected Patriots: London Supporters of Revolutionary America, 1769–1782* (1987). "Indian Labor in Early Rhode Island" appeared in the September 1975 issue of *NEQ*.

WILLIAM S. SIMMONS, formerly Professor of Anthropology at the University of California, Berkeley, is Provost of Brown University. His many publications on the ethnohistory of early New England include *Cautan-*

towwit's House, An Indian Burial Ground on the Island of Conanicut in Narragansett Bay (1970) and *Spirit of the New England Tribes: Indian History and Folklore, 1620–1984* (1986); he coedited *Old Light on Separate Ways: The Narragansett Diary of Joseph Fish, 1765–1776* (1982) and contributed to volume 15 of the Smithsonian Institution's *Handbook of North American Indians*. "Conversion from Indian to Puritan" appeared in the June 1979 issue of *NEQ*.

HAROLD W. VAN LONKHUYZEN, M.D., is a resident in Psychiatry at the University of Washington. He holds an M.A. degree from the University of Pennsylvania, where he completed all work for the Ph.D. except a dissertation. The essay included in this volume, "A Reappraisal of the Praying Indians: Acculturation, Conversion, and Identity of Natick, Massachusetts, 1646–1730," won the 1989 Walter Muir Whitehill Prize in Colonial History, offered by the Colonial Society of Massachusetts, as well as the 1990 Heiser Prize from the American Society for Ethnohistory. It appeared in the September 1990 issue of *NEQ*.

ALDEN T. VAUGHAN is Professor Emeritus of History at Columbia University. His books on Indian-white relations in early New England include *New England Frontier: Puritans and Indians, 1620–1675* (1965; revised edition, 1979; third edition, 1995); an edition of William Wood's *New England's Prospect* (1977); a coedited anthology, *Puritans among the Indians: Accounts of Captivity and Redemption, 1676–1724* (1981); and Part 3 of *Roots of American Racism: Essays on the Colonial Experience* (1995).

Index

Good, Sarah, 160, 162, 163, 173
Goodrich, William, 292, 294
Goodspeed, Obed, 365
Goody, Jack, 229n.38
Gookin, Daniel, 213; on Euroamerican prejudices, 15, 136; on Indian informers, 220; on Indian labor, 90–91, 262; on King Philip, 140; on sachems' power, 5; on Waban, 226n.11
Gookin, Samuel, 220–21
Gorges, Sir Ferdinando, 44–47, 49, 52–54
Gorton, Samuel: followers of, 86, 88, 93, 99
Gosnold, Bartholomew, 48
Goulburn, Henry, 329
Governance (Authority; Political structures): by Algonquians, 4–5, 76, 85, 182–83; Algonquians' resentment of colonial, 10, 11, 66–69, 71–74, 84–108, 145, 187; by Cherokees, 335, 337; of English colonies, 4, 5; and Massachusetts charter revocation, 157–59, 174; of Praying Towns and Indian Reservations, 223, 359–78; by sachems, 4–5, 67, 90, 94, 182–83, 185, 208, 209. See also Law; Political rights; Punishment; Town meetings
Governor Dummer's War, 14
Great Awakening ("New Light"), 18, 246, 247, 269
Great Barrington (Massachusetts), 277
Great Britain. See England
Green, Richard, 265
Green Corn ceremony, 217
Greene, James, 95, 98
Greene, John, Jr., 93, 94
Greene, Lorenzo, 361
"Greenfield Hill" (Dwight), 21
Greven, Philip, 175n.3
Grey Lock's War, 14
Grigory (Indian), 264
Groton (Connecticut), 383–86
Guides (Indians as), 22, 25, 59, 91
Guns. See Firearms
Gyles, John, 15

Haddam (Connecticut), 235
Hallett, Benjamin F., 370, 372, 390–92

Hamilton, Alexander, 312–13
Hamilton, Dr. Alexander, 260
Hamtramck, John F., 317
Handsome Lake (Seneca chief), 380
Hanham, Thomas, 49
Hargreaves, Mary W. M., 351
Harmar (general), 307–9, 317, 322n.11
Harris, William, 148
Hart, William, 176n.8
Hartford (Connecticut), 10
Harvard College, 223; Indian school at, 141, 213; and Phineas Fish, 362, 371, 372, 389
Hassanamesit (Praying Town), 214
Hathorne (judge), 163–65, 167
Haverhill (Massachusetts), 159, 161
Hawley, Gideon, 367, 375n.8
Hawthorne, Nathaniel, 38n.62
Haynes, Charles, 346
Herring Pond (Massachusetts), 360
Hessians, 361, 388
Heydon, William, 117
Hiacoomes (Christian Indian), 187–90, 193, 210
Higginson (captain), 167
Historians: interest in Indians' history by, xi, 84, 85; interpretations of Indian history by revisionists among, xi, 78, 111, 123, 137, 139, 150n.3, 206
Historie of Travell into Virginia Britania (Strachey), 45, 55n.2
History of New England (Winthrop), 112
History of the Indians (De Forest), 112
The History of the Wars of New-England (Penhallow), 14
Hobbomok (Hobbomock). See Abbomocho
Hobbs, Abigail, 164–66
Hobbs, Deliverance, 164, 165
Hobomok (Child), 22
Hoffer, Peter Charles, 174
Hogs. See Livestock
Holden, Randall, 97–98
Holliman, Ezekiel, 93, 94
Holocaust analogies, 125, 127, 129, 131
The Holocaust in Historical Context (Katz), 129, 130
Hope Leslie (Sedgwick), 21